James Mill (1773–1836)
John Rae (1796–1872)
Edward West (1782–1828)
Thomas Joplin (1790–1847)

Pioneers in Economics

Series Editor: Mark Blaug

Professor Emeritus, University of London
Consultant Professor, University of Buckingham
Visiting Professor, University of Exeter

This important series presents critical appraisals of influential economists from the 17th century to the present day. It focuses in particular on those economists who were influential in their own time and whose work has had an impact – often inadequately recognized – on the evolution and development of economic thought. The series will be indispensable for a clear understanding of the origin and development of economic ideas and the role played by the leading protagonists of the past.

A full list of published and future titles in this series is printed at the end of this volume.

James Mill (1773–1836) John Rae (1796–1872) Edward West (1782–1828) Thomas Joplin (1790–1847)

Edited by

Mark Blaug

Professor Emeritus,
University of London

An Elgar Reference Collection

Published by
Edward Elgar Publishing Limited
Gower House
Croft Road
Aldershot
Hants GU11 3HR
England

Edward Elgar Publishing Company
Old Post Road
Brookfield
Vermont 05036
USA

CIP catalogue records for this book are available from
the British Library and the US Library of Congress

ISBN 1 85278 483 0

Printed in Great Britain at the University Press, Cambridge

Contents

Acknowledgements

The editor and publishers wish to thank the following who have kindly given permission for the use of copyright material.

American Economic Association for articles: Paul A. Samuelson (1978), 'The Canonical Classical Model of Political Economy', *Journal of Economic Literature*, **XVI** (4), 1415–34; Samuel Hollander (1980), 'On Professor Samuelson's Canonical Classical Model of Political Economy', *Journal of Economic Literature*, **XVIII** (2), 559–74; Paul A. Samuelson, 'Noise and Signal in Debates Among Classical Economists: A Reply', *Journal of Economic Literature*, **XVIII** (2), 575–78.

Basil Blackwell Ltd. for articles: Edwin R.A. Seligman (1903), 'On Some Neglected British Economists: Parts I & II', *Economic Journal*, **XIII**, 335–63, 511–35; R.D. Black (1945), 'Trinity College, Dublin, and the Theory of Value, 1832–1863', *Economica*, New Series, **XII**, 140–8; S.G. Checkland (1951), 'The Advent of Academic Economics in England', *Manchester School*, **XIX** (1), 43–70.

Duke University Press for articles: Frank W. Fetter (1969), 'The Rise and Decline of Ricardian Economics', *History of Political Economy*, **1** (1), 67–84; William J. Barber (1969), 'James Mill and the Theory of Economic Policy in India', *History of Political Economy*, **1** (1), 85–100; Barry Gordon (1969), 'Criticism of Ricardian Views on Value and Distribution in the British Periodicals, 1820–1850', *History of Political Economy*, **1** (2), 370–87; William D. Grampp (1970), 'Edward West Reconsidered', *History of Political Economy*, **2** (2), 316–43; William O. Thweatt (1976), 'James Mill and the Early Development of Comparative Advantage', *History of Political Economy*, **8** (2), 207–34; Arthur I. Bloomfield (1978), 'The Impact of Growth and Technology on Trade in Nineteenth-Century British Thought', *History of Political Economy*, **10** (4), 608–35; Arthur I. Bloomfield (1981), 'British Thought on the Influence of Foreign Trade and Investment on Growth', *History of Political Economy*, **13** (1), 95–120.

John Wiley & Sons, Inc. for articles: Erskine McKinley (1955), 'The Problem of "Underdevelopment" in the English Classical School', *Quarterly Journal of Economics*, **69**, 235–52; Joseph J. Spengler (1959), 'John Rae on Economic Development: A Note', *Quarterly Journal of Economics*, **73**, 393–406; William D. Grampp (1979), 'The Economists and the Combination Laws', *Quarterly Journal of Economics*, **93** (4), 501–22.

Oxford University Press for article: Samuel Hollander (1977), 'The Reception of Ricardian Economics', *Oxford Economic Papers*, **29** (2), 221–57.

Review of Economic Studies for article: Ronald L. Meek (1951), 'Thomas Joplin and the Theory of Interest', *Review of Economic Studies*, **18** (3), 154–63.

Every effort has been made to trace all the copyright holders but if any have been inadvertently overlooked the publishers will be pleased to make the necessary arrangement at the first opportunity.

In addition the publishers wish to thank the Library of the London School of Economics and Political Science and The Alfred Marshall Library, Cambridge University for their assistance in obtaining these articles.

Introduction

James Mill was one of a number of clever young Scotsmen who emigrated to London around the turn of the eighteenth century to make their way in the world through journalism. He had attended Edinburgh University and heard Dugald Stewart lecture on moral philosophy and political economy. In London, he began to edit a *Literary Journal* writing most of the articles on economic topics and, similarly, in various editions of the *Encyclopaedia Britannica* he wrote the articles on 'government', 'colonies' and 'education'. He became the amanuensis of Bentham, and set to work writing an authoritative *History of British India*, which made his reputation when it appeared in 1817. On the strength of his book, he was appointed Assistant Examiner with the East India Company in 1819, rising to the post of Chief Examiner in 1830.

But James Mill's importance to economics rests, not on his work on India or political Benthanism, or even on his early economic pamphlets capped by his textbook on Ricardian economics, the *Elements of Political Economy* (1821), but rather on the tutoring of his oldest son, John Stuart Mill, and the coaching of Ricardo during the writing of the latter's *Principles*. Mill was never taken seriously as an important economist in his own right until relatively recently. He is now credited with the first declaration in English of Say's Law of Markets and, quite possibly, Ricardo's Principle of Comparative Advantage. It is also he, rather than Ricardo, who was responsible for drawing out the logical implications of Ricardo's theory of rent for the taxation of land rents.

John Rae's *New Principles on the Subject of Political Economy* (1834) was cited and quoted by John Stuart Mill in his *Principals of Political Economy* and rediscovered at the turn of the century as a forerunner of the Austrian theory of capital. Nevertheless, his neglect was so total that the book itself had to be reprinted and edited in 1965. It was neglected in large part because its subtitle — *Exposing the Fallacies of the System of Free Trade, and of Some Other Doctrines Maintained in the 'Wealth of Nations'* — suggested a heavy-going anti-free-trade tract, and free trade after all was an orthodox dogma all through the nineteenth and most of the twentieth centuries. His analysis of the determinants of 'the effective desire of accumulation' and his stress on technical progress rather than capital accumulation as the engine of economic growth in a capitalist regime was far ahead of its time and can be studied with profit even now.

He was born in Scotland, the son of a merchant and shipping magnate, read medicine at the University of Edinburgh but was forced to emigrate to Canada before completing his studies in 1822 when his father's business failed. In Canada he took up school teaching, but sporadically practised medicine. In 1848 he emigrated once again, leaving for California and thereafter Hawaii, where he alternated between teaching, farming and medicine. He came back to the mainland of America in 1868 and died in New York in 1872. He wrote on a large number of scientific subjects in newspapers and magazines, but the *New Principles* was the only book he ever managed to get published.

Edward West is remembered — if he is remembered at all — for having stated the theory of differential rent based on the principle of diminishing returns in a long pamphlet just before

Ricardo did so, and in virtually the same form and language. It appears that Ricardo developed the same idea independently of West and even of Malthus (who also published the idea more or less simultaneously), and at any rate, Ricardo's exposition in his *Essay on Profits* (1815) was clearer than anyone else's, was more carefully set out and went beyond West in spelling out its implications for the distribution of income between wages, profits and rent. In addition to this *Essay on the Application of Capital to Land* (1815), West only wrote one other work on economics, a short book entitled *Price of Corn and Wages of Labour* (1826). At the time of his death, he was working on a treatise in political economy, the manuscript of which has been lost.

West was born in London, educated at Harrow and University College, Oxford, and then went on to study law at the Inns of Court in London. In 1817 he published a major treatise on the law of indemnities against debts to royalty, which earned him a knighthood in 1822 and the appointment of Recorder of Bombay; two years later he was promoted to the post of Chief Justice to the Crown in the Bombay province of India.

Thomas Joplin was a prolific writer of currency and banking tracts in the 1820s and 1830s, advocating joint stock banking alongside a government monopoly of the note issue; this was to replace the Bank of England and the private country banks. The creation of the National Provincial Bank of England in 1833 vindicated his belief that joint-stock banking was feasible. In his *Analysis and History of the Currency Question* (1832) he alleged that Ricardo's posthumous *Plan for National Bank* was taken from his work without acknowledgement. This and other pamphlets by Joplin have been arduously mined by a variety of commentators as containing nuggets of later monetary doctrines.

Note

Several paragraphs in this Introduction were borrowed from my *Great Economists Before Keynes* (Wheatsheaf Books, 1986).

[1]

ON SOME NEGLECTED BRITISH ECONOMISTS.—I

IT is a trite saying that the history of political economy is still to be written. The books that pass under that name contain only the barest outlines of the subject, and they are all especially weak and meagre in that particular division of the field which happens to be distinctly the most fruitful. The literature of economics in Great Britain, from the end of the sixteenth to the middle of the nineteenth century, so far transcends in importance that of other countries that the neglect of all but the great masters of the classical school is as remarkable as it is deplorable. For the period before Adam Smith, so rich that an economist of the period collected no less than fifteen hundred English books and pamphlets prior to 1760, we have only the fragmentary monograph by Roscher, the incomplete and prejudiced bibliography of McCulloch, the short essays by Ashley, Hewins, and Cossa, some allusions in Cunningham, and a few sporadic notices in dictionaries and encyclopædias. For the first half of the nineteenth century there exist, indeed, somewhat fuller, but still quite inadequate, accounts of the great masters, like Ricardo, Malthus, and Senior. Practically the only attempts to include any of the other writers have been made by Foxwell in his masterly sketch of the Socialist Literature, and by Cannan in his excellent history of the Theories of Production and Distribution. Foxwell, however, does not pretend to give more than the barest outline of the subject, and Cannan has not only neglected several writers of at least equal importance with those that he has included, but has failed in some instances to give an entirely fair account of the authors of whom he treats.

It is the object of the present papers to call attention to some of the British writers who undertook to discuss economic theory during the two decades following the appearance of Ricardo's *Principles*. It will perhaps surprise many to find in this literature so much that foreshadows the most recent contributions to economic doctrine. As an introduction to this discussion, we shall say a few words about some of the neglected writers at the close of the eighteenth and beginning of the nineteenth century.

I

In the generation that intervened between the *Wealth of Nations* and Ricardo's earliest tracts, the greater part of the economic literature consisted, as in the preceding period, of pamphlets dealing with current practical problems. In the last quarter of the eighteenth century, some interesting side-lights, it is true, are thrown on economic principles, especially in the discussion of such topics as the commercial relations with the United States, Ireland, and France, the growth of population, the changes in agriculture, the East India trade, the increasing burdens of taxation and the public debt, the relief of the poor, and the rise of prices at the close of the century. The influence of Adam Smith, however, was so preponderant that well nigh the only discussion of economic theory that has come down to us is associated with the names of Godwin, Malthus, and Lauderdale. Yet there are not wanting other discussions of economic theory which have hitherto been overlooked. Of these, it may suffice to mention only two—the controversy over the Physiocratic system, and the treatment of the problem of taxation.

As to the Physiocrats, it is worthy of remark that Oncken, the most scholarly and independent student of the Physiocratic system, has recently made the assertion that the Physiocrats had no followers in England,[1]—this, too, in the face of the discussion by Higgs of the works of William Spence.[2] Yet Higgs also has overlooked two writers, both of them, indeed, anonymous, but each in some respects superior to Spence.

Of these, the first staunch follower of the *Économistes* is the author of a work published in 1797, entitled *The Essential Principles of the Wealth of Nations illustrated, in Opposition to some False Doctrines of Dr. Adam Smith and Others.* In this volume of 144 pages, which displays some acquaintance with the earlier English economic literature, the author states and develops the principal doctrines contained in what he calls "the system of the Economists,[3] or, as he sometimes terms them,

[1] Oncken, *Geschichte der nationalökonomie*, I. *Die Zeit vor Adam Smith*, 1903, p. 422.

[2] Higgs, *The Physiocrats*, 1897, p. 137.

[3] *The Essential Principles, etc.*, pp. 49, 86.

"the political Economists."[1] He takes issue not only with Adam Smith, but more especially with Arthur Young,[2] whose arguments he considers scarcely more solid than the "flimsy productions of the witty Voltaire."[3] In only one point does he balk at the conclusions of the Physiocrats, namely, that of considering the proprietors of land as a productive class. They may, indeed, be made an essential class in the community, says our author, but only the cultivators of the soil are really productive. The way in which the landowners may be made to become an essential class is by putting on them the burdens of the State. Through the adoption of the "single tribute"[4] on land rent, which is the "natural fund for the defence of the community," "the possessors of these rents instantly become not only an essential class in society, but an honourable class as well."[5]

Since the prosperity of England depends, not upon its manufactures or its commerce, but upon the productiveness of its land —this new Potosi, "this mine of riches to which the Economists wish to direct the attention of British patriots,"[6]—it becomes the duty of the Government to help in enhancing the productivity of the soil. "Not only the neglected lands but the neglected cultivators call for the interposition and protection of the Government."[7] Prosperity depends upon high rents, and rent is identified with the "net produce" of the Physiocrats.

"The rise of rents, which is a principal object of the Economists, enlarged the power of the main wheel that moves every other wheel in Society, and is itself set in motion by nature and the industry of man. As the motion of that wheel is progressive or retrograde, so, proportionally, is the prosperity of the State progressive or retrograde."[8] Not all high rents, however, betoken national prosperity. "The increase of produce and not the increase of the price of produce is what a wise agricultural nation will chiefly aim at."[9] And with an enthusiastic statement of what may yet be expected in Great Britain from a complete adoption of the Physiocratic doctrines, the work closes.

The obvious trend of English enterprise, however, at the close of the century was away from the soil, and in the direction of commerce and industry. One last attempt was made to recall the British public to the true path of honour and riches. With this attempt the name of Spence is associated.

[1] *Ibid.*, p. 54. [2] *Ibid.*, pp. 56—81. [3] *Ibid.*, p. 55.
[4] *Ibid.*, pp. 91, 81, etc. [5] *Ibid.*, p. 54. [6] *Ibid.*, p. 115.
[7] *Ibid.*, p. 117. [8] *Ibid.*, p. 118. [9] *Ibid.*, p. 119.

In the controversy between Spence on the one hand, and James Mill and Cobbett on the other, an anonymous author took the part of the theorists who should attempt to remove the controversy from the battlefield of practical politics and relegate it to the quiet and serene field of principle. His work of 115 pages, published in 1809, bears the title, *Sketches on Political Economy Illustrative of the Interests of Great Britain; intended as a Reply to Mr. Mill's Pamphlet Commerce Defended, with an Exposition of some of the Leading Tenets of the Economists.*

The author starts out with a statement of the relation of value to utility, in which he seems to come close to some modern doctrines. In the opening chapter, he points out that "in attempting to establish the criterion of value the first circumstance which occurs is its strict correspondence with want." After speaking of the relation of desires and the means of satisfaction, he goes on to state that "the importance of any object is decreased as the want or desire thereof is diminished, and the value of commodities always corresponds with the proportion which they bear in quantity to our necessities."[1] It is true that in this particular passage he does not use the term utility; but later in his chapter on consumption, he makes it clear that value depends on utility, and he tells us that "we can only deem those things valuable which have an aptitude for consumption, and in this sense it (value) is only another expression for utility."[2] So, again, he tells us that "value is inseparable from utility, and in proportion to its utility will it be estimated."[3] Since want and desire, however, are always in proportion to each other, value arises from the difficulty of obtaining those objects which are calculated to supply want or remove desire. Value, therefore, may safely be defined as "labour or the exertion which is necessary to procure or create any desirable article."[4]

In the course of the argument, the gradation of wants, the satisfaction of which lies at the basis of value, is utilised to prove the dependence of all prosperity upon agriculture, the source of satisfaction of the most urgent wants. Capital, it is conceded, is accumulated labour, but "capital has not the power of reproducing with increase, but can only reproduce itself equal to its original amount."[5] For "it is the effect of a previous cause, and can never be the cause of producing that

[1] *Sketches, etc.*, p. 2. [2] *Ibid.*, p. 74. [3] *Ibid.*, p. 75.
[4] *Ibid.*, p. 3. [5] *Ibid.*, p. 29.

of which it is the effect." This leads him to the ordinary positions of the Physiocrats, which do not call for any special statement. It is, however, interesting to note that in the chapter on consumption he objects to the theory of Adam Smith on productive and unproductive labour, and declares, much in accord with the modern view, that "the distinction between commodities of a durable and perishable character is trifling and futile." On one point, however, he seems to misconceive the conclusions of the Economists, and erroneously states as one of their mistaken conclusions that "an equal division of the land should naturally result from the fact that all wealth is derived from the soil."[1] That our author is still writing under the influence of the domestic system, and that he has no real appreciation of the vast changes which were rapidly transforming the face of British society, appears from his use of the term manufacturer,[2] in its old significance of manual labourer.

With this book, the attempt to introduce and to popularise in England the doctrines of the Physiocrats came to an end—if we neglect, as we may well do, the partial support lent to their theories two decades later by Chalmers. We thus come to the second discussion mentioned above[3]—that of the effects of taxation.

In the field of public finance, easily the most remarkable work is the anonymous *Enquiry into the Principles of Taxation*, published in 1790.[4] With the exception of Petty's essay in the seventeenth century, this is the first English work devoted entirely to taxation.[5] The author sees clearly that the fundamental problem is that of the incidence and effects of taxation. He is the first to make the distinction between "Payers of Taxes" and "Bearers of Taxes," a distinction which slumbered more than a century before it was again introduced into English scientific nomenclature.[6] Although he is well acquainted with the work of Adam Smith, whom he calls in one

[1] *Ibid.*, p. 7. [2] *Ibid.*, p. 39. [3] P. 336.

[4] *An Enquiry into the Principles of Taxation chiefly applicable to Articles of Immediate Consumption.* Printed for J. Debrett, 1790, 4°, 295 pp. The author was probably Andrew Hamilton.

[5] The author explains in the preface that "taxation has long been practised as an art, but has never been fully explained," and that "taxation as a subject of knowledge has never been duly cultivated." He declares the work to be "the first regular attempt which has been made to supply this important chasm in the science of government."

[6] The writer of this essay was ignorant of this remarkable work when preparing the second edition of *The Shifting and Incidence of Taxation.*

place a "very respectable" writer, and in another a "truly ingenious" thinker, he differs fundamentally, not only with Smith, but with Stewart, as well as with the Physiocrats. His analysis of incidence culminates in the statement that the final determinant is the state of demand in relation to supply; and that taxes will be shifted or not according to the conditions of prosperity in each particular class. Where society is advancing, that is where demand is continually increasing, the tax will be "thrown round in a circle" and will be prevented from falling anywhere.[1] The real fund out of which taxes in progressive societies are ultimately paid is the profits resulting from new inventions, subdivisions of labour, and superior dexterity, skill, and exertion.[2]

We can here do no more than barely allude to this interesting author. His importance lies, not only in the fact that he developed the diffusion theory of taxation long before Canard in France, and with a far more rigorous analysis than Verri or his few English predecessors, but that his doctrine constitutes an improvement on the diffusion theory itself. Incidentally, he discloses three mistakes of Adam Smith—first, the assumption that taxes on wages must always be shifted to profits; second, the failure to notice that, even when the conditions are favourable to a shifting of the tax on wages to profits, there is nothing in this process peculiar to wages[3]; and third, the statement of what is now known as the excess-of-price-above-tax doctrine—the doctrine, namely, that when the tax is assessed on the original producer, the price of the article after each exchange will advance by more than the amount of the tax. On the contrary, says our author as a result of his analysis, "when improvements in a State are numerous, when the invention of machines, the subdivision of labour, and greater exertion and skill are taking place in every department, a tax will be lightened, the more hands it goes through. It will be absorbed, as it were, by every improvement, and be lightened or annihilated, according to the degree and number of improvements which it meets with; *i.e.* instead of becoming heavier, taxes will become lighter in proportion to the number of hands through which they pass, in a thriving society."[4] He concludes that "all speculations, whose object is to show on what fixed fund or class taxes must fall, are vain and unsatisfactory, and will be generally disproved (as they almost always have been)

[1] *An Enquiry, etc.*, p. 179.
[2] *Ibid.*, pp. 149—155.
[3] *Ibid.*, p. 178.
[4] *Ibid.*, p. 159.

by experience."[1] It was the failure of Ricardo to notice, and to profit by, this advice which is responsible for much empty discussion in the classical English economists.

II

We come now to several contemporaries of Ricardo, to whom, indeed, we find a few references in economic literature, but whose real importance has not been adequately recognised. Chief among these authors are Torrens and Craig.

Colonel Robert Torrens is treated somewhat cavalierly in Palgrave's *Dictionary*. Not only is the discussion of his writings limited to five lines, but his productions are declared to be, "as a rule, devoid of permanent merit." Yet Ricardo himself entertained a different opinion of Torrens in several matters, and Cannan speaks respectfully of Torrens in the few points discussed by him, even though, as we shall see, he also fails to give Torrens his due place.

There is, indeed, much in Torrens's voluminous writings that is "devoid of permanent merit," and it is incontestable that he is often magniloquent.[2] A careful reading of his productions, however, seems to justify us in making the following claims for Torrens:—

In the first place, he discovered, independently of Malthus and Ricardo, the law of rent.

Secondly, he advanced a theory of wages which was adopted by Ricardo.

Thirdly, he discovered the law of comparative cost, the credit of which is usually ascribed to Ricardo.

Fourthly, he advanced a theory of profits which differed from that of Ricardo, and which is considerably nearer the truth.

With reference to the first point, it is now well known that Ricardo was not the originator of the theory of rent. Not to speak of Anderson in the eighteenth century, the whole theory was implicit, and even to a certain degree explicitly recognised in the Lords' Committee of 1813. The essays of Malthus and West appeared in 1815. The *Essay*[3] of Torrens was published at the beginning of the same year—although it was written in

[1] *Ibid.*, p. 183.

[2] Cannan, *A History of the Theories of Production and Distribution*, p. 123.

[3] *An Essay on the External Corn Trade.* By Robert Torrens, 1815. The preface is dated Feb. 17, 1815.

1814, at a time when the author could not have been acquainted with the works of Malthus and Ricardo.[1] Thus even if the essay of Torrens was not published before those of West and Malthus —although in all probability it did antedate them—Torrens must be credited at least with a simultaneous and independent discovery of the law of rent. For he tells us how the "natural rent of the land proprietor" is always a "net surplus,"[2] and explains later how it appears from the testimony in the Lords' Committee that cultivation proceeds from the better lands to inferior lands. the difference in the produce of "soils of first rate" and of "second rate or third rate quality" appearing in the form of rent."[3] Torrens is accordingly a strong advocate of free trade in corn, for any restriction on importation "forces into cultivation land of inferior quality, and . . . by increasing the natural price of corn, lowers, universally, the productive powers of labour and capital."[4] In a later edition he reiterates some of these views, but thinks that he has made an important emendation of the Ricardian theory, by calling attention to the difference of situation rather than of fertility as an explanation of rent[5]—being here a forerunner of Von Thünen and many later critics.

As to the second point, the proclamation of a theory of wages which was adopted by Ricardo, it will also be seen that Torrens has not received his deserts. Torrens first put forward the theory of the natural rate of wages as influenced by the standard of life, and it is this theory that soon became the stock-in-trade of the classical school. Cannan, it is true, emphasises this,[6] but he exaggerates one alleged point of difference which he thinks he discovers between Torrens and Ricardo, and fails to accentuate the real points of difference. It is claimed by Cannan that by "natural wages" Torrens means the average rate, and Ricardo the minimum rate.[7] Yet when Torrens in a later edition of his work reprints almost word for word the theory first propounded by him, he explains that "the minimum below which the real wages of labour cannot permanently fall consists of that quantity of the necessaries of life which climate and custom

[1] This is so stated in the preface to the later editions. *Cf. e.g.* p. ix of the preface to the 4th edition, 1827.

[2] *An Essay, etc.*, first ed., 1815, p. 60.

[3] *Ibid.*, pp. 212, 256, 325.

[4] *Ibid.*, pp. 73, 74. Cannan quotes this passage on p. 167 of his work, but does not call attention to the emendation in the later edition, referred to in the next note.

[5] *An Essay, etc.*, 4th edition, 1827, pp. 138, 144 *et seq.*

[6] Cannan, *op. cit.*, pp. 243—248.

[7] *Ibid.*, p. 217.

render necessary to support the labourer while at work, to enable him to bring up a family sufficient to preserve the supply of labour even with the demand."[1] Moreover, as regards the alleged distinction between the Ricardian phrase of "perpetuating the race without either increase or diminution" and Torrens's phrase of "preserving in the market an undiminished supply of labour," Cannan himself confesses that when Ricardo applies the theory of wages to taxation, he uses the phrase "to keep up the race of labourers" in the sense of Torrens rather than in his own sense.[2] As a matter of fact, nothing but an over refinement of interpretation can discover any difference between the theory of Ricardo and that of Torrens. Ricardo himself never thought that he was advancing any new doctrine, for he tells us that "the whole of this subject is most ably illustrated by Colonel Torrens."

But while Torrens originated the theory of wages usually ascribed to Ricardo, he did not draw by any means the same conclusions—and it is precisely these conclusions which served later to cast discredit on the political economy of the day. Torrens, for instance, in a subsequent work entitled *An Essay on the Production of Wealth*, strenuously objects to the theory of Ricardo that the introduction of machinery may occasion a permanent diminution in the demand for labour. He declares this doctrine to be "altogether incorrect."[3]

In a still later work devoted entirely to the wages question, where he deals fully with the problem, he claims that Ricardo's conclusions rest upon a "hypothetical case," which "never occurs in practice."[4] On the contrary, Torrens tells us, in advancing the modern doctrine, "all inventions for abridging labour and diminishing the cost of production have the effect of increasing both maximum and actual wages."[5] Torrens, however, does not deny in the least the hardships suffered by those who are for the time being thrown out of employment. It is interesting to find him advocate for the first time the idea of a national insurance fund to be applied to the alleviation of such misery.

"It also appears that the general good which results from the employment of new and improved machinery is accompanied by partial evil. While the public acquires additional wealth, the individuals who are supplanted in their accustomed occupations

[1] Torrens, *op. cit.*, 4th edition, p. 84.
[2] Cannan, *op. cit.*, p. 257.
[3] *An Essay on the Production of Wealth*, 1821, p. ix.
[4] *On Wages and Combinations*, 1834, p. 41.
[5] *Ibid.*, p. 44.

are reduced to poverty. Humanity and justice require that those who thus suffer for the public good should be relieved at the public expense. Whenever a new application of mechanical power throws a particular class of operatives out of employment, a national fund should be provided to aid them in betaking themselves to other occupations. It is a disgrace to the Legislature and to the country, that the numerous body of hand-loom weavers should have been left so long in misery and destitution, and toiling to the death in hopeless competition with the power loom. A comprehensive plan for their relief should be one of the earliest measures of the reformed Parliament." [1]

Even in his earliest works, Torrens was aware of the consequences of the industrial revolution. Whereas all his predecessors had used the term manufacturer in accordance with its derivation in the sense of the manual workman, Torrens distinguishes in 1815 between the "master manufacturers" and the "labouring manufacturers." [2] It was not long before the predominance of the factory system had completed the transition by popularising the term "manufacturer" in its modern sense.

Torrens displays his independence of the classical school in other phases of the labour question. He maintains that combinations of labour might have the effect of increasing the rate of wages. In nations which have some advantage in producing commodities for abroad, this possibility becomes a probability.[3] But after all, thinks Torrens, the limit to which wages may be raised, or even the possibility of raising wages at all, depends on the application of another principle, which he was the first to emphasise, and which we shall now proceed to discuss as the third discovery of Torrens—the principle, namely, of comparative cost.

The doctrine of comparative cost has almost universally been regarded as one of the great achievements of Ricardo. Yet not only the principle itself, but many of its applications, are found in Torrens. Torrens is discussing the influence of a free external trade in corn upon the progress of agriculture. Most people, says he, think that if corn could be grown as cheaply in England as in Poland it would be raised at home.

"But this conclusion, however obvious and natural it may at

[1] *On Wages and Combinations*, 1834, p. 44.

[2] *An Essay on the External Corn Trade*, p. 235.

[3] "In countries possessing superiority in manufacturing for the foreign market, wages may be raised within the limits of such superiority."—*On Wages and Combinations*, p. 73.

first sight appear, might, on a closer examination, be found entirely erroneous. If England should have acquired such a degree of skill in manufactures, that, with any given portion of her capital, she should prepare a quantity of cloth, for which the Polish cultivator would give a greater quantity of corn, than she could, with the same portion of capital, raise from her own soil, then, tracts of her territory, though they should be equal, nay, even though they should be superior, to the lands in Poland, will be neglected; and a part of her supply of corn will be imported from that country. For, though the capital employed in cultivating at home might bring an excess of profit over the capital employed in cultivating abroad, yet, under the supposition, the capital which should be employed in manufacturing would obtain a still greater excess of profit; and this greater excess of profit would determine the direction of our industry." [1]

At a somewhat later date Torrens repeats the principle in the following words [2]:—

"In the earlier edition of the *Essay on the Corn Trade*, it was shown, the Author believes for the first time, that a permanently high scale of general prices, from whatever cause arising, cannot depress domestic industry by encouraging the importation of cheaper foreign articles; and that commodities, the cost of producing which is greater in foreign countries than at home, may, nevertheless, be imported, provided the comparative disadvantage of the foreign capitalist in producing the imported article, be less than the comparative advantage of the domestic capitalist in producing the articles imported in exchange."

Torrens goes on to say that "these principles Mr. Ricardo adopted into his very valuable work upon *Political Economy and Taxation;* and they form, in some measure, the ground-work of his chapters upon foreign trade, and of his doctrines on the influence of taxation upon the export and import of commodities."

Torrens applies this doctrine of comparative cost, not only to the market for commodities, but also to the labour market. Although no enemy of the trade unions, Torrens thinks that the scheme of the eight-hour day in England is at the moment impracticable. He refers to it as the plan propounded by "Mr. Fielden in conjunction with the benevolent monomaniac, Robert Owen.[3] Torrens points out that shorter hours, or what

[1] *An Essay on the Corn Trade*, 1815, pp. 264—5. *Cf.* pp. 48, 222—227.

[2] *Ibid.*, 4th edition, p. vii.

[3] *On Wages and Combinations*, p. 90.

is its equivalent, higher wages, can indeed be secured in a country, but only to the extent that a country possesses peculiar advantages over its competitors in the fabrication of goods for the foreign market; and these advantages may be the result of a natural or of an acquired superiority. But the superiority which England possesses in the greater skill of the workman, in better machinery, and in cheaper fuel, is outweighed by the comparative dearness of food. "No plan for improving the condition of the people can by possibility be effectual, unless it increases the quantity of work which can be executed in a day or year, or the *comparative* cheapness of machinery, fuel, or carriage, or diminishes the *comparative* dearness of food."[1] Hence the first step toward improvement must be the abolition of the corn laws.

The fourth point made by Torrens to which we desire to direct attention is of importance as a criticism rather than as a piece of constructive work. Torrens objects strenuously to Ricardo's doctrine that profits must vary inversely as wages.[2] He terms this "a hasty and premature generalisation," and thinks that Ricardo has over-emphasised the influence of one out of many causes. Profits, according to Torrens, are not a part of the cost of production. Profit is a surplus, not a cost. "The profits of stock never make any part of the expense of production; they are on the contrary, a new creation brought into existence in consequence of this expense."[3] And again, "The profit of stock so far from forming any part of the cost of production is a surplus remaining after this cost has been completely replaced."[4] Hence, while profits constitute a part of the market price of commodities, they do not form part of the natural price.

Torrens seems here to be on the high road to the modern theory. But his own treatment is not entirely satisfactory, for he is unable to analyse successfully the true relation between normal and market price, and tells us, notwithstanding his former statements, that "things equal in natural price will also upon the average, be equal in market price."[5] Whatever we may think of this point, to which attention has been called by others,[6] Torrens shows himself in one respect broader than Ricardo. The rate of profits, according to Torrens, depends, not only on the rate of

[1] *On Wages and Combinations*, p. 99.

[2] *An Essay on the Corn Trade*, 4th edition, p. xi.

[3] *An Essay on the Production of Wealth*, p. 51.

[4] *Ibid.*, p. 54.

[5] *Ibid.*, p. 55.

[6] Cannan, *op. cit.*, p. 208.

wages, as Ricardo thought, but to a much more important extent upon the quality of the soil under cultivation, and above all upon the degree of skill with which labour is applied.[1] The resort to inferior soils, which increases cost, tends to diminish the rate of profits in manufactures as well as in agriculture, but the same increase of population which compels resort to inferior soils leads to more accurate division of employment and to the use of improved machinery, and these lead to an increase in the rate of profit. This last point—" the greater degree of skill and economy in the application of labour "—may completely counteract the effects, not only of the resort to inferior soils, but also of the changes in money wages. High or low profits, therefore, do not necessarily depend, as Ricardo thought, on low or high wages.

We do not stop to dwell on the other contributions which Torrens made to contemporary discussion. Like most of the economists of the day, he had a greatly exaggerated notion of the achievements of the science.[2] But in both constructive and critical powers, Torrens has been much underrated. The future historian of economic theory will have to credit him with the honour of originating several important doctrines which are usually ascribed to his more famous contemporaries.

III

The other contemporary of Ricardo referred to above [3] is John Craig, to whom Palgrave's *Dictionary* devotes just one sentence. Craig was the author of two books—a three-volume work on the *Elements of Political Science*, published in 1814, and a shorter volume of *Remarks on Political Economy*, which appeared in 1821. His *Elements* cover, as the title indicates, a broader field than that of economics, but contain for the economist only two noteworthy points. One is Craig's exposition of the futility of Adam Smith's distinction between productive and unproductive labour.[4] In this, however, Craig had been preceded by Lauderdale, whose criticism of this " extraordinary distinction " is well known.[5] The other point is the attention devoted by Craig to the problems of public finance, and more especially to the question of capitalisation of taxation. As this matter has already been

[1] *An Essay on the Corn Trade*, 4th edition, pp. 117 *et seq.*

[2] " With respect to Political Economy, the period of controversy is passing away, that of unanimity is rapidly approaching. Twenty years hence there will scarcely exist a doubt respecting any of its fundamental principles."—*An Essay on Production*, 1821, xiii.

[3] P. 341.

[4] Vol. 2, pp. 93 *et seq.*

[5] Lauderdale, *An Inquiry into the Nature and Origin of Public Wealth and into the Means and Causes of its Increase*, 1804, pp. 151 *et seq.*

touched upon elsewhere,[1] we shall confine our attention to the later work[2] of Craig devoted specifically to questions of political economy.

Craig starts out by a rather interesting discussion of value. He considers the view of Lauderdale that value in exchange or individual riches should be carefully distinguished from value in use or national wealth. Lauderdale had called attention to the obvious fact that by increasing the quantity of the most useful articles we often diminish its aggregate value in exchange; and like Adam Smith he considered value in use and value in exchange opposed to each other. Craig, on the other hand, finds that utility is the basis of all value. It is undeniable, says he,[3] that relative values of commodities may change, and that "those persons who happen to be possessed of articles which are produced in larger quantities than formerly . . . may find themselves poorer, while the chief uses of the article remain unimpaired." But it would be a mistake, thinks Craig, to conclude that value in use is here opposed to value in exchange. For "in such cases, there are others of its uses which cease to exist. Its possession is no longer a mark of distinction, nor can the additional quantity that has been produced yield to those by whom it must be consumed, gratification equivalent to its former price." If coats fall one half in price, the "exchangeable value" of two coats is now equal to what formerly was the value of one; but neither would their value in use have experienced any perceptible increase.[4] "All of the broadcloth that, in the estimation of purchasers, was worth the former price, had been formerly brought to market, and if more is now to be disposed of, it must be to those who did not reckon its utility equivalent to its former cost. New purchasers indeed will appear in proportion to the reduction of price; because at every step of the decline it is brought down to the estimate which an additional number of persons had formed of its power of producing gratification, or, in other words, to their estimate of its value in use."

This passage is notable because Craig is on the continual

[1] In the writer's work on *The Shifting and Incidence of Taxation*, 2nd edition, 1899, pp. 138—142. It is here stated that Craig was the only early English writer "to devote a separate volume to questions of public finance." But see note above, p. 339.

[2] The full title is: *Remarks on some Fundamental Doctrines in Political Economy illustrated by a Brief Inquiry into the Economical State of Britain since the year* 1815. Edinburgh, 1821.

[3] *Remarks, etc.*, p. 10.

[4] *Ibid.*, p. 11.

verge of expressing the idea of marginal utility. He sees not only that value depends on utility, but that with every decrease in value or price there is a new (marginal) group of purchasers whose lower estimate of utility is now available for disposing of the increased supply. This is practically the basis of the modern doctrine of value.

Craig then proceeds to point out that if the value in exchange of some commodities is decreased by additional supply, the value of other commodities will be increased. For "those who formerly bought the article that is produced in excess, now getting what they want of it at a lower price, will have part of their revenue to expend in some other way; and the new demand thence arising for some other articles will raise their exchangeable value in proportion as that of the other is depressed."[1] It is erroneous to assume, therefore, that increased supply of commodities means a decrease in general values.

Combining these two points, and considering that "by the cheapness of a particular commodity, some of its uses are generally diminished; that by the fall of its price, the demand for some other articles, and consequently their prices, are advanced," Craig concludes that "value in use whether viewed in reference to any single commodity, or to the aggregate possession of a nation, must be very accurately measured by value in exchange."[2] This is not a happy statement. It manifestly confuses total and marginal utility; and, as it stands, seems to be erroneous. But if read in context with the whole explanation it will be seen that Craig is really getting nearer to the truth than most of his predecessors and contemporaries. In another passage he puts the statement in a less exceptionable form. He refers to Say's opinion that value in exchange is "the only kind of value to which the science of Political Economy has reference." "To this," says Craig, "I agree, but only because it is the *exponent* of value in use."[3]

Craig never accepted the fundamental tenets of the Ricardian economics. He is a strong opponent of the labour theory of value, which he declares to be "an ingenious, but unsound theory." In other points, also, Craig takes issue with the dominant school. He does not believe that wages are fixed by the standard of life,[4] nor does he accept the theory that a tax on wages necessarily raises wages.[5] He is equally opposed to the

[1] *Ibid.*, p. 12. [2] *Ibid.*, p. 14. [3] *Ibid.*, p. 14, note.
[4] *Ibid.*, p. 64. [5] *Ibid.*, p. 67.

doctrine that wages and profits must vary inversely to each other. After an analysis of the nature of capital and the relation of profits to wages, he concludes: "It is rather a startling circumstance attending this theory, that what it represents as the necessary effect produced by high wages upon profits in all branches of industry, is directly contrary to the experience in each particular trade. Though it would be going too far to assert that high wages and high profits are always co-existent: yet this proposition would be nearer the truth than that which has been announced by Mr. Ricardo."[1]

Finally, Craig characterises the Ricardian theory of rent as one "which, in so far as it is just, is equally a truism with that opinion which ascribes it to monopoly."[2] He takes exception, moreover, to the historical or dynamic part of the Ricardian theory. But above all, he calls attention to the analogy between returns from the land and from capital, or as he calls them, "rent and the profits of fixed capital." "So much do these sources of revenue resemble each other, that even in ordinary language the return for fixed capital, when the necessary circulating capital is supplied by a different person, is always denominated its rent."[3] Notwithstanding this analogy, however, Craig confesses that in some respects, land must be differentiated from fixed capital. He advances four reasons, of which, perhaps, the chief is the fact that "whereas machinery is gradually deteriorated by use, land is gradually improved."[4]

It is easy from our modern point of view to call attention to the obvious weakness in Craig's exposition, due to his failure to distinguish between interest and profits, although he does make an attempt to do so in another place.[5] But it must not be forgotten that in this respect he did not differ materially from the other writers of the day. It was quite sufficient for one man to have made the valuable suggestions which we find in his work. Craig is the first English economist to emphasise the connection between value and utility, to disclose the fallacy of the supposedly necessary opposition between profits and wages, and to dwell on the analogy between the revenue from land and from capital. All these points, although completely overlooked at the time, have been incorporated into the body of modern economic doctrine. Craig, no less than Torrens, deserves more attention than he has received.

[1] *Remarks, etc.*, p. 90. [2] *Ibid.*, p. 128. [3] *Ibid.*, p. 138.
[4] *Ibid.*, p. 142. [5] *Ibid.*, p. 75, note.

IV

The appearance of Malthus's *Principles of Political Economy* in 1820 seems to have given rise to an active discussion on some of the fundamental topics in dispute between Ricardo, Say, and Malthus. For the next few years we have a number of pamphlets and essays devoted to a consideration of special points of theory. Some of these are of such minor importance as to deserve only a passing reference. Of this nature, are two works published in 1821, one entitled *Observations on certain verbal Disputes on Political Economy, particularly relating to Value and to Demand and Supply*, which seeks to show some inconsistencies in Ricardo, Malthus, and Say; and the other: *An Inquiry into those Principles respecting the Nature of Demand and the Necessity of Consumption, lately advocated by Mr. Malthus, from which it is concluded that Taxation and the Maintenance of unproductive Consumers can be conducive to the Progress of Wealth*. Of somewhat more than ordinary interest is a work which appeared in the following year (1822), designed to enforce the same doctrine as that contained in the last pamphlet, the doctrine, namely, that gluts are possible and can be averted only by an increase of luxurious or unproductive consumption. The title of this is: *Considerations on the Accumulation of Capital and its Effects on Profits and on exchangeable Value*.

A few works of the same period have attractive titles but are somewhat disappointing in contents. The anonymous work of 1821, of almost three hundred pages, entitled *An Essay on the Political Economy of Nations, or a View of the Intercourse of Countries as influencing their Wealth*, is a not over acute book devoted primarily to problems of internal trade. The almost equally voluminous work by Thomas Smith, *An Attempt to define some of the First Principles of Political Economy*, published in the same year, is not what it seems to be. The author tells us, indeed, that "for several years past he has been endeavouring to draw the public attention towards an explanation of the mode of ascertaining value, and of the measures of it, very opposite to what has been assumed by Ricardo." A large part of the work is, in fact, devoted to a discussion of the relation between bank notes and prices—a discussion into which we shall not enter here.

Most of the essays of the time, however, were concerned with the discussion of the nature and measure of value, and of these the majority based themselves on the theory advocated by

Ricardo and McCulloch. The ball was set rolling in 1822 by the author of *An Essay on Political Economy*,[1] who signs himself in the preface, E. R., and who takes exception to the Ricardian labour theory of value. "Commodities are not sold because they are produced, but because they are demanded. Neither does their exchangeable value arise from the cost of producing them, but from the demand for them when produced. . . The quantity of labour only affects the value as it affects the supply."[2]

The author proceeds with his argument to show that high wages do not necessarily mean low profits, but may mean high prices; and he then applies this doctrine to the subject of taxation. It is worthy of note that he here gives a mathematical treatment of the incidence of taxation on land—with one exception the earliest attempt made in England to apply mathematics to economics.[3]

A more acute critic of Ricardo was Samuel Bailey, whose anonymous *Critical Dissertation on Value*[4] exerted considerable influence at the time. This was written as a reply to the familiar *Templars' Dialogues on Political Economy*, which appeared in the *London Magazine* for April, 1824, and in which the author, De Quincey, accepted and amplified the Ricardian

[1] The full title is: *An Essay on some General Principles of Political Economy on Taxes upon Raw Produce, and on Commutation of Tithes*. [By E. R.] London, 1822, 72 pp. The author states in his preface that this work was written before he had seen Malthus's *Principles of Political Economy*.

[2] *An Essay, etc.*, p. 8.

[3] *Ibid.*, pp. 54-66. This earlier attempt was the one contained in *An Essay on the Theory of Money*, London, 1771 (by Major-General Henry Lloyd) referred to by Jevons, *Political Economy*, 2nd edition, xlv–xlvi. The mathematics used in the work of 1771 is of extreme simplicity when compared to that of the essay of 1822, which has escaped the attention of both Jevons and Irving Fisher in their respective bibliographies. A more elaborate effort to apply mathematics to economics, which has also eluded the attention of all writers on the subject, is the interesting work by the American, Samuel Gale, entitled *An Essay on the Nature and Principles of Public Credit*. The original work, a substantial volume of two hundred and thirty-four pages, was published anonymously in London in 1784, although the preface dated at Charles-Town, South Carolina, in 1782, was signed by Gale. A second part, entitled *Essay II. on the Nature and Principles of Public Credit*, appeared in the same year (1784) with a preface dated St. Augustine, East Florida, 1783, and a third part, with a long title of about ten lines, appeared in 1786, not published, but "printed, to save the labour of copying the manuscript." The books by Gale are by all means the most comprehensive and detailed examples of early mathematico-economic literature, and will repay careful examination.

[4] The full title is: *A Critical Dissertation on the Nature, Measures, and Causes of Value, chiefly in reference to the Writings of Mr. Ricardo and his followers, By the Author of Essays on the Formation and Publication of Opinions, etc., etc.*, London, 1825. Bailey is not mentioned by Cannan, much less by Cossa, but a reference to him is found in Palgrave's *Dictionary*.

theory. Bailey does not mince matters. He speaks of the "confusion and obscurity which mark the works of some of the most celebrated writers," [1] and in particular he accuses Ricardo of "elliptical and disjointed reasoning," of "perplexity and confusion," of lack of "analytical subtility," and of "little consciousness of the nature of the operations in which he excelled, and little familiarity with the analysis of terms." [2]

Since value is essentially relative in nature, Bailey objects to Ricardo's attempt to discover a commodity of invariable value.[3] To Bailey, Ricardo's "contradiction involved in affirming the stationary or invariable value of an object amidst the variations of other things, is as direct and palpable" as to constitute a "strange and manifest error." [4] Malthus also is not free from the same mistake. Furthermore, Bailey characterises the alleged distinction between real and nominal value as "arbitrary and incapable of being turned to any use." [5] Above all, he objects to the labour theory of the cause and measure of value Value according to Bailey, although often spoken of as a quality of external objects, really implies a feeling or state of mind.[6] This state of mind is a result of many circumstances, among which, indeed, cost of production is to be included as an important, though not the sole factor. But even if we confine our attention to that class of commodities which is susceptible of increase and subject to the law of competition where the influence of cost of production is so great, it is not true that cost of production is resolvable into mere labour expended. In the first place, it overlooks the co-operation of capital, which cannot be explained away by calling capital "accumulated or hoarded labour."

"This is at best an awkward expression and can answer no good purpose. When we accumulate we add one thing to another, and it is essential to the process, that both should remain in existence. But labour, consisting in the mere exertion of muscular power, or in the equally evanescent motions of the brain, continually perishes in detail, and therefore admits of no accumulation." [7]

Furthermore, apart from this, labour cannot be considered as uniform. Bailey asks:

"What should we think of an assertion that coats are to each other in value as the quantities of cloth contained in them,

[1] *A Critical Dissertation*, p. vii.
[2] *Ibid.*, pp. xvi, xviii, xx.
[3] *Ibid.*, p. 10.
[4] *Ibid.*, p. 16; *cf.* p. 30.
[5] *Ibid.*, p. 38.
[6] *Ibid.*, p. 180.
[7] *Ibid.*, p. 220.

or that their comparative value depends exclusively on the quantities of cloth required to make them.[1]

Above all, the exclusive stress laid upon labour neglects entirely the function of time in economic life. Bailey tells us in almost the same language as Böhm-Bawerk: "We generally prefer a present pleasure or enjoyment to a distant one, not superior to it in other respects."[2] He enters into a consideration of the importance of time in its effects on capital. Time, like labour, is a consideration which may influence both buyers and sellers, and time cannot be resolved into labour.[3]

So that even in the case of continuous production under competitive conditions, value is not resolvable into labour. But there still remain two other great classes of commodities, those subject in part or in whole to the law of monopoly, and those subject to the law of diminishing returns.[4] This leads Bailey to a consideration of the law of rent, in the course of which he asserts the analogy between land rents and labour rents.[5]

"The extraordinary profit out of which rent arises is analogous to the extraordinary remuneration which an artizan of more than common dexterity obtains beyond the wages given to the workman of ordinary skill. In the one case the monopoly is bounded by the existence of inferior soils, in the other of inferior degrees of dexterity."

Here we have the first attempt to generalise the doctrine of rent, an attempt which has usually been associated in English, at all events, with Senior. Over a quarter of a century before Mangoldt and Schäffle, we thus find in Bailey this broadening of the rent concept. Furthermore, Bailey objects to the statement that "rent does not enter into price" as at the best vague and indefinite, and as "one that ought to be banished from the science."[6]

Finally, it must be noticed that Bailey is the first to put his finger on the real fallacy of the doctrine that wages and profits must vary inversely. This error consists in neglecting the fact that "the value of labour does not entirely depend on the proportion of the whole produce which is given to the labourers in exchange for their labour, but also on the productiveness of labour."[7] "The proposition, that when labour rises profits must fall, is true only when its rise is not owing to an increase in its productive powers."[8] . . . "If the productive power of labour

[1] *A Critical Dissertation*, p. 221. [2] *Ibid.*, p. 218. [3] *Ibid.*, p. 219.
[4] *Ibid.*, p. 185. [5] *Ibid.*, pp. 196, 197. [6] *Ibid.*, p. 198.
[7] *Ibid.*, p. 63. [8] *Ibid.*, p. 64.

be augmented, that is, if the same labour produce more commodities in the same time, labour may rise in value without a fall, nay, even with a rise of profits." [1]

This, it will be seen, virtually contains the whole of the modern theory of the economy of high wages.

It will be recognised from this short account how keen and fertile a thinker we have in Bailey. The opposition to the labour theory of value, the emphasis put on time as an element in value, the broadening of the rent concept, the criticism of the statement that rent does not enter into price, and the importance assigned to productivity in affecting value—all these constitute doctrines of importance in the recent phases of the science. That they should have been enunciated in 1825 and then seemingly forgotten is eloquent testimony to the power which is sometimes exerted by a few great names in silencing for a time all criticisms, however sound they may be.

V

The discussion of value was continued in a number of other works. A criticism of Bailey appeared in the *Westminster Review*, and was answered by him in 1826 in a pamphlet entitled *A Letter to a Political Economist*. This, however, does not add anything material to his former exposition. A few years later, the views of Bailey were in part repeated and developed by Cotterill in his *Examination of the Doctrines of Value*.[2] Cotterill makes short work of the labour theory of value, which he deems to have been completely refuted by Bailey, the author of the *Critical Dissertation*, of whose name he seems to be ignorant. He, nevertheless, proceeds to repeat the arguments, "as there are some Ricardians still remaining." [3] De Quincey's dialogues he considers "an ingenious logical legerdemain." [4] Like Bailey, he opposes to the labour theory the cost of production theory of value. He proceeds, however, to criticise Bailey on one point, and in this criticism, he marks a retrogression. Bailey thought that the cause of changes of value "may be correctly stated to arise principally from the cost of production and that cost of production may be either labour or capital, or both." [5] Cotterill contends that this definition of cost is defective, because it does not include profit.[6] It is the

[1] *Ibid.*, p. 66.

[2] The full title of this work is *An Examination of the Doctrines of Value as set forth by Adam Smith, Ricardo, M'Culloch, Mill, the author of "A Critical Dissertation" etc., Torrens, Malthus, Say, etc., being a Reply to those Distinguished Authors.* By Charles Foster Cotterill, London, 1831, 128 pp.

[3] *An Examination*, p. 8.

[4] *Ibid.*, p. 38.

[5] *Critical Dissertation*, p. 205.

[6] *An Examination*, p. 41.

failure of Cotterill, shared by almost all his contemporaries, to distinguish between interest and profits, which is responsible for this confusion of thought. So in criticising the contention of Torrens that profits constitute a surplus, not a cost, Cotterill says triumphantly: "If the profits of stock do not form a component part of cost, the wages of labour cannot, as the former is to the capitalist what the latter is to the labourer. The labourer gives his muscular strength and time, and receives reward under the term wages. The capitalist finds the implements of husbandry, the machines of manufactures, advances the wages of labour, and receives his reward under the term profit." [1]

One other point of interest may be mentioned. Senior's well-known attempt to broaden the rent concept is generally ascribed to the appearance of his *Political Economy* in the fifties. It is found in part, however, in his early lectures at Oxford. A passage from such a lecture, that "much of what properly belongs to profit and rent is generally included under wages," was quoted by Whately in his *Logic*, and led Cotterill to attempt to analyse the rent element in wages.[2] The variety in the genius of different men, thinks Cotterill, is much the same as varieties in the quality of land. The development of the idea, although not very successful, is suggestive, and when we remember the early date of the performance, significant. As we have just seen, however, Senior as well as Cotterill was preceded in this point by Bailey.

VI

In the same year as the work of Cotterill there was published a pamphlet of a very different type, and by a far more original thinker. All the discussions of values during the twenties had revolved around Ricardo, and none of the English writers could see their way to accept the doctrines of Craig and Say as to the dependence of value on utility. This was due chiefly to the failure to analyse clearly and successfully the notion of utility itself. Such an analysis, however, was undertaken in 1834 by W. F. Lloyd, who subscribes himself a student of Christ Church, and Professor of Political Economy at Oxford. The doctrine of final or marginal utility was at one time supposed to be the simultaneous discovery of Jevons in England, Menger in Austria, and Walras in Switzerland, in the opening years of the seventies. Later researches disclosed the fact that the same theory had been developed by Gossen in Germany in the fifties, and even

[1] *An Examination*, p. 46. [2] *Ibid.*, pp. 55–62.

before him by Dupuit in France in the forties. It will come as a surprise to many to be informed that the theory of marginal utility is, after all, an English discovery, and that what is a virtually identical doctrine was advanced by Professor Lloyd in 1834, a decade before Dupuit, two decades before Gossen, and considerably more than a generation before its rediscovery by Jevons, Menger, and Walras.

The title of this remarkable work is *A Lecture on the Notion of Value as distinguishable not only from Utility, but also from Value in Exchange. Delivered before the University of Oxford in Michaelmas Term*, 1833. According to the terms of the professorship held by Lloyd it was required that one lecture at least in each course be published annually. Both before and after 1833 Lloyd published other lectures, such as *Two Lectures on the Checks to Population*, delivered in 1832, and *Four Lectures on Poor Laws* delivered in 1834, each set appearing in the following year. Much as we might be tempted to dwell upon these also, we must content ourselves here with the lecture on value.

The course of 1833 began with a talk on utility in general, and Adam Smith's conception of utility in particular. This lecture is, unfortunately, not preserved, with the exception of a small extract devoted to the latter subject, and published as an appendix to the lecture on value.[1] The work with which we are dealing starts with a reference to this earlier lecture, and repeats the conclusion that Adam Smith evidently used the term value "in the sense of the real importance of an object to the person possessing it, and that he made this importance to depend on the difficulty of attainment." Lloyd now proceeds to a further examination of this view.

He considers first the possibility of a general glut of commodities. Without deciding this, Lloyd maintains that if we look at the matter from the point of view of the consumers, rather than that of the producers, a general glut is impossible, because this is "the same thing as a general superabundance of wealth, and would indicate the full satisfaction of human wants." There is, however, "in fact, no assignable limit to the desires of mankind, for where one inconvenience is removed, others present themselves, which before had never been thought of; and thus the passion for wealth expands with the gratification of existing wants, and, if not absolutely infinite, may, at least, be termed indefinite." [2]

This statement, however, would not be true "if the objects

[1] *A Lecture on the Notion of Value*, pp. 38–40.

[2] *Ibid.*, p. 7.

which can gratify human wants were limited in the number of their kind." "It is only the multiplication of the kinds of wants which renders the passion for wealth unlimited."[1] Savages, for instance, have few wants, but even these are not satisfied. If, however, "the catalogue of their wants could remain invariable," and if they were "fed to satiety and clothed to satiety," then "(all new wants being excluded by the hypothesis) the final sum of their wealth would be reached, and all further production would be useless."[2]

The same is true of more civilised society. "It is the infinite variety of wants, and of the kinds of commodities necessary to their gratification which alone renders the passion for wealth indefinite and insatiable. In the case of each *species infima*, as logicians call it, the desire is limited."

Lloyd now proceeds to apply these observations to the question of utility and value. He has pointed out that "an increase of quantity will at length exhaust, or satisfy to the utmost, the demand for any specific object of desire." What now, he asks, happens, with respect to value, at the time the demand or want is thus fully satisfied. "It will be found that, in the case of every commodity, its value vanishes at the very instant of satisfaction."[3] In the case of water, for instance, when we have more than we need, we have no reason "for being sparing in its use, for hoarding it, or for making a property of it or debarring others from the use of it." These considerations "are sure indications of value, and according to their intensity, so is the intensity of the value."[4] Lloyd concludes, then, that "in the reasons which exist for preserving and for retaining the possession of an object, its value essentially consists. It has with great propriety been defined to mean the esteem in which an object is held."[5]

Our author thinks, however, that some further details are necessary to make this definition complete and easily intelligible. This leads him to give an illustration in almost precisely the same words that were used almost forty years later by the reputed authors of the marginal utility theory. The passage is as follows:

"Let us suppose the case of a hungry man having one ounce, and only one ounce of food at his command. To him this ounce is obviously of very great importance. Suppose him now to have two ounces. These are still of great importance; but the importance of the second is not equal to that of the single ounce.

[1] *A Lecture on the Notion of Value*, p. 8. [2] *Ibid.*, p. 9.
[3] *Ibid.*, p. 10. [4] *Ibid.*, p. 10. [5] *Ibid.*, p. 11.

In other words he would not suffer so much from parting with one of his two ounces, retaining one for himself, as he would suffer, when he had only one ounce, by parting with that one, and so retaining none. The importance of a third ounce is still less than that of the second; so likewise of a fourth, until at length, in the continual increase of the number of ounces, we come to a point when 'through that infallible specific, eating,' the appetite is entirely, or nearly lost; with respect to a single ounce, it is a matter of indifference whether it is parted with or retained. Thus, while he is scantily supplied with food, he holds a given portion of it in great esteem, in other words, he sets a great value on it; when his supply is increased, his esteem for a given quantity is lessened, or, in other words, he sets a less value on it."[1]

Lloyd proceeds to explain the elasticity of wants by a metaphor which is not frequently found in modern treatises:

"The appetite for food may be compared to a spring, to a watch spring for example, which, when fully compressed or wound up, has the greatest tendency to expansion. By degrees as it becomes more and more actually expanded, its tendency to fly out is diminished until at length it ceases altogether."[2]

This is true of every commodity, but not only does the same commodity diminish in importance according to the increase of the supply, but the relative importance assigned to different commodities varies:

"Each different kind of human wants may, like that of food, be compared to a spring; and, in this comparison, the different wants, according to their several differences, will be represented by springs of different degrees of strength. For example, the wants which food can satisfy will be represented by a spring of great power. So also these, to supply which water is required. For representing the wants of clothing and fuel, which are obstacles not as indispensably necessary to human existence, springs of an inferior degree of power may suffice. Passing on to the artificial wants, we may represent them according to their intensities, by lesser springs of various degrees of strength."[3]

There are two ways, thinks Lloyd, in which the same springs may be compared. We may compare them absolutely, as when we say that the main spring of a watch is stronger than the hair spring; or we may compare their expansive forces under some modification of their actual conditions, as when "a watch is nearly run down, we may say that the main spring has scarcely

[1] *Ibid.*, p. 12. [2] *Ibid.*, p. 12. [3] *Ibid.*, p. 13.

B B 2

more strength, that is, in its actual tendency to expand itself, than the hair spring has, when it is most contracted."

Now, utility in the ordinary acceptation of the term is measured in the first way. "We estimate the utilities of objects by the importance of the wants which they are capable of supplying, considered absolutely. . . . Water is no more useful in a ship at sea where it is scarce, than on land where it is plentiful." Here we practically state that the main spring of a watch is stronger than the hair spring. But it is not in this sense that we estimate wants when we speak of value. "The wants, on which value depends, are analogous to the tendencies of the springs, which are already in part extended, to extend themselves further. They vary with every variation in the quantity of commodities, and in the consequent variation of the degree in which the absolute want is satisfied."[1] In this sense, "the want of the most useful may be less than that of the least useful articles. Water is more wanted by a man almost dying with thirst than by another who has quenched his thirst, and desires only to wash himself. It is on want, thus estimated, that value depends."[2]

When people speak of the distinction between utility and value, Lloyd tells us that there is always a peculiar danger of confusion, and it is in his discussion of this point that he reaches the conception of marginal utility. "If, to a man who has already half a dozen coats, you should offer to give another, he might probably reply that he would have no use for it. Here, however, he would speak, not of the abstract utility of the coat, but of its special utility to him under the circumstances of his want of coats being already so far supplied. This, though not quite the same thing as value, approaches very near to it. The coat would be of no use to him; therefore, were he to have it, it would not be valuable in his estimation." "But this is very different from the utility of the coat in the general sense of utility, and ought not to be confounded with it."[3] Lloyd emphasises the fact that when we speak of utility being different from value, we use utility in the abstract sense, not in the special sense. And this special sense is truly a marginal sense, for, says Lloyd, "in its ultimate sense, value undoubtedly signifies a feeling of the mind which shows itself always at the margin of separation between satisfied and unsatisfied wants."[4]

It would be difficult to put in clearer or happier language

[1] *A Lecture on the Notion of Value*, p. 15.
[2] *Ibid.*, p. 16.
[3] *Ibid.*, p. 18.
[4] *Ibid.*, p. 16.

the substance of the modern theory of the relation between value and utility. It is true that we do not find the terminology of the distinction between total utility and final utility; but we find the distinction itself. Total utility is called by Lloyd "abstract utility"; while for the terminal utility of Jevons, or the marginal utility of Menger, Lloyd uses almost the very term suggested by Professor Clark. Professor Clark prefers the term "specific utility"; Lloyd half a century before him used "special utility" to designate precisely the same idea.

It must be confessed, indeed, that Lloyd often contrasts value with utility, as on the title-page and in various other parts of his book. But it is evident that he then always has reference to utility in his sense of "abstract utility." He realised perfectly the veritable relation of value to wants, and the analogy between value and "special utility." Thus to all intents and purposes he discovered the doctrine of marginal utility, even though he did not draw from his discovery all the conclusions which were reserved for economists of a later date.

One conclusion, however, he did draw, namely that the conception of value is something independent of, and anterior to, exchange. In the explanation that he has hitherto given of the nature of value, says Lloyd, there has been no need for a single word about exchanges. Value consists in the real importance of an object to the individual. "Objects may be of real importance to the possessor, as much in the case of an isolated individual, such as Robinson Crusoe, as in the case of a society, such as exists in England."[1] Lloyd proceeds to give such instances, and then adds that a few examples of value, in which the idea of exchange is not concerned, can even be taken from actual life to-day. He here comes near to making what is virtually a distinction between individual and social value.

"We can well conceive an article made expressly for the use of an individual, and to him actually both useful and valuable, when to every other human being it would be absolutely useless and therefore altogether destitute of value in exchange." Such extreme cases he confesses are rare, but it is frequent to find cases in which a great part, though not the whole of the value, is lost in the exchange.[2] So *e.g.*, in the case of a coat made to order, or a seal marked with the crest and initials of the owner. "The same operation which renders the commodity of more value in the estimation of its owner is calculated to render it less valuable in the estimation of all other persons."[3] Thus there

[1] *Ibid.*, p. 20. [2] *Ibid.*, p. 27. [3] *Ibid.*, p. 28.

may be a difference between the individual and the social value, the value to a particular individual and the value to the whole group, which we call value in exchange.

Lloyd calls the distinction one between absolute and comparative or exchangeable value. This is not a happy phrase, for, as it has frequently been pointed out of late, the very conception of value, or the estimate of marginal utility even to the individual, involves a comparison between wants, that is, presupposes the existence of at least two commodities useful to the same person. But in the sense in which value was ordinarily conceived to be relative, *i.e.* dependent on the existence of exchange between different individuals, Lloyd was perfectly correct in denying the relative or comparative nature of value. What he really meant was the distinction between generic and exchange value, or between individual and social value. The distinction itself is sound. Lloyd moreover informs us that in this sense of value—value independent of exchange—the same things are more valuable to a poor man than to a rich one.[1]

Having thus settled to his satisfaction that value, in the sense explained, may be absolute, Lloyd proceeds to discuss whether there can be such a thing as intrinsic value. This he denies:

"The term value does not express a quality inherent in a commodity. It expresses a feeling of the mind, and is variable with the variations of the external circumstances which can influence that feeling, without any variation of the intrinsic qualities of the commodity which is the object of it."[2]

Not only can value not be intrinsic, but the utility of an object is not intrinsic any more than value. Utility, like value, says Lloyd, is predicted of an object with reference to the wants of mankind. Ice is useful in summer, useless in winter. Still the intrinsic qualities of ice are at all times and in all places the same.

Lloyd then proceeds to mention some further problems which flow from these distinctions, but relegates their discussion to future lectures. These other lectures have, so far as we know, not been preserved, or at all events, they have not been published. Yet this single lecture, which seems to have passed entirely unnoticed even by his contemporaries, is sufficient to vindicate for its author the proud position of having been the first

[1] *A Lecture on the Notion of Value*, p. 28. [2] *Ibid.*, p. 31.

thinker in any country to advance what is known to-day as the marginal theory of value, and to explain the dependence of value on marginal utility. With Lloyd and Jevons before us we should no longer speak of the Austrian theory of value. England must henceforth be considered the home, not only of the cost theory, but also of the marginal utility theory of value.

EDWIN R. A. SELIGMAN

(To be continued.)

ON SOME NEGLECTED BRITISH ECONOMISTS—II

V

In the preceding article[1] attention has been directed to the group of writers contemporary with, and immediately subsequent to, Ricardo. Some of these, like Torrens, we have found to be the originators of doctrines usually ascribed to Ricardo, while others like Craig accepted, but only with considerable reservations, the chief Ricardian doctrines. In the controversy that arose during the early twenties on the subject of value we found that important criticisms of the Ricardian theory were advanced by Bailey and Cotterill, and that the foundation stones for an entirely different theory were laid by Lloyd, the originator of the marginal utility doctrine of value.

We come now to another group of writers who flourished during the twenties and thirties, and who, while not neglecting the theory of value, endeavoured to cover the whole field of theory and practice of economics as it was then understood. Most of these were more or less bitter opponents, or at least severe critics, of Ricardo, and some of them made notable contributions to the science—none the less notable because they were passed over at the time, and have for the most part remained unnoticed up to the present.

Beginning with the authors of somewhat less significance in this list, let us turn our attention for a moment to John Rooke, who published in 1824 *An Inquiry into the Principles of National Wealth, Illustrated by the Political Economy of the British Empire*. This volume of almost five hundred pages differs from the ordinary manuals of economics chiefly in the fact that it devotes much space to the historical and practical aspects of the various problems with which it deals. Much of the work is prolix and complicated, but there are a few points of theory which deserve to be mentioned.

In the first place, Rooke sets forth the theory of rent, and

[1] Economic Journal, September, 1903, vol. xiii. p. 335.

claims that he was the first in the field to advance the correct doctrine. In a subsequent tract devoted entirely to the substantiation of this claim, Rooke outlines the details of his discovery.[1]

He tells us that the political events of 1811 and 1812 led him to study closely the economic basis of English prosperity, and to publish in *The Farmers' Journal* in 1814 and 1815 upwards of fifty essays, forming the substance of his *Inquiry*, which appeared a decade later. In his first essay, published in July, 1814, he discusses the cause of the rise in the price of corn. In the fourth essay, written in November, 1814, and published in February, 1815, he maintains the doctrine that "the cost of producing corn on the worst soils is the regulator of natural price," and that "the rent of land is the clear surplus produce which remains after the expenses that conduce to production and the ordinary profits of capital are deducted." In a fifth essay he contends that the price of agricultural labour is a sufficient test of the value of money.

The claim of Rooke seems to be well founded so far as the essays of Malthus and West are concerned. In fact, the essay of Rooke antedates that of Torrens.[2] There seems, in fact, to be little doubt that the doctrine of rent was developed practically simultaneously by Malthus, West, Torrens and Rooke in 1814; but so far as the priority of actual publication is concerned, the above list must be reversed, and in the interests of historical accuracy, Rooke and Torrens must hereafter be accorded the position which they deserve.[3]

Apart from the emphasis laid on the doctrine of rent, the chief claim of Rooke to recognition by modern writers is the fact that he is the first to lay down the rule of marginal cost as a universal principle. He puts the theory in the following words:—

"It is a general rule in the production of every marketable article that the last additional portion, added to the whole supply, will do no more than repay the cost of labour and the remuneration of the capital employed in its production. In case any commodity allows more than this, the supply will naturally

Claim to the original Publication of certain new Principles in Political Economy addressed in a Letter to E. D. Davenport, Esq. By John Rooke, author of *An Inquiry into the Principles of National Wealth.* London, 1825.

[2] See ECONOMIC JOURNAL, vol. xiii. p. 342.

[3] This does not imply any derogation from the reputation of Ricardo. The real ather of a doctrine is, after all, he who sees the important implications of a theory, who works them out in detail, and who makes them fit into his whole system of thought.

increase; and if the market value does not, upon an average, allow these two component parts of cost, the supply will diminish.

"It is this universal and active principle, diffusing and extending itself in every direction, which regulates the relations and proportions of political economy. Necessity marks out the natural bounds of value, and consumption and production are universally accommodating themselves to this first law, constantly regulated by the last additional portion of production, in reference to the demand. . . . The actual demands of the market determine the supply, and the supply is regulated by the lowest cost at which it can be brought to market." [1]

Rooke confesses that this view differs from the principles enunciated by Malthus and Ricardo, but thinks that "these able writers have not paid sufficient attention to the natural predicaments in which man is placed." [2] He shows his independence of Ricardo in other respects also, especially in his criticism of the historical portion of the theory of rent,[3] and in his objection to the neglect by Ricardo of temporary and incidental as opposed to permanent and abstract causes in the settlement of the money problem.[4] Although, like all his contemporaries, he does not make the correct distinction between profits and interest, he comes nearer to it than most of the other writers, and points out that it is a mistake to speak of a general rate of profits as a return for capital. Since risk and expenses of repair vary considerably in particular instances, "the rate of profits is greater or less in proportion to risk and repair." He adds: "It is not then in the actual employment of capital or hoarded labour that we are to look for a general rate of profits; but in the rate of income obtained for the use of it, or the annual interest of money loans." [5]

The fundamental proposition, upon which Rooke's entire volume is based, is that the formation of capital is continually accumulating new stores of wealth, and thereby cheapening the means of living. Although population tends to increase, "capital is constantly setting free the means of subsistence faster than population has advanced." [6] Hence all opposition to the introduction of new machinery is misplaced, even though it frequently happens that the immediate results are distress to the workmen: [7] "It would certainly betray a want of proper feeling

[1] *An Inquiry, etc.*, p. 26.
[2] *Ibid.*, p. 27.
[3] *Ibid.*, pp. 65 and 79.
[4] *Ibid.*, p. 300.
[5] *Ibid.*, p. 38.
[6] *Ibid.*, p. 41.
[7] *Ibid.*, p. 115.

if he did not commiserate the misfortunes of a body of men so numerous as the hand-weavers of plain cotton goods originally were."[1] Rooke tells us that we must look to ultimate, not immediate, results, and adds: "To suppose that man can be injured by forcing the elements into his service betrays a want of those reasoning faculties which enable us to overcome the imposing obstacles in our way."[2]

As against the optimistic conclusions of Rooke and the dominant school of economists there arose during the twenties and the thirties a school of critics known as the Ricardian socialists. These writers have been made familiar to us by Foxwell,[3] and therefore need no detailed mention here. There is, however, one exception, who seems to have escaped the notice of Foxwell—and that one, curiously enough, the earliest advocate of the theory of surplus value subsequently adopted by Marx. Percy Ravenstone wrote in 1821 a volume of almost five hundred pages, entitled, *A Few Doubts as to the Correctness of some Opinions generally entertained on the Subjects of Population and Political Economy*. We shall not stop to dwell on his criticism of Malthus, which does not materially differ from the other works of the kind. In a separate chapter, however, he discusses the rights of property, and finds herein the source of most of the evils which Malthus ascribed to the pressure of population. Ravenstone, indeed, is not a communist, for common property, he thinks, implies tyranny, and would lead to the worst possible form of government. In fact, it could exist only "amongst a small number of crazy fanatics."[4] Nor is private property in itself wrong. The natural right to private property is "the right to the work of one's own hands." "But this right is very different from that artificial right by which a man is enabled to appropriate to himself the ownership of lands which he does not occupy, and on which he does not exercise any industry."[5] "On this pretension of the landowner are built the pretensions of the market-manufacturer, of the tradesman, of the capitalist. All are founded on the same principle."[6] They all claim a share in the earnings of the real producer, and "the labour of the industrious is made subservient to the maintenance of the idle. The labourer must purchase the permission to be useful." The rights of property, says Ravenstone, while undesirable, are far

[1] *An Inquiry, etc.*, p. 117. [2] *Ibid.*, p. 115.

[3] In his Introduction to Menger's *The Right to the Whole Produce of Labour.*

[4] *A Few Doubts, etc.*, p. 197. [5] *Ibid.*, p. 199.

[6] *Ibid.*, p. 200.

less sacred than the rights of industry,[1] for the latter are independent of society, derive from a higher source, and owe their origin to nature itself, being as sacred as our existence. Unfortunately, thinks Ravenstone, in modern society, where property alone confers power, its rights are considered more sacred than those of industry, and the interests of the poor are sacrificed to those of the rich.[2] "Some doubt of the correctness of the modern doctrines of political economy, of the advantages arising from capital, may be suggested by the consideration that in all countries where there is the most wealth, there is the most misery."[3]

This general proposition leads Ravenstone to analyse more carefully rent and profit, which he considers equally indefensible in their modern form.[4] Rent he defines as the idle man's share of the industrious man's earnings. He goes on to explain, however, that it is "the excess of rents, not their existence, which overthrows society."[5] Taxes, again, as they are levied in England, fall chiefly upon the labourer.[6] But the principal enemy of the labourer at present is the private ownership of capital. Profit, like rent, capital, like property in land, "equally arise from the *surplus produce* of the cultivators' labour. The only difference is that rent shares directly, profit indirectly, in the earnings of the productive labourer."[7] It is worthy of remark that while Ravenstone is the first predecessor of Marx to advance the surplus value theory, Marx differs from Ravenstone in that he considers profit to be the direct, and rent the derivative, form of exploitation.

As our concern, however, is here with the economists proper, rather than with their Socialist critics, we shall not dwell longer on the interesting development of the fundamental idea of Ravenstone. Enough has been said to show that in him we have really the earliest of that group of writers who, during the twenties, sought to undermine the very basis of the edifice so carefully erected by the economists.

VI

A few years later than Ravenstone, and doubtless inspired by other Socialist[8] publications, one of which is quoted at great

[1] *A Few Doubts, etc.*, p. 204.
[2] *Ibid.*, p. 206.
[3] *Ibid.*, p. 207.
[4] *Ibid.*, p. 225.
[5] *Ibid.*, p. 229.
[6] *Ibid.*, p. 257.
[7] *Ibid.*, p. 311.
[8] Such publications were at this time called "labour publications." The word Socialist was used for the first time in 1831 in the *Poor Man's Guardian* in a letter

length, Samuel Read wrote *An Inquiry into the Natural Grounds of Right to Vendible Property or Wealth*.[1] This differed in its point of view from the current school of political economy. Read had started out during the currency discussion with several tracts on money and banking, and it was in connection with one of these that he accused McCulloch of plagiarism in a pamphlet of considerable vehemence.[2]

A year or two later he published the reply to Malthus in a tract[3] which advances for the first time the doctrine, anticipating the modern biological theory, that powers of increase in population are themselves weakened and diminished by the force of luxury and refinement. In his larger work, Read claims that he differs from his predecessors in that he discusses not only the question, "what is, or what has been," but also "what should be."[4] Political economy heretofore has been declared to be the science which treats of the production and distribution of wealth; Read wishes to treat of it "as an investigation concerning the right to wealth."[5] These rights, moreover, are not legal rights, for in the existing state of society "a *legal right* is not infrequently a natural and moral *wrong*."[6] It is in accordance with this conception that Read entitles his work an *Inquiry into the Natural Grounds of Right to Vendible Property*. In reading these and similar passages we are forcibly reminded of the

to the editor by an advocate of Owen's social schemes. The name became common in England during the thirties. It is therefore, not, as is currently, but mistakenly, stated, a French term in its origin.

[1] Edinburgh, 1829, 328 pp.

[2] This was entitled *Exposure of certain Plagiarisms of J. R. McCulloch, Esq., Author of two Essays on Reduction of the Interest of the National Debt, committed in the last published of these Essays, the Scotsman Newspaper and Edinburgh Review*. By Samuel Read, author of a *Tract on Money and the Bank Restriction Laws*. *In recto decus*. Edinburgh, 1819. Read pointed out that between McCulloch's two *Essays on the National Debt* which appeared in March and November respectively of 1816, his tract on money had been published in May, and he claimed that the change of front in McCulloch's second essay was due to an unacknowledged appropriation of his own suggestions. These suggestions were first, that in readjusting the currency the rule of justice is that debts should be considered discharged by the offer of the exact weight of bullion represented by the nominal sum of currency stipulated at the time the contract was made (p. 4); and secondly, that the interest on the debt contracted subsequently to the depreciation of the paper money should be so reduced that the creditors would receive precisely the amount of actual bullion which they lent (p. 19). Read also accused McCulloch of borrowing without acknowledgment passages from other authors, including Hume (p. 31).

[3] *General Statement of an Argument on the Subject of Population in answer to Mr. Malthus's Theory*. By Samuel Read. London, 1821. See esp. pp. 13 and 32.

[4] *An Inquiry, etc.*, p. xxvii.

[5] *Ibid.*, p. ix.

[6] *Ibid.*, p. xxiv.

views of Sismondi, as well as of the modern ethical school of economists.

In the body of his work where he attempts primarily to explain "what is," Read shows himself a great admirer of Adam Smith as against the "dogmas and paradoxes"[1] of Ricardo and the "Ricardo school."[2] His excellent definition of wealth deserves to be quoted: "Those external, material objects .... useful to mankind, which it costs some exertion of human labour . . . to produce or acquire . . . and which . . . can be transferred from one to another."[3] In a succession of paragraphs he emphasises, quite in the spirit of the most approved modern treatises, but partly in opposition to most of the text-books of his day, the fact that wealth does not include free, internal, useless, or unappropriable goods.[4] He follows Smith in making the distinction between productive and unproductive labour, but proceeds to explain it away, as in his acceptance of Scott's contention that an author may be a productive labourer.[5] He gives a definition of capital which is of interest in view of the recent theories of Fisher and Cannan, saying that "capital consists of accumulated wealth, which is or may be applied to assist in the work of production, which is nearly equivalent to saying that it consists of all wealth whatever."[6] He adds in a note that "there is no real use in the distinction which has been attempted . . between stock or wealth generally or capital."

Read's opposition to Ricardo is shown in many ways. He criticises unreservedly the statement that labour is the sole cause of wealth. He considers this "a most mischievous and fundamental error,"[7] mischievous largely because of the conclusions that have been drawn from the principle by the "labour writers." Read is the first thinker clearly to perceive that through this theory of value the Ricardian economics leads logically to the Ricardian socialism. Marx, like his predecessors in England, based himself frankly on Ricardo, and drew from Ricardo's labour theory of value a seemingly logical conclusion of social politics, which is at the very antipodes of that of the Ricardian economists.

Read confesses that in his main point of theory he has been anticipated by Bailey, the author of the *Critical Dissertation*;[8] but Bailey, as will be remembered, had paid no attention to the application of the theory made by the Socialists. Wealth is not the result of accumulated labour, says Read, but of labour and

[1] *Ibid.*, p. vi. [2] *Ibid.*, p. 241. [3] *Ibid.*, p. 1.
[4] *Ibid.*, pp. 2—3, 7—9. [5] *Ibid.*, p. 41. [6] *Ibid.*, p. 65.
[7] *Ibid.*, p. xxix. [8] *Cf.* above, p. 353.

capital. Capital is incorrectly described as accumulated labour, for labour cannot be accumulated. Moreover, in every period of society, except in the very origin, all accumulations of wealth have been made with the existence of previous accumulations of capital—accumulations not of labour, nor even of the effects of labour.[1] "If it should be said that capital could not do what is done without the assistance of labour, neither, I reply, could labour do what is done without the assistance of capital."[2] Read confesses, indeed, in another place, that whereas capital can produce *nothing* without labour, labour can produce *something* without capital; but he makes his meaning clear by adding that when we come to ask how much either labour or capital can produce unaided we see at once the futility of the distinction.[3] For it is obvious that in the present state of society far more is due to the productive force of capital than to the productive force of labour. Hence such writers as the author (Bray) of *Labour Defended against the Claims of Capital*, whom Read quotes copiously,[4] are wide of the mark in claiming that since labour, according to the Ricardian theory, is the sole cause of value, the whole produce of labour, that is, all accumulated wealth, belongs to the labourer, and that rent and profits are robbery. It is McCulloch, even more than Ricardo, who, according to Read, is responsible for these perverted views on the part of the Socialists or "Labour Theorists."

While Read criticises the contentions of the Socialists, however, and emphasises the need and efficacy of capital, he is by no means unaware of the exaggeration in the extreme claims of their capitalist opponents. "The labourers have been flattered and persuaded that they produce all, whilst the capitalists on the other hand have combined and established laws of preference and favour which really tread upon the rights of the labourers."[5] "On the contrary," says Read, "while the labourers must be made to understand that they *do not* produce all, whenever they seek the assistance of capital; the capitalists lending that assistance must be equally instructed that . . . no individual can have a right to exclude or interdict others from coming forward or to attempt to enhance their gains by means which are unjust or injurious to their neighbours."[6]

[1] *Ibid.*, pp. 14—15. [2] *Ibid.*, p. 84. [3] *Ibid.*, pp. 129—130.

[4] *Ibid.*, chap. ix., sec. iii., pp. 118—140 *et al.* For Bray's tract see Foxwell's introduction to Menger's *Right to the Whole Produce of Labour.* Foxwell does not refer to Read's criticism.

[5] *An Enquiry*, p. xxix. [6] *Ibid.*, p. xxxiv.

Accordingly, while private property in land is defensible, because of the application of capital to land, there is a certain degree of truth in the contention that there is a common right to the "bare uncultivated earth, unappropriated and unimproved by labour."[1] Read concludes from this that a moderate part of the annual produce of the land should be paid to the Government in the shape of a land tax or quit rent. Such a fund, which should not amount to more than 12 per cent. of the rent would, in Read's opinion, obviate the necessity of any other taxes except in extraordinary emergencies.[2] Another scheme of social amelioration which is suggested by Read is the assertion of a full legal provision for the support of the poor, which should include weekly payments not only to the aged and infirm, but also to the unemployed.[3] "The right of the poor to support, and the right of the rich to engross and accumulate, are correlative and reciprocal privileges, the former being the condition on which the latter is enjoyed."[4]

Read's general opposition to Ricardo is seen in a number of other points. He accepts Adam Smith's theory of rent in preference to that of Ricardo. He characterises as "futile and absurd"[5] the statement of Ricardo that rent is paid for the "original and indestructible powers of the soil," and he points out how, in a later edition, Ricardo has "studied himself fairly out of" this theory.[6] He is unsparing in his criticism of Ricardo for the neglect of the element of situation, rather than of fertility in the rent problem;[7] and he maintains that because rent is the consequence, not the cause, of high price, it by no means follows that rent is not a component part of price. "Rent actually does form a constituent part of the price of commodities."[8] The Ricardian theory of natural wages is equally erroneous, says Read, because Ricardo fails to observe the possibility of a continual rise in the standard of life. "Not only is it *natural* that mankind should increase their numbers and quite possible for them to do so indefinitely, and to increase their wealth and the price of their labour at the same time, but . . . such a progress is the *natural and necessary course of things*, under any tolerable system of liberty or security or good government."[9] "The natural price of labour is, therefore, not a fixed quantity, as Ricardo thought, but a constantly increasing quan-

[1] *Ibid.*, p. 107. [2] *Ibid.*, p. 111. [3] *Ibid.*, pp. 361, 365.
[4] *Ibid.*, p. 375. [5] *Ibid.*, p. 293. [6] *Ibid.*, p. 296.
[7] *Ibid.*, pp. 298–301. [8] *Ibid.*, p. 213. [9] *Ibid.*, p. 252.

tity."[1] This result, in Read's judgment, is very largely due to the increasing productivity of capital. Finally, the effort of Ricardo to show that profits and wages vary inversely to each other is, according to Read, equally unfortunate.[2]

Not the least striking part of Read's constructive work is his attempt to identify profits with interest. He does not, of course, deny the existence of "business gains," but he thinks that all such gain as exceeds the ordinary rate of interest "is either wages—that is, remuneration or reward for labour or industry or ingenuity or skill in the use and application of that capital—or otherwise it is the result of fortune or accident—that is, of secret and unknown causes."[3] Such causes "sometimes occasion greater or less gain in trade, or no gain at all, and sometimes a loss," and ought to be properly considered as a *compensation for risk*. This compensation for risk must not be confounded with the wages of labour or with the "profit ordinarily derivable from capital." Since, therefore, such accidental gain is regulated by no certain principle, it is "without the pale of political science, which is conversant alone with known and determinate causes, rejecting others with disdain."

This passage is interesting. Read indeed uses the word profit as identical with interest for the reason given above, although he at once recognises the objection to this nomenclature, and suggests as a possible substitute the term "rent of capital."[4] But the real importance of the passage lies in the fact that in his description of gain "which lies without the pale of science," we have the origin, in England at all events, both of the modern "risk theory" and the modern "*entrepreneur* theory" of profit. Had Read not been so reluctant to transcend the "pale of science," the analysis at which he hints would doubtless have been developed with his customary acumen and common sense.

In his last chapter Read discusses the subject of public finance. His theory of incidence of taxation is opposed to both the Physiocrats and the Ricardians. "The old French economists who still have a few followers, maintain, that all taxes fall wholly upon the land, or upon rent, denying that either profits or wages afford any; the Ricardo economists again contend that taxes fall entirely upon rent and profit, denying in like manner that wages afford any." Read asserts that both

[1] *Ibid.*, p. 253.
[2] *Ibid.*, p. 249.
[3] *Ibid.*, p. 263.
[4] *Ibid.*, p. 264, note.

these opinions are erroneous, and that the theory set forth by Smith and Hume alone is sound—the theory "that all three distinct sorts of revenue afford taxes."[1] Taxes on wages are shifted only when wages are at the real minimum of subsistence, a condition which is not found in general.[2] Being such an admirer of Hume, it is not strange, perhaps, that Read should accept Hume's theory that taxes when "moderate and laid on judiciously and slowly" may, at first, by exciting a "spirit of industry where it was before wanting, be for a time rather useful and advantageous."[3] Like Hume, however, he thinks that taxation often passes this limit and proves a sensible and even grievous burden on the mass of the people.

It is evident from this review that Read merits further study. Although in the main a conservative and almost an orthodox economist, notwithstanding his objections to the Malthusian theory, Read deserves recognition in four particulars: he is an acute critic of some of the weak points in the classical theory of distribution; he is the first economist to show the connection between Ricardian economics and Ricardian socialism; he is in part the originator of the risk theory of profits, and he is above all the first English economist who, while unreservedly recognising the function of capital, emphasises the fact that the capitalist has duties as well as rights, and that economics is not only a science of what is, but also a science of what ought to be.

VII

Of considerably less originality than Read, but, nevertheless, worthy of mention, is Sir George Ramsay, who published in 1836 *An Essay on the Distribution of Wealth.*[4]

Ramsay's chief claim to attention is to be found in the fact that he attempted, but with meagre results, to introduce into England conceptions which had become familiar to the French economists. He adopts from Destutt de Tracy the consideration that production means either change of form or change of place,[5] although he points out later that there is a third fundamental change, namely, change of time. It is, accordingly, to Ramsay that we must ascribe the first statement in English of the division into form, place, and time value, a distinction which modern

[1] *Ibid.*, pp. 376—7. [2] *Ibid.*, p. 381. [3] *Ibid.*, p. 385.

[4] This was published at Edinburgh as a volume of 506 pages. Ramsay wrote a number of other works, but exclusively on political and philosophical topics.

[5] *An Essay*, &c., p. 17.

writers usually credit to Knies. Ramsay also borrows from the French writers, and especially from Storch, the Russian economist, the conception of the *entrepreneur* as separate from the capitalist. He distinguishes carefully between that part of the gross profits of capital which takes the form of interest or net profit paid for the use of capital, and the remainder which constitutes the "profits of enterprise." Not venturing to use the term *entrepreneurs*, Ramsay suggests the word masters. He is at first inclined to speak of this share in distribution as "Profits of the Master,"[1] but finally decides upon the term profits of enterprize, or, as he spells it elsewhere, enterprise.[2] The masters, he thinks, must not be confused with the capitalists, although when we speak of gross profits, we mean the return of the master-capitalists.[3] The net profits of capital or interest is a compensation for the use of capital while the masters' return or profits of enterprise is the compensation for the trouble and risk incurred, and the skill exerted in the business of direction and superintendence.[4] Ramsay devotes almost a quarter of his entire work to the analysis of these two constituent elements of profit. The return to capital proper, or interest, is not regulated, as the current theory states, by the competition of capitals, but is ultimately fixed by the "productiveness of industry," and not by the productivity of industry in general, but chiefly by the return to those branches of industry employed in producing the necessaries of the labourer and the various elements of fixed capital.[5] "The only competition which can affect the general rate of gross profit is that between master-capitalists and labourers."

The profits of enterprise are made up of three parts—the salary of the master, insurance for risk, and surplus gains.[6] The surplus gains, thinks Ramsay, increase in a greater proportion than the capital employed.[7] This leads him to a consideration of the subject of "concentration of capital." His analysis, quite in the French style, brings him to the conclusion that combination means economy of management and a more rapid increase of natural wealth.[8] But this does not exhaust the question of its desirability, "for we must always bear in mind that the manner in which riches are divided and distributed is a matter of no less consequence than their absolute quantity."[9] It is chiefly because some economists have devoted too exclusive an attention to production, rather than to the question of distribution, thinks

[1] *Ibid.*, p. 193. [2] *Ibid.*, p. 208. [3] *Ibid.*, p. 79.
[4] *Ibid.*, p. 190. [5] *Ibid.*, p. 206; *cf.*, p. 154. [6] *Ibid.*, p. 226.
[7] *Ibid.*, p. 229. [8] *Ibid.*, p. 240. [9] *Ibid.*, p. 243.

Ramsay, that the science of wealth is now beginning to be "covered with unmerited obloquy." [1]

In other points Ramsay is more influenced by the English than by the French writers. He refuses to accept Say's conception of immaterial wealth, and adopts unreservedly Smith's distinction between productive and unproductive labour.[2] In many cases, however, he tempers his approval of the English doctrines with some reservations which seem to show the influence of Read. He follows Ricardo and Malthus in his treatment of the problem of wages and population, but he is careful to emphasise the effect of the standard of life on wages, and he questions the existence of a "natural or necessary price of labour" in the sense of a minimum of subsistence.[3] He shows a commendable sympathy with the factory laws, although he bases his defence on the theory that since the ratio between capital and population remains the same, labourers who work short hours will not receive any less than those who work long hours.[4] He accepts the theory that profits vary inversely as wages, but claims that this is not the whole truth.[5] For since, as has been pointed out above, profit varies directly as the productivity of labour and capital, if productivity increases both profit and wages may be high. High profits due to increased productivity are a benefit to the community; high profits resting on low wages are a menace. For, "the object of political economy being to show, not only how the greatest amount of wealth may be obtained, but also how it may be distributed most advantageously among the different classes of society, that must be allowed to be a strange system which would give as little as possible to by far the most numerous body of all, the labourers."[6] Ricardo's whole theory he deems incomplete, because Ricardo overlooked the fact that "the ultimate cause of the variation in money wages, and hence in profits, is a change in the productiveness of industry." [7]

In two other points Ramsay foreshadows recent discussions. He accepts the classical theory of rent, but maintains that the rent paid on the worst land devoted to a particular use virtually enters into the price of some other use, or the produce of some other use, of the land. "Although rent unquestionably owes its origin to a high price of corn, or whatever may be the principal vegetable food of the people, yet when once created, it prevents the supply of other productions of the soil, such as animals and

[1] *Ibid.*, p. 215.
[2] *Ibid.*, pp. 31—2.
[3] *Ibid.*, p. 133.
[4] *Ibid.*, pp. 100—2.
[5] *Ibid.*, p. 141.
[6] *Ibid.*, p. 143.
[7] *Ibid.*, p. 174—5.

grass for the subsistence of animals, from becoming immediately equal to the demand, and so keeps up the price until they rise sufficiently to give as good a rent as corn. In this manner the rent paid for one species of produce becomes the cause of the high value of others. Rent, then, in its origin is an *effect* of high price, but afterwards becomes itself a *cause* of the high price of various objects of rural industry." [1]

This is the entering wedge of the overthrowal of the doctrine that rent does not enter into price, and is virtually the same theory as that advanced by Prof. Marshall in the later editions of his *Principles*. It is not to be wondered at that Ramsay does not recognise the full bearing of the concession, for neither does his distinguished, but unconscious, follower. It is interesting, nevertheless, to note the origin of the idea.

The second point is the importance attached by Ramsay to the element of time in production. In his discussion of value he maintains that the principle that value depends on the quantity of labour is very considerably modified by the use of capital. Commodities "in which the same quantity of labour has been expended may require very different periods before they are fit for consumption." [2] He takes as an example two casks of identical wine. The cask which is kept in the cellar for several years increases in value; and since the cask of wine "constitutes a fixed capital," the increase of value is due "to a capital withheld." [3] Therefore value depends not only on labour expended, but "on the length of time during which any portion of the product of that labour has existed as a fixed capital." [4] In this, says Ramsay, we see the real importance of capital in the process of production.

Finally, attention must be called to a remarkable passage in the closing chapter devoted to the practical conclusions from Ramsay's principles. Ramsay maintains that were the corn laws to be proposed as a new system, he would certainly oppose them; but now that the whole agriculture of England has been built up on them, he deprecates their entire abolition, because it will mean a sacrifice of agricultural to industrial prosperity. But it is very questionable, thinks he, whether this industrial prosperity, founded on a temporary monopoly, will endure. He adds:

"Mr. Malthus has remarked that it cannot be considered a natural, that is, a permanent state of things, for cotton to be

[1] *Ibid.*, pp. 278—279; *cf.* a similar passage on p. 463.
[2] *Ibid.*, p. 43.
[3] *Ibid.*, p. 44.
[4] *Ibid.*, p. 59; *cf.* p. 29.

grown in the Carolinas, shipped for Liverpool, and again exported to America in its finished condition. The time must come when the United States will fabricate for themselves. The same observations may be applied to other nations. It is quite clear that, unless there be some extraordinary natural advantages peculiar to Great Britain, it cannot have any right to suppose that it shall always supply the greater part of the world with manufactures at a cheaper rate than that at which they can be raised in the respective countries. Much less is it entitled to imagine that *no* other people can ever come into competition with it, and furnish neighbouring or distant lands on as cheap terms as itself." [1]

The question as to how far it was entirely wise for England to sacrifice her agriculture to her industry [2] has not yet been definitely answered. The events of the next quarter of a century will put us in a better position to reply. But in view of the "Back to Protection" or "Retaliation" cry which is now so loudly voiced in Great Britain, the arguments of Ramsay are far from untimely.

VIII

The last of the group of writers to be discussed is one who is in some respects the most remarkable of all—Mountifort Longfield. In 1832 a professorship of political economy was founded by Archbishop Whately under conditions similar to those of the Drummond professorship at Oxford. Whately succeeded Senior in the Oxford position in 1831, and published in the following year his *Introductory Lectures on Political Economy*, in which, as is well known, he proposed to substitute for the name Political Economy that of Catallactics.[3]

[1] *Ibid.*, p. 496.

[2] That this would be the result of the teachings of the Ricardians was clearly perceived at the time in England. One of the most vehement opponents of the "manufacturing economists," as he calls them, was the author of the tract entitled: *Four Letters to Earl Grey, to beware of the Economists.* London, 1830. The author points with withering scorn "to what extent these Economists would change the whole structure of this country; with what cool indifference they would transfer a million of cultivators to the hot steaming atmosphere of a cotton mill, or to the damp weaving room of a Lancashire manufacturer" (p. 24). The author uses as a motto of his work the statement as to rent published by James Anderson in the *Bee* in 1791, which he hints was plagiarised by the "Ricardo school," although he claims that they drew from this theory of rent conclusions exactly opposite to those of the real discoverer of the theory.

[3] Whately's influence may be seen in a number of minor followers, as *e.g.*, in the *Letters on the Rudiments of a Science called formerly improperly Political Economy, recently more pertinently Catallactics, from Patrick Plough, a Yeoman in the country, to his sons, young men in the Town.* 1842.

When Whately was called to Dublin as an ecclesiastical dignitary, his interest in his old subject was so strong that he proceeded forthwith to endow a chair of political economy, of which the first incumbent was Longfield. The eleven lectures which Longfield delivered during his first year were published as the *Lectures on Political Economy, delivered in Trinity and Michaelmas Term*, 1833.[1] Some of his lectures during the two ensuing years also saw the light, but may be passed over here with a bare mention.[2]

Although there is a short notice of Longfield in Palgrave's *Dictionary*, the writer has entirely missed the real contribution of Longfield to economic science.[3]

Longfield adopts many of the doctrines of the classical school, but states that he is compelled to dissent from not a few of their fundamental notions on the distribution of wealth. Above all, he differs from the Ricardians on the theory of profits and its place in the scheme of distribution.[4]

Longfield's general theory of value is noteworthy in that he not only puts very lucidly the influence of cost of production upon the supply side of the equation between supply and demand,[5] but calls attention to the demand side as well. In discussing this part of the subject, he points out that although the intensity of the demand varies with different persons, all will effect their purchases at the same rate, viz., at the market price. "Now if the price is attempted to be raised one degree beyond this sum, the demanders, who by the change will cease to be purchasers, must be those, the intensity of whose demand was precisely measured by the former price." "Thus the market price is measured by that demand, which being of the least intensity yet leads to actual purchases."[6]

Longfield goes on to point out that not only does intensity of demand vary in this way, but "the same person may be said to have in himself several demands of different degrees of intensity." The consumption of food will fall off with every increase of price due to scarcity. "That portion which any person ceases to con-

[1] By Mountifort Longfield, LL.D., Fellow of Trinity College, Dublin, and Professor of Political Economy, Dublin, 1834, 267 pp.

[2] These were *Four Lectures on the Poor Laws*, 1834, and *Three Lectures on Commerce and One on Absenteeism*, 1853. Many years later Longfield wrote an essay on *Irish Land Tenures* for the volume published by the Cobden Club in 1870, on the Land Question.

[3] It is to be noted, that Cannan quotes two passages from Longfield's book. Cannan, *op. cit.*, pp. 266, 309. Cannan, however, seems not to recognise Longfield's importance in other respects.

[4] *Lectures*, preface, p. vii. [5] *Ibid.*, p. 47. [6] *Ibid.*, p. 113.

sume in consequence of a rise in price or that additional portion which he would consume if prices should fall, is that for which the intensity of his demand is less than the high price which prevents him from purchasing it, and is exactly equal to the low price which would induce him to consume it."[1] Pursuing this train of reasoning through successive degrees of high price, Longfield concludes that "each individual contains, as it were, within himself a series of demands of successively increasing degrees of intensity; that the lowest degree of this series which at any time leads to a purchase is exactly the same for both rich and poor, and is that which regulates market price; and that in the case of the rich man the series increases more rapidly, that is to say, the intensity of his demand increases more rapidly in proportion to the diminution of his consumption than in the case of the poor man."[2]

In these passages we see that Longfield virtually expounds the doctrine of marginal demand. It is this marginal idea which he applies to the supply side of the schedule as well, and which results in his most characteristic contribution to economics.

He tells us, for instance, that it is a great mistake to suppose that even if we accept the theory of labour as a proper measure of value, it is "necessary that the whole supply of the commodity should have its value entirely derived from the labour expended in its production. It is sufficient if some part, of equal value with the rest, can thus be as it were resolved into the labour which created it."[3] He goes on to explain that in practically all commodities there exists some such portion. "That portion of every commodity whose value admits of being thus measured is that part which is produced under what I shall call the most disadvantageous circumstances; that is, under those circumstances which require the greatest expenditure of labour in order to produce any certain quantity of that commodity."[4]

In these passages we have an exposition of the theory of marginal cost, as well as that of marginal demand. It is in the theory of profits and interest that we find the application not only of the marginal idea, but of the productivity idea as well, thus combining to form the conception of marginal productivity.

Longfield accepts the theory of rent, as advanced by the Ricardians, but objects to the doctrine that profits are regulated by the fertility of the worst soils under cultivation. He thinks that this "ingenious theory"[5] is destitute of foundation, and that

[1] *Ibid.*, p. 114. [2] *Ibid.*, p. 115. [3] *Ibid.*, p. 34.
[4] *Ibid.*, pp. 34—35. [5] *Ibid.*, p. 182.

the soil has scarcely any direct influence upon the rate of profits. The error rests, in his opinion, upon an incorrect analysis of capital and its return. The essence of the service of capital consists, according to Longfield, in roundabout production. "Let us attend carefully to the important part which capital performs in the work of production, and we shall see how long a period must frequently elapse before certain labour has produced its full effects."[1]

After explaining this at some length, he endeavours to analyse more carefully the conception of production as applied to capital. "Of capital, there is not, properly speaking, any cost of production, except that sacrifice of the present to the future, which is made by the possessor of wealth who employs it as capital, instead of consuming it for his immediate gratification."[2] Longfield recurs continually to the conception of this equalisation of the present and the future as constituting the real function of capital. The more quickly capital is accumulated, he tells us in another place, and the lower the return, "the first direct and most striking effect is to render the future and present period of nearly equal importance."[3] In all questions of the return to capital, we are "comparing present and future advantages."

It is evident from these passages how exaggerated is the extreme contrast sought to be drawn by Böhm-Bawerk between the "productivity," and the "agio" theories of interest. For here, in at least one writer, we have the productivity theory explained in terms of the "agio" theory. All of which impels us to the conclusion that there is far less difference between the brilliant Austrian economist and his English predecessors than is commonly imagined.

It will be seen from the above that Longfield uses profits in the sense of general returns to capital, and that his theory of profits is really a theory of interest. This brings us to the application made by Longfield of the conjuncture of the productivity theory, in his sense of the term, and the marginal theory of cost and demand.

Capital is useful, he tells us, by advancing to the workman the value of his labour before the produce is sold to the consumer, and by supplying the labourer with instruments, tools, and machinery.[4] The owner of the machine will be paid for the use of it in proportion to its value, the injury it receives from use, and the time during which it is lent and "not in proportion to its

[1] *Ibid.*, p. 163.
[2] *Ibid.*, p. 196.
[3] *Ibid.*, p. 230.
[4] *Ibid.*, p. 187.

effect in increasing the efficiency of the labourer." This is a consequence of the principle of competition, for if the owner of one machine could obtain more for its use than the owner of another of equal value and durability, more of the former would be made until the profits of each were reduced to their level. "This level must be determined by the least efficient machine, since the sum paid for its use can never exceed the value of the assistance it gives the labourer." [1]

Longfield is at great pains to explain this process more in detail. He pictures the development much in the same way as do Wieser and Clark in recent years in their description of the "imputation" theory. He uses the hypothesis that the produce of the soil is raised by labourers entirely destitute of capital. Unless they are quickly to relapse into barbarism, some tools must be used. Suppose that the capitalist now puts this first spade "into the hands of the ablest labourer he can find, paying him as wages, so much as, without the aid of such an instrument, he could earn for himself. The profits which the capitalist or owner of this instrument will reap will be the difference between the quantity of work which the labourer can do with and without its assistance. But as the number of such instruments increases, in the hands of the same or different capitalists, other and inferior labourers must be employed to use them, and according to the principle which I have just laid down, the rate of profits must be determined by those cases in which the efficiency of capital is the least; that is, on the supposition I have just made, the profits of a single tool will be equal to the difference of the quantities of work which the feeblest labourer could execute with or without its use." [2]

Longfield applies this reasoning to the profits of capital in general, and concludes that the return to capital is equal to the assistance given to labour "by that portion of capital which is employed with the least efficiency, which I shall call the last portion of capital brought into operation." [3] Or, as he puts it in another place, "the rate of profits may be measured by the efficiency in assisting labour of the least efficient capital." [4]

[1] *Ibid.*, pp. 187—8. [2] *Ibid.*, pp. 191—192. [3] *Ibid.*, p. 194.

[4] *Ibid.*, p. 227. In another passage Longfield puts the same point a little differently. He says: "If a spade makes a man's labour twenty times as efficacious as it would be if unassisted by any instrument, one-twentieth only of his work is performed by himself and the remaining nineteen-twentieths must be attributed to capital. And this is the measure of the intensity of the demand for such an instrument. A labourer working for himself would find it for his interest to give nineteen-twentieths of the produce of his labour to the person who would lend him one, if the alternative

Thus we have in the most unequivocal language the marginal productivity doctrine interest—a doctrine, the origin of which has usually been ascribed to von Thünen, and which has been adopted and adapted by recent thinkers. Yet here again, before von Thünen published his second volume which contains the theory of interest, the identical doctrine had been advanced by an Englishman, or rather an Irishman. Longfield, indeed, did not pursue his analysis so far as to distinguish between profits and interest, and it is for this reason that he argues in opposition to Torrens that profits do form a part of cost of production.[1]

The discovery of the marginal productivity theory of interest is not Longfield's only claim to distinction. In his theory of wages also he marks a decided advance. The accepted theory of wages taught that wages depend on the standard of life, or on the means of subsistence. This whole Ricardian theory seems to Longfield to rest on a mistaken application of the cost of production theory of wages.[2] The cost of production theory is not applicable to labour, according to Longfield, because "the labourer is not produced for the sake of what he can earn."[3] The expression is merely metaphorical, and analogy, says Longfield, is not argument. The standard of life is not the cause, but the result.

The correct theory, according to Longfield, may be summed up in the statement that "the wages of the labourer depend upon the value of his labour, and not upon his wants, whether natural or acquired."[4] He adds, "that if his wants and necessities exercise, as they do, some influence upon the value of his labour, it is indirect, and secondary, produced by their effect upon the growth of the population, and that this effect is not analogous to the effect which the cost of production has upon the price of commodities."

Wages, like the value of everything else, depends upon the relation between the supply and the demand. The supply consists of the existing race of labourers. But "the demand is caused by the utility or value of the work which they are capable

was that he should turn up the earth with his naked hands; or if he worked for another, his employer might pay a similar sum for the purpose of supplying him with an instrument. But this profit is not paid, because on account of the abundance of capital in the country much must be employed in cases where in proportion to its quantity it is not so capable of multiplying the efficiency of the labourer; and the profits on this portion must regulate the profits of the rest." *Ibid.*, p. 195.

[1] *Ibid.*, Appendix, p. 248.

[2] *Ibid.*, p. 202.

[3] *Ibid.*, p. 203.

[4] *Ibid.*, p. 206.

of performing."[1] Hence follows the important conclusion that "wages must be paid out of the produce, or the price of the produce of their labour," and that the real element of significance is "the rate of profit and the productiveness of labour employed in the fabrication of those commodities in which the wages of labour are paid."[2]

The objection might indeed be raised that in this passage Longfield is not quite clear as to the exact relation between profits and wages. Of the truth of his fundamental proposition, however, he is assured. Wages are intimately connected with product. The true theory of wages, in other words, is a productivity theory.

It is for this reason that Longfield denies the possibility of machinery reducing wages. "A machine is never resorted to except for the purpose of producing commodities more cheaply, that is, more cheaply, independent of any reduction in the wages of labour or the rate of profits."[3] New capital means lower prices, not lower wages; and since each man's wages will now purchase more than before, increase of capital virtually leads to higher wages.

A writer who holds as Longfield did to the productivity theory of wages and the marginal productivity theory of interest must necessarily arrive at conclusions as to social progress very different from those of the Ricardian school. He agrees with Ricardo and Malthus that the productiveness of agricultural labour tends to diminish, and that the increase of population tends to raise profits and to lower wages.[4] But, on the other hand, he points out that capital in general tends to increase, and the rate of profits therefore tends to decline, while the evil arising from the necessity of resorting to poorer soils may be neutralised by other circumstances, such as improvements in agriculture. Above all, an improved system of division of labour and the extension of machinery in manufactures will enable the labourer to live more comfortably than before. He will gain more in this way than he will lose by the dearness of food and raw materials. For "in the normal progress of society, if it is well governed, the rate of profits will diminish, labour will become more productive, and the relative value of each man's labour will increase."[5]

With this far from pessimistic conclusion as to the future of industrial society, Longfield closes his remarkable lectures.

The productivity theory of wages and the marginal produc-

[1] *Ibid.*, p. 210. [2] *Ibid.*, p. 215. [3] *Ibid.*, p. 219.
[4] *Ibid.*, p. 235. [5] *Ibid.*, p. 239.

tivity theory of interest as expounded by Longfield seem to have passed unnoticed except in Ireland itself. Longfield was succeeded as Whately professor at Dublin by Isaac Butt, who accepted his predecessor's conclusions as a henceforth well-established part of economic theory. In a monograph entitled *Rent, Profits and Labour*,[1] Butt repeats and develops the doctrine. He speaks of the "most important additions to the discoveries of the science made by my predecessor," and addresses himself in particular to the most difficult question, "What is it that will regulate the exchange between things both produced by the joint operation of labour and capital."[2] Butt proceeds to point out at some length that "by the assistance, the powers of labour are multiplied, in different degrees, in a descending scale, descending as capital multiplies." "The least efficient assistance which the powers of capital actually render to labour is at once the check and the measure of the fall which the competition of capitalists has caused." "The relative value of labour and capital will be determined by that part in the scale at which all the capital in the country can be employed."[3] And after giving numerous examples, Butt claims that what is shown by this method of reasoning is "the relation between the product of the powers of capital and the product of unassisted labour; and this, of course, gives us the proportion in which the joint product is divided between the capitalist and the labourer."[4]

In very much the same way as Professor Clark, Butt contends that "by a parity of reasoning we can calculate the relation between the product, whether of human labour, or of the powers of capital, and the product of a natural agent." For he has already shown how the value of labour can be expressed in that of the powers of capital, or the value of the powers of capital in those of labour. It remains to show "how the value of a natural

[1] The full title of this pamphlet is *Rent, Profits and Labour. A Lecture delivered before the University of Dublin in Michaelmas Term*, 1837. By Isaac Butt, LL.B., Dublin, 1838. Butt also published a larger *Introductory Lecture delivered before the University of Dublin in Hilary Term*, 1837. By Isaac Butt LL.B., M.R.I.A., Archbishop Whately Professor of Political Economy, Dublin, 1837. In this Introductory Lecture, Butt follows Say in defining production as the "creation of utility," rather than the "creation of value" (p. 6), and is especially severe on those economists who wish to limit the term wealth to material objects. Immaterial, like material objects, are equally forms of wealth. The copyright of a book, the pleasures derived from a painting, the command of a pleasant prospect which enhances the rent of a house—all these are immaterial products which constitute wealth (p. 36). (*Cf.* 57—59.) Butt also objects to identifying capital with instruments of production (p. 55). Both here and in other passages he makes long quotations from his unpublished lectures in the same course.

[2] *Rent, Profits, and Labour*, p. 21. [3] *Ibid.*, pp. 23—25. [4] *Ibid.*, p. 26.

agent can be expressed in the terms of either."[1] This he does through the use of the theory of marginal production as contained in the doctrine of rent.

The general principles of exchange are summarised by Butt in the following statement:

"The product of any given quantity of labour will exchange for the product of so much of the powers of capital as render to production an assistance equivalent to that labour, at the lowest rate of assistance to which capital is forced by its abundance to have recourse."

"It will exchange for as much of the produce of the soil as could be raised by that labour, or the equivalent powers of capital, at the least productive expenditure to which the demand for produce has compelled the community to resort."[2]

Butt informs us that in the following lecture he proposes to apply these principles to the condition of the labouring class, and to make other practical applications of the doctrine. So far as we know, however, these lectures, which would assuredly be most interesting, have not been published.

The theory of marginal productivity as applied to capital and labour, Butt tells us, "seems obvious and simple enough, but until the appearance of Dr. Longfield's lectures it was not thought of. With the exception of the discovery of the theory of rent—and, perhaps, even the propriety of this exception is questionable—no such important service has been rendered to the science since the days of Adam Smith."[3] When we reflect that the whole current of modern theory is setting in the direction indicated by Longfield and Butt, these encomiums do not appear to be altogether unmerited.

IX

We stated at the outset of these essays that the history of economics is yet to be written. The slight study that has been made of a period of less than two decades in the history of economic thought in a single country will, we trust, be found to be sufficiently rich in results to lead to a fuller investigation of the same period, as well as of other periods, both anterior and subsequent. British economics during the twenties and the thirties of the nineteenth century, far from presenting the dull level of uniformity and agreement which is usually associated with the name "classical school," abounds in writers, many of

[1] *Ibid.*, p. 27. [2] *Ibid.*, p. 32. [3] *Ibid.*, p. 23.

them of considerable ability, who did not scruple to attack the premisses as well as many of the conclusions of the dominant sect, and who struck out for themselves new paths which have had to be rediscovered by modern thinkers. There are but few recent developments in economic doctrine of which we cannot find the forerunners in this early period. The historical and the ethical conceptions of economics; the emphasis laid on distribution, as well as on production; the opposition to the labour theory of exchange; the accentuation of time as an element in value; the roundabout production theory of capital and the "agio" theory of interest; the broadening of the rent concept and the recognition of the weakness in the statement that rent does not enter into price; the distinction between the capitalist and the *entrepreneur* and the surplus theory of pure profits or business gains; and above all, the theory of marginal utility as the basis of value, and the marginal productivity theories of wages and interest—these are but a few of the doctrines which we have seen advanced and elaborated by the authors of the period. With such a trio as Lloyd, Read, and Longfield—not to mention the others—the so-called "minor" writers of England assume an importance which in some respects transcends that assigned to the "major" writers.

But, it will be asked, how does it happen that all these authors have been so largely overlooked and neglected? For very much the same reason, we answer, that Cournot was passed over in France and Gossen in Germany. Their views were not in accord with those of the dominant school. The practical issues of the time were so momentous that the economic science which taught a doctrine in harmony with these practical demands was accepted as infallible. The economists in England, indeed, were not responsible for free trade and industrial development. Those would have come almost as quickly had economics never existed; for practical policies are the result for the most part of actual interests and not of abstract considerations. But when the demands of the dominant social and political interests were reinforced by the teachings of the scientists, economics leaped with a bound into the position not only of a popular, but almost of a sacrosanct, science. The edifice erected by Ricardo, and elaborated by McCulloch and Mill, became so solid and so stable that it could not be shaken by any current or gust of criticism or opposition. No one would listen to, very few would even read, publications which refrained from entering upon the field of practical discussion, and were content to abide in the realm of theory. A theory that seemed to lead nowhere was not the kind of theory to which the practical age could be expected to lend a ready ear. Discouraged by their reception, most of these writers turned to other lines of activity, and before long their very existence was forgotten. The reputation of the great names was such that any deviation from accepted doctrines was branded as unorthodox. It was reserved for a later age to see the change in economic conditions, which, first abroad and then in England, shattered the old idol of economic orthodoxy, and prepared the way for the newer thinkers who ventured to attack some of the practical conclusions, and not a few of the theoretical positions of the dominant school. From these newer thinkers we must indeed not withhold our tribute of appreciation for their solidity and their originality; but we must likewise not begrudge a generous recognition to the predecessors, whose lot was cast in less fortunate times. When such recognition is accorded, it will be seen that Great Britain is the real mother, not only of classical political economy, but also of that series of newer ideas which is at the present time slowly transforming the face of economic science.

EDWIN R. A. SELIGMAN

[2]

Trinity College, Dublin, and the Theory of Value, 1832-1863

By R. D. Black

The history of economic doctrine is a subject out of which conventional general ideas are very apt to arise. It is a terrain with many varied and complex features, but the majority of those who survey it do so only broadly and recall afterwards merely the general topography and the chief landmarks.

One very prevalent idea resulting from this process is that the period before 1870, in English economic writing at least, marks the dominance of labour or cost-of-production theories of value, whilst the period after that date saw the ascendancy of the " subjective " or " utility " approach to value questions. Of late years, however, this conception has undergone some revision, chiefly in consequence of the pioneer work of Seligman,[1] and it has come to be recognised that even in the British Isles there were a number of economists who rejected the labour theory of value long before the time of Jevons, or indeed even John Stuart Mill. In this and other respects, valuable results have been achieved through the study of the work of " minor economists " of the nineteenth century, but much remains yet to be done.

In particular, it has normally been accepted that the early advocates of the utility approach to value did not constitute a " school of economists " in any proper sense, but were scattered in both time and place and were frequently unaware of each other's work. Yet this view may itself require some modification, for it may be contended that something closely approaching to a " subjective value school " existed at Dublin University in the mid-nineteenth century.

It must be admitted at the outset, however, that this claim involves some misuse of the word " school ", which normally connotes a body of disciples of one teacher or a group having a connected system of doctrine in common. The connection between the group of economists considered here was not so close or complete as this. All were occupants of the Chair of Political Economy in Trinity College, Dublin, but a consideration of the conditions of its tenure makes it evident that no continuous development or dissemination of any single set of principles was possible from it.

The Professorship was founded in 1832 by the Reverend Richard Whately after his appointment as Archbishop of Dublin, a position to which he came direct from the Drummond Chair of Political Economy at Oxford in 1830–31. Throughout the rest of his life Whately paid the salary of the Professor himself, examined candidates for the post, and determined the conditions of office, which he naturally modelled on those of the Oxford Professorship. The most important rules were that no person might hold office for more than five years, or be re-appointed until after the expiry of two years; and the Professor was required to deliver " a Course of Lectures on Political Economy, consisting of *nine* Lectures at the least; and also, during every year, to print and present to the Provost, Senior Fellows, and Visitors, one of such Lectures at the least. The Lectures to be free to all Graduates. Undergraduates to be recommended by their Tutors ".[2]

In consequence, as one of the first holders of the Chair remarked, " The regulations under which this Professorship is placed make it impossible for the person holding it to attempt any thing like a regular course of instruction in Political Economy ".[3] This was indeed almost inevitable in the state of economic knowledge and opinion then prevailing in Ireland, and the general and almost " popular " character of the instruction given, together with the fact that the short term of office at first attracted young graduates who usually had law rather than political economy in view for a permanent

[1] " On Some Neglected British Economists," *Economic Journal*, 1903, Vol. xiii, pp. 335–363 and 511–535. The modified view of value doctrine cited here has been very fully and clearly developed by Miss M. Bowley (*Nassau Senior and Classical Economics*, London, 1937). It is also evident in such works as Roll, *History of Economic Thought* (London, 1938) and Whittaker, *History of Economic Ideas* (New York, 1940).

[2] *Dublin University Calendar*, 1833, p. 130.

[3] Isaac Butt, *Rent, Profits and Labour* (Dublin, 1838), p. 7. The regulations were changed on several occasions after Whately's death.

career, prevented the appearance of any strong teaching tradition. Nevertheless, the regulations had the effect, foreseen, no doubt, by Whately, of bringing a succession of fresh minds in contact with the subject and, still more important, of ensuring the publication of their views. Nor was there a complete absence of continuity in the work of these men; within a comparatively short time after the foundation of the Chair it was being occupied by individuals who had learnt their political economy from their predecessors in it. Apart from this, they were certainly aware of the views published by former Professors. Indeed, under the circumstances, the teachings of the early Professors show a striking degree of unanimity, which yet does not seem to come from any mere uncritical acceptance or expedient following of one's tenets by another.

This unanimity shows most plainly in regard to value theory—not surprisingly, for whilst other subjects might be treated or ignored according to their current importance or the views of the teacher, all felt themselves at some time called upon to lay down principles about this fundamental part of Economic Theory. What is remarkable is that the principles of the Dublin Professors should so steadily have run counter to the trend of received opinion, for from the first labour or cost-of-production theories of value are either directly refuted or given a very subordinate place by them.

Whately himself is well known as an opponent of the labour theory and advocate of the utility approach, having probably been influenced in this by the views of his close friend and predecessor in the Drummond Chair, Nassau Senior.[1] Thus in his lectures at Oxford in 1831 Whately held "Labour not essential to value" and his assertion in support of this—"It is not that pearls fetch a high price *because* men have dived for them; but on the contrary men dive for them because they fetch a high price "[2]—has gained some little fame. He reiterated these views some years later when he wrote his *Easy Lessons on Money Matters ; for the Use of Young People*.[3]

This in itself provides some explanation of the line taken in value theory by the Professors of the period under consideration here. During the whole of that time, Whately assisted at the examinations for the Professorship and took a keen interest in all connected with it. Naturally, therefore, occupants of the Chair would be acquainted with his writings, and further, there is evidence that he had a personal influence on some of them.[4] But equally they were not immune from the powerful influence of accepted classical doctrine, nor was their work a mere reproduction of Whately, whose observations on value in fact constitute no more than a few striking comments. Significant as the influence of the Archbishop may have been in pointing the direction of study—and he was generally regarded as "the father of economic science in Ireland"—he can in no sense be regarded as the founder of a school or creator of a system, for his contributions to Political Economy, though remarkable, are fragmentary, and although he maintained a lifelong interest in the subject his period as a creative economist was brief.

If any one of this group of economists can be called their "Master", it is not Whately, but the man whom he appointed to be the first occupant of the new Chair—Mountifort Longfield (1802—1884). For where Whately had thrown out some illuminating suggestions on the nature of value, Longfield constructed an extra-ordinarily complete marginal value theory, built upon it a Theory of Distribution, and virtually a whole system of economic doctrine.[5]

Indeed, in the work of no other member of this group of Irish economists does the theory of value bulk so large.[6] A large part of Longfield's main work, his *Lectures*

[1] See Bowley, *Nassau Senior*, pp. 106–7; E. Jane Whately, *Life and Correspondence of Archbishop Whately* (London, 1866), references *passim*.

[2] Whately, *Introductory Lectures on Political Economy*, 2nd ed. (London, 1832), Lecture ix, pp. 252–3. These remarks do not appear in the first edition, which excluded this Lecture "as belonging more properly to a second course".

[3] *Easy Lessons*, p. 32. This book was written in 1837 and published "under the direction of the Committee of General Literature and Education, appointed by the Society for the Promotion of Christian Knowledge". It had reached a fifteenth edition in 1858.

[4] Thus W. Neilson Hancock, who was elected Professor in 1846, reveals that the plan of some of his lecture courses was suggested to him by Whately. (See the Preface to his published lecture of 1851, *Is the Competition between Large and Small Shops injurious to the Community?*).

[5] This is admittedly conjectural. Longfield's only other published work which can be regarded as theoretical was his *Three Lectures on Commerce and One on Absenteeism*, delivered in 1834 and published in 1835. He hints in these at further lectures, on production, to come, but these were never published. There is, however, no evidence to show that they were not delivered, for Longfield held office until 1836.

[6] An exception should perhaps be made in favour of Cairnes. But see below.

on Political Economy, delivered in Trinity and Michaelmas Terms, 1833,[1] is occupied by the consideration of it. It cannot be pretended, however, that all of this treatment is original or wholly free from confusion. At the outset Longfield makes no attempt to displace or improve the strict classical analysis, but in fact follows Ricardo in saying that " it is plain that without some utility a thing can have no value . . . But once possessed of any utility, its value will not depend so much upon the extent of that utility as upon other circumstances . . ."[2] Again, the customary classical distinction between " natural " and " market " price figures in Longfield's work; in relation to " natural " price he endeavours at great length to establish the claim of labour to be regarded as the " best " measure of value, although not attempting to make it either an invariable measure or a source of value. In this effort, as might be expected, he is indifferently successful, but in fact it is no more than a side issue in his theory of value; Longfield is much more largely concerned with exchanges and market value and it is in this connection that his theory attains its fullest development and greatest originality.

He gives a clear and attractive account of the manner in which demand and supply affect market price, with abundance of practical illustrations.[3] This is summed up in the statement " that the value of every article depends upon the demand and the supply, and that indirectly the cost of production of any commodity, as well as its utility, has an effect upon its price. The cost of production, by its influence upon the supply, since men will not produce commodities unless with the reasonable expectation of selling them for more than the cost of producing them. And the utility has some effect, although not so easily calculated, since it is to its utility, in the more extended sense of the word, that the demand is to be entirely attributed ".[4]

The further development of this proposition is so placed in the *Lectures* that it has the air almost of an afterthought, but it is really the central feature of Longfield's theory of value and his most remarkable contribution to economic thought. In a revision passage he sets out to explain more fully " the nature of demand, and its influence upon price and value ", and begins with the case of a number of " demanders " for a given article. Here he demonstrates that their demands may be of different intensities and that " the measure of the intensity of any person's demand for any commodity is the amount which he would be willing and able to give for it, rather than remain without it, or forgo the gratification which it is calculated to afford him ". Certain demands may be insufficiently intense to lead to any purchase, whilst on the other hand " there may be, and . . . in fact there generally is, an excess of intensity of demand ". Nevertheless ". . . all will effect their purchases at the same rate, viz. at the market prices . . . Now if the price is attempted to be raised one degree beyond this sum, the demanders, who by the change will cease to be purchasers, must be those the intensity of whose demand was precisely measured by the former price . . . . Thus the market price is measured by that demand, which being of the least intensity, yet leads to actual purchases ".[5]

Advanced as is this analysis, the ensuing passage is even more striking in its anticipation of marginal utility theory. In it, Longfield points out that " the intensity of demand varies not only in different places, and among different individuals, but in many cases the same person may be said to have in himself several demands of different degrees of intensity ". Illustrating this with an example of a change in the supply of provisions, he explains that " that portion which any person ceases to consume in consequence of a rise of prices, or that additional portion which he would consume if prices should fall, is that for which the intensity of his demand is less than the high price which prevents him from purchasing it, and is exactly equal to the low price which would induce him to consume it ". He invites his hearers to reason for themselves ". . . the conclusion, that each individual contains as it were within himself, a series of demands of successively increasing degrees of intensity; that the lowest degree of this series which at any time leads to a purchase is exactly the same for both rich and poor, and is that which regulates the market price ". Finally he adds: " I have chosen the example of provisions as being the most obvious and palpable, and as most frequently affording a practical instance of the principle which it illustrated; but the same observation is equally true, although not so strikingly, in every case in which a

[1] Dublin, 1834. Reprinted in the London School of Economics Series of *Scarce Tracts in Economic and Political Science*, 1931. The pagination is identical in both editions.

[2] *Lectures on Political Economy*, p. 26.

[3] Op. cit., pp. 45–63.

[4] *Ibid.*, p. 110.

[5] *Ibid.*, pp. 111–13.

diminution of supply would occasion a diminution in any individual's consumption, without leading him to give up the use of the article altogether ".[1]

For completeness and clarity this exposition rivals the work of any of that group of nineteenth-century economists whom Miss Bowley has so aptly named " the dissenters ".[2] Such a statement of value theory, evolved quite independently so far as can be ascertained, would give Longfield a strong title to recognition as an economist of the first rank even were it the only novel contribution which he made to the subject. In fact, however, it is but one of a number of original views, often remarkable anticipations of later doctrines. Yet despite this, Longfield still remains definitely amongst the " neglected economists ". It is true that Seligman refers to him as " in some respects the most remarkable of all " the writers whom he " discovered " in 1903—true also that he has received mention from almost all historians of economic theory since that date, but the full extent and importance of his work is still scarcely appreciated.[3]

Nevertheless, history has been kinder to Longfield than were his contemporaries, at least outside his own country. On the more famous economists of the time his work had virtually no effect whatever—it was not even condemned. In Ireland, on the other hand, it was very favourably received. An anonymous reviewer (possibly Isaac Butt) in the *Dublin University Magazine* of June, 1834, had great expectations of Longfield, whom he thought had " shown himself competent not only to understand and elucidate whatever has been written by the ablest men who have heretofore treated of the science of political economy, but to take up the subject in the spirit of an investigator by whom its fundamental principles may be more clearly ascertained, and its boundaries extended ". " It is our belief," he added, " that the living man does not exist by whom political economy may be more advantaged ".[4]

There is evidence too that Longfield and his writings were highly esteemed in the Trinity College of his day. The *Lectures on Political Economy* remained a prescribed text for students of the subject until 1872, and Longfield himself was always spoken of with great respect by his successors, Butt placing his services to Political Economy on a par with those of Adam Smith and Lawson describing him as " one of the ablest writers upon the Science ".[5] It seems clear from all this that Longfield's work played a considerable part in influencing the views of his followers, and to some extent he overshadows them. None the less, the consistency and originality with which they adopted and developed the utility approach to value problems are alike remarkable.

The second occupant of the Whately Chair, Isaac Butt (1813—1879), who took office in 1836, gained lasting fame in later years through his association with the Irish Home Rule movement. As an economist, however, he is not of the calibre of Longfield, to whom he was certainly indebted for many ideas. Yet his work has considerable merit in style and arrangement, and although he has been accused of borrowing from Say and Senior, it is not devoid of originality.

On the subject of value, Butt laid emphasis on the exchange aspect, supporting the view taken by Longfield (but traceable to Samuel Bailey) that " Value is a relation "

[1] Op. cit., pp. 114–15.

[2] Bowley, *Nassau Senior*, p. 67. Perhaps the only members of this group whose work may be compared to Longfield's are Senior and W. F. Lloyd. It seems indisputable, however, that Longfield's anaylsis was evolved independently, for Senior's *Outline of the Science of Political Economy* was not actually published in the *Encyclopædia Metropolitana* until 1836, and Lloyd's *Lecture on the Notion of Value*, delivered from the Drummond Chair at Oxford, where he succeeded Whately, was exactly contemporaneous with Longfield's *Lectures on Political Economy*. (Lloyd's *Lecture* was published in London, 1834, and reprinted by Mr. R. F. Harrod in *Economic History*, May, 1927.)

It is curious that while the influence of Senior, acknowledged or unacknowledged, is plain in the work of most of Longfield's successors, notably Butt and Hancock, that of Lloyd is conspicuous by its entire absence.

[3] Certain parts of Longfield's work have received considerable attention, chiefly his theory of value and his observations on International Trade. The latter have been treated in some detail by Professor Jacob Viner in his *Studies in the Theory of International Trade* (London, 1937) and in his article on " The Doctrine of Comparative Costs " (*Weltwirtschaftliches Archiv*, 36 Band, 1932 II). There is, however, no complete treatment of Longfield's doctrines, which require to be seen as a whole with his theory of value as their foundation. The present writer was led to this conclusion, and became aware of the " value tradition " which forms the subject of this article, through a detailed study of Longfield's work, the results of which are as yet unpublished.

[4] *Dublin University Magazine*, June, 1834, pp. 605 and 618.

[5] Butt, *Rent, Profits and Labour* (Dublin, 1838), p. 23; Lawson, *Five Lectures on Political Economy* (London, 1844), p. 142. For a further account of these works, see below.

Miss Bowley recognises that " In Ireland . . . Longfield bid fair to set up a distinctive school of economists " but mentions only Butt in this connection (*Nassau Senior*, p. 109).

and criticising the idea that labour might be regarded as an invariable or "more real" measure of value—". . . to attempt to fix upon any one article as something that we will assume always bears an invariable value, is to assume, in fact, a contradiction in terms, and to lay the certain ground for errors and mistakes. The whole difficulty of Mr. Ricardo's book arises from the use of the word value in this abstract sense . . ."[1]

Butt himself was severely practical on this subject and cut through all the mazes of the labour theory to answer the question—" What is it that determines the value of commodities ? " in a single statement which few modern economists would care to contradict:—". . . their value appears to be regulated by nothing else than their utility and scarcity ".[2] There is no considerable development of these ideas in Butt's work, but he uses them as an introduction to a novel theory of original prices, based upon productivity considerations, after the method of Longfield.

The same line of thought on value was continued by James Anthony Lawson (1817—1887), who was appointed Professor in 1841, and, like both his predecessors, was a lawyer by training. His *Five Lectures on Political Economy; delivered before the University of Dublin, in Michaelmas Term, 1843*, form only part of a series and unfortunately they do not include the section, to which Lawson refers incidentally,[3] wherein the " nature and production of value " was treated. Some comments in an Appendix constitute the whole of Lawson's published observations on the subject, but these leave no doubt of his adherence to the " subjective " doctrine, and indeed explain it very lucidly within such a small compass.

Lawson holds that " It is a proposition always true, and of universal application, *that the exchangeable value of all articles depends upon their utility*, that is, upon their power to gratify the wants and wishes of man . . . Every other principle which has been assigned as the regulating cause of exchangeable value, is of partial and limited application, and subject to many restrictions and exceptions ".[4]

Explanation of this statement leads Lawson to consider the two " partial principles " commonly employed to account for the values of articles—" the proportion between the demand and the supply " and " the cost of production "—and their relation to his own general principle. In dealing with the first of these, he arrives at the concept of diminishing utility, and states it almost in so many words:—" Demand and supply *generally* influence this utility; for instance, if *A*'s supply of *X* be increased, this will generally diminish its utility to him, or the degree in which he desires its possession, for as our particular desires are capable of being satisfied, it is obvious that we may have more of an article than we wish to use, and therefore the retaining the possession of that surplus is less desirable to us ".

Lawson adds as a rider a point taken for granted by most later writers:—" the exception to this is, when the article is not one which will spoil by keeping, and when we have a prospect of being able, by keeping it longer in our possession, to obtain more of what we want in exchange for it ".[5]

The treatment of the cost aspect is almost more remarkable in its clarity of thought and expression:—". . . as a general rule, the cost of production is not the circumstance which influences a party in determining what he will pay for an article, it is, as I said, the utility of the article . . . It is not true to say that the cost of production *regulates* value, though it is true that in many cases the value, which is determined by other considerations, happens to coincide with the cost of production ". Under the customary mobility assumptions, Lawson then proceeds to show how final prices affect the movement of factors and the supply of goods, and hence concludes that " value is only made to coincide with cost of production *through the medium of a change in supply*, and when this cannot be brought about, there is no such coincidence and no tendency to it ".[6]

The quality of such passages as this makes it a matter for regret that we have not access to Lawson's main work on value, and that he did not devote himself more thoroughly to economic theory. Yet, so far as the present writer is aware, his work has attracted no attention whatsoever since John Kells Ingram wrote his *History of Political Economy* in 1888.[7]

[1] Butt, *Protection to Home Industry; some Cases of its Advantages Considered. The Substance of Two Lectures delivered before the University of Dublin in Michaelmas Term, 1840* (Dublin, 1846), p. 125.

[2] *Rent, Profits and Labour*, p. 18.

[3] Lawson, *Five Lectures* (see note above), p. 26.

[4] and [5] Lawson, op. cit., p. 144. Italics in original text.

[6] Op. cit., p. 145. Italics in original text.

[7] There is one reference to Lawson in Gonnard, *Histoire des Doctrines Économiques* (Paris, 1930), but this refers to his views on method, not value, and appears to be derived from Ingram.

The same is true of the man who succeeded Lawson in the Whately Chair in 1846, William Neilson Hancock (1820–1888). Hancock's main interest was in social problems and what he called "applied Political Economy". He is known as a prolific writer on the Irish economic questions of his time—his many pamphlets and reports are a mine of information for the economic historian—but he is not usually thought of as an economic theorist at all. He was, in fact, the author of only one essay properly concerned with this subject, his *Introductory Lecture on Political Economy; Delivered in the Theatre of Trinity College, Dublin, in Trinity Term, 1848*".[1] This, however, provides one of the most interesting discussions of value theory given by any member of this group of Dublin economists, a discussion particularly noteworthy for its unusual anticipations of modern views.

Hancock begins by pointing out the ambiguity of the word "value", adding that "this ambiguity about value has been increased by some economists using the word as if it were synonymous with cost". But—"Now the word 'price' is fortunately free from all ambiguity, and always means the exchangeable value of a commodity, estimated in the money of the country where the exchange takes place". Consequently, he says, "I propose to substitute observations into the variations in price, for observations into variations in value".[2] The manner in which Hancock sets about doing this is admirably in accord with the methods of modern price theory. He explains that there may be two types of price changes—the familiar "changes from the side of things" and "changes from the side of money" or, as he calls them, "intrinsic and extrinsic changes in prices". The parts of the subject dealing with these "may conveniently be called—the former, the theory of prices, and the latter, the theory of money".[3]

"To proceed then, with the theory of prices, it is found by observation, that no intrinsic variation takes place in the price of any commodity, except from one of two causes; either a change in the degree in which its possession is desired, or in its desirability; or a change in the force of the causes by which its supply is limited, or, in other words, by which it is made scarce."

In developing this statement, Hancock explains his concept of "degree of desirability" by reference to the collective demand of the market:—

> "The degree in which the possession of a commodity is desired, is measured by the number of persons able and willing to purchase at each amount of price. And it is observed that for commodities in general, their desirability increases very rapidly as their prices fall."[4]

At first sight, this phrasing might suggest that Hancock's "degree of desirability" is something very different from Longfield's "intensity of demand" and the normal concept of diminishing utility. In fact, Hancock's approach through aggregate market demand has, as it were, carried him past diminishing utility towards the consequent idea of elasticity of demand, although he does not succeed in expressing this very clearly. Having cited the penny post as an instance of his point, he proceeds without further elaboration of it to indicate the relative importance of demand and supply factors in a passage which inevitably puts one in mind of Marshall:—

> "As very few commodities are capable of an instantaneous increase in supply, the intrinsic variations in prices for short periods depend almost entirely on the changes in the desirability of commodities. But as most commodities can be increased in supply, the permanent intrinsic variations in prices depend almost entirely on changes in the degree of their scarcity."[5]

This leads Hancock to consider the influences affecting the supply of goods, and of these he says:—"The causes, then, which limit the supply of any commodity arise from the necessity of using raw materials and the three instruments of production; and the force of these causes is estimated by the sums which have to be paid for their use, or, in other words, by the respective prices of the materials and of the use of the instruments of production". From the supply side, then, the price of a good depends on the amounts of factors and materials required for its production, multiplied by

[1] Dublin, 1849.
[2] Hancock, *Introductory Lecture*, pp. 9 and 11.
[3] *Ibid.*, p. 13.
[4] *Ibid.*, p. 14.
[5] *Ibid.*, p. 14. Compare Marshall, *Principles of Economics*, 8th ed., Bk. V, Chap. III, p. 349. The contrast between Hancock's emphasis on scarcity and Marshall's on cost of production is noteworthy. Cf. Cannan, *Review of Economic Theory*, p. 212. And see below (p. 146).

their prices, and, following out his general principle, Hancock treats the question of the returns to the factors as entirely a pricing problem. Referring to the theories advanced to explain these returns, he says:—

> " The method of commencing the investigation of these theories is the same in all; namely, by the application of the laws already stated with regard to other prices. The prices of labour, of savingness, and of the assistance of natural agents depend on the causes which make the use of labour, capital, and natural agents desirable, and limited in supply, or scarce."[1]

Naturally, no detailed explanation of these views is undertaken by Hancock in this single lecture. How he may have developed them is a matter for conjecture, and in the light of later knowledge there is some danger of overestimating their depth and significance. Yet it does not seem too fanciful to suggest that here, in 1849, there appears at least the germ of a general interdependence theory of pricing. Certainly it is a theory which, with its emphasis on price instead of value and scarcity instead of cost of production, diverges notably from the classical approach, and in essentially the same fashion as do the doctrines of such modern economists as the late Professor Cassel.

Nevertheless, at the time of Hancock's resignation of the Whately Chair, in 1851, the classical, or more precisely the Ricardian, system was still dominant. Modified and improved, it was gaining new strength and prestige from the publication of J. S. Mill's *Principles*, the influence of which far outweighed and overshadowed that of Longfield's *Lectures*, which had never reached a second edition.

It is scarcely, surprising, therefore, that there appears at this period a reaction from the trend which value theory had been taking at Trinity College. Thus Richard Hussey Walsh (1825—1862), who took Hancock's place in 1851, appears to have accepted the view that value depends upon cost of production. His main work, however, was an *Elementary Treatise on Metallic Currency*[2] and the comments on value in it are so few and so limited in application that it is difficult to speak with any certainty about the true character of his ideas. He gives " a general statement and explanation of the principle that the value of goods is regulated by their cost of production " but says that " it is subject in its application to many limitations ". Most important of these is his statement that " the influence on value of the cost of production is gradual and indirect, being chiefly brought about by the effect exercised on the supply ".[3]

This would seem at first to take the argument somewhat away from the true cost approach, but in reality it seems only to be a use of the term " value " as equivalent to classical " market price ". On the whole, Walsh appears to give the demand aspect of value questions a subordinate place, but he deserves credit for setting out more fully and clearly some of the ideas on demand on which Hancock had touched, for at one point he remarks that ". . . if, from a considerable augmentation in the supply of a commodity, its value falls, the decline will be more or less rapid according to the relation which the commodity occupies with respect to human wants . . . in order that a considerable augmentation of supply should diminish value but slightly, the article should enter very generally into consumption, and be one for which the demand might rise rapidly with every reduction in price ".[4] This promising line of analysis is not continued, however, beyond the point necessary for its application to the question of variations in general prices occasioned by gold discoveries. Indeed, all Walsh's comments on value are intended for use in the study of monetary problems, and in this respect their emphasis on the supply side is natural; yet there seems little justification for regarding him as anything but a supporter of the orthodox doctrine.

Whatever doubts may be entertained as to the position of Walsh, there can certainly be none as regards the views of his successor, John Elliott Cairnes (1823—1875). Cairnes is generally regarded as the " last of the classical economists " in the strict sense, and, in value theory at least, this appears to be one point on which popular views require no modification. The first of the Dublin Professors to devote his life primarily to economic study and teaching, Cairnes remained throughout his entire career a rigid adherent of the cost-of-production theory of value. It is true that his formulation of it was very different and very much more cautious than that of Ricardo

[1] Hancock, *Introductory Lecture*, p. 20. " Savingness " is Hancock's rather clumsy substitute term for Senior's " Abstinence ".

[2] Dublin, 1853.

[3] *Elementary Treatise*, p. 19.

[4] Walsh, op. cit., pp. 77 and 79.

or McCulloch. Yet the greatest change which he made in it was to admit that value was determined by reciprocal demand where the mobility assumption was not fulfilled for factors of production. The concept of non-competing groups which he developed in this connection has found an accepted place in economic theory, and is perhaps the best known part of Cairnes' work. In fact, however, the idea had been fully stated by Longfield,[1] not in relation to the theory of value, but in connection with the theory of wages, where it properly belonged. This was never recognised by Cairnes, who very rarely took any account of the work of his Irish contemporaries on economic theory. The " lack of intellectual sympathy " for the views of others, which shows so plainly in his scathing criticisms of Jevons and the critics of the classical system, is evident here in another form. One cannot but wonder whether, and how, Cairnes reconciled his theories with those in Longfield's *Lectures*, which were prescribed for reading by the students he examined.

At this stage it would certainly appear that the trend which had been so well started by Longfield had been completely reversed after the lapse of twenty-five years. No compromise on value problems was ever essayed by Cairnes, either as a concession to his predecessors in Ireland or his successors in England. Yet in Trinity College this conflict eventually produced one noteworthy result—a " dual theory of value " in which the opposing doctrines were attempted to be synthesised. This was the work of Arthur Houston (1833—1914), who followed Cairnes as Whately Professor in 1861, and published his views under the title of *The Principles of Value in Exchange, explained and expressed in simple and comprehensive formulæ. Two Lectures Delivered in the University of Dublin.*[2]

In this short work, starting from the assumption that the commodities exchanged are produced under completely free competitive conditions and " are naturally of the same degree of utility ", Houston reaches the conclusion that " the value of freely-produced commodities is regulated by their Net Cost of Production ".[3] Developing this, he proceeds to explain that " Net cost of production is the *power* by which value is regulated: *limitation of supply* is the *lever* by which that power is applied. If any force interferes to prevent the free movement of the lever, to prevent its obeying the impulse received from net cost of production, the power fails to produce its proper effect, and value diverges from its natural course "[4] Next Houston abandons the " equal utility " assumption and considers how the value of commodities will be affected by their comparative utility when taken together with the possibilities of varying the supply, concluding:—

> " To sum up, when commodities, the subject of exchange, require some time before a new supply can be procured, scarcity, actual or apprehended, will give rise to a deviation from natural value, greater or less in proportion to their utility, or, in other words, in proportion to the imperiousness of the desire they are adapted to satisfy."[5]

With commendable analytical thoroughness, Houston also removes his assumption of competitive production, and thus carries the study of value a stage further than any of his predecessors before Cairnes by taking in the question of monopoly value also. His treatment of this is especially interesting in the light of modern work, by reason of his recognition of the influence of conditions of demand on the conduct of the monopolist. He points out that beyond a certain point the monopolist by increasing output must " lower the price against himself ". " It must not be supposed, however, that such will necessarily prove a losing speculation for him, as it is possible —nay, probable—that his gains on the larger quantity at the lower value, would be greater than those on the smaller quantity, at the higher." In an Appendix to this, Houston adds: " It is perhaps worth while to inquire what this depends on. It

[1] Longfield, *Lectures on Political Economy*, pp. 83–4. This point has lately received recognition in Whittaker, *History of Economic Ideas* (1940), p. 601.

[2] London, n.d. The exact date of this work is difficult to ascertain. Professor J. G. Smith, in his article " Some Nineteenth Century Irish Economists " (Economica, New Series, Vol. II, p. 30, Feb., 1935) gives the title with the addition *being Two Lectures Delivered in the University of Dublin, 1864*. The copy in the Library of Trinity College has the title given in the text here, but the dedication as a tribute to Whately describes the lectures as " the last delivered in his lifetime from the chair he founded ". This would make the date *of delivery* 1863, and this is therefore the date chosen as marking the end of the period with which this paper deals.

[3] Houston, *Principles of Value*, p. 22.

[4] *Ibid.*, pp. 29–30. Italics in original text.

[5] *Ibid.*, p. 36.

depends, *ceteris paribus*, on the rate at which value falls with increase of supply, in other words, on the extensibility of the demand ".[1]

So here at last that notion about demand which Hancock and Walsh had expressed finds an integral place in value analysis and a name,—a name extraordinarily like that by which it is known to every student of Economics to-day.

In general, there is a noteworthy resemblance between the theory of Hancock and that of Houston, although the latter was certainly strongly influenced by Mill. Like Hancock, Houston emphasises the importance of demand factors in the short period as compared with supply factors in the long, but in Houston's version the emphasis on supply factors—again represented by " cost of production "—is much stronger, the utility aspect being almost incidental. Indeed, so strongly is he imbued with " real cost " ideas that he goes far beyond the classical school in the endlessly disputed matter of measuring values " in real terms ". Making the customary admission that it is impossible to find an invariable measure of value, Houston yet proposes a measure of cost of production in terms of sacrifice " which should enable us to determine the relative values of freely-produced commodities so far, and so long, as the conditions of their production did not vary ". To this end he endeavours to construct a " unit of sacrifice " and even goes so far as to give a hypothetical example of its use, couched in mathematical terms.[2] Criticism would be superfluous, but, despite such defects, Houston's doctrine can bear closer examination at the present day than Cairnes'.

Houston vacated the Dublin Chair in 1866, when the time of the general recognition of the " subjective " approach to value was at hand. As the change is customarily depicted, the work of Cairnes appears as the last statement of the old doctrine, that of Jevons and Menger as the first statement of the new. It is true, indeed, that Cairnes expressed the dominant theory of his day, but equally it appears that his views were more or less alien to the trend of economic thought of the University where he graduated and the Chair he first occupied. Yet perhaps it is true to say that on value questions the work of the early Whately Professors did reflect the general trend of their time. For, after all, in a reflection things *are* reversed.

[1] Houston, *Principles of Value*, p. 44, and Appendix C, p. 90.

[2] Houston, op. cit., Appendix B, pp. 86 *et seq.* In justice to Houston it must be said that he gave other lectures on " value in use ", which he did not publish, but which may have given a more balanced picture of value theory as a whole.

[3]

Thomas Joplin and the Theory of Interest

Keynes' suggestion that savings and investment determine, not the rate of interest as the " Classical " theory had assumed, but the volume of output and employment, was no doubt the most significant feature of his contribution to economic thought. Whereas the " Classical " economists thought in terms of the amount saved out of a given income, with the rate of interest as its most important determinant, we have now become accustomed to think in terms of the amount saved out of a variable income, with the effect of the rate of interest lumped together with that of the other factors upon which saving depends under the general heading of the propensity to save. Most " Classical " economists, of course, recognised that saving actually did vary with income, just as they usually recognised that income varied with investment : what they did not realise was the relevance of these functional relationships to the problems (particularly the problem of employment) which their theory of interest was believed to illuminate. The " Classical " savings and investment curves were actually interdependent, but this did not become clear until the importance and relevance of changes in the level of income had been appreciated. Once the inhibiting assumption of a given income was dropped, income quite naturally began to appear as the primary variable in the savings function. The crucial step had then been taken, and the new model began to fall into shape. If saving is a function of income, then saving and investment can only be kept equal to one another per medium of changes in income.

But Keynes was not, of course, the first economist to insist upon the importance of treating saving as a function of the ability to save : the Classical theory of accumulation also rested upon this basis.[1] Nor was Keynes the first to assert that it was changes in the ability to save which accommodated the supply of savings to changes in the demand for loans : in this respect he had been substantially anticipated by Thomas Joplin in his *Outlines of a System of Political Economy*, which appeared in 1823. The main purpose of the present article is to suggest that most contemporary genealogies of the Keynesian approach—which usually concentrate on the Malthusian underconsumptionist doctrines and the glosses on Say's Law written by the early analysts of forced saving[2]—are seriously incomplete because of their neglect of Joplin's contribution and the tradition in which he wrote. The article begins with a brief discussion of Ricardo's theory of accumulation, designed to place Joplin's work in its historical perspective ; it then passes to a more detailed examination of the relevant passages in the *Outlines;* and it concludes with some speculations (inspired by one of Joplin's later works) as to the reasons for the failure of economists to follow up Joplin's line of approach in the post-Ricardian era.

There are two aspects of the Classical theory of capital accumulation, as it appears in Ricardo's writings, which are of particular significance in the present connection. In the first place, the process of accumulation is visualised by Ricardo (as it had also been visualised by Smith) in terms of the disposition of the social labour force. " When we say that revenue is saved, and added to capital," Ricardo writes, " what we mean

[1] I use the word Classical in quotation marks in Keynes' sense, and without quotation marks in Marx's sense : see *General Theory*, p. 3, footnote.

[2] E.g. Wilson, *Fluctuations in Income and Employment*, Chapter 1. Joplin himself, of course, was one of the most prominent of the " forced saving " writers, but I am not directly concerned with this aspect of his work in the present article.

is, that the portion of revenue, so said to be added to capital, is consumed by productive instead of unproductive labourers."[1] The social surplus, or "net revenue," when it first comes into the hands of the landlord or capitalist,[2] is either expended by its recipient in the employment of unproductive labour (menial servants, entertainers, etc.), or used by him as capital—that is, in the employment of productive labour[3]. If hoarding is regarded as an aberration which for all practical purposes can be ignored, and if full employment is assumed, then the net revenue must necessarily be used to support labour of one of these two types, and an increase in the rate of accumulation, other things being equal, will bring about an increase in the proportion of productive to unproductive labour in the social labour force.

In the second place, Ricardo seems to have taken the view that accumulation could most usefully be regarded as a function of the net revenue—and in particular of that part of the net revenue which took the form of profits. Ricardo, like many of his contemporaries, tended to treat the urge to accumulate on the part of those who had the power to do so rather as a datum presented by nature than as a factor which varied significantly with the rate of reward offered from time to time by the market. "I consider the wants and tastes of mankind as unlimited," he wrote to Malthus in a well-known letter. "We all wish to add to our enjoyments or to our power. Consumption adds to our enjoyments, *accumulation to our power*, and they equally promote demand."[4] If, then, the propensity to accumulate out of net revenue is given more or less independently of changes in the rate of reward, the primary determinant of the volume of accumulation in an advancing economy is likely to be conceived as the *ability* to accumulate, which is measured by the volume of net revenue accruing to the saving classes. "High profits are favourable to the accumulation of capital," wrote Ricardo in the *Principles*,[5] and this was a theme which he repeated again and again. It seems clear that in the great majority of such statements, Ricardo was referring to the effect upon accumulation of a high volume, rather than a high rate, of profits. Accumulation was conceived as a function, not of the incentive, but of the ability to accumulate.[6]

Now if the supply of capital is regarded as a function of the net incomes of the saving classes, it follows that the supply of capital can be accommodated to a change in the demand for it only by means of a change in these net incomes. Ricardo, however, never concerned himself with this problem : he was not particularly interested in the process whereby savings from net revenue were transformed into capital. The word "accumulation" in Classical political economy was a blanket term covering both the action of saving a part of the net revenue and the action of using the savings to employ productive labourers. The Classical economists were, of course, perfectly well aware that the act of saving and the act of investment were often performed by different

[1] *Works* (ed. McCulloch), p. 87.

[2] Ricardo recognised that the labourer might also share in the net revenue (cf. *Works*, p. 210, footnote), but usually assumed that this fact could be neglected (cf. *Notes on Malthus*, pp. 207–8).

[3] "Productive," roughly speaking, meant productive of a surplus over cost. Productive labourers were those employed on a capitalist basis.

[4] *Letters to Malthus*, p. 45 (my emphasis).

[5] *Works*, p. 201.

[6] Cf. G. F. Shove, "The Place of Marshall's 'Principles' in the Development of Economic Theory," *E.J.*, December, 1942, at p. 299, footnote. Some of the relevant passages in Ricardo's writings will be found on pp. 41–2, 53, 67–8, 98, 143, 175, 193–4, 201, 241, 386, 387 and 474 of the *Works*. It is certainly true that in one or two places (notably on p. 68) Ricardo does seem to make explicit reference to a functional relation between the supply of capital and the rate of reward. But the general impression received from Ricardo's work taken as a whole is that he believed the volume of accumulation to be relatively insensitive to changes in the rate of profit—at least until that rate fell so low (near the end of the descent to the stationary state) that the trouble and risk involved in accumulation were not adequately compensated for, when net accumulation would swiftly decline to zero. The notion of a normal supply price of capital was surely quite alien to Ricardo's way of looking at the economic process.

persons and for different motives, but in general they were convinced that what happened in the money market was more or less irrelevant to the main body of economic analysis. This conviction was a natural consequence of their habit of viewing the process of accumulation in " real " terms—that is, in terms of the disposition of the social labour force. If an act of accumulation is visualised primarily in terms of the redisposition of the social labour force which results from it (i.e. essentially *ex post*), there seems to be no good reason for emphasising the distinction between the case where the man who does the saving employs his savings as capital himself, and the case where he lends them to someone else to employ as capital. In either case the saved portion of the net revenue will eventually be consumed " by productive instead of unproductive labourers." Both Smith and Ricardo assumed that it was unnecessary, at least in the main body of their analysis, to treat the two cases separately[1] ; and the controversy between Ricardo and Malthus on the general glut question seems to have been conducted on the same assumption.[2] The question of the transformation of savings into capital was regarded as relevant, strictly speaking, only to the theory of money—a branch of enquiry separate from and definitely subordinate to the " real " analysis in which the Classical economists were chiefly interested. Ricardo's discussion of money, like the discussions on monopoly in modern text-books until recently, tended to be confined to isolated passages bearing little relation to the remainder of the argument. On the one hand, there was the long-period analysis of the economy as a whole, conducted almost entirely in " real " terms on the assumption that money did not matter ; on the other hand, on what was virtually a separate plane of discourse, there was the theory of money. The savings-investment problem could only interest an economist who was concerned with the examination of short-period rather than long-period equilibrium, and who was interested in the theory of the *monetary economy*. Such an economist was Thomas Joplin, who attacked the problem in his *Outlines* in the year of Ricardo's death.

The *Outlines* is a curious and ill-ordered medley of plagiarism, superstition, and intuitive wisdom. It was written, the sub-title tells us, " with a view to prove to Government and the country, that the cause of the present agricultural distress is entirely artificial ; and to suggest a plan for the management of the currency, by which it may be remedied now, and any recurrence of similar evils be prevented in future." Joplin's purpose was to advocate the establishment of English joint stock

[1] Cf. Smith, *Wealth of Nations* (Everyman edition), Vol. I, p. 301, and Ricardo, *Works*, p. 175.

[2] A failure to realise that the Classical economists regarded the act of saving and the act of investment simply as two facets of the single act of accumulation is responsible, I believe, for much over-valuation of Malthus's contribution. Malthus's argument was based on his belief that the amount spent out of income generated by new investment would not necessarily be sufficient to purchase all the new commodities at a profitable price, if the capitalists were committed to a policy of parsimony. The demand of the newly-employed workers would certainly increase by the amount of their wages, but the workers' demand alone was obviously insufficient to absorb the new commodities at a profitable price. And the deficiency of demand, generally speaking, could not be made up by increased consumption on the part of the capitalists, since their very decision to increase investment necessarily implied a corresponding increase in saving on their part, which was conceived by Malthus as involving a *national* diminution of consumption. Under conditions where capital was being rapidly accumulated, therefore, a general glut could only be avoided by an increase in the consumption of the " body of unproductive consumers." It is surely an exaggeration, then, to say that Malthus posed " the whole problem of the balance between Saving and Investment " (Keynes, *Essays in Biography*, pp. 146–7), or that he argued that the trouble was due to " sterile savings " (Wilson, op. cit., p. 4). Some commentators speak as if Malthus visualised the general glut as resulting from a deflationary situation caused by the existence of idle savings, whereas in reality Malthus always regarded " saving " and " the conversion of revenue into capital " as two aspects of the same thing. The difference between the Keynesian and Malthusian systems is indeed striking : in the former, investment is regarded as an invigorating factor necessarily promoting and extending demand, whereas in the latter, under certain conditions, it is regarded as a depressive factor because it is believed to involve a relative diminution of effective demand.

banks, on the Scottish model, and to call for an alteration of the Bank of England charter to enable this to be done. He had begun his campaign in February, 1822, with an *Essay on Banking*, which apparently had a certain amount of success. His view was that the issues of the Country Banks, under the régime which he was attacking, " are not regulated by those of the Bank of England, but are improperly influenced by the pressure and anti-pressure of capital, independently of the Bank of England, or of the Country Bankers themselves."[1] After the publication of the *Essay on Banking*, Joplin seems to have decided that his " plan for a self-regulating system of Currency, which would prevent fluctuations in prices,"[2] would possibly appear more plausible if the theory of money upon which it was based were related to the real analysis with which contemporary economists like Ricardo were primarily concerned. The *Outlines* was the result. The book, as Joplin later admitted, was " composed with a very imperfect knowledge of the writings of others, on the same subject," and did not succeed in attracting much attention. Nevertheless, it is something of a landmark in the history of economic thought. " The title was somewhat ambitious," Joplin himself said of it, " but the opinions were new, whether they were well or ill founded."[3]

The sections of the *Outlines* to which I wish to draw attention commence with a familiar proposition which Joplin calls " the fulcrum of the argument " :

> " The first thing necessary to the annual production of any commodity is, that there should be an annual consumption and demand for it. Its production is, in fact, a proof of its consumption. Without consumption no demand could exist, and no production would take place. Demand, on the other hand, proceeds from income. . . . This conclusion is, therefore, obvious—that if to the existence of an annual income of 430 millions, an expenditure of 430 millions be necessary, in order to cause that demand which gives rise to it, and there is no other source of income from whence this consumption can proceed, every shilling of the 430 millions must be annually spent."[4]

Four short chapters dealing with various aspects of the national income follow. The fourth, dealing with the manner in which the income of society is consumed, is the most interesting. " In whatever way a person acquires the money he receives," Joplin writes, " he must do one of three things with it. He must either hoard it, lend it at interest to others, or expend it himself."[5] If he hoards it—which, as it later appears, he is in fact very unlikely to do—reactions in the sphere of foreign trade will ensure that the " ultimate demand " for commodities is not diminished. If he lends it to others at interest, they will expend it either " commercially " or " actually "—that is, either " in building houses or ships, or digging mines, &c., . . . in the manufacture of goods, or in the purchase and sale of them," or " in the actual purchase, consumption, and enjoyment of the necessaries, conveniences, and luxuries of life." And, finally, if he expends it himself, " it must be either in actual or commercial consumption as above described : so that whether he saves the money, or whether he spends it, consumption is equally produced."[6]

So far Joplin is merely elaborating a number of propositions which had been popularised by Smith and Ricardo.[7] But the terms in which Joplin expressed them, and the purpose which motivated him, resulted in his placing unusual emphasis on a

[1] *Analysis and History of the Currency Question* (1832), pp. 120–1.
[2] Ibid., p. 141.
[3] Ibid., loc. cit.
[4] *Outlines*, p. 33.
[5] Ibid., p. 44.
[6] Ibid., pp. 44–5.
[7] Cf. Smith, *Wealth of Nations*, Vol. I, p. 302, and Ricardo, *Works*, p. 175.

problem which the Classical approach had hitherto tended to conceal—the problem of the adjustment of the supply of savings to the demand for loans. This problem is dealt with in the remarkable chapter entitled " Principles which Regulate the Saving of Money."[1]

Joplin begins as follows : " As all the income of society is, and must be, annually consumed, all the money which is borrowed, in order to be spent by one person, class, or body of individuals, must be necessarily saved by another." If nobody saved, it would be impossible to borrow, and if no one consumed more than his annual income it would be impossible to lend. It follows (if it be assumed that hoarding is " very little practised ") that " the demand for money on the one hand, and supply of it on the other, must be equal. The amount of the savings by those who do not spend their annual incomes, must be precisely equal to the wants of those whose expenditure exceeds them." But this is an *ex post* correspondence. How are supply and demand *made* equal ?

In approaching this problem, Joplin deals in turn with the demand side and the supply side. First, why do people want to borrow ? A " demand for money " (i.e. for loans), Joplin asserts, is produced by four different causes :

> " By the necessity which exists in an improving country for an increased stock of buildings, machinery, commodities, &c., in order to supply the increased population and consumption which its increased fertility creates. By losses in trade and commerce. By the excess of expenditure of those whose expenses exceed their incomes ; and by the wants of government."

After discussing each of these four causes, Joplin proceeds to consider the supply side. First, who supplies the money which people borrow on the money market ? The labourers are usually unable to save, finding their incomes in general " too small to supply their customary wants." Those whose incomes are derived from property are able to save but have little incentive to do so. " Being secure of the annual receipts of their incomes, and in consequence removed from any anxious cares respecting the future, they live in general to the full extent of them." The people who do the bulk of the saving, then—the " economists of society," as Joplin calls them—" principally consist of the mercantile classes." " The capitalists of society," he writes in another place, " are a country's greatest economists."[2] An interesting statement of the motives which induce these " economists " to save part of their incomes now follows :

> " Being dependant upon trades of precarious profit for their support, they learn the inclination of acquiring money from the habit of doing so. It is necessary for every tradesman who means to do well to save money, in order to provide against a future evil day, which the uncertainty of trade often produces. This necessity, the desire for independence, and the ambition to be rich, which the pursuits of trade usually generate, render this class, in general, economists, and the savings of society are principally made by them."[3]

[1] Chapter X, pp. 57–70. Individual page references will not be given for quotations from this chapter. It should be noted that Joplin's analysis in these passages is based on the assumption that his " plan for a self-regulating system of Currency " has actually been put into effect, so that money plays an essentially passive role in the economy, and an increased demand for loans can only be met by an increased supply of savings.

[2] *Outlines*, p. 251. Cf. Ricardo, *Works*, p. 474 : " As all savings are made from profits, as a country is most happy when it is in a rapidly progressive state, profits and interest cannot be too high."

[3] The last part of this statement is somewhat similar to that made by Ricardo in the letter to Malthus referred to in note 4, p. 155. But whereas Ricardo treats the desire for power as an attribute of " mankind " in the abstract, Joplin realises that it is actually generated by " the pursuits of trade."

There is no suggestion in this account that the " economists " are interested in the actual rate of reward for saving, and we are accordingly prepared for the important proposition which follows :

> " The amount of savings by this class must altogether depend upon their power to save. When the interest of money, and profits of trade are large, their power of saving is necessarily greater than when the profits of trade, and interest of money are small. When their income is great, they can of course save more than when it is little."

Joplin's unambiguous acceptance of this Classical concept meant that the terms in which the problem of the adjustment of the supply of savings to the demand for loans could be discussed were fairly rigidly defined. If the demand for loans increased, the supply of savings could increase correspondingly only if the increased demand set up reactions which ultimately increased the *ability* of the " economists " to save—i.e. which increased " the profits of trade, and interest of money." In other words, the supply of savings could be adjusted to a change in the demand for loans only per medium of an induced change in the net incomes of the saving classes.

The mechanism whereby the necessary changes in net incomes occurred, as Joplin described it, was set in motion by changes in the rate of interest. Like the majority of writers in the Classical tradition, Joplin seems to have believed that the rate of interest in the short period was regulated by " the demand for money," but that the *supply* of savings was not directly dependent on the rate of interest.[1] An increase in the " demand for money," therefore, would raise the rate of interest, but, since saving was a function not of the rate of interest but of the net incomes of the saving classes, the rise in the rate of interest would not *directly* affect the volume of saving—that is, it would not affect it per medium of the incentive, as it was conceived to do in the neo-Classical model. The rise in the rate of interest could affect the volume of saving in the appropriate manner only if it initiated an economic change which eventually increased the net incomes of the " economists " to exactly the required extent.

This is precisely what Joplin believed would happen, although the exact manner in which he thought that the mechanism of adjustment would work is not very clearly stated. Suppose, he argues, that the demand for money increases, while the supply of savings remains the same. The rate of interest will then immediately rise, and the following reactions will ensue :

> " Profits are raised with the demand for money, by part of that money being lent for consumption, which would otherwise have gone to replace the stock of the dealer. By this means the consumptive demand is increased, and the prices of commodities raised ; while, by the diminished capital in trade, stocks are kept low, and the prices kept up. Much of the capital employed in trade is borrowed of bankers, and others, by persons in trade, at the market rate of interest ; and the first effect of any increased demand for money, is to induce these bankers to abstract it from its ordinary channels, in order to lend to those who offer better terms for it."[2]

[1] Cf. *Outlines*, p. 62 : " If a person have money, and he cannot get five per cent. interest for it, he must take four ; if not four, three, &c. Any rate of interest, with good security, will be better than hoarding it." Joplin elsewhere recognises that the *demand* for loans will be increased by a reduction in the rate of interest : see the interesting statement in *Outlines*, p. 184.

[2] This argument may become more comprehensible if it is remembered that Joplin is (*a*) placing an emphasis, now unfamiliar, on the demand for loans for consumptive purposes, and (*b*) assuming that the increased demand for loans can be satisfied only by an actual increase in savings.

Suppose, on the other hand, that the demand for money falls while the supply remains the same. In that case a different set of reactions will occur :

> " If a person in trade has saved money, and cannot obtain good employment for it otherwise, he will put it into his trade ; and this being done by all persons in the same trade, who have saved money, and cannot do better with it, the competition will reduce the rate of profits in that trade ; or the lowered rate of interest will drive persons into the trade, as a means of obtaining a better income, who would otherwise have lived upon the interest of their capital without trade. The general effect of this is, that less income is obtained than before; that though there is more capital in trade, less profit, upon the aggregate, is derived from it. Thus the trading part of the community are unable to save money as heretofore. . . ."[1]

These influences affecting the ability to save are reinforced by others which affect the ability to spend in inverse ratio. For example, when the interest rate rises, consequent upon an increase in the demand for loans, the value of land will fall. " An estate which would be worth forty years purchase with the interest of money at 2½ per cent., would be worth only half that with the interest of money at five, and would only have half the spending in it. For this reason, as the demand for government [*sic*] increased, the power of spending by individuals would be diminished." On the other hand, if the interest rate falls, consequent upon a decrease in the demand for loans, " temptations to expenditure are held out by the increased value of landed property."

In both cases, then, the incomes of the " economists " will vary in the right direction, so that the " annual supply of incipient capital " is increased or diminished as required. It is fairly obvious that this analysis, while its ingenuity can scarcely be denied, leaves one asking a number of new questions. But the conclusions which Joplin draws from it are sufficiently remarkable to deserve full quotation :

> " Thus, with the increase or decrease of the demand for money, do interest and profits of trade rise and fall, by which the power of economizing, in order to supply the demand, is exactly proportioned to it.
>
> " The savings of a nation, therefore, diminish the power to save. The incomes of those being reduced, who are the principal economists of the country, their power of economizing is reduced with the excessive supply of money, by which the value of it is diminished.
>
> " The Dutch are the most saving people in Europe ; and with them the profits of trade, and interest of money, are always at a very low ebb. When the bulk of a nation are economists, the difficulty of making money becomes excessive ; and the commercial part of it is ground down to penuriousness by the national parsimony.
>
> " Precisely opposite are the effects produced by an increase of national expenditure. The profits of trade are good, and a free stile of living pervades the mercantile classes ; they not only save more money, but they also spend more.
>
> " Such an unusual increase of expenditure as to raise the interest of money, rarely, however, perhaps never, happens from the expenditure of individuals. It mostly, if not always, arises from the demands of governments."

It is important to note, however, that Joplin did not visualise the process of adjustment of the supply of savings to the demand for loans as necessarily involving

[1] *Analysis*, p. 105. There is no comparable statement in the *Outlines*, but the passage in the *Analysis* seems to express the interpretation placed by Joplin on the quotation from Smith appearing on p. 63 of the *Outlines*.

a variation in the *real* income of the community. He seems to have supposed that any maladjustment would correct itself automatically without affecting "national prosperity." "The profits of trade," he writes, "which fall upon the price of commodities, must be nothing more than a tax paid by the ultimate consumers of them, and . . . just in proportion as the tradesman flourishes the consumer suffers. If the whole income of society must be consumed, it is only a different mode of arranging that consumption, and nationally there is no greater prosperity with great profits than with small ones." The idea that a general depression ever exists, Joplin maintained, was simply a figment of the capitalists' imagination. But it is clear from other passages in the *Outlines* that Joplin was well aware of the fact that the process of adjustment, under certain circumstances, might involve variations in employment. For example, in the first of his chapters on money, he describes how, "in a year of extraordinary abundance," the price of corn will not fall in proportion to the increased supply, and the farmer's profits will accordingly increase. "The surplus above what is necessary for his rent is placed in banks, or lent to those who immediately expend it in the employment of labour ; by which means it makes shorter circuits, more labour is employed, and a greater consumption is created." And the effect of cheap money upon employment is summed up in the following passage :

> "Money, being more abundant, creates itself employment, either by the increased facilities with which it is lent out, or by the reduced interest which is charged for it ; by which means traders are induced to increase their merchant stocks, and people in general to enter into undertakings in which the employment of labour is involved ; but which, with a greater scarcity of money, they would not have attempted."[1]

In his *Analysis and History of the Currency Question*, published in 1832, Joplin included a summary of the doctrines I have just outlined. This summary is interesting because Joplin incorporated certain new features which did not appear in the original presentation of the theory in the *Outlines*—features which may help to account for the failure of contemporary economists to follow up Joplin's line of approach.

Joplin was concerned in the *Analysis* to make a very much sharper distinction between the monetary system he was advocating and the actual system of his own time than he had made in the *Outlines*. His own system envisaged an indestructible metal currency or "a paper currency constructed on similar principles" ; under the prevailing system, on the other hand, the country banks were "issuers of the currency" as well as "dealers in incipient capital."[2] Under the projected system, Joplin argued, "there never is, for any length of time, more money than there is a demand for,"[3] because any discrepancy between the supply of savings and the demand for loans is immediately adjusted by means of the mechanism described in the *Outlines*. Under the actual system, however, the rate of interest charged by the country banks bears little relation to the "true" or "natural" rate, and the adjustment of the supply of savings to the demand for loans may well be achieved only at the expense of violent fluctuations in the value of money.[4]

[1] *Outlines*, p. 184. On the following pages Joplin describes the "opposite effects" produced in "years of scarcity." The analysis is still being conducted on the assumption that the banks cannot meet an increased demand for loans by an extension of their issues : cf. *Outlines*, pp. 214–5.

[2] *Analysis*, pp. 108–9.

[3] Ibid., p. 107.

[4] It was in this connection that Joplin developed his ideas on forced saving, to which a number of writers have drawn attention. See, e.g. Hayek, "Prices and Production," and "A Note on the Development of the Doctrine of Forced Saving," *Q.J.E.*, Vol. 47, p. 123 ; Viner, "Studies in the Theory of International Trade," pp. 190–2 ; and Niebyl, "Studies in the Classical Theories of Money," pp. 109–10.

In the *Analysis*, then, Joplin was more concerned to emphasise the *automatic* character of the process whereby the supply of savings was adjusted to changes in the demand for loans under the " natural " system. In the *Outlines* the whole emphasis had been laid upon the functional connection between saving and the ability to save. In the *Analysis* this emphasis is somewhat less, and Joplin is obviously looking for additional factors which will help to bring the supply of savings back into equality with the demand for loans even more smoothly and harmlessly, if one happens to get out of step with the other. Suppose, for example, that the demand for loans falls. The rate of interest will then fall, and, according to the scheme of the *Outlines*, this will ultimately induce the necessary reduction in the net incomes of the saving classes. In the *Analysis* this same effect is visualised as occurring, but it is reinforced by two additional effects. In the first place, Joplin stresses the fact that a lowered rate of interest will tend to stimulate once again the *demand* for loans. He points out that a fall in the rate of interest " has a general tendency to cause an increase of stocks in all trades ; it induces people to build houses ; and . . . leads to the embarking capital in great public undertakings, which would otherwise not have been ventured upon." In the second place, and more significantly, Joplin for the first time mentions the fact that a lowered rate of interest will tend to reduce the *inducement* to save. When the rate of interest falls, says Joplin, this additional reaction will occur :

> " The man of landed or fixed income is less tempted to save than he was before. Saving is made by a sacrifice of present enjoyment, for a future good, in the shape of an increase of annual income. But as the annual income to be derived from saving diminishes, the temptation to save is reduced. In this way, likewise, a superabundance of the savings of income, or incipient capital, and a fall of interest, will also operate in checking the future supply."[1]

Now Joplin's use of this idea that saving depends not only on the ability to save but also on the incentive was quite clearly associated with a desire to show that the economic system, in itself, was fundamentally sound and self-adjusting. Joplin wanted to demonstrate that if any tendency towards disequilibrium was not swiftly[2] and painlessly corrected, this was the fault of the irrational—and alterable—monetary superstructure. Any trouble which was experienced must be due to something external to the system itself. Such a thesis would obviously be rendered more plausible by any argument which gave added emphasis to the automatic character of the process of adjustment. This suggests one possible reason why the concept of saving as a function of the rate of reward succeeded in becoming popular in the post-Ricardian era—because it could be usefully employed in support of the contention that capitalism was a stable and self-adjusting system.

It is also significant, I think, that Joplin should have associated this new idea with the proposition that " saving is made by a sacrifice of present enjoyment, for a future good, in the shape of an increase of annual income." This notion, which was destined to form the foundation of the neo-Classical theory of interest, had never been emphasised by Smith or Ricardo. It became fashionable only when economists began to feel obliged to demonstrate that interest (or profit) was a *reward* for the act of saving (or accumulation)—an obligation which began to appear particularly pressing after the middle 'twenties, when the " Ricardian socialists " had shown the unfortunate

[1] *Analysis*, p. 106. The statement is expressed to apply only to " the man of landed or fixed income," but it is otherwise perfectly general, and there is no obvious reason why Joplin should not have applied it to *all* savers.

[2] Some of the reactions which Joplin describes are hardly consistent with his suggestion that the process of adjustment was relatively swift. Cf. *Analysis*, p. 106, where the reduction of rents due to an increase in house-building is conceived as an element in the mechanism of adjustment.

use to which the Classical concept of surplus and the labour theory of value could be put. To demonstrate that interest was a reward for the act of saving, rather than an income in the nature of a surplus, it was necessary, first, to discover some aspect of the saving process which could plausibly be presented as involving a real cost or sacrifice on the part of the saver, and, second, to posit a direct functional relationship between the volume of saving and the rate of interest. It is sometimes assumed by historians that the idea of a functional connection between the supply of capital and its return (involving the recognition of a real cost lying behind accumulation) was a necessary element in the Ricardian theory of equilibrium.[1] This does not appear to me to have been the case : the idea was not, in fact, developed until it was found desirable to stress the existence of such a cost.

The tendency to think of saving as a function of the rate of interest, then, may at least in its origin have been associated with the desire to show, first, that the economic system was fundamentally stable, and, second, that it was not founded on the exploitation of the labourer. But one other factor of some importance intensified the tendency, and was largely responsible for the failure of orthodox economics to exorcise it before 1936. Professor Myint has recently drawn attention to the significant difference between the economic problem with which the Classical economists were concerned, and that with which we are mainly concerned to-day.[2] The Classical economists were chiefly interested in the problem of *increasing* the wealth of the nation—in securing abundance. Modern economists, on the other hand (at least since the 1870's), have become interested primarily in the problem of *allocating* a given pool of resources as " efficiently " as possible—in making the best of scarcity.[3] Now, for obvious reasons, the idea that saving should be regarded as a function of the rate of interest has usually been associated with theories which think in terms of the amount saved out of a given income. The idea that saving should be regarded as a function of income, on the other hand, has usually been stressed by economists who were mainly interested in the causes of variations in income. The transfer of attention from the Classical to the modern economic problem, then, meant that the Classical concept of saving as a function of income, upon which Joplin built his analysis in the *Outlines*, began to appear, not only as inferior to its successor from an apologetic point of view, but also as actually irrelevant.

Glasgow. RONALD L. MEEK.

[1] E.g., Marion Bowley, *Nassau Senior*, p. 140.
[2] *Theories of Welfare Economics, passim.*
[3] It is interesting to speculate on the reasons for this change of emphasis. Possibly the crucial point may be that the decade in which the new marginal techniques began to become popular was one in which it was widely believed that the rate of economic growth had at last been checked.

[4]

The Advent of Academic Economics in England

I.

From the fifteenth to the eighteenth century the characteristic economic theory in England was provided by the merchant class; Mun and Child had superseded whatever contribution the schoolmen of the universities might have made through the adumbration of canon law. Their victory had meant the eclipse of the Church and its branch, the universities, as arbiters in economic matters. That claim was not to be renewed until the nineteenth century was well embarked. Though Petty, with his connections with the Dutch universities, Oxford, and the new Royal Society, seems to have merged the academic with the pragmatic, the universities in England took little interest in political arithmetic. Trinity College, Dublin, had by the end of the eighteenth century produced through its Provost, Fellows, and alumni, a number of economic studies arising from the condition of Ireland, but these were factual or prescriptive.[1]

But by the late eighteenth century, Adam Smith, inspired by Hutcheson and Hume, had fully snatched back the initiative from the merchants. Dugald Stewart at Edinburgh, friend and disciple of Smith, followed his lead in teaching the new political economy, not only to native Scots, but to the wave of young Englishmen who went north in lieu of the grand tour, made impossible by the renewal of war with France. On the England of the new century Stewart discharged a group of his pupils, led by Francis Horner and Henry Brougham, who had imbibed political economy along with their moral philosophy and other staples of Scottish academic diet. But there was no unseemly rush on the part of the English universities, still profound in their lethargy, to rival the new light from the north.

[1] R. D. Collison Black, *Economic Studies at Trinity College, Dublin*, *Hermathena*, No. LXX, 1947, p. 65.

To be sure, there had been some donnish dabbling in economic matters at Oxford and Cambridge. As long ago as 1756, William Bell of Cambridge had submitted for one of Lord Townshend's prizes a dissertation on population and trade which succeeded in provoking controversy on the "causes of populosity" and in clearly enunciating the principle of the territorial division of labour.[1] But Bell was soon to busy himself with the proofs of Holy Writ to the exclusion of economic speculation.

The expedients of Pitt's war finance had attracted the attention of two Oxford men—Dr. Tatham, the almost legendary Rector of Lincoln, and Henry Beeke, who as Professor of Modern History from 1801 to 1813 delivered his terminal lecture in Oriel College Hall.[2] Dr. Tatham entertained it as his own sober opinion that to him, and him alone, was owing the overthrow of Bonaparte, and the consequent glory of Great Britain. The Bank, he said, refused Pitt advances, and the war must have dropped, had not a pamphlet of his own, advocating the establishment of a rival bank, frightened the Old Lady of Threadneedle Street into a loan. Nor was this the end of Dr. Tatham's contribution to the financing of the war—he also laid claim to the invention of the property tax. He became a virulent opponent of the Bullion Committee, condemning with characteristic vigour the deflationary policies it proposed.[3] Henry Beeke too had a claim, preferred by some, to the invention of the income tax.[4] He certainly investigated its working, and attempted a calculation of the national income to this end.[5] Somewhat later he was approached by the egregious Vansillart, Chancellor of the Exchequer, for advice. At Cambridge, in part contemporary with Tatham and Beeke, there was Dr. John Symonds, Professor of Modern History 1771-1807. He had spent four or five years studying at first hand agricultural

[1] *What Causes principally contribute to render a Nation Populous, and What Effect has the Populousness of a Nation on its Trade.* Cambridge, 1756.

[2] G. V. Cox, *Recollections of Oxford.* London, 1868, p. 142.

[3] J. R. Green, *Oxford Studies.* London, 1901, p. 186.

[4] D.N.B.

[5] *Observations on the Produce of the Income Tax.* London, 1799.

conditions in Italy in the light of the policies of the several Italian States. He had concerned himself too with the problems of colonisation, and had contributed numerous articles to Arthur Young's Annals of Agriculture.[1]

Academic pronouncements on economic subjects were not without their dangers in the England that confronted Napoleon. The currency was a particularly treacherous subject. Edward Copleston, presiding as Provost over the lively Common Room of Oriel from 1814 to 1827 was a public disputant on the subject, who applauded Ricardo's abilities and the case for resuming convertibility in 1819[2]. Copleston was even thought by some to have inspired the work of Thomas Tooke.[3] But in taking the side hostile to the government's policy of the hour, he prejudiced his prospects to such an extent that when preferment finally came it was to the See of Llandaff, one of the poorest and farthest advanced in decay in the Kingdom.[4]

But the signs that the English Universities were slowly preparing to take a more active interest were gradually beginning to multiply. Sir Edward West, another Oxonian, presented his theory of rent to the world in 1815 under the pseudonym: "A Fellow of University College."[5] At Cambridge, Smithson Tennant, Professor of Chemistry, a visitor to Ricardo's house, was "very well read in political economy,"[6] William Whewell, though not yet Master of Trinity, had by the twenties embraced the subject in the great span of his studies, at one time engaging in discussion "day by day" on Malthus and Ricardo.[7] On the teaching side the

[1]K. T. B. Butler, *A "Petty" Professor of Modern History: William Smyth* (1765-1849). *The Cambridge Historical Journal*, Vol. IX, No. 2, 1948, p. 220.

[2]A Letter to the Right Hon. Robert Peel . . . on the pernicious effects of a variable standard of value.

[3]W. J. Copleston, *Memoir of Edward Copleston* . . . London, 1851, p. 152.

[4]Richard Whately, *Remains of the late Edward Copleston*. London, 1854, p. 28.

[5]*Essay on the Application of Capital to Land.*

[6]*Autobiographical Recollections of George Pryme, Esq., M.A.* London, 1870, p. 115. *Letters of David Ricardo to Thomas Robert Malthus.* ed. J. Bonar, Oxford, 1887, p. 182.

[7]I. Todhunter, *William Whewell, D.D.* London, 1876. Vol. II, p. 346.

study was gradually filtering in. William Smyth, appointed Professor of Modern History at Cambridge in 1807, another partaker of Ricardo's hospitality,[1] did his best not only to revive the subject for which he was nominally responsible, but also to convey to his hearers the importance of the "somewhat repulsive study of Political Economy." [2] George Pryme, partly inspired by Smyth's example, began, though largely on sufferance, a full course of lectures at Cambridge in 1816.[3] Smyth, consistent with his own precept, attended them. At Oxford we hear of Smyth's opposite number, Professor Nares, advertising in 1817 that he will read "during the present term, two courses of lectures, one on History and the other on Political Economy." [4] The conscientious but ineffectual Nares struggled with Smithian indeterminism to a class whose interest in the "curious science" [5] proved difficult to maintain. At Oriel many of the Fellows, including Richard Whately and Thomas Arnold [6] shared their Provost's interest in the subject.

The 'Twenties saw the formal, though still qualified, acceptance of Political Economy by the English Universities. At Oxford, in 1825, the Drummond Chair of Political Economy was founded, with Nassau Senior as the first holder. The University wrote politely to the founder, Henry Drummond, that it anticipated "the happiest effects" from the new Chair.[7] By 1828, Cambridge was prepared to afford Pryme, who by then had lectured for twelve years, an improved status. The courtesy title of Professor was then awarded, though "no duties were annexed to the Professorship," [8] and he was left as best he might to compete for the slender free time of the teaching programme with the Professor of Modern History and Modern Languages and many others, bound, like them, by the under-

[1] *Letters of Ricardo to Malthus.* p. 82.
[2] K. T. B. Butler. *ibid.* p. 220.
[3] *Autobiographical Recollections.* p. 120.
[4] *New Monthly Magazine.* Feb., 1817. p. 46.
[5] C. Mallet, *A History of the University of Oxford.* London, 1927, Vol. III, p. 216.
[6] A. D. Stanley, *Life and Correspondence of Thomas Arnold.* London, 1852, p. 153n.
[7] Mallet. *ibid.* Vol. III., p. 215.
[8] *Cambridge University Commission Report.* 1852, p. 135.

standing that his lectures were not to interfere with "the proper studies of the place." [1] University College, London, as might be expected in an institution with which men like James Mill and Henry Brougham were associated, was soon after its founding in 1826 provided with a Professor of Political Economy. J. R. M'Culloch, as first Professor, began his stormy association with the College. He had failed in 1825 to secure the partition of Dugald Stewart's Chair of Moral Philosophy and Political Economy at Edinburgh, with a view to occupying the latter half himself.[2] King's College, London, followed suit in founding a Chair a few years later, to which Richard Jones, helped by the good offices of Whewell,[3] was appointed in 1833. The Whately Chair at Trinity College, Dublin came in 1832, shortly after Whately's accession to the Archbishopric of Dublin.[4]

So much for chronology. But what were the influences at work which made it possible for political economy to gain this status within the English universities, and which were within some sixty years to make of them the Sinai of the science?

Since the revival of the English universities that began somewhere around Malthus' undergraduate days towards the end of the eighteenth century, the feeling was growing among the creative minority that they owed a general duty to the truth and a persistent enmity to error, not merely in matters of esoteric concern like classical exegesis or dogmatic theology, but also with respect to ideas more directly affecting society,[5] But to meet this reviving sense of obligation two things were necessary. Intellectual discipline in the known fields of study had to be restored, in order that the modes of thought them-

[1] Butler. *ibid.* p. 229.

[2] Mrs. Gordon, *Christopher North, a memoir of John Wilson.* 1879, p. 197.

[3] Todhunter. *ibid.* Vol. II, p. 148.

[4] It was not however until the reforms of the 'Fifties and 'Seventies that the subject played any real part in university examinations, and even then it remained slight. For this reason the attendance at lectures was notoriously slender, and a frequent source of rueful comment by the professors. This was so right through the days of Pryme, Fawcett, Jevons and Cairnes to Marshall's time.

[5] External criticism helped the movement forward. *Edinburgh Review,* October, 1809, p. 40 *et seq.*

selves might be rehabilitated. Beyond this lay the problem of reasoning about society. Philosophy, classics and history had been the traditional guides to social policy, insofar as intuitive judgment had sought criteria beyond itself. But these studies had afforded guidance, if at all, largely in the form of precedent, precept, or disquisition on the ideal form of government. The new natural sciences seemed to offer a new prospect of precise and relevant reasoning. The France of the Enlightenment had caught the vision : the great French thinkers of the eighteenth century had no doubts of the potential value of the abstract method in the study of social phenomena. Montesquieu had argued that a science of society was possible ;[1] Condorcet had repeatedly appealed to scholars in his oration of 1783 "to introduce into the moral sciences the philosophy and the method of the natural sciences." [2]

But the rehabilitation of English university studies was no easy task. Logic at Cambridge, its statutory teaching long defunct, and represented by "a muddy scantling of metaphysic psychology and dialectic," [3] did not recover until well into the century. Mathematics too had fallen on such evil days that when Whewell took his B.A. degree in 1816 the standard of performance was far below that of the continent.[4] But the tradition of Newton was not yet dead. Men like Herschel, Peacock and Babbage repaired the breach in relatively few years. Natural science too was fast reviving under the impetus of Clarke, Malthus' one-time travelling companion, and others. By 1831 Whewell was able to defend Cambridge science to good effect.[5]

The revival in Cambridge of mathematics and natural science was bound to provoke the inquiry in active Cambridge minds, as it had already done at the *Ecole Polytechnique* and

[1]G. de Santillana, *Positivism and the Technocratic Ideal. In Studies and Essays in Homage to George Sarton.* New York, 1944, p. 249.

[2]F. A. v. Hayek, *The Counter-Revolution of Science. Economica,* February, 1941, p. 12.

[3]Sir W. Hamilton, *Discussions on Philosophy, Literature, Education and University Reform.* London, 1852, p. 120.

[4]Mrs. Stair Douglas, *The Life and Selections from the Correspondence of William Whewell, D.D.* London, 1881, p. 401.

[5]*British Critic.* January, 1831, pp. 71-90.

the *Ecole Normale*, should the application of such methods stop short of the study of society itself? There was general agreement that the attempt should be made, though opinion differed of course as to the choice of method and the finality of the conclusions that might be possible. Malthus, ninth Wrangler in his day, was conscious that the mathematical tool-box had applications to economic and social problems,[1] and the great bulk of his writing on population is testimony to his confidence in observation. Richard Jones, Whewell's intimate friend, undertook to apply the methods he had learned at Cambridge to political economy.[2] Perronet Thompson, sometime Fellow of Queen's College, Cambridge, pointed out that political economy "is only another branch of the philosophy of natural phenomena," and that if faulty conclusions relating to tides or telescopes were promulgated, "they (the Universities) would have opposed them by the dissemination of a counter-version of the truth." [3] But, he complained, they were slow in doing their duty in this way by political economy. John Herschel, late Fellow of St. Johns, and a leader of scientific thought, also argued for the application of science to the new field. "Political economy," he wrote, "is found to have sound principles," and " . . . great and noble ends are to be achieved . . . by bringing into exercise a sufficient quantity of sober thought, and by a proper adaptation of means." [4] Whewell himself, greatly concerned, "to procure academic recognition for more modern branches of science and philosophy," was well aware that the new political economy was a subject toward which Cambridge, the great repository of scientific method, owed a duty.[5] Not only so; all universities had the same obligation. Thus we find Adam Sedgwick, sharing with Whewell the leadership of

[1]James Bonar, *Malthus and his Work*. London, 1885, p. 225n.

[2]*Literary Remains of Richard Jones*, ed. Wm. Whewell, 1859, p. xx.

[3]*The True Theory of Rent in opposition to Mr. Ricardo and others* . . . 1826, p. 130. "What is of importance to promote," wrote Thompson, "is the direction of the same rigid processes to this science, that have been extended to the earlier and more forward branches of human knowledge."

[4]*Preliminary Discourse on the Study of Natural Philosophy*. London, 1830, p. 73.

[5]*Stair Douglas. ibid.*, p. 404.

Cambridge natural science, giving his benediction to economics as a fitting academic subject, rejoicing in 1833, perhaps a little prematurely, that "political economy has obtained an honourable seat in most of the academic establishments of the civilised world." [1] To the leaders of Cambridge thought it was clear that if the universities took no part in social thinking, the rule of men's minds would pass to such as had no scruple about claiming scientific sanction for untenable methods and conclusions. "As long as the accredited guardians of learning stand aloof from a branch of learning peculiarly adapted for the exercise of cultivated reason," wrote Thompson, "it necessarily falls into the hands of those who have less power to distinguish fallacies, and less caution to avoid them."[2]

Oxford studies, like those of Cambridge, had much ground to recover.[3] Oxford too had allowed logic to atrophy. Nor was there in the early years of the century any counterpart to Cambridge mathematics, as a form of intellectual discipline aiming at the development of the power of higher generalisation. But the First Examination Statute of 1801 began the remedy by prescribing the teaching of logic. Copleston, lately appointed tutor at Oriel, confronted with the new teaching responsibility, and "having received no instruction in it, and having no living help to apply to, collected and read all the books he could meet with that professed to treat of it." [4] Whately produced his once celebrated "Logic" to fill the gap ;[5] Political Economy was used to demonstrate the technique and problems of precise definition by the addition of Nassau Senior's Appendix of Definitions. But logic, though well embarked by the men of Oriel (their Common Room was said to "stink of logic")[6] found it heavy going against the Oxford addiction to patristic theology, out of which the hubbub of the tractarian controversy was to grow.

[1] *A Discourse on the Studies of the University*. Cambridge, Fourth Edition, 1835, p. 88.

[2] *True Theory of Rent*. p. 31.

[3] Cox. *ibid*. p. 37.

[4] R. Whately, *Remains of Edward Copleston, D.D.* London, 1854, p. 94.

[5] *Elements of Logic*. London, 1826.

[6] W. Tuckwell, *Reminiscences of Oxford*. London, 1900, p. 17.

By the early thirties Oriel, the centre of intellectual life in the University, contained the future leaders of the two factions, Tractarian and anti-Tractarian, whose debates were to pursue their tortuous way through the middle and latter part of the century. But as yet the mystics like Newman had little to say on the subject of political economy. Newman himself had helped Whately to write his logic.[1] The men of "common-sense" school, like Whately and Arnold who were later so strong in their antipathy to the Tractarians, were clear in their minds that the universities should concern themselves with the new discipline. Active minded men like Copleston, Whately and Thomas Arnold were aware that the political economy of the non-Christian Ricardians was fast seizing hold of their generation. But they were greatly struck by the growing significance of the new study in practical affairs. "For it seems to me," wrote Whately, "that before long political economists of some sort or other must govern the world." [2] Men of Whately's mind feared the secularising of political economy. "Now," he said in 1829, "the anti-Christians are striving hard to have this science to themselves."[3] It was not that he was afraid that political economy might become a science in conflict with Christianity or Scripture. Whately was convinced that Scripture would not be damaged by conclusions arrived at by starting from non-Scriptural premises. In this he followed Paley's dictum: "Whatever renders religion more rational, renders it more credible." [4] He was confident in the "argument from design"—his belief in the Divine Order was extended to the economic field. He warned against the *petitio principii* into which the Christian would fall who began by assuming the inspiration of the Bible and judging the fruits of the new science by it.[5] But he did

[1]Whately, *Logic.* p. viii.

[2]E. J. Whately, *Life and Correspondence of Archbishop Whately.* 1866. Vol. I, p. 66.

[3]*ibid.*, p. 67. Much the same view was taken by Thomas Chalmers who desired to "Christianise the science." J. W. Harper, *The Social Ideal and Dr. Chalmers.* Edinburgh, 1910, p. viii.

[4]W. Paley, D.D. *The Principles of Moral and Political Philosophy.* New ed., 1819, p. iv.

[5]*Introductory Lectures on Political Economy.* London, 1832, pp. 29, 31.

greatly fear the gaining of prestige by non-Christians by virtue of their monopoly of political economy :—" . . . if these efforts are not met, the rising generation will be at the mercy of these men in one way or another—as their disciples or as their inferiors."[1] Copleston, Whately and Arnold were Christian pragmatics ; for them 'revelation' was severely limited, certainly stopping far short of guidance in economic matters. Thus they conceived it to be the duty of the Christian to apply his rational faculties to the best advantage to this field, and the University to give all possible assistance.

But though in the early part of the century political economy had to find its way into Cambridge via the scientists like Whewell and into Oxford via the logicians like Copleston and Whately, there was a factor common to both universities—Modern History. We have seen how Becke and Nares at Oxford and Symonds and Smyth at Cambridge had concerned themselves with the new study. The long war with France, with its vast problems of finance and logistics, concurrent with the new industrial inventions were making it abundantly clear that some recognition at least of the economic aspect of history was called for.

Of course there were from the outset grounds for resistance to the proposal that *de jure* recognition should be extended to the *de facto* infiltration. When Dr. Kaye, the Vice-Chancellor, carried George Pryme's proposal to the Heads of Colleges, he found that "some of them wished me to withhold my consent altogether." [2] The post-Waterloo universities were well-nigh Church corporations, and were to remain largely so until the century was three-quarters spent. Malthus had shocked many of his brothers of the cloth with his 'un-Godly' theory of population, and when they perceived that it constituted one of the pillars of the Ricardian system, many leading churchmen were bitter critics. It is significant that Whately and Senior at Oxford and Whewell and Jones at Cambridge were all opposed to Malthus on this score.

[1] *Life*. p. 67.
[2] *Autobiographical Recollections*. p. 121.

Then of course there was the theory of rent. A 'science' that could produce a theory of exploitation of this kind with its plain slight on a major source of college revenues could scarcely expect cordiality. The Heads of Colleges who could inform a Royal Commission as late as 1852 that College rent rolls were their own affair [1] could hardly be enamoured of Ricardianism. Moreover it was not merely the particular vulnerability of the universities to the rent theory that could create a hostile feeling : the Universities and the Church were bound in triple alliance with the landowners. Much opinion in the universities would have included the Ricardians among the malignants described by the Great Johnian, Wordsworth, who were charged with destroying the social fabric, who, "pretending to invigorate the tree, pour scalding water and corrosive compounds among its roots." [2] Peronett Thompson, conscious of this, did his best to amputate the offending concept from the Ricardian corpus.

Such considerations gave further point to the doubts about a subject of such direct significance for social policy. Sydney Smith remarked : "When a University has been doing useless things for a long time, it appears at first degrading to them to be useful. A set of lectures upon Political Economy would be discouraged in Oxford, possibly despised, probably not permitted." [3] So confirmed in his fears of too high a degree of relevance was George Pryme at Cambridge that a major point of pride with him lay in the inability of his students to guess where his sympathies lay, a somewhat curious attitude in one who sat for many years in Parliament and was a vigorous campaigner in the Whig interest.[4] This effect was attained not by assuming a high level of abstraction as is nowadays sometime the practice, but by considering the subject, as one

[1] *Oxford University Commission Report*, 1852, p. 125. Such Colleges as supplied information were overwhelmingly dependent on rents. The Drummond Chair of Political Economy at Oxford was itself a charge on the founder's rent roll. *Westminster Review*, July, 1827, p. 177.

[2] *Second Address to the Freeholders of Westmorland*, 1818. In *Prose Works of William Wordsworth*. Vol. I, p. 252.

[3] Mallet. *ibid*. Vol. III, p. 215.

[4] *Autobiographical Recollections*. p. 123.

student put it, "like Metaphysics, rather in a historical than a partisan light."[1] Even Whewell, noted in his day for directness, knew that caution was called for here. While seeking to persuade the Syndics of the Press belonging to the University of Cambridge to publish Richard Jones' Literary Remains, he confided to Herschel his opinion of the University authorities : "the ominous phrase 'Political Economy' may frighten them beyond all control." [2]

But the general opposition to political economy was less effective than might have been expected. In the years of the supremacy of the Noetics [3] at Oxford and the school of Whewell and Sedgwick at Cambridge, the leaders of both the natural sciences and of the humanities favoured the introduction of the new subject, even though it was on their own terms. Political Economy, an appellant for admission to the English Universities, was tried, in a somewhat absent-minded way, in the balances of contemporary opinion. Some weighed an idealised science, purged of all "non-neutral" elements, some a body of thought that was but the projection of their own philosophy or theology. Most found political economy wanting in greater or lesser degree, yet somehow, by the sum of qualified assents, it was able to insinuate itself.

II.

Two sets of issues dominated the early-nineteenth-century discussion of the functions and future of the English universities. There was the question of the internal organisation of the universities and colleges themselves, the disposition of their respective resources, and the terms of entry. But behind these practical problems, and prior to them in the minds of most disputants, were the claims of the various disciplines, old and new, for attention. At Cambridge, as became its scientific tradition, discussion of the credentials of the fields of study

[1]C. A. Bristed, *Five Years at an English University*. London, 1873, p. 349.

[2]Todhunter. Vol. II, p. 86.

[3]The Fellows of Oriel adopted this title in the first quarter of the century. It signified one "who exercised his highest faculties as opposed to those who let them lie dormant." Stanley, *Life of Arnold*. p. 117.

was relatively free from invocations of the Deity, concerning itself in the main with the kind of issues that would scarcely seem out of place in a modern discussion of the function of the universities. At Oxford in the 'Thirties, the suffocating debates over the Tractarian Movement dominated everything else, providing the principle of selection in such remote matters as the choice of a professor of poetry.

Political Economy, having gained entry to both universities before these debates were really under way, was not obliged to fight the battle of admission in an atmosphere charged with such heady issues. Nevertheless, it was bound to be brought under scrutiny. For on the pedagogical side there were already those like Whately and Senior who saw the value of the new study as a mental discipline and desired for it a larger teaching role. Further, it was becoming increasingly recognised as the beginning of an attempt at the construction of a science of society, and consequently as a sanction for social policies. With this dual character, Political Economy became an important, though subsidiary theme in the contemporary university debates. In these discussions the economists *per se* played but a small part. The status of political economy was a problem of general policy ; the most significant contributions to the discussion came from the leaders of university opinion.

It is possible to identify three leading views. There was the Oxford Noetic view, with Richard Whately, Drummond Professor of Political Economy, 1829-1831, and later Archbishop of Dublin, as its chief spokesman. Whately, the logician, the disciple of Paley, aware of the dangers of political economy, both as sanctioning policies and as colliding with some views of religion, was yet convinced that "we are bound to use our own natural faculties in the search after all truth." [1] There was the view of William Whewell, Master of Trinity College, Cambridge, equally believing that the attempt to construct a political economy must procede, but differing strongly with Whately and his followers both as to the nature of human motivation and the methods appropriate to the new study. Thirdly, there were the Tractarians, with Newman, Pusey and

[1] *Introductory Lectures*. p. 34.

Keble as spokesmen, who differed both with Whately and Whewell, accepting the study grudgingly if at all, maintaining that it, in common with all studies, must be held subservient to theology.

Richard Whately, friend and sometime tutor of Nassau Senior, was one of the founding fathers of the concept of a neutral science of political economy. He knew those who favoured its development in the University to be under jealous scrutiny from several sides. There were those who saw it as impugning the social arrangements of the day. To these Whately extended the assurance that the first half of the title of Political Economy was really a misnomer.[1] There were those who objected to a discipline that isolated out a single field of economic behaviour. With these Whately sought no compromise, expressing the wish "that the complaint against Political Economists of confining themselves to the consideration of wealth were better founded than it is."[2] Thus Whately's choice of the term 'Catallactics' to signify the science of exchanges, was more than a mere curio of nomenclature. It indicated the closely prescribed scope of the subject as Whately conceived it : the market was to supply the basis for political economy.

Then there were those who saw in political economy an illicit, godless science, likely to end in querying the goodness of creation. There were those whom Whately described as censuring political economy "as being connected with *human conduct*, and yet not professing to be *drawn from Scripture*," and who argued that "in the regulation of our conduct, the Bible is the only sure guide ; and a system which professes an independence of this guide in human affairs, is to be regarded as something unholy."[3] To such as these Whately offered the reassurance that the University of Oxford, by appointing himself Bampton Lecturer, and three times Select Preacher, had testified "the most complete dissent from the notion that the studies of Political Economy and of Theology are unfriendly to each other."[4]

[1] *Life of Whately*. p. 142.
[2] *Introductory Lectures*. p. 22.
[3] *ibid*. p. 35.
[4] *ibid*. p. viii.

There had been enough difficulty in reconciling religion and the new physical sciences; a science of society might prove even more intractable. But for Whately the working out of the economic process was a field in which the beneficence of the Creator could be demonstrated with great advantage. He wrote to Senior when he was proposed for the Drummond Chair: "I am thinking . . . of making a sort of continuation of Paley's *Natural Theology*, extending to the body politic some of his views as respecting the natural." [1] Whately would seek economic parallels to Paley's "numerous instances of evident design in the Universe." The bent of his mind is clear when he recommends in conjunction with Paley, *The Theory of Moral Sentiments*, and the *Wealth of Nations*.[2]

But subtle difficulties presented themselves to those who, like Whately, sought to construct mutually consistent chains of reasoning out of economic behaviour. Little progress could be made without entering upon some postulates about human motives. On this matter Whately's generation was strongly divided. There were two contending views on the nature of human conscience, the source of behaviour. The followers of Paley argued that conscience, the sense of right and wrong, were the creatures of experience. As Jevons put it: " . . . it appears that I am decidedly a "dependent moralist," not believing that we have any "moral sense" altogether separate and of a different kind from our animal feelings." [3] The 'independent moralists' maintained that the conscience enjoyed an independent existence, and was not a creature of circumstance. The Paley view of the dependence of conscience (which of course was much older than Paley) was a necessary basis for the utilitarian philosophy—one that argued that the guide to the morality of any act was not some inner light, but the balance of pleasure over pain in which it resulted, and that

[1] *Life*. p. 67. John Bird Sumner, Bishop of Chester and later Archbishop of Canterbury, had anticipated Whately in this in his *Treatise on the Records of Creation and the Moral Attributes of the Creator*. 1816.

[2] Richard Whately, *Miscellaneous Lectures and Reviews*. London, 1861, p. 112.

[3] *Letters and Journal of W. Stanley Jevons*. London, 1886, p. 79.

"conscience" itself was merely the application, often in a habitual way, of this rational calculation. Here too was the clue to man's behaviour as an exchanging animal, as later developed explicitly by Jevons and others. Whately, in this respect, was not an out-and-out follower of Paley. Man did possess a "Moral-faculty by which he is instinctively led to approve virtue and disapprove vice." [1] Yet little could be derived from the contemplation of this entity upon which reasoning about economic choice could be based. The alternative was to by-pass this metaphysical concept, and merely proceed on simplified assumptions of maximising economic gain. As Whewell put it, Whately founded his opinions on the belief that "principles of action are known by consciousness and do not require detailed observation." [2]

The relationship between Whately and the Ricardians was further apparent in his emphasis on the reasoning process rather than on fact gathering. Whately, the leader for a time of English logical thought, uttered warnings to his students in political economy against the "mistake of beginning by a crude collection of facts." [3] "I believe," he said, "it to be a prevailing fault of the present day, not indeed to seek too much for knowledge, but to trust to accumulation of facts as a *substitute* for accuracy in the logical processes." [4] The pitfalls of reasoning on the facts must be faced : "that which demands the principal share of our attention in Political Economy, strictly so called . . . must be the reasoning process :—the accurate and dexterous application of logical principles." [5]

Thus did Whately's theology and his logic hang together. The former sought evidence of harmony and design in creation : the latter was to provide the mode of proof. The provisioners of London demonstrate the marvel : They "combine unconsciously to employ the wisest means for effecting an object, the vastness of which it would bewilder them even to contemplate." [6] Natural Theology could not fail to return

[1] *Miscellaneous Lectures*. p. 95.
[2] Todhunter. Vol. II, p. 123. See *Whately's Logic*, 1826, p. 303.
[3] *Introductory Lectures*. p. 224.
[4] *ibid*. p. 237.
[5] *ibid*. p. 239.
[6] *ibid*. p. 96.

an optimistic verdict : "The apparent design of Providence evidently *is*, the advancement of mankind, not only as Individuals, but as Communities." [1]

At Cambridge the attitude to method was very different. As his biographer has said, Whewell in his celebrated *History of the Inductive Sciences*, and in his other writings "attaches supreme importance to *Induction* : he contrasts this not infrequently with *Deduction* to the manifest disparagement of the latter." [2] The technique of constructing a few definitions and axioms and reasoning therefrom outraged Whewell, particularly where social phenomena were concerned. So strong an advocate of reference to the facts was he that Herschel, who shared many of his views, was criticised for insufficient zeal in his *Preliminary Discourse on the Study of Natural Philsophy*.[3] Definitions and category building ought to be the last stage of inquiry, not the first. On this theme Whewell sent a paper to Malthus, who took it at first as an attack on his own *Definitions in Political Economy*. Malthus agreed that definition could be premature and over rigid, but mildly pointed out that "without some understanding as to the meaning of the words used the advances in knowledge would be very slow." [4] Richard Jones had made this discovery in his own thinking.

But Whewell and Malthus shared the same fear of Ricardo's method. As a scientist, Whewell knew how readily it could yield false conclusions, and as a keen observer he saw how powerful a position such a case could make for itself among those without the perception or training to detect its limitations or pitfalls. The definitions offered by political economists, with their specious air of detachment, were the beginning of deception. "The names about which they contend . . . are in fact . . . goodly spoil." "If rent and taxes, wages and capital, were things with regard to which we might assert our pro-

[1]*ibid.* p. 104.

[2]Todhunter. Vol. I, p. 107.

[3]*ibid.* p. 55. *Compare Whately, Logic*, p. 10 : "The more precise and definite our object, the more likely we are to attain some valuable result."

[4]*ibid.* p. 66.

positions without moving men's minds more than we do when we talk of *lunes*, or the *angle of a semicircle*, we should no doubt be left to make of them what definitions we chose. But the fact is far otherwise." [1]

Cambridge science of the day was hostile to the Ricardians on further grounds. Whewell and Sedgwick in a long crusade had led opinion against the followers of Paley and the felicific calculus. By the same token they were anti-Benthamites. As Sedgwick, with the full support of Whewell put it : "All systems of political philsophy based on the doctrine of utility, and deduced by *a priori* reasoning from assumed simple principles (without comprehending all the great elements of man's moral nature, and without, perhaps, even regarding his social condition) are either mischievous or impracticable . . . The utilitarian scheme starts on the contrary with an abrogation of the authority of conscience . . . virtue becomes a matter of calculation—a matter of profit or loss . . . and among the greatest blunders the economist has committed, has been a hasty spirit of generalisation (and what infant science has not suffered from the spirit ?) an affectation of deductive reasoning, and a rash attempt to usurp, before his time, the chair of the lawgiver." [2] The final aberration of utilitarianism, in Whewell's eyes, would be the attempt, which he foresaw, to apply mathematics to motives. "In dealing with the moral elements of our nature," he wrote, "the laws of space and number bestead us but little." [3]

Whewell and Sedgwick saw the political economy of the Ricardians as a new and dangerous head on the old hydra of utilitarianism. "Pray recollect," wrote Whewell to his friend, James Forbes, Professor of Natural Philosophy at Edinburgh, "that I profess only to trace the consequences of Ricardo's *Principles*—principles which I am sure are insufficient and

[1] *ibid.* p. 53.

[2] *A Discourse on the Studies of the University.* p. 86.

[3] Todhunter. *ibid.* Vol. I, p. 50. Whewell found Say guilty of thinking himself usefully employed in increasing the number of abstract terms in political economy referring to the moral and intellectual qualities of man : he was one of those who "confound the language of the nation with long-tailed words in *osity* and *ation*." *ibid.* Vol. II, p. 49.

believe to be entirely false." [1] Whewell knew that a M'Culloch in Cambridge would have to be numbered among his intellectual enemies, and when a later Ricardian in the person of Henry Fawcett sought the Cambridge Chair he opposed him strongly.[2]

Yet Whewell and those who thought with him were not, as we have seen, averse to political economy *per se.* Richard Jones provided the escape from the apparent dilemma with his Baconian injunction to "look and see." It was to him that Whewell, Sedgwick, Herschel, and other leading Cambridge scientists gave their blessing. Political economy was to serve a long, perhaps indefinite, apprenticeship to the facts. This meant, of course, that to the public their attitude appeared ambiguous, involving acceptance of political economy, but rejection of the leading school, at a time when the two appeared to the indiscriminating to be coterminous. So Whewell prodded and prodded at Jones to produce something which would prick the Ricardian balloon that was blocking the light of reason. "Jones' book," he wrote, "will I expect . . . *faire epoque* in the science when it does appear . . . but he is heinously dilatory." [3]

Cambridge scientists and mathematicians showed no signs of becoming ' social engineers ' of the type that became so influential in France about this time, following the lead of Saint-Simon. By 1830 the *Polytechnique* had produced for Saint-Simon, Comte, and Fourier, something like one hundred disciples.[4] Cambridge science was in fact a bulwark against the illegitimate extension of physical disciplines to society. This was so on the ground both of method and of conscience. The study of society was in its infancy, requiring protection against the "deductive savages" who, over-anxious for the fruit, "cut down the tree to get at it." [5] It was by such abuse of method, claimed Whewell, that the false doctrines of population and rent,[6] the belief in Say's Law, "of which the

[1] *ibid.* Vol. II, p. 122.
[2] Leslie Stephen, *Life of Henry Fawcett.* London, 1886, p. 119.
[3] Stair Douglas, *Life.* p. 137.
[4] Santillana. *ibid.* p. 249.
[5] Todhunter. Vol. II, p. 141.
[6] *ibid.* p. 94.

fallacy appears so very obvious,"[1] and the Free Trade doctrine,[2] as palpably unproven, had gained such strength. Whewell and Sedgwick stood against those, in England or in France, who would "make the first glimmerings of Political Economy a ground of legislation." [3] Not only so, for Cambridge science the guide to conduct was inviolate : freedom of thought and action were paramount. Elaborate social schematics resting on conformity were ruled out. It is curious that John Stuart Mill saw as the great danger of Whewell's view of independent conscience that it could be used to justify coercion. "By the aid of this theory," said Mill, "every inveterate belief and every intense feeling, of which the origin is not remembered, is enabled to dispense with the obligation of justifying itself by reason, and is erected into its own all-sufficient justification." [4] But it was because, in the view of Whewell and Sedgwick, conscience was an independent entity, that it could not be tampered with to remake society, or for that matter, to justify the *status quo*. Thus were method and conscience a double bar to the "esprit polytechnique" in Cambridge.

But Whewell thought Mill and his school in their turn tainted with such ideas. He had noted of Mill in 1843 that : "He is quite subjugated by one whom I think a very bad philosopher, Comte . . . " [5] French positivism and English utilitarianism were, in Whewell's view, of a piece in destroying true science. "Utilitarian philosophers," he argued, "maintain that we cannot have any sufficient inducement for research except the tangible benefit of our expected discovery." [6]

Yet it is clear from Whewell's sermons that for him too political economy could become apologetics. Like Whately he believed that economic thinking could be made to endorse the Christian concept of a beneficent Creator. He too was conscious that "the universe is full of symmetry and order." [7] He

[1]*ibid.* p. 341.
[2]*ibid.* p. 370.
[3]*ibid.* p. 141.
[4]John Stuart Mill, *Autobiography.* London, 1873, p. 225.
[5]Todhunter. *ibid.* Vol. II, p. 314.
[6]*ibid.* Vol. I, p. 56.
[7]*ibid.* Vol. II, p. 330.

prepared a sermon against the population theory of Malthus in order that his hearers might be spared "an oppressive and disquieting thought forced in among their belief and trust in God's goodness." In a veiled tribute to Richard Jones he commended those who combat "those errors by which foolish and unhappy men . . . darken the face of moral nature and divine truth." [1] All this was but part of the broader aim that Whewell sought to serve in contributing to the Bridgewater Treatises and in other works : the reconciliation of the New Science to theology.[2]

Whewell had "a very strong conviction that taking such a line of moral philosophy, political economy, and science . . . we might partly find and partly form a school." [3] But it is plain that neither Jones nor he solved the problem of economic method. Though they could laugh at the conceptions of Senior and Whately of such matters, and "rejoice to have such specimens of what is to be avoided," [4] the alternative was not so clear. Whewell sadly reflected : "Of induction applied to subjects other than Nat. Phil. I hardly know one fair example." Jones' own "Rent" he thought to be such, and perhaps Malthus' population data. "It is not that I do not think induction applicable . . . but I do not yet see my way to anything which I could propound concerning generals."[5] Herschel apparently had some misgivings concerning the mission of Whewell and Jones to produce true doctrines ' capable of being proved at any step of their induction between the most general and the most particular. ' "You will laugh at this criterion," wrote Whewell to Herschel, "but it is capable of being exemplified nevertheless." [6] Whewell was amused to hear of Jones' passages with Whately. But he warned that : "There is no want of abundant means of shewing the actual folly . . . of their method." More effective

[1]*ibid.* p. 331.
[2]E. C. Mossner, *Bishop Butler and the Age of Reason.* New York, 1936, p. 203.
[3]Todhunter. *ibid.* p. 118.
[4]*ibid.* p. 115.
[5]*ibid.* p. 116.
[6]*ibid.* p. 86.

would be examples of the "ascending method applied to moral sciences" [1] whereby general truth could be derived from specified data. But when Jones in his bafflement was caught "relapsing into the human frailty of definitions," Whewell pulled him up sharply.[2]

Adam Sedgwick was even more dubious than Whewell of the methods of inquiry used by Senior and Whately. Like Whewell, he condemned the attempt to transfer, without close discrimination, the methods of physical science to moral philosophy. "One great injury done to moral reasoning," he warned, "has arisen from the attempt to assimilate it too closely to the method of the exact sciences." [3] "Laws for the government of intellectual beings, and laws by which material things are held together, have not one common element to connect them." The error of "confounding moral with physical causation" has led to "the most revolting and unnatural conclusions." [4] In this Sedgwick resembled the German tradition of conceiving of human knowledge as falling into two fundamentally different categories, natural science, and social science, neither of which is amenable to the techniques of the other. The Germans had arrived at this position *via* the philosophy of Kant and Hegel, with its dichotomy between the worlds of matter and of spirit. The doubts of Whewell and Sedgwick about "the identity of the scientific method . . . in physical and moral sciences"[5] sprang rather from the fact that the legitimacy of the transfer had not been demonstrated because of the difficulties and dangers of reasoning on motives. Sedgwick, though he argued with great force that the detectable laws of the physical world afforded powerful evidence of the Divine intelligence, would not allow of attempts to construct laws in the political and economic fields, even for the purposes of "Natural Theology."

When the project was mooted in 1833 that the British Association should form a statistical section, Sedgwick, as

[1] *ibid.* p. 123.
[2] *ibid.* p. 155.
[3] *Discourse on the Studies of the University.* p. 131.
[4] *ibid.* p. 157.
[5] Todhunter. *ibid.* Vol. II, p. 126.

President for the year, pronounced his opinion in such terms that his *caveats* obscured his agreement. "Statistical inquiries might join the rest in harmony if they dealt with matters of fact, with mere abstractions, and with numerical results. Considered in that light they gave what might be called the raw material to political economy and political philosophy." [1] But there were great dangers. These were matters on which self-interest was strong ; attempts to reason on the data could only be disruptive. "These inquiries, however, were most intimately connected with moral phenomena and economical speculations—they touched the mainsprings of passion and feeling—they blended themselves with the generalisations of political science." It would be the end of the British Association's placid deliberations, free from the disturbing contemplation of the laws of economic reward. "Its meetings would no longer be harmonious but would be distracted by the worst human passions." Basically men like Sedgwick (and there were enough of them to fasten a self-denying ordinance for a time both on the British Association and the Statistical Society) really doubted the possibility (or wisdom) of a science of society. Sedgwick remained among those described by Senior, "who admit the importance of the subject, but distrust the conclusions of the science." [2]

Yet it might be thought that Sedgwick, Jones and Whewell could have found a way out of the impasse of method by recourse to statistical techniques of the kind developed by the Belgian Quetelet. He had taken from Laplace and Fourier the idea of applying the law of probability to social and economic statistics. Quetelet was well known to the Cambridge scientific circle and a warm friend of Whewell. But it was not to be. Of the activities of the Statistical Society Whewell wrote to Quetelet : "my opinion at present is that they would go on better if they had some zealous *theorists* among them . . . I believe that without this there will be no zeal in their labours and no connexion in their results." [3] In the end Whewell

[1] *Annals of the Royal Statistical Society*, 1834-1934. London, 1934, p. 5.
[2] *An Introductory Lecture on Political Economy*. London, 1826, p. 9.
[3] Todhunter. *ibid.* Vol. II, p. 229.

himself, perhaps disillusioned with the slow progress of inductive political economy and despairing that the right hypothesis would emerge from the collecting and sorting of the data, tinkered with mathematical models derived from Ricardo, and warming to his task, claimed to have improved on Mill's theory of international trade.[1]

Thus did the Cambridge scientists and the Oxford logicians of the 1830's differ. A third attitude was shortly to be set forth at Oxford. Pusey, Newman and their followers, who supplanted the Noetics in the late 'Thirties, started from the finality of religious truth, and the relationship between man and the Deity by which it was handed down. They maintained that "all sciences move like planets round the run of God's Truth." [2] This was an attitude hardly more favourable to Ricardianism than that of the anti-Paley group at Cambridge. For Ricardo had been clear in his own mind about the relative importance of theology and political economy for human welfare. Of Sumner, who abandoned political economy to devote the whole of his energies to theology, he wrote : "Whether in this latter pursuit he will have an equal chance of benefiting mankind, as in the former, I have great doubts, or rather I have no doubt at all . . . " [3]

Though the Oxford Noetics, led by Copleston and Whately, denounced the Tractarians as "diverting the energies of learners from the humanistic studies into lines mischievous and barren," and as "perpetuating priestly domination," [4] by the late 1830's they were beaten, and the leadership of Oxford thought passed for some years to the followers of Newman. Whately, for his part in the controversy, suffered the fate of one who in a pre-scientific age, sought to tread between the burning ploughshares of the rational and the revealed. He was accused of "Discerning that Revealed Religion . . . was

[1] *ibid.* p. 362.

[2] Mallet. *ibid.* p. 331. Pusey wrote : "All things must speak of God, refer to God, or they are atheistic . . . Political Economy without God would be a selfish teaching about the acquisition of wealth . . . " p. 320.

[3] *Letters of David Ricardo to Hutches Trower and others*, 1811-1823. ed. Bonar and Hollander. Oxford, 1899, p. 47.

[4] W. Tuckwell, *Pre-Tractarian Oxford*. London, 1909, p. 90.

antagonistic of Political Economy," and of permitting "the doubt to rest . . . on the character of Revealed Religion." [1]

Newman's considered views on political economy were enunciated after his departure from Oxford in 1844. They were set forth in his capacity as Rector of the new National University of Ireland. But they are the same views he had held earlier, in common with Keble and Pusey. For Newman, theology was still the queen of the sciences. He argued the danger that many subjects, political economy among them, "may be and are turned against Religion, by being taken by themselves," [2] and that the province of Theology "will be actually usurped by other sciences, which will teach, without warrant, conclusions of their own, in a subject matter which needs its own proper principles for its due formation and disposition." [3] Thus was political economy "a science at the same time dangerous and leading to occasions of sin, . . . if studied by itself, and apart from the control of Revealed Truth." [4] So he was led to set "Scripture and the Fathers over against Political Economy." [5]

The statement of the claims of political economy made by Senior as first Drummond Professor at Oxford is taken as illustrative of the dangers of perversion. In spite of the fact that "if there be a place where Political Economy would be kept in order, and would not be suffered to leave the high road and ride across the pastures and the gardens dedicated to other studies, it is the University of Oxford," [6] yet Senior made untenable claims for the study. This he had done said Newman, mindful of his own travail at Oxford, without causing "any excitement whatever on the part of the academical and religious public." [7] Senior had said "that the pursuit of wealth, that is, the endeavour to accumulate the means of future subsistence and enjoyment, is, to the mass of mankind, the

[1] W. Atkinson, *Principles of Social and Political Economy*. London, 1858, p. 297.
[2] *The Idea of a University. New Impression*, 1929. p. 95.
[3] *ibid.* p. 98.
[4] *ibid.* p. 86.
[5] *ibid.* p. 87.
[6] *ibid.*, p. 88.
[7] *ibid.* p. 89.

great source of *moral* improvement." [1] Against such a claim Newman invokes "our Lord, St. Paul, St. Chrysostom, St. Leo, and all Saints." So Newman represents political economy as saying to the world: "Easy circumstances make men virtuous." [2]

In short, no claims of ' goodness ' may be preferred by the advocates of political economy themselves. Does this then coincide with the desire of Whately for a "neutral" discipline? Not at all. For Whately stood for a science that sought to avoid ethical premises; Newman for one which recognised a single legitimate source of morality. Newman appeals to all specialists, including political economists, "to go on quietly, in a neighbourly way, in their own respective lines of speculation, research, and experiment, with full faith in the consistency of that multiform truth which they share between them, in a generous confidence that they will be consistent, one and all, in their combined results." [3] But the starting point was all-important. Nothing could be done "if any such thinker starts from radically unsound principles, . . . if he be a Hobbes, or a Shaftesbury, or a Hume, or a Bentham." [4] In short, to Newman and his group, political economy, with all other secular conjecture, was subject to the doctrines of the Church.

It would seem easy, at first blush, to confuse the attitude of Newman with that of Thomas Arnold, the Noetic whose imprint on Victorian England was most lasting. As early as 1825, pondering the evils of self-seeking, he had lamented the spirit of self preferment in secular and church affairs, adding, "I think that those one-eyed men, the political economists, encourage this by their language about national wealth." [5] He was strongly averse to the tendency to demarcate certain aspects of *national* life, the economic among them, as secular, and hence immune from spiritual influences. Professor Willey tells us: "The point on which he first attained to clear certainty

[1] *ibid.* p. 91.
[2] *ibid.* p. 97.
[3] *Lectures and Essays on University Subjects.* London, 1859, p. 275.
[4] *ibid.* p. 292.
[5] Stanley. *ibid.* p. 60.

was that the Christian view of the true end of man has a direct bearing on 'our views of national wealth, and the whole question of political economy.'"[1]

Wherein, then, did Newman and Arnold differ? Arnold, of course, was as hostile as Whately and the others to the priestly pretentions of the Tractarians. He would "expel the antichrist of priesthood," and "restore the laity to the discharge of their proper duties."[2] Yet he was dissatisfied with the nature of the influence the teaching of political economy was having on the nation. How then to ensure it against aberration? Arnold would establish no jurisdiction over the construction and teaching of political economy. But he would create a new unity between the true and worthy aims of the Church and the State. The corrective was to be found in a change of national and institutional outlook, from which a new synthesis would emerge, capable of reducing to their proper proportions the claims of economic matters, and making of them an integrated part of the new national outlook. His was a solution in terms of renovating the context within which economic speculation was carried on. He sought to minimise the importance of economic method rather than to indicate the lines it should follow.

The first phase of the debate on political economy in the universities, carrying us to the mid-century, brought out these three distinctive attitudes. It is tempting to see in them, enunciated in a context so different from our own, the trilemma of our own day. Political Economy with Whately, rendered innocuous or at least inoffensive by closely prescribed terms of reference confining it to the apparently narrow phenomena of exchange, and thus emasculated, permitted to use the dangerous techniques of deductive and even mathematical reasoning. From this there could emerge, *ex definitione*, no compulsion to action, merely a set of theorems of exchange. Or Political Economy with Whewell and Sedgwick, regarded as a means of social amelioration, yet forbidden the illicit shortcut of instinctive choice of significant variables. So numerous are

[1]*Nineteenth Century Studies*. London, 1949, p. 56.
[2]*ibid*. p. 59.

the facts to be gathered, and so dangerous any assumptions of human motive, that conclusions of practical meaning are either extremely narrow in their application or indefinitely remote in time. Here was a second road to effective 'neutrality.' Or Political Economy with Newman: a study not neutral indeed, but mystical. The maximising rules of consumer and capitalist must be abrogated, but the alternative seems to get no further than vague hints about self-abnegation and anti-materialism. Could there by a renewal of canon law in economic matters, or an acceptance of Papal prouncements—would theology perform its supervisory role in this way? So, rigidly applied, these three philosophies would produce, respectively, a set of mechanical rules of narrow application, a group of institutional studies incapable of supporting the humblest generalisation, or a political economy that has abandoned the first attribute of science—the refusal to submit to tutelage. The task of selection and reconciliation of method awaits each succeeding generation. And though the task of applying policy might be easier if the kind of nation of which Arnold wrote could be brought to being, the problem of the terms in which it is legitimate and useful to study society would remain.

At this stage the academic economist had not yet fully emerged. Men on the perimeter of the subject, possessed of standards of judgment independent of it,.were still untroubled by the fear of trespass; without diffidence they expressed their views on the problem of procedure. All these men, among the greatest university names of their generation—Whately, Whewell, Sedgwick, Newman, Arnold—were clergymen. Each believed economic truth to be part of the divine order; each had integrated his attitude to economics with his theology. And though they sometimes seem like men with a method seeking for problems, rather than some later specialists—men with problems looking for a method, yet they are worthy of remembrance because they saw that the proper focus of the interest of the universities in the new discipline ought to lie in its organon.

S. G. CHECKLAND.

University of Liverpool.

[5]

THE PROBLEM OF "UNDERDEVELOPMENT" IN THE ENGLISH CLASSICAL SCHOOL*

By ERSKINE MCKINLEY

I. INTRODUCTION

The English classical school[1] wrote at a time when agricultural productivity in England threatened to serve as a severe constraint upon the industrialization of that country. They cast the problem of economic "development" in terms of the displacement of an economy from stationary equilibrium, historical or hypothetical, and its movement towards such an equilibrium.

A stationary economy is characterized by a zero rate of population increase and a zero rate of net investment. Given techniques, the return to a unit of agricultural land at the margin produces just that surplus over labor costs which is regarded by the capitalist-farmer as adequate to keep that unit of land in cultivation but as inadequate to induce further intensive or extensive cultivation. The surplus, or profit, may be large in real terms yet still be regarded in some sense subjectively as "minimum"; or it may actually be very small in real terms. Only in the former case may the economy be regarded as underdeveloped; in the latter, it is mature. It must be presumed that if improved techniques are known but not introduced, they have not served to elevate the schedule of the marginal efficiency of capital enough to induce new investment. The difference between the subjective and objective nature of the rate of profits accounts for the fact that the "observed" minimum rate of profits may vary from economy to economy.[2] China, for example, was cited as a stationary

* This paper, written while the author was a special student at Harvard University under a generous grant from the Earhart Foundation, is largely drawn from a dissertation written under the chairmanship of Professor Howard Ellis and submitted to the University of California, Berkeley.

1. This school is defined to include Adam Smith, Ricardo, Malthus, McCulloch, Senior, and the two Mills.

2. Cf. Lionel Robbins, "On a Certain Ambiguity in the Conception of Stationary Equilibrium," *Economic Journal*, June 1930, esp. pp. 198–200.

economy with a high rate of profits. Adam Smith,[3] McCulloch,[4] and J. S. Mill,[5] all referred to it. But although they agreed to its stationariness, Smith attributed the absence of net investment to monopoly and government interference; McCulloch, to high risk; and Mill, to the overvaluing of present as against future pleasures. Mill also imputed underdevelopment, if not actual stationariness, to Asia, Russia, Hungary, Spain, and Ireland.[6] Ireland was taken as an example of stationary underdevelopment also by Malthus and Ricardo. They referred as well to New Spain.[7]

Since net investment in the classical school meant an advance of wage goods to the labor force which served to raise the rate of real wages above the level of subsistence, a rate of population increase of zero implies that the laboring population is at subsistence whether it be held there physiologically or psychologically. Consequently, the crucial variables for lifting an economy out of underdeveloped stationariness are the level of net investment and the rate of population increase.

II. The Problem: Capital Accumulation and Population Growth

Population will be mentioned only briefly. Even contemporary demographers disagree in their diagnoses and recommendations for underdeveloped areas. With regard to capital, the classical attitude towards (1) its source or supply, (2) the effective desire of accumulation, or the demand for capital, (3) the logical directions of investment for development, or, as one might say today, investment priorities, (4) the rate of investment that is optimal, requires discussion. Only at this point will it be necessary to enter briefly into the classical position on the possibility of factor substitution.

Population: the shift in the classical school.

Malthus' first *Essay* on population posited a principle that is completely physiological, i.e., a vast and constant stream of births feeds a population which must be "tailored" to its physical environment by a death rate which is governed basically by the scarcity of

3. *Wealth of Nations*, Modern Library Edition, p. 72.

4. *Principles of Political Economy* (Edinburgh, 1825), p. 105.

5. *Principles of Political Economy* (London, 1848), I, 128.

6. *Ibid.*, p. 226.

7. Malthus, *Principles of Political Economy* (New York: Augustus Kelley, 1951), pp. 336–41, 345–46 *et passim; The Works and Correspondence of David Ricardo*, ed. Piero Sraffa (Cambridge University Press, 1951–52), VII, 184 and *passim*.

food. Ricardo adopted this position, weakening it somewhat by admitting the possibility, though by no means the inevitability, of a secular upward movement of the level of subsistence. Malthus never, I think, really forsook his early position except to the extent of admitting the possibility, though here again never granting its inevitability, of there arising preventive checks in the course of economic development. One finds in the *Essay* not much hope that such checks will be automatically induced. It is true, however, that in the *Principles* he appears much more sanguine.[8]

The classical school couched the question they put themselves in terms of whether there is a "natural" tendency for capital accumulation to outstrip population increase. It is curious that James Mill and J. R. McCulloch reached totally different conclusions from their observation of the same phenomena. Mill, impressed by the extent of poverty in the world, concluded that there was no such "natural" tendency. McCulloch, impressed by the world's accumulated riches, concluded that there was.[9] The real crux of the matter, we would say today, is not so much the "naturalness" of any tendency but rather the automaticity in the course of economic development of there evolving "a cultural pattern suited eventually to bring population growth to a stand."[1] While not one member of the classical school was completely consistent in this regard, the consensus, after the death of Ricardo, seems to have been that such a cultural pattern would be induced.[2] They would seem, at least at this juncture, to

8. J. J. Spengler argues very convincingly that the *Essay* reveals the causes of poverty; the *Principles*, the causes of its mitigation. See his "Malthus's Total Population Theory," *Canadian Journal of Economics and Political Science*, XI (Feb. and May, 1945), 83–110, 234–64. Senior apparently felt that Malthus, if not abandoning his early position, abandoned at least its more dire results. On balance, I suspect he was mistaken. But cf. James Bonar, *Malthus and His Work*, who more agrees than disagrees with Senior; Marian Bowley, *Nassau Senior and Classical Economics* (London, 1937), pp. 118 ff.; and Kenneth Smith, *The Malthusian Controversy* (London, 1951), pp. 184 ff., both of whom more disagree than agree with Senior.

9. James Mill, *Elements of Political Economy* (3d ed., 1826), pp. 44–45, and McCulloch, *op. cit.*, p. 18.

1. Spengler, *op. cit.*, p. 100.

2. "Far from population having a tendency to increase faster than subsistence, Senior and Tooke held that there were facts enough to prove the reverse was the case; and as to McCulloch, who is always bitter against Malthus, the workings of an envious and mean disposition, he held that there was in human nature a principle of improvement and exertion that was at all times sufficient to counteract and overcome the principle of population, and therefore that Malthus' theory was altogether erroneous, or as he expressed it in his own happy language, false. Torrens likewise attacked the principle. . . ," "From J. L.

have been right. However, there is concern expressed in some quarters today lest any attempt to foster industrialization be overborne by a population explosion, and some doubt as to the transferability of the widespread habit of birth prevention. In any event, the classical school were aware that capital could increase with rapidity but with no repercussions on welfare if that capital increase were matched by an increase in population. And some of them, even granting automaticity of the change in cultural patterns leading to a reduction in the birth-rate, would certainly have approved of positive measures lest the *lag* in cultural adjustments cause any attempt at industrialization to abort.

Capital: its source or supply.

It is possible to distinguish four means of obtaining capital in the classical model. Two of these, the appropriation of rents and inflation, involve the rechanneling or redistribution of existing incomes. Two of them, land reform to eliminate "disguised unemployment," and the evoking of an increased intensity of effort, involve the creation of new capital within existing techniques.

It might be inferred from the Ricardian model that in a stationary state there must be an extreme attenuation of the distribution pyramid with a comparatively small number of landowners receiving a large proportion of the national product. This may indeed be true but it should be pointed out that there is no necessity for such attenuation. For, as James Mill indicated,[3] if the progress towards stationariness has been accompanied by active sales or other legal division of land, there may well have arrived a situation in which there are many landowners each with so small a plot that they are no better off as regards per capita income than other income groups. Further, as Senior made explicit what Ricardo strongly implied, not only the landowners but most individuals in an economy receive incomes in excess of the absolute minimum necessary supply price. These incomes, even when received by the wage-earner, Ricardo

Mallet's Diaries," Political Economy Club, *Centenary Volume* VI (London, 1921), 265–66. See also the statement of a further consensus that "One of the errors of Ricardo seems to have been to have followed up Malthus' principles of population to unwarrantable conclusions," p. 225. Mallet's urbanity, perceptiveness, and occasional waspishness, make the reading of these extracts, ever too brief, a rare delight.

3. *Op. cit.*, pp. 52–53.

called "profits."[4] Senior called them "rents" or "profits." In the event that techniques whereby output may be increased are known and not employed such rents are the logical internal source of the capital necessary to introduce the innovation. The great difficulty is to isolate the element of "pure rent" for if more than this is infringed, supply of the factor will be curtailed with a consequent diminution of output. And even if the rents can be identified, there remains the further difficulty of aggregating them. This may simply be a matter of creating the appropriate credit institutions such as savings banks. Provision of such institutions may, indeed, lead to the automatic inducement into productive channels of otherwise hoarded or squandered funds.[5] Where such hoards and squandered incomes bulk fairly large individually there remains still the problem of why advantage has not been taken of the innovation earlier, in other words why is the entrepreneurial spirit lacking in the economy. This question will arise again.

Accustomed as we are to the cliché that the classical economists thought only in real terms, ignoring money, it may come as something of a surprise to find that they were quite familiar with inflation as a means of capital accumulation. This they saw to operate through favoring the entrepreneurial class to the hardship of the wage-earner and annuitant (or, sometimes, as favoring the first two classes to the detriment of the third). Thus Ricardo, feeling that the entrepreneur alone would benefit by the "depreciation of money" for the purpose of accelerating capital accumulation, rejected the method as augmenting riches only by "diminishing happiness."[6] Malthus, too, explicitly rejected inflation as a method but for a somewhat different reason. Probably, to be sure, he did disapprove of the inequities which inflation works in its course, but his chief grounds was that he feared, in its being carried to excess, the danger of a cyclical downturn of such severity that "landlords, capitalists, and labourers . . . may

4. Sraffa, I, 348 and 348, n. Also, " . . . the wages themselves may be considered as part of the profits of stock, — and are frequently the foundation of new capital." *Ibid.*, VI, 147.

5. Thus, recently we read that in Turkey "the peasant is taking his money out of the mattress and investing it in something other than gold trinkets for his wife. . . . Although the Turkish domestic markets for equities are still in their infancy . . . their growth . . . is . . . one of the most significant developments since Turkey abandoned the policy of state-operated industry in 1950." *New York Times*, Jan. 24, 1954, p. 11.

6. Sraffa, VI, 233.

well wish they had not been subjected to the stimulus."[7] The question came up for discussion at the Political Economy Club. Mallet reported that during the discussion McCulloch, who had none of Ricardo's or Malthus's fears,

> in his sarcastic and cynical manner derided Mr. Tooke's concern for old gentlemen and ladies, dowagers, spinsters and landholders. He cared not what became of them, and whether they were driven from the parlour to the garret, provided the producers — the productive and industrious classes — were benefited, which he had no doubt they were by a gradual depreciation in the value of money.[8]

J. S. Mill did not approve of long-continued forced saving but he did point out the need, implied in all the classical writings, of credit for rendering fixed wealth mobile.[9]

Land reform in underdeveloped areas was a universal prescription of the classical school. That was necessary only where custom had resisted the division of land into the most efficient production unit. Thus, Malthus recommended the breaking up of large landed estates.[1] He cautioned, however, against too great an atomization of the farm unit, which he felt would militate against the great advan-

7. *Op. cit.*, p. 168.

8. *Op. cit.*, p. 219.

9. *Op. cit.*, I, 427 and II, 38. Mill did not go so far as Senior, according to Mallet who reports that " . . . both Mr. Palmer and Senior and the Rev. Sidney Smith, who was our visitor, held that the prosperity of the country (if it be prosperous) was owing to paper money and the facilities of credit afforded by banking. They even went so far as to describe issues of paper money as a *creation of capital*, and Sidney Smith talked of the moral influence country banks had: stimulating industry, encouraging exertions and good character, and so forth; of which anything more incorrect cannot well be conceived; for I take it that the facilities of credit given by country Banks have made ten speculators for one industrious man, and have given a feverish and artificial stimulus to business and agriculture, of which the effects have been anything but salutary. . . . All that a Bank can do — I mean all the good of which it can be the instrument to the community — consists in collecting in the way of deposits accumulations of capital obtained at a low rate of interest, and which would not otherwise be beneficially employed, but might be hoarded or wasted in unprofitable speculations, and distributing these . . . to those who are in want of capital — to the industrious and skillful." *Op. cit.*, p. 240. I think the novelty of this belief of Palmer, Senior, and Smith, that credit facilities can lead to the "creation" of real capital in any sense other than by forced saving can be overemphasized. After all, they were saying that the actual *source* of new capital was "stimulated" industry and "encouraged" exertions. Mallet, on the other hand, underemphasized the *positive* effects — as distinguished from the neutral — on capital formation that may result from the distribution of otherwise squandered or hoarded funds to the "industrious and skillful." Cf. Hayek's "A Note on the Development of the Doctrine of 'Forced Saving', " in his *Profits, Interest and Investment.*

1. *Op. cit.*, p. 373.

tages to be reaped from the division of labor.[2] On this basis, Ricardo, writing to Trower about the condition of Ireland, mentioned in passing that "small farms would be laid into large,"[3] this in the early stage of beginning development. "Disguised unemployment" in the modern sense is perhaps too much to infer from so casual a remark but Arthur Young observed on the continent, and his observation was quoted by J. S. Mill with approval, just such a condition. Thus Mill said that the division of land might be carried so far "as not fully to occupy the time and attention of the family."[4] This quite clearly implies to me a situation such that hands might be transferred from agriculture into industry and, though total food production might not be actually increased it would, at the least, remain undiminished.[5] But here again we have no prescription for how the reform is to be accomplished, much less how the displaced laborer is to be got into industry and the food he formerly consumed channeled back into his possession. McCulloch, somewhat inconsistently with his position on inflation cited above, further cautioned that impoverishment of the landlord in the process of land reform (or suddenly indulged habits of parsimony) might "destroy one of the great incentives to industry and powerful intellectual exertions . . . [since] . . . many a fortune originated in the desire of living like the great of the land."[6]

This leads into a further consideration of the classical school: that there exists a considerable pool of potential capital which can be tapped by simple increased exertion or greater intensity of effort. Just so, since the introduction of cost-reducing innovations in the production of the basic staples may encounter an inelastic demand for the increased output (if population growth does not absorb it) there

2. *Ibid.*, p. 376.

3. Sraffa, IX, 153.

4. *Op. cit.*, I, 326.

5. It might, I think, be said that the unanimous opposition of the school to the Poor Laws was based on a kind of underemployment conception. They felt that the Poor Laws by supplementing submarginal wages to or above the margin, particularly as the rates were based on family size, encouraged the growth of a population beyond its economic justification. This was the sense in which Ricardo and James Mill meant that capital accumulation if continued beyond the economically correct point would result in impoverishment of all classes. Thus Mallet said that " . . . we see that in Ireland, where rent is absorbing everything, in consequence of the immense competition for land, a system of Poor Laws is likely soon to equalize the division." *Op. cit.*, p. 225.

6. Reported by Mallet, *op. cit.*, p. 264. There are echoes here of Malthus' position in deploring actions which might curtail demand and lead to a premature stagnation of the economy.

must be demand-increasing, as well as cost-reducing, innovations.[7] Malthus especially was dubious of the development-promoting efficacy of cost-reducing innovations since he felt that the worker might well spend his increased income on "indolence."[8] And it is quite true that although the wealthy, through the operation of the demonstration of new goods, might be expected to switch from the demand for menial services to that for material luxuries or to have goods produced to exchange for exotic imports, the working classes, having no surplus income to shift, *must* be led to increased effort. Mill even expressed the germ of the Toynbee thesis that obstacles to desire must exist in just the proper degree of stubbornness to evoke such increased effort.[9] We might even go so far as to read into McCulloch the idea that taxes may be beneficial in providing some such necessary stimulus. Thus, Mallet reported of an evening at his Political Economy Club:

> Some things struck me this evening: 1st. The decided opinion which appeared to prevail that taxation and even heavy taxation, under such circumstances as those of the French War, very much tend to stimulate industry, and had in fact led to a much greater amount of savings and accumulation, than would otherwise have been the case. . . .[1]

7. Viewing the matter in retrospect, Warren C. Scoville says: " . . . one must infer that Mr. Brozen thinks purely cost-reducing innovations and imitations are quantitatively more important than hybrid or purely demand-increasing innovations. This may well be the case although some economists may be prone to question the conclusion on empirical grounds." *American Economic Review*, Proceedings, XLI (May 1951), 277.

8. Ricardo agreed in his correspondence however little he may have stressed this in the *Principles*. Thus, very cheap food, in Ireland the potato, in New Spain manioc and the banana, available with little effort, account for the underdevelopment there. He and Malthus seem to have agreed that the cause for the underdevelopment lay in what we would call today a sharply backward-bending supply curve of labor, or in a highly inelastic schedule of the demand for income in terms of effort. See Malthus, *op. cit.*, pp. 336–41 and *passim*. Also, Sraffa, VII, 184, and cf. McCulloch, *op. cit.*, pp. 396–98.

9. *Op. cit.*, I, 122–23.

1. *Op. cit.*, p. 226. Mallet went on to add, and it does not bear out his opinion that taxation leads to a *greater* amount of savings: "McCulloch said in so many words, *that not a farthing more would have been accumulated; that there would not be a farthing more capital in the Country if the National Debt had not been incurred;* which seems to be generally assented to." However, later, p. 271, he says: "But to return to McCulloch — he held that the pressure of taxation was the greatest of all incentives to industry, and during a war, when taxes come pelting in, it stimulates the industrious man to greater and greater exertions; so that 20 years of war were more likely, according to his view, to benefit the country and add to its wealth, than 20 years of peace."

The school saw clearly enough that there must always exist a lag between demand and its gratification and that if an increment to income achieved by increased effort is consumed, no saving can take place. Mill, however, seemed to have believed that the act of saving for the sake of gratifying some consumption desire would lead to a *habit* of saving which would continue even after the objective was achieved.[2] The assumption has been, of course, either that economically warranted resources are available under given techniques or that innovations for increasing output are available. If neither is true, reallocation of income into the hands of the labor force, if it induces further population increase, will simply result in the impoverishment of the expropriated class with no balancing amelioration in the condition of any other class. Thus, for the growth of capital James Mill very boldly suggested an income tax and channeling of the proceeds into entrepreneurial hands. He rejected his own suggestion because, Malthusian that he was, he felt that the effects would be only leveling. Exactly what so-convinced a utilitarian might have thought of this scheme if the existence of innovations at hand were sufficient to produce a virtual explosion of capital formation can only be conjectured.[3]

Capital: the demand side — the effective desire of accumulation.

B. S. Keirstead makes the rather surprising statement that "the orderly and automatic adjustments of Ricardo's market leave no function for the entrepreneur to perform. He has no problem of anticipation, no real risk to bear, no serious charge is put upon his judgment."[4] While it is true that in the *Principles* Ricardo did not discourse at any length upon the duties and functions of the entrepreneur, a not inconsiderable role in the system is assigned to him implicitly. In the first place, he is expected to innovate and the entrepreneur who does not himself innovate is expected to imitate the innovator with remarkable speed. It has been said that the "economic man" does not move of his own volition but gravitates. Ricardo, however, indicated that frictional disorder can be painfully prolonged by an understandable inertia on the part of the entre-

2. *Op. cit.*, I, p. 119.

3. *Op. cit.*, pp. 60–61. In fairness to Mill I must add, lest it be objected that there is nothing intrinsically evil about "leveling," that his fear was that there could be no cushioning of natural disaster should it fall upon a population whose every member was at the level of poverty and barest subsistence.

4. *The Theory of Economic Change*, p. 81.

preneur. The discomforts of the adjustment to structural change are thus prolonged by the "opposition which is naturally given to such change," and the speedy reaction to changes in market indicators depends on "the degree of information, or the strength of the prejudice of those who offer it . . . ." Perhaps for yet unborn econometricians he added: "it cannot be the subject of any thing like accurate calculation."[5] And in the *Principles* he said that the reallocation of capital occasions distress which "will be longer or shorter according to the strength of that disinclination which most men feel to abandon that employment of their capital to which they have been long accustomed."[6] I agree that the function of the entrepreneur may be a gravitational one — the difficulty is that he must know when, how fast, and in what direction to gravitate. It is *difficult* to be an economic man and this has implications for the underdeveloped areas.[7]

Ricardo, Malthus, and the rest of the school saw the entrepreneur as uniquely the economic actor with both the desire and the means to accumulate. And just as J. S. Mill spoke of the "habit" of saving on the part of the wage-earner, so Senior considered entrepreneurial accumulation, too, largely a matter of habituation.[8] The conditions which will induce the growth of this habit are substantially the same as those which will induce increased effort on the part of the labor force. Security in the possession of property is a most important precondition of entrepreneurial activity.[9] McCulloch even listed security as the first of his three conditions for an economy's emergence from barbarism.[1] But this is a precondition and it is

5. Sraffa, VII, 66–67.

6. *Ibid.*, I, 265.

7. Cf. P. T. Ellsworth, "Factors in the Economic Development of Ceylon," *American Economic Review*, Proceedings, XLIII (May 1953), 117: "The Ceylonese peasant is notoriously conservative and guided by tradition; he dislikes change and is not easily moved by economic considerations to alter his customary ways, being far from an 'economic man' in the Western sense."

8. *An Outline of the Science of Political Economy* (New York: Augustus Kelley, 1938), p. 192. "Capitals are generally formed from small beginnings by acts of accumulation which become in time habitual."

9. Senior perhaps quite rightly called this a noneconomic factor but did not hesitate to say that "Ireland is physically poor because she is morally and intellectually uneducated. And while she continues uneducated, while the ignorance and violence of her population render persons and property insecure, and prevent the accumulation and prohibit the introduction of capital, legislative measures, intended solely and directly to relieve her poverty, may not indeed be ineffectual, for they may aggravate the disease. . . ." *Ibid.*, p. 135.

1. *Op. cit.*, p. 73. The second is an exchange economy and the third the accumulation of capital. Cf. p. 112.

again McCulloch who I think summarized the attitude of the school when he said:

> National prosperity does not depend nearly so much on advantageous situation, salubrity of climate, or fertility of soil, as on the adoption of measures fitted to excite the inventive powers of genius, and to give perseverance and activity to industry.[2]

In the earlier stages, at least before industrialization gets well under way, Smith was quoted by Malthus as pointing out the desirability of a shift in taste from personal services to material luxuries. Ricardo also felt it desirable that released menials should produce "lace, china, furniture," as they came, by the induced change in tastes plus a sense of security, to be demanded.[3] But Malthus warned that "most men place some limits, however variable, to the quantity of conveniences and luxuries they will labour for. . . ."[4] New desires, consequently, must be *continuously* generated as the old are gratified. But there need be no qualitative limit to demanded conveniences and luxuries and there would seem to be no limit at all if the desire is for "distinction."[5] This desire for distinction or for "rising in the world,"[6] can manifest itself only in a society where there is vertical social mobility or where, in Senior's words, the "road to social eminence is most open."[7] And the entrepreneurial ability which both permits and is fed by social betterment need not manifest itself only among the wealthy. It was, so far as I know, J. B. Say who first pointed out that

> It is commonly requisite for the adventurer himself to provide the necessary funds. Not that he must be already rich; for he may work upon borrowed capital; but he must at least be solvent, and have the reputation of intelligence, prudence, probity and regularity; and must be able, by the nature of his connections, to procure the loan of capital he may happen himself not to possess. These requisites shut out a great many competitors.[8]

J. S. Mill hoped that education would increase the frequency with which entrepreneurial ability appears. Just as he indicated the neces-

2. *Ibid.*, p. 23.
3. Sraffa, VIII, 102–3.
4. *Op. cit.*, p. 355.
5. Senior, *op. cit.*, p. 12. "The most obvious source of distinction is the possession of *superior* wealth." Italics supplied.
6. McCulloch, *op. cit.*, p. 14.
7. *Op. cit.*, p. 27.
8. *A Treatise on Political Economy*, trans. from the 4th ed. by C. R. Prinsep (Philadelphia, 1857), p. 330.

sity for credit to make capital mobile, so did he look to it to make entrepreneurial ability effective wherever it might appear.[9] His father, too, had stressed heavily the social desirability of a growing middle class. Malthus defended primogeniture as it forced the younger sons of the landed aristocracy to enter the middle and enterprising class. But a certain display was considered necessary to entice the able into wishing to rise into it. It seems reasonably just to say that the desire for material wealth, in the evoking of increased effort on the part of the labor force and entrepreneurial activity among those capable of it, might be regarded as one of the most crucial requirements for the development of an underdeveloped economy.[1]

The directions for investment: priorities.

It was held generally in the classical school that production in agriculture would show historically diminishing returns. By this I mean that upward shifts in the schedule of returns caused by innovations would be compensated for or more than compensated for by the downward movement along the schedule caused by the increasing demand for agricultural products. Production in industry, on the other hand, was thought to be capable of indefinitely increasing returns, either because of economies of scale or because of an indefinite supply of inventions and innovations. This would imply that the terms of trade between agricultural and manufactured goods are turning more and more against the latter. For this reason the rate of return in agriculture was considered in some sense as governing the

9. Credit is, thus, "the means by which the industrial talent of the country is turned to most account for the purposes of production." *Op. cit.*, II, 38.

1. The treatment of a demand for luxuries as an entrepreneurial incentive leads into an obvious dilemma since consumption is in a sense an alternative to saving. I have the impression, however, that it is not so much the matter of a dilemma as of appropriate lags. Thus, it is clear enough that the stimulus to the working class to improve their condition was the emulation of the rich. But just as the level of living of the working class was expected to be rising, so too, surely, was the level of the entrepreneurial class. The crucial shift in demand in a stationary economy was from services to material luxuries. Doubtless, for the sake of *growth* stripped of any welfare significance the prime motive is desire of accumulation. Thus, " . . . the view [was] shared by the early nineteenth-century classicists and Marx, that the almost exclusive source of savings was profits. The workers had no excess income. The landowning gentry lacked a bent toward thrift. But the profit-making commercial classes had both. This heterogeneity in values and aspirations may also explain the alleged paucity of savings in many backward areas in which the richer classes are supposed to lack a bourgeois appreciation of the satisfaction of accumulation. . . ." Moses Abramowitz, "Economics of Growth," in *A Survey of Contemporary Economics,*

rate of return in manufacturing, but it was realized that the two rates were mutually determining and this realization is perhaps more germane to our present inquiry.

It is obviously to the advantage of the economy to have capital-equipped labor move into that sector which shows increasing returns — in the classical model the industrial sector. But any unit of labor must be equipped with food, or, as they would have said, with capital. Here we encounter the fixity of the input of labor and variable capital (in the classical sense). This implies first that food and labor beyond the needs of simple reproduction of the economy be available; second, that the surplus food be advanced to the laborer until his output is produced; and, third, that the output of the laborer be considered as a satisfactory exchange for the originally advanced food. Thus it becomes increasingly clear why it is that the annuitant and landlord must have a demand for industrial products. The validity of the assumption of food as a constraint on industrialization will be mentioned at the conclusion of this paper.

Adam Smith, under the influence of the physiocrats, advocated as most advantageous to an economy the investment of labor on the land. Malthus agreed to the extent at least of wishing, for nationalistic and sociological reasons, to see a balance between agriculture and manufacturing.[2] The more radically classical attitude was, however, that of Tooke and McCulloch:

Vol. II, ed. Bernard F. Haley, pp. 150–51. If we leave aside the somewhat doubtful assertion that the workers had no excess income then it is true that the landowning class's lack of thrift must be compensated by a high degree of it in the entrepreneurial class. But this thrift must, in order to manifest itself, have something to work on, primarily the desire for *material* luxuries on the part of the landowning gentry. Despite the strand in classical thought that extolled parsimony, it was recognized that industry must accompany the parsimony, and that industry must have something on which to work. At all events, I get the strong impression that a rising standard of living was the desideratum for all classes. We have as a much less workable alternative the opinions of Adam Smith and James Mill that social pressure might render frugality just as productive of emulation by the poorer classes as expensive display. Thus Smith, *Wealth of Nations*, pp. 96–97, said of Holland that it is there "unfashionable not to be a man of business. Necessity makes it usual for almost every man to be so, and custom every where regulates fashion." And James Mill, *op. cit.*, p. 59, expected the legislature or social pressure "to render frugality fashionable, and expense disgraceful." Even Malthus, the most demand-conscious member of the school said "when the capital of a country is deficient, compared with the demand for its products, a temporary economy of consumption is required, in order to provide the supply of capital which alone can furnish the means of an increased consumption in the future." *Op. cit.*, p. 326.

2. Cf. Bonar, *op. cit.*, pp. 224 ff. for a reasoned analysis of Malthus' position.

Tooke did not think that we should ever import more than 3 millions of quarters annually, which is little more than was imported in 1830. But I do not see the grounds of such an opinion, with Russia and Poland and North America open. Malthus evidently thought it a very hazardous experiment, but McCulloch was ready to turn the whole country into one vast manufacturing district, filled with smoke and steam engines and radical weavers, and to set adrift all the gentlemen and farmers now constituting our agricultural population. Nor was Tooke at all startled by this *beau ideal* of a country supplied from the fertile lands of North America and Russian Poland; only that he did not think it likely to be realized.[3]

Ricardo, with his eyes too on the food-constraint on industrial development, would have said that the first area for development in a stationary economy (with innovations available) must be agriculture but that the surplus obtained could then be used in manufacturing and that a mutually feeding growth can then proceed.[4] John Stuart Mill, no more protectionist than physiocrat, seems to have agreed. He said:

. . . the best chance of an early development of the productive resources of India consists in the now rapid growth of its exports of agricultural produce. . . . The producers of these articles are consumers of food supplied by their fellow-agriculturalists in India; and the market thus opened for surplus food will, if accompanied by good government, raise up by degrees more extended wants and desires,

3. Mallet, *op. cit.*, pp. 233–34. Mallet's attitude is clear.

4. "It is the accumulation of wealth in Agriculture which first gives the notion and the means of establishing Manufactures. Manufactures which in turn become the cause of new accumulations of capital which tend to produce a fresh demand for labour, an increased population, and a greater consumption of agricultural produce. Thus Agriculture is alternately the cause and effect of manufacturing industry." Sraffa, VIII, 102–3. My belief in Ricardo's assignment of agricultural priority in the developmental process may be challenged. I must adhere to it for two reasons. First, Ricardo's emphasis on the repeal of the Corn Laws would indicate to me that he considered the simplest way of raising profits for increased investment within a given institutional framework would be the lowering of money wages which would be possible in an economy more or less at subsistence only by the cheapening of food. But if this is dismissed as an impracticable means for raising profits, Ricardo seems still to have thought it the readiest fashion for raising the welfare of the subsistence laborers. For he replies to Malthus: "But it may be said that the capitalist's income will not be increased; that the million deducted from the landlord's rent will be paid in additional wages to labourers! Be it so; this will make no difference to the argument: the situation of society will be improved and they will be able to bear the same money burthens with greater facility than before; it will only prove what is still more desirable, that the situation of another class, and by far the most important class in society, is the one which is chiefly benefited by the new distribution." *Ibid.*, I, 424–25. Cf. G. E. Britnell, "Factors in the Economic Development of Guatemala," *American Economic Review*, Proceedings, XLIII (May 1953), 105: " . . . it seems clear that any material improvement in the standard of living in the near future must come about mainly through increased agricultural production."

directed either towards European commodities, or towards things which will require for their production in India a large manufacturing population.[5]

One direction of investment was given high priority by the school, what we might call social overhead capital, of which two examples, educational facilities and means of transportation and communication might be mentioned. Education, they felt, would serve to slow down the rate of population increase but would, at the same time, lead to increased efficiency. Thus Senior referred to "good education" as "a kind of mental raw material."[6] J. S. Mill, as mentioned before, saw a connection between education and entrepreneurial ability and spoke of "intellectual speculation" as "the most influential part of the productive labour of society. . . ."[7] McCulloch, too, saw education both as the source of continuing invention and as "the means for providing for the permanent improvement of the poor."[8] It may be recalled that Adam Smith considered a group of "philosophers" to be one of the fruits of a division of labor but expressed the fear that the same specialization might lead to a loss of general intelligence on the part of the urbanized workman. McCulloch, quite the opposite of an agrarian fundamentalist, surveyed the evidence and reached the conclusion that there is greater gain in education and intelligence from the easy communication which urbanization affords than loss from the particularizing of tasks.[9] Of transport facilities, J. S. Mill held that "good roads are equivalent to good tools."[1] And similarly Senior saw in good transport facilities the means of counteracting the principle of diminishing returns — a hopeful sign for countries without such facilities and which have settled into stationariness because of the operation of diminishing returns.

In sum, I think we might say, the classical school saw the great desirability and indeed necessity of a growing industrial sector in a

5. *Op. cit.*, I, 145–46.

6. And he defined the term as including "Probity, industry, judgment, elementary knowledge, and the other moral and intellectual habits and acquirements to which we give the general name. . . ." *Op. cit.*, p. 220. It may be mentioned again in this connection that Senior considered all this as capital and the material return to it as "profit."

7. *Op. cit.*, I, 53.

8. *Op. cit.*, pp. 118–19, 359.

9. *Ibid.*, pp. 160–61. He asserted, too, somewhat guardedly, that urbanization produces a healthier population. P. 159.

1. *Op. cit.*, I, 219. Notice the *direction* into which the revenue of the rich might be advantageously diverted. "It was admitted on all sides that the application of the revenues of wealthy men to fixed capital such as roads, canals, railways, piers, mills, was advantageous and desirable. . . ." Mallet, *op. cit.*, p. 264.

developing economy. They realized, however, that the growth of this sector was severely limited by the productivity of agriculture and would have recommended first attention to that area. Thus elevating the schedule of returns to land by additional applications of capital, including, perhaps primarily, social overhead capital, might be expected to yield sufficient surplus of food either to feed fixed capital-producing labor directly or to export in exchange for the import of such fixed capital.

The rate of development: the substitution of factors.

Up to this point capital has been considered as composed solely of wage goods, that is to say, capital as the means of *supporting* a unit of labor. This seems to have been Smith's primary meaning. Parsimony meant to him the decision on the part of the owner of a surplus of food not to consume it himself or to assign it to the consumption of menials but rather to "invest" it by paying it out to a laborer occupied in the production of material wealth.[2] Ricardo, emphasizing the increase in variable capital, at first either treated the fixed capital input coefficient as fixed or ignored it. In the third edition, however, he introduced the idea of the possibility of substitution between fixed capital and labor and proposed that labor can be supplanted by fixed capital with which it is in constant price competition. In the event that the introduction of machinery reduces the gross output of an economy, even though the "social dividend" be increased by the substitution, labor may thus become redundant.[3] Here Ricardo is correct in a static context but McCulloch, who accepted the Ricardian logic while denying its applicability to the real world, was correct if progress is assumed. Indeed, short of population increase which may not be desirable, labor-saving innovation is the obvious source of that "surplus" labor which, if equipped with the means of subsistence, can provide the germ of development. The assumption is, of course, that labor which is supplanted in one line of endeavor will be absorbed in another. Senior, like McCulloch taking progress for granted, adopted the notion of price competition between labor and fixed capital and concluded that their relative prices would (and should) determine the

2. Lauderdale was critical, not to say captious, towards this idea and countered that the function of "capital" is not so much to support as to *supplant* labor. Each was, of course, perfectly correct, Smith in a dynamic and Lauderdale in a static context. *Inquiry into the Nature and Causes of Public Wealth* (2d ed., Edinburgh, 1819). For an example of his position see his simile, p. 177 n.

3. Sraffa, I, 386-92.

capital intensity of production.[4] The relevance of this to underdeveloped economies today is clear enough. The classical school would have argued against the too rapid conversion of wage-capital into fixed capital lest, before the fixed capital began to produce, there be experienced a painful shortage of wage goods. Of course, if there is a significant amount of rural underemployment with a large surplus of food this presents no problem. When, however, the creation or increase of the industrial labor force must involve a reduction in the agricultural labor force with consequent diminution of agricultural output, there must be an agricultural surplus available during the period of construction of the fixed capital. And it must, of course, be made accessible to the industrial labor force.

The classical school would have answered the question as to the rapidity with which an economy can industrialize by saying that it depended on the size of the agricultural surplus and the size of the population available to utilize the surplus in new production. The disadvantage here to a stationary and underdeveloped economy is that it is the absence of one of these factors which renders it stationary. But there is a more hopeful aspect. For the school unanimously felt that a country which is not industrialized has a higher degree of flexibility than one which is.[5] This is true since there is little or no "sunk capital" to become obsolete and less chance of technological displacement attendant upon the introduction of new and more efficient techniques of production. This is, I suppose, to underline the obvious: shifts in demand have reverberations throughout the structure of an economy and development involves as an aspect shifts in demand.

The school met this problem by assuming that innovations would be made out of surplus capital and not withdrawn from the existing circular flow. Thus J. B. Say said:

> . . . it is perhaps prudent to defray the charges of experiment in industry not out of the capital engaged in the regular and approved channels of production, but out of the revenue that individuals have to dispose of at pleasure, without fear of impairing their fortune. . . .[6]

4. Senior actually talked of the "length of the period of production," but concludes that this period will be longer where "abstinence . . . is a cheap instrument of production" or, the same thing, where "profits are lower." His example, Holland, made him emphasize commercial rather than manufacturing industry but I do not feel that my inference is improper. Cf. his *Outline*, pp. 195–96.

5. E.g., Ricardo, ed. Sraffa, I, 266.

6. *Op. cit.*, p. 83. Say, by the way, suggested industry as the better sector for investment for quick returns since it ties up capital for a shorter period. While we might not accept this as such, speed of return must be taken into account in planning capital outlays.

If it were claimed that a greater speed were dictated for political reasons they would have answered, then political means must be found for absorbing the shocks. Whether political reasons for rapid industrializations are to be found of such urgency as would have convinced them of the desirability of significant interference I do not know.[7] Malthus, however, spoke of the excitation of new demand as a "plant of slow growth." In general it can be said the classical school thought of capital accumulation as a gradual process.

ERSKINE MCKINLEY.

INDIANA UNIVERSITY

7. At least in the case of England itself, in the conditions of the 1820's, it has been said that "on one thing only could most of them agree — that the pace of industrialization should be slowed down." S. G. Checkland, "The Propagation of Ricardian Economics in England," *Economica*, New Series, XVI (Feb. 1949), 44.

[6]

JOHN RAE ON ECONOMIC DEVELOPMENT: A NOTE

By Joseph J. Spengler

"He formulated the economic theory of new countries. . . ." —R. Warren James[1]

What the historian of thought discovers in a work is determined largely by the questions he brings to its study. Similarly, what the analyst of a treatise notices is governed principally by his interests of the moment. It is not surprising, therefore, that assessments and interpretations of the writings of economists of an earlier era undergo modification as the *Weltanschauung* and the concerns of economists change with the ascent of new problems and the recession of old ones.

A case in point is the work of that remarkable Scotch-Canadian, John Rae. Possibly as brilliant an economist as nineteenth century North America was to produce, his ideas, conceived and formulated in "the solitude . . . of the Canadian backwoods" and supported by homely illustrations drawn from the frontier, have continued to influence economists for more than a century.[2] Thus Nassau Senior, impressed by Rae's account of "the accumulation of capital," recommended his book to Mill who, greatly influenced by it, cited it in his discussions of the division of labor, the disposition to save, indirect taxation, and protectionism.[3] American commentators drew on

1. See R. Warren James, "The Life and Work of John Rae," *Canadian Journal of Economics and Political Science*, XVII (1951), 142.

2. This work, *Statement of Some New Principles on the Subject of Political Economy, Exposing the Fallacies of the System of Free Trade and of Some Other Doctrines Maintained in the "Wealth of Nations"* (Boston, 1834), was edited and reissued by Charles W. Mixter as *The Sociological Theory of Capital* (New York, 1905). Mixter included an acconut of Rae's life which has been supplemented by James (see *op. cit.*) who is preparing an edition of Rae's writings, together with a full account of his life and intellectual achievements. James mentions a doctoral dissertation on Rae's work (Helmut Lehmann's *John Raes Werk, seine philosophischen und methodologischen Grundlagen*, Dresden, 1937), in which Rae's inductive approach and F. Bacon's influence on Rae are treated. Rae was born in Aberdeen, Scotland, in 1796, studied medicine and social and other sciences, came to Canada in 1822, went to California in 1849, lived in Hawaii 1850–70, and then returned to New York where he died in 1872.

3. See J. S. Mill, *Principles of Political Economy*, Ashley ed., pp. 97, 129 n., 165–72, 870 n., 922; James, *op. cit.*, pp. 155–56; unsigned, "John Rae and John Stuart Mill: A Correspondence," *Economica*, X (1943), 254. See also Mixter,

Rae's protectionism and his view of cost-reducing invention;[4] W. E. Hearn seems to have been inspired by his general approach;[5] Thorstein Veblen, by his analysis of consumption;[6] and various interest theorists, by his treatment of capital.[7] F. W. Taussig must have been influenced by Rae's theory of invention.[8]

This note has to do solely with a branch of economic theory that forms the core of Rae's work just as it forms the core of the very work that Rae believed himself to be criticizing, namely, Smith's *Wealth of Nations*. The branch of theory in question is that relating to economic development. Rae's theory will be summarized in Section I; his application of this theory will be examined in Section II.

"Letters of Rae . . . to Mill on the Malthusian Doctrine of Population," *Economic Journal*, XII (1902), 111–20, and *Sociological Theory of Capital*, p. xxxii. Mill's praise of Rae's work led to its translation into Italian by F. Ferrara and its inclusion in his *Biblioteca dell Economisti*, 1st series, XI (Turin, 1856). W. Roscher referred to Rae's views on saving and economizing on tools. See *Principles of Political Economy*, trans. J. J. Lalor (New York, 1878), Book I, secs. 45, 59.

4. See Joseph Dorfman, *The Economic Mind in American Civilization*, II (New York, 1946), 779–89, 795, 835, 838, 940, and p. xiv of "bibliographic notes." See also *ibid.*, III (New York, 1949), 422, where it is said that as late as 1909 the theory of capital formation had not been advanced much beyond Rae's.

5. Mixter believes Hearn, in his *Plutology* (1864), indebted to Rae for "method and spirit." See *Sociological Theory of Capital*, p. xxxii. Hearn wrote this book after removing to Australia; he referred once (*op. cit.*, p. 154) to Rae, but often to Mill.

6. Veblen knew Rae's work but did not cite it.

7. E.g., see E. von Böhm-Bawerk, *Geschichte und Kritik der Kapitalzinstheorien* (Innsbruck, 1900), pp. 375–428; Irving Fisher, unsigned note, "A Neglected Economist," *Yale Review*, V (1896–97), 457, and *The Theory of Interest* (New York, 1930), *passim*, which was dedicated to Böhm-Bawerk and Rae; Gustav Åkerman, *Realkapital und Kapitalzins* (Stockholm, 1923), whose views, partly inspired by Rae, were assessed by K. Wicksell (see appendix to *Lectures on Political Economy*, I (London, 1934), 259–61). Mixter, who had originally looked upon Rae as "A Forerunner of Böhm-Bawerk" (this *Journal*, XI (1896–97), 161 ff.), later described Rae's theory of capital as more complete than Böhm-Bawerk's because it took invention into account ("Böhm-Bawerk on Rae," *ibid.*, XVI (1901–2), 385 ff.).

8. See "Capital, Interest, and Diminishing Returns," this *Journal*, XXII (1907–8), 333–63, esp. 355 ff., 362 ff., also *Principles of Economics* (New York, 1939), p. 32, where the rate of interest is said to depend "on a race between improvement and accumulation." Taussig does not refer to Rae, but knew the latter's work well, having directed Mixter's attention to it. See *Sociological Theory of Capital*, p. xvii. Taussig's 1908 paper may be looked upon as a chapter in a long-continued controversy between J. B. Clark, F. H. Knight, and others, on the one hand, and those who, on the other, supposed the marginal productivity of capital to fall rapidly in the absence of invention. See my "Economic Opinion and the Future of the Interest Rate," *Southern Economic Journal*, III (1936), pp. 19–22.

I

Economic development, Rae argues in his main Book II, depends upon capital accumulation and upon the extent to which man augments his store of technological knowledge and transforms this knowledge into improvements and inventions.[9] It thus depends upon the degree to which man gives expression to the "inventive principle" and to the "accumulative principle"; for the latter prompts man to avoid waste, save at ever lower rates of interest, and form capital, whereas the former enables man to overcome the tendency of returns to capital to fall as the stock of capital increases.[1] Rae says little of that division of labor which, in Smith's work, served, along with capital accumulation, to give rise to economic development. Rae looked upon the division of labor as primarily a result or concomitant rather than as a cause of invention and the growth of intelligence, though he noted that it made possible a fuller use of tools and hence a higher return on capital.[2] Nor did Rae stress population growth which, in Smith's system, became a source of the division of labor.[3]

9. According to E. Cannan, J. S. Mill was the first to note the importance of accumulation of knowledge and progress in the industrial arts. His predecessors had not included technical progress among the highly significant sources of the "productiveness of labour." See Cannan, *A Review of Economic Theory* (London, 1930), pp. 122–24. Cannan seems not to have known Rae's work at first hand. It is quite possible that Rae's work led Mill to appreciate the importance of a community's "skill and knowledge" and its inventiveness (*op.cit.*, pp. 107–9). Mill's appreciation was not shared by his successors, Cannan reports. Mill himself questioned whether mechanical invention had lightened the worker's toil, or could do so, if numbers remained uncontrolled (*ibid.*, p. 751). However, Hearn (*op. cit.*, Chaps. 4, 10–11) devoted three chapters to invention and education.

1. See summary Chap. 14 in Book II of *New Principles.* My references, unless otherwise indicated, are to this edition rather than to Mixter's rearrangement of chapters in his edition, entitled *The Sociological Theory of Capital.* For the purposes of the present discussion the organization of the first edition is superior to Mixter's. A guide to the original is provided, however, on pp. 484–85 of Mixter's edition.

2. *New Principles*, pp. 165, 352 ff., 356–57. Cannan accredits Rae with having been the first to state that the division of labor makes for economy in the use of tools; he cites the quotation from Rae's work used by J. S. Mill to make this point. See Cannan, *op. cit.*, p. 97. Mill who, following E. G. Wakefield, wrote of the co-operation rather than of the division of labor, did not attach so much importance to the division of labor as the source of invention as had Smith (*op. cit.*, p. 128).

3. In the *New Principles* Rae took it for granted that numbers "are kept up to the quantity of materials fit for their subsistence which it affords them" (*ibid.*, p. 96, also pp. 30–31), but he supposed that the standard of life might be higher or lower (*ibid.*, pp. 96–97, 323–25). Eventually, however, as a result of his study of depopulation in the Sandwich Islands, Rae rejected Malthus' explanation and introduced the concept of an "effective desire for offspring" (a companion to his "effective desire of accumulation") which made numbers depend

Rae's Book II is reducible to three principles, according to the first of which the return to capital diminishes slowly but continuously under static conditions and in the absence of new accretions of relevant knowledge and their incorporation in inventions. Having defined the "capacity" of man-made, want-satisfying "instruments" as "their power to produce . . . events equivalent to a certain amount of labor," Rae devised a means of ordering these instruments in terms of their capacity to yield returns over costs per time period.[4] This means, though described by Rae in largely verbal terms, may be reconverted into the quantitative terms he must originally have used when formulating his ideas. Let $e = y/c$ where e stands for efficiency, y for the returns yielded by an instrument during the interval separating its initial formation and its exhaustion, and c for the instrument's initial cost.[5] Furthermore, let $(1 + r)^n = k$, where r stands for rate of return above cost and on cost yielded annually by an instrument; $k = e = 2$; and n stands for the order of an instrument, or the number of years required by it to yield double its cost. Then, if $r = 100$ per cent, $n = 1$, and the instrument is of order A; if r approximates 41 per cent, $n = 2$, and the instrument is of order B; if r approximates 5 per cent, $n = 14$, and the instrument is of order N; and so on. Every instrument falls into an order, or in between two orders.[6] Furthermore, as capital accumu-

upon socio-psychological conditions present within a society as well as upon material conditions external to a population. See Mixter, *Sociological Theory of Capital*, pp. 354–58; also "Letters of Rae. . .", *loc. cit.* That the desire for savings may run counter to the desire for offspring is not gone into.

4. *New Principles*, Book II, Chap. 4, esp. p. 100. Agricultural land also is defined as an "instrument," though, unlike other instruments, it (together with certain improvements in it) is not subject to "exhaustion," or physical depreciation and depletion. *Ibid.*, pp. 100, 107–8; also p. 86 where instrument is defined as any "arrangement" of matter suited to achieve some end.

5. Labor, or a day's wages, is employed as the *numeraire* in terms of which both the cost of an instrument and the returns yielded by it may be represented. *Ibid.*, pp. 91–92; also p. 98 where, after describing "a day's labor as the unit, serving as the base for calculations, concerning the formation and exhaustion of the capacity of instruments," and then finally converting this unit into a day's "wages," Rae points out that such a *numeraire* is not applicable when international comparisons are under consideration.

6. *Ibid.*, pp. 100–106, 194–95. "To simplify the consideration of the matter, we may, for a little, proceed on the supposition, that every instrument is constructed at one precise point of time, and exhausted at another. In that case, every instrument would find a place, in some part of a series, of which the orders were determined by the period of time at which instruments placed in them, issue, or would issue, if not before exhausted, in events equivalent to double the labor expended in forming them. These orders may be represented by the letters A, B, C, * * Z, *a*, *b*, *c*, & *c*." *Ibid.*, pp. 100–101. An instrument in order A yields double its cost in one year; an instrument in order B, does so in two

lates, it must, in the absence of new inventions, yield an ever lower return, that is, assume forms ever deeper in this alphabetical series — forms which belong, not to "the more quickly returning orders," but to "the more slowly returning orders."[7] For, if an instrument's durability is increased, its efficiency e tends to remain unchanged (with costs c and returns y each growing at about the same rate), and, consequently, the value of its n coefficient rises. Even though, given an instrument's durability, existing knowledge can be used to increase its efficiency e and reduce the value of its n coefficient, such extension must presently encounter rising marginal material costs c, with the result that efficiency and return (i.e., e and r) decline.[8] One could infer, from the rate of interest obtaining in a country, "the order in our series, at which instruments are there arrived," since the rate of interest constituted a "fair measure of the real average rate of profits, in any country."[9] One could infer also, and find support in the experience of new and capital-short countries, that in such countries "stock" must be kept employed fully and in "the more quickly returning orders."[1]

Although Rae believed that, "while art itself remained stationary," the "formation of instruments," would "gradually carry instruments to more and more slowly returning orders," he did not suppose that this decline need proceed rapidly, and he took it for granted that vast amounts of capital could be utilized, should it continue to be forthcoming at low rates of return.[2] He was not a stagnationist. Nor did he make use of a stationary state, conceived

years; one in Z, in twenty-six years; and so on. Instruments, whose point of exhaustion fell short of or lay beyond the point in time at which their return was double that of their costs, were reduced to terms of instruments for which these points coincided. See *ibid.*, pp. 102–3.

7. *Ibid.*, pp. 109, 117, 118–19, 195–96.

8. *Ibid.*, pp. 110–14. Rae does not use the term marginal, though it is apparent that, reasoning as had Ricardo, he supposes $\Delta y/\Delta c$ to become a declining quantity. "Neither" durability nor efficiency "can be indefinitely increased, without carrying the instruments constructed continually on, to orders of slower return." *Ibid.*, pp. 113–14. The tendency of returns to decline is less pronounced when a given outlay on an instrument simultaneously increases its durability and efficiency, or when materials are numerous and varied and opportunities for substitution and combination are great. *Ibid.*, pp. 114–15.

9. *Ibid.*, pp. 195–96. A high rate might, of course, reflect either a low rate of accumulation in the past, or a great amount of invention. *Ibid.*, pp. 262, 322.

1. *Ibid.*, p. 207. Nonsavers who migrated to new countries often became savers in these countries because there the interest rate was high enough to evoke savings (p. 199).

2. *Ibid.*, pp. 115–17. It was impossible to fix "any limit" to "the formation of instruments" in a community "where art has made considerable advance." *Ibid.*, p. 117.

of as either an analytical tool, or a possible end result, even though such a result was possible on his premises.

According to Rae's second principle, capital accumulation varied not only with the rate of return to be had,[3] but also with a people's "effective desire of accumulation," with its "determination to sacrifice a certain amount of present good, to obtain another greater amount of good, at some future period," with its ability to perceive the importance of future wants and make provision for them.[4] The more powerful this desire, the "more slowly returning" was the order of instruments which an individual or a society stood willing to construct.[5] Accordingly, the more numerous and the more powerful were the accumulation-favoring elements and motives present in a society, the higher would be its rate of capital formation.[6] Thus, since uncertainty caused man to favor the present over the future, whatever reduced uncertainty (e.g., peace, security, increase of life expectancy) strengthened his desire to provide for the future. And since man as an individual preferred the present to the future even when both were certain, whatever bound man more closely to society and to his fellows (e.g., family ties, "social and benevolent affections," intellectual power to perceive and reflect upon the future) increased his "effective desire of accumulation."[7]

> The desire to accumulate would seem then to derive strength, chiefly from three circumstances.
>
> 1. The prevalence throughout the society, of the social and benevolent affections, or, of that principle, which, under whatever name it be known, leads us to derive happiness, from the good we communicate to others.
>
> 2. The extent of the intellectual powers, and the consequent prevalence of habits of reflection, and prudence, in the minds of members of the society.
>
> 3. The stability of the condition of the affairs of the society, and the reign of law and order throughout it.[8]

3. E.g., see *ibid.*, p. 199, where Rae describes how migrants who had not saved at home begin to save upon moving into countries in which the rate of return to capital is higher.

4. *Ibid.*, p. 119, also pp. 81–83, 87, 89, 322–23.

5. *Ibid.*, pp. 117, 119, 162, 199; also p. 205 where continuing formation of instruments is made dependent on realization of "anticipated returns."

6. He apparently supposed other conditions to be given, since he listed three additional factors which conduced to capital formation by increasing the ratio of capital's return to its cost. These factors are: the "quantity and quality of materials owned" by a society; "progress of the inventive faculty"; and a "lowering in the rate of wages" when it is in excess of the required minimum. Of these three forces, the "advance of invention" was by far the most powerful and unbounded. *Ibid.*, pp. 109, 130–31, 362. Multiplicity of materials was important in that it increased man's range of alternatives (*ibid.*, p. 115).

7. *Ibid.*, pp. 119–25, 128–29. The importance of length of life expected is noted several times (*ibid.*, pp. 119, 123, 155).

8. *Ibid.*, p. 124, also p. 362. See also pp. 275–76, 279, where these circumstances are described as unfavorable to vanity and luxury.

Where opposing circumstances prevailed, the desire to accumulate was weak. For various reasons, among them some that we should label "cultural," societies differed greatly in respect of strength of desire to save: Thus American-Indian hunting tribes were very little disposed to save; Chinese were more disposed to save than were other Asians but less so than Europeans who in turn were somewhat less thrifty than North Americans. Because agriculturalists were relatively inclined to save, capital formation had been fostered by the advent of settled agriculture.[9] Furthermore, consumption habits varied. Vanity, "the mere desire of superiority over others," together with the luxury to which it gave rise, everywhere retarded capital accumulation, but with more force in some countries and regions and classes than in others.[1]

The third of what I have called Rae's three principles amounts to the statement that, in the longer run, it is upon the cumulation of relevant knowledge and its expression in invention that both capital accumulation and the improvement of man's lot ultimately depend. For, in the absence of invention, rising costs and delay in receipt of return cause the return on capital to fall as capital accumulates, until finally capital formation proceeds so slowly, even in countries in which the "effective desire of accumulation" is strong, that it contributes little to the improvement of a society's situation.[2] Normally, however, even though some conditions which conduced to invention were unfavorable to accumulation,[3] Rae believed that

9. On the dispositions of various peoples to save see *ibid.*, pp. 131–42, 147–53, 155–56, 206–7, 239, 278. Individuals and working classes also differed in this respect (*ibid.*, pp. 203–4).

1. Chap. 11 in Book II has to do with "luxury," its genesis, and its effects. See *ibid.*, esp. pp. 265, 266, 268, 271, 283, 285, 290, 292, 311–12, 318. Sometimes vanity encouraged invention which in turn sometimes removed goods from the luxury category by making them common or useful. *Ibid.*, pp. 291–92. Industry and frugality tended to flourish in new countries where, because the population was scattered, vanity could be given little play. "There is hence no better school for the dissolute European than the backwoods." *Ibid.*, pp. 280–81. Rae was not concerned about the possibility of oversaving, since he subscribed to Say's law. *Ibid.*, pp. 203, 310–11.

2. *Ibid.*, pp. 22–24, 113–14, 117, 322. See also p. 31 where invention is described as the "cause of the existence" of capital and population; p. 23 where invention rather than parsimony is said to be the cause of capital accumulation; and p. 264 where it is said that "accumulation of stock diminishes profits" whereas "augmentation of stock" through invention "increases profits." See also p. 13 where it is said that as a nation's capital increases, its composition and quality change.

3. "Intestine commotions, persecutions, wars," etc., either "altogether destroy, or, at least, very much impair the strength of the effective desire of accumulation. On the contrary, they excite the inventive faculty to activity"; for they undermine "the excessive propensity to imitation" and the disposition

many conditions making for capital accumulation were favorable also to invention, among them "a preponderance of the social and benevolent affections," the presence of "reflective men," etc.; that strength of the accumulative principle and strength of the inventive principle tended to co-exist; and that what increased the power of the one principle tended to increase that of the other.[4] Moreover, invention augmented capital accumulation by pushing up the rate of return on capital and causing individuals with a given "effective desire of accumulation" to save more; by increasing output; and by making available new productive objects of desire (e.g., a thresher) whose purchase generally entailed prior and additional saving on the part of would-be purchasers.[5]

Rae's account suggests that the rate of invention tended to be relatively high when inventors were treated well, when the propensity to imitate was weak, and when arts and materials were numerous and diverse. By way of illustration he pointed to the history of the plough, of sacred architecture, of the water mill, of the steam engine, and of printing and banking.[6] As a rule, Rae (himself an inventor) remarked, inventors, though they served all of mankind, were misunderstood, badly treated, and ill-rewarded; it was desirable that their efforts be better compensated.[7] "Servile imitation," the "antagonist" of "change," being the principal immaterial obstacle to

of men to be "so much given to learning, that they do not readily become discoverers." "Whatever, therefore, breaks the wonted order of events, and exposes the necessity, or the possibility, of connecting them by some other means, strongly stimulates invention." "Unexpected exigence" rouses "slumbering faculties." The "palsy of the mind" is undone by "revolutions" and "great changes." *Ibid.*, pp. 222–23; see also pp. 233, 235, 316–19.

4. *Ibid.*, pp. 212, 222, 244; also p. 239 where "the strength of the effective desire of accumulation" is said to have facilitated the passage of various arts into Europe despite the presence of such obstacles as relatively high wages and "stubborn materials." See also *ibid.*, pp. 263, 322. "Were the operation of the principles of invention and accumulation to go on unchecked, the amount of stock of all nations would be gradually and uninterruptedly increased; the one furnishing the means of providing additional supplies for the wants of futurity, the other giving the motives to make the provision." *Ibid.*, p. 265.

5. *Ibid.*, pp. 20, 29–30, 259, 261–63, 321–22. See also *ibid.*, p. 15, where he says that only invention can "create."

6. *Ibid.*, pp. 224–50, on the history of invention.

7. On this last point Rae cited Francis Bacon, on whose comments on invention and induction he often drew. *Ibid.*, p. 216, also pp. 210, 214, 216–17, 219, 222. Rae distinguished sharply between "real inventors" and "mere transmitters of things already known." He described the latter as a "very useful class," but considered their role very inferior to that of inventors, since the latter had to perceive what others could not perceive and, when they made discoveries, had to oppose and "direct the current." It was the inventors, therefore, who brought "visibly before us forms previously hidden" and changed the material world. *Ibid.*, pp. 208, 213–14.

invention, its progress was favored by whatever weakened man's propensity to imitate and dissuaded him from preferring exclusively that which he had always known.[8] Among the circumstances which tended to weaken this propensity he mentioned serious challenges to a people's material welfare (e.g., exhaustion of materials, rising costs), the movement of tools or migrants from one region or country to another, internal disturbances or war, the mingling of peoples with diverse arts and of various cultures, and termination of exclusive dependence on agriculture.[9] Invention tended to flourish when arts were numerous and diverse, because invention often consisted in combining a number of arts and because the intermixture of arts dissipated imitation and gave rise to a kind of cultural heterosis.[1] Similarly, a diversity of materials, by providing men with an opportunity to try out new substances and combinations, encouraged invention.[2]

Unlike early twentieth century writers, Rae did not believe invention itself to be subject to diminishing returns. While the strength of the inventive principle varied from country to country, the role of knowledge was very great, and the force of invention was subject to little or no limit in the long run. "The advance of invention" is a "quantity to the increase of which we can set no bounds." "It is impossible to put any bounds" to the operations of "art." "There are no limits to the inventive faculty."[3] On several occasions he suggested that invention might progress at an increasing rate, after arts and materials had become sufficiently numerous and diverse.[4] Rae was optimistic, therefore, respecting future prospects. "Even the barren deserts of Africa may, in after ages, be fertilized."

8. *Ibid.*, pp. 209, 224–25, 236, 321.

9. *Ibid.*, pp. 224–25, 229, 233, 237–39, 245–46, 251, 255. Of great historical importance was the migration of skilled refugees from religious or political persecution. *Ibid.*, pp. 118–19.

1. *Ibid.*, pp. 225, 237–38, 243.

2. *Ibid.*, pp. 115, 224. Earlier (Book II, Chap. 5, esp. pp. 109, 116–17) he had said that, even when knowledge remained stationary, if materials were sufficiently numerous and a people had acquired "considerable knowledge of the qualities and powers of the materials" they possessed, returns to instruments would not fall very fast as capital accumulated. For there would then be great scope for substituting materials for one another, for exploiting opportunities, and for improvements in one branch of the economy to stimulate improvement in other branches.

3. *Ibid.*, pp. 131, 258, 304, also pp. 55–56, 99, 156; also p. 237 where he speaks of a conditional "continual onward progress."

4. "The productions of the union of arts also propagating others, like all generators, their increase goes on, . . . when there are no retarding checks, not in a simple arithmetical, but in a geometrical progression." *Ibid.*, p. 245, also p. 115.

Yet, judging from his historical account of inventions, he did not soon expect invention to increase at a very rapid rate, though he supposed its progress would be continuous.[5] Because of his confidence in invention, Rae believed that both wages and profits might remain high.[6]

II

Rae's discussion of economic policy, though present in Book I as well as in Book III, was based upon the principles which he developed in Book II. These have been described in the preceding section. An admirer of Francis Bacon whom he frequently cited, Rae believed his principles had been arrived at inductively whereas Smith's principles, against some of which he protested, had been drawn from a philosophical system. Smith's "great work" was intended "to explain known phenomena"; it was not to be considered "an inductive inquiry, leading to the discovery of the real laws determining the succession of those phenomena."[7] Smith's economic precepts did not therefore always fit the requirements of a new country. Thus Rae, believing the relations obtaining between Canada and the rest of the British Empire to be mutually beneficial, rejected the view "that the sooner the connection between them is dissolved the better."[8]

Rae, believing that disparity between "individual and national interests" might be great and taking for granted that the legislator

5. *Ibid.*, pp. 224–30. In one place (*ibid.*, pp. 30–31), however, he commented on the "great productive power of both the population and capital of a country," which, "when room is afforded them to shoot, seems so easily to fill any gap which is made in the national members or stock." He referred to the rapidity with which losses occasioned by great calamities (e.g., war, the fire of London) were made up. But he went on to indicate obstacles to the growth of numbers and capital which could in the end be removed only through invention (*ibid.*, p. 31). Elsewhere (*ibid.*, p. 14) he considered high what we should probably consider a relatively low rate of capital growth: "Within a few centuries the national capital of Great Britain has increased ten fold."

6. *Ibid.*, pp. 263–64. He did not believe that high profits necessarily entailed high prices, since high profits usually were consequent upon invention which served to reduce prices (*ibid.*, p. 263).

7. On Smith see *ibid.*, Book II, Chap. 15, esp. pp. lvi, 332–36, 342, 350–51; and on Rae's approach, *ibid.*, preface and pp. 5–6, 413–14. Rae himself was an experimentalist and a student of natural history, geology, etc., at the time he was formulating some of his economic ideas, and he remained a careful observer and analyst of social phenomena throughout his life. See James's interesting account, *op. cit.* Rae is mistaken, of course, in saying Smith was not much of an empiricist.

8. *Ibid.*, p. 5. Smith had held that, under certain conditions, the American colonies would be better off free. Rae's promised work on these mutual benefits never was printed. See Mixter, *Sociological Theory of Capital*, p. xxx.

was a part of society and an instrument of nature and its processes, indicated that a large amount of state interference in economic life might be called for, above all in new countries. This interference would have economic development as its primary objective.[9] One could not always count upon self-interest to conduce to enough saving, or otherwise to promote economic growth adequately.[1] Private individuals, though well-intentioned, often were unable, or unable compatibly with their own interests, to accomplish, without assistance at the hands of the state, objectives that were to the advantage of the community.[2] A people might lack materials, requisite talents, sufficiently strong accumulative and inventive principles, industries to which its economy was potentially adapted, etc. At the same time it might be possible, through state intervention, to overcome these lackings even though unassisted private individuals could not surmount them.[3] Among the actions open to the state Rae included such as these: rouse the inventive principle; augment capital formation; promote science and art by encouraging the discovery of new arts and improvement of the old; introduce arts and industries from progressive foreign countries; enable private individuals to produce domestically, when feasible, various goods formerly imported, thereby effecting a saving in transportation costs.[4] The various specific actions open to the legislator were grouped by Rae under two headings: (a) introduction of new arts and industries and stimulation of invention; (b) augmentation of the rate of capital formation.[5]

9. E.g., see *New Principles*, pp. 7–8, 358–62; also p. 15 where he says that "the object" of the nation is "to create," which means, to add to the nation's "wealth."

1. *Ibid.*, pp. 15, 125, 343–44; also references cited in next note; also p. xi where he says that "individuals grow rich by the *acquisition* of wealth previously existing; nations, by the *creation* of wealth that did not before exist."

2. *Ibid.*, pp. 32 ff., 48–49, 65 ff., 68, 70 ff., 343–44, 359; also pp. 70–72 where Rae indicates when assistance to private entrepreneurs is warranted.

3. "The whole society, or rather the legislator, the power acting for the whole society, might do so, and in some particular cases has done so, and, to judge of the measure by the events consequent on it, with the happiest success." *Ibid.*, p. 56; also pp. 75–76.

4. *Ibid.*, Book I, esp. pp. 11, 15–16, 31, 45–49, 56, also pp. 368, 377. That new industries could be introduced from abroad despite difficulties (see *ibid.*, pp. 51–55) attendant upon such transfer, was evident from the fact that, when war interrupted commerce, peoples often learned to produce at home what they had theretofore imported from abroad. *Ibid.*, pp. 49–50, 68–71.

5. But see *ibid.*, p. 362, where improvement of cultural factors is treated separately. Presumably Rae also had education in mind, since he wrote or planned to write several pieces on education. Moreover, as has been remarked, he was himself a very learned man, his range of knowledge including mathematics and the classics. See Mixter, *Sociological Theory of Capital*, pp. xxiii, xxxiii, and James, *op. cit.*

The state could foster capital formation in two ways. It could do so indirectly by "the establishment of good laws and the security of the system of government," by preventing crime and waste and destruction, by promoting intelligence and morality, and possibly by facilitating the establishment of such institutional instruments as banking.[6] It could do so directly by curbing the dissipation of funds in luxuries and diverting the amounts thereby saved "to the purposes of the state," that is, "to the construction and maintenance of public works, to the encouragement of science and art by premiums," etc.[7] Duties and taxes might be imposed upon luxuries to accomplish this purpose, or their use might be interdicted, or "the social and benevolent affections and intellectual powers" which were unfavorable to "vanity" might be strengthened.[8]

Rae attached most importance to policies suited to introduce industries, arts, and methods from more progressive countries, or to develop them independently at home, given that a country was sufficiently advanced and suitably equipped with resources for such an undertaking. In essence he was an exponent of infant-industry protectionism. But he rested his case for such temporary protection primarily upon the society-transforming power of invention. There was virtually no limit to what might be accomplished through progress in knowledge and invention, given an adequate supply of capital and requisite raw materials (whose supply also was augmentable through invention). "Because one country now produces particular commodities, we are by no means warranted to conclude that nature intended they should be produced only there"; and he pointed to Great Britain, whose productions were "entirely the work of art."[9] No country was secure in any production monopoly it currently enjoyed. "As there are no limits to the inventive faculty, so no

6. *New Principles*, pp. 318–19, 187 ff., 397 ff.; also p. 312 on losses attributable to fraud and violence and pp. 95 ff. on intercountry differences in societal institutions. See also p. 362 where Rae says that increase of stock is advanced "by whatever promotes the general intelligence and morality of the society; and that, consequently, the moral and intellectual education of the people makes an important element in its progress." See also p. 378 on the role of enlightened public opinion.

7. *Ibid.*, pp. xvi, 318, 362, 369, 377. He devoted two chapters to "luxury," Book II, Chap. 11, and Book III, Chap. 2.

8. *Ibid.*, pp. 279–80, 373–76, 384–85. On p. 318 he states that "the interdiction of a pure luxury occasions . . . no loss whatever to the whole society. It can scarcely fail to produce a gain." See also pp. 289–92 where Rae indicated that invention, by cheapening goods, might remove them from the class of luxuries (*ibid.*, pp. 291–92, 318). Of interest but not relevant to the theme of this paper are Rae's comments on "utility," *ibid.*, pp. 93, 97–98, 300–312.

9. *Ibid.*, p. 258.

community can assure itself that any commodity which it now produces and exports to some other community, may not come to be produced in that community, and so be no longer exported there."[1] It was in order, therefore, "to introduce a manufacture from abroad, by the aid of the legislator, which, when so introduced, will furnish a commodity for home consumption at as low, or at a lower price, than it can be bought for in the foreign country."[2] Such action would have the further effect of saving transport costs, stimulating invention, and making the supply secure in times of war.[3] He argued more generally that "the increase of the wealth of every community is acknowledged to be dependent, not only on the accumulation of capital and division of labor among its members, but also on the progress of arts in other communities, and their subsequent transfer to it"; and he pointed to the favorable experience of England, the United States, and Russia with imported arts and industries.[4] Rae did not discuss the promotion of immigration, perhaps because he thought immigrants would come any way; but he remarked that immigrants bring new methods, and, by making possible a mingling of diverse peoples and arts, gave rise to a situation favorable to invention and inimical to "servile imitation."[5]

III

Rae's place in the history of economic thought is secure, as was indicated at the start of this note.[6] His major contribution consisted

1. *Ibid.*, p. 304.

2. *Ibid.*, pp. 70–71, 76–77; also p. 367 where it is said that the legislator "is never justified" in attempting to introduce arts from abroad when there is no prospect that production costs will fall sufficiently. To this stipulation he made one exception, namely, if a commodity were so essential that interruption of its importation by war would seriously injure the importing nation's economy (*ibid.*, pp. 366–68).

3. *Ibid.*, pp. 364–66. Earlier (*ibid.*, pp. 173–74) Rae had said that men had assembled in towns and villages to reduce transport costs consequent on the division of labor.

4. *Ibid.*, pp. 76–77, 264, also 312, 367–68; also 316–17 on the introduction of improved British agricultural methods into Norway.

5. *Ibid.*, pp. 237–38. Respecting Britain and the United States he said: "Servile imitation can there have no place, for there is no common standard to imitate" (*ibid.*, p. 238). Cf. A. Marshall, *Industry and Trade* (London, 1927), p. 146. Rae could not foresee that, as Marshall observed (*ibid.*, p. 146), ethnic heterogeneity makes for homogeneity "in matters of consumption." At one time Rae prepared a work intended in part to inform immigrants to Canada of its resources. See James, *op. cit.*, p. 144.

6. Schumpeter, the apostle of innovation, in his *History of Economic Analysis* (New York, 1954), touches a number of times upon Rae's work. Rae had a "conception of the economic process, which soars above the pedestrian view

in his recognition of the importance of the role of technical knowledge and invention in economic development, a role he was able to appreciate, however, only because he clearly recognized both the tendency of capital's productivity to fall and the limitations to which man's disposition and capacity to form capital were subject. Invention served in his system, as the division of labor did in Smith's, to prevent the advent of a stationary state at least so long as the inventive principle continued in effect. His contribution to *political* economy consisted in his appreciation of the role of the state in economic development, a role which, as many studies have since demonstrated, has been great and continues to be great in countries that are relatively backward as was Rae's Canada. In the course of his discussion of "luxury," a discussion apparently somewhat influenced by H. Storch's work, Rae contributed to the understanding of the formation of habits of consumption, remarking in particular the role of "vanity," the circumstances which strengthened or weakened it, and the place of serviceableness of commodities in fixing their rates of exchange. Here again his experience in a new country made him aware that there the scope for luxury was necessarily limited. Methodologically, Rae was quite modern in that, though he sought continually to seek explanation in terms of his theoretical organon, he accommodated his organon and his interpretations to his inductive findings. Had he had at his command the opportunity for study which he craved, he might have greatly accelerated the progress of the economics of development.[7]

Duke University

that it is the accumulation of capital per se that propels the capitalist engine." His theory of capital was "conceived in unprecedented depth and breadth." It included the two cornerstones of Böhm-Bawerk's structure: the proposition that 'lengthening' the process of production (postponement) will usually increase the physical amount of final product"; and the proposition that man prefers an object immediately present to the same object certainly available at some future date. See *ibid.*, pp. 468–69; also p. 846 where it is said that Mixter "greatly overstates the case for Rae" in respect of Böhm-Bawerk's work.

7. Rae's influence upon Canadian economic thought is treated by Crauford Goodwin in a study scheduled to be completed in 1960.

[7]

The Rise and Decline of Ricardian Economics

Frank W. Fetter

EVERY economist has heard of "Ricardian economics," and it is a rare one who has not talked about it. But if one compares the various statements about Ricardian economics, a newcomer to the field that Ricardo and his contemporaries referred to as their "science" would be hard put to it to say what its distinguishing theoretical content was, how much of this theory was Ricardo's and how much was taken over from those who went before, what its achievements were in the field of policy, and when it was superseded by some other kind of economics. The one point on which there seems to be agreement is that Ricardian economics did not begin until Ricardo's first published writing in 1809.

Ricardian economics has many facets, and the one that at any time has shone most brightly has depended on the light in which it was placed and the position of the observer. Or to shift the metaphor, the judgments of economists on Ricardo suggest the opinions of the nine blind men who felt various parts of the elephant and then described the animal. We have the view of Keynes, and (since few economists of the younger generation have read Keynes, and the rest only articles by their colleagues about Keynes) a quotation is in order:

> The idea that we can safely neglect the aggregate demand function is fundamental to the Ricardian economics, which underlie what we have been taught for more than a century. . . . Ricardo conquered England as completely as the Holy Inquisition conquered Spain. . . . The completeness of the Ricardian victory is something of a curiosity and a mystery. It must have been due to a complex of suitabilities in the doctrine to the environment into which it was projected. That it reached conclusions quite different from what the ordinary uninstructed person would

MR. FETTER *is Professor of Economics Emeritus of Northwestern University and now lives in Hanover, New Hampshire.*

> expect, added, I suppose, to its intellectual prestige. That its teaching, translated into practice, was austere and often unpalatable, lent it virtue. That it was adapted to carry a vast logical superstructure, gave it beauty. That it could explain much social injustice and apparent cruelty as an inevitable incident in the scheme of progress, and the attempt to change such things as likely on the whole to do more harm than good, commended it to authority. That it afforded a measure of justification to the free activities of the individual capitalist, attracted to it the support of the dominant social force behind authority.[1]

Elsewhere I have questioned whether Keynes correctly interpreted the failure of economists after Ricardo to concern themselves with effective demand.[2] But regardless of that question, there is no doubt but that Keynes believed that the essence of Ricardian economics was lack of concern about effective demand and that Ricardian economics thus defined was dominant until he escaped from the bondage of Marshallian teaching.

James Mill had expounded the view that supply creates its own demand before a word of Ricardo's had ever appeared in print. Aside from that point, contemporaries of Ricardo, veterans of the doctrinal wars of the time, would have been astonished to learn that the decisive battle that established a *Pax Ricardiana* in economic theory was the victory of Ricardo's ideas on demand over the ideas of Malthus on demand. And they, as well as economists of the decades following Ricardo, would have been incredulous at the idea that Ricardo's economics—whatever that was—had won such a triumphant victory over rivals.

Shortly after Ricardo's death James Mill had written to McCulloch that they were Ricardo's "two and only genuine disciples."[3] And one would never have guessed, from the words of William Thompson, four years after Ricardo's death, that Ricardian economics, or for that matter any particular brand of economics, had won any such victory as Keynes later ascribed to it:

1. J. M. Keynes, *General Theory of Employment, Interest and Money* (London, 1936), pp. 32-33.
2. F. W. Fetter, *The Development of British Monetary Orthodoxy, 1797-1875* (Cambridge Mass., 1965), pp. 142-143; idem, "The Relation of the History of Economic Thought to Economic History," *American Economic Review* 55 (May 1965): 138-39.
3. Piero Sraffa, ed., *The Works and Correspondence of David Ricardo* (Cambridge, 1951-1953), 9:391. Cited below as Ricardo *Works*.

> We shall find as many sects in the schools of political economy as in the schools of religion, each of them relying on his own peculiar doctrines as the exclusive means of salvation for the operative, or industrious classes.[4]

And two years later Samuel Read wrote:

> By all who are acquainted with the most recent and most noted works on Political Economy, it will be readily admitted that the science is at present in a very unsettled and unsatisfactory state. There is indeed scarcely a single doctrine—if we except that of *commercial* freedom, as expressed long since by the French economists—upon which there is a perfect and uniform, or even a *general* agreement, among the various sects and schools into which the science is now divided.[5]

In contrast to this picture of an economic Tower of Babel, Robert Torrens, often thought of as an upholder of the major Ricardian doctrines, wrote two years before Ricardo's death: "With respect to Political Economy the period of controversy is passing away, and that of unanimity rapidly approaching."[6] Yet in the same volume Torrens expressed doubts as to the adequacy of the ideas of James Mill and Say that supply creates its own demand;[7] and in later years, although he always considered himself a Ricardian, he expressed increasing doubts about supply creating its own demand, took a hopeful view of the population problem that certainly differed in emphasis from the Ricardian view, and advanced a favorable position on retaliatory tariffs that was contrary to the Ricardian tradition.

More recent judgments leave one in fully as much doubt as to the essential features of Ricardian economics and the date of its demise. In the eyes of Herbert Foxwell, Ricardo's economics had as baneful an influence as Keynes later pictured, but the nature of the teaching and the nature of the damage were of a quite different sort than Keynes had in mind. It was that Ricardo, by his unfortunate phrasing of the labor theory of value, had encouraged socialism:

> I am more and more impressed, as I study the literature of socialism, with the far-reaching, disastrous consequences of the

4. William Thompson, *Labor Rewarded* (London: 1827), p. 39.
5. Samuel Read, *An Inquiry into the Natural Grounds of Right to Vendible Property or Wealth* (London, 1829), p. v.
6. Robert Torrens, *An Essay on the Production of Wealth* (London, 1921), p. xiii.
7. Ibid., p. ix.

> unfortunate colour given to economic teaching by Ricardo. . . . it was Ricardo's crude generalizations which gave modern socialism its fancied scientific basis, and provoked, if they did not justify, its revolutionary form. . . . [Ricardo] did more than any other intentionally socialist writer to sap the foundations of that form of society which he was trying to explain. . . .[8]

Mark Blaug in a chapter, "The Heyday of Ricardian Economics,"[9] said: "By 1827 every leading writer denied the Ricardian maxim 'that profits depend on wages' except of course as a truism about relative shares." Yet in a later book Blaug wrote: "Until 1870 Ricardo thoroughly dominated British economic thought."[10] When Schumpeter wrote: "Ricardo's system failed from the first to gain the assent of a majority of English economists,"[11] it is clear that to him Ricardo's system meant something very different than to Keynes. Schumpeter went on to say:

> Ricardo died in 1823. In 1825, Bailey launched an attack that should have been decisive on the merits of the case. Actually it was not, for schools are not destroyed so easily. But the decay of the Ricardian school must have become patent shortly after, for in a pamphlet published in 1831 we read that 'there are some Ricardians still remaining.' In any case, it is clear that Ricardianism was then no longer a living force.[12]

For those who were raised on Keynes, the economics over which Ricardian economics triumphed was that of Malthus. But a large proportion of Ricardo's contemporaries would have found bizarre the idea that Ricardo and Malthus were engaged in a doctrinal battle of the giants over aggregate demand. It was not as the leaders of rival schools, but as theoretical brothers in arms, that a large part of the generation of Ricardo, and of the decade after his death, regarded Malthus and Ricardo. Ricardo in his formal theory drew heavily on Malthusian population ideas; Ricardo's and Malthus's technical analyses of land rent were very similar, much as their policy conclusions might differ; their views on the Poor Laws were marked more by agreement than by differences; and on monetary matters, despite differences in ex-

8. Herbert Foxwell, Introduction to Anton Menger, *The Right to the Whole Produce of Labour* (London, 1899), pp. xl-xli.
9. Mark Blaug, *Ricardian Economics* (New Haven, 1958), p. 61.
10. Blaug, *Economic Theory in Retrospect* (Homewood, Ill., 1962), p. 127.
11. Joseph A. Schumpeter, *History of Economic Analysis* (New York, 1954), p. 478.
12. Ibid.

plaining balance-of-payments adjustments, they were both of the Bullionist School, and they both favored the reestablishment and maintenance of the gold standard.

It is true that there was a head-on theoretical difference over the problem of aggregate demand and on the causes of unemployment as between Ricardo's *Principles* of 1817 and Malthus's *Principles* of 1820, and for economists of today, privileged to read the exchanges of letters between the two men, these differences have been brought into sharp relief. But lest we lose our sense of proportion it is well to keep two points in mind. For about six years after the death of Ricardo economic conditions in England were substantially better than from 1815 to 1822, and this not only blunted the force of Malthus's view that lack of aggregate demand was the great economic problem but to a large degree stopped discussion, by Malthus or anyone else, of the theoretical difference between Ricardo and Malthus on this issue. It was not so much a matter of Ricardian ideas on aggregate demand crushing Malthusian ideas, but of economists and laymen alike, and above all Malthus himself, losing interest in the problem. From 1824 until his death Malthus wrote hardly a line on aggregate demand; and the posthumous second edition of his *Principles* that came out in 1836 reveals no evidence that Malthus in the last ten years of his life was much concerned, one way or the other, about the problem.

Vigorous attacks on the Ricardian idea that employment would take care of itself came from George Poulett Scrope and Thomas Attwood, as well as from the poet laureate Robert Southey. These men were almost equally critical of Ricardo and Malthus, whom they seemed to regard as the two principal figures of the economists' establishment that they wanted to overthrow. Scrope, discussing population, headed a section of his *Principles of Political Economy* as "Folly, mischief, and impiety of the Malthusian doctrine";[13] yet he wrote elsewhere at about the same time:

> The economists have nowhere committed greater errors than in discussing the relations of the demand to the supply of commodities. . . . We have shown, however, that the real demand being for final consumption only, a general increase in the propensity to save, as compared with that to spend, would

13. George P. Scrope, *Principles of Political Economy* (London, 1833), p. 12.

> proportionately diminish the demand as compared with the supply, and occasion *a general glut.*[14]

Southey, without benefit of economic analysis, in 1812 in discussing the Poor Laws spoke of "Malthus' system [of population]" as "worthless," and as appealing to "the shallow, the selfish, and the sensual."[15] Four years before the appearance of Malthus's *Principles* Southey made suggestions for public works, in times of "stagnant manufacture, and languishing agriculture, and a population suddenly turned loose from the military or naval services of the country,"[16] that have the flavor of Malthus's ideas on demand. Southey continued such proposals for the next fifteen years, and at the same time denounced Malthus along with the rest of the economists.

If to contemporaries and immediate successors of Ricardo his economic system—whether triumphant or dying—meant something very different than to Keynes, just what was the Ricardian system? Discussions of the contribution and influence of Ricardo have been muddied by a failure to distinguish between three things:

1. The broad economic and philosophical notions that were current at the time, and that Ricardo took over with little critical appraisal of his own and used as the basis of his own analysis.

2. The technical analysis that he developed, within the framework of these tacitly accepted assumptions.

3. His policy proposals and their influence.

Ricardo's first interest in economics came from reading Adam Smith; his broad philosophical assumptions were those of Smith; and his technical analysis was in large part an attempt to extend, amend, or correct the master. He adopted, and strengthened, Smith's belief that the desire of men for economic gain provided a self-regulating mechanism for the economy. Walter Bagehot said that Adam Smith's economics assumed that there was a Scotchman in every man. It might seem impossible to gild that lily of the economic man, but I would suggest that Ricardo did so by his assumption that there was also a stockbroker in every man. In much of what Smith said was an implication—probably reflecting his observation of economic behavior in his native Kirkcaldy, in Glasgow, and in France—that tradition and institutional barriers prevented instantaneous adjustments. Ricardo, on the other hand,

14. Scrope, "The Political Economists," *Quarterly Review* 44 (Jan. 1831): 23.
15. Robert Southey, "Inquiry into the Poor Laws," ibid., 8 (Dec. 1812): 321.
16. Southey, "Parliamentary Reform," ibid., 16 (Oct. 1816): 277.

usually assumed that even in industry and agriculture, adjustment took place on the basis of as small price differences, and almost as quickly, as did arbitrage in government securities and in foreign exchange. And Ricardo's belief that self-interest was the wellspring of economic development also went beyond Smith in Ricardo's almost pathological feeling that the government did everything badly. The difference between Smith and Ricardo on the role of government was a subtle but nevertheless important one, and one that I believe most economists have neglected or underplayed. *The Wealth of Nations* has far more examples than has the *Principles of Political Economy* of appropriate fields for government action. But this was not the whole difference. Smith, as Professor Stigler pointed out in his Presidential Address before the American Economic Association, distrusted government not so much because it was inept but because it was "the creature of organized, articulate, self-serving groups."[17] Ricardo gives the impression of the universal ineptness of government, although rarely expressed as bluntly as in a letter to James Mill, written from Carlsruhe in 1817: "We were very much delayed by the dilatoriness of the German Post, which being a monopoly, is of course very much mismanaged. . . ."[18]

On two other matters Ricardo drew heavily on those who had gone before: the Malthusian principle of population, and the theory of money and the foreign exchanges. However, whether it was the Malthus of the first edition or the Malthus of the second edition on whom Ricardo drew cannot be answered unequivocally even by a meticulous line-for-line examination of every word that Ricardo wrote on population. You can find what you look for. As I read it, Ricardo's formal model of income distribution was based on population behavior of Malthus's first edition of the *Essay*; but much of what Ricardo said, when not constrained by the rigors of his model, robbed Malthus's ideas on population of their perpetual poverty note and would allow for the "lower orders of society" enjoying the comforts of today's American suburbanite. If wages at the minimum of subsistence was Ricardian economics, as much of what Marx wrote assumed, then Ricardian economics started on its downward path with the publication of Malthus's second edition of 1803, was given a body blow by Nassau Senior in

17. G. J. Stigler, "The Economist and the State," *American Economic Review* 55 (March 1965): 3.

18. Ricardo *Works*, 7:163.

his exchanges of letters with Malthus,[19] and had ceased by the 1830's to play a part in a theory of distribution.

The third major point where Ricardo drew on the common economic thinking of his day was the theory of money and the foreign exchanges, and more particularly the idea of an automatic adjustment of exchange rates in response to changes in the money supply. The mercantilist idea that government should do something about the money supply and the balance of payments had, beginning with David Hume in mid-eighteenth century, been the subject of extensive analysis and criticism. Adam Smith paid little attention to Hume's analysis but agreed with his conclusions, and in typical Smithian style appealed to the laws of nature and the lessons of history to support the view that the best policy of monetary regulation and exchange regulation was masterly inactivity. Following the suspension of cash payments by the Bank of England in 1797, a number of English writers had expanded and refined the Hume-Smith approach, bringing out that factors unrelated to the money supply, or even to prices, such as crop failures, foreign-war expenditures, and foreign loans and subsidies, might, at least in the short run, affect the flow of specie and the movements of the foreign exchanges. The most notable of these contributions came from Henry Thornton in his classic *Paper Credit of Great Britain*, but Sir Francis Baring, Walter Boyd, Henry Parnell, John Leslie Foster, and John Wheatley also made stimulating contributions to the discussion before Ricardo began his carrer as an economist in 1809 with his letters to the *Morning Chronicle* on the price of gold.

When one speaks of the Ricardian "contribution" to the analysis of money and the foreign exchanges, the idea of "contribution" has a Pickwickian touch. What Ricardo did, in the heat of controversy over the credit policy of the Bank of England, was to strip from existing theory Thornton's refinements on Hume and come up with a simplistic proposition that had a tough cutting edge in the polemics of the day: depreciation of English money on the foreign exchanges was entirely the result of the expansion of the note issues of the Bank of England. This was not the theory of Henry Thornton, it was not the theory of the Bullion Report. But with the increasing public opposition to the doubtful wisdom with which the Bank of England had used its discretion in the 1820's and 1830's Ricardian monetary economics

19. Nassau Senior, *Two Lectures on Population. . . to Which Is Added, a Correspondence Between the Author and the Rev. T. R. Malthus* (London, 1829), pp. 55-90.

finally won its triumph in the Bank Act of 1844. Ricardo was the doctrinal father of the Currency Principle that wished to tie changes in the currency supply to changes in the specie holdings of the Bank of England; whereas Henry Thornton, and the Bullian Report of which he was a coauthor, anticipated much of the Banking Principle in their recognition of the need for discretionary action by the Bank of England.

Ricardian economics embraced two other major concepts that were more peculiarly Ricardo's own contribution than were his ideas on effective demand, laissez-faire, population, or the foreign exchanges: viz., his theory of international trade, and his theory of value and distribution. So many great names in economics have worked the vineyard of Ricardo's theory of international trade that I shall be brief and perhaps dogmatic. This was a magnificent intellectual tour de force and a landmark in the history of economic analysis. It is true that Torrens had expressed the general idea of comparative costs as early as 1808 in *The Economists Refuted.* But it was Ricardo who spelled out the argument in detail, drove home its practical application, and made it his own. No idea of Ricardo's has stood up so well against critical attack, or has so powerfully influenced policy, as did this analysis. The argument was phrased in terms of labor costs, but I would like to add my protest to that of Haberler against the idea that Ricardo's theory of international trade depended on a labor theory of value.[20] The basic idea was difference in the ratios of production as between countries; the phrasing of these ratios in terms of labor was simply a technique of exposition. It could just as well be phrased in terms of opportunity costs. Far from the Ricardian theory of comparative costs being dependent on the labor theory of value, it was the other way round: from its association with the Ricardian theory of international trade the labor theory of value was given a vitality that it would never have had otherwise.

If we regard Ricardo's theory of international trade as peculiarly his, we have here a case of Ricardian economics with a greater influence after Ricardo's death than during his lifetime, that influence culminating in the repeal of the Corn Laws in 1846. It is true that Mark Blaug has argued with persuasiveness that the campaign of the Anti Corn Law League made almost no use of Ricardian analysis: "The campaign which finally secured the repeal of the corn laws in 1846 based itself,

20. Gottfried Haberler, *The Theory of International Trade* (New York, 1936), pp. 175-97.

more often than not, on arguments directly contrary to the spirit and letter of Ricardo's works. The free traders of the 1840's were the progeny of a parent they disowned."[21]

I would suggest, however, that the Ricardian notion of the expansion in productive power with a geographical division of labor based on different ratios of exchange had by the 1840's permeated the thought of many British who may never have heard the name of Ricardo. For every Britisher who read Ricardo there were scores who read the essence of his free trade ideas in the *Edinburgh Review*, in the *Westminster Review*, in pamphlets of Peronett Thompson, and in the writings of Harriet Martineau. The general idea that free trade increased national production was the basis from which more technical arguments or political arguments proceeded, even though these arguments may have been at odds with a purist version of Ricardian analysis. And Ricardo's analysis of international trade is still a force to reckon with: it strengthens the faith of anyone who argues in favor of freer international trade, no matter what technical analysis he may use. And its strength is shown by the way that those making a theoretical case in favor of a more restrictive policy still consider the Ricardian analysis as the roadblock that must be blasted away.

It is a futile type of scholasticism to argue which feature of Ricardian economics was the most Ricardian. But, with the possible exception of international trade theory, probably the Ricardian analysis most closely associated with his name—or at least until Keynes taught us that the neglect of aggregate demand and the assumption of full employment were the hallmark of Ricardo's system—is his theory of value and the distribution theory associated with it. Marx repeatedly suggested that he was the doctrinal heir of Ricardo's labor theory of value, and he, and even more his followers, have given the impression that the theories of surplus value and of worker exploitation somehow or other follow from Ricardo's exposition of a labor theory of value. I am unable to discover any logic that associates the labor theory of value of Ricardo with the conclusions that Marxists claim spring from it.

As a result of the claims that Marxian doctrine has a Ricardian pedigree and of the attacks on these claims, probably more words have been used, and more nonsense written, about Ricardo's labor theory of value than about any other single idea in the history of economics.

21. Blaug, *Ricardian Economics*, p. 209.

And as a consequence of this overproduction of words, in the interests of setting the records straight we have had further words to bring sense to the discussion. I have in mind particularly Professor Stigler's admirable critique, "Ricardo and the 93 Per Cent Labor Theory of Value."[22] Ricardo was trying to explain the *ratios* at which goods exchanged, not the price, *in terms of labor input*, at which goods should sell. There is no statement in Ricardo that goods do or should sell for a sum equal in value to the labor that went into them; nor any suggestion that there was any reason why labor was entitled to or could receive a wage equal to the sales price of the goods. Throughout the Ricardian analysis ran the argument, sometimes spelled out, sometimes implicit, that some return must go to those who supplied the capital and directed the operations, if production was to continue. Schumpeter did not fall into vulgar error on this point; but in his admiration for Marx as a social thinker his writings are filled with statements linking the labor theory of value of Ricardo to that of Marx.[23] Schumpeter is technically correct—he never says the two labor theories of value are the same or that the Marxian theory follows logically from the Ricardian theory, much less that Marx's surplus value stems from Ricardo's labor theory of value. But many an eager graduate student or even a seasoned Ph.D. might easily get the impression from Schumpeter that Marx's labor theory of value was the legitimate offspring of Ricardo's labor theory of value.

Furthermore, Ricardo never claimed that goods exchanged exactly in proportion to the labor that went into their production, but merely that this was, in most cases, a reasonably close approximation to the situation, and hence he would make this assumption in his model.[24] It was comparable to the assumptions in the Keynesian model that savings are a function of income and are uninfluenced by the rate of interest; or that changes in the money supply have an inverse effect on interest rates but no effect on prices. Keynes never claimed that this is always the case, but it made a nice working model. Ricardo

22. Stigler, "Ricardo and the 93 Per Cent Labor Theory of Value," *American Economic Review* 48 (June 1958): 357-67.

23. An example is in Schumpeter's *Capitalism, Socialism, and Democracy*, 3d ed. (New York, 1952) p. 23: "His [Marx's] theory of value is the Ricardian one." Elsewhere Schumpeter wrote: "Actually, however, there is nothing mystical or metaphysical about the Marxist theory of value. . . . It is nothing but Ricardo's real value fully worked out and fully made use of." *History*, p. 598.

24. This is developed in detail in G. J. Stigler, "Ricardo and the 93 Per Cent Labor Theory," n. 22.

then developed a theory of value and distribution that eliminated rent at the margin, and made the total return to profits what was left of total price after rent and wages at the minimum subsistence had been deducted.

It was a neat model, but with assumptions piled so high that it came under attack from many quarters. Probably, although it would be hard to prove, it was Ricardo's labor theory of value and his distribution theory that James Mill had in mind when he told McCulloch that they were Ricardo's only disciples. And probably many of the remarks, in the 1820's and 1830's, about the decline or demise of Ricardian economics had reference to the undermining of the factual assumptions and logic of this model. I have always been puzzled as to why such importance has been attached to a model that had so marginal a relation to the hard core of Ricardian policy. It is true that the idea that, with rising real costs of food, labor and rent would eat up such a large proportion of the national product as to impair the national supply of savings added force to the argument for reduction or abolition of the Corn Laws. Yet Ricardo's analysis of the benefits of international trade was in no substantive way tied up with his theory of value or his theory of distribution. Similarly his belief in the free market and his extreme distrust of government, his views on monetary policy, and his lack of concern with aggregate demand or measures to secure full employment stood on their own feet and were not dependent upon the Ricardianism of value and distribution. When Schumpeter wrote that in 1831 "it is clear that Ricardianism was . . . no longer a living force," he must have had in mind the Ricardianism of this formal model, and not the Ricardianism that inspired the Bank Act of 1844, contributed to the repeal of the Corn Laws two years later, or according to Keynes "conquered England as completely as the Holy Inquisition conquered Spain."

Richard Jones in 1831 challenged the realism of the Ricardian rent picture,[25] and William Whewell's prefatory notes to Jones's *Literary Remains*, although written nearly thirty years later, expressed well the spirit of Jones's criticism of the rent concept of the Ricardian model: "And the reader might be left to decide for himself which subjects of inquiry may be better worth his notice—the rents that are actually paid in every country, or the Ricardian rents which are *not* those paid

25. *An Essay on the Distribution of Wealth, and on the Sources of Taxation* (London, 1831), pp. xii-xiii.

in *any* country." The best organized and most effective attack on Ricardo's theory of value and distribution came in Samuel Bailey's anonymous book of 1825, *A Critical Dissertation on the Nature, Measures and Causes of Value.* This book has received high praise from Schumpeter: "Bailey . . . attacked the Ricardo-Mill-McCulloch analysis on a broad front and with complete success."[26] Herbert Foxwell, that great collector of economic libraries, whose likes and hates were of major dimensions, wrote in his copy of the book that is in the Kress collection at Harvard: "A crushing refutation of Ricardo, by the ablest economist of his day." But what Bailey was refuting was not Ricardo's views on the foreign exchanges, international trade, laissez-faire, or full employment. His criticism was primarily of Ricardo's search for an invariable measure of value, of Ricardo's failure to recognize that value has meaning only as a relative concept, and of Ricardo's theory of the inverse relation of profits and wages. In Bailey's dissection of Ricardo's theory of the inverse relation of profits and wages (Chap. 4, "On Profits") he brought out the dependence of the Ricardian conclusion about inverse relation upon the assumption that "the productive power of labour continues the same" (pp. 65-66).

Bailey's book was a powerful critique not just of the labor theory of value, but also of the whole idea of a simplistic explanation of value. The final paragraph of his book opens with a passage that has its message even for 1969:

> On a review of the subject [of value] it appears, that economists attempt too much. They wish to resolve all of the causes of value into one, and thus reduce the science to a simplicity of which it will not admit. They overlook the variety of considerations operating on the mind in the interchange of commodities. These considerations are the causes of value, and the attempt to proportion the quantities in which commodities are exchanged for each other to the degree in which one of these considerations exists, must be vain and ineffectual [p. 231].

Important and telling as was much of Bailey's criticism, one may question to what extent it was an "overthrow" of the Ricardian system. As suggested earlier, there is serious doubt whether the Ricardian theory of value and distribution, despite the theoretical controversies that it spawned, was in any way fundamental to Ricardo's analysis of

26. Schumpeter, *History*, p. 486.

the economic problems of England or to the policies for which he argued. It was rather a gadget created by Ricardo's fertile and orderly mind to help him think through the problems.

If, as was the general impression by the 1830's, Ricardo's theoretical framework had been largely rejected, there is a mystery as to why the name of Ricardo was so closely associated with the economic theory of John Stuart Mill and English neoclassical economics. Why should Keynes, born half a century after the reputed death of the Ricardian system, have felt that the baneful economics on which he was raised, and against which he reacted so vigorously when he became a Keynesian, was Ricardian? As suggested at the beginning of this paper, his feeling was due in part to his belief that Ricardo's lack of concern with aggregate demand was the essence of Ricardian economics. This was only a part of the picture, however. To Keynes's generation, Ricardian ideas were often almost a synonym for economics—even for ideas that were not Ricardo's or, as in the field of balance-of-payments adjustments, for ideas that Ricardo had opposed. For this rehabilitation of Ricardo I would suggest two major causes that sprang from quite different circumstances but nevertheless had the same result—the belief that Ricardo, if properly interpreted, had really been right. These causes are outside the framework of formal economics: one was basically a matter of political propaganda; the other a matter of personal piety, whose explanation can come more appropriately from the psychoanalyst than from the economist. These causes were Marxian socialism; and the respect of John Stuart Mill for the memory of Ricardo, and the respect of Alfred Marshall for tradition.

The constant suggestion of Marx, and even more the claims of his followers, that the Marxian labor theory of value, and, at least by suggestion, surplus value, were the legitimate heirs of Ricardian theory, placed the name of Ricardo once more in the center of discussion, by Socialists and non-Socialists alike. The two great schoolmasters of English-speaking economists from the 1850's to the 1920's, John Stuart Mill and Alfred Marshall, contributed greatly to the impression that Ricardo, if *properly interpreted*, really had given the right analysis. Mill has been thrown to the Freudian lions so often that there is no point in retracing his early education in the eternal verities of Ricardo under that severe taskmaster, James Mill, and his later emancipation and the emotional crisis that accompanied it. John Stuart Mill of the

Principles appeared to be an impartial and objective critic of Ricardo; yet with all his disagreement and criticism there is left the impression that insofar as Ricardo erred, it was in minor details, not in the fundamentals of analysis. On the relation between profits and wages Ricardo's words are reinterpreted to express "what Ricardo meant"[27]; of Ricardo's theory of rent Mill said, "It is one of the cardinal principles of political economy."[28] And the whole picture, even when the analysis was quite contrary to Ricardo's is to suggest that the Ricardian framework remains almost unaltered. No one would suspect, from reading Mill's *Principles*, the criticism to which Ricardian ideas on rent, value, wages, and profits had been subjected in the previous twenty years.

Just before Mill's death Stanley Jevons launched an all-out attack on Ricardian value theory. His general position is indicated by an oft-quoted passage:

> When at length the true system of Economics comes to be established, it will be seen that that able but wrong-headed man, David Ricardo, shunted the car of Economic science on to a wrong line, a line, however, on which it was further urged towards confusion by his equally able and wrong-headed admirer John Stuart Mill.[29]

Jevons also spoke of "casting ourselves free from the Wage-Fund Theory, the Cost of Production doctrine of Value, the Natural Rate of Wages, and other misleading or false Ricardian doctrines. . . ."[30] This seemed to set the stage for a return to the situation before Mill's *Principles*—a rejection of the Ricardian ideas on Wages, Rent, Profits, and Value. But Jevons died in 1882 at the age of forty-seven, and his counterrevolution was in England short-lived.

Alfred Marshall soon took up and amplified the work of Mill—of showing that if one understood what Ricardo *really meant*, then the Ricardian structure was intact, although many details had to be modified. Marshall's approach is indicated by a passage in Appendix I, "Ricardo's Theory of Value":

> If we seek to understand him rightly, we must interpret him generously, more generously than he himself interpreted Adam

27. *Collected Works of John Stuart Mill*: *Principles of Political Economy* (Toronto, 1965), 1:413.
28. Ibid., p. 419.
29. Stanley Jevons, *The Theory of Political Economy*, 2d ed. (London, 1879), p. lvii.
30. Ibid., p. l.

> Smith. When his words are ambiguous, we must give them that interpretation which other passages in his writings indicate that he would have wished to give them. If we do this with the desire to ascertain what he really meant, his doctrines, though very far from complete, are free from many of the errors that are commonly attributed to them.[31]

It is awesome to contemplate what would happen to the supply of economists with Ph.D.'s if teachers in graduate schools used these Marshallian standards in reading qualifying examinations and theses.

W. J. Ashley's article, "The Rehabilitation of Ricardo,"[32] shortly after the appearance of the first edition of Marshall's *Principles*, with a wealth of illustrations documented Marshall's *apologia* for Ricardo. And there is the judgment of Schumpeter on Marshall's *Principles*: "the rooms of this new house are unnecessarily cluttered up with Ricardian heirlooms, which receive emphasis quite out of proportion to their operational importance."[33] Many economists, particularly in the United States, objected to Marshall's picture of his own economics as Ricardo brought up to date, but they were in the minority. The prestige of Marshall did not destroy this opposition; it kept it in the position of a guerrilla force making raids, but never capturing the main bases of the Marshallian economic establishment. The surprising thing was not the victory of Ricardian economics as Keynes conceived of Ricardian economics—lack of concern with aggregate demand and with unemployment. It was rather the victory of the idea, for which John Stuart Mill and Alfred Marshall, with an assist from the Marxians, are largely responsible, that Ricardian economics, generally repudiated by the 1830's, was still a potent force from mid-19th century until the 1920's. Ricardian economics was in decline, if not rejected, but the idea that the ideas of neoclassical economics, as adumbrated by Mill and expounded by Marshall, were really Ricardian, was victorious. No wonder that economists who had read too deeply in Mill and Marshall were confused as to when, if at all, Ricardian economics had gone into decline. If we assume that Ricardian economics is not what

31. Alfred Marshall, *Principles of Economics: Ninth Variorum Edition, with Annotations by C. W. Guillebaud* (London, 1961), 1:813. This passage, which appeared in the first edition of 1890, remained unchanged in the subsequent seven editions published during Marshall's lifetime.

32. W. J. Ashley, "The Rehabilitation of Ricardo," *Economic Journal* 1 (Sept., 1891): 474-89.

33. Schumpeter, *History*, p. 837.

Ricardo wrote but what Mill and Marshall said Ricardo *really meant*, then the task of dating the decline of Ricardian economics is indeed is a hunt for a will-o'-the-wisp.

There is a further consideration in this quest for the essence of Ricardian economics and the date of its demise. If we take the view that Ricardo's great contribution to economics was his explanation of a particular problem, be that international trade, exchange rates, the relation of wages and profits, the influence of taxes, or the role of government, then the essence of Ricardian economics and the date of its demise have an elusive and ever-changing character. What to one man, or to one generation, may appear to be Ricardo's great contribution, may in another setting seem trivial or only an antiquarian episode. A strong case can be made that the most distinguishing feature of Ricardo's economics, and his most lasting contribution to economics, was not his treatment of a particular problem, but his use of a technique of analysis: his stress on the importance of production conditions at the margin; his recognition, in connection with the theory of rent, that there were economic returns not functionally necessary; and his use of a simple macroeconomic model as the basis for arriving at broad policy recommendations. Ricardo made assumptions, which whether realistic or not, he carried through to their logical conclusions. In individual statements he sometimes recognized the artificiality or dubious validity of his assumptions, but that rarely stopped him from going ahead with his analysis and presenting his conclusions as if there were no doubt about his assumptions.

No economist who preceded Ricardo, and no other economist of the English-speaking world from his time until Keynes, so delighted in making sweeping policy recommendations from assumptions of his own choosing. The London *Economist*, in reviewing Sraffa's edition of Ricardo, said: "The classical economists in general, and Ricardo in particular, discovered something more important than any single economic generalization; they discovered the technique of economic analysis itself."[34] The kinship between the techniques of Ricardo and Keynes, and the confidence they both display in drawing policy conclusions from the theory, are striking. Schumpeter has pointed out that in "Ricardo's and Keynes' methods of securing the clear-cut result . . . they were brothers in the spirit."[35]

34. *The Economist*, Sept. 1, 1951, p. 502.
35. Schumpeter, *History*, p. 475, n.3. He makes much the same point on p. 1171.

In the century after Ricardo economists gave relatively greater attention to microeconomics than had Ricardo, and in the macroeconomic field the popularity of Ricardo-type model building was weakened by the importance attached to institutional factors, even by his admirers John Stuart Mill and Alfred Marshall. If one regards Ricardo's handling of economic analysis as the most distinctive feature of his economics, then Keynes in the *General Theory*, although he may have thought that he was demolishing Ricardian economics by his criticism of Ricardo for his neglect of aggregate demand, was in fact by his own method of analysis reviving in its full flower the most distinctive feature of Ricardian economics.

[8]

James Mill and the Theory of Economic Policy in India

William J. Barber

I

On assuming his duties in the London headquarters of the East India Company in 1819, James Mill did not underestimate the importance of his office. As he then described his functions:

> It is the very essence of the internal government of 60 millions of people with which I have to deal; and as you know that the government of India is carried on by correspondence; and that I am the only man whose business it is, or who has the time, to make himself master of the facts scattered in a most voluminous correspondence, on which a just decision must rest, you will conceive to what an extent the real decision on matters belonging to my department rests with the man who is in my situation.[1]

Moreover, he was convinced that those who held senior positions in the East India Company could contribute enormously to the increase of human welfare. When appealing to Ricardo in 1820 to stand for election to the Company's Board of Directors, Mill argued that "it would put you in a situation where your means of doing good to your fellow creatures would be prodigious" and urged a favorable reply "on account of the millions. . .over whose happiness and misery you would be invested with so much power . . ."[2]

In Mill's view, an enlightened and intelligent administration of the territories under the jurisdiction of the East India Company was all the more important because of the entrenched stagnation of Indian society. Mill had emerged from a decade spent in preparing his massive

Mr. Barber *is Professor of Economics in Wesleyan University.*

1. James Mill to Dumont, 13 December 1819, in *The Works and Correspondence of David Ricardo*, ed. P. Sraffa (Cambridge, 1952), 8:40 n.
2. Mill to Ricardo, 23 September 1820, ibid., 8:251.

three-volume *History of British India* (published in 1817) with the conclusion that "the progress of knowledge, and the force of observation, demonstrated the actual state of the Indians as little removed from that of half-civilized nations."[3] In his view, Indian society had been decadent for centuries. He was thus not bothered by a question which had perplexed many eighteenth-century minds: what, they had asked, accounted for the decay of Indian civilization from its past glory and for its failure to resist the encroachments of a handful of merchant adventurers? In Mill's view, the question itself was a mistake, and those who had raised it had failed to interpret the evidence correctly. Sophisticated skill in weaving, for example, was not an indicator of high civilization; to an Indian, he argued, such an activity recommended itself because it was a sedentary occupation and "thus in harmony with his predominant inclination." Further, it required little bodily exertion "of which he is always exceedingly sparing, and the finer the productions, the more slender the force he is called upon to apply."[4] Nor was he prepared to regard the invention of the game of chess (which reputedly had sprung from ancient India) as testifying to cultural achievement. "The invention of ingenious games," Mill asserted, "is a feat most commonly displayed by nations in their rude condition. It is prior to the birth of industry that men have the strongest need for games, to relieve them from the pain of idleness. . . ."[5]

The central problem facing the man responsible for the "very essence" of the internal government of British India was one of devising policies to elevate the masses of the population. Mill welcomed the challenge—and he brought to his endeavor a reasonably clear set of goals. In the first instance, the economy should be organized to foster economic growth. As a utilitarian liberal, he also attached importance to a satisfactory distribution of income. Aggregative economic expansion would ultimately be self-defeating if the masses failed to share in its fruits. But success could not be measured solely in terms of advancing material standards. No less important was cultural change which would liberate the bulk of the population from the chains of superstition. Mill did not expect such a transformation to come quickly; but he was convinced that an environment of economic expansion would improve its prospects.

3. James Mill, *History of British India* (London, 1817), 1:436.
4. Ibid., 1:342.
5. Ibid., 1:350.

How were these goals to be reached? A sceptic among his contemporaries might argue, with considerable plausibility, that the institutional framework within which Mill operated was uniquely ill-suited for the purpose. Was not a government in the hands of a private monopoly a most unpromising vehicle? Adam Smith had certainly thought so when writing that "the government of an exclusive company of merchants is, perhaps, the worst of all governments for any country whatsoever."[6] In the *History*, Mill had voiced much the same views about the Company's behavior in the eighteenth century. By 1819, however, the more serious reservations that a man of Mill's persuasion might have held toward association with the East India Company had been moderated. The Charter Renewal Act of 1813 had stripped the Company of its monopoly trading privileges with India (though not with China). Its role in India had thus been reduced primarily to that of a sovereign. But another development was perhaps as significant: the emergence on the scene of the theory of differential rent.

II

Ricardian rent theory was the linchpin of Mill's strategy of economic policy for India. It provided the design for a "scientific" tax: i.e., one which insured an elastic revenue base but which in no way distorted the costs of production. So long as the revenue demand did not exceed the portion of the social product attributable to the differential fertility of the soil, wages and profits would approach their natural level. Meanwhile, the state—by drawing off the rental share—would acquire the resources needed to promote public improvement and uplift. As Mill described the relevance of the theory to India to the Select Committee on the Affairs of the East India Company in 1831:

> I conceive. . .that the peculiarity of India, in deriving a large proportion of its revenue from the land, is a very great advantage. Nine-tenths probably of the revenue of the government in India is derived from the rent of land, never appropriated to individuals, and always considered to be the property of government; and to me that appears to be one of the most

6. Adam Smith, *The Wealth of Nations*, ed. Edwin Cannan, 6th ed. (London, 1950), 2:72. It is of interest to note that at one stage in his career, Smith had no scruples about enjoying the East India Company's patronage. In 1772 he actively sought a position on a commission the company was planning to form; the commission, in fact, was never created. See John Rae, *Life of Adam Smith* (London, 1895), esp. p. 254.

fortunate circumstances that can occur in any country; because in consequence of this the wants of the state are supplied really and truly without taxation. As far as this source goes, the people of the country remain untaxed. The wants of government are supplied without any drain either upon the produce of any man's labour, or the produce of any man's capital.[7]

In the context of Indian tax discussions, the doctrine of differential rent performed a further important function: it provided the basis for an analytical critique of Cornwallis's Permanent Settlement in Bengal in 1793. Under this arrangement, tax collectors (or zemindars) who had been engaged by traditional Indian rulers were treated as "owners" of substantial blocks of land; retention of their property rights, however, was contingent on the delivery of specified amounts of tax revenue to the East India Company's administrators.[8] These sums were fixed in perpetuity—hence the permanence of the Permanent Settlement—but no limit was set on the demands landowners could place on the cultivating tenantry.[9] Before the rent doctrine was available, criticisms of the East India Company's land revenue policies had been directed to their social and distributional consequences. Thereafter, the critique could be substantially broadened. With the aid of the theory of differential rent, it could be argued that the Bengal settlement was unfortunate on two further grounds: (1) the failure of the authorities to appraise the taxable potential of land with reference to the fertility of the soil; and (2) the shortsightedness of the authorities in making the tax settlement permanent, a decision which meant that the government could not tap subsequent increases in the rental share of income.

With the insights supplied by Ricardo at his disposal, it is not surprising that James Mill should have warmed to his task. A scientific formula was now available to guide the construction of an ideal tax

7. Mill, "Minutes of Evidence Before the Select Committee on the Affairs of the East India Company, 2 August 1831," *Parliamentary Papers, 1831*, 5:292.

8. For additional background on this point, see Eric Stokes, *The English Utilitarians and India* (Oxford, 1959), esp. chap. 2.

9. With some justice, officials of the East India Company could claim that they had drawn on the best economic thinking of their day in constructing the "Permanent Settlement." Thomas Law, one of Cornwallis's principal advisers, invoked *The Wealth of Nations* in defense of the Bengal system, citing Smith's view that taxes which were not defined and fixed were subject to abuse. See *Remarks on the Ryotwarree and Mocurrery Systems*, a pamphlet attributed to Thomas Law, no place or date. As John Stuart Mill later remarked, "The architects of the Bengal settlement flattered themselves that they had created, throughout the Bengal provinces, English landlords, and it proved that they had only created Irish ones." *Principles of Political Economy*, ed. W. J. Ashley (London, 1926), pp. 326-327.

system in the Company's domains beyond Bengal; and though the mistakes of Cornwallis in Bengal could not be completely corrected, the state could improve matters there by buying out the zemindars and becoming itself the owner of the soil. Not only did Mill's situation at India House place him in a position to enlarge the sphere of human happiness, it also provided him with an opportunity to apply and test the latest advances in economic theory. Moreover, he could operate with much greater freedom of maneuver than would have been possible in his home country. In India, policies of economic reform could be implemented with minimal political constraints. The use of India as a laboratory for Western social scientists considerably antedates the Ford Foundation.

III

The creation of the ideal tax system—crucial though it was—was only one component of Mill's thinking about policies for Indian development and uplift. The other side of the coin was a strategy for public expenditure. Mill's approach to this matter is likely to be regarded by mid-twentieth-century students as quite unimaginative. His program called for heavy outlays for the provision of administrative services and for the maintenance of law and order. Measured against post-World War II standards, a very low priority was attached to the provision on public account of capital works which would now be treated as more economically productive.

Within Mill's frame of reference, however, provision of security for person and property and of a judicial system which was non-arbitrary and non-corrupt was held to be fundamental to economic progress. Indeed, it was the dynamic agent of change. Most of the ills of the traditional Indian economy could be traced to the "subjection of the population to a rigid government under which the fruits of labour were never secure."[10] Correction of this intolerable situation was the overriding imperative of British administration. If this mission could be faithfully discharged, Mill had no doubt that healthy growth would naturally follow. "Elevation," he told the Parliamentary Committee on the Affairs of the East India Company in 1831, "is the natural state of a man who has nothing to fear; and the best riches are the

10. Mill, *History of British India*, 2:314.

effects of man's own industry; effects which never fail when the protection is good."[11]

Mill's faith in the growth potential associated with the provision of security and justice was, of course, linked with his thinking on the land revenue question. The theory of differential rent offered not only the design of a program for acquiring revenue; it also set clear limits to the tax obligations the government could impose. Tax demands which exceeded the true rent would impinge on costs of production and frustrate the accumulation of capital. Moreover, in Mill's terms, taxation beyond the bounds of the net rent would be patently unjust. The failure of traditional Indian rulers—who levied their claims on the basis of a share of the gross product of the land, rather than on the net rent—to appreciate this point went a long way toward explaining the backwardness of the Indian economy. To avoid repetition of such mistakes, Mill instructed the company's revenue officers to err on the side of underassessments. Thus, he concluded that "if it were limited to the rent merely, and the collection were not carried beyond the limits of a moderate rent . . . then I should say that the revenue system in India is the best in the world."[12]

This perspective, in turn, was closely associated with the general mould of the classical economic mind on the appropriate division between the private and the public sectors. The state was responsible for creating an institutional framework favorable to economic expansion, and it was uniquely qualified to supply certain of the required supporting services. Though governments should open space for private initiative, it was alien to their role to provide the resources to foster growth in the private sector. The primary responsibility for accumulation should be left in private hands. The government's role—though vital—was thus limited. This meant, as Mill put it, that "it is through

11. Mill, "Minutes of Evidence, 25 August 1831," *Parliamentary Papers, 1831,* 5:396. While Mill called for the highest standards—whatever the cost—in the provision of security and justice, he was no champion of military expenditures to enlarge the company's territorial domain. As his testimony before the Select Committee in 1831-1832 reveals, he was convinced that direct British administration of the "Native States" would enormously enhance the welfare of their inhabitants. He opposed annexation, however, primarily on the grounds that the political storm which could be expected to follow in England would be distracting and unproductive.

12. Ibid., p. 336. Within Mill's terms it would also be unjust to substitute other forms of taxes for a tax on rents: "if the government were to give it up, and to supply the deficiency by taxes, it must bestow the rent in gift upon certain individuals, and make up for the want of it by taxing others; it would be a plan to enrich a portion of the people by impoverishing the rest." Mill, "Observations on the Land Revenue of India," ibid., vol. 11, app. 7, p. 48.

the ryots [the small cultivators], and by giving a proper protection to their property and to themselves in the exercise of their industry, and through that mainly, that the improvement of India must take place."[13]

On one count, Mill might have been expected to prescribe a more ambitious form of intervention by the state. In the light of his diagnosis of the degraded condition of Indian culture, it would seem to follow that a major program of educational uplift would be called for. He fully endorsed the desirability of such an enterprise: "on every account," he maintained, "I consider the improvement of the natives in education as an object of paramount importance; and that it ought to be forwarded by every possible means."[14] But he was doubtful about its feasibility. India was too vast and the number of Englishmen in direct contact with the population too small. Educational resources could, of course, be concentrated and directed to training a class of Oriental Englishmen who could, in turn, serve the administration at lower costs than their English counterparts. Mill saw risks in this course. He put his case as follows:

> The idea generally entertained is, that you would elevate the people of India by giving them a greater share in their own government; but I think that to encourage any people in a train of believing that the grand source of elevation is in being an employé of government, is anything but desirable. The right thing, in my opinion, is to teach people to look for their elevation to their own resources, their industry and economy. Let the means of accumulation be afforded to our Indian subjects; let them grow rich as cultivators, merchants, manufacturers; and not accustom themselves to look for wealth and dignity to successful intriguing for places under government; the benefit from which, whatever it may be, can never extend beyond a very insignificant portion of the whole population.[15]

This form of high paternalism emerged from Mill's blending of the teachings of classical political economy and of utilitarian social philosophy. In its essential intellectual ingredients, the conceptual framework though which policy in India was interpreted was no different from the one developed for English conditions. On points of detail, some adjustments were made for the peculiarities of Indian circumstances.

13. Mill, "Minutes of Evidence, 4 August 1831," ibid., 5:309.
14. Mill, "Minutes of Evidence, 21 February 1832," ibid., 9:55.
15. Mill, "Minutes of Evidence, 25 August 1831," ibid., 5:396.

The scale of the country being governed – as well as the low level of its civilization –meant that the appearance of impressive evidences of economic and social improvement might be delayed. Yet there was no doubt among those who formulated the strategy that the course they had charted was correct. With only minor adaptations, the model developed for English conditions could be used to put India on the path of sustained economic progress.

IV

On several grounds, a critic of Mill's position might well have challenged the suitability of the classical framework of economic analysis to the Indian economy. While it was true that the organizing question of classical theorizing—namely, the analysis of economic expansion over the long period—was clearly relevant to the central Indian problem, it did not necessarily follow that analytical tools worked out in England could readily be transferred to an institutional environment so radically different.

At one point in particular, Mill's contemporaries were alert to the possibility that the prospects and circumstances of the two countries diverged fundamentally. The mere existence of the imperial connection meant that economic events were being diverted from their natural course. Smith had interpreted the relationship between the East India Company and India as one which necessarily implied that the growth prospects of the Indian economy were severely handicapped. Much of India's surplus product, which might otherwise have supported accumulation in the home economy, was transferred abroad by the East India Company and its agents.[16] Indeed, in Smith's day, the promise of a vast tribute flowing from territorial acquisitions in India was being advertised by directors of the East India Company as a national asset to Britain.

When discussing this phase of the Company's experience in his *History*, Mill offered conclusions similar to those Smith had reached. But at least by 1800 the flow of transfers had been reversed. Unscrupulous trading on private account by the Company's agents in the field had been curbed. More important, the evidence supplied by the East India Company's accounts indicated that the company had

16. Smith, *Wealth of Nations*, vol. 2, esp. pp. 137-38. Smith proposed that the "tribute," rather than being left in private hands, should be appropriated by the British crown.

incurred enormous deficits as its administrative responsibilities had increased. In 1826 Mill made a vigorous statement of his position:

> Under the ignorance in which Englishmen have remained of East India affairs, it floats in the minds of a great many persons, that, some how a tribute, or what is equivalent to a tribute, does come from the East Indies. Never did an opinion exist, more completely without evidence, contrary to evidence, evidence notorious, and well-known to the persons themselves, by whom the belief is entertained. India, instead of yielding a tribute to England, has never yielded enough for the expence of its own government. . . . So far is India from yielding a tribute to Great Britain, that, in loans and aids, and the expence of fleets and armies, it has cost this country enormous sums.[17]

It is perhaps worth noting that Mill arrived at this general position before he joined the service of the East India Company. In 1813, he wrote:

> Now, on the score of surplus-revenue,—of any share of the taxes levied on the people of India being ever brought to this country, —if our minds could even reconcile themselves to the justice of it, our experience tells us that nothing of the sort has ever yet happened; and all that we know of human affairs combines to assure us, and with a force which few assurances can boast, that no such event will ever come to pass. Neither we nor our posterity shall ever see any share of the revenues of India brought to this country.[18]

Mill supported these conclusions with the argument that all governments necessarily spend all the revenues they can extract from the public. In a colonial situation, governmental expenditures were likely to be less closely supervised than was the case in England; moreover, the costs of many public services were likely to be higher. Hence, there was a "moral impossibility" that India could ever yield a permanent tribute to England from its territorial revenues.

Not all observers of the Indian scene could be expected to find these arguments completely persuasive. It could be reasonably maintained that the costs of government—and, no less important, the leakages

17. Mill, "Colony," an article in the supplement to the *Encyclopedia Britannica*, 1826, p. 17.

18. "Bruce's Report on the East-India Negotiation," *Montlhy Review* 70 (1813): 35.

from the Indian economy—could be substantially reduced if qualified Indian administrators replaced expensive English ones. There was no necessary reason why Britain should be a monopoly supplier of administrative services. Mill, though opposed to a color bar, saw no prospect that the requisite talents could be supplied from within India for a considerable time ahead. "It appears to me," he asserted, "ten thousands time more important, with respect to the good of the population in general, that the business of the Government should be well done, than that it should be done by any particular class of persons."[19] At least for the time being, good government had to be imported.[20] Its costs were more than compensated by the contributions it made to the moral and material progress of India.

But not all of the troublesome points could be so tidily disposed of. As the Earl of Lauderdale had argued in a tract published in 1809, sizable transfers from India to England—however legitimate they might be—imposed strains on the economies of both countries. Under the prevailing system, the government of India was obliged to discharge certain obligations in sterling: service charges on the India debt held in Britain, pensions and allowances of its servants, and payment for government stores acquired in England, as well as other "home charges." If these commitments were to be met, an Indian export surplus was required. For these reasons, Lauderdale held that the Indian trade in the hands of the East India Company was a "trade of pure remittance,"[21] conducted without regard to normal commercial considerations. Lauderdale was more concerned with the implications of such arrangements for British manufacturers than with its impact on India. The forced importation of Indian goods, he feared, would place British competitors at a disadvantage. The same line of argument suggested (though Lauderdale did not develop the point) that the nature of the transfers shifted India's terms of trade to her disadvantage.

Mill offered no rejoinder to this line of criticism. Lauderdale's reputation as a maverick was sufficiently well established that few of the classical economists felt compelled to take his arguments seriously.

19. Mill, "Minutes of Evidence, 21 February 1832," *Parliamentary Papers, 1831-32*, 9:56.

20. It should also be observed that Mill was a strong advocate of improved standards for Englishmen in the Indian Service. He sought tighter selection procedures and more rigorous training than the East India College at Haileybury supplied.

21. Lauderdale, *An Inquiry into the Practical Merits of the System for the Government of India* (Edinburgh, 1809), p. 163.

At least to his own satisfaction, Mill was convinced that no tribute existed and that the payment of substantial administrative costs in foreign exchange was a good bargain for India.

V

The applicability of classical economic theorizing to India was more seriously threatened by another challenge. As developed in England, classical reasoning was built around the implicit presuppositions of a well-articulated and predominantly monetized economic structure. How satisfactory was this conceptual kit to India, which was not only poor, but overwhelmingly traditional and agrarian in its structure? It is by no means self-evident that concepts suited to one set of institutional circumstances are useful in another.

In the first instance, questions might be raised about the adequacy of the classical conceptual kit to the analysis of Indian agriculture. Mill was acutely aware that Indian land tenure systems and agricultural practices differed radically from those in England. Nevertheless, recognition of this fact did not diminish his insistence that Indian tax policy should be built around the Ricardian concept of differential rent. He held that in all societies rent arose from the differential fertility of the soil. All that was required for the successful implementation of his land revenue program was a technique to evaluate the natural productive powers of the land.

In English conditions, such a problem might have been handled with relative ease. Land had been alienated in private hands; a broad division between classes of landowners, tenants, and agricultural laborers had been established; and regular markets for both the inputs and outputs of the agricultural sector were in being. The natural flow of market forces thus established income shares which (apart from the exceptional case of the small owner-operator) could be broadly identified with the classical concepts of wages, profits, and rents. Moreover, for most practical purposes, a classical economist might reasonably regard rental payments as approximate measures of the differential fertility of the soil.

The investigator of differential rent in Indian conditions encountered much more formidable difficulties. The institutional supports which would aid him in his search in England were not available. In Mill's view, this was an unfortunate circumstance, but not one which precluded the ultimate success of his land revenue program. In the Indian situation, implementation of his policies required surveys of individual plots in order to assess their natural productive powers. Mill did not expect this technique—though the best available—to yield precise results.

He recognized some of the difficulties when he observed:

> We have none but very imperfect instruments to employ; with the total absence of a moral feeling in the country to aid us, it is not shameful to be dishonest in a public trust; no discredit attaches to a man in such a situation for robbing either his fellow subjects or the government. . . .When we consider, in addition to these circumstances, how imperfectly any one European with an imperfect knowledge of the natives, their language and circumstances and with a large extent of country to attend to, can watch over the numerous individuals that he employs, it will be easily understood that the difficulty is exceedingly great of limiting the exaction upon the ryot to the rent. . . .[22]

By trial and error methods, he saw no reason why the system could not overcome these obstacles:

> The best mode of approximating to correctness, will probably be an attentive observation of the effect of any particular amount collected; whether the payment is made with difficulty or with ease; to watch carefully till evidence is obtained, that what is exacted of the ryot is only a moderate exaction.[23]

Despite temporary frustrations, his faith in the ultimate outcome was unshaken:

> I have no doubt that means will be found of limiting the demand upon the ryot to a moderate rent, and then I conceive that the prosperity of that country will be as fully secured as it can be.[24]

Thus, though he appreciated that the transfer of the rent model to India involved administrative strains, Mill denied that any problem of principle arose. If reality diverged from the requirements of the model, reality, not the model, should be adjusted to produce a closer fit.

22. Mill, "Minutes of Evidence, 11 August 1831," *Parliamentary Papers, 1831*, 5:334-35.
23. Ibid., p. 335.
24. Ibid., p. 335.

Was the Indian economy sufficiently plastic to permit this operation to be performed? It was, of course, possible for the administrative officers to specify a rental charge and levy it on those recognized as owners of land. It did not follow—even when assessment had been made with care—that the state's claim would be as neutral in its effects on costs as the more enthusiastic advocates of the differential rent theory had maintained. In Indian agriculture, conducted as most of it was with unpaid family labor, the income shares written about in classical theory did not visibly emerge. On such grounds, Richard Jones, the lonely critic of the extension of the Ricardian theory to Indian conditions particularly (and to peasant economies more generally), had argued that the procedures recommended by Mill led to results counter to those intended.[25] The theory presupposed that rent was the residual after costs of production had been covered. But in the absence of organized markets for capital and labor, the state's claim on rent took precedence. Only the remainder was available for wages and profits. Thus, a fixed demand by the state—which Jones held could never be set with the standards of perfection Mill hoped to achieve[26]—was likely to cut into other income shares. Not only would the peasant's level of living be depressed, but both his ability and his will to accumulate would be curtailed.

This was not the end of the difficulties. The rent obligation set by officers of the East India Company was to be paid in cash. Fulfilling this condition was not always easy in much of rural India, where organized markets for agricultural products were far from fully developed. Nor did a tax obligation fixed in money terms make adequate allowance for two of the basic facts of agrarian economic life: seasonal fluctuations in output and wide variations in market prices. Disturbances of either variety—when combined with an unchanged cash assessment—could produce severe hardship in peasant households.[27]

25. Richard Jones, *An Essay on the Distribution of Wealth and on the Sources of Taxation* (London, 1831), *passim*; the issue is further explored in his *Literary Remains*, ed. William Whewell (London, 1859).

26. The required mapping and measurement of individual plots was an exercise which Jones described as "a gigantic task, that never could be efficiently done!" Richard Jones, *Literary Remains*, p. 288.

27. Mill attempted to deal with this issue as follows: "We may hope, at no very distant period, to see so great an improvement in the circumstances of the ryots, and in their education and state of mind, as that they will know how to reserve the surplus of one year for the deficiency of another, and whenever they come to be in a condition of that sort, then a lease, with a moderate rent, will be an adequate protection for them." "Minutes of Evidence, 9 August 1831," *Parliamentary Papers, 1831*, 5:324.

The subsequent evolution of those parts of the Indian agrarian structure which were subjected to the treatment recommended by Mill suggests that policy makers in his time might have been well advised to heed the cautions Jones had urged upon their attention and to have been less dogmatic in their views. In his lifetime, Jones's sceptical message largely fell on deaf ears. Though the answers he supplied were imperfectly worked out, the questions he raised were pertinent in his day, and for that matter, have not lost their relevance. Later theorists of agrarian economies have appreciated the importance of the issues he raised.[28]

Yet another structural objection might have been raised against the transfer of classical models to India. Classical growth theory, it will be recalled, placed heavy reliance on the accumulation of capital by members of a capitalist class. In India in the early nineteenth century, such a class was virtually non-existent. Men with high income could be found—particularly among the zemindars of Bengal—but they could not be relied upon to behave as productive investors. In Mill's view, the zemindars were "notoriously not accumulators" and he added that as a class they were "habitually and even proverbially improvident and spendthrift."[29] Nor could a large volume of saving be expected from the peasantry. Even if the state was moderate in its exactions, peasant incomes were too low to permit productive saving in significant volume. Moreover, the encouragement to improvidence latent in traditional behavior patterns had not yet been eradicated. As Mill lamented: "notwithstanding the simplicity of their habits, they find means very easily of spending what comes into their hands, for they run to immense expences at marriages, and at the births of children, in religious obsequies, and in feeding Brahmins, which is their great delight."[30]

On the surface, this state of affairs would not appear to have been highly favorable to the realization of the classical vision of economic growth. The absence of an indigenous capitalist class, however, could be offset by foreigners. Mill was sympathetic to this solution. Not only would foreign investment remedy at least part of the problem arising from local capital deficiency; he hoped also that it would provide

28. For example, A. K. Sen, "Peasants and Dualism With or Without Surplus Labor," *Journal of Political Economy* 74 (1966): 425-50.
29. Mill, "Minutes of Evidence, 9 August 1831," *Parliamentary Papers, 1831,* 5:313.
30. Ibid., p. 316.

external benefits by exposing Indians to European industry and organization. He was not prepared, however, to make special concessions to foreigners to induce them to invest in India. He firmly opposed the requests of the small European community for segregated courts of law in India.

One other approach to India's capital deficiency was conceivable: the use of the powers of the government to perform the functions of a capitalist class in a growing economy. Mill was eager to have the Indian government take on the role of a landlord as a rent recipient. But he shrank from expanding the state's role to that of a capitalist. His thinking was too much in the mould of classical liberalism to permit him to entertain this possibility seriously. Though he supported the Indian government's retention of its monopolies in salt and in the opium trade, he did so on grounds of expediency rather than conviction. The revenue base, he argued, was not yet sufficiently secure to permit a change in well-established arrangements.

VI

As an official of the East India Company, James Mill left an important legacy: he devised a theoretical structure to underpin the economic policies pursued by the government of India. Within its own terms, this theory was coherent and internally consistent. The influence of the doctrines he espoused was formidable. Not only did they mould approaches to Indian problems long after Mill's death; they were also sufficiently alive at the end of the nineteenth century to be seriously proposed as a strategy for economic policy in West Africa.

These considerations deserve emphasis as counters to two widely held interpretations of British imperial practice in India in the first half of the nineteenth century. One school has maintained that the system was deliberately structured to exploit India for the benefit of the mother country; another has argued that no consistent thread of policy can be detected. Both interpretations are incorrect. Mill had developed a well-thought-out strategy—and one which set the uplift of the Indian masses as its primary objective.

The most serious challenge to Mill's strategy must be leveled from a different direction. Like most of his contemporaries, he was the captive of the assumptions of classical political economy. Whatever the merits of this mode of analysis in English conditions, its applicability to India was highly questionable. On some points of detail, he was prepared to modify and adapt his doctrines to bring them more closely in touch with his appraisals of Indian reality. But on the crucial point of his strategy—the doctrine of differential rent as a basis for the tax system—he was inflexible.

Keynes's reference was intertemporal when he attributed much economic error to the tendency of men to be the "slaves of some defunct economist." Perhaps no less important—though less commented on—is error which may arise at any given moment in time when men who interpret economies different from their own are the intellectual slaves of live economists.

[9]

Criticism of Ricardian Views on Value and Distribution in the British Periodicals, 1820–1850

Barry Gordon

In the three decades which followed the publication of David Ricardo's *Principles of Political Economy and Taxation* (1817), his views and those of his followers were subject to widespread criticism in contemporary journals. One facet of this criticism concerned the adherence of the Ricardians to Say's law of markets, a facet which was surveyed by the present writer in an earlier paper.[1] However, only a fraction of the opposition encountered by the Ricardians was directed at Say's law, as such. The greatest weight of critical comment involved their views on value, the distributive shares, and the rates of return to land, labor, and capital. For example, the labor-embodied approach to value determination came under repeated attack. Again, Ricardian rent theory and the doctrine of "the necessary opposition" of wages and profits were rejected vehemently in most of the periodicals examined. It is the purpose of this paper to outline the dimensions of such anti-Ricardian sentiment and to describe the content of some of the more notable contributions to the debate.

Mr. Gordon *is Associate Professor of Economics in the University of Newcastle, New South Wales.*

1. "Say's Law, Effective Demand and the Contemporary British Periodicals, 1820-1850," *Economica*, n.s. 32, no. 28 (Nov. 1965): 438-46. The periodicals surveyed in both this and the above article are *The Bankers' Magazine* (London), *Blackwood's* (*Blackwood's Magazine*), *The British and Foreign Review*, *The British Critic*, *The British Quarterly Review*, *The Dublin Review*, *The Dublin University Magazine*, *The Eclectic Review*, *The Edinburgh Review*, *The Foreign Quarterly Review*, *Fraser's* (*Fraser's Magazine*), *The Gentleman's Magazine*, *The London Magazine*, *The Monthly Review*, *The North British Review*, *The Quarterly Review*, *Tait's* (*Tait's Edinburgh Magazine*), *The Westminster Review*. With respect to the identification of authorship of anonymous contributions, both articles are indebted mainly to the published researches of Professor Frank W. Fetter and of Professor Walter Houghton. Professor Houghton was kind enough to supply the present writer with identifications not yet published.

The Discussion of Value Theory

The *British Critic* was the first of the journals surveyed to publish a critique of Ricardo's value theory. In December 1819, a review of Ricardo's *Principles* contends that utility, not labor, is the foundation of value. The concept of an invariable measure of value is described as "a pure chimera," and Ricardo's failure to incorporate demand factors in his theory is seen as a major error.[2] A second article dismisses the Ricardian position as an "extravagance" which has resulted from an undue extension of Adam Smith's "pretty piece of romantic hypothesis" concerning the dependence of real value on the toil and trouble of acquisition.[3]

In May 1821 the *British Critic* reviewer expanded his treatment of value. Demand as well as supply conditions must be taken into account because "the value of a thing consists in those properties which make it sought after; and . . . the said value is measured by the quantity of commodities, which is given in exchange for it."[4] Cost of production cannot serve as a measure of exchange value, although that cost might be relevant to value determination in that it could exert a long-run influence on supply. Such influence, the reviewer believed, is often remote, because of the immobility of factors of production. He wrote:

> In the transactions of the buyer and seller in these great departments, the cost of production is never once thought of, as the basis of exchangeable or market value. That cost will no doubt ultimately, after the lapse, perhaps, of several years, determine the quantity brought to market, so as to obtain the ordinary return for capital and labour expended; but, so difficult is it to remove capital from one employment to another and to change the habits and residence of workmen, that nothing is more common than for farmers and other capitalists to continue in their line of business, long after the cost of producing their commodities has ceased to be the measure of their exchangeable value.[5]

2. *British Critic* 12 (Dec. 1819): 564. This and subsequent articles on political economy in the *British Critic* may have been written by John Craig, author of *Elements of Political Science*, 3 vols. (Edinburgh, 1814) and *Remarks on Some Fundamental Doctrines in Political Economy* (Edinburgh, 1821).
3. *British Critic* 14 (Aug. 1820): 130-31.
4. Ibid., 15 (May 1821): 450.
5. Ibid., 17 (Feb. 1822): 140-41.

Thomas Malthus was the next to attack Ricardo's value theory. In his *Quarterly Review* articles of April 1823 and January 1824 he contends that labor-commanded, not labor-embodied, is the most accurate measure of exchange value. He attempts to demonstrate that both in the short run and the long run, demand factors will influence commodity prices. Profit, he affirms, is "a component part of price," and the rate of profit depends upon the state of demand. Long-run price trends are conditioned by the movement of the "natural" or long-run rate of profit. Hence, demand as well as cost of production has a bearing on the formation of normal or long-run price.[6]

In the *Monthly Review* of February 1826, J. R. McCulloch's adherence to a labor theory of value was identified as the major fault underlying his reasoning. The reviewer declares that "this initiating principle of political science is the most complicated and the most insidious and consequently the most dangerous of its many errors."[7] His line of attack is rather different from that of Malthus, and suggests that he may have been influenced by Physiocratic and other Continental writing. He argues that Ricardian value theory has originated in Adam Smith's "too unqualified rejection" of Quesnay. Hence, labor alone is considered in the assessment of cost by the Ricardians. In reality, they should also take account of the variable productivities of different qualities of soil and of different forms of capital. Further, they neglect demand considerations which, because of the vagaries of consumption, are relevant to the question of value determination. He concludes: "provided nature was alike bountiful, industry alike productive and consumption exactly in the ratio of production, we might admit that the cost of growing and manufacturing was the principal regulating principle of price."[8]

During the next decade, criticism of Ricardian theory was continued in a series of articles for the *Quarterly Review* by George Poulett Scrope. His article of January 1831 is outstanding and must rank as one of the most important periodical contributions to the literature of political economy. Scrope asserts that value in exchange and value in use are, in fact, identical; that the former is measured by the latter; and that any cost of production approach fails to provide a measure of relative

6. *Quarterly Review* 30 (Jan. 1824): 314-16.
7. *Monthly Review*, n.s. 1 (Feb. 1826): 118.
8. Ibid., p. 120.

value. He begins with the proposition that the wealth represented by any group of objects consists of

> the qualities possessed by those objects of gratifying man; and the degree in which they are to be reckoned as wealth; in other words, their value, he must estimate by the intensity of these qualities.[9]

It follows that

> value, in exchange or in general estimation, (they are the same thing), must vary with the fluctuations of human wishes and caprices, fancies and fashions. . . . It has been said with metaphysical refinement, that value means not only value in exchange but also the estimation in which a thing is held and that the two are not identical. If they are not with regard to property voluntarily exchanged by its owners, we know not where lies the difference.[10]

Finally, he observes

> it has been argued that, in the long-run, the values of all objects are equal to the costs of producing them, or their production would be discontinued and that the costs of production are therefore their real value. This is true; but since these costs include a variety of sorts and quantities of labour and capital, all themselves of undetermined value, how are they to form a standard for reference?[11]

Another critic adopted an approach similar to that of Scrope in a review of Mountifort Longfield's *Lectures on Political Economy* for the *Dublin University Magazine* of June 1834. He dismisses Adam Smith's distinction between value in use and value in exchange:

> Smith describes it [value] as two-fold; value in use and value in exchange. He thus distinguishes use from exchange in a manner that appears to us illogical; as exchangeability is but a mode of usefulness, or a species of utility. We are, therefore, inclined to think that his meaning would be more accurately expressed if, instead of the above, he had adopted as his division value as a means and value as an end.[12]

9. *Quarterly Review* 44 (Jan. 1831): 4.
10. Ibid., p. 14.
11. Ibid., p. 16.
12. *Dublin University Magazine* 3 (June 1834): 609-10.

Thus, as exchangeability is derived from usefulness, utility is the basis of all value, although cost of production also plays a significant role:

> Value, in the abstract, means estimation. Nature has implanted in all men a desire for the necessaries and conveniences of life, which is in fact, the foundation of the value which we set upon them. The utility of any particular product may be resolved into its aptitude to satisfy this natural desire; and its value will be directly as its utility and the difficulty of its attainment.[13]

Although cost is relevant, the writer agrees with Longfield that the labor element can have no valid status as the measure of value. In fact, it is impossible to find a fixed standard which can act as a satisfactory measure.

Thomas Perronet Thompson of the *Westminster Review* believed that a fixed measure of value could not be established. In a review of McCulloch's edition of the *Wealth of Nations*, he contends that value and cost of production are never, or very rarely, the same. According to Thompson the disparity of cost and price is a necessary feature of contemporary markets. He writes: "this perpetual oscillation on both sides of the cost price, instead of being an inconsiderable accident, is in reality the great agent by which the commercial world is kept in motion."[14]

In 1842 *Blackwood's* published a three-part series in which value theory was extensively discussed by Thomas De Quincey. Although he pays due deference to Ricardo, De Quincey is not uncritical, and he complains that "Ricardo never admits the thought that possibly, when the price of the products comes to be settled, this price might be influenced by affirmative value."[15] For De Quincey, "affirmative value" is the equivalent of value in use, and this will coincide with value in exchange: "from the moment when the value in use comes at all to challenge attention from the economist, it has ceased to divide against exchange value; on the contrary, it is value in exchange—it has coalesced with value in exchange—it has become the value in exchange."[16]

De Quincey then considers the traditional argument used to refute any such identification of the two values. In this argument the relatively

13. Ibid., p. 610.
14. *Westminster Review* 17 (Oct. 1832): 295.
15. *Blackwood's* 52 (Dec. 1842): 737.
16. Ibid., p. 725.

high use-value of water was contrasted with its low exchange-value and the high exchange-value of diamonds with their value in use. The wide disparities involved were thought to demonstrate the impossibility of forging any link between the two types of valuation.

De Quincey explodes the myth of the supposed insolubility of the so-called water and diamonds paradox, and in so doing establishes two of the principles that were widely recognized later as basic to any discussion of economic value. In the first place he claims, "before it can enter the field of political economy, a commodity must enter, or be capable of entering the market."[17] The point is then made that entry into market calculations is dependent upon the supply of the commodity concerned not exceeding the maximum possible effective demand for it. For example, if water is so abundantly available as to satisfy every expressible desire for its use, then it will command no price. He next points out that intensity of desire for a commodity is a declining function of the quantity obtained. He brings together the two principles as follows:

> Each [water and diamonds] must be tried sub conditione of its being wanted and on a graduated scale expressing the intensity of that want. Forty gallons of water, if offered to Governor Howell and party in the "Black Hole" of Calcutta . . . would have borne a higher premium than ever yet did diamonds. You must have a case in which water is actually wanted, in which the affirmative value is sustained by a pressure then resting upon men, or else you cannot try the question in its exchange value.[18]

Dissatisfaction with Ricardian value theory was also expressed during the late 1840s in the *Westminster Review*. Mary Elizabeth Mill (sister of J. S. Mill) complained of inconsistencies in Ricardo's use of the term "value."[19] An editorial note appended to this article states: "What a commodity will 'bring' is dependent upon supply and demand; and supply is, of course, regulated by cost; but 'cost of production' alone is not value; for that which has cost the most often produces the least."[20] Later, similar sentiments were expressed in the July 1847 article on the Bank Charter Act;[21] and in the subsequent currency article of January

17. Ibid.
18. Ibid., p. 729.
19. *Westminster Review* 48 (Oct. 1847): 111.
20. Ibid., p. 118.
21. Ibid., 47 (July 1847): 448.

1848, Ricardo's adherence to a cost criterion of value is seen as having "added nothing to the science but the perplexity of a verbal puzzle."[22]

The Discussion of Rent Theory

Even before the publication of Ricardo's *Principles of Political Economy*, the *British Critic* expressed opposition to the idea that rent was a return determined independently of the prevailing rate of profit. In a review of Malthus's *Essay on Rent* it is argued that "the rent of land . . . will never rise above the ordinary rent or interest of other fixed capital, unless indeed it be artificially raised by legislative interference."[23] Rents and profits are simultaneously determined because land is merely one type of fixed capital and because investment is mobile between the agricultural and nonagricultural sectors. Investment will be distributed so as to equalize the returns on fixed capital in all productive pursuits:

> Land is thus regarded as an instrument, for the loan of which, during a specified time, a certain hire is obtained; which hire, of course, will be greater or less according to the goodness of the said instrument and to the extent of the competition for possessing it. In fact, it stands in the same point of view as fixed capital of all kinds, which if the owner does not choose to employ it himself, he lets out to others at the current price which the market brings.[24]

Subsequent articles contend that Ricardian rent theory reverses the real causal sequence involved in agricultural pricing. The amount of land in use, and hence the marginal cost of agricultural production, does not determine the price of food, as Ricardo maintains. Rather, it is market price which determines how much land will be brought into production. Rents are also determined by market prices:

> poorer soils are taken into cultivation, not in order to raise rents on the more fertile, but because prices are high and rents already raised; and, moreover, . . . the prices of land-produce are not regulated by the produce of any species of soil, either the best or the worst, but by the more general principle of supply and demand.[25]

22. Ibid., 48 (Jan. 1848): 465.
23. *British Critic* 3 (April 1815): 395.
24. Ibid., p. 391.
25. Ibid., 15 (May 1821): 461.

This line of argument was to become the standard mode of "refuting" Ricardo's theory.

Nassau Senior, although sympathetic to many aspects of Ricardo's thought, nonetheless felt obliged to object to the causal sequence used by Ricardo to relate the price of corn to the extension of cultivation into marginal land.[26] He suggests that it is only as "an index" that the cost of producing corn on marginal land might be associated with the general price of corn. Price is determined at the margin, not by the margin. Senior writes:

> to say that it is the price of this last portion of corn, which governs that of the remainder, is to mistake the effect for the cause. The price of other corn does not rise because the last portion has been produced at a greater expense, but the last portion is produced, because the proportion of demand to supply has previously occasioned such a rise in the price of corn already produced, that additional capital laid out in producing additional corn, at a greater proportionate expense, will return the average profit of capital. . . . And it is in this sense only (and it must be acknowledged to be very obscurely pointed out), that the corn raised at the greatest expense can be said to fix, or govern, or regulate the price of all other corn; not as an efficient cause, for it must always be subsequent in time, but as an Index.[27]

Then, even as an index, the status of the marginal cost is open to question. Its usefulness depends upon the postulation of certain static conditions which are rarely encountered in reality:

> But this Index will be correct only in a stationary economy, a market neither rising nor falling. If the market price be rising from an increased demand, it will outrun the natural price even of the corn produced at greatest expense. . . .[28] [As] every country is, in fact, either advancing or declining, . . . there is no country in which the cost of the production of any portion of corn can be said correctly, even to indicate much less to govern, or regulate, or fix, that of the rest. Our readers will perceive that we are opposed on this point, as well as on some others, to Mr. Ricardo.[29]

26. *Quarterly Review* 25 (July 1821): 466-504.
27. Ibid., p. 476.
28. Ibid.
29. Ibid., p. 477.

During this period *Blackwood's* joined in the general criticism. William Stevenson, in the course of his series "The Political Economist," wrote: "It has been well observed that the chapter of Ricardo on the subject of rent is perhaps the least satisfactory and intelligible of his whole work."[30] In 1827 two short articles were devoted to the fallacies of Ricardian rent theory. Then, in 1829 David Robinson also declared the theory invalid.[31] None of these articles displays any depth of analytical insight on the subject of rent, but their authors are vehement in their opposition to Ricardo.

Throughout the early 1830s the opposition continued in a variety of journals. The most common line of criticism was to affirm that corn prices and rents were not high because additional, poorer land had been brought into cultivation. Rather, this land was cultivated because of high corn prices and a rise in rents. This argument was promoted especially by T. P. Thompson in the *Westminster Review*[32] and in his widely read pamphlet, *The True Theory of Rent*. His views were echoed by Mountifort Longfield in the *Dublin University Magazine* and by Samuel O'Sullivan in *Blackwood's*.[33] Even in the *Edinburgh Review*, Herman Merivale allowed that Ricardian rent theory was "a lapis offensionis, startling and offending many, partly from the exaggerated results which, undoubtedly, Mr. Ricardo and his followers have drawn from it; and partly from the apparent contradiction which it offers to phenomena familiar to most observers."[34]

In the *Quarterly Review*, G. P. Scrope argued that the Ricardian conception of rent was far too narrow. He wrote:

> This description entirely omits what in reality constitutes by far the greater part of all rent, namely:—(1). The interest of capital expended on houses, farm-buildings, fences, drains, roads, the original clearing, and the manure or other additions by which the original powers of the soil have been improved. There can be little doubt that more than one-half of the gross rental of the country is of this nature—(2). The value of position, with respect to markets, purchasable manures, and supply of labour.[35]

30. *Blackwood's* 15 (June 1824): 654.

31. Ibid., 21 (Jan. 1827): 74-79; 21 (March 1827): 311-14; 26 (Sept. 1829): 512-13.

32. *Westminster Review* 17 (Oct. 1832): 267-311.

33. *Dublin University Magazine* 1 (April 1833): 469; 3 (June 1834): 612; *Blackwood's* 33 (March 1833): 222-23.

34. *Edinburgh Review* 66 (Oct. 1837): 96.

35. *Quarterly Review* 44 (Jan. 1831): 33-34.

Scrope finds himself in agreement with the views of Richard Jones. Reviewing Jones's treatise on rent, Scrope affirms that the author "has dealt the finishing stroke to the miserable 'theory of rent' of the Ricardian school of economists."[36]

During the 1840s there was little discussion of this theory which had been so widely disowned. In his series of three articles for *Blackwood's* during 1842, Thomas De Quincey was still prepared to defend the doctrine, but in the *British and Foreign Review* T. C. Banfield was most critical. Banfield champions Richard Jones against Ricardo and goes on to examine Von Thunen's *Der isolirte Staat*. The importance and novelty of the latter is emphasized.[37] In the *North British Review* Thomas Chalmers repeats the point made some years before by Nassau Senior, that Ricardo is mistaken in believing that the cost of production of corn on marginal land determines, rather than merely measures, the price of corn.[38] In general, it is apparent that, as in the case of value theory, there were few supporters of Ricardo on rent to be found among periodical contributors after some thirty years of debate.

The Determination of Wages and the Wage-Profit Relationship

The relationship of the wage and profit shares in income was discussed frequently by the periodical writers. However, little attention was paid to the examination of the factors determining wages. A contributor to the *Dublin University Magazine*, one of the few to take up this second issue, reveals an explicitly anti-Ricardian approach. The author contends that labor productivity is the chief determinant of wage rates. The Ricardians have failed to perceive this fact and have fallen into further error by adherence to the idea of an equilibrium "natural rate" of wages. Such a rate, he suggests, is quite indeterminate, especially if it is thought to be governed by a minimum subsistence standard which is socially derived. He writes:

> Mr. McCulloch even approves of Adam Smith's definition of it [the natural rate], to be such a rate as may enable them to obtain not only the commodities which are indispensably necessary for the support of life but whatever the custom of the country renders

36. Ibid., 46 (Nov. 1831): 81.

37. *British and Foreign Review* 16, no. 31 (1844): 30-71. Banfield's authorship in the case of this article is not certain.

38. *North British Review* 6 (Nov. 1846): 105.

it indecent for creditable people, even of the lowest order, to be without. In this there is an obvious confusion between cause and effect. Custom renders it discreditable to be without that which every man can earn; but whenever the rate of wages is altered, the custom will follow it. . . .[39]

Custom, the writer continues, is influenced by the actual market rate of wages, so any "natural rate" would be dependent on market rates. Hence, the natural concept points to no necessary equilibrium position of wages.[40]

The lack of explicit discussion of wage determination suggests that there was widespread tacit acceptance of the notion of wages constantly tending to a natural level through wage-induced increases and decreases in the population. However, it is of some significance that the Malthusian assumptions upon which this notion was based were attacked in at least four of the journals. In the *Monthly Review* it is suggested that, far from bearing any direct relationship,

> the law of increase (of population) operates in an inverse proportion to the acquisition of wealth; . . . it is only when people become more luxuriant, when those engagements which form the principal charm in humble life lose their attractions by the substitution of habits of refinement, that the increase becomes progressively less.[41]

This type of argument is repeated by *Fraser's* in 1832 in an attack on Harriet Martineau's Malthusian propaganda.[42] Other attacks on Miss Martineau's efforts about this time came from G. P. Scrope in a highly satirical review[43] and from Charles De Coux in the *Dublin Review*, who, with well-turned phrase, suggested that "if the propagation of our species could be stopped by subtlety and talent, the works of Miss Martineau would entitle her to the especial gratitude of that posterity—whose existence she would have prevented."[44]

Although offering little on the actual determination of wages, almost all of the journals were extremely hostile to the Ricardian dogma that a rise or fall in wages must lead to a corresponding fall or rise in profits.

39. *Dublin University Magazine* 26 (July 1845): 10.
40. Ibid., p. 11.
41. *Monthly Review*, n.s. 1 (Feb. 1826): 124.
42. *Fraser's* 6 (Nov. 1832): 408.
43. *Quarterly Review* 49 (April 1833): 151.
44. *Dublin Review* 3 (July 1837): 168.

Reaction began very early, objections being raised in the October 1817 issue of the *British Critic*.[45] Two years later the same periodical again condemned the dogma as a prime example of what in more recent times has been dubbed "the Ricardian Vice":

> Assuming these facts as a first principle in all cases and taking for granted, as usual, that money never changes in value and the proportion between the supply and demand of any given commodity never alters, (which is as if the astronomer were to assume as the basis of his calculations, that all the planets stand still and that they all stand still to all eternity), he assigns a specific sum to be divided between the master and the workmen, as the unalterable price of the goods which they produce; from which adaptation of hypothetical conditions, it naturally follows, that, if the workmen get more, the master-manufacturer must receive less, there being only a certain sum to divide between them.[46]

In the same year, a similar argument was put forward in *Blackwood's*. The author claims that in most cases, profits and wages increase or decrease together.[47]

Throughout the 1820s this last proposition was repeated on numerous occasions. Both the *Monthly Review* and the *British Critic* take James Mill to task for his adherence to a wage-profit opposition in *Elements of Political Economy*.[48] Malthus joined in the general criticism in his *Quarterly Review* article of January 1824,[49] and in *Blackwood's* David Robinson employed a rudimentary multiplier concept to demonstrate the stimulating effects on business activity, employment, and profits that could flow from a higher level of consumption based on wage increases.[50] Ricardo had also been attacked along similar lines in this same journal some years before by William Stevenson in his series, "The Political Economist."[51] The succeeding two decades saw a rapid decline in the volume of controversy on this issue, the majority of journals seeming to have taken the view that this particular aspect of Ricardian doctrine had been well disposed of.

45. *British Critic* 8 (Oct. 1817): 355.
46. Ibid., 12 (Dec. 1819): 570.
47. *Blackwood's* 5 (May 1819): 171-73.
48. *Monthly Review* 48 (May 1822): 19; *British Critic* 17 (Feb. 1822): 141.
49. *Quarterly Review* 30 (Jan. 1824): 315-16.
50. *Blackwood's* 26 (Sept. 1829): 513-18; and 27 (Jan. 1830): 30.
51. Ibid., 15 (June 1824): 651.

The Determination of Profits and the Profit-Interest Relationship

During the 1820s, the *British Critic* opposed the idea of profits as mere residuals and urged the view that they depended essentially on the demand and supply of capital.[52] In the same period the *Monthly Review* questioned the validity of the idea of a tendency for equality of profits to be established throughout industry. Ricardo and later Torrens are accused of assuming too great a mobility of capital and, hence, of expounding "the doctrine of the impossibility that two rates of profit can co-exist in a country, when everybody knows that there are twenty, arising from the impracticability of transferring capital and the personal acquirements of skill from one business to another."[53]

Malthus was one of the first to move away from the residual treatment of profit when he considered the valuation problems raised in Torrens's discussion of the pricing of well-matured wine. Writing in the *Quarterly Review*, Malthus suggests that part of the profit earned by sale of the wine will be due to the period of delay in earning a return on capital while the wine matures. This period of "waiting" will earn for the capitalist a margin over and above that of normal profit; and the longer the delay, the greater the margin. He writes:

> the increased value which the wine acquires is in no degree proportioned to the efficiency of her [Nature's] workmanship, as is mainly the case in rents, but is entirely regulated by the time during which the returns of the capital are delayed and by the ordinary rate of profits.[54]

An outstanding contribution was made by William Ellis in his lengthy article on machinery for the *Westminster Review* of January 1826. Unlike nearly all his contemporaries, Ellis is not deceived by the blanket term "accumulation," and he sees that saving and investing are distinct processes for which "two sets of motives are necessary": saving is induced by "the expectation of greater enjoyment from deferred than immediate consumption,"[55] and investment is induced by the expectation of profit. Such a recognition opens the way for a risk-effort theory of profits, with emphasis on the first element: "The largeness of

52. *British Critic* 14 (Sept. 1820): 276; and 17 (May 1822): 462.
53. *Monthly Review* 98 (Aug. 1822): 370; and 99 (Nov. 1822): 266-67.
54. *Quarterly Review* 30 (Jan. 1824): 312.
55. *Westminster Review* 5 (Jan. 1826): 106.

the profit must be proportioned to the risk incurred in drawing treasure from the hoard and employing it in production."[56]

Ellis believes that the risk element involved in investment, especially investment of an innovative character, has been ignored by most writers. Hence, the basis for an explanation of profit is lacking. He writes:

> The loss of superseded machinery, the want of skill and practice, in workmen and the uncertainty of the result, all unite in preventing the adoption and application of that which is untried. These difficulties doubtless, are constantly overcome, so constantly that to many, perhaps, they may appear unworthy of notice. They are only conquered, however, by the prospect of the great additional profit, with which the adopted invention is expected to be accompanied.[57]

Ellis's concern for a theory of profit leads him to attempt a distinction between profit and interest. Interest is a return on "the productive employment" of savings and may also carry a risk premium. Profit is a return to risk taking and managerial effort. It also includes interest only where the entrepreneur is using his own capital:

> Where an individual employs his own savings productively, in the profit which he obtains is included, after deducting an adequate allowance for the risk to which his capital may have been exposed in his particular business, the remuneration for his time and skill, which remuneration may be called agency for superintendence; and the remuneration for the productive employment of his savings, which is called interest. The whole of this remuneration we may call gross profit. Where an individual employs the savings of another he obtains, after deducting the same allowance, the agency only. Where an individual lends his savings to another, what he obtains is interest. This interest may, without impropriety, for our present purpose, be designated as neat profits.[58]

The most important journal analysis of profits throughout these decades was provided by G. P. Scrope in the *Quarterly Review* for January 1831. Deploring the absence of any profit theory in Ricardo, and anticipating the published views of Nassau Senior, Scrope expounds an

56. Ibid., p. 111.
57. Ibid., p. 117.
58. Ibid., pp. 107-8.

"abstinence" theory. Profit is "the compensation for abstinence from immediate gratification" involved in investment expenditure rather than consumption.[59] But this is "profit" only in the narrow sense of the term where it is identical with "interest." In the wider and more usual sense of "profit," the two are far from identical:

> what is thus vulgarly called profits, or living profits, comprehends much more besides the strict current profit on stock. . . . If we analyse the surplus produce defined above, which corresponds to the vulgar notion of the living profits of capital employed in an active business by the owner and which the economists universally speak of as the "profits of stock," we shall find them in all cases to be made up of, 1. Interest of capital, or what can be got for its use without personal labour or risk; 2. Insurance against the risks incident to the particular business in which the stock is employed; 3. Wages of labour for the personal superintendence, skill, or talent of the capitalist; 4. Monopoly gains, arising from the possession of exclusive advantages, such as secret or patented processes or instruments, superior connexions, facilities of local position, of soil, mines collieries, &c. Of these elements, the last comprehends rent itself, or that portion of it at least, to which as we shall shortly see, the economists have confined the term and which solely arises from monopoly.[60]

What emerges then, is an abstinence theory of interest, and a risk-effort theory of profit which is linked with a quasi-rent approach. In all, this is a performance superior to Senior's in some respects and carrying the great advantage of a reasonably firm distinction between profit and interest.

In the *Westminster Review* of January 1848, William E. Hickson took up the question of the relationship of profit and interest rates. Dissenting from the view shared by Ricardo and Smith, Hickson affirms that interest rate movements are governed exclusively by developments in the money market. He writes: "The doctrine that a high rate of interest is only proof, not of an enhanced value of money but of a scarcity of capital, we think may be shown to be palpably at variance with a plain sense view of the matter."[61] The rate of interest is seen as

59. *Quarterly Review* 44 (Jan. 1831): 18.
60. Ibid., pp. 19-20.
61. *Westminster Review* 48 (Jan. 1848): 463.

a function of the demand and supply of money, and rates of profit and rates of interest will often move strongly in opposite directions. For example, in periods of buoyant business activity when profits are high, the supply of money is likely to be more than adequate in terms of demand, and interest rates are consequently low.[62] Unfortunately, the author does not explore the nature and origin of profit in any depth, but his discussion of interest determination constitutes a lively critique of popular Ricardian monetary thought.

If periodical opinion is useful as an index in such a matter, it would seem that near the end of the 1840s the reputation of the Ricardians was at a low ebb. However, in 1848 a remarkable revival was set in motion though the publication of John Stuart Mill's *Principles of Political Economy*. As the present writer has remarked elsewhere:

> This work was widely acclaimed on all sides, from the moment of its appearance in 1848. In truth, there was something in it for everyone. Mill sought to qualify the more "dismal" predictions of political economy, and a good many of the common objections to hard line Ricardianism were granted. At the same time, the reader was left in no doubt as to Ricardo's preeminence as an economist; in the surge of critical approval, Mill's high opinion of Ricardo was accepted. Throughout the next twenty to twenty-five years, the many students who came to economics by way of Mill's book learned to place Ricardo in the pantheon together with Adam Smith.[63]

Favorable reactions to Mill's *Principles* were evident even in journals which had usually opposed most doctrines of the political economists. In *Blackwood's*, William Henry Smith praised Mill for "demolishing, on the ground of still more scientific principles—the value of which time, however, must test—those arguments by which his scientific predecessors had attempted to mislead the man of experience or of empirical knowledge."[64] Smith continues:

> There are things in these volumes as may easily be conceived, in which we do not concur—views are supported, on some subjects, to which we have been long and notoriously opposed;

62. Ibid., p. 473.

63. B. J. Gordon, *Non-Ricardian Political Economy: Five Neglected Contributions*, Kress Library of Business and Economics Publication No. 20 (Boston, 1967), p. 2.

64. *Blackwood's* 64 (Oct. 1848): 407.

> but there is, in the exposition of its tenets, so accurate a statement, so severe and lucid a reasoning, and, withal, so genuine and manly an interest in the great cause of humanity, that we cannot hesitate a moment in awarding to it a high rank amongst the sterling literature of our country.[65]

Fraser's Magazine was another to welcome Mill's work. Yet, during the 1830s, this journal had repeatedly attacked the "set of shallow pretenders, who luxuriate upon the muddy economy of the quack schools of Edinburgh."[66] One contributor had gone so far as to describe Ricardo as an "enormous and overgrown capitalist" enriching himself through currency legislation which "has thrown the capital of the country into a few hands; giving, as it were, a monopoly to the holder of stock and ready money."[67] In contrast, Mill's reviewer castigates "the large, unthinking, ignorant majority [who] scout every appeal to the authority of political economists, [and] fiercely impugn every one of the important doctrines of political economy itself."[68] Current debate in the House of Commons is cited as evidence of the continuing "strength of this dislike and distrust of political economy and its professors."[69] This writer expects Mill's *Principles* to aid materially in correcting the widespread antipathy: "His work forms an epoch in the science, by collecting, arranging, and explaining with perfect clearness, and the ease which power confers, all that other inquirers have discovered and established with respect to its general principles."[70]

The *Westminster Review* and the *Edinburgh Review* were journals which had frequently provided venues for the exposition of Ricardian doctrine in the 1820s and 1830s. James Mill and his son contributed to the former, while J. R. McCulloch had established a virtual monopoly of the political economy reviewing in the latter for some years. It is not surprising, then, to find that J. S. Mill's *Principles* was welcomed warmly by both of these periodicals.

In the *Edinburgh Review*, Nassau Senior declared:

> Mr. Mill's book is not intended to serve a temporary purpose, and to be thrown aside when that purpose has been attained.

65. Ibid., p. 411.
66. *Fraser's* 2 (Nov. 1830): 420.
67. Ibid., 2 (Dec. 1830): 575.
68. Ibid., 38 (Sept. 1848): 246.
69. Ibid., p. 246.
70. Ibid., p. 260.

> It is not an attempt to advance human knowledge in one direction, to be superseded hereafter by more comprehensive treatises. It is . . . a magazine of truths and of precepts from which philosophers and statesmen will, for centuries to come, draw theory and practice.[71]

Such expressions of general enthusiasm are tempered by criticism of Mill's views on some specific points. Senior does not think that land, considered as an agent of production, "is quite fairly treated by Mr. Mill, or indeed by any economist of the Ricardo School."[72] Again, he objects that Mill's use of the term "wages" is often ambiguous, and that the exposition of the wages fund theory is deficient in that it neglects thorough discussion of the factors determining the size of the fund.[73] However, despite such particular criticisms, Senior's review lends strong support to the authority of Mill.

An unidentified contributor in the *Westminster Review* was even less willing than Senior to express disagreement with individual aspects of Mill's treatise. He concludes his laudatory remarks as follows:

> It is a book of all others the most required for the present time; certain to be recognised by all as the production of a master mind pregnant with thought in every line and perhaps unrivalled in modern literature for the comprehensiveness of its philosophical survey of the highest subjects of human interest.[74]

The repetition of such sentiments throughout a wide range of previously conflicting periodical opinion is indicative of the transformation which Mill's *Principles* helped effect. One facet of this transformation was a renewed luster for the somewhat tarnished reputation of Ricardo, since Mill was careful to pay his predecessor the deference he felt he deserved.

71. *Edinburgh Review* 88 (Oct. 1848): 339.
72. Ibid., p. 317.
73. Ibid., pp. 320-22.
74. *Westminster Review* 49 (July 1848): 314.

[10]

Edward West Reconsidered

William D. Grampp

EDWARD WEST has a small but distinguished place in the history of economics, and it rests on his having stated the idea of diminishing returns before Ricardo did. However, there is information in Sraffa that indicates Ricardo developed the idea independently of West and at about the same time or possibly a bit earlier. West, we are given to believe, is no longer to be called, as Cannan called him, the first of the Ricardian school, first before even Ricardo himself.

Yet if this distinction is taken from West, he ought to be given another. It would rest on the other contributions he made. They have, with a minor exception, gone unnoticed. The purpose of this article is to describe them. They are (i) a conception of international trade that anticipates Heckscher and Ohlin, (ii) a theory of prices and wages that anticipates Marshall, (iii) a hypothesis of how a change in the money stock causes a change in income and, what is unusual, how it causes relative as well as absolute prices to change, and (iv) some diverse but by no means random observations about unemployment, forced saving, the rate of return, and economic development.

Personal History

If there is a particular reason why these contributions were unnoticed, it is that they were put before the world at a time when there no longer was an interest in the problem which gave rise to them. That problem was the decrease in the price of corn between 1817 and 1822. West analyzed it in his *Price of Corn*, published in 1826.[1] His other economic work was the *Essay* on diminishing returns,

MR. GRAMPP *is Professor of Economics at the University of Illinois, Chicago.*

1. West wrote only two works on economics: The first is *Essay on the Application of Capital to Land, with Observations Shewing the Impolicy of any Great*

published in 1815; it had explained why the relative price of corn had risen.

West signed the *Essay* "By a Fellow of University College, Oxford" on the advice of friends who said his career in the law might suffer if he were known to be in other pursuits as well.[2] He had been educated at Harrow before Oxford, had excelled in classics and mathematics in college, and after leaving had received private instruction in the latter from a noted actuary. His mathematical training, however, does not show itself in his writings (except perhaps in the ease with which sentences can be converted to curves and equations). He was born in 1782 in Middlesex and raised in the country near Kings Lynn in Norfolk. These years may account for his being temperate and conciliatory toward landlords, as Ricardo certainly was not. West spoke of their kindly feudal feelings, their sense of duty, their altruism. He wanted them to know that some landlords actually would benefit by a freer trade. He was not rebuked for a "violent" manner as Ricardo was.[3]

Restriction of the Importation of Corn, and that the Bounty of 1688 Did not Lower the Price of It (London, 1815), 70 pages. This was reprinted as *Sir Edward West on The Application of Capital to Land 1815*, ed. Jacob H. Hollander (Baltimore, 1903), 54 pages. All references to the *Essay* in this article are to the Hollander edition.—West's second book is *Price of Corn and Wages of Labour, with Observations upon Dr. Smith's, Mr. Ricardo's, and Mr. Malthus's Doctrines upon those Subjects; and an Attempt at an Exposition of the Causes of the Fluctuation of the Price of Corn During the Last Thirty Years* (London, 1826), viii + 150 pages.—In the field of law West wrote *A Treatise of the Law and Practise of Extents in Chief and in Aid* (London, 1817), 336 + 152 pages.—The principal commentary on West's economics is by Alfred Plummer, "Sir Edward West: 1782–1828," *Journal of Political Economy* 37, no. 5 (Oct. 1929): 573–82. Of the many references to his contribution to the ideas of diminishing returns and rent, the most complete is probably that in Edwin Cannan, *A History of the Theories of Production and Distribution in English Political Economy from 1776 to 1848*, 3d ed. (London, 1924). The only reference to his other contributions is in the present writer's biographical article on him in *International Encyclopedia of the Social Sciences* (New York, 1968), vol. 16. However, William Breit has commented on an aspect of West's wage theory. See below, n. 46.

2. The only biography is F. Dawtrey Drewitt, *Bombay in the Days of George IV: Memoirs of Sir Edward West*, 2d ed. (London, 1935). There is an article by W. A. S. Hewins on West in the *Dictionary of National Biography*, vol. 20, and an extended unsigned notice in *The Annual Biography and Obituary, of 1829* (London, 1830), 14: 104–20.

3. Arthur Young, *An Inquiry Into the Rise of Prices in Europe, etc.* (London, 1815), p. 188.

West moved ahead swiftly in the law and in 1817 published a work on the law of extents. A writ of extent (as one economist might explain it to another) is an order directing the seizure of the person or property of an individual who is in debt to the king (an extent in chief) or such an order directed against an individual who is in debt to a debtor of the king (an extent in aid). The latter was abused by collusion or legal fictions, so much so that a change was demanded. The use of extents became restricted by legislation and by reform of the Court of Chancery. West's treatise became standard in the field and had a part in the reform. In 1822 he began the last phase of his career when he was appointed Recorder of Bombay; and in 1824, on the establishment of the Supreme Court of Judicature in the Bombay Presidency, he became the first chief justice. He was one of the "king's judges," presiding over a court established by the British government rather than by the East India Company. He was made a baronet in 1822.

West insisted on the independence of the crown court from the Company, and wherever his decisions were known, so was his personal authority. The Company's views were not his, and he did battle with it almost from the day of his landing. The governor-general, Lord Elphinstone, sought to obstruct West and even challenged him to a duel. West declined on the ground that judges do not engage in duels, not even with governors-general, and persevered in his course. He conducted his court with impartiality towards the natives and the British, he made natives eligible for jury duty, he reduced judicial delay, caused the jails to be reformed, stopped the flogging of prisoners, ruled against censoring the press, and in these and other ways tried to establish British justice—or, one should say, the Radical Whig view of it. In this, he was much like other economic writers of the day. If West were to be called a Ricardian, the reason would have to be his politics, not his economics.

Through the difficult years in India he maintained his interest in economics and wrote what may have been a general treatise.[4] It is

4. West in *Price of Corn* wrote, "This subject the author means to attempt to illustrate in a future publication" (p. 85). The antecedent of "this subject" is unclear. In *The Annual Biography* is the statement that West at the time of his last illness "was engaged . . . with a new work on political economy . . . It would, probably, have amounted to a general treatise" (p. 109). Drewitt stated: "The book is still in manuscript" (p. 249 n).

believed to have survived, but I have not been able to find a trace of it. A continuing search is in order, because it would be a precious addition to the archives of economics. West found economics and the law to be taxing. His wife recorded in her diary (in 1827): "Poor Edward is very unwell. He has, I think, fagged too much at Political Economy."[5] The next year he contracted the fever and after a brief illness died. His obituarist wrote:

> They [economics and the law] are evidently the pursuits of a powerful understanding; but they are also characteristic of a mind disposed, even in moments of relaxation, to look for its resources rather in the severer parts of human knowledge, than in those light and trifling occupations which engage the attention of the generality of mankind. This tendency to deny himself complete repose, when business ceased to employ him, was much to be regretted, especially in the latter moments of his life; for all serious application brought on palpitation of the heart, and increased the tendency, to which he was constitutionally liable, of blood in the head. Political economy, and other grave studies, were as objectionable in this point of view as business; and, in fact, he was frequently compelled, for a time, to relinquish them.[6]

Soon after West's death, there were established, by Indian merchants and others, "Chief Justice West's Scholarship and Prizes," with an endowment to the Native Education Society. The society seems to have been the origin of what (ironically) was named Elphinstone College.

Lady West died two months later of the same cause. They left a daughter, Fannie Anne, who was brought to England. In 1842, on her sixteenth birthday, she was given a copy of her father's second work on economics, inscribed by her aunt, which has come to rest in a library in Chicago and seems not to have been often disturbed. Neither has the book been much read elsewhere. That is a pity; had it been, economics could have taken a different course in the nineteenth century and have attained its present position much sooner.

5. Drewitt, p. 250.
6. *Annual Biography*, pp. 109–10.

West would then be remembered for many more ideas than the idea of diminishing returns.

Diminishing Returns

The idea was the centerpiece of West's *Essay,* published 13 February 1815, and also of Ricardo's *An Essay on . . . the Profits of Stock,*[7] published only eleven days later. Each author developed the idea independently of the other, explained it in his own way, and drew his own particular conclusions from it. Ricardo had put it forward in 1814 in some papers on profit which have not survived and in a letter to Trower which has.[8] West said he had had the idea for some years before writing his *Essay.* So had others: it is in writings by Turgot and James Steuart of 1767 and by James Anderson, an Edinburgh contemporary of Smith, of 1777.[9] There is no indication that West knew any of these writings. Ricardo knew of Turgot and Steuart, but made the surprising statement that they had been uninformative about rent.[10] Actually Turgot had explained

7. *An Essay on The Influence of a low Price of Corn on the Profits of Stock; etc.* (London, 1815), reprinted in *The Works and Correspondence of David Ricardo,* ed. Piero Sraffa (Cambridge, 1951), 4:1–41.

8. *Works,* 4:3. On the place of West and others in the enunciation of diminishing returns at this time, see the editor's "Note on 'Essay on Profits,' " 3–8.

9. Cannan states that Turgot enunciated the principle in *Observations sur le mémoire de M. de Saint-Péravy en faveur de l'impôt indirect, couronné par la société royale d'agriculture de Limoges* and quotes extensively from it, including a paragraph in which Turgot states that incremental returns increase before they diminish. Edwin Cannan, "The Origins of the Law of Diminishing Returns," *Economic Journal* 2, no. 1 (March 1892): 54–55. That Turgot noticed the rising as well as falling portion of the marginal product curve got him very high marks from J. A. Schumpeter, *History of Economic Analysis* (New York, 1954), p. 260, who also cited (p. 259) James Steuart's *An Inquiry Into the Principles of Political Economy* as a predecessor of Ricardo's *Essay.*—James Anderson in *An Enquiry Into the Nature of the Corn Laws, With a View to the New Corn Bill Proposed for Scotland* put forward the idea of differential returns on land, according to Plummer, pp. 575–76. Cannan is of two views about this, stating that Anderson did put forward the idea of differential returns but did not believe diminishing returns were a fact of agriculture, rather that increasing returns were. Cannan, "Origins of Law," p. 53, and *History,* pp. 145–46, 371–74, 371 n.

10. David Ricardo, *The Principles of Political Economy and Taxation* (London, 1911), p. 1.

diminishing returns and also had deduced from it the idea of differential returns, which is rent. So had Malthus in 1815.[11] The two ideas are so closely related that they are usually thought of as one. They are not. Ricardo was familiar with diminishing returns for at least a year before he related it to rent.

West did not instruct Ricardo in either idea. The belief that he did is inferred from a remark Ricardo made in the preface to his *Principles,* that West and Malthus had "presented to the world, nearly at the same moment, the true doctrine of rent."[12] The remark was generous, misleadingly so. This does not mean that West, though he cannot be placed ahead of Ricardo, had an insignificant part in the development of the idea. Shall he then be placed alongside him, perhaps just a trifle ahead, *primus inter pares?* One would think yes, after reading Cannan and Hollander.[13] But they wrote some seventy years ago. A reader today would probably think otherwise and would be inclined to add a few words to the history of diminishing returns, long though it already is.

Ricardo's pamphlet was more carefully reasoned, was very much clearer, and worked out in a consistent way the implications of the idea for the distribution of income (though not for policy). He had two purposes: to explain a new economic idea and to apply it to the

11. Thomas R. Malthus, *An Inquiry Into the Nature and Progress of Rent, etc.* [1815], ed. J. H. Hollander (Baltimore, 1903), p. 21 and passim; and Malthus, *The Grounds of an Opinion on the Policy of Restricting the Importation of Foreign Corn* (London, 1815), p. 21 n. Hollander believed that Malthus had stated the idea of diminishing returns as early as the second edition of the *Essay on Population* and had suggested the idea of rent in *Observations on the Effects of the Corn Laws, etc.* (1814). See Hollander's preface to *An Inquiry*, pp. 4, 5.—In the *Inquiry,* Malthus wrote that rent varies with fertility and that a high price of corn causes more land to be cultivated (pp. 18, 22, Hollander edition). That he had diminishing returns in mind is clear from his stating in the *Essay* that as "cultivation [is] extended, the additions that could yearly be made to the former average produce, must be gradually and regularly diminishing" (chap. 1). This statement, in the second edition, carries a step further the suggestion of diminishing returns that is in the first (1798), viz., "A demand for [manufactured goods] will not fail to create them in as great a quantity as they are wanted. The demand for food has by no means the same creative power. In a country where all the fertile spots have been seized, high offers are necessary to encourage the farmer to lay his dressing on land from which he cannot expect a profitable return for some years" (chap. 5).

12. Ricardo, *Principles,* p. 1.

13. Cannan, *History,* p. 160, Hollander, *West,* p. 3.

Corn Laws. West, for his part, wanted to explain why the rate of profit had been falling. The reason, he said, was diminishing returns in agriculture. His discovery had a bearing on the Corn Laws, and he made the connection explicit. In applying the idea to policy, although he made a noteworthy slip, his work was superior to that of Ricardo. His exposition of the idea of diminishing returns was inferior, even though the idea appears in the two essays in identical form. West did not explain it as adequately or as clearly (although his work was of about the same length as Ricardo's), and he was mistaken in saying the idea implied that landlords were made worse off as more capital was brought into agriculture. This cannot be.

Rent, we will recall, was the difference between the net product and the amount of profit in any use of capital. The net product was the difference between the gross product (our total revenue) and capital (total cost). The amount of profit was its rate times capital. The rate was the ratio of the net product to capital at the margin. The rate of profit on all capital was the sum of the individual amounts over total capital, and the rate fell as capital increased. The rate of rent was the ratio of the sum of individual rents to total capital. To this point, the two men were in agreement. As neither had the faintest notion of the other's work, the agreement is startling. One can understand why Ricardo, when he did see West's pamphlet, wrote on the cover, "it never came into my hands till after I had published my Essay."[14] But the two works differed about how the rate of rent changes when there is a change in the amount of capital in agriculture. Ricardo said it must rise, and landlords become better off, while West in his *Essay* mistakenly said it must decline. (In the *Price of Corn*, however, he had it increase.)

If the slip had been left at that, it would call for only the briefest mention. But it was carried on. West said the decrease in the ratio of rent was the explanation for what many witnesses had told parliamentary inquiries—that the ratio of rent to gross produce had been falling. An alternative explanation was the increase in taxes falling on the landlords. The explanation suggests that the witnesses were speaking of rent after taxes, which conceivably could fall relative to capital while rent before taxes rose. However that may be, the belief

14. Ricardo, *Works*, 4.

in a falling rate of rent would have a surprising effect on landlords. Those with the better lands would have an interest in the inferior lands being taken out of cultivation, as they would be if Britain increased its imports of corn. In other words, free trade would increase the rate of rent. That is just what West said when he turned to the question of policy, as described below. The landed interest, one remembers, did not take offense at West's pamphlet as it did at Ricardo's.

To explain what had happened, what was happening, and what was likely to happen, was the intention of West. It was not to add to the stock of economic knowledge for the sake of that stock. Most of his *Essay* is given over to showing the empirical foundation for his ideas.

This is not to say that Ricardo was indifferent to the factual basis of diminishing returns. We will do well to recall that the idea was put forward as an empirical, not as a logical, proposition. It said, "The world is thus and so, and hence this and that will happen." It did not say, "If the world were thus and so, then this and that would happen." West and the Ricardians believed agriculture was subject to diminishing returns, not only while technology is constant but also when it improves. They did not expect that technological progress would be great enough to offset diminishing returns. They were wrong, and by the standards of warrantability they employed, the mistake should have made the idea invalid and have dismissed it from economics. Nothing of the sort happened. The reason is that later economists have regarded the idea primarily as a logical proposition, one to be used mainly for analytical purposes. The earlier economists, to be sure, did use it analytically also, but they believed it rested on fact, and from it they drew some of their most familiar views—their case for a freer trade, their forecast that income would be redistributed in favor of landlords, the belief in falling profits and constant real wages. Diminishing returns was implied by the population theory of Malthus, and he was, fittingly, the first to make it explicit. The assumption that it was a fact, along with the ideas about population, is what gave economics its pessimistic chill. It lay behind the iron law of wages, the doom-saying of the Malthusians, the nay-saying of the Ricardians to reform, the mournful faces of the dismal scientists who in time became notorious as the pests of the people and the persecutors of the poor. . . . All because of the way they perceived reality.

They clung to that perception as if to give it up meant giving up the principle of diminishing returns as a logical proposition. West, in his second work, wrote that "new inventions of machinery and improved modes of husbandry . . . may at one stage enable the same labour to raise as much from inferior soils as it could in a former stage from the better."[15] But he thought this would "merely retard, and not entirely prevent" the operation of diminishing returns. He believed moreover that many of the improvements presupposed a high price of corn and so were the effect of diminishing returns and not a force to offset the tendency.[16]

Those who denied the idea of diminishing returns did so on factual grounds. They said agricultural productivity could increase sufficiently to offset the tendency, indeed to produce a condition of increasing returns. This was the belief of Arthur Young when, great in years and esteem, he wrote one of the first replies to West and Ricardo.[17] An economist today might wonder why those who rejected the idea made so much of its empirical and so little of its analytical content. It was the theoretical achievement of the age. Yet we find Young saying West and Ricardo did not know all they should about open fields, salt land, stiff clay, hedges, ditches, hollow drains, and what happens to turnips on chalky loam, as if the issue was the facts of farming. That indeed is just what it was at the time. West and Ricardo were wrong about it, and they are remembered. Young and his party were right, and they are forgotten. Not so today, of course, when the issue is the logical correctness of the marginal principle. West would have been pleased had he known to what far reaches his

15. *Price of Corn*, p. 46.

16. *Price of Corn*, p. 134. Malthus considered the possibility of increasing returns in a surprising passage in *Grounds:* "There is even a chance (but on this I will not insist) of a diminution of the real price of corn owing to the extension of those great improvements and that great economy and good management of labour, of which we have such intelligent accounts from Scotland" (p. 21). This implies that an increase in population is possible, and Malthus assures the reader that is just what he meant to imply: "I feel persuaded that the country has ample resources for a great and continued increase of population, of power, of wealth, and of happiness" (p. 48).

17. Young, pp. 187–89.

principle would be taken. He was given to pride of place, as his biography suggests and he himself made clear. He was also most honest and he would have been surprised, perhaps have felt a little guilty. Thomas Henry Huxley said the great tragedy of science is "the slaying of a beautiful hypothesis by an ugly fact"—one of those fictions that sustain an empiricist and are not sustained by the fate of diminishing returns. That fate recalls instead the lines of Eliot about history having many cunning corridors and contrived passages.

Trade History

West applied diminishing returns to the Corn Laws. If they were repealed, would rent disappear? If not, would the rate of rent decrease? Would the rate of profit fall? No, was his answer to all of these questions. It rested on what he believed the idea implied about the distribution of income, including his slip about the rate of rent. There was another question, and it troubled the public mind. If the laws were repealed, would England import all of its food and hence become wholly dependent on foreign supplies? West answered by reversing the operation of diminishing returns. As England imported more grain, the cost of producing grain would fall at home and would rise in the exporting countries. The total consumption of England would be supplied by both domestic and foreign farms. The implication is that if imports were completely unrestricted, the amounts produced by each would be those that equalized costs at home and abroad. The idea will be recognized as a simple form of the principle put forward a hundred years later by Heckscher in 1919 and then enlarged upon by Ohlin, that trade equalizes marginal costs in increasing-cost industries.[18] Here is the principle in West's words:

> I come now to the consideration of some of the consequences of a free importation of foreign corn; . . . It would appear to cursory observation that the whole of our agriculture would,

18. Eli F. Heckscher, "The Effect of Foreign Trade on the Distribution of Income," in *Readings in the Theory of International Trade*, ed. Howard S. Ellis and Lloyd A. Metzler (Philadelphia, 1950), translated from the Swedish of *Ekonomisk Tidskrift*, vol. 21 (1919).

> in time, be superseded. And such would inevitably be the case if our expenses of cultivation should not diminish as our growth diminished, nor the expenses of foreign growth increase as their produce increased. . . . But . . . the principle will show that in such case, as the growth of the foreigner increased the proportionate expense of his growth would increase, and as the home growth was diminished, the proportionate expense of the home growth would also be diminished. . . . The actual price of both in the market must meet.[19]

Actually West did not anticipate an equalization of prices because like most economists of the day he was opposed to completely free trade. Nevertheless, the idea of equalization had a bearing on policy. West ingeniously used it to remove what was a major argument for protection: that protection guaranteed England would produce at least some of its food and would not become entirely dependent on foreign supplies. To say that this was one, if not the most, compelling argument is no overstatement. Malthus found it more compelling than the economic arguments for free trade and said so in the pamphlet to which Ricardo paid tribute for its rent theory.[20] Ricardo, although he did not favor eliminating the corn duties, did favor reducing them. In the essay on profit, he stated that lowering them would increase total output and the rate of profit. The statement was the stronger part of his argument, and out of it grew *The Principles*. But it was not an answer to Malthus. It could have been made into one, and West made it so. But Ricardo did not; instead he tried to refute Malthus with ideas taken from not only economics but psychology, political theory, technology, and even Deism.[21] He was a stranger in these worlds and awkward in them: some of the things he said were embarrassing. Malthus won the day even though, by his own principle of diminishing returns, he was wrong. However, Ricardo did use the principle later when he argued against dependency in *On Protection to Agriculture* in 1822.[22]

19. Hollander, *West*, pp. 36–37. West did not have the idea of marginal cost.
20. Malthus, *Grounds*, p. 38.
21. Ricardo, *Essay on Profits*, in *Works*, 4:27–31; e.g., "Providence has bountifully secured us from the frequent recurrence of dearths."
22. *Works*, 4:265.

Price Theory

The other contributions of West are found in the *Price of Corn*. This book was a critical analysis of Ricardo's explanation of why the price of corn had fallen, relatively and absolutely, between 1817 and 1822.[23] Ricardo said the supply had increased; West said the demand had decreased.

That does not sound like an argument that promises to be instructive. But it was. The issue itself was significant, because it was about price and not value. West invited the reader away from the search for an essential quality like labor or land whose use imparts value or provides a way of measuring it or both. He invited the reader to consider the prosaic but more useful question of why the price of corn had fallen 50 percent in five years.[24]

23. The *Price of Corn* was directed mainly at Ricardo's *On Protection to Agriculture* and only incidentally at the *Principles.*

24. Just who was right is not terribly important, since the controversy is remembered for the ideas it generated and not for the facts they affected to explain (which is an aspect of it that contains a methodological lesson). Still, one is naturally curious about whose facts were accurate. We might know if we knew something about the quantity exchanged between 1818 and 1822. We do know that the price of wheat in each of these years was lower than in the preceding year. If the quantity exchanged in any one year was more than in the preceding year, that would suggest (although certainly not prove) that the price had fallen because the supply had increased, as Ricardo contended. But if the quantity was less, that would suggest that demand had fallen, which was West's explanation.—There is some information about the quantity, and it is inconclusive. I report it nevertheless. If it signifies nothing about the controversy, it does signify something about the difficulty of making an empirical judgment concerning historical controversies: Ricardo (*On Protection to Agriculture, Works,* 4:270) supplied information on the quantity of domestically produced corn sold on Mark Lane, the principal London market. The quantity exchanged of wheat was higher each year than in the preceding year from 1819 to 1822 inclusive, but lower in 1818 than in 1817. Joseph Lowe, *The Present State of England in Regard to Agriculture, etc.* (1823; reprinted, New York, 1967), p. 132, presented information on whether the wheat crop was average, above, or below, and from it one can conclude that the crop was greater than in the preceding year in 1818 and 1820, less in 1819 and 1821, and about the same in 1822. His data are consistent with Ricardo's for only one year. There is a tabulation similar to Lowe's in a parliamentary paper ("Third Report from the Select Committee on Agricultural Distress," *British Sessional Papers, House of Commons,* 1836, 8, pt. 2:558), and it indicates that the crop was higher than in the preceding year in 1818, 1820, and 1822, lower in 1821, and about the same in

What he said was, briefly, that price is determined by demand and supply, each of them considered as functions. Demand is determined by the wants and means of buyers, and their means are determined by employment, which in turn depends on the rate of return on capital. Supply is determined by average cost of production, which is regulated by diminishing returns in agriculture and increasing returns in manufacturing. Demand is subject to short-run fluctuations, because employment and income are. A short-run change in price and output can be caused by a change in either demand or supply, the short run being a period when population is constant.[25]

In Ricardo's system, only a change in supply (as a function) can change both price and quantity in the short run. A change in demand can change only price in the short run, and even this is exceptional. A change in the money stock causes demand and prices to change in the same direction, but output does not change because all prices are assumed to change proportionately. In the long run a

---

1819. The data are consistent with Ricardo's for two years. What each of the sources suggests—and I would put it no more strongly than "suggests"—as the cause of the price decrease is summarized below, where ΔD is a change in demand, ΔS is a change in supply, and N indicates that the information does not permit any inference however tentative.

	RICARDO	LOWE	SELECT COMMITTEE
1818	$\Delta D < 0$	$\Delta S > 0$	$\Delta S > 0$
1819	$\Delta S > 0$	$\Delta D < 0$	N
1820	$\Delta S > 0$	$\Delta S > 0$	$\Delta S > 0$
1821	$\Delta S > 0$	$\Delta D < 0$	$\Delta D < 0$
1822	$\Delta S > 0$	N	$\Delta S > 0$

An oddity is that the data of Lowe and the Committee supported Ricardo's contention for 1818, while his own data did not.—West himself presented no information and merely called attention to the fact that in a parliamentary inquiry of 1821 some witnesses had said the crop of 1819 was average, others that it was above average, and still others that it was below. *Price of Corn*, p. 5. Actually the conclusion of the inquiry was that the crop of 1819 was abundant in Ireland and that of 1820 was abundant everywhere in the United Kingdom; the latter finding is consistent with all three sources above. "Report from the Select Committee of the House of Commons, to whom the several Petitions complaining of the depressed State of the Agriculture of the United Kingdom were referred," Hansard, *Parliamentary Debates*, n.s. 5:lxxiv.

25. This summary paragraph is based on chap. 2. "Analysis of Price," chap. 3. "Demand for Corn, How Regulated," and chap. 5, "Supply of Corn," of *Price of Corn*, except for the idea that manufacturing is subject to increasing returns which is in Hollander, *West*, p. 19. Specific citations for ideas from the *Price of Corn* are given below.

change in demand will affect output as well as price because the change will have been caused by a change in population.[26]

West employed the idea of demand as a function. He said that for any good there are classes of buyers and a maximum price each class will pay: "Let the first class be willing to give 10 s. a pound for a certain quantity of it, the next class 9 s. for a given quantity, and so on to the lowest, whose maximum of price is 1 s. the pound."[27] The implication is that the amount bought at any price is the amount bought by the class for whom that price is the maximum plus the amounts bought by the classes for whom the price is below their maximum. West made this clear when he wrote that the market price is that demand price at which one or more classes will take all that is offered for sale.[28]

Usually West used "demand" to mean demand price, but he sometimes used it to mean quantity demanded. That may have puzzled some of his readers and explain why they did not recognize his innovations. A reader today would be put off by the usage and also by West's saying supply can "be considered as an element of demand."[29] Nevertheless, his ideas about demand and supply were a contribution. Although he did use "demand" to mean price at one time and quantity at another, he was on each occasion consistent in the way he used it. He never on any one occasion used it to mean both and he never confused a point on the function with the function itself. When he wrote that supply was a part of demand, all he meant was that given the demand schedule, the market price will be determined by the quantity offered for sale. This is a legitimate analytical device, used before him by Ricardo and after by Jevons, the Austrians, Marshall, and economists today.

One must note that West may not have been the first to describe a demand schedule. He was not the first to suggest the idea, although he did so much more plainly than anyone I know of. Malthus seems to have had the idea.[30] Smith and Ricardo may have also. But none gave it an important place in their systems. They did write that

26. Ricardo, *Principles*, esp. chaps. 1, 4, 30.

27. *Price of Corn*, p. 28.

28. *Price of Corn*, pp. 28–29.

29. *Price of Corn*, p. 29.

30. T. R. Malthus, *Principles of Political Economy* (London, 1820), chap. 2, sec. 2.

demand and supply are the determinants of price in the short run and they used the words in the flexible sort of way which produces plausible statements, but not the precise statements which the analysis of price requires.[31] What they did had been done by the English mercantilist writers before them and still earlier in some medieval tracts.[32] But the first closely reasoned statement about price of which I know was made by West.

About supply he was less impressive than about demand, but he did make some instructive statements. He implied that the amount offered for sale at any given demand price would in the long run be the amount that could be produced at an average cost, including profit, equal to that price. (Here the long run is a period when output, not population, can change.) He distinguished between what today would be called fixed costs and variable costs. He remarked that once a cost was incurred it had no effect on output, that is, he expressed the idea that a firm should operate so long as market price covers average variable cost. Speaking of how a farmer who has improved his land when prices were high will continue to utilize it when they are low and do not cover the cost of the improvement, he said, "it may answer, when the chief expense is once incurred, to take advantage of it whilst the effects continue."[33] This is a curious way of putting the principle, perhaps; but he might have found our way stilted.

In the long run, market price equals average cost. If they are unequal, output will change until they become equal. "The supply is regulated . . . by the proportion which the demand bears to the cost of production."[34] The sentence is less odd if one knows he meant

31. See, e.g., bk. 1, chap. 7, of *The Wealth of Nations*, "Of the Natural and Market Price of Commodities," or Ricardo in chap. 30 of the *Principles*, where in addition to his own "plausible" statements he quotes those of Buchanan, Say, and Lauderdale.

32. As an example of the mercantilists, see Nicholas Barbon, *A Discourse of Trade* [1690], ed. Jacob H. Hollander (Baltimore, 1905). The notion that price is determined by demand and supply is contained, I suggest, in the medieval view that price is determined by the "common estimation" of buyers and sellers. For examples of this view, see Raymond de Roover, "The Concept of the Just Price: Theory and Economic Policy," *Journal of Economic History* 18, no. 4 (Dec. 1958): 422, 424.

33. *Price of Corn*, pp. 108–109.

34. *Price of Corn*, p. 92.

quantity supplied and demand price, and it is a suggestion of the idea of a supply schedule. The idea is suggested again in his statement that in manufacturing, all firms in an industry produce at the same cost (or in today's language, they have identical schedules relating output and supply price).[35] About the supply of agricultural products he made the interesting observation that there are two kinds of improvements, one that enables the farmer to raise more but at a higher cost and another that enables him to raise a given amount at a lower cost—a distinction, of course, between a movement within the function and a movement of the function.[36]

There is the idea of equilibrium in his saying that output is constant when demand price and average cost are equal. He was not the first to say it; it had been said before by Smith, who like most British economists, including Marshall at times, defined equilibrium as the equality of demand and supply prices at a given quantity rather than as an equality of quantities at a given price.[37]

In the matter of equilibrium, West was no better or worse than his time. In other matters he was ahead of it. He treated profit as an explicit cost of production, as Ricardo had done, but without any of the ambiguities to which the labor theory of value gives rise and which Ricardo cannot be said to have avoided. West avoided them by simply setting aside the labor theory of value. Had he been asked, What does determine value if labor does not? he would have said, "Demand and supply," and probably would have used the word "price" instead of "value."

Elasticity

In analyzing the effect on price of changes in supply (as a function), West used the idea of price elasticity of demand.[38] That is a curious use and may be the reason why his part in the development of the idea has been overlooked. He said a decrease in the quantity supplied of bread, say 50 percent, will cause a rise in price of a magni-

35. *Price of Corn*, pp. 94-95. 36. *Price of Corn*, pp. 98–99.

37. See, e.g., *Wealth of Nations* (New York, 1937), p. 57, and Marshall, *Principles of Economics*, 8th ed. (London, 1938), p. 345.

38. *Price of Corn*, pp. 54–56.

tude that depends on the proportion of income that was spent on bread before the quantity changed. If the laborer spent his entire income on bread before the quantity changed, he can spend no more now. The price then will rise in "exact proportion to the deficiency." (He meant, the ratio of the new to the old price is equal to the ratio of the old to the new quantity, which follows from expenditure being constant.) But if the laborer has been spending only half his income on bread, he can now spend twice as much, and if he does, the price will be "quadrupled." West cited the calculations of Gregory King (c. 1696) that a 10 percent decrease in the output of corn would raise its price 30 percent. We can get from West's notion of elasticity to ours by making the change in quantity demanded equal to that in quantity supplied and then inverting his ratio. Although his use of the idea is unusual, the use was entirely appropriate to the question he was analyzing.

That question—How will a change in supply affect price?—was more interesting to West's contemporaries than the question of how a change in price will effect quantity demanded. Ricardo had asked it earlier, and in answering it he too had used the idea of elasticity.[39] He came to the same conclusion as West later came to, that (i) the price of corn will change relatively more than the change in the crop, and (ii) the amount spent on a large crop will be less than the amount spent on a small crop. The idea of elasticity may have been suggested to West by his reading of Ricardo, but could have been no more than suggested. From Ricardo's remarks, one does not know whether he believed all goods were like corn or only agricultural goods were like corn, and so one does not know whether price and expenditure move

39. *On Protection to Agriculture*, *Works*, 4:220. Both West and Ricardo were anticipated by W. Jacob, *An Inquiry Into the Causes of Agricultural Distress* (London, 1816), where this remarkable passage occurs: "Although the price at which productions will sell, is in some measure regulated by the proportion betwixt demand and supply, yet it is by no means in the ratio of the excess to the demand in times of super-abundance, or in the ratio of deficiency to demand in times of scarcity. Thus, if the demand be as ten, and the supply as eleven, the price will be depressed more than ten per cent. If, on the other hand, the demand be as ten, and the supply as nine, the price will be raised more than ten per cent" (p. 22). After this description of inelasticity, Jacob goes on to observe that it is characteristic of goods that cannot be put in inventory because they are perishable or bulky and expensive to store. The observation about inventories also anticipates West (see the next paragraph below).

in opposite directions in all markets or only in agricultural markets. Ricardo does not refer at all to goods on which expenditure changes in the same direction as price. West does. Moreover, West distinguishes between necessities and other goods according to whether price and expenditure move in the same or the opposite direction. There is nothing of this in Ricardo's pamphlet.

West, in explaining elasticity, made a puzzling observation about inventories. He said an increase in the crop causes price to fall by less than a decrease of equal size causes price to rise. The reason, he said, is that a part of a bumper crop is placed in inventory. This makes one ask why inventories could not be drawn down when the crop was deficient and so moderate a rise in price. He was silent on the point.

West used the idea of income elasticity as well as of price elasticity. He did so in analyzing how a change in working-class income would affect the price of bread. The price would rise, because workers, though they may have enough bread to live on, never have all they want. This is not true of some others. "Increase the incomes of those who always have as much bread as they desire, and you will not at all affect the demand for corn."[40] Simple as the idea is, Smith had it wrong; and he constructed a theory of the origin of rent on the mistaken assumption that as the productivity of agriculture increased, its output remained the same and labor was released to manufacturing industries. This is so because "the desire for food is limited in every man by the narrow capacity of the human stomach."[41] West had only to remark that "the limits . . . of desire and necessity, are very different."[42] The observation led him to the rationing function of prices; the statement is worth quoting for that reason and because it indicates his use of the demand function:

> It is by the rise of price and consequent contraction of consumption of the poorer classes that a scanty crop is made to last throughout the year, and by the fall of price and consequent expansion of the consumption of those classes, that an abundant crop is disposed of.[43]

40. *Price of Corn*, p. 32.
41. *Wealth of Nations*, p. 164.
42. *Price of Corn*, p. 32.
43. Ibid.

Wage Theory

West began with the proposition that "the price of labour is regulated by the same law as all other price"—by demand and supply. He meant by "price" the amount paid the workers for a unit of output or for a given amount of time worked (i.e., the wage rate). It is, he stressed, different from the wage income of the worker —he called this the "wages of labour"—which is price multiplied by the quantity of labor employed (measured either in work units or in time). The wage income of all workers can also vary independently of average wage income, because employment can vary independently of the price of labor or wages.[44]

These distinctions made West's wage theory more useful for short-run analysis than that of the Ricardians. They assumed full employment and so made the wage income of each worker and of the working class vary in the same proportion as the wage rate, which in real terms was constant and equal to the cost of subsistence. Taken in this simple form, the theory was rigid and unhelpful. It did not admit of changes in employment without prior changes in population. It did not allow real wages to change without the change being reversed by a subsequent change in population. It implied a close connection between prices and wages, and hence between product and labor markets; thus it did not allow for changes in the allocation of labor and the composition of output. The constancy of real wages, taken together with diminishing returns, doomed the rate of profit to decline, and the decline limited the fund for the support of labor. One must add, to be fair, that the theory was not initially meant to be used for short-run analysis, but to explain long-run changes in the distribution of income. In time it came to be used for short-run analysis as well.

In both uses it was wholly unfactual, West said. Observation showed that real wages had changed in the past thirty years in Britain and also showed that they differed at any one time among countries. He did acknowledge that Ricardo had allowed for the possibility of real wages rising for an "indefinite" time because the stock of capital, and hence the demand for labor, might increase indefinitely. But that

44. *Price of Corn*, pp. 62, 67.

view, West said, involves another mistake—the belief that the demand for labor can increase only if there is a prior increase in capital. The belief was the wage-fund doctrine.[45]

What West said about the wage-fund doctrine (unlike what he said about most other things) has not been entirely ignored.[46] He has recently been praised as one of its first critics, as indeed he was; but the praise would puzzle him. He is said to have agreed with the Ricardians that an increase in the capital stock will increase the demand for labor, but to have added, as they did not, that there must first be an increase in the aggregate demand for output in order for an increase in the demand for labor to be profitable. For this he has been called a forerunner of Keynes. The temptation to call him so is great. Still, what he said was, "So increase the demand for and the price of labor [,] and the necessaries which the labourers require will soon be raised and manufactured."[47] What he meant was, I suggest, the un-Keynesian idea that the demand for output depends upon employment, that an increase in the demand for labor will justify itself by inducing an increase in the demand for goods—not the other way around. On this point, West was hopelessly classical.

West's most telling criticism of the wage-fund doctrine was to explain how it failed to notice that the demand for labor can increase without there first being an increase in the capital stock. The demand for labor can increase because of what he called commercial fluctuations and what we would call the upswing of the cycle (see below). Another reason is a greater demand for labor by the government. There is still another reason, and it is more interesting. He said the demand for labor can increase because "paper credit" (currency) increases.

45. *Price of Corn*, pp. 74, 77, 79.

46. William Breit, "Some Neglected Early Critics of the Wages Fund Theory," *Southwestern Social Science Quarterly*, June 1967, p. 55.

47. *Price of Corn*, p. 81. Actually, West was a little obtuse, or more than a little unfair, about the wage-fund doctrine, which was not altogether as absurd as he and other critics have made it out to be. If labor cannot be substituted without limit for other resources, there must be a stock of them before employment can increase. If labor must be supported during the production period, there must be a stock of wage goods before employment can increase, except if real wages can be reduced, as in the classical system they cannot be. All of this was made clear by Smith in his exposition, with which West affected to be familiar and even quoted.

Money

West's ideas about money were a part of his argument that the price of corn had fallen because there had been a decrease in the demand for corn and for all goods.[48] One reason for the decrease in demand was the decline in the money stock after 1819, which produced what he called "the elevation of the value of the currency." He addressed himself to two questions: What are the "modes in which any alteration of the currency affects the whole commerce of the country," i.e., what is the mechanism by which a change in the value of money causes a change in income? Can the alteration affect the "real" as well as the "nominal" price of a good, i.e., can a change in the value of money affect relative as well as absolute prices?

Suppose, he said, that the value of money falls 10 percent. The prices of all final goods will rise that much. But the average cost of production will rise 10 percent only in industries that are not subject to a tax or other fixed charges, like rent or interest. In industries where there are such charges, cost will rise less than 10 percent, and hence profit will increase. "New activity and vigour would be infused into trade and manufactures, and more employment furnished to the labouring population, which would be attended by larger wages and an increased demand for corn." The price of corn will rise, and the increase will be more than that of other prices, because (as explained above) the demand for it is more sensitive to income changes than is the demand for other goods. A decrease in the price level would raise the ratio of cost to price on goods subject to fixed charges, would lower the profit on them, and would cause a "stagnation of trade and manufactures," and a decrease in employment, in wages, and in the demand for corn and its relative price. (One may note that the critical assumptions were differences among industries in the ratio of fixed to total cost and in the income elasticity of demand for their products.)

West's analysis of the relation between changes in absolute and changes in relative prices was noteworthy. Indeed, if he had done no more than make an effort to analyze the relation, he would have been unique. So far as I know, no one else even mentioned the topic in his day, or before it, or in his century. In our time the point seems

48. *Price of Corn*, chap. 6, "Effects of the Alteration of the Currency."

to have been shunted off into statistics, where it appears as the problem of price dispersion in the construction of index numbers. There is the ratchet effect in macroeconomics, but it is an institutional notion. West explained the relation by employing a purely theoretical consideration (income elasticity). His analysis is of more than historic interest. It suggests a way of bringing together the theory that explains the price level with the theory that explains relative prices and of going on to integrate ideas about what determines total output with the ideas that explain the composition of total output. That is a complex undertaking and may have been more than his contemporaries cared to attempt.

Those contemporaries found the question of how money and income are related to be more manageable. It has been the subject of economic speculation for centuries, and the results are odd. Nearly everyone has answered the question in the same way, namely, by saying that income and money move in the same direction. And nearly everyone has given a different reason. A celebrated explanation is in Hume's essay *On Money*. It was of some moment to West. He quoted Hume's statement that when the money stock increases "everything takes on a new face"—output and employment increase, the worker becomes more diligent, the businessman more enterprising, the farmer more attentive to the plow. Just what Hume had in mind is not clear. He seems to have begun with a condition of unemployment and to have assumed that an increase in the money stock first causes an increase in income and after some time an increase in prices. In the interim, profits rise and bring employment and output up with them. Yet Hume went on to say that the best policy with respect to money "consists only in keeping it if possible still encreasing" because that keeps the spirit of industry alive and increases the stock of labor. Conceivably, he had growth in mind; he may even have supposed that ever-increasing prices would make people work harder. Or he simply could have been mistaken. West thought he was. But that is a desperate conclusion to draw about one who reasoned as carefully as Hume did. Sophist he could be, and elusive to others; but hardly to himself. West did not share Hume's conclusions that the money stock should be increased continuously and did not even consider the long-run effect of changes in the money stock. He was indeed somewhat infirm of purpose even about the short-run effects. After quoting in a sympathetic way the heretical ideas of Thomas Attwood, to whom gold was anathema, West concluded by praising the Gold Resumption Bill of 1819. He may have believed it would prevent a recurrence of deflationary movements.

Another of West's ideas about money is forced saving. It appears in his explanation of how an increase in the amount of paper money causes a change in the size of the capital stock and in the distribution between the productive and unproductive classes of what he called "capital" and we would call the real value of money balances. The increase in money raises prices in England relative to those abroad and sends gold abroad to buy foreign goods which then become a part of England's capital. In the process, the distribution of real balances changes twice. When the price level increases, there is a redistribution in favor of those whose borrowing caused the money stock to increase. They are usually merchants and manufacturers, members of the productive class. The amount of money held by country gentlemen and other members of the unproductive class does not change, and they are made worse off by the price rise. But the export of gold restores the original price level and hence the original command over goods held by the unproductive class. They then have the same absolute real balances they initially had and their relative balances, though lower than initially, are higher than after the rise in prices. The productive class is better off, because it now owns more capital. That capital would not have been imported had the redistribution been in favor of the unproductive class, because that class consumes more of its income than the productive class does.[49]

The System of West

The ideas of West, each in itself, invite our interest, and most of them our respect, a few our admiration. So I suggest, and would add that this fact entitles him to a place in the history of economics, different from the place he now has but no less worthy, indeed rather

49. *Price of Corn*, p. 44. One cannot help but wonder if West recognized that behind all of this was simply an exchange of gold for imports. One also wonders why he did not believe domestic prices at one point would fall below their initial level because, by his quantity-theory reasoning, they would be affected by two changes, the export of gold and the import of goods.

more. Whether his ideas constitute a system should not regulate our historical judgment. If it were to do so, the history of economic thought would be very different and far shorter than it now is. Those who have a place in it are most of them remembered for particular ideas and not for systems. One hesitates to cite examples for fear of not knowing where to stop. Yet consider a few: Hume for the specie-flow mechanism, Mun for the export of bullion, Hales for the allocative function of profit, Cairnes for noncompeting groups, Senior for abstinence, Mill for reciprocal demand, Böhm-Bawerk for time preference, Pareto for optimality, Clark for marginal productivity, Malthus for population. One could go on and on.

At one time economists thought the history of the subject could be studied topically as well as chronologically, and a distinguished text arranged the ideas by topics—Edmund Whittaker's *A History of Economic Ideas* (1943). The arrangement has fallen out of favor. The change reflects the change in economics itself. It has so far progressed that it constitutes a logically complete body of knowledge, or so some would claim. Each idea is to be understood in relation to the others and all of them together as a model of the economic system. The achievement has affected our view of the past. We are inclined to judge our predecessors according to whether their ideas constitute an integrated whole.[50] "Old X, yes, a clever fellow and more right about some things than Ricardo. Interesting bits and pieces, but what can you do with them? Did he have a system? Ricardo did, you know." Thus in this generation we have had studies of Ricardian economics as a paradigm, a dynamic model of Malthusian population theory, a geometric exposition of Marxian macroeconomics, a growth model read from *The Wealth of Nations*.

What can be said of West? He had a system; it can be stated in our language and logical categories or in his own. How he viewed it is indicated in the concluding chapter of *Price of Corn*. "We will now apply the principles which we have endeavored to explain in the foregoing pages to the present state of the country," he wrote (and actually added two principles more, about the cycle and development).

50. "But although his [West's] insights were acute, he failed to expand his ideas into [a] rounded system from which politically relevant inferences could be drawn. That task fell to David Ricardo." Joseph S. Keiper et al., *Theory and Measurement of Rent* (New York, 1959), p. 33.

He assumed that the demand for corn would continue to increase. If imports were prohibited, the relative price of corn would rise because its production was subject to diminishing returns. Whether the absolute (i.e., nominal money) price would rise would depend on ventures of the moment in the mining of monetary metal in South America. Whatever the absolute or the relative price of corn came to be, it would be more unstable than in the past. The reason was the growing instability of the British economy. That, he said in a digression that constituted a simple theory of the cycle, was caused by the increase in the output of manufactures relative to total output. The demand for them is more unstable than the demand for agricultural goods because the former is determined not only by need, which is predictable, but also by taste, which is capricious. Manufacturing firms unavoidably produce too much of some things and not enough of others. The overproduction in some markets depresses income more than the underproduction in others raises it. Why the effect was not symmetric, he did not explain—an omission that was typical of nineteenth-century writing on the cycle. He did go on to say that as the number of markets for manufactured goods increases, the instability of the system becomes less because ''the gain in one may compensate the loss in another.''

In examining the course of agriculture, West noticed that as the population of Britain had increased, there had been an increase in the amount of capital in agriculture and land in cultivation just as the principle of diminishing returns would lead one to expect. But there had not been the expected increase in the proportion of the labor force employed in agriculture. The proportion in fact had decreased. He explained the paradox by the improvement in the skill of agricultural labor and an increase in its exertions, ''increase'' here meaning that each laborer was working longer hours and more members of each farm family were working. The greater participation in the labor force was the result of farm families buying on the market what they once had produced in the household, a change, he said, that came of an extension of specialization and exchange (or economic development).

As Ricardo had done, West made predictions about the distribution of income and said the money price of labor would rise, but not as much as the price of corn. The consequent decline in the real price of labor was something that his system admitted but Ricardo's did not. The latter held that wage income is strictly proportional to the price of labor and in the long run cannot fall below the cost of subsistence. The effect of diminishing returns is to reduce the real *price* of labor as well, West said, although he did not expressly say real wage *income* would fall.

The amount of rent would increase, West said. Landlords could benefit in two ways: by receiving a larger proportion of the total output of agriculture and by the higher price of agricultural output. Each change indicates an increase in their share of the output of the economy. The former implies an increase in the rate of rent, thus correcting the slip made about it in the *Essay*. Landlords, although they could benefit, probably would not, because as they obtained a larger share of total income they would have to bear a larger share of taxation. "Landlords in such case would suffer in common with the rest of the community," he said, which implies that their taxes would rise as much as their income. Here one notices another appeal to the landlords which, again, is most un-Ricardian.

About the effect of diminishing returns on the supply of resources, West wrote that "the addition of each year to the capital and population of the country, must bear a less and less proportion to their whole amount." This decline in the rate of capital accumulation would be intensified, West wrote, by capital leaving the country as the rate of profit fell. The export of capital seems to have perturbed him, as it did Ricardo and Smith. Ricardo wrote of the commendable feelings that induce people to keep their capital at home. Smith was just as much of a nationalist, at least on this point. Although its context is hardly ever noted, he made his most noted and notorious statement—that about the invisible hand, no less—in the course of explaining why free domestic exchange will keep capital at home. West hoped this could be done by an improvement in economic policy, and he proposed four measures, one of them being Smith's free domestic exchange.[51]

Thus did West see his system. How might it be seen today? Consider first its microeconomic aspect. (1) The demand function treats quantity as dependent on price while taste and income are con-

51. *Price of Corn*, p. 143; cf. Smith, p. 423, and Ricardo, *Principles*, p. 83.

stant; the supply function treats it as dependent on the price of resources and their productivity. (2) Productivity in agriculture is subject to diminishing returns, and in manufacturing to increasing returns. (3) Product markets are in equilibrium when the demand price for a given stock of goods is equal to the supply price. If the latter is also equal to average cost, there is long-run equilibrium. If supply price and average cost are not equal, output will change until they are. (4) Price and expenditure also change then, in the same direction if demand is inelastic and oppositely if elastic. (5) A firm is in long-run equilibrium when the price of its product equals average total cost, including normal profit, and will operate so long as price is not less than average variable cost. In manufacturing, all firms in an industry have equal average costs. In agriculture, average costs are unequal and are highest for the marginal farm. (6) In labor markets, the wage rate is determined by the demand for and supply of labor, and wage income by the wage rate times employment. Demand is a function of the profit of the firm. Supply, given the population, is a function of the participation rate, which increases as the extent of market activity increases. (7) The normal rate of profit for the economy is the ratio on the marginal farm of its net product (total revenue minus total cost) to its total cost. The amount of profit of a firm or farm is the rate of profit times its total cost. (8) The amount of rent is the net product of a farm minus the amount of its profit. (9) In foreign trade the average cost of marginal farms is the same everywhere, and a given good is produced in both the net importing and net exporting countries. In manufacturing (because manufacturing operates at decreasing cost) the entire output of a given good is produced in the country where average cost is lowest.

In its macroeconomic aspect, the system consists of these elements: (10) It explains the long-run distribution of income. The rate and amount of real wages can rise or fall. The amount of profit increases, but the rate falls. Both the amount and the rate of rent increase, but landlords cannot benefit because their taxes are expected to rise proportionately. (11) Total output is subject to fluctuations which can be endogenous, because of disequilibrium in individual markets, or exogenous, because of changes in the money stock. (12) Changes in the money stock cause output to change in the same direction if not all prices (including costs) change in the same proportion. (13)

The consequent change in income affects particular goods differently depending on their income elasticities and hence alters their relative as well as their absolute prices. (14) A change in the money stock can affect exports and imports and so alter the distribution of income between agriculture and manufacturing. (15) Changes in output, irrespective of their origin, cause total employment to change. (16) In consequence, there can be a change in the wage rate, wage income, and total wage bill.

A monitory word seems the proper way to conclude. This paraphrase, even though it is simply a restatement of West's ideas, is so different from his language and his way of looking at things that he probably would not recognize the system it describes as his. One recalls a story about Eliot being shown an arcane interpretation of one of his poems. "Did I say that? Thank you very much!"

[11]

James Mill and the early development of comparative advantage

William O. Thweatt

I

This essay explores anew the early development and subsequent incorporation into the main body of economic analysis of the law of comparative advantage. The main characters in this account are familiar—Torrens, Ricardo, McCulloch, and later, John Stuart Mill, but the hitherto unrecognized crucial role played by James Mill is shown and emphasized.

Modern texts in beginning economics and international trade credit David Ricardo with the formulation and development of the law of comparative advantage.[1] Specialized works in the history of economics do the same.[2] Frank Fetter's recent summary of "Ricardian economics" epitomizes the present consensus on Ricardo's supposed contribution to the theory of comparative advantage.[3]

WILLIAM THWEATT *is Professor of Economics at Vanderbilt University.* *A shortened version of this article was given as a paper at the Second Annual Conference of the History of Economics Society, at the University of North Carolina, June 1974.*

1. Cf. P. A. Samuelson, *Economics*, 9th ed. (New York, 1973), pp. 668, 670–71, and R. G. Lipsey and P. O. Steiner, *Economics*, 4th ed. (New York, 1975), pp. 737 and 740, for two popular beginning textbooks; Roy Harrod, *International Economics* (Cambridge, 1948), p. 20; S. Harris, *International and Interregional Economics* (New York, 1957), p. 15 and chap. 2, entitled "Ricardo and Comparative Advantage"; C. Kindleberger, *International Economics* (Homewood, Ill., 1968), p. 21; J. Viner, *Studies in the Theory of International Trade* (New York, 1937), p. 442; J. W. Angell, *The Theory of International Prices* (Cambridge, Mass., 1926), pp. 66, 82—to name but a few.

2. L. Rogin, *The Meaning and Validity of Economic Theory* (New York, 1956), p. 144; J. A. Schumpeter, *History of Economic Analysis* (New York, 1954), p. 607; M. Blaug, *Economic Theory in Retrospect*, rev. ed. (Homewood, Ill., 1968), pp. 126–30; H. W. Spiegel, *The Growth of Economic Thought* (Englewood Cliffs, N.J., 1971), p. 328.

3. F. W. Fetter, "The Rise and Decline of Ricardian Economics," *History of Political Economy* 1 (1969): 75–76. Fetter is not being novel, he is simply echoing long-held views such as: "The Law of Comparative Cost was a great, if not *the* great discovery made by Ricardo." E. D. K. Gonner, Introductory Essay to Ricardo's *Principles of Political Economy* (London, 1891), p. vii. "Ricardo's chapter is dominated by the new doctrine." J. H. Hollander, *David Ricardo: A Centenary Estimate* (Baltimore, 1910), p. 91. ". . . in April, 1817, appeared Ricardo's *Principles*, with the

Fetter tells us that Ricardo's theory of international trade, a contribution "peculiarly" his own, was a "magnificient intellectual tour de force." Although Robert Torrens had "expressed the general idea of comparative costs as early as 1808 . . . it was Ricardo who spelled out the argument in detail . . . made it his own . . . and drove home its practical application. . . . No idea of Ricardo's has stood up so well against critical attack, or has so powerfully influenced policy . . . culminating in the repeal of the Corn laws in 1846 . . . as did this analysis [which] by the 1840's permeated the thought of many [Britishers including the] scores who read the essence of his free trade ideas in the *Edinburgh Review* [and] in the *Westminster Review*."[4] Such is the state of the current myth.

Contrary to Fetter's caricature we hope to show that Ricardo's writings on the law of comparative advantage were not "peculiarly his own," nor that what Torrens wrote in 1808 should give him priority, any more than James Mill's simultaneous and equally valid statement. Furthermore, Ricardo did not spell out the argument in detail, did not make it his own, nor drive home its practical application. Also, Ricardo's analysis could hardly have "stood up so well against critical attack," since in the contemporary literature there was no criticism of what little Ricardo did write on the theory of comparative advantage—his theories of value and distribution were the chief targets of attack. And, interestingly, there was little anyone could have read in the *Edinburgh Review* or the *Westminster Review* about the law of comparative advantage. Indeed, so few of the arguments for free trade were based on comparative advantage, as distinct from a Smithian-derived "territorial division of labor" argument based squarely on absolute cost differences, that it is misleading to say the doctrine of comparative costs was influential in the discussion leading to the repeal of the Corn Laws in 1846.

Before examining the evidence for this position it may be helpful if first we briefly outline the concept of comparative costs. As Viner pointed out, as early as 1701 trade was seen as beneficial to a nation when it provided commodities "which could not be produced at home at all or could be produced at home only at costs absolutely greater than those at which they could be produced abroad."[5] Let us call this

---

theory of comparative cost set forth in classical detail." Idem, *Economic Journal* 21 (1911): 462. And Alfred Marshall, in his *Money, Credit and Commerce* (London, 1923), said Ricardo made comparative advantage into a "coherent doctrine," and "integrated it into an organic whole" (p. 41). Similar statements are contained in Seymour Harris, Schumpeter, and Viner cited supra nn. 1 and 2.

4. Fetter, pp. 75–76.

5. Viner, pp. 439–40.

notion, following Viner, the "eighteenth-century rule." In effect, the "rule" states that trade is beneficial whenever the resource cost of obtaining commodity A, in terms of commodity B, is lower when obtained through trade than when produced domestically. The "eighteenth-century rule," however, is compatible with explaining trade on both an absoute and on a comparative basis, and while not inconsistent with, does not necessarily imply, comparative costs.[6]

The further notion that, under these cost conditions, it still might be profitable to import commodity A even though it "could be produced at less cost at home than abroad" has to be considered "the essence" of the doctrine. Viner stressed that the explicit statement of "the essence" was the "sole addition of consequence which the doctrine of comparative costs made to the eighteenth-century rule."[7] Thus, "the essence" completes the explanation of the gains from trade in terms of comparative, as distinct from absolute, costs.

The full statement of the law of comparative advantage requires an explanation of the division of the gains from trade. There is, however, no dispute as to who first published a complete account of how the gains are divided in terms of reciprocal demands. John Stuart Mill first wrote it out sometime during 1829–30, but published it only in 1844 and later repeated it almost verbatim in his *Principles*. While there is still some unraveling to do with this part of the story, this will have to wait for another time, since there is enough to unravel with respect to the *early* development of the theory of the gains from trade. We therefore concentrate on the history of the "rule" and the "essence" components of the law of comparative advantage in attempting to ascertain the roles James Mill, Robert Torrens, and David Ricardo played in their development.

II

The occasion for the introduction of the eighteenth-century rule into what was to become the emerging orthodoxy of the British classical school was Napoleon's 1806 Berlin decree as he attempted to shut off England from trade with the Continent. Many an Englishman shuddered at the thought. It was in such an atmosphere of national concern that William Spence, who has been described as an English

6. The *locus classicus* of the "rule" is the remarkable pamphlet, *Considerations Upon the East-India Trade*, published anonymously in 1701. W. L. Barber, *British Economic Thought and India, 1600–1858* (Oxford, 1975), provides an excellent account of the role of this "remarkable document" in the history of trade theory in the eighteenth century, although he implies that the "eighteenth-century rule" is a "clear statement of the doctrine of comparative advantage" (p. 63), which it is not.

7. Viner, p. 441.

Physiocrat and an early underconsumptionist,[8] wrote his 1807 tract whose very title (*Britain Independent of Commerce or, Proofs Deduced from an Investigation into the True Causes of the Wealth of Nations, That Our Riches, Prosperity, and Power, are Derived from Sources Inherent in Ourselves, and Would Not be Affected even though Our Commerce Were Annihilated*) apparently was designed to assure his compatriots that they had no reason to fear Napoleon from this cause.

Spence's main contention was that since a nation's agriculture is the source of its wealth, a blockade of trade could not injure the national economy. He coupled this with the idea that it was essential for the landed proprietors of the country to spend all their incomes, lest prosperity be diminished through underconsumption. More than thirty books and pamphlets rapidly appeared in print—some, like Cobbett's *Political Register*, supporting Spence,[9] while most others attacked his ideas. One of the latter of particular importance was written by James Mill, who, for the first time in England, made use of the "law of markets" to dispose of the "dangerous doctrine" requiring landed proprietors to spend all their incomes "for the encouragement of agriculture."[10] Then making use of the eighteenth-century

8. Both B. Corry, *Money, Saving and Investment in English Economics, 1800–1850* (London, 1962), pp. 121–25, and B. Semmel, *The Rise of Free Trade Imperialism* (Cambridge, 1970), pp. 56–60, depict Spence as a follower of the French "Economistes"—an English Physiocrat. Spence did accept the Physiocratic "grand axiom" that agriculture creates all wealth, but their application of the axiom —government should favor agriculture at the expense of the "unproductive" manufacturing sector—he termed "erroneous," at least with respect to the great commercial states of Britain, France, and the Netherlands, wherein "agriculture has thriven only in consequence of the influence of manufactures." He insisted "agriculture *and* manufactures are the *two* chief wheels in the machine which creates national wealth. . . of these two . . . it is the latter which communicates motion to the former." *Britain Independent of Commerce*, pp. 16 and 24; emphasis added. This, of course, was a very un-Physiocratic approach. In urging the necessity of an expanding landlord expediture of the social surplus for the continued prosperity of manufactures and thus the national economy, Spence was more in the long line of earlier British writers such as Cantillon, Sir James Steuart, and T. R. Malthus. Cf. R. Meek, *The Economics of Physiocracy* (London, 1962), pp. 322–28.

9. Cobbett devoted over fifty pages to Spence's tract in the November and December 1807 issues, and another twenty pages in the early months of 1808. That Cobbett's series of "Perish Commerce" articles popularized Spence's position has often been noted. Cf. L. Robbins, *Robert Torrens and the Evolution of Classical Economics* (London, 1958), p. 12; B. Semmel, p. 56; and D. Winch, *James Mill: Selected Economic Writings* (Edinburgh, 1966), p. 29. They fail to mention, however, that Spence felt compelled to reply to Cobbett's bitter charge of plagiarism. See Spence's letter in the *Political Register* (Dec. 1807), pp. 922–28.

10. "Spence's Britain Independent of Commerce," *Eclectic Review* 3 (Dec. 1807): 1056. James Mill's lifetime effort of establishing and defending a conservative politico-economic orthodoxy against "dangerous doctrine" probably makes him the

rule, he went on to show that a nation can benefit from "the trade of export and import." Mill's booklet was entitled *Commerce Defended*, and it appeared in early 1808, a few weeks after he had reviewed Spence's work.[11] The other important critique of Spence in terms of the emerging orthodoxy was Robert Torrens' *The Economists Refuted*, published almost at the same time as Mill's essay.

Torrens opened his work by attacking Spence's "idea of agriculture being the only source of wealth."[12] He then went on to refute the notion that foreign trade did not augment a country's wealth, using as proof an example also based on the eighteenth-century rule. It is interesting that most writers concerned with the origins of the "law of markets" concentrate on Mill's reply to Spence, while those concerned with the origins of the law of comparative advantage quote only what Torrens wrote, leaving the wrong impression that Mill had not written in this latter regard.[13] To show that this is not the case let

---

ideological founder of the British classical school. In a later study we hope to document this assertion.

11. Ibid. In his study on James Mill, D. Winch (p. 444) shows the date of Mill's *Commerce Defended* as 1807, but this surely is incorrect. Winch reproduces the 2d edition, of 1808, which is only slightly different from the A. M. Kelly photocopy reprint of the 1st edition (New York, 1965), the titlepage of which gives the correct date as 1808. A recent acquisition by the author, a copy of *The Economic Library of Jacob H. Hollander* (Baltimore, 1937), confirms on p. 193 the 1808 date for both the 1st and 2d editions.

12. *Economists Refuted*, p. 6. All references to this extremely rare pamphlet are to the 1857 reprint in R. Torrens, *The Principles and Practical Operation of Sir Robert Peel's Act of 1844 Explained and Defended* . . . 2d ed. (London, 1857). As Robbins, p. 260, and Corry, p. 158 n., have pointed out, this reprint omits a final chapter on making peace with France, but the main text contains only "numerous minor differences."

13. See, surprisingly perhaps, J. S. Mill, *Principles of Political Economy*, ed. Ashley (rpt. New York, 1965), p. 576 n., where he gives Torrens credit, along with Ricardo, for the doctrine of comparative costs based on what Torrens wrote in 1808, i.e., only the eighteenth-century rule. J. A. Schumpeter (p. 607) follows J. S. Mill in making this error, as indeed, does B. A. Corry (p. 122 n.). Even John Chipman's masterly "Survey of the Theory of International Trade: Part I, The Classical Theory," *Econometrica* 33 (1965): 479–83, the best account of the early development of the law of comparative advantage, completely overlooked Mill's *Commerce Defended*, by beginning: "Historians of economic doctrine have debated whether priority for the law of comparative advantage should go to Ricardo (1817) or to Torrens (1808, 1815)." Interestingly, William Spence himself never once mentioned Torrens, directing his reply to "Mr. Mill and the Edinburgh Reviewers." The review of Spence in the *Edinburgh Review* (Jan. 1808) most likely was by Henry Brougham, as noted by Semmel, (p. 56 n.), who, rightly, we think, takes issue with F. W. Fetter, "The Authorship of Economic Articles in the Edinburgh Review, 1802–47," *Journal of Political Economy* 61 (1953): 246, who ascribed the review to "T. R. Malthus (probably)." Semmel is exceptional in his treatment of James Mill, noting both his early formulation of the law of markets and his hint of the "principle of comparative cost," in *Commerce Defended*. Actually, Mill, like Torrens, in 1808 presented only the eighteenth-century rule.

us quote the eighteenth-century rule examples of both Mill and Torrens to establish Mill's equal priority along with Torrens.

In Mill's *Commerce Defended* (pp. 36–37), we read:

> On making a ton of iron in Great Britain, let us suppose, that the labourers, etc. employed in providing the ore and the coals, and in smelting and preparing the metal, have consumed ten quarters of corn. Every ton of iron therefore prepared in Great Britain costs ten quarters of corn. Let us suppose, that in the preparation of a certain quantity of British manufactures, nine quarters of corn have been consumed; and let us suppose, that this quantity of [manufactured] goods will purchase in the Baltic a ton of iron, and afford, besides, the expense requisite for importing the iron into Britain. Is there not an evident saving of a quarter of corn in the acquisition of this ton of iron? Is not the country one quarter of corn the richer, by means of its importation?

And, in Robert Torrens' *The Economists Refuted* (p. 53), we read:

> . . . if I wish to know the extent of the advantage which arises to England, from her giving France a hundred pounds' worth of broad cloth, in exchange for a hundred pounds' worth of lace, I take the quantity of lace which England has acquired by this transaction, and compare it with the quantity which she might, at the same expense of labour and capital, have acquired by manufacturing it at home. The lace that remains, beyond what the labour and capital employed on the cloth might have fabricated at home, is the amount of the advantage which England derives from the exchange.

Surely there is not much to choose between these two 1808 statements. Chipman's comment that what was being compared was the "cost ratio in one country with the international price ratio . . . but [that] the comparison of cost ratios (or rates of transformation) between two countries was lacking"[14] holds for both examples. If anything, Mill's presentation seems superior, particularly since he avoided Torrens' further ideas (i) that à la Adam Smith, trade by extending the division of labor increases productivity and creates a *surplus* above home requirements which foreign trade eliminates,[15] (ii) that an exchange of equivalents yields greater benefits to the nation receiving durables rather than perishables (hardwares as against

14. Chipman, p. 480.
15. *Economists Refuted*, pp. 15–26.

wine and fruit)[16] and necessaries rather than luxuries (woolen cloth as against lace),[17] (iii) that the advantages stemming from the home trade are more permanent than those of foreign trade, which are of "uncertain tenure" due to the "caprice of strangers and the hostility of rivals,"[18] and (iv) that "in every exchange of the home trade, the *whole* of the benefit remains in the country; in every exchange of the foreign trade a *part* of the benefit goes to enrich foreigners."[19]

Additionally, it surely distorts the story to proceed directly from 1808 to Torrens' February 1815 *Essay on the External Corn Trade*,[20] where, by adding the "essence" to the "rule," he stated for the first time the *complete* explanation of the gains from trade based on comparative advantage. To do so overlooks James Mill's important *Eclectic Review* article on the Corn Laws which appeared in July 1814. In this article Mill, again using the eighteenth-century rule, defended the orthodox position of free trade against Malthus' *Observations on the Effect of the Corn Laws*. Mill stressed the need for foreign trade in terms of efficiency, stating:

> If we import, we must pay for what we import, with the produce of a portion of our labour exported. But why not employ that labour in raising the same portion at home? The answer is, because it will procure more corn by going in the shape of commodities to purchase corn abroad, than if it had been employed in raising it at home. . . . A law, therefore, to prevent the importation of corn, can have only one effect,—to make a greater portion of the labour of the community necessary for the production of its food.[21]

Mill then goes on to take Malthus to task for his pro-Corn Law stance, making five main points in so doing: (i) a better regularity of food supply is secured via importation from various nations rather than from only the domestic economy, (ii) if a major exporter withholds supplies, the "world is wide" and another exporter will be forthcoming, (iii) the exporting nation which does restrict exports has more to lose than the importer because of its investment and specialization in corn production, (iv) the gain from trade can be measured by

16. Ibid., p. 50. Spence (pp. 47–48), also held this misconception, and Mill in his *Commerce Defended*, pp. 37 and 45, took him to task for it.
17. *Economists Refuted*, pp. 50–51.
18. Ibid., p. 31.
19. Ibid., pp. 30–31.
20. As does, for instance, Robbins, pp. 22–23, and Chipman, 480–81.
21. *Eclectic Review* N.S., 2 (July 1814): 4–5.

the difference between the domestic price of corn and the imported price (the eighteenth-century rule), and (v) in any event, historical facts show that Holland, with little domestic corn production, has attained opulence, relying upon imported corn for its food supply.

Interestingly, and hitherto unnoticed in the literature, all these arguments reappear, seven months later, in the replies of Torrens and Ricardo to Malthus' February 1815 pamphlet defending the Corn Laws.[22] Although Ricardo does not cite Mill explicitly, the last half of his *Essay on Profits* is so closely patterned on Mill's attack on Malthus' defense of the Corn Laws that we may take it that he had read Mill's article and discussed the issue with him in the Winter of 1814 while composing his own seminal essay.[23] As for Torrens, he *was* explicit. His Preface states: "one or two of [my] arguments . . . have been suggested by . . . an excellent article which appeared in the *Eclectic Review*."[24] This must be a reference to Mill's July 1814 article, since at that time Mill wrote all the articles on economic topics for the *Eclectic Review*.[25]

Notwithstanding the above remarks, it is true that up to February 1815 neither James Mill nor David Ricardo had gone beyond the eighteenth-century rule as an analytical argument in favor of repealing the Corn Laws. This Torrens did in his *External Corn Trade* essay

22. Cf. ibid., pp. 5–13, and Ricardo's *Essay on Profits*, pp. 27–32 and 39, as reprinted in *The Works and Correspondence of David Ricardo*, ed. P. Sraffa (Cambridge, 1951–1973), IV. In Torrens' "pamphlet" of over 360 pages, *An Essay on the External Corn Trade* (London, 1815), see "Part the First," chap. 2, esp. pp. 24, 35, 39–42, and 48.

23. Leaving open the question of the nature and extent of Mill's influence on Ricardo, the July 1814 Corn Law article shows clearly that both Stigler, "Sraffa's Ricardo," *American Economic Review* 43 (1953): 588, and T. W. Hutchison, "James Mill and the Political Education of Ricardo," *Cambridge Journal* 3, no. 2 (Nov. 1953): 81, are wrong when they maintain that "on matters of economics . . . Mill was inactive . . . during most of the period" (Stigler). Hutchison quotes a part of a sentence from a letter of Mill to Ricardo dated 9 Nov. 1815 in which he said, "for a good many years I have not been able to think of [political economy]." This of course, is belied by the Corn Law article, and furthermore, during this period, when Mill and Ricardo were both in London and much involved in matters economic, it was not quite cricket of Hutchison to omit the remaining portion of Mill's sentence, ". . . except when I was excited by your instructive conversation or by your writings." Sraffa, *Works*, VI, 320–21. This just might have been most of Mill's time!

24. *Essay on the External Corn Trade*, p. xiv. Torrens said, "one or two of the arguments contained in the Second Part," but much of the contents of chap. 2 of the First Part fall into this statement of indebtedness.

25. Although J. J. Spengler, "The Physiocrats and Say's Law of Markets, II," *Journal of Political Economy* 53, 4 (Dec. 1945), long ago said the article was written by "an anonymous reviewer," the more recent research of A. L. Lazenby, *James Mill: The Formation of a Scottish Emigré Writer* (D. Phil. diss., University of Sussex Library, Sept. 1972), p. 255, definitely attributes it to Mill. Donald Winch in a letter to the author dated 24 Aug. 1972 concurs in this.

published, Sraffa tells us, on the same day as Ricardo's *Essay on Profits*.[26] But he did not announce the "new doctrine" on the first page nor, for that matter, in the opening chapters. Not until after some 260 pages when, for the third time, he gave an explanation of the gains from trade based on the eighteenth-century rule,[27] did he finally add the further point, which we have called "the essence," enabling him to convert the long-known and often-used "rule" into the full statement of comparative costs:

> If England should have accquired such a degree of skill in manufactures, that, with any given portion of her capital, she could prepare a quantity of cloth, for which the Polish cultivator would give a greater quantity of corn, than she [England] could, with the same portion of capital, raise from her own soil, then, tracts of her territory, though they should be equal, nay, *even though they should be superior*, to the lands in Poland, will be neglected; and a part of her supply of corn will be imported from that country.[28]

So Robbins surely is right when, after quoting the above, he concluded Torrens was the "first in the field." He immediately added, however: "But as pure analysis it still lacks the final emphasis upon the comparison of ratios which is the ultimate essence of this principle."[29] It was to be 1827 before Torrens added this final touch, but by then both Ricardo in 1817 and, at greater length, James Mill in 1818 and 1821 had published complete statements embellished with the comparison of the cost ratios.[30] Nevertheless, by 1815 Torrens was on record. What about Ricardo?

Is it true, as Marshall was to put it in 1923, that "Ricardo took the fragmentary truth of his predecessors [Torrens and Mill?] and made them into a coherent doctrine," or as Schumpeter was to say, Tor-

26. *Sraffa*, Works, IV, 5.

27. *External Corn Trade*, pp. 48, 221–22, and 263–64. The initial use of the "rule" on p. 48 seems to have escaped the notice of E. R. A. Seligman and J. H. Hollander, "Ricardo and Torrens," *Economic Journal* 2 (1911): 448–68, and more recently that of Chipman, pp. 480–81. Lord Robbins (p. 23) cites only the example on pp. 263–64.

28. Ibid., pp. 263–64; emphasis added.

29. Robbins, p. 23.

30. For Torrens see the 4th edition of his *External Corn Trade*, and for Ricardo, *Works*, I, 135–36. For James Mill, see his Feb. 1818 article "Colonies" in the *Encyclopaedia Britannica*, Supplement to the 4th, 5th, and 6th eds. (Edinburgh, 1824), pp. 257–73, and his *Elements of Political Economy* (London, 1821), pp. 84–88. That Mill first published his "Colonies" article in early 1818 and not in 1824, the date of the reprint of the Supplement usually given as the date of publication of the article itself, I owe to the unpublished, meticulous study of A. L. Lazenby, pp. 301 and 42.

rens only "baptized the theorem," while Ricardo "elaborated it and fought for it victoriously"?[31]

In his *Essay on Profits* Ricardo too was urging freer trade, but on a completely different basis, as part of what has been called his "Corn Model" of economic growth.[32] Chipman, in his careful assessment of this period, concludes that the *Essay* "contains scarcely any recognition of the principle of comparative advantage."[33]

The reason why this is so becomes apparent once we determine the role foreign trade was to play in Ricardo's thinking. The hitch in Ricardo's growth theory was the shortage of land, setting a "limit upon the expansion of agriculture, and therefore, by implication . . . upon that of economy generally."[34] Foreign trade, acting as a substitute for the shortage of land, would convert diminishing returns in agriculture into constant returns. No need for *comparative* advantage here, and, as we shall see, no need for it later in his *Principles*.[35]

Ricardo, in this early period, was still groping, but despite the unfortunate loss of his "papers on the profits on Capital,"[36] we can see the direction of his thinking from what he wrote to Trower in March 1814:

> . . . in short it is the profits of the farmer which regulate the profits of all other trades,—and as the profits of the farmer must necessarily decrease with every augmentation of Capital employed on the land . . . all other profits must diminish.[37]

And, again in December of 1814, he insisted to Malthus:

> Accumulation of capital has a tendency to lower profits. Why? Because every accumulation is attended with increased difficulty in obtaining food. . . . If there were no increased difficulty, profits would never fall, because there are no other limits to the profitable production of manufactures but the rise of wages.[38]

31. Marshall, *Money, Credit and Commerce* (London, 1923), p. 41 n.; Schumpeter, p. 607. Cf. also Viner, p. 442, where he said: "Torrens clearly preceded Ricardo in publishing . . . the doctrine . . . however . . . Ricardo is entitled to the credit for first giving due emphasis to the doctrine, for first placing it in an appropriate setting, and for obtaining general acceptance of it by economists."

32. See Sraffa, *Works*, I, xxxi–xxxii. Cf., however, S. Hollander's critique of Sraffa in his "Ricardo's Analysis of the Profit Rate, 1813–15," *Economica* NS, 40, 159 (Aug. 1973): 260–82.

33. Chipman, p. 481.

34. Sir John Hicks, *Capital and Growth* (New York, 1965), p. 44.

35. Stigler sensed this, as can be seen in his remark, "the principle of comparative cost . . . had no special relevance to the politically strategic commodity, food." *Essays in the History of Economics* (Chicago, 1965), p. 274.

36. Sraffa, *Works*, IV, 3.

37. Ibid., VI, 104.

38. Ibid., p. 162.

This represents the essentials of Ricardo's analytic vision: profits are inversely related to wages, and wages are a function of the cost of producing food and necessaries. Because of diminishing returns, economic expansion, entailing an increase of capital and population on a fixed supply of land, caused these expenses to increase, driving wage costs higher and thus lowering agricultural profits. Since "it is the profits of the farmer which regulate the profits of all other trades," the limitation of land stops economic expansion as profits continue to fall.

What to do? In the very next sentence in this letter to Malthus, Ricardo supplied the answer: "If with every accumulation of capital we could tack a piece of fresh fertile land to our Island, profits would never fall."[39]

From this notion it was but a short step to the recommendation that the import duties of the Corn Laws be reduced so that low-cost, presumably constant-cost food could be imported from abroad, thereby averting diminishing returns, rising wage costs, and falling profits. Two months later, in February 1815, immediately after having finished reading Malthus' new pamphlet on rent, Ricardo incorporated the differential theory of rent into his own embryonic theory of profits and in a matter of three weeks published his *Essay of Profits*.[40]

With his theory of rent, profits, and wages now in place, Ricardo there concluded: "Profits of stock fall only, because land equally well adapted to produce food cannot be procured . . . . If, therefore, in the progress of countries in wealth and population, *new portions of fertile land could be added to such countries*, with every increase of capital, profits would never fall."[41] Additional portions of fertile land being impossible to come by, Ricardo, as a second-best alternative, recommended foreign trade as a device to overcome the land shortage so that through importation, corn could continue to be supplied "at a cheap price." The *Essay* concluded: "If by foreign commerce . . . the commodities consumed by the labourer should become much cheaper, wages would fall; and this . . . would raise the profits of the farmer, and therefore, all other profits."[42]

This straightforward analysis leading to a recommendation of free trade in commodities "consumed by the labourer" does not require

39. Ibid.

40. That it was Malthus' theory of differential rent and *not* Ricardo's, notwithstanding the note written by J. S. Mill for McCulloch's edition of the *Wealth of Nations*, is made clear in Sraffa, I, 6–7, as well as Ricardo's explicit acknowledgment in his *Essay*: "In all that I have said concerning the origin and progress of rent, I have briefly repeated, and endeavoured to elucidate the principles which Mr. Malthus has so ably laid down." (p. 15 n.).

41. Sraffa, *Works*, IV, 18; emphasis added.

42. Ibid., p. 26 n.

nor involve comparative advantage. Indeed, it is an argument which quite comfortably can be couched in terms of differences in absolute costs, with England specializing in manufactures, in which she had an absolute advantage, and her trading partners specializing in food and raw materials, their line of absolute advantage. What is surprising perhaps, and what we intend to demonstrate, is that Ricardo's view of foreign trade essentially never went beyond this conception—the three-paragraph illustration of comparative advantage in the *Principles* notwithstanding!

That free trade was needed primarily as an offset to diminishing returns in agriculture, Ricardo, in the *Essay*, made quite clear by restricting this "wise policy" to a nation "already wealthy"—a society "advanced in wealth and population." "It is *only* when a country is comparatively wealthy, when all its fertile land is in a state of high cultivation, and [it] is obliged to have recourse to its inferior lands to obtain the food necessary for its population . . . that it can become profitable to import corn."[43]

Ricardo, in early 1815, was urging a very restricted form of free trade—freer trade in food and necessaries for advanced, wealthy countries experiencing sharply diminishing returns, as progress forced the cultivation of wheat up the "bleak hillsides" of Ricardo's England.[44] But was his position any different when, after two years of Mill's constant badgering and tutoring, Ricardo completed his *Principles*? To see that the answer essentially is no, let us examine Ricardo's chapter on foreign trade; a chapter which J. Hollander, long ago, assured us was "dominated" by the principle of comparative costs as Ricardo set it out "in classical detail."[45]

After a few introductory paragraphs, Ricardo reasserted his basic theorem and the strategic role foreign trade played in averting diminishing returns:

> It has been my endeavour to shew throughout this work, that the rate of profits can never be increased but by a fall in wages, and that there can be no permanent fall of wages but in consequence of a fall [in the price] of the necessaries on which wages are expended. If, therefore, by the extension of foreign trade . . . the food and necessaries of the labourer can be brought to market at a reduced price, profits will rise . . . *but* if the commodities

43. Ibid., p. 27; emphasis added.

44. Cf. A. Marshall, *Principles of Economics*, variorum edition (London, 1961), I, 673.

45. See supra n. 3.

obtained at a cheaper rate, by the extension of foreign commerce . . . be exclusively the commodities consumed by the rich, no alteration will take place in the rate of profits. The rate of wages would not be affected, although wine, velvets, silks, and other expensive commodities should fall [in price] 50 per cent, and consequently profits would continue unaltered.[46]

Ricardo, obviously, was advocating the repeal of the Corn Laws, not free trade in general. Freer trade was espoused only insofar as wage goods, needed to spur industrialization, could more readily be obtained. If England, the "richest country in Europe," could but obtain its food and raw produce "from abroad in exchange for manufactured goods" it would be difficult, Ricardo later maintained, "to say where the limit is at which you would cease to accumulate wealth."[47] This was so, providing, as he wrote in the *Principles*, the "commodites imported be of that description on which the wages of labour are expended."[48] Trade in such luxury goods as wine and velvets was irrelevant, since it left profits unaffected.

So, free or freer trade for Ricardo meant a policy appropriate to an advanced manufacturing nation in its relations with countries supplying it with food and raw materials. That Ricardo was still thinking of absolute cost differences based upon natural and human endowments peculiar to each country is clear from his description of the benefits to be derived from an international system where "each country naturally devotes its capital and labour to such employments as are most beneficial to each." Such a system "determines that wine shall be made in France and Portugal, that corn shall be grown in America and Poland, and that hardware and other goods shall be manufactured in England."[49]

Up to this point in the chapter on foreign trade Ricardo had, as it were, restored the original optimism of Adam Smith, notwithstanding the pessimism generated later by Malthus' introduction into the science of incessant population growth and diminishing returns in agriculture. And he had accomplished this on what was essentially the Smithian notion of absolute cost differences arising from the "peculiar powers bestowed by nature" upon the various regions of the globe. Had he stopped at this point, the doctrine of comparative advantage would have had to be passed along to subsequent genera-

46. Sraffa, *Works*, I, 132; emphasis added. Cf. also p. 118.
47. Ibid., IV, 179.
48. Ibid., I, 133.
49. Ibid., pp. 133–34.

tions by someone more interested in what is a piece of comparative statics, and not the rough dynamics, of Ricardo's classical trade-growth model.

But on the very next page, Ricardo, incongruously we think, inserted three paragraphs outlining the principle of comparative costs:

> England may be so circumstanced, that to produce the cloth may require the labour of 100 men for one year; and if she attempted to make the wine, it might require the labour of 120 men for the same time. England would therefore find it her interest to import wine, and to purchase it by the exportation of cloth.
>
> To produce the wine in Portugal, might require only the labour of 80 men for one year, and to produce the cloth in the same country, might require the labour of 90 men for the same time. It would therefore be advantageous for her to export wine in exchange for cloth. This exchange might even take place, notwithstanding that the commodity imported by Portugal could be produced there with less labour than in England. Though she could make the cloth with the labour of 90 men, she would import it from a country where it required the labour of 100 men to produce it, because it would be advantageous to her rather to employ her capital in the production of wine, for which she would obtain more cloth from England, than she could produce by diverting a portion of her capital from the cultivation of wines to the manufacture of cloth.
>
> Thus England would give the produce of the labour of 100 men, for the produce of the labour of 80. Such an exchange could not take place between the individuals of the same country. The labour of 100 Englishmen cannot be given for that of 80 Englishmen, but the produce of the labour of 100 Englishmen may be given for the produce of the labour of 80 Portuguese, 60 Russians, or 120 East Indians. The difference in this respect, between a single country and many, is easily accounted for, by considering the difficulty with which capital moves from one country to another, to seek a more profitable employment, and the activity with which it invariably passes from one province to another in the same country.[50]

Notice the brevity. The doctrine hardly "dominates the chapter," nor is it laid out in "classical detail," as J. Hollander would have it.[51] And from an analytic point of view, Chipman noted that the first

50. Ibid., pp. 135–36.
51. See supra n.3.

paragraph taken by itself is a "*non sequitur*, since nothing so far has been said about Portugal," and the second paragraph is "equally unsatisfactory, except when read in conjunction with the first."[52] Ricardo "saves himself," however, in the passages contained in the third paragraph, but at best his version of the doctrine is "carelessly worded." Indeed, it is Chipman's considered opinion that "Ricardo's . . . statement of the law is quite wanting, so much so as to cast some doubt as to whether he truly understood it."[53] How do we explain that Ricardo did not "truly understand" what Samuelson, in attributing the doctrine to him, called his "greatest tour de force"?[54]

Does it seem likely, in view of Ricardo's admitted analytic talents, that had he stumbled upon the new doctrine just prior to composing his *Principles*, as legend seems to have it, and having decided to develop and spell it out in detail by working it into a theoretic "organic whole," the end product of his labors—what he put into the chapter on foreign trade in his *opus magnum*—would have been wanting in the extreme? And, further, it is not the case that what he wrote in the *Principles* was not his *best* account of the doctrine. On the contrary, and this seems significant, it is the *only* account of it Ricardo ever wrote.[55]

In view of Ricardo's very brief and almost casual treatment of comparative costs, it seems doubtful whether his concern with the doctrine was serious. Certainly it did not fit in easily with the Ricardian theoretic structure of trade and development. Could it be that the idea for its inclusion in the chapter came from James Mill, being yet another, albeit more important, instance of his direct influence on Ricardo? The next section examines the likelihood of this possibility, and the concluding section explores how it was, in view of Ricardo's marginal relationship to the doctrine, that comparative advantage became a central plank in the core of classical political economy.

III

Is it so unlikely that Mill could have been responsible for the inclusion of the page-long account of the principle of comparative

52. Chipman, pp. 479–80.

53. Ibid., p. 480.

54. P. A. Samuelson, "Economists and the History of Ideas," *American Economic Review* 52 (1962): 9.

55. There is only one entry under "comparative costs and foreign trade" (to the three-paragraph example in the *Principles*), in the newly issued "General Index" of the Sraffa edition of Ricardo's *Works*. See, *Works*, XI, 19. Cf. also Carl Shoup, *Ricardo on Taxation* (New York, 1960), p. 169 n., where he stated: "it is in fact surprising how little use Ricardo makes of the doctrine of comparative costs in analyzing the effects of import and export duties and bounties."

costs in Ricardo's chapter on foreign trade? We know Ricardo already had used "Mill's words" in his *Economical and Secure Currency* pamphlet in dwelling upon the "*moral* part of the argument against the Bank," and Sraffa noted that the wording of the long final paragraph of that essay suggested "it was drafted or revised by Mill."[56] And Mill, it appears, may have played a similar role in the composition of the *Principles*.

Long ago, Simon Patten believed that "James Mill wrote or at least inspired the first three paragraphs of the Preface. They have his tone and style, and not Ricardo's."[57] And, of interest, Sraffa cites this approvingly,[58] before noting Mill's hand in the translations from J. B. Say and the "unmistakably characteristic" phrases of Mill in the three-page conclusion on the poor laws in the chapter "On Wages." That Mill's assistance to Ricardo often included the drafting and revising of various passages in the *Principles* we may take as established.

Furthermore, by referring to the Mill-Ricardo correspondence for the period between the *Essay on Profits* and the *Principles*, we can observe Mill's tactics as he went about attempting to "make of Ricardo the Quesnay of nineteenth century England."[59] This effort, by 1819, would culminate in Ricardo becoming, as Mill was to put it, the undisputed "head of Political Economy" in England.[60] In 1816 Mill, with this objective in mind, can be envisioned scanning the manuscript of the first seven chapters Ricardo had sent to him, making certain that all the original and sound doctrines of the emerging

56. Sraffa, *Works*, IV, 47 and 46 n. Mill's assistance here and, as noted above (see n.23) the similarity between Mill's (1814) and Ricardo's (1815) replies to Malthus' arguments in favor of the Corn Laws would seem to contradict Stigler's statement: "We must recall that Ricardo wrote the two pamphlets on the bullion controversy and the *Essay* (1815) without apparent intervention by Mill." See "Sraffa's Ricardo," p. 590.

57. "The Interpretation of Ricardo," *Quarterly Journal of Economics* 7 (1893): 338. For example, Ricardo opened his *Essay on Profits* with: "Mr. Malthus very correctly defines 'the rent of land,' " etc. The fourth paragraph of the Preface to the *Principles*, probably the first paragraph written by Ricardo begins: "In 1815, Mr. Malthus, in his 'Inquiry into the Nature and Progress of Rent,' " etc. In what probably are Mill's first three paragraphs we read of changes in income distribution during the "different stages of society," which Mill, as a student of the Scottish Historical School easily could have written, whereas it is doubtful if Ricardo would have begun in this fashion. There are other telltale traces of Mill's hand. For example the Mr. "Stuart" mentioned in the third paragraph. For an attempt to answer the minor, but intriguing, question of who "Stuart" was, see my "Will the Real Mr. Stuart Please Stand Up." *Annals Mid-South Academy of Economists* 3 (Nov. 1975).

58. Sraffa, *Works*, I, xxi–xxii.

59. E. Halévy, *The Growth of Philosophic Radicalism*, English ed. (1928, New York, 1965), p. 273.

60. Sraffa, *Works*, VIII, 10.

science were incorporated. Thus, in judging the seventh chapter on foreign trade, in addition to Ricardo's own trade-growth model making England the "workshop of the world," he would insist on having added the "four magic numbers that constitute the core of the doctrine of comparative advantage theory."[61] Otherwise the brief, but complete, statement of it by Torrens in February 1815 would analytically still have been superior. Mill would have been aware of this, in view of his long-time effort at spelling out (in 1808) and utilizing (in 1814) the gains-from-trade argument, and so most likely would have insisted on its being included in Ricardo's major work, which was soon to become the "Text Book" of the new school of political economy.[62]

This view imputes to Mill a considerable influence on Ricardo as he prepared the manuscript of the *Principles*. But the correspondence between the two, in 1815–16, gives support to this suggestion. For example, shortly after Ricardo published his *Essay on Profits* we find him writing to J. B. Say, telling him he understood from "Mr. Mill many able persons think . . . I have not been sufficiently diffuse. . . . Mr. Mill wishes me to write it over again more at large. I feel the undertaking exceeds my powers."[63] But Mill would not let Ricardo rest, being resolved he must write the primer for the new science "on which the progress of human happiness to a singular degree depends"; after which he must present its policy implications in Parliament![64]

Despite Mill's insistence that he persevere in composing the manuscript, Ricardo balked, and in October 1815 as the "affairs of the Bank are to be considered next session," he lost interest in the "great work," spending his time putting his "thoughts on paper respecting their [the Bank's] concerns."[65] Nevertheless Mill, in the role of persistent taskmaster, insisted that his plan—having Ricardo first write out a draft of his thoughts on each subject, and then send it to him for an analytical commentary, paragraph by paragraph, a procedure which Mill had earlier suggested Ricardo should use in composing his forthcoming book—now be the method Ricardo should use in preparing his currency essay. By the end of November Ricardo agreed he

61. P. A. Samuelson, "The Way of an Economist," reprinted in *The Collected Scientific Papers of Paul A. Samuelson*, ed. R. C. Merton (Cambridge, Mass., 1972), 3:678.

62. As it was described by Ricardo's stockbroker friend, Hutches Trower. See Sraffa *Works*, VII, 309.

63. Ibid., VI, 249.

64. Ibid., pp. 250–54 for Mill's letter of 23 Aug. 1815.

65. Ibid., p. 312.

would certainly practice "Mill's suggested procedure in any future performance."[66] In replying, Mill insisted "this is what you must do with the *opus magnum*."[67]

Even before the currency pamphlet was off the press, in late December, Mill again wrote Ricardo "in anticipation of the M.S. which I expect soon to receive as part of the great work."[68] But Ricardo, the following February, after having read his latest work on currency, lamented he had made "no progress in the very difficult art of composition," and a little later he told Malthus, "I have the greatest disinclination to commence work again. . . . I do not think I shall ever proceed further."[69]

Almost by way of apology Ricardo, in August 1816, explained to Mill that his "procrastination has not proceeded from not having you in my thoughts."[70] In an unusually sharp tone Mill retorted: "Why should a man that is not afraid to talk upon a subject before any body, be afraid to write . . . Another command of mine, is, that—as I know you have by this time, a pretty mass of papers, written first and last upon the subject—you put as much of them as possible . . . up in a parcel, and send them here . . . you should include those which you read to me in London."[71]

So we know that sometime between February and July (after which they both usually left London[72]), Ricardo had worked closely with Mill on an early draft-manuscript of the *Principles*. Presumably, Mill then had made suggestions requiring revisions, and so by August, hoping the revisions completed, Mill again wrote Ricardo to send him posthaste the "pretty mass of papers" for his further scrutiny and correction.

But it was to be October before Ricardo's parcel containing the first seven chapters of the manuscript was received by Mill. Ricardo's excuse was the "pretext that he must copy it out," but the real reason for the delay, Sraffa tells us, "was that he had been very much impeded by the question of price and value."[73] Ricardo asked Mill specifically to give him his "well considered opinion on this difficult point."[74] The papers were in such a "rough state" that Ricardo could only hope Mill would be able to make out what he had said, since he

66. Ibid., p. 324.
67. Ibid., p. 330.
68. Ibid., p. 338.
69. Ibid., VII, 19, 28.
70. Ibid., p. 53.
71. Ibid., p. 60.
72. Ibid., VI, p. xvi.
73. Ibid., I, p. xv.
74. Ibid., VII, 83.

was "desirous of ascertaining how far your opinion coincides with mine of the correctness of the views which I have taken. A hint or two of yours will enable me to make the next copy much more perfect."[75] Ricardo then waited "patiently for the further instructions which I am prepared to follow."[76]

Mill kept the manuscript for over three weeks, later making no apology to Ricardo, for he "wished to read it carefully, writing marginal contents for my own use, as I went along. . . . I now have got through the whole, and have the contents of each paragraph, regularly numbered, before me."[77] We can glean an idea of the impression Mill had of the work from the letter he sent to Ricardo after completing his study of the first seven chapters. Overall, Mill obviously was pleased, saying, "you have made out all your points."[78] He noted Ricardo's propositions on value, and his fundamental theorem on the inverse relationship between wages and profits, and was "very much struck" by Ricardo's paradoxical "curious effect."[79]

As to the analysis contained in the chapter on foreign trade, Mill said it was "original, and sound, and excellently demonstrated." He approved of Ricardo's opening—"no extension of foreign trade will immediately increase the amount of value in a country,"[80] and he continued almost triumphantly, "that it may be good for a country to import commodities from a country where the production of those same commodities costs more, than it would cost at home: that a change in manufacturing skill in one country, produces a new distribution of the precious metals, are new propositions of the highest importance, and which you fully prove."[81]

Mill was prescient in emphasizing the importance of Ricardo's now classic explanation of the way the "precious metals tend to be distributed so as to bring it about that trade takes place as if under conditions of barter." As Lord Robbins emphasized, Ricardo's contribution in this respect was "the basis of all further developments in

75. Ibid., p. 90.

76. Ibid. A perusal of this correspondence gives the definite impression that Ricardo held Mill's analytical powers in considerably higher regard than recent assessments of "Mill the economist." See, e.g., Sraffa, *Works*, I, p. xx; Stigler, "Sraffa's Ricardo," p. 588; D. Winch, p. 186; T. W. Hutchison, p. 81. Stigler does add, however: "Ricardo had a great respect for Mill, and so should we."

77. Ibid., p. 97.

78. Ibid., p. 98.

79. I.e., the *fall* in the exchange value (prices) of commodities produced by capital-intensive methods, due to a general *rise* in wage rates.

80. A statement the truth of which, Malthus would later claim, would stop commercial "intercourse between nations." See his *Principles of Political Economy* (London, 1820), p. 450 n. (390 n. in the 2d ed. of 1836).

81. Sraffa, *Works*, VII, 99.

this connection."[82] Indeed, if any theoretic analysis or concept which Ricardo developed on foreign trade can be said to have been integrated into an organic whole, or to have dominated the chapter, and if any could be looked upon as an intellectual *tour de force*, peculiarly Ricardo's own, then surely the last half of his chapter on foreign trade, containing the account of the relationship between prices, money incomes, and specie flows which underpins the *real* analysis of comparative costs, must be it. And that Mill had this lengthy analysis in mind when he credited Ricardo with "new propositions of the highest importance which you fully prove" is indicated by his laudatory reference to this part of Ricardo's chapter when shortly thereafter he wrote his article "Colonies"—an article written in late 1817 and published the following February. There Mill, after showing the benefits from trade on the basis of comparative advantage, using the "four magic numbers," said it "would take too many words" to describe how the "precious metals distribute themselves so as to leave the motives to this barter exactly the same as they would be," and referred the interested reader to Ricardo, "the first author of it."[83]

But it is significant that Mill also recognized the importance of including in the *Principles* a brief statement containing the "essence" of the doctrine of comparative advantage—of when it is profitable to import a commodity whose domestic labor costs are lower than those abroad. Apparently, in Mill's mind a complete account of the benefits stemming from trade required, at least, a brief mention of the comparative-cost ratios. Consequently, it appeared sandwiched in between Ricardo's interesting account of foreign trade averting growth-induced diminishing returns and his original and "excellently demonstrated" explanation of the movements in prices, incomes, and specie flows needed to obtain the mutual advantages of trade as if occurring under conditions of barter. According to Mill's lights, the chapter would then be fully consistent with the principles of the "new political economy."[84] And so Mill wrote approvingly to Ricardo, saying he had indeed "made great progress toward the production of a most admirable book."[85]

Of course, the above remarks are speculative. Perhaps the brief and poorly composed illustration of comparative advantage was all Ricardo's own doing. But if so, this makes it very difficult to account

82. *Robert Torrens*, p. 25.

83. "Colonies," p. 269.

84. S. G. Checkland, "The Propagation of Ricardian Economics in England," *Economica* n.s. 16, no. 61 (Feb. 1949): 40.

85. Sraffa, *Works*, VII, 99.

for two interesting and peculiar aspects of the particular example that appears in the *Principles*.

First, why the "odd geography" which had Portugal more efficient than England in producing both the cloth and the wine? Samuelson suggested[86] that Ricardo was trying to convince readers of mercantilist persuasion that England could gain from trade even if its labor costs all-round were higher than its trading partners'. And since Ricardo immediately added (in an attached footnote) that England possessed absolute advantages in machinery and skill and so could export manufactures at lower labor costs than obtained abroad, the argument for freer trade was just that much stronger. Perhaps so. On the other hand Ricardo could have gone along with Mill's suggestion to include the comparative-cost illustration, but chose this unrealistic example to intentionally belittle the importance of it. The reader, apparently, was not to take these three paragraphs too seriously.[87]

Further evidence that this may have been the case is the peculiar set of commodities Ricardo chose to illustrate the gains from trade under comparative advantage—cloth and *wine*! In all other places in the *Principles* when Ricardo discussed the gains from international trade, he did so in terms of being able to import "cheap" corn from America and Poland. And in his three major essays, written before and after the *Principles*, whenever Ricardo proposed freer trade, the reduced cost of corn was always emphasized.[88] In the comparative-advantage illustration, however, he selected not cloth and corn, "the commodities in common use" at the time,[89] but cloth and wine. In this famous example, therefore, on the basis of his "four magic numbers" England could export cloth and thereby import wine 20 percent cheaper than otherwise. But of what relevance was cheaper wine to Ricardo's trade-growth model, in which foreign trade was crucial because by averting diminishing returns it prevented wages from rising and profits from falling? None whatever, and he said so explicitly only three pages earlier when he declared that the rate of profits, the key variable deter-

86. *Collected Scientific Papers*, 3:679. For a similar view see Joan Robinson, *Reflections on the Theory of International Trade* (Manchester, 1974), p. 4.

87. Cf. Stigler's comment on this point, supra n. 35.

88. *Essay on Profits* (1815), *Funding System* (1820), *On Protection to Agriculture* (1822). See Sraffa, *Works*, IV, 22, 23, 179, 237.

89. J. Hollander, "Ricardo and Torrens," p. 461. It is strange that Seligman, in trying to establish Torrens' priority over Ricardo for the first statement of the theory of comparative advantage, should say that Ricardo employed the identical example utilized by Torrens, "namely, the corn trade between Poland and England." Ibid., p. 448. Equally strange is Hollander's reply, when he agrees with Seligman conceding only that this "can hardly be deemed evidence of plagiarism" (p. 461).

mining England's economic future, would not be affected even if the price of wine "should fall 50 per cent."[90] That the comparative-advantage example was irrelevant to the rest of the chapter can be seen from Ricardo limiting his recommendation for freer trade to the case where the commodities imported were "of that description on which the wages of labour are expended." And further, the recommendation was valid only for an economically advanced nation, such as the England of his day, where further economic expansion was threatened by the "scarcity, and consequently high value, of food and other raw produce."[91] Not the price of wine, but the problem of averting diminishing returns from the shortage of land was for Ricardo "a question of the utmost importance in political economy."[92]

That an analysis in terms of comparative costs had little to offer Ricardo in answering this important question he thus made clear in the one instance he had occasion to comment briefly on it. He did this by describing how it would result in a reduced cost of wine, a "nonbasic" good, changes in the price of which, like "velvets, silks, and other expensive commodities . . . consumed by the rich," in no way affected the level of profits.[93] So the famous example was, if nothing else, irrelevant to the general scheme of Ricardo's theories of trade, distribution, and economic growth. As Joan Robinson recently has stressed, there is "no need to argue against protection for a commodity [such as wine] which is useful and which cannot be produced at home . . . . What Ricardo was really concerned about was to abolish the corn laws so as to lower the real cost of *wage goods* and raise the rate of profit . . . . This was the desideratum of the whole argument."[94] The above remarks do seem to support the hypothesis that the idea for including the analysis in the *Principles* was not Ricardo's and therefore must have been James Mill's.

But Mill's idea or Ricardo's, the truth of the matter is that the statement of the law of comparative advantage as it appeared in Ricardo's *Principles* was very brief, poorly worded, the example unrealistic, and, more important, irrelevant and not part of Ricardo's general trade-growth model. Also Ricardo himself probably did not "fully understand" it. How then did the myth that it was Ricardo who "chanced upon," "developed," and "elaborated . . . and fought for" the doctrine of comparative advantage come about? To provide a

90. Sraffa, *Works*, I, 132.
91. Ibid. p. 133 and IV, 179.
92. Ibid., IV, 179.
93. Ibid., I, 132.
94. Joan Robinson, pp. 4 and 6; emphasis added.

possible answer to this intriguing question we examine the writings of James Mill and John Ramsey McCulloch—Ricardo's "two and only two genuine disciples," as Mill described himself and McCulloch just a week after Ricardo had passed away.[95]

IV

If it was not Ricardo who was responsible for incorporating the law of comparative advantage into mainstream political economy, it must have been one of his disciples—and so it turns out. But surprisingly (although not as surprisingly as it would have been prior to Denis O'Brien's definitive study on McCulloch, in which he shows that the notion McCulloch was "more Ricardian than Ricardo" is itself a complete myth[96]) it is not McCulloch, the popularizer of Ricardian doctrines and his most vociferous convert, but instead the lesser-known James Mill. In view of O'Brien's detailed study, we can be brief in commenting on McCulloch and comparative advantage.

O'Brien has made clear that "trade originated in McCulloch's view, as in Smith's, in a 'vent for surplus,' " and consequently, "McCulloch *never accepted the theory of comparative costs* as expounded by Torrens and Ricardo."[97] Apparently McCulloch, although accepting the Hume-Ricardo "theory of the distribution of the precious metals," nevertheless "clung firmly to *absolute* advantage as providing the basis for trade and indeed publicly rejected Ricardo's formulation."[98] In all of McCulloch's briefs for free trade in his many *Edinburgh Review* articles he relied upon absolute, not comparative, advantage. And in his influential review of Ricardo's *Principles*[99] there was barely any mention of Ricardo's chapter on foreign trade, still less of comparative advantage. Indeed, the subject of foreign trade, said McCulloch, formed a "subsidiary" part of the work! Explaining and defending Ricardo's value and distribution theories were the principal burdens of the review.

Furthermore, the absence of any mention of comparative advantage in McCulloch's review was of no concern to either Ricardo or Malthus, or, it appears, to anyone else. In another major review of Ricardo's *Principles* which appeared in the May 1817 issue of *Blackwood's Edinburgh Magazine*, the only reference to foreign trade was to Ricardo's 1815 *Essay on Profits*, in which he had shown the

95. Sraffa, *Works*, IX, 391.

96. D. P. O'Brien, *J. R. McCulloch: A Study in Classical Economics* (New York, 1970), p. 15.

97. Ibid., pp. 197, 191; emphasis added.

98. Ibid., pp. 192–93.

99. "Ricardo's Political Economy," *Edinburgh Review*, June, 1818, pp. 59–87.

"folly of restricting the corn trade."[100] Indeed, practically all the literature critical of Ricardo was confined to his labor theory of value and his "fundamental theorem of profits depending upon wages."[101] His views on foreign trade received scant attention, and the three-paragraph illustration of comparative advantage went completely unnoticed. Whether Ricardo intended it or not, his readers did not take the comparative-cost example seriously. In fact, it is amazing how very little comment it attracted.

Since McCulloch wrote so many of the articles on political economy in the *Edinburgh Review* during this long period of the Corn Law debate (78 of 133 articles between 1818 and 1837), it is not surprising that *no mention of the law of comparative advantage appeared in that prestigious journal*. What is surprising is how Fetter in his account of the "general idea of comparative costs" could write of the "scores" who read in the *Edinburgh* of Ricardo's "notion of a geographic division of labor based on different ratios of exchange."[102]

Indeed, other than Torrens' *Essay on the External Corn Trade*, and his verbatim quotation of Ricardo's comparative cost example in "Letter X" of *The Budget*, and two brief references to comparative advantage by Pennington and Longfield,[103] the only serious discus-

100. "Ricardo on the *Principles of Political Economy and Taxation*," p. 178.

101. M. Blaug, *Ricardian Economics* (New Haven, Conn., 1958), p. 209.

102. Fetter, pp. 75–76.

103. Pennington, *A Letter to Kirkman Finlay Esq.* (1840), reprinted in *Economic Writings of James Pennington* ed. R. S. Sayers (London, 1963), pp. 29–46; M. Longfield, *Three Lectures on Commerce* (Dublin, 1835) as reprinted (New York, 1971). Both Torrens and Pennington simply quoted the comparative advantage examples of Ricardo and James Mill. Longfield made up his own examples, but in one, in "Lecture III," p. 53, he had England twice as productive in one commodity and France twice as productive in the other—a special case of absolute advantage used by, among others, McCulloch, *Principles of Political Economy* (Edinburgh, 1825): 126, and William Ellis, "Exportation of Machinery," *Westminster Review*, 3 (April 1825): 388–89. Viner, *Studies*, p. 446 mistakenly cites these as examples of *comparative* advantage. O'Brien, pp. 192–93 has made it clear that McCulloch used only absolute advantage in explaining the gains from trade. Actually, in the example cited by both Viner and O'Brien, we find McCulloch in 1825 (*Principles*, p. 126) stating the example incorrectly by claiming that England could "manufacture 10,000 yards of cloth, *and* raise 1,000 quarters of wheat" (my emphasis), instead of 10,000 yards of cloth *or* 1,000 quarters of wheat, as he correctly wrote it in the 1843 edition of the *Principles* (p. 142). By the time of the 5th edition in 1864, the edition readily available to modern readers since it has been reprinted (New York 1965), McCulloch omits the numerical example, concluding that the gains from international trade arise from "enabling each country to obtain commodities which it could either not produce at all, or if at all, then only at a vast expense." (p. 94). This, as Viner long ago noted, does not go beyond the eighteenth-century rule, with all products being produced "where their real costs were lowest" (p. 440). Viner added that Adam Smith never advanced beyond this notion—neither did McCulloch! The abstract and mathematical account of

sions and use of the law of comparative costs, prior to the repeal of the Corn Laws in 1846, were by members of what might be called the Millian group. Besides Ricardo and James Mill, this would include William Ellis, George Grote, and James' son, John Stuart.

But first, what role did Torrens play in furthering the development and acceptance of the comparative-costs doctrine? He had, of course, contributed to the early development of the new doctrine, but in later years Torrens often merely repeated what Ricardo and Mill had already published. Lord Robbins in his commentary on Torrens' contribution to the development of classical international trade theory seems not always to have realized this.

For example, in giving priority to Torrens for the complete statement of the gains from trade on the basis of comparative advantage, Robbins admitted Torrens' 1815 analysis lacked the "final emphasis upon the comparison of ratios which is the ultimate essence of this principle."[104] This omission, Robbins assured us, "disappears completely in the extended version of the theory which is to be found in the fourth (1827) edition of the same essay. Here the exposition explicitly starts from the demonstration that if all cost differences are equal, then there is no incentive for trade." He then quoted: "No difference however great, in the cost of production universally in one country, and the cost of production universally in another can occasion an interchange of commodities between them . . . . On the contrary, a difference in the cost of production between two countries, affecting commodities in each, not universally but partially, gives immediate occasion to an interchange of commodities."[105] And Robbins concluded: "It is difficult to think of any passage in the whole literature of the subject before Taussig in which the essence of the doctrine is more forceably presented."[106]

With all deference to the scholarship of Lord Robbins, this statement does overlook the earlier expositions of the new doctrine in its "comparison of ratios" form in James Mill's *Encyclopaedia Britannica* article "Colonies" (1818) and in his 1821 *Elements*, as well as the unpublished and apparently completely unknown essay on comparative advantage of George Grote, a prominent member of the

---

comparative advantage contained in the anonymous *A Letter on the True Principles of Advantageous Exportation* (London, 1808) received no notice at the time of its publication and almost none since. Cf. *Economica*, no. 39 (Feb. 1933): 40–50. We owe this last reference to Barry J. Gordon.

104. Robbins, *Robert Torrens*, p. 23.

105. Ibid., pp. 23–24, quoting Torrens, *Essay on the External Corn Trade* (1827), as reprinted (Clifton, N.J., 1972), pp. 402–03.

106. Ibid., p. 24.

"Millian group."[107] Torrens probably was not aware of the Grote manuscript, but surely he knew of Mill's important publications.

Mill began with the obvious case of commodity interchange based on absolute advantage. He then considered, exactly as Torrens did later, the case in which Poland, though having the advantage over England in both cloth and corn, had the advantage in each commodity to the same degree. Under these conditions "Poland will have no motive to import either from England." But "if two countries can both of them produce two commodities, corn, for example, and cloth, but not both commodities with the same comparative facility, the two countries will find their advantage in confining themselves, each to one of the commodities, and bartering for the other."[108] As for describing the gains from trade on a comparative-cost basis, it would certainly appear that in 1827 Torrens simply was repeating the earlier analysis of James Mill. Torrens, a believer in the "great benefits of international division of labor" in his younger days, was later to break away from the orthodox trade policy of "unilateral lowering of obstacles," basing his own advocacy of freer trade upon reciprocity, colonization, and "the establishment of an imperial Zollverein."[109] There was no need for comparative costs in this approach. Viner sensed this when he concluded, "the doctrine was never an integral part of Torrens's thinking."[110]

If then we do not owe the early development of the doctrine of comparative advantage to Ricardo, Torrens, or McCulloch, then almost by elimination it must be due to the efforts of James Mill. And that this was indeed the case, the evidence presented above has attempted to demonstrate.

To summarize the case for Mill's crucial role in the early development of the doctrine, let us list his contributions. First, we had

107. The story of the discovery in 1930 of the Grote manuscript as part of what Sraffa refers to as the "Ricardo Papers," after having been lost for almost a century, is in Sraffa, *Works*, VI, p. xxxiv, where he also quotes from Grote's diary, which gives the exact date Grote sent the manuscript on foreign trade to Ricardo—Saturday, 27 March 1819. This was during a time when Grote often breakfasted with Ricardo and Mill and enjoyed, as he told his diary, "some most interesting and instructive discourse with them." See, Mrs. Grote, *The Personal Life of George Grote* (London, 1873), pp. 32–37. Grote's other manuscript papers on political economy, consisting of some 230 pages, are in the British Museum (Add. MSS. 29, 530). These essays, which form a fairly complete set of notes of a book on Political Economy, contain a further essay on foreign trade, somewhat shorter than the manuscript in the "Ricardo Papers." Both essays on trade are similar to Mill's 1821 presentation in the *Elements*. We are presently preparing the Grote manuscripts for publication.

108. *Elements of Political Economy* (London, 1821), pp. 84–85.

109. Robbins, *Robert Torrens*, pp. 255–56.

110. *Studies*, p. 443.

his *Commerce Defended*, published in 1808, in which he reintroduced into mainstream economic thought the "eighteenth-century rule," simultaneously with Torrens' *Economists Refuted*. Second, was Mill's use of "the rule" in his July 1814 *Eclectic Review* article to attack Malthus' views favoring the retention of the Corn Laws—an article which influenced both Ricardo's and Torrens' February 1815 contributions to the Corn Law debate, and yet an article the importance of which has gone virtually unnoticed since 1815.[111] Third, there was Mill's influence on Ricardo during the writing of the latter's *Principles*, culminating, we have maintained, in Ricardo inserting a brief mention of comparative costs into a chapter which would be complete without it in terms of Ricardo's dynamic model of trade and economic expansion. Finally, there was the publication of Mill's *Encyclopaedia Britannica* article "Colonies" in 1818 and the *Elements* in 1821, both of which contained the first extended discussions of the law based on a comparison of cost ratios—expositions which completely anticipated the 1827 "extended version" of the doctrine by Torrens. Mill's efforts were thus not inconsiderable, and surely outweigh those of Ricardo, Torrens, and McCulloch.

Ironically, Mill's last contribution to the development of the doctrine of comparative costs was to be of a negative kind. It will be recalled that Ricardo did not discuss the problem of how the gains from trade were distributed between the trading partners, assuming they were divided equally between them.[112] Mill, apparently intending to do the same, blundered into awarding the total gain to each of the trading bodies.[113] We now know the attempt to correct this blunder by J. S. Mill's group of "younger Utilitarians" led to J. S. Mill's eventual solution of the division of the gains on a basis of reciprocal demands. Published first in 1844 as Essay I in J. S. Mill's *Essays on Some Unsettled Questions in Political Economy*, it was reproduced almost verbatim in his "splendid edifice of theory" in the "great chapter" on international values in his 1848 *Principles*.[114]

So in a backhanded fashion James Mill also was instrumental in

111. Halévy, supra n. 59, p. 278, and Winch, *James Mill: Selected Economic Writings*, p. 199, refer very briefly to the *Eclectic Review* article without commenting on its importance.

112. Viner, pp. 444–45.

113. *Elements* (1821), pp. 85–87. Interestingly, Mill had *not* made this blunder three years earlier (February 1818) in his *Encyclopaedia Britannica* article on "Colonies" (p. 269), where he correctly, but arbitrarily, divided the gain according to the rule he later enunciated in the 3d edition of the *Elements* (1826), i.e., "the result of competition would be to divide the advantage equally" (p. 122).

114. F. Y. Edgeworth, *Papers Relating to Political Economy*, II (1925), pp. 22 and 9, as reprinted by B. Franklin (New York, n.d.).

the final elaboration of the comparative-cost doctrine by his son. And inasmuch as it was from John Stuart Mill, and not from McCulloch, Longfield, Torrens, or Pennington, "that later economists took over the doctrine,"[115] the modern theory of international trade is indebted to the "Millian group" in a way which up to now has not been recognized or appreciated.

When the ancestry of the doctrine becomes better known, the crucial role of James Mill in developing the concept, in recognizing its importance to orthodox theory and policy, and therefore in seeing that it was fully integrated into standard economics, will surely be better appreciated than it is at the present time.

115. Viner, p. 447. See also, C. F. Bastable, *Theory of International Trade* (Dublin, 1887), p. 22.

[12]

THE RECEPTION OF RICARDIAN ECONOMICS[1]

By SAMUEL HOLLANDER[2]

I AM concerned in this paper with two central themes of the modern literature on classical economics: The supposed early demise of 'Ricardianism', and the related notion of a 'dual' development of nineteenth-century theory entailing, on the one hand, typically Ricardian procedures and on the other embryonic neo-classical procedures. My investigation reveals an impressive resilience of the fundamental Ricardian theorem on distribution, and its derivation in terms of the standard measure of value, amongst the so-called 'dissenters' as well as those traditionally classified as members of Ricardo's school; and it casts doubt on the historical accuracy of a well-defined duality of analytical development. An introductory word is in order regarding the secondary interpretations, and the precise scope of the present article.

The key features of the Ricardian theory of distribution, as it is now generally expounded, are its conception of real wages as a social or institutional datum, and that of profits as a form of residual. (In the more complex models attributed to Ricardo—in contrast to the simple single-sector models—distribution is said to have logical priority over exchange values in the sense that the price structure is known only after the prior and independent determination of the wage and profit rates.[3]) Ricardian procedure is sharply contrasted with that of the neo-classical (general equilibrium) economists either to its advantage or to its disadvantage. Thus from one perspective it is said that scientific economics requires the treatment of productive organisation within a general-equilibrium context wherein the returns to the productive factors are envisaged as the competitively-determined prices of services; Ricardian procedure thus appears to constitute the *arbitrary* reduction of the number of variables in the system leaving one variable (profits) to be determined residually.[4] But from another perspective it is the general equilibrium approach that is defective; the function of the economist is seen to consist precisely in

[1] I am indebted to Walter Eltis and Lawrence Moss for constructive criticism.

[2] Professor of Economics, University of Toronto, Canada.

[3] M. Dobb, *Theories of Value and Distribution since Adam Smith* (Cambridge, 1973), 35; 'income-distribution (e.g. the profit–wage ratio) was a pre-condition of the formation of relative prices.' (Also ibid., pp. 169, 261, 266.) And see p. 116: *Given* the wage rate 'the conditions of production in the industry of industries producing necessities for wage-earners played a key role in determining the ratio of profits or surplus to wages, and hence (given necessary labour-expenditures in various lines of production) relative exchange values'.

[4] J. A. Schumpeter, *History of Economic Analysis* (New York, 1954), 568 f.; F. H. Knight, *On the History and Method of Economics* (Chicago, 1956), 37–88.

the specifications of 'causal' or one-way relations where appropriate,[1] and great merit is attached in particular to the specification of the real wage in cultural or institutional terms and the treatment of profits as residual.

Now the notion of a *dual development* of nineteenth-century analysis is shared by modern commentators from whichever of the diametrically opposed perspectives they may view the early literature. One stream of nineteenth-century doctrine—the non-Ricardian stream—is said to originate in Adam Smith's 'adding-up-components' theory whereby competition, through the operation of supply and demand, assures that market prices gravitate towards 'natural' prices defined as the sum of unit wage, profit and rent costs; in this scheme the factors themselves are paid at their natural rates determined, in their turn, by the general conditions of demand and supply in factor markets. The embryonic neo-classical approach of Smith is identified in the work of Turgot, J. B. Say, Lauderdale and Malthus, and in the later writings of the Longfield–Senior group of 'dissenters' from Ricardianism, J. S. Mill, Jevons and Marshall.[2]

The second or Ricardian line, runs the argument, was short lived although revitalised decades later by Marx. According to the reading of the record by Schumpeter the Ricardian system 'failed from the start to gain the assent of the majority of English economists', and by the early 1830's 'was no longer a living force'.[3] This position is much the same as that of Marx, although for Schumpeter Ricardo's poor fortune was a welcome sign while for Marx the (supposed) early demise was a symptom of the degeneration of economic science; 1830 was for Marx the dividing line between 'scientific' and 'apologetic' economics.[4]

It was in fact Schumpeter's belief that J. S. Mill must be excluded from

[1] L. L. Pasinetti, *Growth and Income Distribution* (Cambridge, 1974), 44.

[2] Schumpeter, *History of Economic Analysis*, 465, 474, 568, 673 n.; Dobb, *Theories of Value and Distribution*, 44 f., 112 f.

[3] *History of Economic Analysis*, 478. See also T. W. Hutchison, 'Some Questions About Ricardo', *Economica*, XIX, November 1952, 428–9: 'nearly all the great economists of the second quarter of the 19th century, especially those regarded as significant and original today, abandoned the main Ricardian questions and the main Ricardian answers (with the very doubtful exception of J. S. Mill). The obvious examples are Bailey, Longfield, the Oxford group of Whately, Senior and Lloyd and also Richard Jones . . . to take only the main English names.'

[4] Afterword to the second German edition (1873) of *Capital*, vol. 1 (Moscow, 1965), 14–15; Marx's rough draft notes (written 1857) *Grundrisse: Foundations of the Critique of Political Economy* (Pelican Marx Library, London, 1973), 883. (See also R. L. Meek, *Economics and Ideology and Other Essays* (London, 1967), 54.)

T. W. Hutchison has observed that by adopting this position Marx placed all his 'bourgeois' contemporaries 'beyond the pale of serious scientific discussion'—thus representing the development of economics 'as a process uniquely culminating in, and consummated by, the writings of Marx himself.' See (unpublished *University of Birmingham* working paper, 1974) 'The Cambridge version of the History of Economics', 14.

that group which constitutes Ricardo's 'school'.[1] This evaluation, is equally characteristic of Marxist interpreters. Marx himself speaks of Mill's work as an example of the 'eclectic, syncretistic compendia' which characterized the period after the collapse of 'scientific' political economy in 1830.[2] Along these lines Maurice Dobb has observed of Mill: 'when looking back on him from a distance one can see quite clearly that in major respects his own work was much nearer to Marshall than it was to Ricardo; and that so far as his theory of value was concerned, on the contrary to continuing and improving on Ricardo, in essentials he took his stand on the position of Smith where Ricardo had been opposing him.'[3]

In his recent volume on J. R. McCulloch, Professor O'Brien has added his authority to the view that the central Ricardian model suffered a serious decline soon after Ricardo's death. For it is the general theme of this work that while McCulloch 'did much to popularize economics . . . it was not Ricardo's economics that he was popularizing . . .'[4] McCulloch, runs the argument, must be considered as full square in the Smithian tradition. A similar revisionist interpretation has recently been put forward regarding De Quincey.[5]

We shall be concerned with the two issues raised in the preceding account: the supposed early demise of Ricardianism and the related notion of a dual development in nineteenth-century economics. Needless to say it is impossible to approach these matters without a rather precise specification of the Ricardian paradigm, extending beyond the general questions of doctrinal position and archetypal method. Investigation not only of the *content* but also the *origins* of Ricardo's *Principles*—particularly the process whereby Ricardo, in Spring 1813, commenced to discern what he considered to be a number of logical errors in the Smithian position—suggests that what is *characteristically 'Ricardian'* is the use of a special theory of value involving an absolute standard in the derivation of the inverse relationship between wages and profits—the famous fundamental theorem on distribution.[6]

[1] 'From Marshall's *Principles*, Ricardianism can be removed without being missed at all. From Mill's *Principles* it could be dropped without being missed very greatly.' *History of Economic Analysis*, 529.

[2] *Grundrisse*, 883.

[3] But see the position of Pedro Schwartz, *The New Political Economy of John Stuart Mill* (London, 1972), 16–17 which places Mill more firmly in the Ricardian tradition at least as far as concerns analysis: 'The sway of Ricardian doctrine over British economic thought was in some way restored with the publication of John Stuart Mill's *Principles* in 1848. From an analytical point of view, Mill's treatise followed the pattern of the master, while the doctrinal changes that Mill introduced made it easier to accept the Ricardian heritage.'

[4] *J. R. McCulloch: A Study in Classical Economics* (London, 1970), 402–3. The treatment of the invariable measure of value, which is said to be 'central to Ricardo's system,' we are told 'never interested McCulloch at all' (ibid., 146).

[5] P. W. Groenewegen, *Economic Journal*, LXXXIII, March 1973, 193.

[6] Insofar as concerns the theory of value the essential point to keep in mind is its function

In the Ricardian structure, an increase in the proportionate share of wages appears as an increase in wages, expressed in terms of the measure of value—a commodity produced with constant labour input and thus constituting a labour-embodied unit. An increase in *per capita* 'gold' wages implies a rise in the labourer's share in *per capita* output which is necessarily of constant 'value'. The entire Ricardian scheme is thus designed to relate the rate of return on capital to the 'value' of *per capita* wages (Ricardian 'real' wages)—which in effect amounts simply to the proportion of the work-day devoted to the production of wages—and variations in the rate of return to (inverse) variations in the 'real' wage rate.

It follows from the basic analysis that—assuming unchanged input coefficients in the production of the monetary metal, or ruling out nominal changes in money values—wage-rate increases are noninflationary and at most generate an alteration in relative prices within limited bounds; capitalists are unable to pass on increased wage costs in the form of generally higher prices. This fundamental conception, it must be emphasized, was initially formulated as a direct challenge to received doctrine based upon Adam Smith's analysis whereby wage-rate increases *are* passed on by capitalists in the form of higher prices in manufacturing industries and lower rents in agriculture. Here lies the essence of the Ricardian contribution. The significance—indeed the objective—of Ricardo's work cannot be accurately evaluated unless placed in this historical context.[1]

It is my primary conclusion that the Ricardian theorem on distribution —the inverse wage–profit relationship—left a firm and positive impression on the work of a number of authors normally regarded as 'dissenters' *par excellence*—including Malthus, Bailey, Torrens and Longfield—and this despite their frequent formal criticisms of Ricardo and his followers and their declared objective to break new ground or at least to refute the merit

as a necessary preliminary for the analysis of distribution, particularly the analysis of profit-rate determination and the effect of wage-rate changes upon the rate of profit. Ricardo was preoccupied with the problem of defining the minimum conditions required of a medium of exchange—at least in principle—to assure approximate constancy in the value of the output to be shared between the recipients of income net of rent in the face of changes in distribution. Cf. editor's introduction, to the *Principles of Political Economy* in *Work and Correspondence of David Ricardo* (Cambridge, 1951), I, xlviii. For accounts of the Ricardian procedure see also G. J. Stigler, *Essays in the History of Economics* (Chicago, 1965), 156–97; and Mark Blaug, *Ricardian Economics* (New Haven, 1958), esp. pp. 23–5.

[1] The weakness of the Smithian position came to the fore partly in consequence of preoccupation with the great monetary issues during the early years of the century. And it should be remarked that, despite the attention paid to the problem of constructing a suitable measure of value, the conclusion that wage-rate increases are non-inflationary was maintained quite generally and applied to the 'real world' where the conditions required of the theoretical measure are not fulfilled.

of Ricardo's divergencies from the *Wealth of Nations*.[1] Although I shall only briefly consider the status of McCulloch, J. S. Mill and Thomas De Quincey, it is my belief that to play down their adherence to Ricardianism and place them in Smith's camp as far as concerns the theory of value and distribution is unjustified.[2]

A demonstration of the resilience in the works of the dissenters of the Ricardian distribution theorem raises some serious questions regarding the legitimacy of the notion of a dual development in the course of nineteenth-century economic analysis. These doubts are reinforced by two further circumstances. My investigation reveals a very considerable degree of disagreement *within* the group of dissenters. The fact is that there occurred no concerted attack on Ricardo. Of particular significance for an accurate perspective is the weight of objection directed by various 'dissenting' writers against Bailey, frequently regarded as the head of the line of Ricardo critics. Secondly, it becomes clear that in many cases the criticisms constitute a misunderstanding of Ricardo's position, while in others the contributions of the dissenters would not have been considered objectionable by Ricardo. I have in mind particularly in this latter category the emphasis upon the relativity dimension of exchange value (Bailey); the scarcity theory of rent (Thompson, Senior); the insistence that the cost determination of price operates by way of demand–supply variation (Malthus); the principle of diminishing marginal utility (Lloyd); and the abstinence approach towards interest (Longfield, Scrope, Read, Senior). But of outstanding significance is the application of market demand–supply analysis to long-run wage determination (Malthus, Longfield, Torrens, Read, Scrope, Senior). Ricardo I believe stood squarely in the *Smithian* tradition regarding wage theory. The notion of a subsistence wage as central feature of his system, the key theme in modern representations of Ricardian economics, has been seriously exaggerated.[3]

[1] Professor Jacob Viner observed many years ago that any investigation of the extent and nature of the dissension requires that attention be paid to the replies of the Ricardians to their critics, for 'some of the criticisms directed against the Ricardian analysis were either based on misinterpretations of it or would have been accepted by the Ricardians . . .' (*The Long View and The Short*, Glencoe, 1958, 419–20.)

[2] In his *Ricardian Economics* Mark Blaug has also argued the case for the resilience of 'Ricardian' economics using the term, however, in this context in a sense different from ours. Blaug has in mind 'the proposition that the yield of wheat per acre of land governs the general return on invested capital as well as the secular changes in the distributive shares' (ibid., 3). See also ibid., 61: 'The rate of capital formation was still held to be governed by returns in agriculture, and the core of the Ricardian system, the law of diminishing returns, continued to dominate the body of economic thought.'

[3] Ricardo's emphasis upon the role of demand–supply analysis in both product and factor markets is substantiated more fully in my forthcoming *Economics of David Ricardo*. See also John Hicks and S. Hollander, 'Mr. Ricardo and the Moderns', *Quarterly Journal of Economics* (forthcoming 1977).

I. The dissenting critics

I shall give some indication in this section of the extent of adherence to the inverse profit–wage relationship amongst several of the main writers usually classified as dissenters. As already indicated, the acceptance of Ricardo's position implies—and this implication was usually well understood by nineteenth-century economists—the rejection of key features of Smithian analysis.

I wish first to emphasize that Malthus himself, who is commonly taken for granted to be a severe critic of the Ricardian theory in fact accepted much of its substance. It is a serious error to neglect the extent of his accord with the inverse theorem. Thus in his famous *Quarterly Review* article for 1824 treating McCulloch's *Encyclopaedia Britannica* contribution of the previous year Malthus wrote: 'Of all the truths which Mr. Ricardo has established, one of the most useful and important is, that profits are determined by the proportion of the whole produce which goes to labour. It is, indeed, a direct corollary from the proposition, that the value of commodities is resolvable into wages and profits; but its simplicity and apparent obviousness do not detract from its utility.'[1] Similarly: 'We fully agree with the author of the present treatise, that when it is said that profits depend on wages, they must not be understood to depend on wages estimated in money, in corn, or in any other commodity, but on proportional wages, that is, on the share of the commodities produced by the labourer, or of their value, which is given to the labourer.'[2] His only substantive criticism is of the unsatisfactory manner in which the divison is actually determined by Ricardo. The inverse profit–wage relationship, he insisted, is 'only one important step in the theory of profits, which of course cannot be complete till we have ascertained the cause, which under all circumstances, regulates this proportion of the whole produce which goes to labour immediately and accumulated'.[3] Malthus also believed that his own doctrine relating to the role of aggregate demand stood up empirically better than the Ricardian emphasis upon the difficulty of production on the land in accounting for the (supposed) historical decline in the profit rate, but at the same time insisted that the evidence accorded 'most perfectly with the more general proposition of Mr. Ricardo respecting profits, namely that they are determined by the proportion of the whole produce which goes to labour'.[4]

That Malthus accepted the substance of Ricardo's position is also confirmed by a note of fundamental import attached to his *Measure of*

[1] 'Political Economy', *The Quarterly Review*, January 1824, Vol. XXX, No. 60, in Bernard Semmel, ed., *Occasional Papers of T. R. Malthus* (New York, 1963), 189.

[2] Ibid., 199. [3] Ibid., 189.

[4] Ibid., 198. See also *Principles of Political Economy*, 2nd (posthumous) edn. (1836; New York, 1964), 260–1.

Value (1823). Malthus had observed in the text that 'it may be laid down . . . as a general proposition, liable to no exception, that when the value of any produce can be resolved into labour and profits, then as the *proportion* of such produce which goes to labour increases, the proportion which goes to profits must decrease in the same degree, and as the *proportion* which goes to labour decreases, the proportion which goes to profits must increase in the same degree'.[1] To this he added: 'This proposition is essentially the same as that which is very clearly and ably expressed by Mr. Ricardo in his chapter On Profits in the following terms: "in all countries and at all times profits depend on the quantity of labour requisite to provide necessaries for the labourers on that land, or with that capital which yields no rent;" a proposition which though incomplete in reference to the ultimate causes of the variations of profits, contains a most important truth. From this truth the legitimate deduction appears to me to be, the constant value of labour; but Mr. Ricardo has formed his system on a deduction exactly opposite to it. He has, however, in my opinion, amply compensated for the errors into which he may have fallen, by furnishing us, at the same time, not only with the means of their refutation, but the means of improving the science of Political Economy.'

The criticisms alluded to briefly in the foregoing passage relate to Ricardo's (supposed) failure to deal satisfactorily with real (basket) wage-rate determination and to the tortuous issue of the *measure of value*. Communications virtually broke down between the correspondents on the latter issue. But from our present perspective one outstanding fact remains—namely, Malthus's insistence that by the relationship which he envisaged between the constancy of the value of a given command over labour and the proportionate shares, he was attempting to get across precisely the same conception of things as Ricardo himself.

* * *

Schumpeter gave the central place to Samuel Bailey amongst those who reacted against orthodoxy: 'Bailey,' he maintained 'attacked the Ricardo–[James] Mill–McCulloch analysis on a broad front and with complete success. His *Dissertation*, which said, as far as fundamentals are concerned, practically all that can be said, must rank among the masterpieces of criticism in our field, and it should suffice to secure to its author a place in or near the front rank in the history of scientific economics.'[2] More specifically, he showed convincingly 'the defects of the concept of real value and of the Ricardian theory of profit'.[3]

[1] *The Measure of Value Stated and Illustrated* (1823; New York, 1957), 28-9. See also *Principles of Political Economy*, 2nd edn., 88.

[2] *History of Economic Analysis*, 486.

[3] Ibid., 599.

Let us consider this evaluation. While Bailey maintained that the notion of an invariable standard 'amidst universal fluctuations' involves an inherent contradiction, it is quite clear that this follows from his own definition of value as price, or *exchange value.* His case turns out to be a purely terminological one:

> The specific error of Mr. Ricardo on the subject of invariable value consists . . . in supposing, that if the causes of value affecting one commodity remained the same, the value of that commodity could not vary, overlooking the circumstance, that value denotes a relation between two objects, which must necessarily alter with an alteration in the causes affecting either of them. He incessantly identifies constancy in the quantity of producing labour with constancy of value. Hence he maintains, that if we could find any commodity invariable in the circumstances of its production, it would be in the first place invariable in value; and, 2ndly, it would indicate, or would enable us to ascertain, the variations in value of other commodities.[1]

In point of fact a commodity produced with a constant labour input, Bailey observed, 'would enable us to ascertain, not the fluctuations in value between two or more commodities (for these are facts to be gathered from appropriate evidence), but the fluctuations in the quantity of labour which produced them'.[2] Alternatively expressed, we would be enabled to establish in which commodity 'those [observed] fluctuations had originated'.[3] *Now this renders precisely the purpose of Ricardo's measure, and the critique amounts to no more than an unwillingness to use the term 'value' in the Ricardian fashion.* Bailey himself seems to concede as much:

> Many of the strictures, which have been made on Mr. Ricardo's writings . . . would be in some degree obviated if two things were conceded, namely, if we assumed that he was constantly speaking of real value, and if we were to grant him the absurdity which we have shown this expression to imply; or, in other words, if we were to consider it as importing [*sic*] cost of production, without relation to the power of commanding in exchange.[4]

The terminological penchant of the book is also evident from Bailey's comments upon Ricardo's identification of a change in the 'value' of wages—*wages in terms of the invariable measure*—with a change in the proportion of wages in aggregate output, that is the representation of labour as rising or falling in value 'only when a larger or smaller proportion of the commodity produced goes to the labourer'. For Bailey simply

[1] *A Critical Dissertation on the Nature, Measure and Causes of Value* (London, 1825), 121.

[2] Ibid., 124.

[3] Ibid., 121.

[4] Ibid., 253. However, Bailey continues rather less generously: 'But then, although some inconsistencies would by this means be obviated or explained away, we should obtain in their place a number of other sequally irreconcilable, and also a series of unmeaning and identical propositions. For instance, the proposition that a million of men always produced the same value, but not the same riches, would be reduced to this, that what a million of men produced always cost the labour of a million men: $a = a$. The truth appears to be, that the idea of real value was seldom distinctly present to his mind, although there was almost constantly an obscure reference to it.'

altered the sense of the term 'value' to refer to exchange-value; from which it followed that a change in the proportion of wages in total output was only one among several possible causes of variation in the 'value of labour', that is Bailey's term for *commodity wages*.[1] On this terminological usage, when allowance is made for changes in aggregate output generated by increased labour productivity, and neglecting rent, wages and profits may both vary in the same direction.[2] As Bailey pointed out towards the close of his work his contention was simply 'that in cases of improved productive power, the product might be so divided, that the rate of profits [identified with the profit share in output] should be increased while the value of labour [the commodity wage] was enhanced'.[3]

This conclusion, however, is totally in accord with Ricardian analysis. Bailey's criticisms of the inverse profit–wage relation were evidently not directed at Ricardo's position *as Ricardo understood it*. When in fact Bailey actually considered this matter he conceded frankly enough the legitimacy of Ricardo's case:

> Mr. Ricardo's inference is a legitimate deduction from his premises, if we concede certain postulates. Grant him the kind of value called *real*, which has no relation to the quantity of commodities commanded, but solely to the quantity of producing labour, and it inevitably follows, that there could be no alteration in the *real* value of labour, but from an alteration in the proportion of the product which went to the labourer. Neither, if money were always produced by a uniform quantity of labour, could there be any alteration in the money-value of labour.[4]

Indeed, Bailey's recognition that the profit rate falls when commodity wages rise (given labour productivity) runs along strictly Ricardian lines, involving as it does the proposition, which conflicts with that of Adam Smith, that capitalists cannot pass on the higher wage costs to consumers in the form of higher prices, since the prices, that is the exchange values, of *all* commodities cannot logically be raised simultaneously:

> If labour rises while [its] productive powers remain the same, profits will inevitably fall. This may be easily proved from the principles already advanced; for if labour rises in value, whoever purchases labour must give a greater quantity of other things for it, and as the capitalist purchases labour, he must pay more for it. It will be said, perhaps, that he may raise the value of his goods, that is, he may require a greater quantity of other commodities than before, in exchange for his own. But the capitalist who produces these other commodities is in the same predicament, and they cannot both raise their goods . . . it is a contradiction to maintain, that a universal rise in the value of labour can increase the value of commodities.[5]

[1] Ibid., 46.

[2] It should be carefully noted that Bailey retains the Ricardian usage of profits as a share in aggregate output while at the same time he utilizes the conception of commodity wages —concluding, not surprisingly, that in the case of constant output an increase in the commodity wages paid to a given work force *must* involve a decline in the profit share (Bailey's 'rate of profit'); while in the case of an increasing output due to technical progress an increase in the commodity wages *need not* have this effect (ibid., 64 f.).

[3] Ibid., 241.

[4] Ibid., 58 n.

[5] Ibid., 64–7.

Bailey's acceptance of this basic Ricardian objection to Smith cannot be ignored.

It follows from all this that Schumpeter's high praise for Bailey on the grounds that he showed convincingly the 'defects of the concept of real value and of the Ricardian theory of profit' is scarcely justified. Bailey failed on the whole to analyse Ricardo's objectives in devising his measure, concentrating as he did upon terminology, but he nonetheless accepted the accuracy of Ricardo's position regarding the profit–wage relationship on Ricardo's use of terms and rejected Smith's view of the relation between wages, profits and prices. The entire Bailey episode has been overdone as an indication of revolt against Ricardo.

It is also pertinent that Bailey himself presented no alternative model[1] although he did show a preference for far greater 'generality' than was apparent among the Ricardians, and in his conclusion he emphasized the oversimplification characteristic of Ricardian method. Even in this regard he made allowances, conceding that Ricardo himself had recognized increasing costs and therefore elements of 'scarcity' or of 'partial monopoly' —utilizing the early nineteenth-century term for less than infinitely elastic supply—at least in the case af corn and gold. He took issue with Ricardo's formal position that 'commodities can be classified according to the "source" of their exchangeable value'—namely 'scarcity' and the quantity of labour embodied—and attention focused upon the latter since this group is quantitatively the most significant; and in dealing with price formation he talked of the role of 'considerations acting on the human mind.'[2] Yet at the same time the 'main considerations' in this context are said by Bailey himself to be production costs.[3]

In fact, insofar as concerns matters involving the so-called 'causes of value'—that is the theory of price—*there is no divergence of substance between Ricardo and Bailey.* Bailey generalized the conception of differential rent to apply to labour but also adopted the position that rent is not a 'cause' of value,[4] while his insistence that rent may be generated even in the absence of differential land qualities, by dint of land scarcity, was conceded also by Ricardo. Bailey forcefully rejected statements of the labour theory of James Mill, De Quincey and McCulloch,[5] but was less harsh with respect to Ricardo himself who, he recognized, qualified the theory.[6]

* * *

[1] He asserted (ibid., xii) that 'the science cannot yet be exhibited in a regular and perfect structure'.

[2] Ibid., 227–8.

[3] Ibid., 199.

[4] Ibid., 197.

[5] Ibid., 207–8.

[6] Ibid., 213–14. His concession was, however, made rather grudgingly. In this context, Bailey praised De Quincey's analysis of the severe problems relating to qualitative differences in labour and the use of the wage scale to obtain units of standard labour (214 f.). Bailey recognized Ricardo's concession that a variation in wages will influence relative

C. F. Cotterill's famous comment that there are 'some Ricardians still remaining' led Professor Schumpeter to conclude that 'the decay of the Ricardian school must have became patent' shortly after Bailey's contribution.[1] It is not, however, difficult to show that it is unjustified to draw such broad implications from what in any event is a most ambiguous statement, for the fact is that Cotterill also refers to variations of exchange value proportionate to alterations in relative labour input as a proposition which 'most economists maintain'—in contrast to Smith's position relating increases in prices 'to the rise in wages'.[2]

Space limitation precludes a full demonstration of the fact that much of Cotterill's criticism of Ricardo was misplaced. We wish, however, to emphasize Cotterill's recognition of the *need for* an 'invariable standard', and his belief in *the possibility of its construction.* Amongst the most important features of his pamphlet Cotterill himself counted the statement of 'the conditions necessary to a standard of value' and the refutation of 'the erroneous doctrine that the supposition of such a standard involves contradictory conditions'.[3] And it was Bailey (as well as Torrens) whom he largely had in mind by this latter statement.[4] His main objection as far as concerned Ricardo himself was to the specific character of Ricardian 'money' as an invariable standard—in his estimate it was impossible to talk meaningfully of exchange value in terms of such a medium—but not to the principle of the matter. In fact Cotterill himself provided illustrations of the 'correct' procedure designed to guarantee that aggregate money value remains unchanged in the face of an alteration in distribution.[5] And he candidly recognised Ricardo's contribution to the proposed solution: 'The conditions, however, essential to an invariable standard, do appear to me so very obvious, especially upon Mr. Ricardo's own principles in opposition to Adam Smith.'[6]

* * *

H. Merivale's single adverse comment on Ricardian rent theory—'a lapsis offensionis, startling and offending many'—cannot safely be regarded as indicative of a generally hostile position as is sometimes maintained.[7] The review in question considered in its entirety is not hostile. On the contrary, Merivale supported Ricardian method which he talked of as the

prices in the event of differing factor proportions but asked: 'Why persist in calling quantity of labour the sole determining principle of value?' (ibid., 217).

[1] *History of Economic Analysis*, 478.

[2] *An Examination of the Doctrines of Value* (London, 1831), 107.

[3] Ibid., v.

[4] See ibid., 99. He might have included Say, in principle, who thought of the invariable standard as a 'chimera'.

[5] Ibid., 76. [6] Ibid., 75 n.

[7] Barry Gordon, 'Criticism of Ricardian Views on Value and Distribution in the British Periodicals, 1820–1850', *History of Political Economy*, I, Fall 1969, 378.

method of the 'modern English school',[1] and was very favourably disposed to McCulloch's edition of the *Wealth of Nations* since it indicated 'the principal notions of an erroneous character which pervades the whole of the great work of Dr. Smith'. By contrast, 'Mr. Ricardo investigated the fundamental truths of the science with singular profoundness; his theories, while they have led many followers astray, have nevertheless penetrated thoroughly into all subsequent lucubrations on the subject and he may be regarded, more justly than any other, as the real founder of the school which at present exists in England.'[2]

* * *

We turn now to Longfield. Mountifort Longfield probably represents for historians of economic thought the most original of that group of writers known variously as 'the Dissenters', 'the Men who Wrote above Their Time', and 'Voices in the Wilderness'. Professor Seligman referred to him in his celebrated paper 'On Some Neglected British Economists' as 'in some respects the most remarkable of all'; and Professor Schumpeter wrote of Longfield that 'he overhauled the whole of economic theory and produced a system that would have stood up well in 1890'. More recently Professor Blaug has maintained that 'of all the treatises on political economy which appeared in the 1830's the most original was Longfield's *Lectures*', and Professor Bowley awards Longfield 'the title of the first of the Victorian economists, or perhaps the first of the neo-classics'.[3] We may also refer to the following evaluation by Professor Black in his Introduction to the recently published *Economic Writings of Mountifort Longfield*: 'It would certainly be wrong to represent Longfield's analysis as a complete anticipation of neo-classical pricing and distribution theory. Yet whatever limitations it may have, whatever classical elements may be left, incompletely integrated, within it, the fact remains that it is a fundamentally and systematically different analysis from the Ricardian one . . . Only Longfield, amongst those who wrote in English at this period, offered his readers a theory of value which was complete—and completely original.'[4]

In our view the flavour of much of the discussion of the *Lectures* is unmistakably 'Ricardian'. We have in mind the emphasis upon long-run cost price, the choice of a labour measure of value, the rationale given

[1] 'Senior on Political Economy', *Edinburgh Review*, No. 133, October 1837, 77, 79–80.

[2] *Edinburgh Review*, No. 142, January 1840, 429.

[3] E. R. A. Seligman, 'On Some Neglected British Economists, II', *Economic Journal*, XIII, December 1903, 525; J. A. Schumpeter, *History of Economic Analysis*, 465; M. Blaug, *Ricardian Economics*, 159; M. Bowley, *Studies in the History of Economic Theory Before 1870* (London, 1973), 217.

[4] R. D. C. Black, 'Introduction', *The Economic Writings of Mountifort Longfield* (New York, 1971), 15–16.

for such choice in terms of the overwhelming role played in price determination by alterations in labour input, and the exclusion of alterations in relative wages or relative profits as a source of disturbance. It has been observed of some of these Ricardian features that they appear in the early lectures given at Dublin in the Trinity term of 1833, while all Longfield's really 'original contributions' occur in the sixth and later lectures given in the Michaelmas term. His conception of things, runs this argument, altered as the year progressed and only by late 1833 was he in a position to formulate the subjective theory of value and the productivity theory of distribution. It was during the period between terms in mid-1833 that Longfield 'seems to have decided to break away from classical distribution theory and from Lecture VI on his analysis proceeds with impressive originality'.[1]

If, however, we consider this hypothesis closely it will be found wanting in several respects and it is our view that, on the whole, Longfield retained a Ricardian structure throughout. At the very commencement of Lecture VI—where the fullest treatment of demand is undertaken—the main Ricardo-like propositions regarding value are *re-stated*. Thus the labour measure is again justified as a suitable (though not unique) measure: 'as most of the commodities in which the wealth of the country consists are produced by labour, political-economists make use of it as a measure of value.'[2] And it is in Lecture VIII where we read that 'all the commodities which men consume, and which can be made the subject of exchanges, owe their existence and their value to labour. The exceptions to this are very trifling, and are of such a nature that they do not vitiate any of the conclusions drawn from it.'[3] Moreover, the assumption of a *constant* wage and profit structure is maintained throughout the book. The secondary importance of demand theory as far as concerns the main issue of distribution is also quite apparent in the sixth Lecture, which is largely devoted to the theory of rent.

The differential rent theory served for Longfield precisely the same function as for Ricardo, namely to permit the focus of attention upon the wage–profit relationship: 'This analysis I shall enter upon, merely for the purpose of disengaging the cost of production from this element of complexity, and thus of rendering questions concerning wages and profits more simple, by freeing them from a source of confusion and vicious reasoning, in circles to which they are particularly liable.'[4] (The same theme is reiterated in the seventh lecture.)[5] We must here take into

[1] R. D. C. Black, *The Economic Writings of Mountifort Longfield*, 13.

[2] *Lectures on Political Economy* (Dublin, 1834), 109.

[3] Ibid., 164.

[4] Ibid., 116.

[5] Ibid., 132. Here Longfield insisted that differential land fertility was not *per se* the 'cause' of rent, since 'whatever is useful, and is limited in quantity is capable of possessing

consideration also Longfield's rejection of Malthus's insistence—evidently derived from Smith—upon the multifold uses of land which renders rent a cost in any single use: 'I cannot agree with Mr. Malthus, in supposing that the rent which the worst land could pay, as pasture land, should be deemed part of the cost of production of corn.'[1]

Thus the standard rent theory presented in Lecture VI was not only accepted by Longfield but defended competently along lines which, for the most part, would have been favoured by Ricardo. The only matter with which Longfield took issue related to some formal data in the *Principles* which imply a continually increasing proportion of rent in total produce.[2] Yet we know that Ricardo himself did not stand by this relationship and altered his text at various points in the third edition to avoid any such implication.

Longfield defined profits as a 'discount which the labourer pays for prompt payment', or as the 'sacrifice of the present to the future' by the possessor of wealth 'who uses it as capital'. But he recognized that these expressions merely constitute a definition of 'what profits are'.[3] He also attempted to show 'how their amount is calculated', and in the course of this exercise he was led to define—as he phrased the issue in the Preface—'the meaning of proportional wages as they regulate profits',[4] and *to defend the Ricardian conception against criticisms by Torrens and McCulloch.* We are faced with a quite extraordinary reversal of roles.

Assuming that all advances are made for one year, and also that all advances constitute wages, the rate of profit can be defined as 'the proportion in which the value of any commodity is divided between the labourer and the capitalist'.[5] 'This proposition,' he conceded, 'may be considered useless or untrue, as depending upon false suppositions. It is, however, true in those cases in which it does apply, and all other cases may, with a little care, be reduced to them.' And now it becomes clear for what ultimate purpose the measure of value was devised. 'Such reduction,' he continued, 'must be made, whenever we resort to labour as a common measure for comparing the values of commodities. Whatever advances are not made in labour must be reduced to the measure of labour. If a capitalist expends £50 in raw materials, it must be considered as so much advanced on account of labour. In order to make use of labour as a measure of value, we, as it were, reduce every thing else of value to that denomination.'

value, if it can be made the subject of exchange . . .' (134). Ricardo would have accepted this proposition.

[1] Ibid., 148.
[2] Ibid., 153 f.
[3] Ibid., 179.
[4] Ibid., xi.
[5] Ibid., 171. Longfield uses the term 'depends upon' but he obviously intended an identity relation.

The object of all this was to confute Torrens's assertion that the doctrine according to which profits depend on wages 'is equally untenable, whether the terms alteration of wages, alteration of profits, are employed with a reference to proportions, or whether they are used in relation to quantities'.[1] Torrens based his objection upon an arithmetical illustration purporting to show that proportional wages may remain unchanged while the rate of profits increases. The error of the calculation lay, Longfield insisted, in a failure to recognize that all inputs other than labour may be reduced to labour so that the only payments to be taken into consideration are wages and profits.[2]

Longfield thus accepted the Ricardian proposition that the profit rate 'depends upon the proportion of the shares of the final value received by the labourer and the capitalist'. Indeed in an Appendix he formulated, *and justified*, Ricardo's isolation of the conditions required to assure that changes in *money* wages will reflect changes in *proportionate* wages:

> Mr. Ricardo frequently asserts that wages and profits together are always of the same value, and that nothing but a rise in one can produce a fall of the other. He uses the term '*wages*', sometimes to signify the absolute wages which the labourer receives, and sometimes as the proportional wages. *This did not arise from an abuse of words or a confusion of ideas, it was the natural and necessary consequence of a hypothesis, which for simplicity of illustration, he laid down at the commencement of his work.* He assumes that any given quantity of gold, or the metal of which money is made, is always produced by the same quantity of labour, with the same interval of time before its production. On this hypothesis, if gold is raised from mines within the kingdom, absolute money wages will be identical with, and be measured by, proportional wages, and a rise of wages, that is of money wages, will always be accompanied by a fall of profits.[3]

The entire discussion thus far has merely provided a definition of profits and a statement of how the rate of profits is to be calculated. The ninth Lecture is devoted 'to the investigation of the laws which determine their actual amount',[4] wherein Longfield finally set out his objections to his conception of orthodox theory and advanced his alternative. And although he fails to state precisely how his own theory was related to the preceding defence of the Ricardian inverse profit–wage relationship, *it seems clear enough that he envisaged the latter as a valid framework for a satisfactory theory* built around the efficiency of capital (envisaged as

[1] *An Essay on the External Corn Trade*, 3rd edn. (London, 1826), xv–xvi.

[2] *Lectures on Political Economy*, 172 f.

[3] Ibid., 266–7. (Author's emphasis.) Despite his adherence to the main propositions of the Ricardian position, Longfield simultaneously ascribed in the same lecture (VIII) to Smith's view that an increase in wages will generate a general rise in the level of prices. The latter argument was not, however, soundly based upon a specific theory of value. And since he ends the lecture with a defence of Ricardo's inverse profit–wage relationship we conclude that in adopting the Smithian position he fell into serious error from the perspective of his own argument.

[4] Ibid., 179.

'machinery') in its least productive application within a demand–supply context.[1]

* * *

Longfield's market-price analysis, involving the notion of marginal demand price, had rather limited direct influence upon subsequent subjectivist economic thought even in Ireland. And those writers, such as Butt and Lawson, who drew upon elements of Longfield's distribution analysis did not appreciate its relationship with an archetypal supply–demand theory.[2] Nonetheless, the positive influence of Longfield was profound for his lectures elicited a formal retraction from Torrens of his severe critique of Ricardian distribution theory as we shall now see.

In his third edition (1826) of the *Essay on the External Corn Trade* Torrens had described the Ricardian inverse wage–profit relationship as 'equally untenable, whether the terms alteration of wages, alteration of profits, are employed with a reference to proportions, or whether they are used in relation to quantities'.[3] Yet the fact is that there probably exists no clearer statement in the entire literature of the period of the pure Ricardian theory of distribution involving the proportions-measuring 'gold' than that presented, favourably, by Torrens in his *Colonization of Southern Australia*.[4] Similarly, in 1844 Torrens candidly withdrew his earlier objections: 'Some of the commentators on the doctrines of Ricardo appear to have fallen into the misconception, that, in altering his nomenclature and in modifying his principles as varying circumstances required, they refuted his theory of profits. In this censure I include myself.' He had in mind precisely the Ricardian principle that 'profits rise or fall only as wages fall or rise',[5] and provided a defence of the proportions measuring money against a number of strictures by Senior and Jones.[6] The change in position was attributed by Torrens himself to Longfield's lectures which had 'succeeded in removing the main objection to the reception of Ricardo's theory of profit, by showing . . . that the cost of production is to be measured by the single standard obtained by reducing previous and proximate labour to a common denomination.'[7]

* * *

[1] Ibid., 187 f.

[2] Lawrence Moss, 'Mountifort Longfield's Supply-and-Demand Theory', *History of Political Economy*, VI, Winter 1974, 427 f. Butt's combination of the utility teaching of Say and Senior with aspects of Longfield's theory of distribution to arrive at an early statement of the marginal utility theory of imputation seems to be one of the most impressive outcomes but it is only in this century that Butt's work is becoming generally known. See Moss, 'Isaac Butt and the Early Development of the Marginal Utility Theory of Imputation', ibid., V, Fall 1973, 317–38.

[3] Above, p. 235.

[4] *Colonization of Southern Australia* (London, 1835), 22–35.

[5] *The Budget: On Commercial and Colonial Policy* (London, 1844; New York, 1970), xxxvi.

[6] Ibid., xxii f.

[7] Ibid., li–lii. For a full discussion of this matter see Lionel Robbins, *Robert Torrens and the Evolution of Classical Economics* (London, 1958), 53 f. This evidence has largely been

The Ricardian frame of reference is less marked in the works of Samuel Read—which Schumpeter noted 'bears witness to the influence of Bailey'[1] —and G. Poullet Scrope than in that of the other 'dissenters' we have considered so far. But even in their cases the evidence is mixed: Read insisted upon an inverse relationship between the wages of regular labour and the wages of management,[2] and Scrope's objections relate not so much to the inverse relationship as such but to the precise differential effects exerted by wage changes—a characteristic Ricardian problem.[3] To take this position, is in effect to concede a very great deal of the Ricardian position. And the fact is that Scrope formally granted the validity of the inverse relationship on Ricardo's own use of terms albeit as an uninteresting truism.[4]

As far as concerns increases in wages in 'the correct and ordinary sense of the word', Scrope insisted, the proposition that a wage increase will leave unaffected the price level is 'directly false'.[5] Unfortunately Scrope does not justify this assertion. What he presumably meant by the 'ordinary' sense of the term is 'the money-price of labour', and even Ricardo agreed that a money-wage increase, if merely nominal, will be accompanied by a general price rise.[6]

* * *

It is commonly asserted that R. Whately's celebrated suggestion to rename political economy 'Catallactics', or the science of exchanges, implies a significant indication of a deflection of classical economics from its primary preoccupations to a narrowly constrained emphasis upon the 'sphere of circulation'. But this interpretation does not accurately reflect Whately's intentions. His purpose in proposing the change of

overlooked; cf. Black, *The Economic Writings of Mountifort Longfield*, 26; Blaug, *Ricardian Economics*, 127, 159. Lord Robbins conjectures that Ricardo would probably not have welcomed the Longfield–Torrens defence in so far as it was based upon a theory of value depending on quantity of capital, or accumulated labour, which Ricardo had turned down in earlier debate with Torrens. (*Robert Torrens*, 57.)

[1] *History of Economic Analysis*, 488.

[2] *Political Economy* (Edinburgh, 1829), 249; 'The more the inferior labourer gets as *his* wages, the less will remain to the superior labourer as his . . .'

[3] 'The political Economists', *Quarterly Review*, Vol. XLIV, No. 87, January 1831, 29.

[4] 'Having persuaded themselves of the truth of these false conclusions, our economists go on, in the most self-satisfied way, to draw from them several corollaries, such as, "It is abundantly certain, therefore, that no rise of wages *can* ever occasion a general rise of prices, and no fall of wages a general fall of prices" (*McCulloch*, . . .). Why certainly, when wages are defined to be merely the labourer's share, as compared to that of the capitalist, their fall or rise can have no influence on the value of the joint return . . .. We need no professor of political economy to announce, as a recondite proposition, what is identical with their own postulate' (ibid., 3).

[5] Ibid., 3.

[6] It is an increase in wages expressed in money of unchanged general purchasing power—either because of constant real costs of production of the metal or because of a constant supply of money—which cannot be accompanied by a general price rise.

nomenclature was to assure that a study of the wealth of nations should be limited to exchangeable commodities and exclude, for example, the analysis of problems relating to a 'Robinson Crusoe' type economy.[1] That the emphasis was not on the phenomenon of exchange *as such* is clear from his rejection of the term 'philosophy of commerce' as a designation of the subject matter.[2] Whately's suggested redefinition cannot be interpreted as a sophisticated attempt to redefine the scope and nature of political economy. In the final resort he remained concerned with 'the nature, production, and distribution of wealth',[3] and regarded the study of what wealth 'consist[s] in' and what are 'the fundamental laws that regulate its distribution' as essential for an understanding of topical questions.[4]

* * *

It will be clear that the extent of *substantive* hostility towards Ricardo is considerably less than is generally maintained. In concluding this section it may be in place to refer to the history of thought written by Travers Twiss, who, as Professor of Political Economy at Oxford, held the same chair as Senior, Whately and Lloyd.

Twiss in 1847 accepted Ricardo's position that rent is not an element in price.[5] He adopted the view, in sharp contrast to Smith's, that 'variations in the rate of wages and profit, where the proportion of fixed capital is unchanged, affect all commodities in the same degree, so that their relations, in respect of such variations, would remain undisturbed, and their exchangeable value not be altered'.[6] And he accepted Ricardo's distinction between circulating and fixed capital in terms of durability observing that 'variations in the rate of wages or the rate of profits, will . . . affect the cost of production very differently, according as the use of perishable or durable capital preponderates in any branch of manufacture'.[7] There was certainly no general Oxford revolt against Ricardo.

II. Some reactions by 'dissenters' to Bailey

We return now to consider Bailey's place in the dissenting literature. That Bailey cannot legitimately be regarded, as is so common, as standing

[1] *Introductory Lectures on Political Economy*, 2nd edn. (London, 1832), 8. (Whately does not, however, limit the investigation to material objects.)

[2] Ibid., 9.

[3] Ibid., 26.

[4] Ibid., 223. It is certain that opponents of Ricardianism writing from an inductivist or historical point of view, would have read Whately's work as a defence of Ricardian procedures.

[5] *View of the Progress of Political Economy in Europe since the Sixteenth Century* (London, 1847), 169–70.

[6] Ibid., 170–1.

[7] Ibid., 188.

at the head of a line of anti-Ricardians is clear if we consider a little more closely some reactions to his work by other so-called 'dissenters'.[1]

Professor Schumpeter commented of Samuel Read's work that it 'bears witness to the influence of Bailey whom Read followed in his Ricardo criticism . . .'[2] Now this comment is quite inaccurate. The fact is that, on the contrary, Read explicitly took Bailey to task in very strong terms for neglecting to consider the value of commodities in terms of 'their relation to mankind and to human labour':

> Notwithstanding the very high respect I entertain for this author, it will be seen in the following pages, that I find occasion to differ from him very widely in his main positions in the 'Critical Dissertation'. It appears to me that the fundamental error in that work, and that from which all the others to be found in it flow, consists in his treating of value as if it were *a mere relation of commodities between themselves*; whereas it appears to me that the idea of value in commodities *cannot even be conceived* without being mingled with the idea of their relation to mankind and to human labour, of which *some portion* must always be employed in producing or procuring them originally.[3]

Professor Meek in his study of the 'decline of Ricardian economics in England' refers to this same passage relating value to 'mankind and human labour' but mistakenly understands it as a position rejected by Read who attributed it to Ricardo, rather than one *maintained by Read himself*, and observes that 'it was this vital concept which virtually vanished from English political economy after Ricardo's death'.[4] The evidence to the contrary speaks for itself at least as far as concerns Read.

Criticism of Bailey was in fact widespread amongst the dissenters. It is not apparently common knowledge that Cotterill was dissatisfied with significant parts of Bailey's performance regarding the 'cause' of value: 'the causes of value, as stated by the author of the "*Critical Dissertations*

[1] Despite his assertion that 'the decay of the Ricardian School must have become patent' soon after 1826 Schumpeter (*History of Economic Analysis*, 478) hedged his account with multifold qualifications: The influence of Bailey 'was much greater than appears on the surface'; 'though but few contemporaries did justice to him, it became clear in time that he had turned the tide and dealt a fatal blow' (ibid., 599). Similarly, while Bailey's critique did not 'pass unnoticed', and while 'it is safe to presume that his influence extended beyond the range of explicit recognition,' and although 'a poll of writers on value from 1826 to 1845 would produce a considerable majority for Bailey', nevertheless there occurred no 'spectacular victory', Bailey's '*defeat*' (our emphasis) being accounted for on two grounds, that his challenge was 'premature' and that Bailey failed to show how Ricardo's system might be replaced. Thus Bailey and those who followed his example helped 'undermine' the system 'but they did so by a slow process of attrition' (ibid., 487).

[2] *History of Economic Analysis*, 488.

[3] *Political Economy*, viii. The same kind of criticism is directed by Read against Lauderdale's *Inquiry* of 1804. Any attempt 'to reduce the idea of value to a mere *relation of commodities between themselves*, without any connexion with mankind, with labour, or with cost of production' is fatal, since 'the connexion of the exchangeable value of commodities with labour and cost of production is indeed the only circumstance which confers any importance on the connexion of the exchangeable value of commodities between themselves' (ibid., 221).

[4] *Economics and Ideology*, 67.

&c" are extremely unsatisfactory: notwithstanding many parts of that work cannot but be admired by everyone friendly to the science of political economy.'[1] Similarly, he did not think that Bailey's work constituted 'a performance likely to set the controversy at rest; on the contrary, I consider the Author's use of the term value, on many occasions, inconsistent with its obvious meaning, and the chapter on the causes of value, in my opinion, leads to nothing less than complete scepticism. So that, however certain I am, that the work has done much to evolve the difficulties in which the subject was acknowledged to be enveloped, and however dexterously I conceive the author detected the double meaning in which Ricardo used the term I cannot but regret the appearance of these blemishes.'[2] He was equally critical of Bailey's position on the measure of value as we have seen.[3]

Lloyd is quite specific as to the doctrine he objected to. His criticisms are not directed against Ricardo at all, although of course Ricardo's definition of 'value' differed from his own. The purpose of his pamphlet was to demonstrate the legitimacy of saying of a commodity that it varies in value 'without any reference to other objects'.[4] He rejected the assertion (which in fact was by J. S. Mill) that 'value is a relative term: if it is not this, it is nothing: if any one talks about absolute value, or any other kind of value than exchangeable value, we know not what he means.'[5] He took J. B. Say to task for his analogy between motion and value in his argument that 'all value is relative'. And he found fault with the pamphlet entitled *Observations on Some Verbal Disputes in Political Economy*

[1] *An Examination of the Doctrines of Value*, 53. In his chapter dealing with the causes of value Bailey (*Critical Dissertation*, 185) had distinguished between 'commodities which are monopolized, or protected from competition by natural or adventitious circumstances'; those 'in the production of which some persons possess greater facilities than the rest of the community, and which therefore the competition of the latter cannot increase, except at a greater cost'; and those 'in the production of which competition operates without restraint'. The general notion is that 'their respective causes of value cannot be the same'.

[2] Ibid., 40–1. Thus if Cotterill was critical of Ricardo in the context of the cause of value, he was equally dissatisfied with the treatment of Bailey whose explanation of long-run exchange value in terms of cost of production was 'defective': 'it does not include profit, and therefore never can determine value, because, though the labour or capital should not vary, the profit may vary, and consequently the value of any commodities.' (On similar grounds Cotterill objected also to Torrens (ibid., 46).)

[3] See above (p. 231).

[4] *Lecture on the Notion of Value* (London, 1834), 28.

[5] Ibid., 34. The citation is from J. S. Mill's (unsigned) review of Malthus's contribution of 1824, 'Periodical Literature—Quarterly Review'. Cf. *Westminster Review*, Vol. III, No. 5, January 1825. Mill by his assertion intended to deny Malthus's conception of aggregate demand not, as is often maintained, to challenge the Ricardian position regarding absolute value. Lloyd, however, took the statement out of context and applied it generally.

Bailey himself in *A Letter to a Political Economist on the Subject of Value* (London, 1826), 37, applauded the sentiment of the article but expressed surprise at finding an insistence upon value as a relative conception in the *Westminster Review* which in 1826 had published an attack—which we know to be by James Mill—upon his own *Critical Dissertations*. If the respective contexts are borne in mind the apparent inconsistency of position between the journal volumes creates no difficulty.

(1821), which, as we shall see, bears a close resemblence in many respects to Bailey's *Critical Dissertation.*[1]

III. The Ricardians

We devote this section to a brief consideration of the 'Ricardians themselves, specifically McCulloch, J. S. Mill and De Quincey, and their relationship with Ricardo.

Recent commentaries on McCulloch perform a 'disappearing trick', as it were, in his case. He is either dismissed, as by Schumpeter, as a 'henchman' of Ricardo and therefore apparently not worthy of much attention, or as by O'Brien he is classified as a 'Smithian'. Neither position seems adequate. In particular the argument of Professor O'Brien according to which McCulloch was not essentially Ricardian at all but directly in the Smithian tradition is over-stated. The treatment of the invariable measure is taken—with considerable justification—to be the hallmark of Ricardianism; it is the statement that the invariable measure 'never interested McCulloch at all'[2] which I believe involves a misreading of McCulloch's position.

McCulloch's *formal* denial of the existence of an invariable measure of value must be seen in proper perspective. In all editions of his *Principles* the existence of such a measure is denied on the empirical grounds that all commodities are subject to 'perpetual variations' in the quantities of labour required to produce them.[3] Yet the fact remains that money *was* assumed to have the mean factor proportions so that at least *one* of the Ricardian prerequisites for a suitable measure is presumed to be actually satisfied in practice. Moreover, McCulloch distinguished *conceptually* between the case of a nominal wage change, and that of a 'real' wage change reflected in an altered wage in terms of money of 'invariable value', and it is the latter which concerned him. Equally significant is McCulloch's insistence that while it could be demonstrated that a rise in wages would leave unchanged the level of prices, yet even in the event that the price level did rise the real value (in the sense of purchasing power) of profits must fall. And, finally, and I believe conclusively, since Ricardo also had forcefully insisted that his 'fundamental theorem of distribution' (to the effect that the burden of a wage increase falls on capitalists) held good whether or not the conditions required for a suitable measure of value

[1] See below p. 245 regarding this pamphlet.

[2] *J. R. McCulloch: A Study in Classical Economics*, 146. Cf. Schwartz, *The New Political Economy of J. S. Mill*, 15: 'After reading Dr. O'Brien, one might even say that in a short time he [James Mill] was the only one left in the Ricardian succession—together with John Stuart Mill.'

[3] *Principles of Political Economy*, edn. 1, 1825 (London, 1872), 119; edn. 5, 1864 (New York, 1965), 243.

were satisfied in practice, I conclude that McCulloch's position in all essentials is identical with that of Ricardo.

Schumpeter shares with Marxist interpreters the view that J. S. Mill must be excluded from that group which constitutes Ricardo's 'school' namely James Mill, McCulloch and De Quincey.[1] It is contended in particular that Mill rejected on Bailey's grounds the conception of a measure of absolute value.[2] We have considered this view elsewhere and found it to be untenable: Mill accepted the Ricardian theory in the strict sense outlined earlier, specifically the derivation of the theorem about profits and wages from the concept of the invariable measure.[3]

It may not appear necessary to demonstrate De Quincey's loyal adherence to Ricardo. But the tide is so strong in favour of the view that the Ricardian influence was short-lived that even he is being pushed into the opposition.[4] We must, however, keep in mind the opening declaration in the first part of the three-part essay for *Blackwood's* in 1842 that 'David Ricardo made the first and last effort that can be made to revolutionize that science which, for nations, professes to lay bare the grounds of their prosperity, and for individuals, as distributed by nature into three great orders of proprietors, the grounds of their expectations'.[5] There can be no doubt of his continued allegiance to Ricardo as will be made clear in the discussion which follows of the *Logic of Political Economy*.[6]

De Quincey's dissatisfaction with the treatment in the literature of market prices diverging from long-run costs is quite apparent and Ricardo is indeed included amongst the culprits; Ricardo's fourth chapter is termed 'a very short chapter and a very bad one.'[7] But it is Adam Smith who throughout bears the brunt of the criticism for his statement of the 'paradox of value',[8] as well as those who 'fancy that the relation of Supply and Demand could by possibility, and that in fact it often *does*, determine separately *per se* the selling price of an article'.[9] Furthermore, De Quincey

[1] *History of Economic Analysis*, 476.

[2] Ibid., 589, 603. See also Blaug, *Ricardian Economics*, 172–3.

[3] On Mill see my 'Ricardianism, J. S. Mill and the Neo-Classical Challenge', in M. Laine and J. M. Robson, eds., *Essays on James and J. S. Mill* (Toronto, 1976), 67–85.

[4] Groenewegen, *Economic Journal*, LXXXIII, March 1973, 193, refers to De Quincey's remarks on the mutual determination of exchange value by 'intrinsic utility' and 'difficulty of attainment' as a 'change of heart in favour of the Smith tradition in value theory'.

[5] *Blackwood's Edinburgh Magazine*, Vol. LII, No. 323, September 1842 in Masson, ed., *Political Economy and Politics*, Vol. X of *Collected Works of Thomas de Quincey* (1897; New York, 1970), 113.

[6] De Quincey wrote a three part essay for *Blackwood's* in 1842 entitled 'What is the Radical Difference between Ricardo and Adam Smith? With an occasional Note of Ricardo's Oversights'. This essay was recast and expanded as *The Logic of Political Economy* (1844).

[7] Cf. *The Logic of Political Economy* (1844) in Masson, ed., *Political Economy and Politics*, 200.

[8] Ibid., 144–5, 188–90.

[9] A view attributed to 'almost every journal in the land' which he knew Ibid., 121.

spoke very warmly of Ricardo's chapter 'On Value and Riches', writing of it as 'essentially novel' and worthy of 'special admiration'.[1] More significantly, when he turned to consider the case of long-run price—and without question this constituted his main concern in value theory—Ricardo is allowed to come fully into his own. Thus the chapter 'On Value', upon which is based 'a total revolution of political economy', is described as 'Ricardo's great reform',[2] his 'great inaugural chapter',[3] after which 'the powerful hand of Ricardo, will be felt in every turn and movement of economy'.[4] It is in fact the labour theory which De Quincey had in mind modified by the complication created by different proportions of fixed and circulating capital.

Moreover, De Quincey's distribution theory is strictly Ricardian, as indeed is the relationship between distribution and value. Ricardo's illustrative data on wages and rent are fully reproduced.[5] The emphasis is upon the inverse profit–wage relation which in Ricardian fashion is set squarely upon the labour theory: 'Even the novice is now aware that a rise in wages would leave prices undisturbed' in contrast to the position of 'the superannuated economic systems smashed by Ricardo' which envisaged wage increases passed on in the form of higher prices.[6] More specifically:

> In one brief *formula*, it might be said of profits that *they are the leavings of wages*: so much will the profit be upon any act of production, whether agricultural or manufacturing, as the wages upon the act *permit* to be left achieved . . . But do not the wages and profits as a whole, themselves, on the contrary, predetermine the price? No; that is the old superannuated doctrine. But the new economy has shown that all price is governed by proportional quantity of the producing labour and by that only. Being itself once settled, then, *ipso facto*, price settles the fund at which both wages and profits must draw their separate dividends . . .

[1] Ibid., 127. [2] Ibid., 181. [3] Ibid., 200.

[4] Ibid., 179. De Quincey also referred to his early work *Dialogues of Three Templars on Political Economy*, which originally had appeared in three successive numbers of the *London Magazine* in 1824 (see Masson, ed., *Political Economy and Politics*, 37) and which had been considered with some respect by Bailey in his *Critical Dissertations*. The object of this early work, De Quincey observed, (*Political Economy and Politics*, 119) had been 'to draw into much stronger relief than Ricardo himself had done that one radical doctrine as to value by which he had given a new birth to Political Economy'. And while he has been pleased with the attention given to the work by Bailey, nevertheless 'with all his ability, that writer failed to shake any of my opinions. I continue to hold my original ideas on the various aspects of this embarrassing doctrine.'

[5] Ibid., 224–5, 246.

[6] Ibid., 248 n. In the *Logic* reference is also made to an earlier demonstration in the 'Templars' Dialogues' that the concept of a stable measure of value was 'demonstrably a chimera, an *ens rationis*, which never could be realized' (ibid., 151–2). In the 'Dialogues' Ricardo himself is cited to the same effect, the third edition of his chapter on value 'having for its direct object to expose the impossibility of any true measure of value' (ibid., 93). Yet Ricardo used the notion of a constant measure as a conceptual device, and De Quincey followed the same procedure: Ricardo's practice was to 'neglect the variations in the value of money . . . he made it understood, that . . . he would always assume money as ranging at its stationary natural value . . .' (*Logic*, ibid., 201–2).

But if *that* be true, then it follows that wages and profits vary inversely . . . Any other rise in profits, such as would leave wages virtually undiminished, could be only an apparent rise through some depreciation in the currency; and that depreciation, changing any one thing nominally, must change all things: affecting all apparently, really it would affect none.[1]

Finally we recall De Quincey's adherence to Ricardian rent theory and more specifically Ricardo's analysis of its consequences for profits, wages, and prices, which placed economists 'irredeemably' in his debt.[2] There can surely be no question of De Quincey's continued adherence to strict Ricardianism.

IV. Some Ricardian reactions to their critics

In many important instances the post-Ricardian critics simply misinterpreted Ricardo. Malthus, for example, believed quite erroneously that Ricardo maintained his cost theory of exchange value as an *alternative* to demand–supply theory.[3] Both Malthus and Longfield asserted without justice that in Ricardo's system rising capital with population unchanged leaves the profit rate unaffected—that the only cause of falling profits was resort to inferior land.[4] Bailey implied that Ricardo failed to appreciate the relativity dimension of exchange value. Senior's objection to Ricardo —adopted also by Bailey and T. P. Thompson—that to say 'it is the price of [the] last portion of corn, which governs that of the remainder, is to mistake the effect for the cause' and his adoption, as an *alternative*, of a demand–supply or 'monopoly' explanation[5] falls into the same category. The fact is that the Ricardians—and to a considerable degree Ricardo himself confirms the point—accepted much of the *substantive* argument of the 'critics'. We consider first some Ricardian reactions to Bailey.

A *Westminster* reviewer, possibly James Mill, made the point that Ricardo would not have objected to the principal theme of the first

[1] Ibid., 257–8. De Quincey emphasized the fundamentally important feature of Ricardian economics that 'a change cannot commence in profits; that function of industry is not liable to any *original* affection of change' (ibid., 277); see also ibid., 258–9; 'Any change that can disturb the existing relations between wages and profits must originate in wages: Whatever change may silently take place in profits always we must view as recording and measuring a previous change in wages . . . Ricardo's chapter upon profits is substantially no more than a reiteration of his two chapters upon wages and rent.'

[2] But De Quincey at the same time criticized Ricardo for playing down 'that eternal counter-movement which tends, by an equivalent agency, to redress the disturbing balance' (ibid., 249). Accordingly, he denied that one could speak of an 'immovable law of declension' of the profit rate. (Ibid., 294.) Yet oddly enough he also conceded that technical progress 'may be altogether torpid' while diminishing returns is a phenomenon which 'is sometimes for a century together proceeding with activity' (ibid., 259). But it is doubtful whether De Quincey's charge can be sustained; see my 'Ricardo and the Corn Laws: A Revision', *History of Political Economy*, IX, Spring 1977.

[3] 'Political Economy,' 181–2.

[4] Malthus, ibid.; Longfield, *Lectures on Political Economy*, 184 f.

[5] Nassau W. Senior, 'Report on the State of Agriculture', *Quarterly Review*, Vol. XXV, No. 50, July 1821; T. P. Thompson, *The True Theory of Rent in Opposition to Mr. Ricardo and Others* (London, 9th edn., 1832).

chapter of the *Critical Dissertation* relating to the nature of value: 'This chapter is logamarchy, simply and purely. It makes profession, or rather ostentation and parade, of being a controversy with Mr. Ricardo. But it contains not an assertion, to which, as far as *ideas* politico-economical are concerned, Mr. Ricardo would not have assented; it contains, not indeed, as far as such ideas are concerned, an assertion which is not implied in the propositions which Mr. Ricardo has put forth. It is a criticism of some of Mr. Ricardo's forms of expression . . .'[1] And that this would have been Ricardo's view is clear from the latter's reaction to the anonymous *Verbal Disputes* of 1821, which in its essentials is so similar to the *Critical Dissertation* that Bailey feared he might be accused of plagiarism.[2] Writing to Trower in August 1821 Ricardo observed:

> With respect to our difference of opinion on the subject of exchangeable value it is more an apparent difference than a real one. In speaking of exchangeable value you have not any idea of real value in your mind—I invariably have. Your criticisms on passages in my book are, I have little doubt, correct, because they are also the criticisms of others on the same passages. A pamphlet has appeared 'On Certain Verbal Disputes in Polit. Econ.' where the same ground of objection is taken as you take; the fault lies not in the doctrine itself, but in my faulty manner of explaining it.[3]

J. S. Mill, in a Note attached to McCulloch's edition of the *Wealth of Nations* (1828) alluded to Senior's objections to Ricardo's rent theory when he wrote of those 'who affect to suppose that Sir Edward West, Mr. Malthus, and Mr. Ricardo, considered the cultivation of inferior land as the *cause* of a high price of corn'. The argument that 'the cultivation of inferior soils is not the cause but the effect of high price, itself the effect of demand' was, he insisted, a doctrine 'explicitly laid down by the distinguished authors previously referred to, and particularly by Mr. Ricardo'.[4] Much the same argument would apply to the strictures of T. P. Thompson.[5]

[1] 'On the Nature, Measures, and Causes of Value', *Westminster Review*, Vol. V, No. 9, January 1826, 157. (Reprinted with the London, 1967 (Cass) edition of the *Critical Dissertation*.) For the attribution of the review to James Mill see Frank W. Fetter, 'Economic Articles in the *Westminster Review* and their Authors, 1824–51', *Journal of Political Economy*, LXX, December 1962, 584.

[2] The authorship of *Observations on Certain Verbal Disputes in Political Economy* (1821) has not yet been ascertained. The Cass edition of Bailey's works (London, 1967) includes the pamphlet but see the note by Ken Dennis on 'The Bailey Notebooks and Authorship of "Verbal Disputes"'. *History of Economic Thought Newsletter*, Autumn 1973, No. 11, 17–18. Karl Marx, *Theories of Surplus Value*, Part III (Moscow, 1971), 125, commented on the similarity between the works in question.

[3] Letter of 22 August 1821, *Works*, IX, 38.

[4] 'On the Nature, Origin, and Progress of Rent', *Collected Works*, IV (Toronto, 1967), 174.

[5] Thompson himself (*The True Theory of Rent*, 12) raised the question whether there was, in fact, any substantive difference between his approach and that of the Ricardians, and gave a rather unconvincing answer to the affirmative: 'If it is urged that both the present writer and Mr. Ricardo from whom his theory is derived, have distinctly represented the cultivation of the inferior soils as flowing from the appropriation of land and the limitation of its quantity, and that to affirm that rent proceeds from the secondary cause is tantamount to affirming that it proceeds from the first;—the answer is, that it is one thing to affirm that

Mill's reaction was perfectly justified. Ricardo himself said (to Trower) of Senior's article: 'I am glad to have got so good an ally, for what I think the correct principles, and you must partake of the pleasure which I feel in observing that they are every day making way.'[1] The fact is that in the *Principles* Ricardo had shown a thorough awareness that differential rent is but a special case of a more general phenomenon. In his discussion of early settlements, he observed, 'no one would pay for the use of land, when there was an abundant quantity not yet appropriated, and, therefore, at the disposal of whosoever might choose to cultivate it'.[2] The further extension of this statement runs explicitly in terms of demand-and-supply (and refers to the authority of J. B. Say): 'On the common principles of supply and demand, no rent could be paid for such land, for the reason stated why nothing is given for the use of air and water, or for any other of the gifts of nature which exist in boundless quantity . . .; as the supply is boundless, they bear no price. If all land had the same properties, if it were unlimited in quantity and uniform in quality, no charge could be made for its uses unless where it possessed peculiar advantages of situation.'[3] Indeed Ricardo takes Smith to task for failing in his occasional emphases upon the *physical* contribution of the land factor to appreciate the dependency of the *value* dimension of rent upon scarcity: 'Dr. Smith does not reflect that rent is the effect of high price . . . It is . . . from the price at which the produce is sold, that rent is derived; and this price is got not because nature assists in the production, but because it is the price which suits the consumption to the supply.'[4]

It should be added that it is perfectly consistent with the Ricardian position that rent may be generated even in the absence of differentials. We have in mind not merely differentials reflecting differences in the 'qualities' of successive plots, for it is diminishing returns at the *intensive* margin which constitutes a more general case,[5] but the increase in rent due to a constraint upon output expansion of any kind—whether at the extensive or intensive margins—in the face of rising demand.[6]

the competition is the simple cause of rent in all cases, and would equally cause it if no difference in the qualities of soils and no knowledge of the art of forcing crops were in existence,—and another thing to affirm, that it causes rent through the intervention of these circumstances, and would not cause rent without them.'

Thompson, it may be added, commended Ricardo for his proposition that 'rent will be paid because corn sells high; and not corn sell high because rent is paid', which ordered the causal sequence correctly (ibid., 8).

[1] Letter dated 11 December 1821, *Works*, IX, 122.

[2] *Works*, I, 69. Conversely, '[if] air, water, the elasticity of steam; and the pressure of the atmosphere, were of various qualities; if they could be appropriated, and each quality existed only in moderate abundance, they, as well as the land, would afford a rent, as the successive qualities were brought into use' (ibid., 75).

[3] Ibid., 69–70. [4] Ibid., 71 n. [5] Ibid., 71, 72.

[6] See J. S. Mill, *Collected Works*, II, 428. Ricardo on various occasions explained in great detail the process of output expansion in response to rising demand. Within his structure,

We turn next to the Ricardian response to Malthus. In his *Encyclopaedia Britannica* contribution of 1823, commenting upon Malthus's *Principles* of 1820, McCulloch observed that while 'some of the subordinate doctrines respecting value advanced by Mr. Ricardo in the first and second editions of his *Principles of Political Economy and Taxation* were opposed by Mr. Malthus in his recent publication', yet 'Mr. Malthus does not attempt to invalidate the leading principles established by Mr. Ricardo, and the alterations and corrections which the latter has made in the third edition of his work have gone far to remove the objections of Mr. Malthus.'[1] And that this is indeed so is clearly revealed by Malthus's remarks, as we have already noted, which suggest that he adopted much of the Ricardian inverse profit–wage relationship.

How did Ricardo himself view Malthus's position on distribution published in 1820? The treatment of the Profits of Capital in Malthus's *Principles* met with Ricardo's approval. Ricardo observed in his *Notes* that 'I maintain no other doctrine than that which has been well explained by Mr. Malthus in the 2 first sections of 5th chapter. His own statements are sometimes at variance with it, mine I believe never.'[2] More specifically, Ricardo commented favourably on Malthus's analysis of the adverse effects upon the profit rate generated by increased difficulty of producing wage goods, *and* by increased commodity wages and concluded:

> These 2 causes may both be classed under the name of high or low wages. Profits in fact depend on high or low wages, and on nothing else ... In all this Mr. Malthus and I appear to concur. Whenever the difficulty of production on the land is such that a greater proportion of the value of the whole produce is employed in supporting labour, I call wages high, *for I measure value by these proportions*; and from Mr. Malthus's language here, everybody would think he agreed with me . . .[3]

Ricardo's great complaint was that Malthus unjustly insisted that his analysis failed to allow for the effect of real (basket) wage variation upon the profit rate: 'I have invariably insisted that high or low profits depended on low and high wages, how then can it be justly said of me that the only cause which I have recognized of high or low profits is the facility or difficulty of providing food for the labourer. I contend that I have also recognized the other cause, the relative amount of population to capital, which is another of the great regulators of wages.'[4]

Ricardo also saw eye-to-eye with Malthus in the *Principles* regarding the effects of changes in distribution upon prices. On reading of Malthus's acceptance of the proposition that a fall in profits will generate a decline in the prices of capital-intensive goods, Ricardo observed: 'Now I confess

permanent constraint on such expansion must imply an increase in rents to prevent the profit rate in agriculture remaining permanently in excess of that in manufactures.

[1] See *Outlines of Political Economy* by John McVickar (1825; New York, 1966), 135.

[2] *Works*, II, 288. [3] Ibid., 252. [4] Ibid., 264. See also ibid., 285, 446.

that I feared Mr. Malthus himself would have found the proposition paradoxical, because in some of his works he has maintained that a rise in the price of corn will be followed by an equal rise in the price of labour, and an equal rise in the price of *all* commodities; and it was only after further consideration that he thought it fit to reduce the proportion in which commodities would vary when corn varied, and to fix it at 25 or 20 p.c., when corn varied 33⅓—that is to say when corn varies 100 p.c. commodities are to vary 75 to 60 p.c.'[1] In point of fact Ricardo saw his position as closer to that of Malthus than to that of McCulloch in the light of the extreme position sometimes adopted by the latter regarding the labour theory.[2] It has recently been observed, quite correctly we believe, that while Ricardo was on good terms with both McCulloch and Malthus 'he did not value their opinions equally . . . Malthus seems to be the person whom Ricardo took more seriously than he did anyone else.'[3]

As for Malthus's contention in the *Quarterly Review* of 1824 that the New School—unlike Adam Smith whose position 'strongly savours of the effects of demand and supply'[4]—rejected demand and supply in accounting for competitive long-run price, Mill insisted that in fact the very opposite was the case. *All influences upon price operated by way of demand and supply, and the cost theory was dependent thereupon.*[5] Mill's insistence that there is no conflict between cost and demand-supply analyses reflects precisely Ricardo's position: 'Mr. Malthus mistakes the question', Ricardo protested of the formulation in Malthus's *Principles*, 'I do not say that the value of a commodity will always conform to its natural value without an additional supply, but I say that the cost of production regulates the supply and therefore regulates the price.'[6]

[1] Ibid., 60–1. (The reference is to the *Grounds of an Opinion*, 1815.) Malthus's emphasis upon the disturbance to the price structure of a wage-rate is reiterated, ibid., 285–6.

[2] Thus he wrote to McCulloch (9 October 1822, *Works*, IX, 279): 'You go a little further than I go in estimating the value of commodities by the quantity of labour required to produce them: you appear to admit of no exceptions or qualification whatever, whereas I am always willing to allow that some of the variations in the relative value of commodities may be referred to causes distinct from the quantity of labour necessary to produce them.' Here he had in mind the effects of changing wages: 'To this second cause I do not attach near so much importance as Mr. Malthus and others but I cannot wholly shut my eyes to it.' To Malthus himself, he insisted that their difference was only one of degree, that is to say, that the effects of a variation in wages were limited: 'no great effects can follow because profits themselves constitute but a small portion of price, and no great addition, or deduction can be made on their account' (9 October 1820, ibid., VIII, 279).

[3] W. D. Grampp, 'Malthus and his Contemporaries', *History of Political Economy*, VI, Fall 1974, 284.

[4] *Occasional Papers of T. R. Malthus*, 189. Malthus had in mind Smith's notion of the 'natural prices' of commodities determined by the natural rate of wages and profits or 'the ordinary or average rate which is found in every society or neighbourhood, and which is regulated . . . by the general circumstances of the society, their riches or poverty, their advancing, stationary, or declining conditions . . .'

[5] *Collected Works of J. S. Mill*, IV, 33–4.

[6] *Works*, II, 48–9.

J. S. Mill's reaction to De Quincey is also pertinent. In his review of De Quincey's *Logic* for the *Westminster* of June 1845, he observed that 'the larger half of the volume is occupied with the theory of Value; which he rightly esteems the master key to the principal difficulties of the science'. But Mill denied that De Quincey's observations on the relation between value-in-use and value-in-exchange had 'all the originality which he ascribed to them', for he had merely brought 'into full theoretical explicitness what was known to all clear thinkers . . .'[1] He also believed that De Quincey had not given due credit to received doctrine relating to prices diverging from cost: 'Have not all political economists distinguished between articles which can be multiplied to an indefinite extent by labour, and articles naturally or artificially limited to a quantity short of demand, and have they not all, from Ricardo downwards, affirmed that in the former, and more common case, the value conforms on an average to the cost of production, while in the latter there are no limits to the value except the necessities or desires of the purchaser?'[2] But considering the work as a whole, Mill found little to object to and his recognition of De Quincey's allegiance to Ricardo is clear, as indeed is his own position: 'One of [De Quincey's] merits is his early and consistent appreciation of Ricardo, the true founder of the abstract science of political economy, and whose writings are still, after all that has been written, its purest source.'[3] On matters of distribution in particular 'De Quincey thoroughly understands his master, and is therefore able to supply new developments and illustrations of his master's doctrines'.[4] This general evaluation by Mill seems quite accurate as we have seen above.

V. The consistency of Ricardian and 'dissenting' propositions

That the Ricardians were able to see eye to eye with so much of the apparently critical work on value is not surprising. As already remarked Ricardo did not envisage his cost of production theory as an *alternative* to supply–demand analysis.[5] Conversely, it should be emphasized that the majority of 'dissenters' continued to emphasize the cost determination of price. This is true of Bailey himself and Longfield, both of whom spoke of production costs as the main consideration in price determination. It

[1] *Collected Works of J. S. Mill*, IV, 395–6.

[2] Ibid., 398. De Quincey actually recognized the distinction in question but believed that the literature treated the matter at a superficial level (*Political Economy and Politics*, 155). In point of fact De Quincey was much concerned with bilateral monopoly while J. S. Mill operated in terms of a competitive structure and wished to fit De Quincey's case into demand–supply analysis (*Collected Works*, IV, 399 f).

[3] *Collected Works*, IV, 394.

[4] *Collected Works*, IV, 401.

[5] Extraordinary as it may seem Read went so far as to charge the 'Ricardo School' for following Lauderdale's lead in *emphasizing* utility and scarcity or supply–demand rather than cost analysis (*Political Economy*, 220–1).

is true also of Cotterill who included in costs only wages and profits and like Bailey excluded rent. Read adopted a cost theory although he was inconsistent in emphasizing in some circumstances Smith's conception, while elsewhere he accepted the opinion that 'rent is the consequence, not the cause, of high price of raw produce'. Scrope, following Read, also adopted a theory of cost price which was an amalgam of that of Smith and Ricardo, and rejected the 'vulgar opinion' that rent affects price. In Longfield's analysis of *changes* in relative prices the emphasis, as with Ricardo, was upon variations of the labour input, and here too was seen to lie the justification of a labour measure.[1] Much weight is sometimes placed on Whately's criticism of the labour theory.[2] But to our mind, it would be unjustified to exaggerate its import. For his criticism explicitly limits the discussion to the case of given supplies. No labour theorist would have quarrelled with Whately's observations since they do not relate to long-run equilibrium values in the case of infinitely elastic supplies, and are thus not inconsistent with a labour or cost explanation of long-run value. Indeed Whately himself conceded that 'valuable articles are, in *almost* all instances, obtained by Labour'.

* * *

What, however, of Lloyd's contribution to marginal utility or Longfield's conception of intensity of demand? In this context the recent researches of Dr. Marian Bowley are particularly pertinent. As she puts the matter 'no revolutionary significance' was attached to discussions of the law of diminishing marginal utility and related conceptions. Moreover, 'these contributions did not affect the main classical conclusions as to the nature of market and natural prices and their determination'.[3] Her remarks are

[1] Several of the dissenters accorded labour a special role in their *definitions of wealth*. Thus Read defined wealth as 'those external, material objects, necessary, useful, or agreeable to mankind which it costs some considerable exertion of human labour or industry to produce or acquire originally, and which once acquired can be transferred from one to another—appropriated or alienated'. Further, he concluded that 'as the existence of all value in exchange is wholly dependent on the necessity of some portion of human labour being employed in the production of those commodities in which value in exchange forms an attribute, so labour is the only certain measure of that value'. Longfield, for his part, observed that 'as most of the commodities in which the wealth of the country consists are produced by labour, political-economists make use of it as a measure of value', and also that 'all the commodities that men consume, and which can be made the subject of exchanges, owe their existence and their value to labour. The exceptions to this are very trifling, and are of such a nature that they do not vitiate any of the conclusions drawn from it.' Whately, for his part, asserted that 'valuable articles are in almost all instances, obtained by labour'. And while Scrope spoke harshly against the notion of labour as the 'only source of wealth', he nonetheless chose to describe capital as the 'result of previous labour'.

[2] *Introductory Lectures on Political Economy*, 2nd edn. (London, 1832), 252–3; 'It is not that pearls fetch a high price because men have dived for them; but on the contrary, men dive for them because they fetch a high price.'

[3] 'The Predecessors of Jevons: The Revolution that Wasn't', *The Manchester School*, XL, March 1972, 27.

made with reference to attempts 'to clear up particular problems' generated in the *Wealth of Nations*, but in our view Ricardo would not have objected to the developments. While, of course, his main interests lay in long-run price determination, his economics required and, implicitly at least, hinged upon the operation of the competitive mechanism involving demand–supply analysis. His rejection of demand–supply theory did not apply to the particular version elaborated by Longfield, and Longfield himself appreciated Ricardo's objections to the 'indefinite' and 'vague' expression 'proportion between the demand and supply' as unhelpful in the prediction of market price.[1] It may also be remarked that Lloyd's famous analysis of marginal utility is not inconsistent with a cost or even a labour theory, *and was not so envisaged by Lloyd himself*: 'if labour becomes more effective, so that commodities of all kinds shall be produced in a degree of abundance greater in proportion to the wants of mankind, all sorts of commodities, though exchangeable in the same proportions as before for each other, could be said to have become less valuable.'[2] This statement is quite consistent with a cost or labour theory of exchange value.[3]

* * *

To what extent may the conception of interest as a return to 'abstinence' developed by Scrope, Read and Longfield be interpreted as a sharp break with Ricardian procedures? To what extent would Ricardo have objected to an analysis of the precise nature of the savings supply function? The conception in Ricardo's work of profits as residual is we believe little more than a formal consequence of the implicit presumption that the only contractual payment is that made to labour. There can be no doubt that Ricardo recognized the necessity of interest in the limiting case. More importantly, he took into account the effect of a declining profit rate on accumulation. It is true that he gave no *name* to the effect but it is by no means certain that he would have objected to the investigation of the time preference notion which the so-called 'dissenters' insisted upon. J. S. Mill, of course, found no difficulty in ascribing at one and the same time to the inverse wage–profit relationship *and* to the abstinence conception.

* * *

[1] *Lectures on Political Economy*, 247.

[2] *Lecture on the Notion of Value*, 28.

[3] In a recent study of Lloyd ('W. F. Lloyd—A Non-Ricardian?') R. M. Romano observes that Lloyd adopted an approach to rent as residual which grows in the course of secular expansion; however, he ascribed to the 'scarcity' theory of rent developed by Thompson and Senior according to which differential productivity is not a necessary condition. He made only scattered references to profits but suggests that profit rates had fallen due to increased 'competition of capitals'—the Smithian position.

What finally of the widespread application of market demand–supply analysis to long-run wage determination, as for example by Malthus, Longfield, Torrens, Read, Scrope and Senior? Here too there occurred no breakaway. The story would be a different one were it the case, as is apparently quite generally believed, that the subsistence wage played a key role in Ricardo's work, not only in the context of his growth model but also in basic applications such as wage taxation. But this is far from an accurate perspective. Ricardo's model was a growth model in the true sense with wages and profits *above* their respective minima which become relevant only in the stationary state; while the taxation theorems were applied by Ricardo to the case of above-subsistence wages.

It is of great historical significance that Longfield did not actually attribute to Ricardo a subsistence theory of wages. On the contrary, he recognized Ricardo's ascription to a model entailing secularly falling wages.[1] There can be no doubt that Longfield hit upon one of the most complex issues of Ricardian growth theory when he objected that, in principle, there is no reason why wages cannot bear the full brunt of secularly rising food prices since, in a context of *on-growing* population expansion, real (commodity) wages must initially exceed the 'subsistence' level.[2] Yet Ricardo did address himself to this issue and attempted to justify the secular decline in the rate of profit in circumstances of declining commodity wages, and Longfield failed to consider Ricardo's case which turns upon the effect of a declining wage upon the population growth rate, and the presumed operation of a *market process* which assures that the population growth rate is kept in line with a secularly falling capital growth rate.[3]

VI. The review literature: a second view

A widespread hostility to the Ricardian theory of value and distribution has been discerned by a recent investigator of the review literature of our period.[4] This position, we believe, cannot be substantiated as far as concerns the four major journals. In the first place twelve (supposedly) 'hostile' writers—of whom only seven (De Quincey, Ellis, Malthus,

[1] But the charge of inconsistency on Ricardo's part—having maintained simultaneously the conception of declining secular wages and the proposition that custom and habit assured *constant* wages—is quite unjustified. (*Lectures on Political Economy*, 205.) There is *nothing* in the orthodox position which requires secular *wages* to be a constant in a growing economy.

[2] Ibid., 182 f.

[3] Torrens, quite independently, formulated in his fifth edition of the *Essay on the External Corn Trade* (London, 1829), 468–9, a statement of the theory of development with special reference to the course of wages and profits, which reflects, we believe, Ricardo's own position on the matter. (See also *On Wages and Combination* (London, 1834), 21–2 for the same passage.)

[4] Barry Gordon, 'Criticisms of Ricardian Views on Value and Distribution in the British Periodicals', op. cit.

Merivale, Scrope, Senior and T. P. Thompson) can be strictly speaking described as economists—writing no more than sixteen articles over almost three decades constitutes too small a sample to permit any strong generalizations. In any complete evaluation it would certainly be necessary to allow for the contributions by such 'pro-Ricardians' as James and J. S. Mill and also the articles by McCulloch in the *Edinburgh Review*—and his influence on editorial policy—which 'by the standards of the time, and also by the judgements of later economists' had the reputation of being the leading economic journal.[1] Professor Fetter, writing of the *Edinburgh Review* during the period 1818–37, has described McCulloch as 'preaching the Ricardian doctrine with almost fanatical discipleship'—a phenomenon which did much to bring about 'the victory of Ricardian dogmatism'; over this period, 'McCulloch's virtual monopoly of economic articles enabled him to throw the influence of the *Edinburgh* back of the doctrines of the Ricardian system and also to keep out of the *Review* articles critical of the Ricardian system.'[2] Its readers would have had scarcely a hint of anti-Ricardian sentiment.[3]

But even this takes for granted that we can accept the seven economists named above as hostile to Ricardian theory as far as concerns its key propositions. We have shown in this study that this would be a questionable position to take. Merivale and De Quincey positively supported Ricardo. The positions of Senior and Thompson on rent do not conflict with Ricardian principles—indeed Ricardo welcomed Senior's article of 1821. And Malthus recognized the value of the inverse profit–wage relationship in his *Quarterly Review* contribution of 1824, a position consistent with various other statements.

VII. The Political Economy Club: a second view

Our investigation leads us to question the accuracy of J. L. Mallet's famous account of the position of leading members of the Political Economy Club as conclusive evidence of a decline in Ricardo's influence.[4]

[1] F. W. Fetter, 'Economic Controversy in the British Reviews, 1802–1850', *Economica*, XXXII, 427.

[2] 'The Authorship of Economic Articles in the *Edinburgh Review*, 1802–1847', *Journal of Political Economy*, LXI, June 1953, 234, 238.

[3] In point of fact very little appeared on the specific issue of value and distribution. But one such article by Empson ('Life, Writings, and Character of Mr. Malthus', *Edinburgh Review*, No. 130, January 1837) was very well disposed towards Ricardo. Empson refers to Ricardo's 'masterly criticism', in his last letters, of Malthus's pamphlet of 1823; and observed (correctly) that the influence of Ricardo remained strong with Malthus (ibid., 470–2).

[4] The proceedings of the Political Economy Club, particularly those of 13 January 1831, are frequently cited as evidence of widespread hostility amongst economists towards Ricardian economics. The debates in question turned on the question put by Torrens: 'What improvements have been effected in the science of Political Economy since the publication of Mr. Ricardo's great work; and are any of the principles first advanced in

When we find that so much of the fundamental Ricardian position relating to the specific matters of the measure of value and the inverse profit–wage relationship—and not merely to general matters of method—left a strong positive impression on Longfield, and brought about a concession of error on the part of Torrens, and that even Bailey and several other 'dissenters' writing during the early 1830's recognized the logical validity of Ricardo's basic theoretical structure, provided his use of terms is accepted, we are obliged to conclude that Mallet's report fails to reflect the state of opinion during the post-Ricardian period as-a-whole even if they do provide an accurate account of the mood of particular Club meetings early in 1831.

But even when we limit our attention to early 1831, and set aside the change in opinion on Torrens' part under the influence of Longfield, there are reasons not to exaggerate the import of Mallet's report. The account is ambiguous. If *Torrens* took a negative view of Ricardo's stature, Mallet makes it clear that both Tooke and McCulloch 'considered that Rent was in point of fact the effect of differences in the productiveness of soils, because inferior soils were not brought into cultivation until the demand for food and the increased price enabled the cultivator to bring those soils into culture with a fair profit. McCulloch [unlike Tooke] stood up vigorously for Value as well as Rent, and paid very high compliments to Ricardo, whom he still considered as right in most points, and at all events as having done the greatest service to the science, his methodical and scientific way of treating it, so that even where he was mistaken, his errors could be detected by a subsequent and more accurate analysis. He was not an inventor, and no more was Bacon; and their merits in McCulloch's opinion had very much the same character.'[1] Now according to Mallet '*This seemed to be generally assented to*'.[2] Similarly, at the second of the two meetings in question Mallet noted: 'It was generally admitted that Ricardo is a bad and obscure writer, using the same terms in different senses; but that his principles are in the main right. Neither his Theories

that work now acknowledged to be correct?' (*Centenary Volume of the Political Economy Club* (London, 1921), 35.) According to J. L. Mallet's account it was Torrens's opinion that 'all the great principles of Ricardo's work had been successively abandoned, and that his theories of Value, Rent and Profits were now generally acknowledged to have been erroneous. As to value the dissertation on the Measure of value published in 1825 by Mr. Baillie [Bailey] of Leeds has settled that question. As Thompson had shown that Rent was not the effect of differences in the relative productiveness of soils, but the effect of demand and price, and as to profits, it is clear that the part that goes to replacing the capital employed, which Mr. Ricardo had omitted to take into the account, was decisive of the unsoundness of his views.' Ibid., 223–4.

[1] *Political Economy Club: Centenary Volume*, 224. (Cf. also McCulloch's 'boldly standing by Ricardo's doctrine, that equal quantities of labour are equal in value all over the world' —in opposition to Torrens and Malthus.) However, both McCulloch and Tooke are reported as accepting the criticism that Ricardo's theory of profit was vitiated by the failure to allow for the replacement of fixed capital; while Tooke took exception to Ricardian value theory.

[2] Ibid.

of Value nor his Theories of Rent and profits are correct, according to the very terms of his propositions; but they are right in principle.'[1]

Torrens (according to Mallet) referred both to Bailey and to Perronet Thompson as conclusively refuting Ricardo on Value and Rent respectively. Now we have already suggested that such an evaluation of Bailey's work as far as concerns value is an exaggeration. As for the matter of rent, it is clearly the case that several of the so-called 'dissenters', in addition to Tooke and McCulloch who spoke favourably at the Club meetings, supported Ricardo's position. We have in mind Cotterill and Longfield and also Malthus who, in correspondence during 1829 and 1831, rejected T. P. Thompson's position that contemporary rent must be accounted for in terms of a monopoly theory rather than the principle of diminishing returns.[2] Indeed it is of some interest that Malthus expressed displeasure at Torrens' particular formulation of the question debated by the Political Economy Club: 'I was hardly prepared to expect that in so short a time as has since elapsed [since his debates with Ricardo], one of the questions in the Political Economy Club should be 'Whether any of the principles *first* advanced in Mr. Ricardo's work are now acknowledged to be correct?' My apprehension at present is that the tide is setting too strong against him . . .'[3]

VIII. Conclusion: A 'dual' development?

Acceptance of the Ricardian theorem on distribution—the inverse profit–wage relationship—was far more widespread during the post-Ricardian period than is generally believed. But it is important to recognize that Ricardo obtained his results, paradoxical as it may appear, by a more consistent and rigorous use of the conception of *relative* value than appears in the *Wealth of Nations* or for that matter in Bailey's work. For the demonstration of Ricardo's main theme obliged him to pay considerable attention to inter-industry linkages. It is in fact impossible to do justice to Ricardian economics without keeping to the fore the micro-economic or allocative foundations thereof; indeed it is helpful to envisage Ricardo as engaged in an effort to distinguish between a disturbance (such as a tax) affecting a *single* industry which will leave the general profit rate unaffected—this conclusion stands even if the industry in question happens to be agriculture—and a disturbance (such as a general wage increase) affecting *all* industries which will reduce the general profit rate.[4]

[1] *Political Economy Club: Centenary Volume*, 225. (Author's emphasis.) Mallet himself took a more reserved view.

[2] Neil de Marchi and Sturges, 'Malthus and Ricardo's Inductivist Critics', *Economica*, XL, November 1973, 385, 386.

[3] Letter to Whewell, 31 May 1831, in de Marchi and Sturges, ibid., 391.

[4] Despite Schumpeter's strong 'indictment' of Ricardo on the grounds of a failure to

Here we note that even those sections on the *Wealth of Nations* most consciously preoccupied with resource allocation are severely constrained from this very perspective. For the average returns to the factors are not themselves determined in the adjustment process set in motion, for example, by demand disturbances; the movement of factors between industries acts upon product prices and the prices of factors in particular industries but the average returns remain unaffected. His procedures in formal analysis—as distinct from applied studies—imply identical factor proportions between sectors. Furthermore, Smith neglected the matter of variable proportions in any productive unit. In much of this Ricardo followed Smith. But he was much more conscious of the analytical problems created in the pricing process by the existence of differential factor proportions and was preoccupied by the *relative* dimension of price to a very marked degree. Similarly, he was in a large part of his work engaged in the rejection of Smith's isolation of the pricing of corn for special treatment, insisting that corn must be treated in the same manner as every other product of the system. Ricardo thus corrected a variety of deficiences in Smithian allocation economics along what were to be the 'neoclassical' lines.

As far as concerns the matter of abstinence or recognition of a supply price for capital, it would appear that Ricardo as well as J. S. Mill, Senior, Read, Scrope and Longfield abandoned the standard eighteenth-century position according to which savings are institutionally determined. In this regard too Ricardo—unlike Smith—stands on the neoclassical (Marshallian) road.

Most striking of all is Ricardo's adherence to a supply–demand analysis of long-run wages. In this respect, and also in his analysis of wage taxation Ricardo was wholly dependent upon Smith.

From all these perspectives—and bearing in mind the relationship between the dissenters and Ricardianism outlined in this paper—it appears unhelpful to think of a 'dual development' of economic analysis during the nineteenth-century, involving on the one hand Smith, the dissenters, Mill and Marshall; and on the other Ricardo and Marx. We do not intend, of course, to suggest an identity of objective or of procedure between Ricardo and Marshall but the picture is far too complex to permit a neat and clear-cut categorization such as that outlined at the outset.

In conclusion we wish to consider a recent remark by Professor Frank Fetter to the effect that 'if, as was the general impression by the 1830's, Ricardo's theoretical framework had been largely rejected, there is a mystery as to why the name of Ricardo was so closely associated with

appreciate the production–distribution process as a 'web of exchanges', on occasion he was less severe. See *History of Economic Analysis*, 568, 590.

the economic theory of John Stuart Mill and English neoclassical economics'.[1] A number of explanations for the phenomenon alluded to are offered, amongst which are the respect of Alfred Marshall for tradition, and Mill's respect for the memory of Ricardo which left the impression that 'even when the analysis was quite contrary to Ricardo's . . . the Ricardian framework remains almost unaltered. No one would suspect, from reading Mill's *Principles*, the criticisms to which Ricardian ideas on rent, value, wages, and profits had been subjected in the previous twenty years.'[2] But in the light of our own discussion it is not at all clear that there is a problem to resolve. For J. S. Mill did not ignore the criticisms of the preceding quarter century; the point to keep in mind is that he did not believe these criticisms to be destructive of the main Ricardian theoretical structure. His position is very clearly formulated in his review of De Quincey's *Logic* in which he comments on De Quincey's belief that there had occurred little advance since the 1817 'revolution':

> We dissent from the opinion that political economy does not advance. We think it is in a state of most rapid progression. But . . . the superstructure seems to be overgrowing the foundation. The science is growing at the extremities, without a proportional and suitable enlargement of the main trunk. Many important new views—new, at least, in having been previously overlooked—have dawned upon political economists during the last twenty years. But for want of sufficiently careful habits of systematic thought, these new views have been too frequently promulgated as contradictions of the doctrines previously received as fundamental; instead of being, as they almost always are, *developments* of them; corollaries flowing from these fundamental principles, certain conditions of fact being supposed . . . What has been added to the science since Ricardo, does not need to be substituted for his doctrines, but to be incorporated with them. They do not require alteration or correction, as much as fuller exposition and comment.[3]

Our analysis of the monograph and periodical literature suggests that J. S. Mill was quite justified in taking this view. Many of the criticisms of Ricardo turn out in fact to be quite in accord with Ricardian theory and *Riçardo himself*, to the extent that he was familiar with the critical literature, took a view quite consistent with that of Mill.

[1] F. Fetter, 'The Rise and Decline of Ricardian Economics', *History of Political Economy*, I, Spring 1969, 80.

[2] Ibid., 81. See also P. Schwartz, *The New Political Economy of J. S. Mill*, 236–7.

[3] *Collected Works of J. S. Mill*, IV, 394.

University of Toronto

[13]

History of Political Economy 10:4

The impact of growth and technology on trade in nineteenth-century British thought

Arthur I. Bloomfield

A criticism often raised against the classical theory of international trade is that it was essentially static in character and with few exceptions disregarded the interrelations between trade and growth.[1] Some commentators have even found this feature of the theory rather puzzling in view of the strong interest displayed by the classical economists in problems of economic growth generally.[2] By contrast, we have a recent authoritative opinion to the effect that "there are many elements in Classical trade theory, particularly in its interconnection with growth and development, which have been almost entirely neglected in modern treatments of that theory"[3]—although we are given few hints as to what those elements were.[4] In a similar vein Viner had noted twenty years earlier that what the classical writers had to say about the growth aspects of trade (and certain other problems in trade theory) "has never been carefully surveyed and if so surveyed might surprise by its extent and pertinence."[5]

There is some truth in both of these contrasting positions. On the one hand, there can be no doubt that the core of classical trade theory—and in fact trade theory generally up to the early 1950's—was fundamentally static in its assumptions and approach. On the other

Arthur I. Bloomfield *is Professor of Economics at the University of Pennsylvania.*

1. This, for example, was the main thrust of the criticisms raised by J. H. Williams, "The Theory of International Trade Reconsidered," *Economic Journal*, June 1929, pp. 195–209.

2. M. Blaug, *Economic Theory in Retrospect*, rev. ed. (Homewood, Ill., 1968), p. 211: "It is curious that classical theory, generally oriented as it was to problems of long-run development, should have developed an almost wholly static theory of international trade."

3. D. P. O'Brien, *The Classical Economists* (Oxford, 1975), p. 200. There is a misleading "its" in the quotation which I have removed, with Professor O'Brien's permission.

4. Ibid., pp. 172, 181–82.

5. J. Viner, "International Trade Theory and Its Present Day Relevance," in *Economics and Public Policy*, Brookings Lectures 1954 (Washington, 1955), pp. 113–14.

hand, a detailed examination of nineteenth-century British writings indicates that the relations between trade and growth were a subject of considerable if peripheral interest and discussion, especially in the first half of the century. Most of the classical economists and many of the lesser writers of the period displayed a lively awareness of the variety of growth-stimulating effects that foreign trade could exert on domestic economies. Conversely, many of them examined the impact of the growth process, and the factors propelling it, upon the pattern of comparative advantage, the terms of trade, and the volume of trade. Some of these discussions anticipated present-day theories of trade and growth, especially in the area of technological change and trade. For example, nearly all of the elements of the so-called technological-gap theory of trade are to be found in these earlier writings.

What the classical economists and their contemporaries had to say on the relations between trade and growth was usually in the form of comparatively brief observations and *obiter dicta* scattered throughout their writings, generally in the course of historical digressions, discussions of current policy issues, or forecasts of future trends. These views were seldom the subject of systematic or sustained analysis and were rarely integrated into the main body of classical trade theory. Taken together, however, they add up to a not insubstantial volume of material that has never been brought together and analyzed.

This article will confine itself to examining the views of nineteenth-century British writers on only one of the various aspects of the trade-growth relationship that they discussed, namely, that involving the impact of growth and technological change on comparative advantage and trade patterns.[6] A number of questions were raised in this broad area. For example, what are the factors determining changes in comparative advantages? What is the influence of technological advance and its diffusion on trade? How does the commodity composition of a country's foreign trade change with growth? What are the implications of changes in the pattern of international specialization for the volume of world trade? For the position of an individual country such as Great Britain? The answers to these and related questions by the writers concerned should be of interest in the

6. The period covered will be roughly 1800–1914, with emphasis on writings in the first half of the period when greater interest was displayed in these problems. Adam Smith is of course excluded. I have examined Smith's views on trade and growth in "Adam Smith and the Theory of International Trade," *Essays on Adam Smith*, ed. A. S. Skinner and T. Wilson (Oxford, 1975), esp. pp. 467–73.

light of the attention given in more recent years to "dynamic" theories of comparative advantage.[7]

Most of the classical economists made some references to the forces determining the nature of comparative advantages *at any given time*. To be sure, in Ricardo's famous illustration no reason was explicitly given for the postulated difference in the comparative costs of producing wine and cloth in Portugal and England. Yet he, as well as Malthus, McCulloch, Cairnes, and others, revealed in scattered passages of their writings some understanding of the role of relative abundance and relative prices of productive factors in determining the pattern of international specialization.[8] More frequent was the stress placed on differences in soil and climate, labor skills, and technology. John Stuart Mill, for example, spoke of a country's superiority in particular export commodities as arising from "greater natural advantages (such as soil, climate, richness of mines); superior capability, either natural or acquired, in the labourers; better division of labour, and better tools or machinery."[9] Torrens, Malthus, McCulloch, and others explained England's superiority in manufactures in terms of such factors as availability of coal and iron, better machinery and technology, greater skill and energy of labor, and geographical position.[10] In general, the factor most commonly stressed in explaining comparative advantages at any time was differences in natural conditions.[11]

In a recent article, Johnson has stated that the Ricardian trade model, "based as it was on differences in comparative cost created by nature . . . implied a static and permanent distribution of comparative advantages and disadvantages which economic policy could do little

7. For an invaluable survey and synthesis of the recent literature in this field, see H. G. Johnson, *Comparative Cost and Commercial Policy Theory for a Developing World Economy*, Wicksell Lectures (Stockholm, 1968). See also R. E. Findlay, *International Trade and Development Theory* (New York, 1973), chs. 7–9.

8. J. Viner, *Studies in the Theory of International Trade* (New York, 1937), pp. 504–7.

9. John Stuart Mill, *Principles of Political Economy* [1848], ed. W. J. Ashley (London, 1909), p. 681, and ibid., pp. 102–15 for a more detailed discussion.

10. Robert Torrens, *Letters on Commercial Policy* (London, 1833), pp. 36–42; Thomas R. Malthus, *The Grounds of an Opinion on the Policy of Restricting the Importation of Foreign Corn* (London, 1815), p. 31; and John R. McCulloch, *Treatises and Essays*, 2d ed. (Edinburgh, 1859), pp. 444–47. McCulloch, incidentally, subscribed to a theory of absolute, not comparative, advantage, as has been noted by D. P. O'Brien, *J. R. McCulloch: A Study in Classical Economics* (New York, 1970), pp. 191–94.

11. See, e.g., Mountifort Longfield, *Three Lectures on Commerce and One on Absenteeism* (Dublin, 1835), p. 59: ". . . of all the causes which have given rise to commerce, the most striking is the difference of soil and climate, and the variety which exists in the natural productions of different countries."

but accept gracefully or seek to alter with the outcome only of a pointless reduction of real income and economic welfare"; and he also speaks of comparative advantage in the Ricardian model as being "ineluctably fixed by nature."[12] As it so happens, in discussing the international distribution of specie in the very chapter in which he expounded his trade model, Ricardo referred several times to situations in which comparative advantage could change because of improvements in the arts and machinery, discovery of new processes, or other factors. He even discussed a case where, because of the assumed discovery in England of a process for making wine, it might become profitable for England and Portugal "to exchange employments; for England to make all the wine, and Portugal all the cloth consumed by them."[13] It seems clear, then, that Ricardo did not believe the pattern of comparative advantage to be immutably fixed, even within the framework of his model. Nor for that matter did other writers of the period take comparative advantages as given.

Comparative Advantage and Technological Change

There are many possible explanations for *changes* in pattern of a country's comparative advantage over time. These would include such factors as technological change and its diffusion, changing relative factor proportions, discovery or exhaustion of important natural or mineral resources, opening of new markets for exports or sources of supply of imports, shifts in tastes, and so on. Nineteenth-century British writers put considerable stress on the first of these.

The classical economists discussed various aspects of technological change in general (or "improvements" as they were usually called), but never developed a systematic theory in this area. They assigned only a subsidiary role to technical change in the growth process, which they regarded as propelled mainly by capital accumulation and population growth. Nevertheless, they actively debated the effects on employment of the introduction of new machinery. They examined the effects of innovations on distributive shares. They drew distinctions between process and product innovations, though not in those terms, and between various kinds of factor-saving inventions. A few even examined the role of innovations in inducing cyclical upswings.

12. H. G. Johnson, "Technological Change and Comparative Advantage: An Advanced Country's Viewpoint," *Journal of World Trade Law*, Jan.–Feb. 1975, pp. 4, 5.

13. David Ricardo, *The Works and Correspondence of David Ricardo*, ed. P. Sraffa (Cambridge, 1951–55), I, 137–38. See also ibid. pp. 141–42, 144, 145.

In the international area an aspect of technological change that attracted much attention was its effect upon the terms of trade. The customary procedure here was to assume an improvement in a country that had the effect of cheapening the cost of production of an existing export commodity, or of creating a new branch of exports, and to trace through the resulting impact on the terms of trade. The seminal contribution in this field was that of John Stuart Mill;[14] and the issue was also analyzed by Scrope, Cairnes, Pennington, Bastable, Nicholson, Flux, and Edgeworth, among others.[15] Since the focus of these discussions was on the terms of trade rather than on comparative advantage, they will not be examined here. The assumption that improvements characteristically occurred in the export industries, however, implied the view that technical change would tend to widen rather than narrow international differences in comparative cost, and thereby enlarge rather than reduce the scope for and extent of gain from trade.[16]

A number of writers in addition to Ricardo in the example just mentioned explicitly referred to the fact that technological change could alter a country's comparative advantage. Longfield, after noting that continuing improvements in England's manufactures might be expected to bring about continuing changes in its foreign trade, indicated that a significant increase in its manufacturing skills could induce a shift of resources into the production and export of manufactures and away from shipbuilding, in which he assumed it previously had had a comparative advantage and still had an absolute advantage.[17] Cairnes outlined in more detail how a mechanical invention in

14. Mill, *Principles*, pp. 593–96, 622–25; and *Essays on Some Unsettled Questions in Political Economy* (London, 1844), p. 30. The *Essays* were actually written in 1829–30. A detailed examination of Mill's analysis is to be found in Viner, *Studies*, pp. 535–41.

15. [G. Poulett Scrope], "The Political Economists," *Quarterly Review*, Jan. 1831, pp. 23–25; John E. Cairnes, *Some Leading Principles of Political Economy Newly Expounded* (New York, 1874), pp. 337–39; James Pennington, *A Letter to Kirkman Finlay, Esq.* (London, 1840), pp. 41–45; Charles F. Bastable, *The Theory of International Trade*, 4th ed. (London, 1903), pp. 185–87; Joseph S. Nicholson, *Principles of Political Economy*, II (London, 1897), 310–11; Alfred W. Flux, *Economic Principles* (London, 1904), pp. 213–14; and Francis Y. Edgeworth, "The Theory of International Values—I," *Economic Journal*, March 1894, pp. 40–41. Some of the finer points in the Bastable-Nicholson-Edgeworth exchange have been analyzed by J. Bhagwati and H. G. Johnson, "Notes on Some Controversies in the Theory of International Trade," *Economic Journal*, March 1960, pp. 79–83; and by M. C. Kemp, "Technological Change, the Terms of Trade, and Welfare," ibid., Sept. 1955, pp. 467 ff.

16. See H. G. Johnson, "Effects of Changes in Comparative Cost as Influenced by Technical Change," in *International Trade Theory in a Developing World*, ed. R. F. Harrod and D. C. Hague (London, 1963), pp. 97–98.

17. Longfield, *Three Lectures*, pp. 62–64.

England that greatly reduced the cost of its woollen goods would set into motion forces affecting not only its terms of trade but also the pattern of its comparative advantage. He concluded: "Every new invention, every happy discovery, that cheapens the cost of producing particular commodities, and so alters their comparative cost, sets into action forces which operate in the directions I have indicated."[18]

Cairnes had made these observations following a brief summary of the results of an earlier study in which he had tested the theory of comparative advantage in connection with the Australian gold discoveries in 1851. He had there outlined in detail the pattern of change in wages, prices, and resource allocation whereby those discoveries had shifted that country from the position of an exporter of various agricultural products to that of exporter of gold and an importer of foodstuffs in many of which it had an absolute advantage over the countries from which they came.[19] He had concluded that "the essence of the gold discoveries, regarded economically, consisted . . . in the reduction in the cost of raising gold which was thereby effected,—a reduction which, not shared by other countries, involved a change in the comparative costs of Australian and foreign productions. The consequence of this has been a change in the character of her foreign trade."[20]

There was general agreement that technological change, and scientific discoveries generally, tended to be diffused rather speedily and that no nation could expect for any length of time to keep new inventions secret. For example, in listing among the benefits of foreign trade the diffusion of new techniques of production, McCulloch wrote:

> Were any considerable improvement made in any important art, either in China or Peru, it would very speedily be understood and practised in England. It is no longer possible to monopolize an invention. The intimate communication that now obtains amongst nations renders any important discovery, wherever it may be made, a common benefit.[21]

The same idea was expressed by many others. Malthus, for example, noted "how difficult it is to confine improvements in machinery

18. Cairnes, *Some Leading Principles*, pp. 337–39.

19. J. E. Cairnes, *Essays in Political Economy* (London, 1873), pp. 20–52. Also Cairnes, *Some Leading Principles*, pp. 312–15, 335–36.

20. Cairnes, *Essays*, p. 37.

21. J. R. McCulloch, *On Commerce* (London, 1833), p. 9. This idea had been stated earlier by David Hume, *Writings on Economics*, ed. E. Rotwein (Madison, Wis., 1970), pp. 14, 78–79.

to a single spot."[22] Torrens argued that in the actual state of knowledge and international communications "the adoption of the latest improvements in scientific power cannot be confined to a particular country."[23] Still another writer noted: "Improvements in the sciences and arts, by which the fruitfulness of the sources of wealth is heightened, are sure to diffuse themselves."[24] There appears, on the other hand, to have been relatively little discussion of the process of diffusion or of the particular channels whereby new techniques were transmitted internationally.[25] Nor was the distinction between invention and innovation clearly drawn in this connection. But at least a clear implication was that any comparative advantages derived from an improvement in one country would be eroded or lost as it was diffused to other countries.

One writer went to pains to emphasize that the countries which borrowed technology from abroad had a much easier task than the countries in which the technological change had originally occurred. In a remarkable series of passages that anticipate some of the recent discussion of the "handicap of the early start,"[26] William Playfair wrote in 1805:

> The nation that is highest treads in discovery, inventions, &c. a new path, and is never certain how far she can go, nor how to proceed. Those who follow have, in general, but to copy, and, in doing that, it is generally pretty easy to improve. . . .
>
> So far as methods of working and machinery are connected, the imitating nation has the advantage; it copies the best sort of machine, and the best manner of working at once. The workmen have neither an attachment to the old inferior methods, nor do they use old inferior machines, to avoid the expense of new ones. In short, they adopt all improvements without much additional expense. . . .

22. T. R. Malthus, *Additions to the Fourth and Former Editions of an Essay on the Principle of Population* (London, 1817), p. 108.

23. R. Torrens, *The Budget. On Commercial & Colonial Policy* (London, 1844), p. 235.

24. J. S. Eisdell, *A Treatise on the Industry of Nations* (London, 1839), I, 352. For similar ideas, see Robert Hamilton, *The Progress of Society* (London, 1830), p. 296; Thomas Hodgskin, *Popular Political Economy* (London, 1827), pp. 162–63; and G. K. Rickards, *Three Lectures Delivered Before the University of Oxford* (Oxford and London, 1852), p. 63.

25. The export of machinery was one channel that attracted frequent notice. See infra.

26. Some of the recent literature is examined in C. P. Kindleberger, "Obsolescence and Technical Change," *Bulletin of the Oxford University Institute of Statistics*, Aug. 1961, pp. 281–97.

> As to the difficulties in rivalling a nation in skill, in any mechanical art, there are none. The only difficulties in manufactures are in the inventions and improvements, and these have been overcome by the leading nation, and are no difficulties to that which follows.
>
> . . . the nations that follow others in arts are not always confined to imitation, though . . . even there they have a great advantage. It frequently happens that they get hold of some invention which renders them superior, in a particular line, to those whom they are only intended to imitate.[27]

For these and other reasons, Playfair concluded that a country which got an early lead in the arts of manufacturing was likely eventually to be overtaken by other countries that got a later start. He cited the cases of Holland, Flanders, and France, which he claimed were all originally superior to England in manufacturing; and he argued that England, "without care and attention," could not itself be expected for long to maintain its present degree of manufacturing supremacy as its technical advances were diffused to other nations and perhaps even improved upon by them.[28] He noted that "the nation the farthest advanced in invention has only to remain stationary a few years, and it will soon be overtaken, and perhaps surpassed";[9] and he expressed the view that Britain could not in fact expect indefinitely continuing inventions.[30] On the other hand, there were those who argued that there *would* be a continuing stream of innovations in Britain on a scale that would keep it well ahead of potential rivals, i.e., that technical change would proceed at a faster rate than its diffusion. One writer put it this way: "The latest improvements we at present enjoy may in a few years have found their way to our rivals; but, as these will probably have given place, in the progress of improvement, to further changes, we shall still continue in advance of them."[31]

27. William Playfair, *An Inquiry into the Permanent Causes of the Decline and Fall of Powerful and Wealthy Nations* (London, 1805), pp. 208, 210, 212.

28. Ibid., pp. 203–4. Playfair made one general exception to his rule. He seems to have believed that "southern" nations could not be expected to rival "northern" countries in manufactures. Ibid., p. 210. The adjectives are his own.

29. Ibid., p. 203.

30. Ibid., p. 282: "Our inventions, to abbreviate labour, cannot be perpetual, and, in some cases they can go no farther than they have already gone." A similar view was expressed by another writer who, in noting that Britain's superiority had hitherto been supported by "continually succeeding improvements in mechanics," cautioned that "there is a point at which invention must cease, and new improvements are soon copied and transferred to other nations." [Anon.], *Remarks on the Commercial Policy of Great Britain, Principally as it Relates to the Corn Trade* (London, 1815), p. 64.

31. John Kennedy, *On the Export of Machinery* (London, 1824), p. 23. Eisdell,

The fear expressed by Playfair that England's superiority in the production and export of manufactures would tend gradually to be weakened was echoed by other nineteenth-century British writers, but for reasons not always explicitly associated with the diffusion of technology abroad. These views will be examined in a later section. What is relevant here is to emphasize that just as improvements affecting British exports tended to widen international differences in comparative-cost ratios and to increase the volume of trade in the commodities affected, so did subsequent diffusion tend to reduce or eliminate the trade so generated as the initial advantage was eroded or lost. This was well expressed much later in the period by Marshall:

> Every improvement in the manufacturing arts increased England's power of meeting the various wants of backward countries. . . . the progress of invention opened a wider field for the sale of her special products. . . . But this good fortune has been short-lived. Her improvements have been followed, and latterly often anticipated, by America and Germany and other countries; and her special products have lost nearly all their monopoly value.[32]

In the statements of Playfair, Marshall, and others we have the essential elements of the so-called technological-gap theory of trade.[33] A country develops a new export product or a new process that lowers the cost of an existing export (the focus today is usually on the former). A special advantage is thereby conferred on the innovating country and the volume of its exports increases. But that advantage,

---

Treatise, I, 345, similarly noted that "invention [in Britain] . . . is still going on. It seems even to proceed at a more rapid pace than that at which other countries are able to follow." A similar point was made in 1903 by Marshall, but with regard to France's continuing superiority at the time in many goods on the border line between art and luxury. He noted: "New Parisian goods are sold at high prices in London and Berlin for a short time, and then good imitations of them are made in large quantities and sold at relatively low prices. But by that time Paris . . . is already at work on other things which will soon be imitated in like way." Alfred Marshall, "Memorandum on the Fiscal Policy of International Trade," *Official Papers*, ed. J. M. Keynes (London, 1926), p. 404. Whether or not one country could indefinitely maintain its superiority in manufacturing and trade over others had been the subject of an earlier debate in a wider context between Josiah Tucker and David Hume. Tucker took the position that it could, Hume that it could not. See J. M. Low, "An Eighteenth Century Controversy in the Theory of Economic Progress," *Manchester School*, Sept. 1952, pp. 311–30.

32. A. Marshall, *Principles of Economics*, 5th ed. (London, 1907), p. 674.

33. See, e.g., I. B. Kravis, " 'Availability' and Other Influences on the Commodity Composition of Trade," *Journal of Political Economy*, April 1956, esp. pp. 153–55; M. V. Posner, "International Trade and Technical Change," *Oxford Economic Papers*, Oct. 1961, pp. 323–41; and G. C. Hufbauer, *Synthetic Materials and the Theory of International Trade* (Cambridge, Mass., 1966) pp. 23–34.

and the trade that it generates, are gradually lost as the new technology is imitated or otherwise diffused abroad. Indeed, if foreign countries have relative factor endowments and factor prices that make them more suitable producers of the commodity in question—or if they improve upon the initial innovation—they could successfully compete in the commodity concerned in third markets or even begin exporting it back to the innovating country itself.[34] The international shifts in the location of production and the changing patterns of international specialization involved in this process constitute the basis for a truly dynamic theory of comparative advantage.

It was noted earlier that nineteenth-century British writers, when analyzing the international effects of techological change, focused on improvements that affected countries' export industries and thus expanded the scope for trade. It was of course implicitly recognized that the improvements, when and if imitated abroad, would strengthen the position of import-competing industries in the imitating countries, leading to a reduction of trade. Marshall, however, was the only earlier writer of whom I am aware who *explicitly* distinguished between these two kinds of improvements that were later to be called "export-biased" and "import-biased."[35] And he did not specifically regard the latter as stemming solely from the adoption of technological advances made by other countries; they could be autonomous to the countries concerned. In 1903 he wrote: "Other things being equal, an increase in the efficiency of those industries in which a country is already leading will increase her foreign trade more than in proportion. But an increase in the efficiency of those in which she is behind will diminish her foreign trade."[36] Marshall went on to make it clear by some examples that by leading industries he meant export industries and by lagging industries he meant import-competing industries. He made a much more explicit distinction between these two kinds of improvements in a later work, where he also distinguished the case of improvements which were of a sort that equally affected both a country's export industries and its import-competing industries.[37]

Analogous to export-biased innovations are improvements in international transport, since these likewise tend to expand the volume of trade. John Stuart Mill observed that some goods may not enter

34. This possibility was also recognized by Playfair himself, *Inquiry*, p. 282: "Our inventions, to abbreviate labour . . . [when] copied by nations where labour is cheaper, give them a superiority over us."

35. J. R. Hicks, "The Long-Run Dollar Problem," *Essays in World Economics* (Oxford, 1959), pp. 73 ff.

36. Marshall, *Official Papers*, p. 406.

37. Alfred Marshall, *Industry and Trade*, 2d ed. (London, 1919), pp. 15–16, 64–65.

into international trade because their transport costs normally more than outweigh the differences in their production costs in the various countries.[38] It would seem to follow that transport improvements involving a reduction in costs of carriage would widen the range of goods capable of moving into international trade—although this was not explicitly noted—and also tend to increase the volume of trade in goods already being traded. This is a direct application of the logic of comparative advantage. Nineteenth-century writers did in fact make frequent references to the reductions in transport costs that were occurring and recognized their significance for trade. Scrope, Torrens, and Marshall, for example, referred to the trade-stimulating effects on Britain of transport improvements through reducing the costs of imported foodstuffs and raw materials or enlarging markets for British exports.[39]

Stages in the Evolution of a Country's Foreign Trade

A number of writers distinguished various "stages" through which a country's foreign trade would pass—the changing commodity composition of its trade—in the course of the country's economic evolution. In doing so, they revealed an awareness of the changing pattern of international specialization with growth. It is not clear, however, whether they subscribed to the theory of comparative advantage as such or indeed to any particular theory of trade at all. And they seldom explained in any detail the forces propelling a country from one stage to another.[40]

An early nineteenth-century statement of the "stages" approach to foreign trade was provided succinctly by Sir Edward West:

> Such is the course in which improving nations seem destined to move. They begin by exporting raw produce for manufactures; as they grow more wealthy they export less corn, and fabricate more manufactures at home; in a further stage they export manufactures only, and receive rude production from nations less

38. Mill, *Principles*, pp. 589–90.

39. G. Poulett Scrope, *Principles of Political Economy* (London 1833), pp. 380–81; Torrens, *The Budget*, p. 74; and Marshall, *Official Papers*, pp. 402–3.

40. The idea of stages of growth in general goes back to the eighteenth century and was later developed in the writings of Friedrich List and the German historical school in particular. See B. F. Hoselitz, "Theories of Stages of Economic Growth," in B. F. Hoselitz and others, *Theories of Economic Growth* (Glencoe, Ill., 1960), pp. 193–238. The notion of stages in the evolution of a country's foreign trade was often implicit and sometimes explicit in these writings. For an earlier explicit and detailed treatment, see Sir James Steuart, *An Inquiry into the Principles of Political Œconomy* (London, 1767), vol. I, book II.

advanced than themselves, and these manufactures change in kind, containing less and less of rude material, and more and more of manufacturing skill.[41]

There is nothing in this passage, or in the context in which it appears, to suggest any possible explanation of this changing sequence of stages. It is possible, however, that the law of diminishing returns, which West was one of the first to formulate in the very book in which this passage occurs, was one of the main causal factors that he had in mind.

Thomas Smith, another writer of the period, was somewhat more explicit as to causes when outlining a similar pattern of stages. A newly settled country, he noted, will devote its energies almost entirely to agriculture as long as land is abundant and fertile; and it will export its surplus primary produce in exchange for manufactures which it can acquire in this way more cheaply than if made at home. But as population grows and cultivable land becomes fully occupied, part of the increased population can no longer be profitably employed in agriculture and will turn to manufacturing. The growth of the manufacturing population will eventually become greater than can be supported by the country's agricultural produce, and the country will begin to export manufactures to obtain needed food and raw materials.[42] The two key elements in the causal chain so outlined are the "need" to establish manufactures to keep the growing population fully employed and the "need" to export manufactures to acquire the agricultural produce that, implicitly because of diminishing returns, is becoming insufficient at home to support the growing population.[43]

Almost an entire book was devoted by still another writer to a detailed elaboration of the stages in the development of a country's foreign trade.[44] The argument is very obscurely worded, but the same general sequence of stages emerges. The role of diminishing returns in

41. [Edward West], *Essay on the Application of Capital to Land* (London, 1815), pp. 38–39.

42. Thomas Smith, *An Attempt to Define Some of the First Principles of Political Economy* (London, 1821), pp. 64–65. Smith concluded: "This appears to be the natural progress of all nations, and a reference to history will show, that it has taken place in every country that has been civilized." A similar pattern of stages was outlined by an anonymous writer, S. T., believed to be the same Thomas Smith, in *An Address to the Merchants and Manufacturers of Great Britain on the Present State of the Country* (London, 1817), pp. 24–25.

43. Precisely the same two elements were stressed in another brief description of the stages of foreign trade in [Jane Marcet], *Conversations on Political Economy* (London, 1816), p. 367.

44. Thomas Sharpe Smith, *On the Economy of Nations* (London, 1842). This author should not be confused with the Thomas Smith just cited.

agriculture was explicitly stated and made an integral part of the evolving sequence. The writer even suggested that the whole process could be reversible if for some reason "decay" overtook the country and its population contracted.[45] The author also made the interesting point that during the process, before the country shifted to the role of exporter of manufactures, foreign trade would come virtually to a halt for a period of indefinite length: "foreign commerce, which was at first an exchange of raw materials for wrought commodities, shall become little more than a mere barter of articles peculiar to, or more advantageously furnished by either of the countries for those of the other."[46]

Industrializaion and World Trade

Another aspect of the changing patterns of international specialization that drew the attention of various writers was the probable effect of the industrialization of the less developed countries on the volume of world trade. A common conclusion to which many were led, although not always for the same reasons, was that spreading industrialization would reduce the basis for world trade and lead to an actual or at best relative decline in its volume.

One stark argument—in effect, an extreme version of the technological-gap theory—was made in 1828 to the effect that trade would virtually cease when techology had been equally diffused throughout the world. The author wrote:

> All useful distant commerce is founded on inequality in the knowledge of the useful arts; and it is impossible to prevent this knowledge from diffusing itself. When the knowledge of the arts is equally diffused, nearly all commerce between distant towns will cease, and every country or small territory will be independent of all other countries. At no distant period, England will cease to manufacture for the rest of the world, and every nation will find it most profitable to manufacture for itself.[47]

This argument seems to assume that differences in technology are the only cause of trade and apparently of differences in comparative ad-

45. Ibid., pp. 91–92.

46. Ibid., pp. 52–53.

47. T. R. Edmonds, *Practical Moral and Political Economy* (London, 1828), pp. 86–87. A more reasonable statement of this point of view was made by Hamilton, *Progress of Society*, p. 282, in which, after referring to the diversity of skills in particular arts among countries as one of the causes of trade, he noted: "In process of time, other nations may acquire that skill in which they are at present deficient, and then commerce, *so far as it arises from this source*, will be discontinued" (italics supplied).

vantage. It also seems implicitly to assume that at some point technological change comes to an end and that the process thereafter is solely one of diffusion, so that all nations will eventually "catch up" with each other.

A more common line of argument was based on the view that less developed countries as they industrialized (which itself implied drawing to some extent on foreign technology) increasingly would absorb for domestic use primary produce that would otherwise be available for export and would replace manufactures imported from abroad with those made at home. Since world trade was assumed to consist predominantly of an exchange of manufactures for primary produce, the result would be a decline in the volume of trade.

An early statement of this argument was made by an anonymous writer in 1821 and the conclusion explicitly drawn. In discussing the evolution of "less civilized" countries that started out by exporting raw produce for manufactures, he noted that population growth would in time absorb the larger part of that produce for consumption at home. These countries would thus have diminished means for acquiring imports at a time when demand for them was growing. At the same time the desire to give employment to a population that was pressing on the land and becoming redundant would induce them to begin to produce their own manufactures. He concluded that "in the end, all commerce must cease, except in those commodities which can only be produced in particular countries."[48] This argument is similar to the "stages" approach outlined in the preceding section, but the latter was carried one step farther.

A similar type of argument was used by Malthus in the course of his discussion of the relative merits of what he called agricultural systems and commercial (or manufacturing) systems.[49] He noted that one of the problems posed for a "commercial" country was its heavy dependence on imports of primary produce, the purchase of which depended on the country's ability to export manufactures. Those exports, he argued, would be subject to "a necessary and unavoidable diminution" in the "natural progress" of foreign countries. For when agricultural profits in the "landed nations" began to fall (because of diminishing returns), those nations would turn to manufacturing. As a result, the "commercial" countries would find their exports of manufactures falling and their ability to import needed raw produce impaired. An implication of this argument was that the industrialization

48. [Anon.], *Notices on Political Economy* (London, 1821), pp. 61–62.
49. Malthus, *Additions*, pp. 115–17, 133–34.

of primary-producing countries would result in a reduction in the volume of world trade.

McCulloch regarded this argument—"that ultimately every agricultural nation will manufacture for itself, and will cease purchasing from abroad"—as perhaps "the most imposing of all the arguments which Mr. Malthus has urged against the policy of allowing an unrestricted corn trade." But he went on to add:

> . . . surely Mr. Malthus does not mean to insinuate, that, in the progress of society, there will be no interchange of manufactured commodities for raw produce carried on between different countries! It is evidently impossible such a state of things can ever be brought about until the cost of raising raw produce in all the different commercial countries of the world shall be the same.[50]

In this rather ambiguous passage McCulloch appears once again to have been expressing his belief that the pattern of foreign trade is determined by differences in absolute real costs rather than by differences in comparative costs.

The prediction that world trade would become of diminishing importance as nations developed was also made by Torrens in somewhat different terms. He argued that, as a new countries grew in population, increasing resort to less fertile soil would raise the cost of raw produce, while extension of the division of labor would reduce the cost of manufactures. He concluded:

> Hence, in all new settlements the increasing value of raw produce must gradually check its exportation, and the falling value of wrought goods progressively prevent their importation; until at length the commercial intercourse between nations shall be confined to those peculiar articles, in the production of which the immutable circumstances of soil and climate give one country a permanent advantage over another.[51]

Torrens' conclusion is clear enough, but his reasoning is not entirely free of ambiguity. A reasonable interpretation of the passage

50. J. R. McCulloch, "Corn Laws and Trade," *Supplement to the Fourth, Fifth, and Sixth Editions of the Encyclopaedia Britannica* (Edinburgh, 1824), III, 362. Another writer thought that Malthus' argument, if valid at all, would be valid only in the very long run. See J. Clay, *A Free Trade Essential to the Welfare of Great Britain* (London, 1819), pp. 62–63.

51. R. Torrens, *An Essay on the Production of Wealth* (London, 1821), pp. 288–89. This passage was reproduced in almost the same language, but without acknowledgment to Torrens, by Eisdell, *Treatise*, I, 389.

would be that the rise in the cost of agricultural produce relatively to that of manufactures in newer countries as they grew would involve—on the implicit assumption of slower growth or no growth in the industrial countries—a narrowing of comparative-cost differences as between the two sets of countries[52] and thus a reduction in the basis or scope for trade between them. In other words, with increasing pressure of population on land and growth of manufactures in the agricultural countries, relative cost and production structures would become internationally more similar.[53]

Arguments of the kinds raised by Torrens, Malthus, and others were based on the assumptions that imports of manufactures into industrializing countries would decline, that world trade was mainly an exchange of primary products for manufactures, and that agriculture would run up against diminishing returns. The reasoning also implicitly assumed a kind of two-commodity, two-country model. When these assumptions are relaxed, the conclusion can quickly change.

Industrialization does indeed involve some import substitution and to that extent imports tend to fall. But the higher level of real income associated with industrialization increases the demand for imports in general, including manufactures; while the higher level of domestic investment involves increased imports of machinery and industrial materials.[54] On balance, therefore, the industrialization of agricultural

52. Clearly "comparative-cost differences" as used here and elsewhere in this article mean those that would exist in the absence of trade. For with trade, given variable costs and no tariffs or transport barriers, (marginal) comparative-cost ratios become equal in the trading countries. Torrens himself was implicitly aware of this. See *An Essay on the External Corn Trade*, 4th ed. (London, 1827), pp. 80–81. See also the related exchange on this matter between Bastable and Edgeworth in *Economic Journal*, Sept. 1897, pp. 401–2; Sept. 1900, p. 391; June 1901, pp. 227–28; and Dec. 1901, p. 589; and Bastable, *Theory of International Trade*, pp. 196–97.

53. Some years later Cairnes noted that "in proportion as countries approximate to each other in natural resources or in the industrial qualities of their inhabitants, the scope for international trade is narrowed: it is even possible that it should fail altogether." *Some Leading Principles*, p. 300. Unlike Torrens, Cairnes does not appear to have been making a prediction. Variations of the Torrens argument were advanced in more recent years by D. H. Robertson, "The Future of International Trade," *Economic Journal*, March 1938, pp. 1–14; J. G. Smith, "Economic Nationalism and International Trade," ibid., Dec. 1935, pp. 624–25; and E. A. G. Robinson, "The Changing Structure of the British Economy," ibid., Sept. 1954, pp. 455–56.

54. See, e.g., E. A. Staley, *World Economic Development* (Montreal, 1944), pp. 135, 152–43; and A. J. Brown, *Industrialization and Trade* (London, 1943), pp. 47–48. Some later nineteenth-century writers were well aware of these points. See, e.g., Robert Giffen, "Foreign Manufactures and English Trade," *Essays in Finance*, 2d series (London, 1886), pp. 240–74. For similar recognition by some earlier English writers, see infra.

countries could well raise the level of their imports and in fact historically appears to have done so.[55]

Once one drops the assumption that world trade is primarily an exchange of manufactures for raw produce, moreover, it is evident that growth can involve an expansion in trade of manufactures for manufactures—both between agricultural and industrial countries and between industrial countries themselves—with individual countries specializing in particular lines of manufactures in keeping with their comparative advantages and with manufactured exports becoming increasingly differentiated. Indeed, for some time this has been the most rapidly expanding part of world trade. There could also be an expansion of trade in some kinds of primary produce for others. Thus a decline in world trade as a whole need not necessarily follow. Moreover, diminishing historical returns in agriculture, an integral part of the nineteenth-century argument regarding the putative tendency for world trade to decline, could be offset by agricultural improvements.[56] Finally, since there are a great many factors affecting long-term trends in world trade (and in the relation between world trade and world production),[57] attention cannot properly be directed only to the effect on trade resulting from the industrialization of agricultural countries.

The conclusion that world trade was destined to become of decreasing importance was also stated in 1904 by John A. Hobson, but on grounds having nothing to do with changing patterns of comparative advantage. He argued that as per capita incomes rose consumers' expenditures on services would rise faster than on material products, and that a growing fraction of the latter would consist of goods catering to the special tastes and habits of local consumers. As a result, a smaller proportion of aggregate output would be capable of "forming the material of international trade." Foreign trade, while continuing to grow in absolute terms, would not keep pace with the growth of

55. See especially A. Maizels, *Industrial Growth and World Trade* (Cambridge, 1963), pp. 2–14, 415–16.

56. Many of the nineteenth-century writers were of course aware of this as a theoretical possibility, but believed that the offset could be only temporary. Some, although not among those who had predicted a declining trend in world trade, believed that in actual practice this offset had already occurred. See Mill, *Principles*, pp. 193, 704; and Alfred Marshall, "Social Possibilities of Economic Chivalry," *Economic Journal*, March 1907, p. 10.

57. J. Viner, "The Prospects for Foreign Trade in the Post-war World," *Transactions of the Manchester Statistical Society*, June 1946; and R. N. Cooper, "Growth and Trade: Some Hypotheses about Long-term Trends," *Journal of Economic History*, Dec. 1964, pp. 609–28, and *The Economics of Interdependence* (New York, 1968), ch. 3.

production or of internal trade.[58] He regarded this, like several German writers of the period, including Sombart, as an "economic law," the only British writer before 1914 who seems to have done so.[59]

Britain's Comparative Advantage and Foreign Competition

If world trade should indeed contract as industrialization abroad spread, as Malthus, Torrens, and others had predicted, it was clear that Great Britain would be the country most adversely affected, in view of its leading position as an industrial and trading nation. Considerable concern was in fact expressed in the first half of the century on the part of many writers that Britain's supremacy would be eroded by industrialization abroad and by other factors weakening its industrial leadership. It was feared that Britain would face increasing competition from continental countries[60] in their own markets, in third markets, and even in the British market itself, and that its exports of manufactures would decline either absolutely or as a share of world exports in such products. Many believed that apart from the adverse direct effect of such developments on the industries concerned, Britain's overall rate of economic growth would thereby be reduced and its ability to import impaired. These discussions will be briefly surveyed here because they reflected, from yet another angle, awareness of the prospective changes in the pattern of international specialization that growth could bring.[61] It is not suggested, however, that all of the writers concerned were familiar with the theory of comparative advantage as such.

The fear that British exports of manufactures would decline under the impact of increasing foreign competition was one of the factors

58. John A. Hobson, *International Trade* (London, 1904), pp. 5–9. A similar argument to Hobson's was made years later by J. M. Keynes, "National Self-Sufficiency, *Yale Review*, June 1933, p. 760.

59. For this he was chided by Bastable in a review of Hobson's book in *Economic Journal*, Dec. 1904, pp. 610–12.

60. The focus at the time seems to have been mainly on these countries rather than on the United States and other overseas areas.

61. The issue again came into prominence in the latter part of the century, especially after the 1860's, with the actual rise and growth of competition in manufactures from Germany, the United States, France, and other countries, and with the decline in the rate of growth of British exports and in Britain's share in world exports of manufactures. The issue spilled over into parliamentary debates and papers. In addition, a number of valuable empirical studies of the actual extent and effects of foreign competition were made by private investigators, such as Sidney J. Chapman, *Work and Wages: Part I. Foreign Competition* (London, 1904) and Thomas Brassey, *Foreign Work and English Wages* (London, 1879), pp. 118–50, 157–96. But much of the literature of this later period often constituted rather crude pleas for tariff protection, imperial preference, or colonial expansion.

that led to support among some economists for continued agricultural protection as a means of avoiding excessive dependence on manufacturing and on imports of primary produce. John Barton, for example, argued that it was "more than probable that the channels of commercial industry, at all times liable to the most capricious and inexplicable changes, will one day desert us; and this whole kingdom would then become one great decayed manufactory."[62] George Ramsay, another agricultural protectionist, wrote that Britain "cannot have any right to suppose that it shall always supply the greater part of the world with manufactures at a cheaper rate than that at which they can be raised in the respective countries." He spoke of the "dangers of an overgrown manufacturing population" and of the uncertainty of "that fabric of prosperity, built upon a vast manufacturing industry destined to supply foreign nations."[63]

Several elaborated on the gradual erosion that they expected to take place in the various sources of Britain's superiority in manufactures. In an earlier section reference has been made to the view that Britain's industrial leadership would wane as its technology was diffused abroad and as its pace of invention slackened. Other citations to that effect could be made. Malthus argued, with Britain undoubtedly in mind, that advantages based on capital and skill could not in their nature be permanent, since both could be acquired, and that it was unreasonable to expect "that any one country, merely by the force of skill and capital, should remain in possession of markets uninterrupted by foreign competition."[64] Others contended that Britain's advantages resulting from its abundant and cheap coal would be offset as coal mines on the continent were worked more intensively and new mines discovered; and reference was also made to the fact that water power could be used to great advantage in many places abroad.[65] In 1844 Torrens noted that since 1815 continental countries had in fact been approaching nearer and nearer to an equality with England with respect to its superior advantages in mechanical inventions, manual

62. John Barton, *An Inquiry into the Expediency of the Existing Restrictions on the Importation of Foreign Corn* (London, 1833), pp. 42–43.

63. George Ramsay, *An Essay on the Distribution of Wealth* (Edinburgh, 1836), pp. 496, 497, 499. Similar views were expressed by J. B. Holroyd, Lord Sheffield, *A Letter on the Corn Laws*, 2d ed. (London, 1815), pp. 25–26. These views essentially repeat the argument of Malthus, who, as noted above, applied it to "commercial" countries generally.

64. Malthus, *Additions*, p. 108. See also [Anon.], *An Essay on the Political Economy of Nations* (London, 1821), p. 236; and William Spence, *Britain Independent of Commerce* (London, 1807), pp. 73–76.

65. Ramsay, *An Essay*, 496–97; and *Remarks on the Commercial Policy of Great Britain*, op. cit., p. 65.

dexterity, and productive coal mines.[66] At about the same time, a number of economists were arguing that Britain was even then already being undersold in third markets in many of its staple items of manufacture.[67]

Several took a more optimistic view of Britain's export prospects, but on grounds often as impressionistic as those of the pessimists. Thus McCulloch, in listing the sources of Britain's manufacturing superiority, found it difficult to believe that foreign countries could easily match them.[68] One commentator even spoke of Britain's superiority as constantly increasing and dismissed as groundless the fears that it would be left behind in a competitive race.[69] Thomas Tooke is reported to have said in 1839 that he believed it impossible that Britain would not for long maintain its superiority in manufacturing against foreign competition.[70] There were some who recognized that if continental countries displaced some British manufactures as they industrialized, the greater income and wealth associated with their industrialization would mean that "the more will they, on the whole, buy from us, from their using a greater variety of articles, as well as a larger average quantity."[71] Others argued that there could be a greater degree of international specialization in different kinds of manufactures so that Britain, while yielding markets in some, would develop or expand markets in others in which it had some natural advantages or which could not be produced elsewhere.[72] Finally, there were many who simoly contended that exports would take care of themselves if only Britain removed its import barriers and bought freely from abroad.[73]

66. Torrens, *The Budget*, pp. 234–35, and his similar statement in *Tracts for Electors in Finance and Trade*, no. 2 (London, 1852), pp. 28–29.

67. William R. Greg, *Not Over-Production But Deficient Consumption, The Source of Our Sufferings* (London, 1842), pp. 21–25. See also [W.R. Greg], "Emigration or Manufactures," *Westminister Review*, Aug. 1843, pp. 118–19; and J. Broadhurst, *Political Economy* (London, 1842), p. 239.

68. [J. R. McCulloch], "Rise, Progress, Present State, and Prospects of British Cotton Manufacture," *Edinburgh Review*, June 1827, pp. 26–27.

69. Eisdell, *Treatise*, I, 345.

70. As reported by J. L. Prévost in Political Economy Club, *Minutes of Proceedings, 1899–1920, Roll of Members, and Questions Discussed, 1821–1920, With Documents Bearing on the History of the Club* (London, 1921), pp. 277–78. For extreme optimism, see William T. Thornton, *Over-Population and Its Remedy* (London, 1846), pp. 445–46: "Britain may yet, for aught that human eye can discern, retain her manufacturing prosperity till the end of time." This comes immediately after a discussion of the reasons why Britain allegedly had nothing to fear from foreign competition.

71. George Purvis [Simon Gray], *All Classes Productive of National Wealth* (London, 1817), p. 208.

72. [Henry Parnell], "Effects of the Protective System," *Edinburgh Review*, Jan. 1841, p. 454; and Purvis, *All Classes*, pp. 206–7.

73. See, among others, Ricardo, *Works*, II, 363, and VI, 108–9. A number of writ-

It was inevitable that the question of relative money wages in Britain and on the continent would be introduced into the discussion as a factor affecting Britain's competitiveness. As early as 1803, Malthus had expressed the fear that the price of labor and food at home "must soon increase in a manner out of all proportion to their price in the rest of Europe; and it is impossible that this should not ultimately check all our dealings with foreign powers, and give a fatal blow to our commerce and manufactures."[74] He later took a more balanced view of foreign competition and in particular distinguished manufactures in which Britain had special advantages and those in which it did not. He wrote in 1815:

> . . . if we look at the probable effects of returning peace to Europe, it is impossible to suppose that, even with a considerable diminution in the price of labour, we should not lose some markets on the continent, for those manufactures in which we have no peculiar advantage; while we have every reason to believe that in others, where our colonies, our navigation, our long credits, our coals, and our mines come in question, as well as our skill and capital, we shall retain our trade in spite of high wages.[75]

In the first edition of his *Essay on the External Corn Trade*, Torrens had emphasized that higher food prices meant higher money wages, which in turn meant higher prices of manufactures and other goods generally; and he had argued for removal of the Corn Laws partly on the ground that by bringing down food prices and thereby wages and prices generally, it would improve Britain's competitive position in world markets.[76] However, by the third edition in 1826 the references to rising wages having the effect of increasing prices in general were eliminated. Torrens continued to argue, however, that increases in money wages could have an injurious effect on Britain's competitive position.[77] Many other writers emphasized the alleged

---

ers, notably Bowring, Jacob, and MacGregor of the Board of Trade, argued that free trade by Britain would also help its exports of manufactures by slowing down the development of manufacturing on the continent. On this, see C. P. Kindleberger, "The Rise of Free Trade in Western Europe," *Journal of Economic History*, March 1975, pp. 33–34.

74. T. R. Malthus, *An Essay on the Principle of Population*, 2d ed. (London, 1803), pp. 443–44. This sentence was removed from later editions of the *Essay*. Spence, *Britain Independent*, pp. 69–72, also laid great stress at about the same time on high British wages in his pessimistic forecast of British exports.

75. Malthus, *Grounds of an Opinion*, p. 31.

76. Torrens, *Essay*, 1815, esp. pp. 226–44, 298–99.

77. R. Torrens, *On Wages and Combination* (London, 1834), pp. 60–80. See also L. Robbins, *Robert Torrens and the Evolution of Classical Economics* (London, 1958), pp. 58–60.

competitive advantage to continental exporters because of their lower wage levels.

In response, there were those who argued that the higher money wages in Britain were simply a reflection of the higher productivity of British labor and did not imply higher unit labor costs. Mill, for example, expressed doubts that British wages were higher than those on the continent if allowances were made for differences in efficiency.[78] He further argued that low wages, even when corrected for productivity, would not help a country's competitive position in world markets if they were common to all branches of a country's industry. For, he said, low or high wages were not a cause of low or high prices: they simply made profits high or low.[79] An earlier version of this argument, with a decidedly "Heckscher-Ohlin" flavor, had been presented by McCulloch to the effect that higher wages paid in England compared (by way of illustration) with France, by causing lower profits, would give Britain an advantage in the export of those manufactures that used relatively much machinery, while giving France an advantage in those goods that used relatively much labor. He concluded that a rise in wages could never be fatal to a country's foreign trade: if it raised the price and checked the export of certain goods, it would lower the price and stimulate the export of others.[80]

With regard to later nineteenth-century discussions of foreign competition and of actual or prospective changes in the pattern of Britain's comparative advantage, brief reference will be made only to Jevons and Marshall. In his *The Coal Question* in 1865, Jevons cautioned against the assumption that the growth of commerce ensured Britain everlasting riches and industrial supremacy. Like Torrens over forty years earlier, he was deeply concerned with the longer-run prospect of industrialization abroad, especially in the United States, and with its effect on British trade; and he anticipated a narrowing of comparative-cost differences as resources were shifted from primary production to industry abroad under the impact of population growth and diminishing returns in agriculture. He predicted gloomily:

78. Mill, *Principles*, p. 681. See also Purvis, *All Classes*, pp. 205–6.

79. Mill, *Principles*, pp. 682–85. This was of course the Ricardian position. Edgeworth later criticized Mill on the ground that he had underrated the danger to the home country arising from foreign competition. F. Y. Edgeworth, "The Pure Theory of International Values, III," *Economic Journal*, Dec. 1894, pp. 613–15.

80. J. R. McCulloch, *The Principles of Political Economy*, 2d ed. (London, 1830), pp. 335–57. Broadhurst (op. cit., p. 281) noted that Britain could not hope to compete in labor-intensive manufactures with those continental markets where labor was relatively cheap.

> Corn will be growing dearer in the States, while coal and iron are growing dearer here. The industrial conditions of England and the States will thus approximate to equilibrium, and the advantages of trade will diminish. We shall neither buy corn from them, nor sell iron articles to them. And at the same time America will tend to supplant us in the European market for iron and other crude materials, and in all parts of the world in the market for textiles and useful manufactured articles in general.[81]

Such a development, coupled with declining coal resources at home, would check the continuous growth of British population and industry (if that had not occurred earlier), necessitate wholesale emigration, and lead to economic retrogression.

The changing international position and prospects of Britain were also discussed by Marshall in the course of a far-ranging survey in 1903 of British trade policy in the light of the economic changes of preceding sixty years.[82] Among other things, he called attention to the relative retrogression of Britain compared with the United States and Germany, to the fact that the "progress of the arts and resources of manufacture" had in nearly all respects benefited England less than other countries, to the comparative ease with which its industrial processes and technology had been adopted and in many cases improved by other nations, to the growth of foreign tariffs against its manufactures, and to the effects that all these and other developments were exerting upon the character and prospects of British trade. He noted that

> England will not be able to hold her own against other nations by the mere sedulous practice of familiar processes. These are being reduced to such mechancial routine by her own, and still more by American, ingenuity that an Englishman's labour in them will not continue long to count for very much more than that of an equally energetic man of a more backward race. Of course, the Englishman has access to relatively larger and cheaper stores of capital than anyone else. But his advantage in this respect has diminished. . . . and must continue to diminish. . . . England's place among the nations in the future must depend on the extent to which she retains industrial leadership. She cannot be *the* leader, but she may be *a* leader.[83]

81. W. Stanley Jevons, *The Coal Question*, 2d ed. (London, 1866), p. 346.
82. Marshall, "Memorandum on the Fiscal Policy of International Trade."
83. Ibid., p. 404.

Elsewhere he pointed out that the real danger from foreign competition is "that we shall be undersold in the product of high class industries, and have to turn more and more to low class industries . . . that our industries will become of a lower grade relatively to other countries."[84]

Britain's Comparative Advantage and Restrictions on the Export of Machinery

In the 1820's to 1840's there was a lively debate in Britain on the pros and cons of removing the various restrictions that had been imposed in the eighteenth century on the export of machinery and the emigration of artisans—a debate in which many of the leading economists of the day participated. These restrictions were mainly designed to forestall competition in manufactures from potential foreign rivals. Between 1824 and 1841 the subject was explored in detail by no less than three Select Committees of the House of Commons, which collected voluminous testimony and issued several excellent reports.[85] The ban on the emigration of artisans, almost wholly ineffective in any case, was lifted in 1824 following the recommendation of the first Select Committee, but the restrictions on the export of machinery were not fully lifted until 1843.

Economic writers focused their attention mainly on the question of the export of machinery.[86] Their views are of relevance here because the issue at stake in effect involved Britain's comparative advantage in manufactures and the possibility of its impairment. Four differing attitudes to the restrictions can be distinguished.

One position was that the restrictions should be continued on the ground that although they were not wholly effective and continental

84. Letter to Bishop Westcott, 20 January 1901, in *Memorials of Alfred Marshall*, ed. A. C. Pigou (London, 1925), p. 393.

85. House of Commons, *Reports from the Select Committee on Artizans and Machinery*, 23 Feb.–21 May 1824, 6 parts (#51); *Report from the Select Committee on the Laws Relating to the Export of Tools and Machinery*, 30 June 1825 (#504); and *Reports from the Select Committee Appointed to Inquire into the Operation of the Existing Laws Affecting the Exportation of Machinery*, 2 parts, 1 April 1841 (#201) and 11 June 1841 (#400). These voluminous studies consisted mainly of testimony collected from engineers, merchants, customs officials, manufacturers, and others. The only two economists of note who testified were McCulloch and Malthus.

86. A recent writer has called attention to the fact that Manchester manufacturers inconsistently demanded removal of import duties on imports of raw cotton and the abolition of the Corn Laws, while remaining stubbornly protectionist in opposition to removal of restrictions on the export of machinery. A. E. Musson, "The 'Manchester School' and Exportation of Machinery," *Business History*, Jan. 1972, pp. 17–50. Musson's article gives some details regarding the background of the debate on the restrictions. See also B. Semmel, *The Rise of Free Trade Imperialism* (Cambridge, 1970), pp. 181–83; and Kindleberger, *Journal of Economic History*, March 1975, p. 29.

countries would eventually be able in any case to construct similar machines themselves, there was no reason why Britain should make it any easier for these countries to acquire British technology and to compete that much sooner with British manufactures. To be sure, British machine-makers were being hurt by the restrictions—to the extent that they were effective—but it was implicitly assumed that manufacturers of the products made by the machines would be hurt far more if the restrictions were removed.

This was the position taken by Torrens in an early statement of his views on the subject. He argued that the principle of free trade should be limited by the principle that each country should reserve to itself the sole benefit of those exclusive advantages that it happened to enjoy. Why, he asked, should Britain permit the free export of its superior machinery, which made its manufactures cheaper and better than those of its rivals?[87] Another writer similarly asked why Britain should sell to foreigners machinery that had taken her, and might take them, years to acquire, and in so doing adversely affect those of her industries that in large part owed their continued existence to the superiority of that machinery.[88] Senior also seems to have been of the same mind. In dissenting from the view that England would not be injured by the improvement of its neighbors—noting that England and the continent were competitors in the general market of the world—he pointed out in a footnote that his reasoning bore materially on the question of the export of machinery.[89]

A second approach to the problem was to argue for a removal of the export restrictions, not because they were necessarily objectionable in themselves, but because in actual practice they were ineffective in achieving their purpose. McCulloch, the chief proponent of this point of view, argued in fact that a monopoly of machinery, if it could be achieved, would redound considerably to Britain's benefit. But he was aware, as were Malthus and others—and as testimony before the Select Committees had confirmed—that there was extensive smuggling out of machinery that could not be curbed, that plans, models, and specifications of machines could easily be acquired by foreigners, and that scientific knowledge could readily be transferred

87. Torrens in *Parliamentary Debates*, n.s., XVI, 6 Dec. 1826, col. 294–95.

88. [Sir William Sleeman], *On Taxes or Public Revenue* (London, 1829), p. 200.

89. Nassau W. Senior, *Three Lectures on the Cost of Obtaining Money* (London, 1830), pp. 25–26. For further expressions of opposition to the removal of restrictions on these lines, see [Charles Ross], "Artizans and Machinery," *Quarterly Review*, March 1825, pp. 418–19; Kennedy, *Export of Machinery*; pp. 23–25; J. Syme, *The Principles of Political Economy Applied to the Financial State of Great Britain* (London, 1821), p. 320; and Edmonds, supra n.47, pp. 91–92.

abroad in a variety of ways. As they saw it, the main result of the restrictions—to the extent that they were effective—was to encourage the production of machinery abroad and to cut down a profitable market that British machine-makers would otherwise have had, without necessarily helping the British manufacturers whom the restrictions were designed to help. Under the circumstances it seemed wisest to eliminate the restrictions altogether. The stress, however, was on their ineffectiveness and their side-effects rather than on any strong objection to the principle underlying them.[90]

A third point of view, also in favor of removing the restrictions, was based on the belief that foreign countries, even if they could import British machinery freely, would probably still be unable to compete effectively with or pose a serious challenge to British manufactures. For Britain's superiority in manufactures depended not only on the possession of superior machinery but also on a wide variety of other factors influencing its comparative advantage in this area. This point of view was well expressed in the report of one of the Select Committees in the following words:

> Supposing, indeed, that the same Machinery which is used in England could be diffused on the Continent, it is the opinion of some of the most intelligent of the witnesses that the want of arrangement in foreign manufactories, of division of labour in their work, of skill and perseverance in their workers, and of enterprize in the masters, together with the comparatively low estimation in which the master manufacturers are held on the Continent, and with the comparative want of capital, and of many other advantageous circumstances detailed in the evidence, would prevent foreigners from interfering in any great degree by competition with our principal manufacturers.[91]

90. McCulloch's views on the export of machinery were scattered widely throughout his writings. See especially *On Commerce*, pp. 66–67; *Treatises and Essays*, pp. 448–49; "Restraints on Emigration, &c.," *Edinburgh Review*, Jan. 1824, p. 345; and his testimony on 7 May 1824 before the Select Committee on Artizans and Machinery, *Sixth Report*, 21 May 1824, pp. 582–98. Malthus' views were expressed in his testimony before the same committee on 10 May 1824, ibid., pp. 598–601. Torrens, whose earlier views have been noted above, had also accepted this point of view by the time he wrote *The Budget*. He there noted that laws against the exportation of machinery could only retard, not prevent, the inevitable transfer of scientific power abroad under the existing state of international communication, and that in the long run "we should lose the advantage of manufacturing superior machines for the foreign market without being able to secure their exclusive application." Ibid., pp. 235–36.

91. *Report from the Select Committee on the Laws Relating to the Export of Tools and Machinery*, supra n.85, p. 15.

In short, the thrust of this point of view was that restrictions on the export of machinery were not really needed to protect British manufactures from foreign competition and could therefore be abolished without any serious consequences. It is of interest to note that this position was also taken by McCulloch and Malthus in their testimony before the 1824 Select Committee already cited, although its logic was to some extent inconsistent with that underlying the other argument they had expressed in favor of removing the restrictions.

Finally, there were those who supported removal of the restrictions on the ground of the positive benefits that would accrue from the free export of machinery. John Stuart Mill, for example, argued that it was in "the common interest of all nations that each of them should abstain from every measure by which the aggregate wealth of the commercial world would be diminished." He noted that machinery made freely available to foreign countries would be employed above all in the production of those goods in which they already had the greatest natural advantages, so that if the country which made the machines available lost by their improvements in the production of the goods which it sold, it would gain by their improvements in those which it bought. Even so, Mill had several reservations and, while favoring the removal of the restrictions, concluded that the "exportation of machinery may . . . be a proper subject for adjustment with other nations, on the principle of reciprocity. Until . . . all restrictions upon trade are done away with, a nation cannot be required to abolish those from which she derives a real advantage, without stipulating for an equivalent."[92]

William Ellis argued the case for free export of machinery on the ground that the benefits of trade lay not in a country's exports but in its imports, and that restrictions on the export of machinery, by restraining productive improvements abroad, made imports more expensive than they would otherwise be. He illustrated his argument by an arithmetical example purporting to show that countries would be better off with free rather than restricted export of machinery.[93]

According to Sraffa, Ricardo shortly before his death had promised his friend Joseph Hume that he would assist him in his proposed motion before the House of Commons, subsequently introduced on February 12, 1824, against the laws restricting the export of machin-

92. Mill, *Essays on Some Unsettled Questions*, pp. 30–32.

93. [William Ellis], "Exportation of Machinery," *Westminster Review*, April 1825, pp. 386–94. See also Charles Babbage, *On the Economy of Machinery and Manufactures*, 4th ed. (London, 1846), pp. 364–78.

ery, the emigration of artisans, and combination of workers.[94] We do not know for sure what the basis for Ricardo's support would have been.

Conclusion

Nineteenth-century British economic writings reveal ample awareness of the fact that patterns of comparative advantage and of trade flows were changing over time and would continue to change under the impact of economic growth and other dynamic forces. Technological advance and its international diffusion were widely regarded as among the leading forces propelling these changes and were examined in some detail. Recognition was also given to the role of such factors as population growth, diminishing returns in agriculture, increasing capital supplies, and discovery or exhaustion of important natural resources.

Analyses were made of the implications of changes in comparative advantage for world trade and for individual countries. Some writers argued that the growth of less developed countries would reduce the volume of world trade by narrowing comparative-cost differences among nations or for other reasons. Others distinguished more or less predictable "stages" in the evolution of the commodity composition of trade of individual countries as they developed. Still others stressed the factors acting on and potentially weakening Britain's comparative advantage in manufactures as foreign countries grew. Many participated in discussions of the pros and cons of maintaining the restrictions on the export of machinery that had been imposed in an attempt to preserve Britain's trade superiority in manufactures.

In the process of elaborating these ideas, many of the writers anticipated concepts and models that have been used in modern analyses of the impact of growth and technological change on comparative advantage and trade. Although these various ideas were seldom developed systematically or integrated into the main body of classical trade theory, the range and breadth of the discussions on these problems, as well as on other related trade issues of a "dynamic" sort that will be examined in later articles, indicate that the classical economists and their contemporaries were much more interested in the relations between international trade and economic growth than is commonly believed.

94. Ricardo, *Works*, V, xx.

I am indebted to Wilfred Ethier, Irving Kravis, and Sidney Weintraub for helpful comments. I also wish to express my indebtedness for their many courtesies to librarians of the Goldsmiths' Library, the British Museum, the London School of Economics and Political Sciences, the Kress Library, the New York Public Library, and the Special Collections of the University of Pennsylvania Library.

[14]

Journal of Economic Literature
Vol. XVI (December 1978), pp. 1415–1434

The Canonical Classical Model of Political Economy

By PAUL A. SAMUELSON
Massachusetts Institute of Technology

I owe thanks to the National Science Foundation for partial financial aid, and thanks also to helpful criticisms from George Stigler, William Baumol, and Mark Blaug, most of which I took to heart.

1. Adam Smith, David Ricardo, Thomas Robert Malthus, and John Stuart Mill shared in common essentially one dynamic model of equilibrium, growth, and distribution. When the limitation of land and natural resources is added to the model of Karl Marx, he also ends up with this same canonical classical model.

In its present version the model is stripped down to its minimal essentials. For brevity I employ modern mathematical tools, but only to characterize in modern terms the relations that were actually common to all these writers.

The reader should of course be warned that any simple codification of the classical economists' discursive writings must be an oversimplification: in some of their passages they qualify what they have written elsewhere; in some they provide negations and contradictions. Not a few of the stereotypes about the classical writers are, to paraphrase Voltaire, myths agreed-upon by later commentators—distortions that both improve and libel the originals. The relevant object of study for a modern scholar is the corpus of original texts and the commentaries on them, the latter not being genuinely of less interest than the former once we have succeeded in telling them apart.

To the fascinating question of whether classical political economy does, or can be made to, offer an *"alternative paradigm"*—in the sense of Thomas Kuhn [11, 1962]—to modern mainstream economics, the present investigation provides an instructive answer. So to speak, within every classical economist there is to be discerned a modern economist trying to be born. A Ricardo or Mill did not so much replace supply and demand by quite different mechanisms but rather sought to be able to say something significant and limiting about their properties, quite in the same way that we moderns endeavor to do. I describe and analyze here the basic classical model in its essential form.

2. Real output is divided interchangeably between *consumption* and *capital formation* (on a net or gross saving-investment basis). Ignoring details concerning the input-intensity differences between goods of different industries (much as can be done in a modern one-sector one–capital-good model), the classicists in effect assume that output is produced by a pro-

duction function involving land input and a *dose* of labor-*cum*-capital input. Competition among (1) landowners, (2) entrepreneurs who hire labor and needed raw materials to work with hired land, and (3) owners of labor and capital goods out to make the most favorable terms for themselves—all this leads to a determinate breakdown of competitive earnings and cost between (a) land rent and (b) the *combined return to the composite dose of labor-capital.* The breakdown of the combined return to the dose between its two components would be indeterminate as far as the demand side of the problem is concerned (at least this would be so if we stick literally to the fixed-proportions assumption usually alleged to be adhered to by the classical writers). The needed conditions come from the supply side.

3. The classical long-run theory postulates that the workers' wage rate is ultimately determined by (α) the real *subsistence* level needed to ensure reproduction and maintenance of the working population. Just as the classicists had a long-run horizontal supply curve for the subsistence wage, so they had a long-run horizontal supply curve for capital at (β) the *minimum-effective rate of accumulation,* that profit rate just low enough and just high enough to cause capital to be *maintained* with zero net algebraic saving. The long-run equilibrium number of total doses, with the implied long-run plateau of population and of capital stock, is just big enough so that the law of diminishing returns brings down the combined return of the dose to the *sum* of the needed wage-subsistence and needed minimum-profit rates. When accumulation has gone that far and population has grown in balanced proper degree, then in the absence of further technical change total land rent is *maximal.* Equilibrium prevails forever. (Mill went on to emphasize that technological innovation, continued in the long-run steady state, would imply *rising output forever;* we can show on Mill's behalf that, if the technical change is *land-augmenting* at a steady exponential rate, then labor and capital will grow forever at the same balanced exponential rate, just enough to match the growth of land measured in "efficiency units" and with the long-run wage rate and profit rate each just high enough above their respective bare minima to elicit the implied growth rates of the factors.)

4. The long-run equilibrium is stable in the sense that the system, if disturbed from it, will spontaneously return toward it. To grasp the short-run transient development of the system, suppose labor and capital goods begin in the balanced proportions needed for the technological dose, but with each at a level short of the long-run equilibrium level. Land rent then will begin below its long-run equilibrium; by the same token, the aggregate return to the composite dose will begin in excess of the long-run subsistence levels. The short-run breakdown of the dose's aggregate return among capital and labor will be determined by competitive auctioneering at that fractional breakdown just *needed to keep the two components of the dose growing at the same balanced rate* (which will be a uniquely determinate growth rate).

Thus, if population adjusts so rapidly to any surplus of real wage above subsistence that we can practically assume the truth of (what can be termed) Ricardo's "short-circuited" approximation, then the transient wage rate will be insignificantly different from the long-run subsistence level. The rate of profit is then determinate as a *residual* in the short run. And being thus determined *above* the long-run minimal profit rate, the system's saving propensities will determine the rate at which capital accumulates and population grows apace. Asymptotically, the growth of doses of capital as applied to a limited supply of land leads down the trail of diminishing returns to the rendezvous of long-run equilibrium.

Suppose we go beyond the short-circuited version and recognize that just as it takes an increment of profit rate to elicit positive saving and growth of capital, so too there must be an increment of real wage rate over the subsistence level to elicit the needed transient growth in population. Still, we shall find that there is a determinate short-term breakdown between the components of the dose's aggregate return that will be just enough to keep both labor and capital growing in the needed fixed-proportions way. The only difference in this more realistic scenario is what Smith envisioned so much more clearly than Ricardo—namely, that the real wage is higher in the transient state of progressive growth. Only in the final equilibrium when growth ceases is society in Smith's *dull* state of minimal real wages. Ricardo's predecessor and successor, Smith and Mill, are both more realistic than is Ricardo himself on wages adjustments. (By contrast, Ricardo is more realistic in 1817 [21] than Smith in 1776 [29] when it comes to recognizing that continuing new inventions will greatly delay the fall of the profit rate to its minimum and perhaps continue to do so permanently.)

Even Mill is not realistic enough in his modelling of innovation and the lagging supply of population in advanced economies. What observers like Kuznets have observed this past century is that the growth of technology has been enough *to keep the real wage growing at something like an exponential rate,* with the growth in population and saving not being fast enough to wipe out the rising trend in real wages. By contrast, the rate of profit has meandered more or less trendlessly depending on the qualitative structure of technical change, much as if population growth were more a bottleneck than were saving. It is curious that the Marxian variant of classicism, with its soft-pedalling of the limitations of land and natural resources, ought logically to have led to an even more optimistic scenario for the laws of motion of capitalistic profits than the Ricardo-Smith version.

Long-Run Equilibrium Diagrammed

5. *Figure* 1 shows the canonical classical equilibrium in the long run or steady state. The *DD'* relation, which looks like a modern demand relation, gives the competitive return to the composite dose of capital-*cum*-labor: the greater the number of doses competing for the same fixed supply of various qualities of land, the higher will be bid up land rents and the lower will be the dose price available to be divided between labor's wage rate and capital's profit-or-interest rate.

The *DD'* relation looks like a Clarkian neoclassical marginal-product curve for the variable composite doses applied to fixed land(s). But we shall be more in tune with the classicists' own mode of thinking if we delay giving *DD'* that admissible interpretation.[1] Perusal of the accompa-

[1] The numerical tables in the last part of Chapter II on rent of Ricardo [21, 1817] leave sketchy his notion that "successive portions of capital [doses 1, 2, 3, and 4] yielded 100, 90, 80, 70 [with total rent therefore being (100−70) + (90−70) + (80−70) + 0 = 60 and the total return to the 4 units of doses being [(100+90+80+70) − 60]/4 = 280/4 = 70]." It is clear that Ricardo believed that extra available doses would both work with lands of lower quality not previously worth cultivating and work old lands more intensively, thus altering both the *extensive* and *intensive* margins of cultivation.

Until the last half century, no one seems to have worked out rigorously the processes going on implicitly in the background, although Mountifort Longfield [12, 1834] came close to doing so as far as "reduced-form" descriptions are concerned. We shall outdo the classicists and underplay neoclassical versions of marginalism by first utilizing the following model, which is analyzed in Samuelson [24, 1959; 28, 1977].

(a) A strip of land declines continuously "eastward" in "fertility." (b) Every grade of land is cultivated

LONG-RUN EQUILIBRIUM

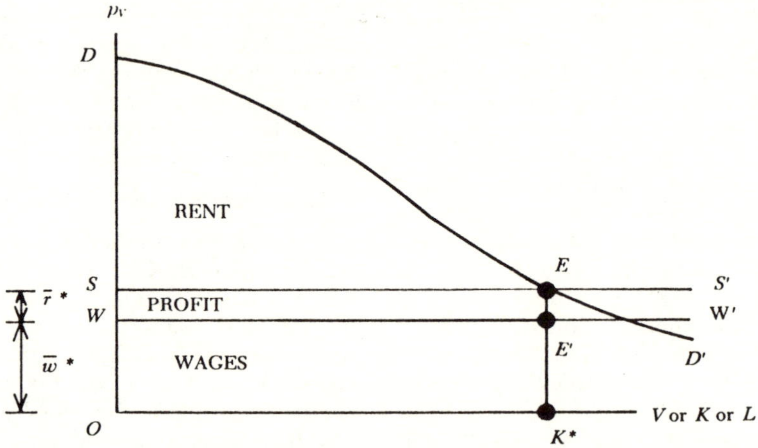

Figure 1. Long-run equilibrium is at *E*, where the *DD'* curve of return to the doses of *V*, made up of balanced proportions of *L* and *K* applied to a fixed profile of lands, just intersects the *SS'* supply curve that measures the wage subsistence and the minimum profit rate needed for steady reproduction of labor and capital. The equilibrium long-run wage rate is $\bar{w}^*$ and the long-run profit rate is $\bar{r}^*$, both exogenous parameters. Distribution of total product, *OK*ED*, is between the residual rent triangle *SED* and the dose's rectangle *OK*ES*. The breakdown between wages and profit is given by the rectangle's breakdown into *OK*E'W* and *WE'ES*. (Possibly $\bar{r}^*$ could be zero. *DD'* can be given the ultra-classical interpretation as the *average product* of the dose on the *external* margin of a continuum of lands of different grades; but, also, it could be the dose's common *marginal product* at the varying *intensive* margins of all lands used.)

nying footnote shows how we might also interpret *DD'* as the curve of *average product of the varied dose* out at the moving external frontier of zero-rent grade of land.

6. The supply of labor is given by the horizontal line *WW'*, representing the subsistence cost of reproduction of labor in steady-state numbers. Followers of Smith, Ricardo, and Mill were prepared to recognize non-physiological components in the subsistence level of wages required by workers before their patterns

by composite doses of exactly the same internal *relative* labor-capital proportions. (c) Fixed proportions of dose to land prevail at each grade's longitude, with (d) return of product per doses applied declining continuously as we move eastward. Then, when total available doses are few, all land to the east is not worth cultivating; as doses increase in availability, they all are applied ever further eastward (with no change in density of doses on prime westward land, but of course with increased *differential rent* earned on those prime acres). For each total of doses available, there is an external frontier of zero-rent land: the height of *DD'* at any given *V* is the *average product* (not the yet-to-be invented "marginal product") of output per unit of *V*, namely *Q/V* there. Footnote 7 below will show when *DD'* also can be interpreted as a true marginal product of the variable composite dose, *V*.

of marriage, procreation, migration, and labor-force participation were just adequate to keep total labor employed constant. Marx shifted the determinants of *WW'* away from Malthus's emphasis on biological elements of marriage, procreation, and mortality toward his own emphasis on the reserve army of the unemployed, labor-saving inventions, and inmigration to the industrial regions from the over-populated rural areas.

So long as we choose conventional units for labor, capital goods (or "leets"), and composite doses that agree in numerical magnitude, the height of *WW'* represents the *real wage rate* per unit of labor, $\bar{w}^*$, that must prevail when labor power's cost of reproduction is just achieved and its long-run total is in stationary equilibrium.

7. Superimposed on *WW'*, to achieve the long-run supply response *SS'* for the composite dose, is the long-run profit per unit of capital goods needed if the profit rate per annum is to be at the effective rate of accumulation, $\bar{r}^*$, just enough to choke off further net saving but not so low as to cause dissaving and eating up of the previously existing stock of capital goods.

8. The distance *WS*, or *E'E*, represents both the rental rate of capital goods *and* the ("own") profit rate per unit time (such as .10 when 10 percent is the rate of profit to be earned on assets) when our numeraire for output is capital-goods per unit time. When differences in factor intensities between the consumption- and the capital-goods industries are ignorable, as in *Figure* 1, there is no difference between using consumption goods or capital goods as numeraire provided both kinds of goods are actually being produced—as will be the case for any stationary or growing system.

This long-run profit rate might, in some theories, be zero (after, of course, all allowances for depreciation and replacement of principal have separately been allowed for; after any needed actuarial premia for probable accidents and losses had been properly allowed for; and after any wages of managing capital assets had been provided for). If $\bar{r}^*$ is zero, *SS'* would coincide with *WW'* and *E* with the intersection of *DD'* and *WW'*: the vertical distance between them measures the long-run *perpetual net rental* (if any) to be earned by owners of maintained capital-goods (leets) in the steady state when they are just motivated to cease net saving or dissaving.

9. The *residual of land rent* is measured on the diagram by the curvilinear triangle *SED*. It is what is left of total product, *OK*ED*, after the composite doses are paid their needed long-run aggregate of *OK*ES*. Whereas J. B. Clark and such neoclassicals as Philip H. Wicksteed, Knut Wicksell, Léon Walras, and Paul Douglas would split up the non-rent aggregate between labor and capital by a marginal-product calculation in which variability of the labor-to-leets components is brought to the optimal degree of substitution, the present classical paradigm denies such smooth substitutability *within* the composite dose and at best tolerates it between land and the composite of the fixed-components dose.

From the horizontal long-run supply curves of the components, *WW'* and *SS'*, and from them alone comes the classical system's determinate *long-run* distribution theory of the non-land factor shares.[2]

[2] If $V = \text{Min}[L, K]$ were replaced by a neoclassical-first-degree-homogeneous smooth function, $v[L, K]$ with well-defined partial derivative, $\partial v[L, K]/\partial L$, the same $\bar{w}^*$ and $\bar{r}^*$ levels would prevail in the long run: but now the 2-dimensional *Figure* 1 would be inadequate to depict the determination of the resulting L^* and K^* levels: marginal productivity conditions, involving *DD'* and $\partial v[L, K]/\partial L$ would be the necessary and sufficient conditions to determine the extra unknowns of the rephrased problem, as in §19 below.

10. As noted in the Physiocratic version of the classical system of Samuelson [23, 1959], under long-run equilibrium all goods can be decomposed into their (marked-up) socially-necessary *land* contents: a shift in tastes and final demand from one good to another, toward more cloth and less corn, would have no effect on long-run prices. But such a shift toward less–land-intensive and more–labor-intensive goods would lower rent's share in ultimate national income; it would also raise the plateaux of population and of capital in any model where they combine in doses of the same proportions in all industries (an implausible special case). The point is obvious that any classicist who thinks he can separate "value" from "distribution" commits a logical blunder. He also blunders if he thinks that he can "get rid of land and rent as a complication for pricing" by concentrating on the external margin of no-rent land: where that external margin falls is an *endogenous* variable that shifts with tastes and demand changes so as to vitiate a hoped-for labor theory of value or a wage-*cum*-profit-rate theory of value.

11. For given technological knowledge, there is defined a unique steady-state ("factor-price") frontier relating (α) the *profit or interest rate* to (β) the *real wage rate* (expressed in terms of market basket of subsistence goods or in terms of any specified good) and (γ) the *rate of land rent* earnable by a composite unit of *all* grades of land weighted by their actual importance in the system. With the profit rate and the real wage given at their long-run supply levels, the rent rate is maximal at the long-run rendezvous of the system. (For fixed profit rate, the trade-off between real wage and rent rates can be shown to be convex, no matter how many the sectors or capital goods.)

Any reader uninterested in the rigorous analysis of this classical model may skip the next section's mathematical exposition and concentrate on the subsequent section's graphical analysis of classical growth and development.

Mathematical Version of the Canonical System

12. To define the system's behavior both in long-run equilibrium and also in transient movements toward equilibrium, here are the equations implied by this version of the classical system.

Real output, Q, is divided into real consumption, C, and net capital formation, dK/dt. It is produced at time t out of land and a composite dose of labor and capital goods ("leets"), $V_t = \text{Min}[L_t, K_t]$, where the units in the dose and in L_t and K_t are related so that one dose involves one unit of labor and one unit of capital goods. With land (possibly of various grades) fixed, we can omit the symbol for it (T, standing for a scalar, a vector, or even possibly a function of a parameter denoting a continuum of grades) in the economy's production function.

The basic production function becomes

$$Q = 1(C) + 1(dK/dt) = f(V). \quad (1)$$
$$V = \text{Min}[L, K], \quad (2)$$

where $f(V)$ is a *concave* function with $f'(V) \geq 0, f''(V) \leq 0$. [Warning: only the expositional need to compress the model into a single sector and the desire to exaggerate the differences between classical and neoclassical writers can justify so simple and strong an axiom of fixed proportions. When we relax this by quoting passages in classical writings, we need to augment the system with extra equations that help determine the extra unknowns.]

Total land rent, R, is given residually by

$$R = f(V) - Vf'(V). \quad (3)$$

The non-rent real return to the total dose, p_V, expressed in output units as numeraire, is equal to the sum of the wage component and the profit component: it is given by

$$f'(V) = p_V = 1w + 1r, \qquad (4)$$

where w is the real wage in output units, r is both the own rate of interest and the real rental rate of capital goods expressed in output units (*i.e.*, interchangeably in capital-good or consumption units), $f'(V)$ is the increment in product resulting from an extra dose of V, applied to fixed land(s); its reciprocal is the competitive marginal cost of output in terms of extra needed V requirements.[3]

13. As *Figure* 1's WW' and SS' horizontal lines indicated, w and r have to be at the well-defined $\bar{w}^*$ and $\bar{r}^*$ levels in long-run equilibrium. Thus, *Figure* 1's E is defined by the long-run equilibrium equations:

$$f'(V^*) = \bar{w}^* + \bar{r}^* = p_V^* \qquad (4^*)$$
$$R^* = f(V^*) - V^*f'(V^*) \qquad (3^*)$$
$$L^* = K^* = V^* \qquad (2^*)$$
$$Q^* = C^* + 0 = f(V^*). \qquad (1^*)$$

Any increase in the subsistence wage, $\bar{w}^*$, or in $\bar{r}^*$, must lower V^*, R^*, K,* and L^*, Q^*, and C^*. The absolute shares ($\bar{r}^*K^*$, $\bar{w}^*L^*$) can move in either direction relative to R^*: if $\bar{r}^*/\bar{w}^*$ rises, the profit/wage share rises, but how a change in $\bar{w}^*+\bar{r}^*$ affects the $(\bar{w}^*+\bar{r}^*)V^*/R^*$ ratio must depend on how changes in V affect the elasticity of the $f(V)$ curve (more precisely, on what we today call the elasticity of substitution of the $f(V)$ production function).

[3] As will be seen later, when one of the L or K inputs exceeds its needed proportions—*i.e.*, when $L/K > 1$ or $K/L > 1$—the price of the redundant's input in (4) is zero, corresponding to a free good. So (4) must be augmented under ruthless perfect competition by

$$w = 0, \quad L > K \qquad (4a)$$
$$r = 0, \quad K > L \qquad (4b)$$
$$w + r = f'(\text{Min}[L, K]), \quad L \gtreqless K. \qquad (4c)$$

For all their talk about the importance of the problem of distribution between land rent, labor wages, and profits, the classicists succeeded in saying little definite (and correct!) on levels of and changes in relative factor shares.

14. The dynamic laws of growth of population, $(dL/dt)/L$, and of the accumulating stock of capital, $(dK/dt)/K$, must be specified for the canonical model. When the real wage rate, w, is above the subsistence real wage rate, $\bar{w}^*$, the population grows—and grows at a greater rate the greater is the excess in wage rates:

$$\epsilon(dL/dt)/L = \lambda[w - \bar{w}^*]; \qquad (5)$$
$$\lambda[0] = 0, \quad \lambda'[\ ] > 0.$$

Here ϵ is a non-negative parameter determining the slowness of the growth response of labor supply to surpluses over subsistence wages: if $\epsilon = 0$, the adjustment is instantaneous of short-run w to long-run $\bar{w}^*$ level of subsistence as L grows at whatever pace is needed to achieve $\bar{w}^*$; this is what I call the Ricardian "short-circuited" version of dynamics. If ϵ is a large positive parameter, evidently the more realistic case historically, the population grows only slowly during a high-wage era. By definition, in the long run, $(dL/dt)/L = 0$ when $w = \bar{w}^*$.

15. For Smith, Ricardo, and Mill, saving and investing never fail to be equated at full-employment conditions; only Malthus expressed doubts, envisaging in 1820 [15] the possibility of oversaving and violation of what we know loosely as "Say's Law." The rate of saving-investment is positive when r exceeds $\bar{r}^*$, the effective rate at which net accumulation ceases. Crudely, we write:

$$(dK/dt)/K = \sigma[r - \bar{r}^*]; \qquad (6)$$
$$\sigma[0] = 0, \ \sigma'[\ ] > 0,$$

where $\sigma[r - \bar{r}^*]/r$ is the fraction that saving will bear to total profit incomes.

16. Our dynamic canonical classical system is almost complete.[4] If it *always* started with initial L_0/K_0 in the balanced configuration of unity and remained always in a balanced configuration, it would in fact generate determinate motions of all our variables: $L(t)$, $K(t)$, $V(t)$, $w(t)$, $r(t)$, $p_V(t)$, $C(t)$, $Q(t)$.

One such complete version is the "short-circuited" case already referred to. In it, we make the unrealistic polar Ricardian assumption that population adjusts virtually instantly, so that w falls or rises immediately to the $\bar{w}^*$ subsistence wage rate. Now (5) is replaced by:

$$w = \bar{w}^*, \quad L(t) \equiv K(t) \equiv V(t) \qquad (5')$$

Our new system [(1)–(4), (5′), (6)] can now be reduced to

$$(dK/dt)/K = \sigma[f'(K) - \bar{w}^* - \bar{r}^*], \quad K(t_0) = K_0 \qquad (7.1)$$
$$Q = f(K) \qquad (7.2)$$
$$C = f(K) - dK/dt \qquad (7.3)$$
$$L = V = K \qquad (7.4)$$
$$w = \bar{w}^* \qquad (7.5)$$
$$R = f(K) - Kf'(K). \qquad (7.6)$$

The equilibrium at the K^* root of $f'(K) = \bar{w}^* + \bar{r}^*$ is globally stable: for any initial positive K_0,

$$\lim_{t\to\infty} [K(t), L(t), r(t), R(t), \ldots] = [K^*, L^*, \bar{r}^*, R^*, \ldots], \qquad (7.7)$$

where the starred long-run equilibria are precisely those of (1*)–(4*). The global stability follows from the fact that $\sigma[x]$ always has the sign of x and $-dK/dt$ therefore always the sign of $K - K^*$.

17. Not even Ricardo adhered to the short-circuited version in which the population is instantly variable so that the wage rate could be regarded as adjusting to the long-run $\bar{w}^*$ rate instantaneously. Ricardo realized that labor as well as capital would have to share in the transient surplus of the dose's return: how much of the maximum "wage fund" that could go to wages rather than to profits was never worked out in proper supply-and-demand detail by the classical writers but was left implicit by Ricardo and his contemporaries. Our supply relations (5) and (6) explicitly bridge the logical gap. (See ***Figures*** 3(a) and 3(b) for the diagrammatic details.) The full classical system of (1)–(6), if started out with initially balanced (K_0, L_0) sufficiently near to (K^*, L^*), will forever after grow with K/L in the needed balance and with neither factor redundantly free. Subject to such balanced conditions, the canonical system of (1)–(6) can be reduced to the determinate dynamical system:

$$(dK/dt)/K = \sigma[f'(K) - w - \bar{r}^*], \quad K_0 = L_0 = V_0 \qquad (8.1)$$

$$(dK/dt)/K = (dL/dt)/L = \sigma[f'(K) - w - \bar{r}^*] = \epsilon^{-1}\lambda[w - \bar{w}^*]. \qquad (8.2)$$

Between (8.1) and (8.2) we can eliminate w as an unknown, solving for it uniquely in terms of K:

$$w = \omega(K; \epsilon) \qquad (8.2')$$
$$\partial w(K;\epsilon)/\partial K < 0,$$
$$\omega(K^*;\epsilon) \equiv \bar{w}^*.$$

The less is ϵ, the faster w approaches final equilibrium, the sign of $\partial\omega/\partial\epsilon$ being that of $-(K - K^*)$.

Our determinate system becomes:

$$(dK/dt)/K = \sigma[f'(K) - \omega(K;\epsilon) - \bar{r}^*] \qquad (9.1)$$
$$0 \equiv \sigma[f'(K^*) - \omega(K^*;\epsilon) - \bar{r}^*]$$
$$\lim_{t\to\infty} K(t) = K^*$$

for all K_0 near enough to K^* for (8.2) to have the solution of (8.2′). The smaller is ϵ, the closer the solution of the full-fledged canonical system (1)–(6) to the short-circuited version.

[4] With the (4a) and (4b) relations of footnote 3, the dynamic system would be complete (as will be discussed later in footnote 6).

18. There remains only the task of showing that the canonical system is determinate and globally stable from any *initial conditions* of positive K and L, balanced or unbalanced.[5]

Suppose we start the system off with excess supply of one of the factors—say with more of capital goods (leets) than can be manned by labor. With $K_0 > L_0$, the short-term rentals of redundant capital goods would fall to zero under ruthless competition. At a current profit rate of zero (really negative if we recognized depreciation), there would be no profit income to save, and presumably there would be every incentive for all holders of capital assets to want to dissave at as rapid a rate as possible. Meantime labor's wage is getting all of the gross return to the composite dose, and population growth will be rapid. Therefore, very quickly, K/L will diminish toward balanced proportions without redundancy— the case already analyzed in (8) or (9).

Similarly, if we begin with redundant L/K, labor will be a free good with a zero competitive price or wage. Under laissez faire, people will die like flies; even if poor-law relief slows down the process of genocide, after an interval L/K will have dropped to balanced proportions suitable for the earlier analysis. (If one more realistically replaces perfectly fixed proportions by some variability of techniques, the r/w factor-price ratio will not gyrate so violently to zero or infinity and the more neoclassical model of §19 will better approximate reality.)

In every case, ours is a deterministic system for $(L, K, dL/dt, dK/dt)$ and the other variables.[6]

Digression on Neoclassical Elaboration of the Classical Model

19. Ricardo and Marx were not so naive observers as to believe literally in fixed proportions between capital goods and labor. Their knowledgeable commentaries on current events presuppose recognition that, at certain price and profit rates, substitutions will be made that would not be competitively viable at other price and profit rates. So it is a caricature to insist on fixed-proportion doses, $V = \text{Min}[L,K]$.

On the other hand it would be ahistorical to read into the classicists a full-fledged post-Clarkian model of neoclassical type. Nonetheless, if we wish to flesh out the torsos of their logically incomplete models, we must supply the equations missing for their additional unknowns. And, once we commit ourselves to (α) free-entry and widely-shared knowledge, (β) constant-returns-to-scale technology, and (γ) smooth variability of the (L_t, K_t) components of the V_t dose, ruthless competition will enforce the neoclassical marginal productivity relations in the canonical model whether or not the classicist is yet aware of those relations and is able to apprehend them. (Before Isaac N.'s birth, apples and the moon fell toward the earth in accordance with inverse-square-of-distance gravitational laws!)

To evaluate the question of how different the classical paradigm was from to-

[5] Strictly speaking, if initial L_0 is astronomically large, starvation and insurrection might kill off the system in one fell swoop. To do justice to this realism, we would have to make $\lambda[w - \bar{w}^*]$ minus infinity at $w = 0$ and perhaps make $f(V)$ turn down for overly large V. Along with the classical writers, I forbear from modelling scenarios of *extinction* from overpopulation. Darwin would no doubt deem this a fault.

[6] The dynamic system is most generally defined by

$$dL/dt = \epsilon^{-1}\lambda[g_1(L, K) - \bar{w}^*]$$
$$dK/dt = \sigma[g_2(L, K) - \bar{r}^*]$$

$$g_1(L, K) + g_2(L, K) = f'(\text{Min}[L, K]), \quad K \gtreqless L$$

$$g_1(L, K) \equiv 0, \quad L > K; \quad g_2(L, K) \equiv 0, \quad K > L.$$

For any initial (L_0, K_0), this system will approach §13's (L^*, K^*) asymptotically.

day's mainstream economics, it is worth sketching briefly the consequences of replacing $f(\mathrm{Min}[L,K])$ by smooth constant-returns-to-scale technology. To relate the discussion more easily to classical "wage-fund" notions, I work with discrete-time variables, $K_{t+1} - K_t$ instead of dK/dt, and so forth. Writing $(T_1, T_2, \ldots) = \mathbf{T}$ for prescribed amounts of different grades of land, we have:

$$Q_{t+1} = C_{t+1} + K_{t+1} - K_t = F(L_t, K_t; T_1, T_2, \ldots), \quad (10.1)$$

where $F(\ )$ is a first-degree-homogeneous, concave function.[7] For this section, F's partial derivatives are assumed to be well-defined everywhere, in contrast to $\mathrm{Min}[L_t, K_t]$'s assumed non-substitutability. The present section does not rule out that $F(\ )$ might have the separability property of $F(v[L,K]; T_1, T_2, \ldots) \equiv f(v[L,K])$, where $v[L,K]$ is now a smoothly substitutable first-degree-homogeneous and concave function. In this last case, $\partial F/\partial L$ and $\partial F/\partial K$ would be equivalent to $f'(v[L,K])\,\partial v[L,K]/\partial L$ and $f'(v[L,K])\partial v[L,K]/\partial K$, with $wL + rK = f'(v[L,K])\,V$ still.

We complete our system with the relations:

$$r_t = \partial F(L_t, K_t, T_1, \ldots)/\partial K_t \quad (10.2)$$

$$w_t = \frac{\partial F(L_t, K_t, T_1 \ldots)/\partial K_t}{1 + r_t} \quad (10.3)$$

$$R_{t+1} = F(L_t, K_t, T_1, \ldots) - r_t K_t - w_t L_t(1 + r_t). \quad (10.4)$$

Note that the workers who are paid *at the beginning* of the period receive only their *discounted* marginal productivity. Note that the total of profit includes (α) interest on wages advanced to the workers (in consumable output) plus (β) the interest earned on the capital-goods used in production K_t. Land gets as residual rent under competitive bidding that part of end-of-period product not preempted by competitive bidding for laborers and capital goods; if rent is payable in advance, competitive arbitrage will ensure that it too will be discounted by the $1/(1 + r_t)$ factor.

Long-run equilibrium comes when all dated variables are starred constants determined by (10.1)–(10.4), when (10.2)–(10.4) have had inserted inside them $\bar{w}^*$ and $\bar{r}^*$ exactly as in §13.

To generate the dynamic growth path of the classical system, we complete it by the supply conditions of saving and of population growth:

$$\frac{K_{t+1} - K_t}{K_t} = \sigma[r_t - \bar{r}^*], \quad (10.5)$$

$$\sigma[0] = 0 < \sigma'[\ ]$$

[7] As Ricardo and J. H. von Thünen understood, larger totals of L and K involve more intense cultivation of previously cultivated grades of good land—say of T_1, at the same time that T_2 newly comes into cultivation. In the background, the function $F(\ )$ has been defined implicitly *as if* by a maximization process. Thus

$$F(L, K; T_1, T_2, \ldots) = \underset{L_i, K}{\mathrm{Max}}\{F_1(L_1, K_1, T_1) + F_2(L_2, K_2, T_2) + \ldots\}$$

subject to

$$L_1 + L_2 + \ldots = L,$$
$$K_1 + K_2 + \ldots = K.$$

If $F_i(\ )$ are concave in (L_i, K_i) and $\partial F_i(\ )/\partial L_i$ and $\partial F_i(\ )/\partial K_i$ are well-defined, or if, for the composite dose $V_i = \mathrm{Min}[L_i, K_i]$, $\partial F_i(V_i, T_i)/\partial V_i$ is well-defined for $F_i(\ )$ concave in V_i, then for all lands actually in use, there will be common marginal productivities of the transferable factors, equal as the case may be to $\partial F(L,K; T_1, T_2, \ldots)/\partial L$ or $\partial F(L,K; T_1, T_2, \ldots)/\partial K$ or to $\partial F(V; T_1, T_2, \ldots)/\partial V$. Therefore, in *Figure* 1 and later figures, the DD' curve of $f'(V)$ represents not merely the *average* product at the *external margin* of continuous-grade lands (as in my footnote 1's' ultra-classical interpretation); DD' alternatively represents the true *marginal* product (at the *internal* margin on every land used of whatever grade) of the variable dose there applied. Note that residual rent, $R = F(V; T_1, T_2, \ldots) - V\partial F(V; T_1, T_2, \ldots)/\partial V$, can *also* be given the post-classical interpretation as being a *marginal-product imputation to lands:* it is logically $R = [T_1 \partial F(V; T_1, T_2, \ldots)/\partial T_1] + [T_2 \partial F(V; T_1, T_2, \ldots)/\partial T_2] + \ldots$ when $F(V; T_1, T_2, \ldots)$ is smooth and obeys constant-returns-to-scale—whether or not Adam Smith had ever known anything of the work of his contemporary, Leonhard Euler!

$$\frac{L_{t+1} - L_t}{L_t} = \lambda[\mathrm{w} - \bar{w}^*], \qquad (10.6)$$

$$\lambda[0] = 0 < \lambda'[\ ]$$

$$\lim_{t\to\infty} [L_t, K_t, r_t, w_t, \ldots] = [L^*, K^*, \bar{r}^*, \bar{w}^*, \ldots]. \qquad (10.7)$$

The stability property of (10.7) holds under wide conditions.[8]

It would not be hard to include in (10.5) explicit handling of the wage-fund component in the total asset base upon which capitalists earn profits. For that matter, the capitalized value of land could, in the fashion of A. R. J. Turgot [34, 1770] and Franco Modigliani [18, 1966], be included in the asset base of life-cycle saving. But to handle these items and the public debt rigorously would be to mete out more than justice to the classical writers.

Actually, the classical economists did less than justice to their own model. To suppose that the real wage of any period must merely be the ratio of however many workers present themselves for jobs, divided into that part of C_t which capitalists have decided not to consume but instead have dedicated to the wage fund is not so much a falsehood as a triviality. There could be a period so short in which that version of the wage fund might even be formally correct. (But even this is dubious: the potatoes coming into Manchester need not go by that night into some worker's belly; they might be stored for another day or be destined for the stomach of one of Jane Austen's genteel rentiers.) For a more sympathetic appraisal of wage-fund, see George Stigler [32, 1976].

In the long-run steady state, the fraction of C^* that is adapted to wage-earner's consumption will have been *endogenously* determined. In the transient growth phase of the classical system where each month or year is not very different from its predecessor or successor, the competitive system will anticipate and forestall unpleasant surprises: so the "wage fund" will have been adapted to the viable real wage and total of employed population rather than itself constituting a *deus ex machina* to predetermine wages. John Stuart Mill had reason to dither when various of his wage-fund expositions came under attack—which is not to disagree with the attack in Frank W. Taussig [33, 1896] on the vulgar view of Henry George that

---

[8] For $\sigma'[\ ]$ and $\lambda'[\ ]$ sufficiently small, the difference equations of the above neoclassical model will be at least locally stable. For any number of factors, $(T, L, K, \ldots) = (x_0, x_1, x_2, \ldots)$, the following version will be stable:

$$(dx_i/dt)/x_i = s_i[p_i - \bar{p}_i^*], \quad (i = 1, \ldots, n)$$

$$p_i = \partial F(1, x_1, \ldots, x_n)/\partial x_i = \partial f(x_1, \ldots, x_n)/\partial x_i$$

$$s_i[0] = 0 \leq z s_i[z] x_i, \qquad x_i > 0$$

$$F(x_0, x_1, \ldots, x_n) = x_0 f(x_1/x_0, \ldots, x_n/x_0)$$

$f(x_1, \ldots, x_n)$ a strictly-concave function.

We may set $x_0 = 1$; and denote by $(x_1^*, \ldots, x_n^*)$ the unique roots of

$$\bar{p}_i^* = \partial f(x_1, \ldots, x_n)/\partial x_i, \quad (i = 1, \ldots, n).$$

Then, for all positive (x_i^0),

$$\lim_{t\to\infty} x_i(t) = x_i^*, \qquad (i = 1, \ldots, n).$$

To prove this theorem on global stability, consider

$$R(x_1, \ldots, x_n) = F(\bar{x}_0, x_1, \ldots, x_n) - \sum_1^n \bar{p}_j^* x_j$$

$$\dot{R} = \sum_1^n [F_j(\bar{x}_0, x_1, \ldots, x_n) - \bar{p}_j^*]\dot{x}_j = \sum_1^n [F_j(\ ) - \bar{p}_j^*]x_j$$

$$s_j[F_j(\ ) - \bar{p}_j^*] > 0 \text{ when } x_j \neq x_j^*$$

$$\therefore \lim_{t\to\infty} R(t) \equiv \text{Max } R = R^*$$

$$\lim_{t\to\infty} x_j(t) = x_j^*, \ (j = 1, \ldots, n).$$

Note that $\dot{R} = dR/dt$, etc., and that the sign-preserving property of $z_j s_j[z_i] x_j$ has been exploited in the above proof of global stability. I owe thanks to Hiroaki Nagatani of the MIT graduate school for suggesting that $d[R^* - R(t)]/dt$ be used as a Lyapunov function for this stability proof. When dx_i/dt is replaced in this footnote's first equation by $x_i(t + 1) - x_i(t)$, it can be shown that the resulting difference equations will assuredly be locally stable provided

SHORT-CIRCUITED CASE

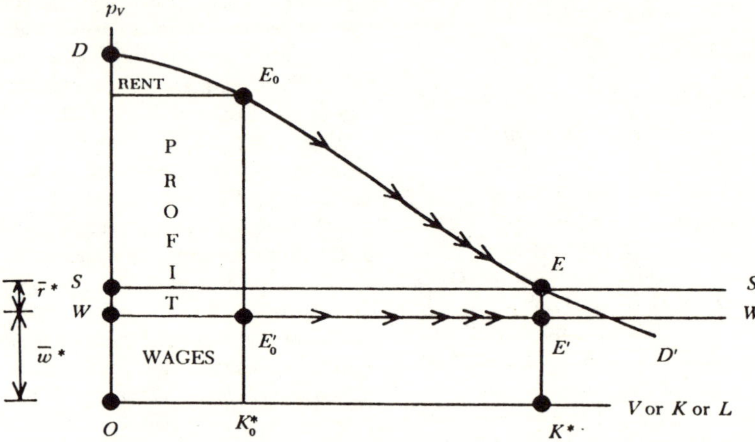

Figure 2. When population supply adjusts virtually instantly, $w(t)$ is always at $\bar{w}^*$ along WW'. With capital (and labor) initially scarce at K_0, rent begins low as shown by the small triangle at E_0: *all* the gain to the composite dose goes to profit as a short-term residual, as shown by E_0' being down on WW'. But the excess of $r(t)$ over $\bar{r}^*$ generates accumulation, as shown by the growth arrows at E_0 and E_0'. Gradually, as $E_0 \rightarrow E^*$ and $r(t) \rightarrow \bar{r}^*$, growth shuts itself off as shown by the shortening of the arrows near the long-run equilibrium E.

production of outputs by inputs is instantaneous and automatically synchronized, a view that seemed to have been surprisingly condoned by J. B. Clark [7, 1899] and Frank Knight in his many writings of the 1930's, and a view properly questioned in Eugen von Böhm-Bawerk [2, 1906; 3, 1907] and echoed a generation later by Fritz Machlup [13, 1935] and Friedrich von Hayek [9, 1936].

* * *

After this neoclassical digression, the reader may return to the canonical classical system. Whether or not he has sampled the mathematical expositions of §12–19, he should be able to follow the next section's graphical depiction of the canonical classical model's path of dynamic development.

Diagrammatics of Classical Growth Theory

20. *Figures* 2, 3(a) and 3(b) provide a self-contained derivation of how the classical system is self-propelled into development by capital accumulation and parallel population growth whenever it initially starts from scarcity of capital and labor relative to their long-run equilibrium rates when they barely earn their costs of reproduction.

For pedagogical simplicity, it is well to begin with the "short-circuited" version of virtually instantaneous population adjustment and the real wage practically always at the subsistence level $\bar{w}^*$. *Figure* 2 portrays this archetypical case, essentially embodying the equations of (7) from §16. The legend should be self-explana-

CANONICAL GROWTH

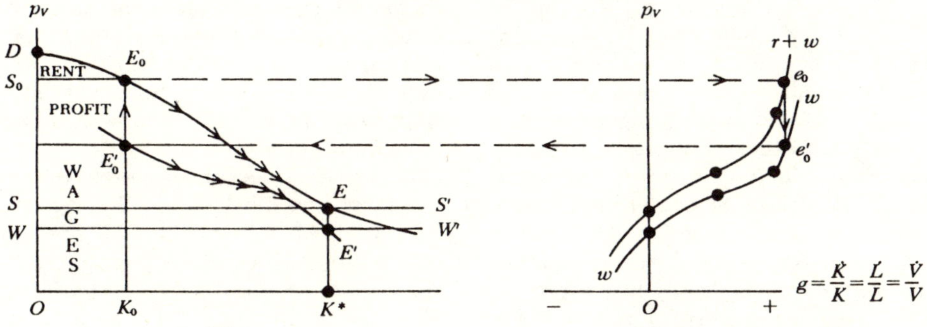

3(a) 3(b)

Figure 3. Labor and capital grow in concert from initial E_0. But now competition determines a fractional breakdown of the dose's surplus return between *both* components of the dose, $w(t) - \bar{w}^*$ as well as $r(t) - \bar{r}^*$, at those fractions that just succeed in evoking the same balanced growth in the supplies of the respective factors $L(t)$ and $K(t)$. The $E_0'E'$ locus in 3(a) gives the breakdown of the fruits of transient progress between capitalists and laborers: the faster the relative supply responsiveness of population, the nearer will $E_0'E'$ be to WW' and the greater profit's transient share; the steeper is $E_0'E'$ northwest of E', the greater the transient share of labor in the above-subsistence surplus. (Short-run distribution of total product, of OK_0E_0D, is shown by the rent triangle S_0E_0D; the dose's remaining rectangle $OK_0E_0S_0$ is divided between profit share and wages share by E_0' on the $E_0'E'$ locus.)

3(b) shows exactly how the $E_0'E'$ locus is determined. The locus ww shows the real wage needed to elicit each algebraic growth rate of labor in balance with the composite dose, $g = \dot{K}/K = \dot{L}/L = \dot{V}/V$ (where $\dot{L} = dL/dt$, etc.). The $r + w$ locus shows the p_V composite returns needed for the combined dose to grow, its needed wage rate plus needed profit rate, to induce balanced growth g—with $w(t)$ read from the lower curve and $r(t)$ from the interval between the curves. One begins at the computational cobweb E_0 in 3(a) then moves horizontally to e_0 in 3(b) and down to e_0'. Going back to 3(a) gives appropriate height of E_0' in 3(a) and appropriate short-run distribution of non-rent income between profit and wages, thus filling in at each new time any logical gaps in the "wage-fund" palaver of the classicists.

tory, as the system moves the short-run equilibrium point E_0 down the path of diminishing returns on fixed land: as E_0 approaches E^*, with $w(t)$ always on the WW' level of $\bar{w}^*$ and $r(t)$ therefore falling toward $\bar{r}^*$, the motive for saving shuts itself off and the system eases itself asymptotically into long-run equilibrium with minimal profit and wage rate and maximal land rent.[9]

[9] If scarcity of land is ignored, the law of diminishing returns is negated and DD' becomes a horizontal line above WW'. This yields the perpetual exponential growth of Marx's *Tableau of Extended Reproduction*, with the growth arrows never shortening and with finite E undefinable.

21. *Figures* 3(a) and 3(b) are interrelated diagrams that handle the more general case. Eschewing the naiveties of the short-circuited pole, they portray the short-term equilibrium in which the transient shortfall of capital and labor leads to both wage and profit being above their ultimate subsistence levels in relative degrees determined by the short-run elasticities of these factors' growth responses: the auction markets for goods, lands, labor, and capital determine short-term equilibrium factor and goods prices that provide allocation between profits and wages of the composite dose's transient surplus return.

To supplement the legends of *Figures* 3(a) and 3(b), the reader will want to understand what determines the dynamic path $E_0'E'$ in 3(a), the path that summarizes how much goes to above-subsistence wages and how much to what Schumpeter would have called *transient* profits (which, he thought, would soon cease to exist in the absence of technical change and entrepreneurial innovation because $\bar{r}^* = 0$ for Schumpeter).

To test his understanding, the reader should be able to realize that Smith's cheerful rise in real wages would be enhanced if the ww curve were made more vertical in 3(b) and the $r + w$ curve were made virtually parallel to it.[10] By contrast, the short-circuited case will be understood as that in which ww is virtually horizontal while $r + w$ is not. In every case, the dashed-line cobweb $E_0e_0e_0'E_0'$ determines the position of the points on the $E_0'E'$ path of wage-profit allocation and the decelerating growth rate of the classical system as land scarcity invokes the law of diminishing returns and the relapse into long-run equilibrium.

Ricardo's readers should not have been shocked by his third edition discovery that invention of machinery could depress the real wage and lower the population and the total of product in the short and long run. Already in his earlier editions, and quite independently of the *durability* of capital goods, there was present to a truly sophisticated eye the possibility that *DD'* could twist *upward and inward*, the *only* limitation on the *long*-run viability of an invention being that it *raise* the *SED* rent triangle!

[10] *Figures* 3(a) and 3(b) in effect solve the simultaneous equations (8.1) and (8.2) for each inherited level of K and its accompanying balanced L. In the pre-balanced stage where one of L or K might be redundant, the diagrams must be reinterpreted. Thus, suppose K/L initially unbalanced above unity. Then only the ww curve in 3(b) is relevant: we run from E_0 over to it and short-run E_0' coincides with E_0; V_t grows with L_t and, being redundant, K_t's level is irrelevant. Once L_t rises to K_t, 3(a) and 3(b) apply as shown. To handle the case of initially redundant L_0, the reader should vertically subtract ww from $w + r$, labelling the result as rr; then, erasing ww, he should proceed as in the previous several sentences but with the factors being interchanged in the logically obvious way.

Final Qualifications and Extensions

22. The classicists earned for our subject Carlyle's title of the dismal science precisely because their expositions erred in overplaying the law of diminishing returns and underplaying the counterforces of technical change. They lived during the industrial revolution, but scarcely looked out from their libraries to notice the remaking of the world.

Thus, as innovation plucks the *DD'* string outward, it would in all likelihood lift real wages and profit rates above their minima. Before they and the string can dampen down, a new invention plucks again the string. Therefore, a Brownian dance or Schumpeterian fluctuation of real wages and profits at average levels *above* the minima would be the proper and realistic generalization of the notion of gloomy equilibrium. Indeed, if one steps up the rate of innovation enough, an upward trend in the level of E_0' and real wage may be called for as the putative laws of motion of developing capitalism, which could have made economists in

Carlyle's eyes the complacent scientists and the apologists for the system.

Just as one example, suppose land-augmenting technical change takes place according to Malthus's *arithmetic* progression. Then if he could analyze correctly his version of the canonical system, he would find that population comes to grow in an *arithmetic* and not in a *geometric* progression [14, 1798]. An amusing irony? Perhaps, but not a joke on Malthus: for, asymptotically, the real wage would then indeed approach his subsistence wage, $w(t) \rightarrow \bar{w}^*$. But, whatever the warrant for geometric progressions in biological reproduction, Malthus never had any plausible reasons behind his gratuitous effusions about arithmetic progressions. If the wrangler had remembered from his Cambridge education three rather than two kinds of progressions, Malthus's impact would have been weakened, but his analysis would have been less special.

23. The present model narrows the classical focus to a single sector. Thereby, one succeeds in freeing their distribution theory from the dreaded complications of value theory. Thereby, one fabricates the Ur-Ricardo model, which determines the system's profit rate from the corn sector alone: having only one sector, it is the corn sector that Ladislaus von Bortkiewicz [5, 1907], Piero Sraffa [30, 1951], Nicholas Kaldor [10, 1956], and others liked to think about; and, contrary to enemies of neoclassicism, there is nothing in the model of a corn-sector-that-determines-its-own-profit-rate which is alien to neoclassicism.

But of course many of the classical problems—as for example the actual share of wages to profits or rent—were recognized by them to depend on many-sector demands. Reducing the Corn-Law tariff on imported food shifted the mix of English production to less land-intensive goods and lowered rent's share. Ricardo knew that in 1815 and 1821: no external margin can logically save his pseudo-labor-theory-of-value from "the complications of value theory and resource scarcities." In my bicentennial appreciation of Smith [28, Samuelson, 1977], I sketched a many-commodity version of the present system, and in my classroom lectures on Ricardo, I show how a 2-primary-factor time-phased system *must* depart from the simplicities of a labor-only technology. It would be easy here to deal with many capital goods of differing durabilities.[11] But it is ludicrous to think that problems that haunt a post-neoclassical writer today—the 1966 Hahn problem of foresight to determine the warrantable allocation among microsectors and durable goods, reswitching, *etc.* [8, 1966]—were themselves absent from the century of 1750–1850 or were better handled by some lost paradigm of the capitalist writers. Under a powdered wig you find the usual head, like yours and mine, sometimes inflated and sometimes sage, but quite innocent of magic charms and skeleton keys to banish complexity.

24. Much of what has been called history of economic thought deals with questions like, "What did Ricardo mean when he said . . . ?" And "Was Smith right and Malthus wrong in alleging . . . ?" On this occasion it has not been my purpose to find and quote the pages in which Smith or Marx or Mill did or did not define an exogenous reproduction wage or profit rate, $\bar{w}^*$ and $\bar{r}^*$. Like the Bible, the canon of classical political economy contains passages that seem to assert and to deny the same thing. If, in some mood or for some problem, an ancient writer denies some axiom of what has here been called the canonical classical system, that does not

[11] Thus, we might replace K in (2) by the vector $\mathbf{K} = (K_1, K_2, \ldots)$ and dK/dt in (1) by $\Sigma c_j(dK_j/dt)$, recognizing that depreciation of each K_i occurs at the rate $\delta_i K_i$.

dispose of the problem. It raises the question of what he then intended to provide for the now-missing equation of the new system.

The canonical model is not so realistic in its features or pretty in its logic that any classicist, if he really understood it in all its, interrelations and implications, would want to go into a very hot oven to defend it. As you read the letters of debate and agreement between Malthus and Ricardo, the treatises of Smith and Mill, you realize that theirs was not an age where one set out in Whitehead-Russell or even Spinoza purity the structures of their models. Their quarrels lasted because often they were quarrels over misunderstandings and definitions. (I was intrigued a few years ago when Professor Dorfman came from Harvard to my MIT seminar to report on Malthus's theoretical system: it turned out—Say's Law aside—to be isomorphic with my earlier report to the seminar on Ricardo's system, even though Dorfman and I had never compared notes! Yet Ricardo and Malthus thought they had different and irreconcilable views on microeconomics, and most commentators have judged Ricardo the victor in the debate.)

On reflection, I think that the present version of the classical system agrees in behavioral essentials with that understood by John Ramsey M'Culloch, William Nassau Senior, Samuel Bailey, Karl August Dietzel, Francis Y. Edgeworth, Edwin Cannan, Frank W. Taussig, Jacob Viner, and Piero Sraffa. I have checked my relations and behavior equations against those of Nicholas Kaldor [10, 1956], Luigi L. Pasinetti [20, 1960], Mark Blaug [1, 1978], Hans Brems [6, 1960], and Samuelson [22, 1957; 23, 1959; 24, 1959; 25, 1971; 26, 1974; 27, 1977] and believe they all tell essentially the same classical story. Left to the Appendix is a cursory sampling of the semantic quarrels of the classical writers.

Literary Appendix on Doctrinal Disputes Among Classicists

I ought to address myself, even if briefly, to the following queries. "Have you not minimized the basic differences between the classical writers in formulating for them a common canonical model? After all, didn't Ricardo set out to write his *Principles* in considerable degree because he thought Smith in error on important matters?"

The considered answer I would give is this: "Yes, Ricardo differed with Smith; and thought those differences important. But upon detailed examination, we find that their differences do not mainly involve differences in their behavior equations, short-run or long-run, but rather involve their semantic preferences about what names could be given to the same agreed-upon effects. To moderns, it is for the most part a quarrel about nothing substantive, being essentially an irrelevant argument carried out by Ricardo, often with somewhat unaesthetic logic."

I shall illustrate with no less than Ricardo's Chapter 1, Section 1 [21, 1817]: Here Ricardo wishes to relate changes in any good's "value" to changes in its embodied labor content alone; and here he chides Smith for replacing embodied labor content by how many hours of labor a good can command (or, in some Smithian moods, by what need not be quite the same thing, by the amount of corn or means-of-subsistence goods basket that the good in question may trade for or command).

A 3-good version of the canonical model will show Smith and Ricardo in absolute agreement on *all* substantive facts. Corn, ballet, and gold are each producible by land, labor, and possibly out of themselves as needed raw materials or durable goods in a time-phased way. Here are test cases.

Case 1. Land is redundant and rent

zero. The profit rate is zero ($\bar{r}^* = 0$). In this initial rude state, each good has a market price in proportion to its labor contents; each good commands precisely those same labor contents. A drop in labor requirements for a good like gold cheapens gold relative to corn and ballet and relative to a day's labor. Gold has dropped in "value," both writers agree. (Note: "money prices" expressed in gold rise for corn, ballet, and a day's labor.)

Case 2. Replace the invention in gold production by a similar one in corn production only. Now only corn has dropped in "value" for Ricardo. Gold and ballet have remained unchanged. The same holds for Smith's labor-command version of value. But now of course Smith's corn-command measure of value must diverge from Smith's labor-command measure: in terms of the former, Smith would say that gold, ballet, and a day's labor have risen in "value" and corn by definition has not changed.

If this were the end of the matter, despite Einstein's shrugging of shoulders, Ricardo's terminology and Smith's here-identical first-version terminology would seem slightly preferable to Smith's second-version terminology. I suspect Smith would agree for this case.

Case 3. But Smith—and Ricardo in Chapter 1, Section 1—would not expect the matter to end with this new short-run equilibrium. With the real wage now above the (previous) subsistence level, population would grow and in *Figures* 2–3 we would move along E_0E'. With land superabundant and the population adjustment parameter ϵ in (5) very fast (as suggested by Ricardo's words "in no long time" or "probably at the end of a very few years"), the corn invention would raise the profit rate above zero (actually to 100 percent per period if the labor requirements for corn halved) keeping the corn wage down near $\bar{w}^*$ and making Smith's two versions now agree with each other. But now they differ from Ricardo's version.

And which is semantically more appealing? I believe the jury will say, if *case* 3 is at all the common one in history, then Smith's terminology is more appealing: For Smith, the rise in the prices of gold and ballet in terms of both corn and a day's work (these last are in the same exchange rate as before) represents an increase in their "value." Moreover, Smith's quantitative degree of rise in their "value" does *exactly* match their rise in relative price. By contrast, Ricardo says that gold and ballet are completely unchanged in "value," while corn has halved in "value"; relative to corn's "value," they have exactly doubled in "value"—whereas actually, both men agree that their prices could have increased respectively by 10 percent and 999 percent or by 99 percent and 1 percent or by *any* quantitative degrees, depending on what a 100 percent profit rate does in marking up their competitive prices!

Ricardo's debating gaffe is to chide Smith for departing from concepts appropriate only for a $r = 0 = R$ world, and then in Section 1 himself adopting such departures as the ammunition for his criticisms of Smith.

Case 4. To amplify the point, let's suppose land is scarce and rent no longer zero. For simplicity, posit $\bar{r}^* = 0$ and concentrate on comparing long-run equilibria. Suppose all wages are spent on subsistence corn, which is produced by land and labor. Suppose all rent is spent on a luxury good (say gold), which is produced by labor alone. *Figure* 1, with WW' and SS' coinciding, determines the corn employment level at E (and coinciding E'). Knowing the ratio of the SED rent triangle to the wage rectangle formed by E, we know the ratio of labor employed in gold to that employed in corn. So our 2-good canonical long-run equilibrium is determinate in all details.

Now let a labor-augmenting invention in the corn industry make one laborer be the equivalent to two laborers. After a transient rise in profit and wage rates, $r(t)$ and $w(t)$ settle back to 0 and $\bar{w}^*$ by that determinate change in corn labor that reflects the shifted E intersection. In the end, the prices of corn, a day's labor, and gold are in *exactly the same ratios* as they started out. Both of Smith's verbiages well describe the facts: neither corn nor gold have changed in command over a unit of labor; gold is unchanged in its command over corn; only rent has risen in its command over everything else, corn, gold, and a unit of labor.

Ricardo, by contrast, is in a pickle. Gold's embodied labor is unchanged; but corn's embodied labor, measured by *total corn labor/total corn,* rises if rent's share of corn cost rises and falls if that rent share falls: either case is possible depending on a 1932 elasticity-of-substitution undreamed of by Ricardo or Mill. Who would find it useful to follow Ricardo in saying that corn's "value" has changed when *all* (P_c, P_g, W) ratios are unchanged?

There is one way out for Ricardo—a disastrous one. Suppose Ricardo measures corn's embodied labor content, not by *average* labor content, L_c/Q_c, but by *"marginal* labor content"—measured by labor per corn output on *external* margin land, or on the *internal* land margin's $1/(\partial Q_c/\partial L_c)$. To coin a phrase, this neoclassical version of Ricardo (call it Clark-Ricardo) is a disaster for his debate with Smith *because, using it, Ricardo finds himself here in exact agreement with* the labor-command *doctrine of Smith* that *Section* 1 is attacking![12]

[12] As Viner [35, 1930, pp. 79–80] pointed out in his famous review of Cannan, a marginal-labor theory of value is isomorphic with a marginal-land theory of value or with a marginal-fertilizer theory of value: when n goods are each producible out of transferable-indifferent labor and transferable-indifferent fertilizer, it is as trivial to say that any competitive price ratio, P_i/P_j, is equal to relative marginal-fertilizer–requirement ratios as to marginal-labor–requirements. It would be anticlimactic if the labor theory of value, from John Locke through Marx, reduced down to this (envelope) triviality.

[13] One such is Ricardo's accusation that Smith makes land rent price determining. After a careful audit, we should agree with the dissenting verdict of Stigler [31, 1952, p. 205]: ". . . the tenor of Smith's theory of rent, which was not given a coherent statement, was that aggregate rents are a residual, but that the rent of any one use of land is a cost determined by alternative uses of land. Ricardo ignored the multiplicity of uses of land." Another Ricardian *non sequitur*, Sraffa [30, 1951, p. xxxvii], is his invalid inference that Smith's equating of price to the *sum* of wages + rent + profit implies that Smith believed that such a price was necessarily higher than in the rude state (when productivity was so low as to make rent zero and the earnable-profit zero). Again, it is the critic, Ricardo, who seems to have nodded.

Professor Stigler points out to me that I have been rather charitable to Smith in attributing to him knowledge of diminishing returns; and less than just to Ricardo in not crediting his Chapter 1 with having succeeded in showing that changes only in wage rates will not affect relative values. I ought to mention that the similarity of Ricardo and Malthus ends when we deal with the macroeconomics of Say's Law. Professor Blaug also doubts that the differences between Ricardo and Smith are usefully dismissed as being merely semantic; in any case, upon review, I find no thought experiments proposed by Ricardo to which he has given a different substantive answer than would Smith's system; outright slips by Smith seem if anything less than those in Ricardo and are of secondary importance in both cases.

* * *

Other beefs with Smith by Ricardo reduce to similar semantic snarls.[13] We are left with the essential unity of the classical model, the progressions and retrogressions being primarily in the modes of explanation.

References

1. Blaug, Mark. *Economic theory in retrospect.* Third edition. London; New York and Melbourne: Cambridge University Press, [1962, 1968] 1978.
2. von Böhm-Bawerk, Eugen. "Capital and Interest Once More: I. Capital vs. Capital Goods," *Quart. J. Econ.*, Nov. 1906, *21*, pp. 1–21.
3. ______. "Capital and Interest Once

More: II. A Relapse to the Productivity Theory," *Quart. J. Econ.*, Feb. 1907, *21*, pp. 247–82.

4. ______. "The Nature of Capital: A Rejoinder," *Quart. J. Econ.*, Nov. 1907, pp. 28–47.
5. VON BORTKIEWICZ, LADISLAUS. "On the Correction of Marx's Fundamental Theoretical Construction in the Third Volume of 'Capital,'" *Jahr. Nationalökon. Statist.*, 1907, *89*, pp. 319–35; reprinted in English in *Karl Marx and the close of his system, by Eugen von Böhm-Bawerk and Böhm-Bawerk's criticism of Marx, by Rudolf Hilferding; with an appendix by L. von Bortkiewicz.* Edited by PAUL M. SWEEZY. New York: Kelley, 1949.
6. BREMS, HANS. "An attempt at a Rigorous Restatement of Ricardo's Long-Run Equilibrium," *Canadian J. Econ.*, Feb. 1960, *26*, pp. 74–86.
7. CLARK, JOHN BATES. *The distribution of wealth: A theory of wages, interest and profits.* New York: Macmillan, 1899.
8. HAHN, FRANK H. "Equilibrium Dynamics with Heterogeneous Capital Goods," *Quart. J. Econ.*, Nov. 1966, *80*, pp. 633–46.
9. VON HAYEK, FRIEDRICH A. "The Mythology of Capital," *Quart. J. Econ.*, Feb. 1936, *50*, pp. 199–228.
10. KALDOR, NICHOLAS. "Alternative Theories of Distribution," *Rev. Econ. Stud.*, 1956, *23*, pp. 83–100.
11. KUHN, THOMAS S. *The structure of scientific revolutions.* Chicago: University of Chicago Press, 1962.
12. LONGFIELD, MOUNTIFORT. *Lectures on political economy.* Dublin: R. Milliken and Son, 1834.
13. MACHLUP, FRITZ. "Professor Knight and the 'Period of Production,'" *J. Polit. Econ.*, Oct. 1935, *43*(5), pp. 577–624.
14. MALTHUS, THOMAS R. *An essay on the principle of population* [First Essay on Population]. London: J. Johnson, 1798.
15. ______. *Principles of political economy.* London: J. Murray, 1820.
16. MARX, KARL. *Capital: A critique of political economy.* Vol. 1, 1867; Vol. 2, 1885; Vol. 3, 1894.
17. MILL, JOHN STUART. *Principles of political economy.* Boston: Little & Brown, 1848.
18. MODIGLIANI, FRANCO. "The Life Cycle Hypothesis of Saving, the Demand for Wealth and the Supply of Capital," *Social Res.*, June 1966, *33*, pp. 160–217.
19. MORISHIMA, MICHIO. *Marx's economics: A dual theory of value and growth.* New York and London: Cambridge University Press, 1973.
20. PASINETTI, LUIGI L. "A Mathematical Formulation of the Ricardian System," *Rev. Econ. Stud.*, Feb. 1960, *27*, pp. 78–98.
21. RICARDO, DAVID. *On the principles of political economy and taxation.* London: J. Murray, 1817.
22. SAMUELSON, PAUL A. "Wages and Interest: A Modern Dissection of Marxian Economic Models," *Amer. Econ. Rev.*, Dec. 1957, *47*, pp. 884–912; reprinted in *The collected scientific papers of Paul A. Samuelson.* Vol. 1. Edited by JOSEPH E. STIGLITZ. Cambridge, Mass.: MIT Press, 1965, pp. 341–69.
23. ______. "A Modern Treatment of the Ricardian Economy: I. The Pricing of Goods and of Labor and Land Services," *Quart. J. Econ.*, Feb. 1959, *73*, pp. 1–35; reprinted in *The collected scientific papers of Paul A. Samuelson.* Vol. 1. Edited by JOSEPH E. STIGLITZ. Cambridge, Mass.: MIT Press, 1965, pp. 373–407.
24. ______. "A Modern Treatment of the Ricardian Economy: II. Capital and Interest Aspects of the Pricing Process," *Quart. J. Econ.*, May 1959, *73*,

1434 Journal of Economic Literature, Vol. XVI (December 1978)

pp. 217–31; reprinted in *The collected scientific papers of Paul A. Samuelson*. Vol. 1. Edited by JOSEPH E. STIGLITZ. Cambridge, Mass.: MIT Press, 1965, pp. 408–22.

25. ______. "Understanding the Marxian Notion of Exploitation: A Summary of the So-Called Transformation Problem between Marxian Values and Competitive Prices," *J. Econ. Lit.*, June 1971, *9*(2), pp. 399–431; reprinted in *The collected scientific papers of Paul A. Samuelson*. Vol. 3. Edited by ROBERT C. MERTON. Cambridge, Mass.: MIT Press, 1972, pp. 276–308.

26. ______. "Marx as Mathematical Economist: Steady-State and Exponential Growth Equilibrium," in *Trade, stability, and macroeconomics: Essays in honor of Lloyd A. Metzler*. Edited by GEORGE HORWICH AND PAUL SAMUELSON. New York: Academic Press, 1974, pp. 269–307; reprinted in *The collected scientific papers of Paul A. Samuelson*. Vol. 4. Edited by HIROAKI NAGATANI AND KATE CROWLEY. Cambridge, Mass.: MIT Press, 1977, pp. 231–69.

27. ______. "A Modern Theorist's Vindication of Adam Smith," *Amer. Econ. Rev.*, Feb. 1977, *67*(1), pp. 42–49.

28. ______. "Correcting the Ricardo Error Spotted in Harry Johnson's Maiden Paper," *Quart. J. Econ.*, Nov. 1977, *91*(4), pp. 519–30.

29. SMITH, ADAM. *An inquiry into the nature and causes of the wealth of nations*. London: W. Strahan and T. Cadell, 1776.

30. SRAFFA, PIERO. "Introduction," in *Works and correspondence of David Ricardo*. Vol. 1. Cambridge: Cambridge University Press, 1951, pp. xiii–lxii.

31. STIGLER, GEORGE J. "The Ricardian Theory of Value and Distribution," *J. Polit. Econ.*, June 1952, *60*, pp. 187–207.

32. ______. *The scientific uses of scientific biography*, with special reference to J. S. Mill. Toronto: University of Toronto Press, 1976, pp. 55–66.

33. TAUSSIG, FRANK W. *Wages and capital: An examination of the wages fund doctrine*. London and New York: Macmillan, 1896.

34. TURGOT, ANNE ROBERT JACQUES. *Réflexions sur la formation et la distribution des richesses* (1770). Translated as *Reflections on the formation and the distribution of riches*. New York: Macmillan, 1898.

35. VINER, JACOB. "Book Review of Edwin Cannan's *A Review of Economic Theory*," *Economica*, 1930, *10*(28), pp. 74–84.

[15]

Journal of Economic Literature
Vol. XVIII (June 1980), pp. 559–574

On Professor Samuelson's Canonical Classical Model of Political Economy

By SAMUEL HOLLANDER
University of Toronto

IT IS PROBABLE that Professor Samuelson's statement of the "canonical classical model of political economy" will become the *locus classicus* for the next generation of textbook writers; teachers of the history of thought would be advised to familiarize themselves with the ingenious diagrams in particular. But the author, who himself warns of the dangers of myth-making in undertaking such reconstructions (1978, p. 1415)—particularly (I would add) such *Gestalt* reconstructions—has provided no means whatsoever whereby the reader is enabled to evaluate the historical accuracy of the formulation.[1] It is to repair this deficiency, in part at least, that I devote the present note, attending largely to Adam Smith and David Ricardo.

By adopting a historical approach, some quite tricky problems of interpretation raised in the article are avoided. Professor Samuelson alludes to a number of modern authorities who take issue with his view that the principle of diminishing returns features prominently in the *Wealth of Nations* (Samuelson, 1978, p. 1432*n*). Now this is surely a matter that can be answered by careful textual analysis. There is in fact a great deal that can be said in a formal sense in favor of Professor Samuelson's reading of Adam Smith; for it is indeed possible to build up *from the texts* a model wherein the profit rate tends to decline secularly in consequence of extensions to increasingly inferior land. But all this would be "irrelevant"[2] if contemporary and near-contemporary economists were totally unaware of Smith's position. And such indeed seems to have been the case. The outstanding *historical* fact, which is in danger of being overlooked, is the failure of late-eighteenth and early-nineteenth century writers to recognize the presence in Smith's work of diminishing returns and its implications for distribution.

The significance of this fact, which certainly requires explanation, cannot be overstated. It colors the reading of the early nineteenth-century literature; in

[1] Apart from an extraordinary appeal to authority, including his own (1978, p. 1430). The same deficiency characterizes Samuelson (1977).

[2] "Irrelevant" in the special sense suggested by George J. Stigler (1976). Stigler makes the point that if we seek to understand the *scientific* role played by a figure in the history of economic theory, what is relevant is how his work "appeared to his contemporaries," for "science consists of the arguments and the evidence that lead *other* men to accept or reject scientific views" (1976, p. 60). The ideas they may have *intended* to express are not relevant from this perspective.

particular, an entire range of difficult questions arises relating to the nature and timing of what Ricardo considered, with reason, to be his *break-away* from Smith regarding profit rate determination and the rationalization of the profit-rate trend. For despite the presence in Smith's work of allusions to the implications of increasing land scarcity, the evidence reveals that Ricardo was totally *unaware* of Smith's discussions. The significance to Ricardo of the principle of diminishing returns lay less in any resultant "prediction" of a declining rate of profit and more in the negative proposition that in its absence there would be no other conceptual reason for a decline; in short, *he regarded his argument as a counterfoil to Smith's analysis in terms of "competition of capitals," which had to be ruled out of court because it flew in the face of the law of markets—to which Smith himself subscribed.*

Now if Ricardo misunderstood Smith's intentions, Smith himself must bear a large part of the responsibility, for his notion of "competition of capitals" occurs repeatedly in the analysis of the profit rate and is presented as the general theory into which diminishing returns may be fitted as a special case. Smith's own responsibility in this regard is further compounded by the presence in his work of propositions (conspicuously formulated) relating to corn pricing that actually imply a denial of the principle of diminishing returns.

Professor Samuelson has asserted at one point of his argument that the differences between the classical authorities were matters of *semantics* alone (1978, pp. 1430, 1432); and more specifically that there are "no thought experiments proposed by Ricardo to which he has given a different substantive answer than would Smith's system . . ." (1978, p. 1432*n*). It will become clear in what follows that this is simply not the case. Neither is it true that the contradictions in the *Wealth of Nations* can be regarded as "insignificant" (1978, p. 1415); they were significant enough to have caught the attention of contemporary commentators.

Before we proceed to substantive matters, it should be emphasized that Professor Samuelson's *short-circuited version* of the "canonical" classical model, attributed to Ricardo, is a serious and regrettable case of myth-making; and so too is his (related) assertion that Ricardo failed to appreciate as clearly as did Smith the demand–supply determination of wages (1978, pp. 1416–7; also Samuelson, 1977). It is unnecessary to provide verse and line references for all of this. The case has been fully documented recently by David Levy (1976), Sir John Hicks and Hollander (1977), and Carlo Casarosa (1978).

In what follows I outline the textual evidence suggesting the presence of the "canonical" model in the *Wealth of Nations.* In *Section* II, I attempt to account for its neglect by Smith's contemporaries and near-contemporaries. *Section* III discusses the Ricardian theory of profits envisaged as a *challenge* to Smithian doctrine; reference is made also to the position of Sir Edward West from the same perspective. Further objections to Smith in terms of the conflict between the principle of "competition of capitals" and the law of markets are taken up in *Section* IV. The final section discusses Ricardo's fundamental innovation on distribution—the inverse profit-wage relationship.

I. *The Canonical Model in the "Wealth of Nations"*

The celebrated notion "competition of capitals" occupies the center of the stage in the profit-rate analysis of Smith's first Book and appears as the general theory into which the implications of diminishing returns are fitted as a special case. This section is devoted to an exposition of the textual evidence.

The "ordinary" rate of profit, in Smith's account, is "every where regulated by the quantity of stock to be employed in proportion to the quantity of the employment, or the business which must be done by it" ([1776] 1937, p. 799). Accordingly, the rate tends to fall with accumulation in consequence of "increased competition" between capitalists: "The increase of stock, which raises wages, tends to lower profit. When the stocks of many rich merchants are turned into the same trade, their mutual competition naturally tends to lower its profit; and when there is a like increase of stock in all the different trades carried on in the same society, the same competition must produce the same effect in them all" ([1776] 1937, p. 87).

The phenomenon is related in Smith's Book II to what would now be called an increasing paucity of investment opportunities; it will be noted that the pressure on profits manifests itself in the forms both of rising wages and falling final prices:

> As the quantity of stock to be lent at interest increases, the interest, or the price which must be paid for the use of that stock, necessarily diminishes, not only from those general causes which make the market price of things commonly diminish as their quantity increases, but from other causes which are peculiar to this particular case. *As capitals increase in any country, the profits which can be made by employing them necessarily diminish. It becomes gradually more and more difficult to find within the country a profitable method of employing any new capital. There arises in consequence a competition between different capitals, the owner of one endeavouring to get possession of that employment which is occupied by another.* But upon most occasions he can hope to justle that other out of this employment, by no other means but by dealing upon more reasonable terms. He must not only sell what he deals in somewhat cheaper, but in order to get it to sell, he must sometimes too buy it dearer. The demand for productive labour, by the increase of the funds which are destined for maintaining it, grows every day greater and greater. Labourers easily find employment, but the owners of capitals find it difficult to get labourers to employ. Their competition raises the wages of labour, and sinks the profits of stock. But when the profits which can be made by the use of a capital are in this manner diminished, as it were, at both ends, the price which can be paid for the use of it, that is, the rate of interest, must necessarily be diminished with them. [(1776) 1937, p. 336; my emphasis.]

The only specific instance of such increasing paucity of investment opportunities is an allusion in the basic chapter on profits to *diminishing agricultural returns.* The passage in question, which deals specifically with "new colonies," is important for the reference to both high wage and profit rates at an early stage of development, and a *rising* wage rate but *falling* profit rate during the course of subsequent progress:

> *High wages of labour and high profits of stock, however, are things, perhaps, which scarce ever go together, except in the peculiar circumstances of new colonies.* A new colony must always for some time be more under-stocked in proportion to the extent of its territory, and more under-peopled in proportion to the extent of its stock, than the greater part of other countries. They have more land than they have stock to cultivate. What they have, therefore, is applied to the cultivation only of what is most fertile and most favourably situated, the land near the sea shore, and along the banks of navigable rivers. Such land too is frequently purchased at a price below the value even of its natural produce. Stock employed in the purchase and improvement of such lands must yield a very large profit. . . . Its rapid accumulation in so profitable an employment enables the planter to increase the number of his hands faster than he can find them in a new settlement. Those whom he can find, therefore, are very liberally rewarded. *As the colony increases, the profits of stock gradually diminish. When the most fertile and best situated lands have been all occupied, less profit can be made by the cultivation of what is inferior both in soil and situation. . . . [But] the wages of labour do not sink with the profits of stock.* The demand for labour increases with the increase of stock whatever be its profits; and after these are diminished, stock may not only continue to increase, but to increase much faster than before. [(1776) 1937, pp. 92–93; my emphasis.]

In the chapter specifically devoted to colonies in Book IV the high wages and profits characterizing new establishments are discussed in the following terms:

> Every colonist gets more land than he can possibly cultivate. He has no rent, and scarce any taxes to pay. No landlord shares with him in its produce, and the share of the sovereign is commonly but a trifle. He has every motive to render as great as possible a produce, which is thus to be almost entirely his own. But his land is commonly so extensive, that with all his own industry, and with all the industry of other people whom he can get to employ, he can seldom make it produce the tenth part of what it is capable of producing. He is eager, therefore, to collect labourers from all quarters, and to reward them with the most liberal wages. But those liberal wages, joined to the plenty and cheapness of land, soon make those labourers leave him, in order to become landlords themselves, and to reward, with equal liberality, other labourers, who soon leave them for the same reason that they left their first master. . . .
>
> In other countries, rent and profit eat up wages, and the two superior orders of people oppress the inferior one. But in new colonies, the interest of the two superior orders obliges them to treat the inferior one with more generosity and humanity; at least, where that inferior one is not in a state of slavery. Waste lands of the greatest natural fertility, are to be had for a trifle. The increase of revenue which the proprietor, who is always the undertaker, expects from their improvement constitutes his profit; which in these circumstances is commonly very great. But this great profit cannot be made without employing the labour of other people in clearing and cultivating the land; and the disproportion between the great extent of the land and the small number of the people, which commonly takes place in new colonies, makes it difficult for him to get this labour. He does not, therefore, dispute about wages, but is willing to employ labour at any price. [(1776) 1937, pp. 532–33.]

The foregoing passages must, however, be read in conjunction with Smith's allusions to a "stationary state" marked by wage and profit rates at their respective minima:

> In a country which had acquired that full complement of riches which the nature of its soil and climate, and its situation with respect to other countries, allowed it to acquire; which could, therefore, advance no further, and which was not going backwards, both the wages of labour and the profits of stock would probably be very low. In a country fully peopled in proportion to what either its territory could maintain or its stock employ, the competition for employment would necessarily be so great as to reduce the wages of labour to what was barely sufficient to keep up the number of labourers, and, the country being already fully peopled, that number could never be augmented. In a country fully stocked in proportion to all the business it had to transact, as great a quantity of stock would be employed in every particular branch as the nature and extent of the trade would admit. The competition, therefore, would every-where be as great, and consequently the ordinary profit as low as possible. [(1776) 1937, pp. 94–95.]

Reference has just been made to a *rising* trend of real wages and an ultimate state of stationariness when wages are at their *minimum* or subsistence level. Evidently a stage of *falling per capita* wages must be envisaged along the route. *Smith did not spell out the logic behind this downward trend in his analysis of the falling profit rate,* but there are pertinent materials from which to draw elsewhere and these perhaps allow us to fill in the picture.

The characteristic feature of Smith's analysis of wages is the role accorded to the rate of capital accumulation as an "independent" variable governing the demand for labor, upon which depends the (long-run or secular) real wage rate and the growth rate of population; to each growth rate of labor demand there corresponds a long-run real wage rate, which assures an equivalent rate of growth of population, and therefore of the work force: "It is not . . . in the richest countries, but in the most thriving, or in those which are growing rich the fastest, that the wages of labour are highest" ([1776] 1937, p. 69)[3] According to the Smithian position, an increase in the (long-run)

[3] See Hollander (1973), p. 157.

wage rate will occur in consequence of a *change* in the rate of capital accumulation; a steady rate of increase of capital would not alter (long-run) *per capita* wages. By extension it may, therefore, be fair to attribute to Smith the view that the implied *falling* trend of real wages, alluded to earlier, is attributable to a *declining* rate of capital accumulation, itself a reaction to the falling profit rate. This interpretation, however, begs many key questions as will shortly become clear.

The foregoing textual analysis brings together much of the primary evidence, of which I am aware, in support of Professor Samuelson's argument that the "canonical" classical model appears in the *Wealth of Nations.* It is indeed quite an impressive case.[4] *Yet from the point of view of the intellectual historian the disturbing fact must be faced that Smith left no impression whatsoever on his contemporaries regarding his formulation.* On the contrary, as we shall see, commentators focused on aspects of Smith's work that point conspicuously away from the phenomenon of diminishing returns.

II. *Some Characteristics of the Smithian Presentation and the Neglect of Smith's Canonical Model*

I shall attempt in what follows to explain the neglect of Smith's discussion of land scarcity and its implications for distribution by subsequent commentators.

Some allowance should perhaps be made for matters of exposition. The discussion is not concentrated in one location; it is scattered and, most significant, much of the evidence given above derives from the analysis of *colonies* where institutional arrangements differed, in some important respects, from those in the competitive exchange system, which primarily concerned contemporaries. These formal matters may well have played a part in disguising Smith's argument.

More important is the fact that Smith, unlike Ricardo, did not establish land scarcity as the *sine qua non* for a secularly falling profit rate. If we take into account disturbances that check or reverse the regular downward trend of the profit rate, it becomes apparent that increasing land scarcity—diminishing agricultural returns—is not a *necessary* condition for the supposed trend. Thus the trend would be checked not only by the "acquisition of new territories" but also *by the "acquisition of new branches of trade,"* which reduces the pressure of "competition" in community markets, thus permitting final prices and thus profits to rise:

> The acquisition of new territory, or *of new branches of trade,* may sometimes raise the profits of stock, and with them the interest of money, even in a country which is fast advancing in the acquisition of riches. The stock of the country not being sufficient for the whole accession of business, which such acquisitions present to the different people among whom it is divided, is applied to those particular branches only which afford the greatest profit. Part of what had before been employed in other trades, is necessarily withdrawn from them, and turned into some of the new and more profitable ones. In all those old trades, therefore, the competition comes to be less than before. The market comes to be less fully supplied with many different sorts of goods. Their price necessarily rises more or less, and yields a greater profit to those who deal in

[4] There is no obvious relationship between the Smithian analysis of "investment priorities" and his "forecast" of a secular downward trend in the average rate of profits in a growing economy. I have argued (1973, pp. 281–83) that the relatively high profit rates available in the agricultural sector, frequently emphasized in the *Wealth of Nations,* reflects the extreme cheapness of land, which is regarded as typical in an economy at an early stage of development. Economic growth tends to alter the factor endowments such that the agricultural profit rate falls *relatively to that potentially available in manufacturing.* There does not seem to be any necessary implication for the profit rate trend since, in principle, increasing labor supplies might counterbalance the effect on profitability of increasing land shortage.

them, who can, therefore, afford to borrow at a higher interest. [(1776) 1937, p. 93; my emphasis.]

The analysis is, incidentally, applied to explain an upward movement in interest rates in London after the peace of 1763. "New business" was provided by the British "acquisitions" in North America and the West Indies, and capital was diverted away from the Mediterranean and European branches of trade: "So great an accession of new business to be carried on by the old stock, must necessarily have diminished the quantity employed in a great number of particular branches, in which the competition being less, the profits must have been greater" ([1776] 1937, pp. 93–94).

I conclude that Smith's rationalization of the falling profit rate included considerations apart from land scarcity. The combining of such distinct phenomena could not have helped the case.

In any event the argument is vitiated by severe ambiguities. It is not even clear whether the pressure exerted upon the profit rate by increased "competition of capitals" takes the form of rising wages in addition to falling prices. Smith is sometimes circumspect on this matter; as we have already seen "the increase of stock, which raises wages, tends to lower profit" —a fall which is then apparently related formally to competition in *commodity* markets.[5] We must here keep in mind that capitalists are frequently accorded the ability to *escape* the burden of rising wages by way of increased manufacturing prices and reduced rents (see below). It is difficult in any event to appreciate why the wage rate tends ultimately to *fall;* to explain it in terms of a *declining* rate of accumulation as provisionally suggested above does not really solve the problem, for Smith explicitly asserts that "the demand for labour increases with the increase of stock whatever be its profits; and after these are diminished, stock may not only continue to increase, but to increase much faster than before" ([1776] 1937, p. 93). Finally, and most important, it is not made clear why, if indeed there is scope for a decline in the real wage (and setting aside pressure on final prices), there is any necessary reduction on the profit rate at all. *It was Ricardo who ultimately developed a model where all these issues are resolved.*

These considerations suggest that the main case was not well thought through or clearly argued in the *Wealth of Nations.* But the failure to leave any impression on the main issues that concern us can be better appreciated if we also keep in mind the common belief that *Smith had actually ruled out diminishing returns.*

This may be illustrated from the *Inquiry into the Nature and Progress of Rent* (1815) where Malthus set out the principle of differential rent, which he contrasted with the notion of rent envisaged as a "monopoly" return by Smith, Say, the Physiocrats, Sismondi, and Buchanan.[6] What is particularly striking from our present perspective is the interpretation and critical assessment of the Smithian approach to corn-price determination in a secular context:

> Adam Smith has very clearly explained in what manner the progress of wealth and improvement tends to raise the price of cattle, poultry, the materials of clothing and lodging, the most useful minerals, &c. &c. compared with corn; but he has not entered into the explanation of the natural causes which tend to determine the price of corn. He has left the reader, indeed, to conclude that he considers the price of corn as determined only by the state of the mines which at the time supply the circulating medium of the commercial world. But this is a cause obviously inadequate to account for the

[5] See above, p. 561.

[6] Malthus also took Smith to task for the view "that all land which yields food must necessarily yield rent," but recognized that Smith sometimes "contemplates rent quite in its true light" (1815, p. 180).

> actual differences in the price of grain, observable in countries at no great distance from each other, and at nearly the same distance from the mines. [1815, p. 209.][7]

For his own part Malthus accounted for a "high comparative money price of corn" in terms of its "high comparative real price, or the greater quantity of capital and labour which must be employed to produce it" (1815, p. 210).

Ricardo made precisely the same point. It is appropriate to keep in mind the strength of his objections to Smith's position on corn pricing whereby "if you except corn and such other vegetables as are raised altogether by human industry, . . . all other sorts of rude produce, cattle, poultry, game of all kinds, the useful fossils and minerals of the earth, &c. naturally grow dearer as the society advances in wealth" ([1776] 1937, p. 217). "Why should corn and vegetables alone be excepted?" he protested. "Dr. Smith's error throughout his whole work, lies in supposing that the value of corn is constant; that though the value of all other things may, the value of corn never can be raised" (1817, p. 374).

There is a closely related aspect of Smithian theory that next requires attention. I have referred to Smith's *apparent* denial of a secular increase in the corn price due to the pressure of growing land scarcity. But more generally it was his position that a rise in the price of corn in consequence of government intervention in the corn trade, for example by the corn export bounty, can have no *allocative* implications; the argument presumes that an increase in the price of corn will be translated by way of the money wage rate to the prices of manufactured goods, leaving unchanged the *relative* profitability of agricultural activity.

The model is laid out in the chapter "Of Bounties," although the various constituent elements are established in the theoretical chapters of Book I:

> . . . the money price of corn regulates that of all other home-made commodities.
>
> It regulates the money price of labour, which must always be such as to enable the labourer to purchase a quantity of corn sufficient to maintain him and his family either in the liberal, moderate, or scanty manner in which the advancing, stationary or declining circumstances of the society oblige his employers to maintain him.
>
> It regulates the money price of all the other parts of the rude produce of land, which, in every period of improvement, must bear a certain proportion to that of corn, though this proportion is different in different periods. It regulates, for example, the money price of grass and hay, of butcher's meat, of horses, and the maintenance of horses, of land carriage consequently, or of the greater part of the inland commerce of the country.
>
> By regulating the money price of all the other parts of the rude produce of land, it regulates that of the materials of almost all manufactures. By regulating the money price of labour, it regulates that of manufacturing art and industry. And by regulating both, it regulates that of the complete manufacture. The money price of labour, and of every thing that is the produce either of land or labour, must necessarily either rise or fall in proportion to the money price of corn. [(1776) 1937, pp. 476–77.]

The outstanding theoretical conclusion is that an increase in the wage rate can be passed on by employers in the forms of higher final prices in the manufacturing sector, and lower rents in agriculture (e.g., [1776] 1937, pp. 816, 824). As for matters of policy, Smith's fundamental conclusion is that government intervention designed to raise agricultural profits by means of a corn export bounty must fail in its objective because of the effects of a higher corn price upon money wages and therefore

[7] *Cf.*, Smith's discussion in the "digression on silver" (particularly [1776] 1937, p. 191) regarding the determination of the corn price (also p. 36); and p. 217 regarding the relative prices of agricultural products other than corn to that of corn (also pp. 174–76).

manufacturing prices in general: "The real effect of the bounty is not so much to raise the real value of corn, as to degrade the real value of silver; or to make an equal quantity of it exchange for a smaller quantity, not only of corn, but of all other home-made commodities . . ." ([1776] 1937, p. 476). Similarly, a few pages later, in the first two editions, we find an equally strong statement: "[Our country gentlemen] did not perhaps attend to the great and essential difference which nature has established between corn and almost every sort of goods. . . . The nature of things has stamped upon corn a real value which no human institution can alter. No bounty upon exportation, no monopoly of the home market, can raise that value" ([1776] 1937, p. 482).

This feature of Smith's work was remarked upon repeatedly by contemporary and near-contemporary commentators. Critical reference to it is the most striking feature of the literature during the period 1776–1815. It seems scarcely surprising that late-eighteenth and early-nineteenth century critics were unaware of what Adam Smith wrote about land scarcity and its consequences given his treatment of corn pricing and its apparent denial of the possibility of real changes in the price of corn. I wish to elaborate upon this feature of the historical record.[8]

In his *Observations on National Industry*, James Anderson developed a case—precluded as we have just seen by Smith—for government intervention to encourage domestic agriculture by means of an export bounty. In the course of an attempt to fix upon the precise magnitude of the subsidy required, Anderson utilized the principle of diminishing returns—from which he deduced the conception of rent as an intramarginal surplus—on the grounds that it is the level of *marginal costs* that is relevant for the calculation. The exposition of the principle is striking (1777, pp. 207–09). Anderson did not formally emphasize that his rent conception differed from that of Smith, and he did not base a full-fledged "Ricardian" system upon it; but the principle of diminishing returns from which the rent concept derives is used nonetheless to counter Smith's position on the bounty. In effect, the entire body of Smithian theory, according to which variations in the price of corn can only be *nominal* variations, in consequence of the general effect upon prices as a whole, is turned down.

The same case was presented by Anderson in his *An Enquiry into the Nature of the Corn-Laws*. Here he observed in criticism of Smith's general analysis of price in Book I, chapter 7 of the *Wealth of Nations* that "it is not . . . the rent of land that determines the price of its produce, but it is the price of that produce that determines the rent of the land . . ." (1777, p. 45*n*).[9] Accordingly, to fix a low corn price would mean not merely a fall of rent but *a reduction in agricultural output* despite the "popular objection . . . that the price to the farmer is so high only on account of the high rents and avaricious extortions of proprietors. Lower (say they) your rents, and the farmer will be able to afford his grain cheaper to the consumer." The notion of no-rent land at the (extensive) margin of cultivation is expounded with most impressive clarity in an account that has much in common with that regarded as "revolutionary" nearly forty years later.

On Anderson's *Enquiry*, let us note, J. R. McCulloch later wrote that its publication "marks an important era in the history of economic science, from its containing the earliest explanation that is any-

[8] I draw freely from Hollander (1979), chap. 1.

[9] *Cf.*, also David Hume ([1776] 1932, p. 311): "I cannot think," he wrote to Smith, "that the Rent of Farms makes any part of the Price of the Produce, but that the Price is determined altogether by the Quantity and the Demand."

where to be met with of the real nature and origin of rent" (1845, p. 68).

Malthus provides a conspicuous illustration of the present theme. In the second edition of his *Essay on Population* he added a chapter "Of Bounties on the Exportation of Corn"—a subject of the "highest importance"—which took strong exception both to various aspects of Smith's analytical treatment of the issue, and to his policy conclusions (1803). Here he insisted *inter alia* that an export subsidy would in fact raise the agricultural profit rate and thus encourage expansion, denying the existence of any "great and essential difference" between corn and other goods such as that emphasized by Smith:

> When Dr. Smith says that the nature of things has stamped upon corn a real value, which cannot be altered by merely altering the money price; and that no bounty upon exportation, no monopoly of the home market, can raise that value; nor the freest competition lower it; it is evident, that he changes the question from the profits of the growers of corn in any particular country, to the physical and absolute value of corn in itself. . . . I certainly do not mean to say, that the bounty alters the physical value of corn, and makes a bushel of it support a greater number of labourers for a day, than it did before: but I certainly do mean to say that the bounty to the British cultivator does, in the actual state of things, really increase his profits on this commodity; and by thus making the growth of corn answer to him, encourages him to sow more than he otherwise would do, and enables him in consequence to employ more bushels of corn in the maintenance of a greater number of labourers. [1803, pp. 461–62]

In the later *Observations on the Effects of the Corn Laws* (1814), formally designed as an impartial evaluation of the merits of protection and of free trade, the discussion again turned on Smith's treatment of the corn-export bounty and in particular the special treatment accorded corn prioing: "I have always thought, and still think, that this peculiar argument of Dr. Smith, is fundamentally erroneous" (1814, pp. 96–97). The issue at stake, as in the *Essay on Population,* was Smith's assertion that "corn is of so peculiar a nature, that its real price cannot be raised by an increase of its money-price; and that, as it is clearly an increase of real price alone, which can encourage its production, the rise of money-price, occasioned by the bounty, can have no such effect" (1814, p. 98). Here too Malthus insisted that the money wage rate does not rise proportionately with the corn price, and this because of the existence in the wage basket of home and imported goods other than corn (1814, p. 99). Moreover, the reaction of money wages to an increase in the price of corn occurs in consequence of a *slow* response of labor supply so that "corn and labour rarely keep an even pace together; but must often be separated at a sufficient distance and for a sufficient time, to change the direction of capital" (1814, p. 100). In brief, "the price of corn does not immediately and generally regulate the prices of labour and all other commodities; and . . . the real price of corn is capable of varying for periods of sufficient length to give a decided stimulus or discouragement to agriculture . . ." (1814, p. 106). *It is worth adding that Malthus considered Smith's theoretical position to fly in the face of the general theory of resource allocation:* "it cannot be maintained without violating the great principles of supply and demand, and contradicting the general spirit and scope of the reasoning, which pervade the 'Wealth of Nations'" (1814, p. 97). The Smithian approach excluded corn from those normal supply responses which flowed from changes in the relative demands for commodities and constituted an unjustifiable exception to "the operation of that principle, so beautifully explained and illustrated by Dr. Smith, by which capital flows from one employment to another, according to the various and necessarily fluctuating wants of society" (1814, p. 101).

Francis Horner, in his well-known article for the *Edinburgh Review* of 1804 adopted (though with qualifications) the Smithian position in his analysis of the corn export legislation of that year, asserting that "the real price of corn will be maintained the same, notwithstanding a nominal variation," and adding that "without a just apprehension of this fundamental truth, it is impossible to reason with accuracy upon the subject" (1804, p. 106). Now Horner's article was subsequently described by Ricardo, in his chapter dealing with "Bounties on Exportation" as subject to the "common error which has misled Dr. Smith, and, I believe, most other writers on this subject," namely that "because the price of corn ultimately regulates wages, . . . it will regulate the price of all other commodities" (1817, p. 302). Indeed, Ricardo maintained that "perhaps in no part of Adam Smith's justly celebrated work, are his conclusions more liable to objection, than in the chapter on bounties" (1817, p. 304). It is precisely in the context of corn legislation—it must be remembered that what is said of a corn export subsidy had clear implications for corn import duties as well—that we can perceive most clearly the differences between the Smithian and the Ricardian theoretical models.

The point in question is reiterated in one form or another throughout the entire range of Ricardo's writings. It is worth recalling, for example, Ricardo's repeated denial, in debate with Malthus, that it is possible to identify a change in the corn price with a change in money value as Smith, we have seen, did: "Money I think only falls in value, when it will exchange for less of all things; not when it will exchange for less of one thing, or of two things, or of a dozen things" (1820, p. 144). While Ricardo believed that corn was "the most important commodity of all others" (1820, p. 180), he nonetheless insisted that it must be treated merely as one among the others. Similarly, in the *Essay on Profits:* "It has been thought that the price of corn regulates the price of all other things. This appears to me to be a mistake. If the price of corn is affected by the rise or fall of the value of the precious metals themselves, then indeed will the price of commodities be also affected, but they vary, because the value of money varies, not because the value of corn is altered" (1815, p. 21*n*).

The turning point in the transition between the *Essay* and the *Principles* came at the end of 1815 when Ricardo, having commenced the expansion of the pamphlet, wrote to James Mill: "I know I shall be soon stopped by the word price." Ricardo then expanded his argument in terms relevant for our case:

> [My readers] must know that the prices of commodities are affected two ways one by the alteration in the relative value of money, which affects all commodities nearly at the same time,—the other by an alteration in the value of the particular commodity, and which affects the value of no other thing, excepting it enter into its composition.—This invariability of the value of the precious metals, but from particular causes relating to themselves only, such as supply and demand, is the sheet anchor on which all my propositions are built; for those who maintain that an alteration in the value of corn will alter the value of all other things, independently of its effects on the value of the raw material of which they are made, do in fact deny this doctrine of the cause of the variation in the value of gold and silver. [*Letters, VI* (1815), p. 348–49.]

Ricardo reacted quickly enough to what he regarded as the Smithian error in J. R. McCulloch's essay on the national debt: "Your system proceeds upon the supposition that the price of corn regulates the price of all other things, and that when corn rises or falls, commodities also rise or fall,—but this I hold to be an erroneous system, although you have great authorities in your favour, no less than Adam Smith, Mr. Malthus, and M. Say" (*Letters, VII* [1816], p. 105). And there can be no question that one of his main objectives in the *Principles* itself was to demonstrate the error of Smith's position (common "to all the writers who have followed him"), according to which an increase in wages generates an increase in the prices of *all* commodities: "I hope I have succeeded in showing, that there are no grounds for such an opinion, and that only those commodities would rise which had less fixed capital employed upon them than the medium in which price was estimated, and that all those which had more, would positively fall in price when wages rose" (1817, p. 46. *Cf.*, pp. 302, 307, 315). "These results," Ricardo insisted, "are of such importance to the science of political economy, yet accord so little with some of its received doctrines, which maintain that every rise in wages is necessarily transferred to the price of commodities" (1817, p. 61).

III. *The Ricardian Break-away on the Theory of Profits*

It is scarcely surprising that an economist who denied the possibility of a relative increase in the price of corn during the course of secular expansion should have been understood as neglecting the implications of increasing land scarcity—whatever he might have written about the matter in the context of new colonies. And it is also scarcely surprising that Ricardo should have referred to *his* theory of profit-rate determination in the first extant Ricardo documents touching on the "classical" approach to the problem. I allude here to the famous letter to Malthus of 10 August 1813: "On further reflection I am confirmed in the opinion which I gave with regard to the effect of opening new markets or extending the old. I most readily allow that since the war, not only the nominal but the real value of our exports and imports has increased,—but I do not see how this admission will favour the view which you take of this subject. . . . [Extension of trade] does not prove a general increase of profits nor any material growth of prosperity" (*Letters*, VI, p. 93). In a second letter Ricardo explicitly stated the position that attention should be directed at agricultural productivity to understand trends in the rate of profit:

> That we have experienced a great increase of wealth and prosperity since the commencement of the war, I am amongst the foremost to believe; but it is not certain that such increase must have been attended by increased profits, or rather an increased rate of profits, for that is the question between us. I have little doubt however that for a long period, during the interval you mention [1793–1813], there has been an increased rate of profits, but it has been accompanied with such decided improvements of agriculture both here and abroad,—for the French revolution was exceedingly favorable to the increased production of food, that it is perfectly reconcileable to my theory. My conclusion is that there has been a rapid increase of Capital which has been prevented from shewing itself in a low rate of interest by new facilities in the production of food. [*Letters*, VI, pp. 94–95.]

This formulation, it must be emphasized, was regarded by Ricardo as an *alternative* to the Smithian view of profit-rate determination and rationalization of the profit-rate trend, running in terms of "competition of capitals," which he himself had once held. For each of the extracts is followed by a statement insisting that *an increase in general prices occurs only in consequence of a rising money supply (or velocity), while only a falling level of prices can induce a monetary inflow.* It is most likely that the statements alluding to the profit rate and those relating to the monetary mechanism are connected. If this is so, Ricardo appears to be objecting to a formulation by Malthus very similar to that which was to appear later in the latter's *Principles* of 1820—namely that an increase in the value of aggregate output from given resources may be "occasioned by commerce" and will be associated with a rise in profits of those engaged in the new or expanded trade, which extends to the general rate of return. It would seem to be this body of doctrine—which attributes the rising value of national product since 1793 and a correspondingly upward trend in the profit rate to the opening of new markets for British goods—with which Ricardo took issue in 1813, on the grounds that the expansion of the means of finance required to assure a higher level of prices and profits, of which Malthus was very confident, would not in fact be forthcoming. In short, the argument was seen to be inconsistent with Hume's specie-flow mechanism. *But Ricardo's rejection of Malthus's position implies the rejection of the standard Smithian view referred to above according to which "the acquisition of . . . new branches of trade, may sometimes raise the profits of stock . . . even in a country fast advancing in the acquisition of riches," in consequence of the reduction in the pressure exerted by "competition of capitals."*

It is in this light that one may best understand the objective of the *Essay on Profits* itself: "Profits of stock fall because land equally fertile cannot be obtained, and through the whole progress of society, profits are regulated *by the difficulty or facility of procuring food. This is a principle of great importance, and has been almost over-looked in the writings of Political Economists. They appear to think that profits of stock can be raised by commercial causes, independently of the supply of food"* (1815, p. 13*n;* my emphasis). And the central theme of the famous chapter on Foreign Trade in the *Principles* is important from the same standpoint: "extension[s] of foreign trade" in themselves alter neither the "value" of the national product nor the general return on capital (1817, p. 128). Smith's contention that such extensions—by attracting funds from alternative (domestic) projects thereby reducing the pressure of "competition between capitals"—raise the general return on capital is firmly rejected: "I am of opinion, that the profits of the favoured trade will speedily subside to the general level." His concern was to provide an "independent" refutation of Smith's position rather than merely to assert the validity of his own theory of profit rate determination, according to which foreign trade can play a part only in the special case that real wage-goods prices are affected. Nonetheless, the latter proposition is strongly formulated: "It has been my endeavour to shew throughout this work, that the rate of profits can never be increased but by a fall in wages, and that there can be no permanent fall of wages but in consequence of a fall of the necessaries on which wages are expended. . . . Foreign trade, then, . . . has no tendency to raise the profits of stock, unless the commodities imported be of that description on which the wages of labour are expended" (1817, pp. 132–33).

The extent of the break-away from Smith may be guaged also by reference to Sir Edward West's pamphlet of February 1815, famous for its formulation of the principle of diminishing returns (allowing both for the intensive and extensive margins) and for the use of the principle in the analysis of the declining secular return on capital. What concerns us most here is *West's rejection of the Smithian position, which runs in terms of increasing "competition of capitals," on the grounds of fallacy of composition:*

> Smith therefore attributes this decline in the rate of profit to increased competition. But the slightest consideration will detect the fallacy of this opinion. If the capital employed in one branch of trade alone be increased, doubtless the increased competition of the dealers in that branch will lower the price of their articles, and consequently the profits of those dealers. But why is the price lowered except because that article is now more abundant than others, and could not be sold without such diminution of price. But if the capital in all the different branches of trade, and consequently the quan-

> tity of all the articles of these respective trades be increased in the same degree, the same ratio between each and all the rest remains, and each article must sell for the same *real* price as it fetched before. If the competition be increased in any one article, it for the same reason is increased in all; and as it exists in the same degree in each, it cannot alter the real price of any one. It is only the relative alteration of the demand and supply which can increase the price, and here there is no such alteration. [1815, p. 21.]

West's implicit distinction in the foregoing passage between relative and absolute prices is of the first importance. It is conceded that there would be a temporary decline in *general* money prices in the case at hand which would, however, be corrected by a monetary inflow: "The money price of all articles would no doubt be diminished, and therefore the money-profits of stock; but this would not lower the real price of those articles, nor the real profits; even the money price would soon be raised to a level with the real price, by a favourable balance of trade and the consequent introduction of bullion."

In all this West's argument bears a close resemblance to that of Ricardo, who also insisted that a disturbance affecting all commodities can have no real consequence, while a change in the general level of prices (in any single country) will be temporary only in the light of money flows.

IV. *The Law of Markets*

Ricardo's objections to the Smithian analysis of the profit rate extended further. For, on his reading, the principle of "competition of capitals" conflicted also with the law of markets to which, of course, Smith subscribed. This aspect of the criticism is made very clear in the chapter of the *Principles* specifically devoted to the effects of accumulation on the profit rate.

The chapter is designed to demonstrate that the *only* cause of a falling profit rate is an upward trend in "wages": "If the necessaries of the workman could be constantly increased with the same facility, there could be no permanent alteration in the rate of profits or wages, to whatever amount capital might be accumulated." Similarly, "whether these increased productions and the consequent demand which they occasion"—in the course of accumulation—"shall or shall not lower profits, depends solely on the rise of wages. . . ." Adam Smith's ascription of the declining secular return on capital to "increased competition" between capitalists is rejected as in conflict with the law of markets, for "at the same time that capital is increased, the work to be effected by capital, is increased in the same proportion" (1817, pp. 289, 292, 289–90). Smith's contentions regarding the effects on profits flowing from "competition" for *labor* are accepted by Ricardo but only in so far as concerns the short run. The weight of emphasis is upon "competition" in product markets, and Smith's approach is rejected entirely.

Ricardo clearly conceived his chapter as a demonstration of the untenability of the notion of secular stagnation—or an approach to stationarity—independently of the considerations given pride of place in his own model. Accordingly, the only conceivable (permanent) constraint on growth is that deriving from a rising real cost of producing wages, which reduces profits to their minimum: "there cannot, then, be accumulated in a country any amount of capital which cannot be employed productively, until wages rise so high in consequence of the rise of necessaries, and so little consequently remains for the profits of stock, that the motive for accumulation ceases" (1817, p. 290). But provided the profit rate yields an adequate motive to accumulate, expansion of capacity will occur without check, since demand expands *pari passu*.

Now in support of his general position

in the chapter, Ricardo drew upon Say's authority. Specifically, in support of the case against Smith's doctrine relating to "competition of capitals," Ricardo observed that "M. Say has . . . most satisfactorily shewn, that there is no amount of capital which may not be employed in a country, because demand is only limited by production." And regarding Smith's statement to the effect that "the more disposable capitals are abundant in proportion to the extent of employment for them, the more will the rate of interest on loans of capital fall," Ricardo, in the light of "M. Say's Principle," asked rhetorically: "If capital to any extent can be employed by a country, how can it be said to be abundant, compared with the extent of employment for it?"

V. *The Inverse Profit-Wage Relationship*

The implications of Smith's "error" were profound. For if, as Smith believed, the impact of a rise in the price of corn and accordingly in the money wage rate were upon prices (in the manufacturing sector) and rents (in agriculture), there need be no fall in the profit rate during the course of secular expansion; capitalists could "pass on" the burden imposed by land scarcity.

The appearance of Robert Torrens's famous *Essay on the External Corn Trade* in February 1815 provided an ideal opportunity for Ricardo to state this case. For Torrens repeated Adam Smith's belief that increases in the price of corn are passed on to consumers in consequence of rising money wages. Ricardo simply insisted that Torrens "on this part of the subject appears to me defective, as I think that the price of commodities will be very slightly affected either by a rise or fall in the price of corn. If so every rise in the price of corn must affect profits on manufactures, and it is impossible that agricultural profits can materially deviate from them" (*Letters,* VI, p. 213). A year later, however, he was pleased to find that Robert Torrens had apparently accepted the *"Ricardian"* position on the main issues at stake. "Have you seen Torrens' Letter to Lord Liverpool?—He appears to me to have adopted all my views respecting profits and rent; and in some conversation which I had with him a few days ago, he unequivocally avowed that he was now of my opinion, that the price of labour, arising from a difficulty of procuring food, did not affect the prices of commodities. He confessed that his former view on that subject was erroneous" (*Letters,* VII, p. 24). And a little later he repeated that Torrens had become "quite a convert to *all* what you have called my peculiar opinion on profits, rent, &c." (*Letters,* VII, p. 36).

The general argument may be briefly summarized: Wages expressed in terms of "money" of constant "value" depend upon both the commodity wage and the price of wage goods. But in consequence of the rising real cost of producing wage goods—a reflection of diminishing returns—money wages will rise secularly. The secular increase in money wages—despite a reduced commodity wage—in turn has the effect of reducing the profit rate in manufacturing, since manufacturing prices are not raised by the wage increase: "Notwithstanding, then, that the labourer would be really worse paid, yet this increase in his [money] wages would necessarily diminish the profits of the manufacturer; *for his goods would sell at no higher price, and yet the expense of producing them would be increased"* (1817, p. 102; my emphasis). The same conclusion is repeated in the chapter "On Profits": "Supposing corn and manufactured goods always to sell at the same price, profits would be high or low in proportion as wages were low or high. But suppose corn to rise in price because more labour is necessary to produce it; that cause will not raise the price of manufactured goods in the production of which no additional quantity of labour is required. If, then, wages continued the same, the profits [of manufacturers] would remain the same; but if, as is absolutely certain, wages should rise with the rise of corn, then [their] profits would necessarily fall" (1817, pp. 110–11).

All of Ricardo's theoretical efforts were in fact devoted to demonstrating that a general increase in wages implies an inverse fall in the profit rate leaving general prices unaffected. (In the reconstruction, it would seem, the differential rent theory played a key but nonetheless *supplementary* role. The point here is Ricardo's insistence that the existence of rent in no way disturbed the inverse wage-profit relationship; the importance of the rent doctrine should be evaluated within the context of the fundamental theorem on distribution.)

It was Ricardo's great achievement to demonstrate that what is at stake in profit-rate analysis is *proportionate* wages; to this end he sought an appropriate measuring device in terms of which a rise in "money" wages would imply a rise in the proportionate share of wages in the net product to be distributed between laborers and capitalists. On these terms it became quite clear how even a falling commodity wage—which characterizes the trend path of an economy subject to diminishing returns—might be consistent with a rising "money" (Ricardian "real" or "proportionate") wage and thus entail an inverse profit-rate change.[10]

VI. *Conclusion*

To conclude: The "canonical" model can only be said to be present in the *Wealth of Nations* on the basis of a very selective choice of texts. Even this selection is largely constrained to the special context of colonies and leaves much to be desired in terms both of internal consistency and consistency with central Smithian propositions relating to corn pricing. As for "influence," there was none. On a balance of considerations I suggest that the model was a Ricardian construction insofar as concerns both pure logic and intellectual indebtedness.

[10] See Hicks and Hollander (1977).

References

ANDERSON, JAMES. *An enquiry into the nature of the corn-laws.* Edinburgh, 1777.

———. *Observations on the means of exciting a spirit of national industry* [1777]. Vol. II. Dublin, 1779.

CASAROSA, CARLO. "A New Formulation of the Ricardian System," *Oxford Econ. Pap.*, March 1978, *30*(1), pp. 38–63.

HICKS, JOHN [SIR] AND HOLLANDER, SAMUEL. "Mr. Ricardo and the Moderns," *Quart. J. Econ.*, August 1977, *91*(3), pp. 351–69.

HOLLANDER, SAMUEL. *The economics of Adam Smith.* Studies in Classical Political Economy, Vol. 1. Toronto and Buffalo: University of Toronto Press, 1973.

———. *The economics of David Ricardo.* Studies in Classical Political Economy, Vol. 2. Toronto and Buffalo: University of Toronto Press, 1979.

HORNER, FRANCIS. "Observations on the Bounty upon Exported Corn," *Edinburgh Rev.*, Oct. 1804, *5*(9). Reprinted in *The economic writings of Francis Horner in the Edinburgh Review 1802–6.* Edited by F. W. FETTER. New York: Kelley and Millman, 1957, pp. 96–114.

HUME, DAVID. *The letters of David Hume.* Vol. II. Edited by J. Y. T. GREIG. Oxford: Oxford University Press, Clarendon Press, 1932.

LEVY, DAVID. "Ricardo and the Iron Law: A Correction of the Record," *Hist. Polit. Econ.*, Summer 1976, *8*(2), pp. 235–51.

MCCULLOCH, JOHN R. *The literature of political economy.* London: Longman, Brown, Green, and Longmans, 1845.

MALTHUS, THOMAS R. *An essay on the principle of population.* Second edition. London, 1803.

———. *Observations on the effects of the corn laws.* Second edition. London, 1814; reprinted in *Pamphlets of Thomas Robert Malthus.* New York: Kelley, 1970, pp. 93–131.

———. *An inquiry into the nature and progress of rent.* London, 1815; reprinted in *Pamphlets of Thomas Robert Malthus.* New York: Kelley, 1970, pp. 175–225.

———. *Principles of political economy.* London, 1820.

RICARDO, DAVID. *Works and correspondence.* Vol. I. *On the principles of political economy and taxation.* Edited by PIERO SRAFFA with the collaboration of M. H. DOBB. Cambridge: Cambridge University Press for the Royal Economic Society, [1817] 1951.

______. *Works and correspondence.* Vol. IV. *Essay on the influence of a low price of corn on the profits of stock.* [1815] 1951.

______. *Works and correspondence.* Vol. VI. *Letters, 1810–1815.* 1951.

______. *Works and correspondence.* Vol. VII. *Letters, 1816–1818.* 1951.

______. *Works and correspondence.* Vol. II. *Notes on Malthus's "Principles."* [1820] 1951.

SAMUELSON, PAUL A. "A Modern Theorist's Vindication of Adam Smith," *Amer. Econ. Rev.*, Feb. 1977, *67*(1), pp. 42–49.

______. "The Canonical Classical Model of Political Economy," *J. Econ. Lit.*, Dec. 1978, *16*(4), pp. 1415–34.

SMITH, ADAM. *An inquiry into the nature and causes of the wealth of nations.* Modern Library edition. New York, Modern Library [1776], 1937.

STIGLER, GEORGE J. "The Scientific Uses of Scientific Biography, with special reference to J. S. Mill," in *James and John Stuart Mill: Papers of the Centenary Conference.* Edited by JOHN M. ROBSON AND MICHAEL LAINE. Toronto: University of Toronto Press, 1976, pp. 55–66.

TORRENS, ROBERT. *An essay on the external corn trade.* London, 1815.

WEST, SIR EDWARD. *Essay on the application of capital to land.* London: T. Underwood, 1815; Baltimore: Lord Baltimore Press, 1903.

[16]

Journal of Economic Literature
Vol. XVIII (June 1980), pp. 575–578

Noise and Signal in Debates Among Classical Economists: A Reply

By PAUL A. SAMUELSON
Massachusetts Institute of Technology

1. It is high praise when so expert a scholar as Samuel Hollander (1980) hails my canonical classical model (1978) as likely to become "the *locus classicus* for the next generation of textbook writers." Like Fletcher I care not who makes a nation's laws if I can shape its textbook writers' songs.

But with power comes responsibility. I must weigh and respond to the doubts Dr. Hollander raises about some positions I took in the three-seventeenths of my positivistic text that digresses to interpret particular historical controversies.

I shall be brief and deal only with most essential points.

2. I am glad that Dr. Hollander does find in the *Wealth of Nations* the canonical model that I attributed to the classical writers and to it. My readers will be grateful to him for documenting the case that it is there.

3. Ricardo and his contemporaries may, however, be in no need of enemies if their defenders must write on their behalf that they missed what was in the *Wealth of Nations* because the relevant material was "scattered" and appears in out of the way chapters where such esoteric subjects as colonies are discussed. To say that something in an earlier well-known author is "irrelevant" because it was "overlooked" seems just another way of saying it has been overlooked—a *description* of a misdemeanor and not an *extenuation*. A stronger defense of Smith against such misunderstandings can be provided by modern economics, I believe, and now wish to explain.

4. Experienced readers know that Ricardo all too often (1) does not succeed in expressing what he means to say. And (2) that which he does mean to say is often *not* correct until properly qualified. What complicates the matter is that (3) Ricardo often reveals somewhere in his work that he has glimpsed the needed qualification.

Thus, the following Factor-Price–Frontier Theorem was certainly glimpsed by Ricardo.

THEOREM. (α) In a given competitive technology, there is a trade-off relation between the equilibrium (1) *profit* rate, (2) *real wage* rate (in terms of any good or subsistence basket of goods), and (3) *real rent* rate (or set of real rent rates if, instead of a single homogeneous land, we assume a vector of heterogeneous lands). Mathematically,

$$0 = \text{profit rate} + f(\text{real wage, real rent})$$
$$= p + f(w,r)$$

where $f(w,r)$ is a quasi-concave monotone-increasing function—i.e., one with convex contours. (See *Figure* 1 for plots of this trade-off.)

(β) It follows that, if the real wage stays *in the long run* at a prescribable subsistence level as the result of population adjustment, there can be no decline in the profit rate unless land's scarcity rent rises.

FACTOR-PRICE–FRONTIER TRADE-OFF

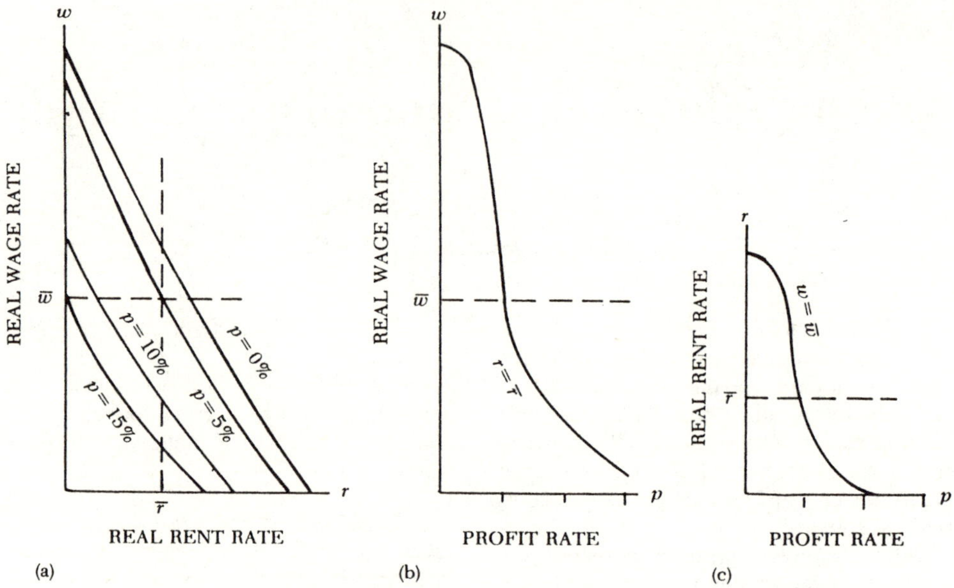

Figure 1. Competitive equilibrium requires that, when any two of (w,r,p) are higher, the remaining one must be lower. With technology unchanged, the iso-profit contours in (a) must be convex, but no such curvature restrictions need occur in (b) and (c). In Ricardo's longest run in which the subsistence wage is kept by population adjustment to $\bar{w}$, (c) depicts the trade-off that Ricardo perceived. Smith also perceived this. So long as we avoid the unrealistic "short-circuited version of the Ricardian system," in which population adjusts infinitely quickly, capital accumulation that outpaces population can move the system upward on (b)'s contour (or even *north*west-ward of it); so Smith is free of logical error in having accumulation bid down the profit rate without regard to land and diminishing returns. He would, however, be wrong if he thought that labor could command the same amount of subsistence corn while the profit rate was falling, technical change was possibly going on, and the scarcity rent of land was not rising; but can such a belief be fairly pinned on Smith?

Ricardo never stated the above post-1953 truth in my clear language. But, to repeat, he obviously did grasp it.[1] What

[1] To illustrate my remark that what Ricardo wants to say is often not true without qualification, let me mention the case well known to the classical writers of *joint production*. The above Factor-Price–Frontier Theorem is *not* true for it. Thus, when capitalists and rich landowners shift their tastes for shoes made of hides that are jointly produced with workers' meat, Ricardo must concede that the profit rate, real subsistence wage rate, and real rent rate could *all simultaneously fall*. In what follows I explicitly rule out joint production as the disputants would obviously want me to.

we grant to him, Ricardo was unwilling to grant to Adam Smith. However, when I read what the *Wealth of Nations* has to say about the rude state, about China, Bengal, and other regions whose fertile lands get "filled up" with their complements of people, I find Smith's understanding to be commendable. (Book I seems by itself adequate. But so are later Books.)

5. I must now investigate the possibility that what Smith does at times grasp, he at other times denies or at least overlooks.

In particular, was Adam Smith at fault in speaking so often of a process whereby extensive accumulation of capital will bid down the profit rate without Smith's making explicit or implicit reference to diminishing returns on fixed land?

My verdict is in Smith's favor. The following valid third paragraph of the Factor-Price–Frontier Theorem demonstrates why.

> (γ) It also follows that, whenever the accumulation of capital (or the vigorous attempt to accumulate it) sufficiently exceeds the pace of population growth, there can be a decline in the rate of profit and a rise in the real wage during whatever run of time the process is continuing—and this even in a colony without land scarcity or even where the existent land scarcity is not becoming more pressing, and indeed even where land rent were to be forced *down* by the creation of new capital items that happen to be competitive in production with land. [Thus, envisage a movement northwest along or near a contour in *Figure* 1b.]

If Ricardo denies this truth, he errs. If he and other contemporaneous readers affirm it, they must withdraw their charge and absolve Smith of *logical error* in numerous passages where he writes that an increase in capital can bid down the profit rate (and can cogently claim this even in the absence of mention of the fact of diminishing returns and of such diminishing returns being present).[2]

Once Dr. Hollander acquits Dr. Smith of logical error, Smith's "celebrated notion of 'competition among capitals'" is seen to have little cogent bearing on Ricardo's quashed indictment. It is like the red herring of whether Smith momentarily deviated into the heresy of questioning what is today called Say's Law (or James Mill's Law, or Francis Hutcheson's, or Smith's, or Ricardo's). You can affirm Say's Law and still agree with Adam Smith's contention that fast capital accumulation can depress the profit rate without necessarily raising remuneration of land.

6. Patently, Smith's terminology is not that of modern purists. I would not call land's return a "monopoly" return—even

[2] Only in what I called the "short-circuited version" of the Ricardian system will we be moving *in every run* on a contour of *Figure* 1c and would Ricardo's indictment of Smith be strictly sustained. I must mildly protest that Dr. Hollander does me an injustice in saying that my article fabricated a myth in discussing this short-circuited version. I presented that version as a pedagogic device; the fact that this polar case contained the prefix "Ricardian" was not meant to indicate that Ricardo himself believed in it but rather that it applied to Ricardo-like systems. However, I do not mind doing here what I refrained from doing in the article on the canonical model, namely joining with the host of commentators on Ricardo who complain over his exaggerating the speed with which long-run relations are realized. Schumpeter, not unfairly, called this "the Ricardian vice"—one of several such. Citing some sentences where Ricardo lapses into good sense will not wash away the stain. I should add that other classicals, Smith not excepted, sometimes perpetrate similar misjudgments about the long and short run—as some writers now living have been observed to do. It is an interesting curiosity that Ricardo himself criticized Adam Smith's facile assumption that population adjusted quickly enough to make it approximately true that labor always commands about the same ration of subsistence corn. (In the 1980 Eleventh edition of my textbook, *Economics* [1980, p. 257], I reproduced the behavior of the subsistence wage rate calculated by E. H. Phelps Brown and S. V. Hopkins [1956], and I was surprised to see how well Adam Smith's doctrine of "labor command" stood up empirically in the period 1550–1800.)

if its return covers no cost—so long as no landowner is big enough to affect market rents. But substantively Smith's rent theory and mine are one.

Similarly, when a plentiful rye harvest bids down the price of rye, I would not speak of "an increase in competition" for fear that a modern reader of Chamberlin might infer that I was asserting that the degree of *market imperfection* had changed. But, still, Smith's theory of what is going on in the rye market and mine are the same one.

Therefore, I am not tempted to throw a very large stone when Smith indulges in expressions like "increased competitions of capitals." He and I are agreed that the equilibrium interest or profit rate is likely to be lowered when the investment-saving rate soars and biological reproductive propensities remain the same. And so should Ricardo when we call to his attention the facts that it takes nine months to make a baby and more than a decade for that baby to ripen into a worker.

I put to the counsel for Ricardo the following questions: "Will you please shift downward in *Figure* 3(b) of Samuelson's canonical classical model the $r + w$ locus to reflect a sudden increase in thriftiness. Now I ask you to state the answers to these three questions: (i) What happens to the rent rate? (ii) What happens to the profit rate? (iii) What happens to the real wage rate? Must you not agree with the answers: (i) Rent changes not at all in the first instance. (ii) The profit rate is bid down. (iii) The real wage is bid up." I rest Adam Smith's case.

7. In conclusion, I want to make clear that I believe West, Malthus, and Ricardo did in 1815 add much value to the classical doctrines. Every historian of science appreciates how vague are the brilliant perceptions of the earliest writers and how constructive is the achievement of later writers in synthesizing and clarifying ideas. I do not wish to say, "It was all in Adam Smith from the beginning," but to rescue him as I would John Stuart Mill from the discount that they suffer as theorists on the bourse of posterity opinion. Puffing Ricardo simply sets him up as a great short sale.

Still, I must say, *"Touché,"* when Dr. Hollander gently reproves me for my incautious boyish words alleging that all classical writers believed in the same behavior equations. Like us, they were too human to be above error and self-contradiction.

References

Hollander, Samuel. "On Professor Samuelson's Canonical Model of Political Economy," *J. Econ. Lit.*, 1980, *18*(2), pp. 559–74.

Phelps Brown, E. H. and Hopkins, S. V. "Seven Centuries of the Prices of Consumables Compared with Builders' Wage-Rates," *Economica N.S.*, Nov. 1956, *23*, pp. 296–314.

Samuelson, Paul A. "The Canonical Classical Model of Political Economy," *J. Econ. Lit.*, Dec. 1978, *16*(4), pp. 1415–34.

——. *Economics*. Eleventh edition. New York: McGraw-Hill, 1980.

[17]

THE ECONOMISTS AND THE COMBINATION LAWS

WILLIAM D. GRAMPP

The Combination Laws of Great Britain prohibited workers from organizing to fix wages and imposed the same prohibition on employers. The repeal of the laws in 1824 was an important event—both curious and instructive.

It has been represented as a triumph of classical economics.[1] That is curious because the effect was to reduce competition in labor markets. Actually, the influence of the economists, although noticeable, was small. There were three other groups that influenced the event much more: One was the leadership of political parties, especially the Tory; another was the radical reformers; the third was the working class.

One finds that there was a similar grouping when other economic policies were enacted: a party leadership that was looking for the

1. The following are representative statements of almost all that has been written about why the laws were repealed:

"... Place's efforts would have failed had not the *laissez faire* ideas embodied in the *Wealth of Nations* gradually found acceptance by the governing class." A. Aspinall, *The Early English Trade Unions, Documents from the Home Office Papers in the Public Record Office* (London: 1949), p. xxv.

"Place's remarkable achievement carried through on the principles of *laissez faire*, with the help of M'Culloch and Joseph Hume. ..." Mary Dorothy George, "The Combination Laws," *Economic History Review*, VI (April, 1936), 178.

"But both Place and Hume were devotees of orthodox 'political economy,' and had given active assistance in the dismantling of *all* legislation restraining the 'freedom' of capital or of labour." E. P. Thompson, *The Making of the English Working Class* (New York: 1964), p. 517.

"A large body of opinion, which was in sympathy with the new economic theory of *laissez-faire*, realized that the right of combination could not be denied to the artisan classes while it was freely afforded in practice to employers, and was convinced, moreover, that some measure of combination should be allowed both to labour and to capital." R. Y. Hedges and Allen Winterbottom, *The Legal History of Trade Unionism* (London: 1930), p. 34.

"By 1824 reformers imbued with Benthamite philosophy campaigned for repeal of the Combination Laws on the ground that 'all artificial restraints should be lifted.'" K. W. Wedderburn, *The Worker and the Law* (London: 1965), p. 208.

The Combination Law of 1800 "was removed in the name of Laissez-faire in 1824." S. B. Clough and C. W. Cole, *Economic History of Europe*, rev. ed. (Boston: 1947), p. 522.

"As a result of the efforts of Benthamite reformers, such as Joseph Hume, Francis Place, and J. R. McCulloch, a Select Committee on Artisans and Machinery in 1824 recommended that employers and workmen should be free to make such agreements as they thought fit, ..." N. A. Citrine, *Trade Union Law* (London: 1950), pp. 6–7.

The Quarterly Journal of Economics, November 1979 0033-5533/79/0093-0501$01.00

sensible thing to do; a reform movement that was driving the leadership to do it; and a group in the economy that believed it stood to gain if the thing were done. The Corn Laws were repealed by the Tory government under Peel in 1846, and he also was responsible for seeing the Resumption Act through the House of Commons in 1819. The repeal of the Corn Laws was preceded by a massive public campaign under middle-class leadership and was supported by the factory owners who believed they stood to gain.

The working class believed it would benefit by the repeal of the Combination Laws. That is not surprising except in one respect. Some of the workers would have preferred the laws to continue—and the right to organize denied—if in return the government would fix wages as by law it was directed to do but had not done. The repeal of the Combination Laws is in this respect instructive. It uncovers one of the origins of trade unionism: a second-best method of wage-fixing.

The repeal of the laws is instructive in other ways also. It shows that the reformers in getting what they wanted were not overly scrupulous in the way they went about getting it. Much of what has been written about the repeal is by historians and lawyers who have regarded it as enlarging the freedom of the working class and hence a good thing. They have not taken much notice of the questionable way the good thing was gotten. They probably would not change their opinion of it even if they did. But the record would be more accurate. This paper, while not a study of the event in its entirety but of the place of the economists in it, does contain information that belongs on the record.

The Laws and the Reasons for Them

The act of repeal in 1824 expressly exempted combinations from indictment or prosecution for conspiracy under the common law and under thirty-five statutes that were repealed wholly or in part. They had been enacted over a period of 520 years. The common law prohibition was even older.

Under it, the restraint of trade was a conspiracy, and combinations were restraints of trade. Some of the statutes were directed solely at making combinations illegal. Those of 1799 and 1800 did that and also made them a summary offense; they were the first actually to be called "Combination Laws," the others thereafter being renamed. Some did not have as their main purpose the prohibiting of combinations but did so because combinations interfered with the main purpose. For example, the statutes that directed public authorities to fix wages could also include a prohibition against workers or employers combining to secure different wages.

An economist looking at the history of the laws would notice that four distinct arguments were made for them. (A lawyer might notice more.) (1) They prevented a particular combination from having a damaging effect, as the combination of London millwrights in 1799 was said to have. (2) Combinations, as a restraint of trade, enabled sellers to take advantage of buyers or vice versa, as workers were accused of doing when wages were rising and employers when wages were falling. (3) Combinations, as a restraint of trade, were inconsistent with competition. (4) Combinations interfered with the exercise of public authority, as in the fixing of wages.

The importance of each argument depended on the times. When markets were regulated, as in the sixteenth century, or when men said they should be, which was often, the second and the fourth were important. When labor was militant, as in 1799, the first was. How important at any time was the third, which is the reason a classical liberal could advance, I would like to know but do not. In 1824 there was much talk that men and masters should be free to make whatever bargains they pleased. The talkers, one would suppose, favored competition and opposed combinations. Actually, they favored both.

Why they opposed prohibiting combinations is explained below. Their claims will be seen to have met directly only the first of the arguments above. Much more was said, but it did not join issue squarely with the others.

THE ECONOMISTS AND REPEAL

The economists did not say much. Still, it should be described. One reason is to set the record straight. Another is to suggest how it got to be wrong. Another is to provide information about a topic that today is of particular interest: the relation of economists and their ideas to the making and unmaking of policy.

When the economists of the classical period (from Smith to John Mill) did have an effect on policy, the fact made itself known in particular ways. They usually had written something about the issue, not just a passing comment but a considered statement. Examples are what Smith wrote about the Corn Laws, what Ricardo wrote about them and what he wrote about the currency question, and what

Malthus wrote about poor relief.[2] This writing elicited a response from outside of economics, like the reply of Arthur Young to the *Essay on Profits* in which Ricardo made the theoretical case for reducing the tariff on grain.[3] When the economists were influential, their authority was invoked, their opinions cited, and their names held up for all to see and to rally around. This was sometimes done by both sides to the debate.[4] What was attributed to an economist might actually be an opinion he held or it might not, and he could be misrepresented by both sides of a controversy.[5]

When the economists were influential, they made their interest in the issue known in a clear and public way. They published their opinions in the newspapers and quarterlies; they sent letters to the great; they put their views before Parliament; they drafted legislation; and from 1821 onward they discussed the issue in the Political Economy Club. They did not always agree among themselves, and hence their influence could be felt on both sides of an issue as it was when Malthus supported the Corn Laws and the Ricardians opposed them.[6]

By this definition one may say that the economists had an influence on the Corn Laws, the resumption of gold payments, and the Poor Laws. One also may say they did not have an influence on the

2. Adam Smith, *The Wealth of Nations* (New York: 1937), Bk. III, Ch. 5.

David Ricardo, *An Essay on the Influence of a Low Price of Corn on the Profits of Stock; etc.*, *Works*, Vol. IV, Piero Sraffa, ed. (Cambridge: 1951), pp. 1–41; and *On Protection to Agriculture, ibid.*, pp. 207–66.

Thomas R. Malthus, *An Essay on the Principle of Population, etc.*, 6th ed. [1826] (London: 1890), Bk. III, Chs. V–VII.

3. Arthur Young, *An Inquiry into the Rise of Prices in Europe, etc.* (London: 1815).

4. An early instance was the debate in 1796 over the bill to fix the wages of agricultural laborers. The Tories opposed the bill in the name of free labor markets, and the Whigs supported it, while insisting that they too favored free markets. *The Parliamentary History of England, etc.*, Vol. XXXII (London: 1818), pp. 703, 706 (Feb. 12, 1796).

The most important instance was the debate over the Corn Laws. See the present writer's, *The Manchester School of Economics* (Stanford: 1960), pp. 17–18.

5. An example of misrepresentation, and of ambiguity also, is the debate in 1824 over the usury laws. Serjeant Onslow for years had asked for their repeal because, among their effects, they restricted the economic freedom of the individual. But Alderman Heygate objected and said Smith favored some control of the rate of interest, which Smith did (*Wealth of Nations*, pp. 339–40). C. W. W. Wynn replied to Heygate and correctly said Bentham had objected to Smith's policy. John Calcraft followed and opposed repeal, citing figures of Ricardo showing the effective rate of interest paid on government securities to be much above the nominal rate. Hansard, Vol. X, pp. 559–63 (Feb. 16, 1824). No one that day troubled to refer to Ricardo's stated views. He had in 1818 testified against the usury laws before a Select committee and in 1821 had spoken against them in the House. Ricardo, *Works*, Vol. V, pp. 337–47, 109–10.

6. Thomas R. Malthus, *Observations on the Effects of the Corn Laws, etc.* (London: 1814); *The Grounds of an Opinion on the Policy of Restricting the Importation of Foreign Corn* (London: 1815); *An Inquiry into the Nature and Progress of Rent, etc.* (London: 1815).

Factory Acts before 1837 (when Senior wrote his celebrated letters). On the repeal of the Combination Laws they had a small influence.

M'Culloch

It was mainly that of M'Culloch. He made a substantial effort on behalf of repeal and is the only economist who did. But his interest seems to have been created by Francis Place and not to have come from M'Culloch's own ideas or those of other economists of the period. Of course, Place knew the economists well and subscribed to their doctrine as he understood it. But he was not one of them. He supplied M'Culloch with information about the Combination Laws, how they operated, and what their effect had been. Not all of the information was correct, but it convinced M'Culloch the laws were unjust and ineffective. He wrote on them extensively from 1818 to 1824; his major article was in the *Edinburgh Review* in 1824, a few months before the issue was put before Parliament.[7]

He made two arguments. One seems to have come from Place who had said the laws were unfair because they punished labor more severely than they punished employers. The inequity provoked the workers into combining out of resentment. They also combined to protect themselves against the combinations of masters. Because the unions were illegal, they were necessarily conspiratorial, and conspiracy bred violence.[8] All of this was repeated by M'Culloch, and he made an extension. It was a venture into criminal psychology. If a man wants to steal a lamb but knows he may be punished as much as if he stole a sheep, he will steal the sheep, not because the "return" is greater, but in order to "deserve" the punishment and to show his outrage over its injustice. The repeal of the laws, M'Culloch continued, would cause combinations to disappear and would bring about a "free and unrestrained competition" in labor markets.[9]

In this way did he connect repeal with competition, and in this sense are the historians correct when they say he did. But they fail to say his argument was made only at the urging of an outsider and that

7. [J. R. M'Culloch] "Art. III. 1., Draft of proposed Bill . . . Relating to Combinations of Workmen, etc.," *Edinburgh Review*, XXXIX, No. 77 (Jan. 1824), 315–45. This was enlarged and became *An Essay on the Circumstances Which Determine the Rate of Wages and the Condition of the Labouring Classes* (London: 1826; 2nd ed., 1854). For the complete bibliography of M'Culloch's writings on the Combination Laws, see D. P. O'Brien, *J. R. McCulloch A Study in Classical Economics* (New York: 1970), pp. 366–70.

8. See the testimony of Place, *First Report from Select Committee on Artisans and Machinery. British Sessional Papers, House of Commons*, Vol. V (Feb. 23, 1824), pp. 44, 45.

9. M'Culloch, *Edinburgh Review*, pp. 330–32.

the outsider seems to have supplied him with it. If we learned that Ricardo proposed a change in the Corn laws only after an outsider had suggested it to him and provided him with the idea of diminishing returns, we would attribute less influence to him in the ensuing debate.

M'Culloch did not rely entirely on Place. He used another and more substantial argument. It was that competition usually makes peaceable combinations ineffective. (He strongly opposed those that were violent and urged strong penalties against them.) If wages are below equilibrium, a union can raise them, thus doing what ought to be done and in time would be done by the market itself. A union, then, can do no harm and may do some good.[10]

What he said gratified the unions of the day (though ours would find it poor stuff). Two of them cited his opinion in their bylaws and used it to advance their cause. There was no other economist of the time whose authority they could invoke. M'Culloch was looked upon as their "champion" and "ardent defender." So Patrick O'Brien states in his valuable book on M'Culloch.[11] The statement does M'Culloch too much honor. He appears to have done so much for the unions because the other economists did so little.

Ricardo

The idea that combinations are powerless in a competitive market was stated by Ricardo in a letter to M'Culloch in 1820.[12] Ricardo said he had not studied the Combination Laws closely. His impression was that they were unjust to labor and yet did not protect employers from intimidation by it. "The true remedy for combinations," he wrote, "is perfect liberty on both sides, and adequate protection against violence and outrage. Wages should be the result of a free compact. . . ." He wished M'Culloch well in his efforts but said he did not himself expect much from Parliament until it was reformed. This could mean that he believed M'Culloch should have been working for Parliamentary reform (which, incidentally, M'Culloch did not favor nearly as much as Ricardo did) or could mean that Ricardo himself did not care to spend his time on repeal. One has the impression Ricardo did not think there was much in the issue. Later he may have come to think otherwise. Joseph Hume has been understood to say that Ricardo did believe repeal was important. But

10. *Ibid.*, p. 323.
11. O'Brien, *op. cit.*, pp. 370, 369.
12. Ricardo, *Works*, Vol. VIII, p. 316.

we shall do well not to rely much on what Hume said or seemed to say.[13]

Malthus

Malthus was the only other economist who, to my knowledge, expressed an opinion during the campaign. He favored repeal but was reserved. He appeared before the Select Committee of the Commons named to inquire into the laws and also into those that prohibited the emigration of skilled workers and the export of machinery. Hume was the chairman. M'Culloch had appeared a few days earlier. His manner was different from that of Malthus, just as his economics was. M'Culloch came through clearly, categorically, and no doubt at full volume in the Scots for which he was noted. He rang out his answers with, "To be sure"—"Certainly"—"Unquestionably"—"Precisely so."[14]

The witnesses were asked rhetorical questions. Place said he prepared them for Hume and coached the working class witnesses in how to answer them.[15] Occasionally a witness would be difficult. He would be brought into line by being asked if he did not believe men and masters should be at "perfect liberty" to make whatever wage bargains they pleased.

Then Malthus appeared.[16] The rhetorical questions came forth in due course. The desired answers did not. He replied, "Not particularly"—"On the whole, perhaps"—"I have not data."[17]

He was asked if he had paid any attention of the Combination Laws. "No particular attention; a general one of course." The questioner imprudently drove on:

> Is it your decided opinion, that masters and men, upon all occasions, should be left to make what bargains they please?

The question did not intimidate Malthus. Infirm of speech he was but not of mind or character. He answered:

> I think so; but it is very important that any sort of force used on the part of the men, to prevent others taking lower wages, should be punished severely, such as acts of intimidation either towards the masters or other men.[18]

13. See below, pp. 513–14, 520.
14. *First Report, etc.*, pp. 592–98.
15. Graham Wallas, *The Life of Francis Place*, 4th ed. (London: 1925), pp. 212–13.
16. *First Report, etc.*, pp. 600–01.
17. He was sometimes mistaken as when he said masters could combine "without being liable to punishment." They could not. *Ibid.*, p. 601.
18. *Ibid.*, p. 601.

Now Hume and Place had been at pains to assure everyone that violence would not increase if the laws were repealed, that violence indeed could be expected to diminish, and that in any event there were other laws to prevent it. The last thing either man wanted was a witness to warn against it, especially a witness who was supposed to be friendly. After putting another question or two, the Select Committee dismissed Malthus, and he was heard from no more.

Smith

Neither Malthus nor his contemporaries, not even M'Culloch, had an important influence. Many years earlier, when the Combination Law of 1799 was before the Commons, the authority of Adam Smith was invoked. The ideas attributed to him appeared again in the hearings of Hume's committee. Smith had been dead thirty-four years. Even more curious is the fact that he really had not written anything about whether or not the laws should be repealed. One may infer he believed they should be. He was opposed in principle to interference by the government (though not always in practice) and he was sympathetic to labor and the common people. Yet these ideas were not used by the opponents of the laws, in 1799 or 1824, except possibly by Burdett. Three other ideas of Smith were used. One was that the property each man has in his own labor is the foundation of all property. Another was that workers have less bargaining power than masters. The third was that masters always are in a tacit combination not to raise wages.

Smith actually did say these things.[19] But none has much to do with the Combination Laws. The first was a reason he gave for opposing the law that regulated apprenticeship. The second and third he stated in the course of explaining that in the short run wages are determined by bargaining. He was represented, by those who cited him, as saying that masters always combine to lower wages. He did not really. What he did say was that they tacitly combine in order not to raise wages above their "actual rate"; that they sometimes combine to reduce wages "even below this rate"; but that they cannot do so "for any considerable time." What he meant, I suggest, is that employers keep an eye on each other so that none need pay more than the competitive or "actual" wage (an interpretation with which W. H. Hutt concurs[20]); that they sometimes combine to pay even less; but that

19. Smith, *op. cit.*, pp. 122, 66, 67.

20. W. H. Hutt, *The Theory of Collective Bargaining* (London: 1930), pp. 32–33.

they succeed only in the short run—this last, an idea that the advocates of repeal of course did not utilize.

The labor historian Aspinall was so impressed by what they did use that he reported Smith advocated the repeal of the Combination Laws.[21] Smith did not. The mistake of thinking he did may have come from the report of a speech Francis Burdett made in the Commons on the law of 1799. He is reported in Woodfall's *Debates* as saying he objected to the bill because he was in favor of "having all things of this kind, as well as articles of any marketable nature, to find their own level" and also because combinations of masters, being more numerous and dangerous than those of workers, ought to be the concern of Parliament. Woodfall adds, "For the support of this reasoning he quoted the authority of Dr. Adam Smith on the Wealth of Nations."[22] The report does not make clear how much of this was attributed to Smith by Burdett. He could not have correctly attributed all of it. While Smith did say combinations of employers were more effective than those of workers, he did not say that Parliament should be concerned only with the former. Or did he say it should ignore the latter?

Of course, he was inclined to "having all things of . . . any marketable nature, to find their own level." However, he also was inclined to make exceptions to the principle, which if it is to be used as a summary statement of his economic policy, must be used with care. Even more care is needed if it is to be taken as evidence that Smith influenced a particular person or policy. Pitt invoked the principle in 1796 when he opposed a bill to fix the wages of farm workers. The unwary will suppose he also must have opposed the Combination Law of 1799 and to have stood by the side of Burdett. Actually, Pitt supported it.

The Political Economy Club

So much use, and misuse, was made of the principle and of other ideas of Smith because (I suggest) there was so little else to use. The repeal of the Combination Laws simply did not interest most of the economists. Why it did not is puzzling. Certainly it was important in a practical sense, and it could have directed the economists to a valuable inquiry about the effect of organizations of workers and employers on the market for labor. This did not occur. The economists

21. Aspinall, *op. cit.*, p. ix.
22. William Woodfall *et al.*, *Debates . . . in the Two Houses of Parliament, etc.* (London: 1799), Vol. III (June 10, 1799), p. 235.

had their minds on other things. What these other things were is suggested by the agenda of the Political Economy Club.[23] Nine years after the laws were repealed, combinations themselves were a topic, but not the laws affecting them, and it was put in an interesting form: "Have combinations which keep up the rate of Wages of Workmen the effect of distributing among the working classes a greater aggregate amount than if the competition were perfectly free?" The record does not say who proposed the topic but does say Malthus and M'Culloch were present when it was discussed.[24]

Torrens and Senior

After the laws were repealed, there were a few pamphlets and periodical articles about them. A writer in *Blackwoods* in 1825 said repeal had been a mistake and was responsible for the strikes and disorders that followed it. He singled out "the Political Economists" for particular blame. They had led Parliament astray.

There actually was considerable labor trouble, and it probably was greater than it would have been if the laws had not been repealed. But a part of it had a quite different cause: The cyclical increase in the demand for labor that occurred at the time of repeal and brought with it the familiar increase in labor militancy. The article is rich in invective, is not particularly informative, and is poor beside the writing of the thirties on the issue. There is no mention of M'Culloch by name, which is surprising because *Blackwoods* was then given to abusing him.[25]

A much better statement is in *The Law Magazine* of 1834. It is informative and judicious. It also is critical of the economists who, the writer said, had assured the public that once the laws were repealed, combinations would cease to be a problem. "On this subject the unanimity of the wise and liberal, such as Mr. Francis Place and others, was as wonderful, as it has since proved erroneous."[26] In the same year a pamphlet by E. E. Tunfell, *Character, Object, and Effects of Trades' Unions*, states the case against labor combinations in a

23. *The Political Economy Club, Minutes of Proceedings, 1821–1882, Rolls of Members, and Questions Discussed*, Vol. IV (London: 1882), pp. 41–70.

24. *Ibid.*, p. 114.

25. "The Combinations," *Blackwoods*, XVIII (Oct. 1825), 463–72. The magazine was the voice of the Edinburgh Tories, and they could not be expected to be as gentle with the editor of the Whig *Scotsman* as M'Culloch had been. He complained in 1821 of the "blackguard" behavior of Lockhart, the editor of *Blackwoods* and son-in-law of one of its new owners, Sir Walter Scott. "So," M'Culloch observed, "the libels of the son-in-law will be printed by the father-in-law." (A letter to John Scott in the Scottish National Library, MS 1706, f. 75.)

26. "Art. VII, Combinations and Combination Laws," *The Law Magazine*, XI (Feb. 1834), 155.

clear, cogent way. Three years earlier there had been another pamphlet, and it had made the same case. It was the anonymous *On Combinations of Trades*.

Neither is the work of an economist. *On Wages and Combinations* [1834] by Robert Torrens is. It is skillful but rather too intricate and is meant to show that only in special circumstances can unions raise wages permanently (if they can limit the supply of labor or if productivity increases). Usually they are powerless in the long run, Torrens wrote. The pamphlet is addressed to the electors of Bolton whom Torrens represented in the House. If they understood it, they were exceptional citizens. Torrens' conclusion was similar to that of Ricardo and M'Culloch. He reached it by a route different from that taken by M'Culloch. How Ricardo reached the same conclusion we do not know, since he did not explain himself.

The interest of Senior was engaged in 1830. Melbourne, then Home Secretary, asked him and a legal expert to report on union activity, which was considerable and militant. Senior and his colleague reported that if it was not stopped, Britain would lose its industrial superiority. They recommended legislation that would have drastically restricted the activities of unions and of employers, not as much as the Combination Laws had done but far more than the Whig Government cared to do. It was of the opinion (according to the Webbs) that what was recommended was a "serious infringement upon the constitutional liberties of the country."[27] The report was never published, which may be just as well for the memory of Senior, who has enough odium attached to his name for his part in the Poor law of 1834, his letters on the Factory Act of 1837, and his Report on the Handloom Weavers of 1839. Had his policy for unions been put into effect, they truly would have needed a champion and one stronger than M'Culloch.

Misreading the Evidence

The foregoing is meant to show that there is no evidence the economists had an important part in repeal or had any significant effect on the issue for the next decade. The belief they did have an important part is a mistake that comes, I believe, from a misunderstanding of our information about the period.

Francis Place managed the campaign for repeal. He is known to have been friendly with the Ricardians, to have professed their doc-

27. Sidney and Beatrice Webb, *The History of Trade Unionism* (New York: 1894), pp. 126–27.

trine, and to have been a familiar of James Mill and Bentham. How natural it is then to conclude that he was putting the doctrine into practice. The truth is nearer to the opposite, which is that an economist proposed to put an idea of Place into practice: the idea M'Culloch got from Place. Whether Place discussed the laws with any of the other economists, I do not know. I have found no evidence that he did but have found evidence of his having discussed other issues with them, such as a discussion with Ricardo about the repayment of the national debt.[28]

Place himself left behind misleading information. In 1826 in a labor newspaper, he wrote in praise of political economists, saying, "To them we owe the repeal of the manifold laws which constituted the obnoxious laws known by the name of the Combination Laws."[29] Now this statement is not borne out by the account Place wrote of the repeal campaign and which is given at length in the biography of him by Wallas.[30] Either the account is to be rejected, or the statement in the labor paper is to be rejected. There is nothing to corroborate the latter, and there is much to refute it. The issue is complicated slightly (but no more) by a statement in the account concerning the *Edinburgh Review* article of M'Culloch. Place said that several members of the House told him the article had persuaded them to support repeal and that one said he was going to make it the substance of a speech.[31] Hansard does not report such a speech, but this is not proof it was never made. Yet if it were, it would not be evidence of the economists' having had an important effect on the issue. Why Place should have given the economists more than their due is an interesting question. The answer is probably in the nature of the man. He had a high opinion of himself, but not being inclined to strut or swagger, he kept it to himself, one of the few opinions that he did. What he said of the economists was, as noted above, also said in *Blackwoods* and *The Law Magazine*. The writers of those articles may have gotten the idea from the speeches of Joseph Hume.

Those speeches are the most misleading of all of the information from the period. Hume addressed the House early in 1824 and moved the appointment of a Select Committee on the laws affecting combinations, the export of machinery, and the emigration of skilled

28. The letters that passed between Place and Ricardo on this issue in November, 1819, are in Ricardo's *Works*, Vol. VIII, pp. 118–25.

29. *Trades Newspaper and Mechanics Weekly Journal*, no. 52, June 18, 1826, quoted in Wallas, *op. cit.*, p. 161.

30. Wallas, *op. cit.*, Ch. viii.

31. *Ibid.*, p. 208.

workers. He opened by saying the House had suffered a great loss when his friend, Ricardo, had died five months before. ("Hear, hear," Hansard records.) He said Ricardo had advised him to propose an inquiry and he, Hume, had hoped Ricardo would assist him with it. He reminded the House that Ricardo had spoken against the Spitalfields Acts, and they were among the laws Hume now proposed to investigate and to repeal.[32]

When he finished speaking, William Huskisson rose.[33] He too paid his respects to Ricardo and referred to him as a friend. Huskisson declared himself in favor of repealing the laws concerning machinery and artisans. He was guarded about the Combination Laws. He said that when he had more information he might favor their repeal also. His declaration, although it was qualified, was important. As President of the Board of Trade, he spoke for the Tory Government. Later he did support the repeal of the Combination Laws.

What was said in the House that day seems to justify the conclusion that Ricardo had a particular interest in the Combination Laws and that his ideas and authority were a major reason why later they were repealed. Just such a conclusion has been drawn, but I have found no evidence to support it.

Hume began his speech by saying he was going to fulfill an "undertaking" of which he had given notice in the last session and that he was doing so "by the advice, and in the hopes of the assistance, of a distinguished individual, whose recent loss the kingdom had to deplore." Just what the undertaking was is not explicitly stated in the accounts of the speech in Hansard and the *Morning Chronicle* but is inferred to be the repeal of the laws against exporting machinery and the emigration of artisans. This is explicitly stated in the account in the *Times*.[34] What this suggests is that Ricardo had advised Hume to put before Parliament only the issues of machinery and artisans. Hume had been understood to say that Ricardo advised him to put before it the issue of combinations also. So we read in *The Law Magazine*.[35] So even do we read in Sraffa who in this instance does not follow his usual practice of giving us a telling citation.[36]

Early in 1824 Place wrote to Hume, "It was generally understood

32. Hansard, Vol. X (February 12, 1824), p. 141.

33. *Ibid.*, Vol. X, p. 150. *The Morning Chronicle* (February 13, 1824) reported that Huskisson also invoked the name of Smith and in doing so elicited cries of "hear, hear."

34. *The Morning Chronicle*, February 13, 1824; *The Times*, February 13, 1824.

35. "Art. VII, etc.," Vol. XI, p. 155.

36. Piero Sraffa, "Introduction to the Speeches in Parliament," *Works*, Vol. V, p. xx.

that you would move for a repeal of the Combination Laws in this session. . . . You and I had a similar understanding, and I acted upon it very extensively."[37] Was the understanding the same as the understanding to which Hume referred in his speech to Parliament? Probably not. Later in that speech Hume said he wished to add another issue to the undertaking he had pledged, and the additional issue was the repeal of the Combination Laws.

Of course, Ricardo conceivably could have advised Hume to seek the repeal of the Combination Laws, but that he may have done so is not proof that he did. Yet if he did not, the fact does not mean he was opposed to repeal. Quite the contrary. We know he had a good word for M'Culloch's efforts. He very likely would have had another for Hume's. The question is whether he believed the issue was important and whether he had any influence on the outcome. The answer, in my opinion, is no.

Yet what shall we make of Hume's connecting Ricardo with the Spitalfields Acts? They did, *inter alia,* prohibit combinations. Ricardo did speak against the acts and said they should have been repealed long ago.[38] However, what he objected to was their fixing of wages, and that was their more important provision. Some in the House agreed with Ricardo, but they did not want to repeal the laws until action first had been taken on the emigration of artisans. Such action was a part of what Hume now proposed. He then could say quite properly that by allowing emigration the House would prepare the way for doing what Ricardo had wanted done. The House indeed did repeal the laws against emigration. The decision, along with the repeal of the Combination Laws, suggests that Hume had two-thirds of a triumph (the other third being Parliament's declining to repeal the laws against the export of machinery). But in fact the decision was something less and was a rejection of a measure Ricardo had proposed. He had on occasion spoken against the truck system (the payment of wages in goods instead of in money). He believed (as Smith did not) that wages should be paid in whatever form the workers and employers agreed upon. Many of the Combination Laws prohibited the truck system because it was believed to provoke the workers into combining. When the laws were repealed, those prohibitions were in most instances allowed to remain.

The speech of Huskisson is not evidence that the economists were influential on this occasion. Although he held many of Ricardo's ideas

37. Letter of February 7, 1824, Wallas, *op. cit.*, pp. 210–11.

38. Ricardo spoke against the Spitalfields Acts on four occasions. *Works*, Vol. V, pp. 292, 295–97, 306–09.

of economic policy, they differed over when the ideas could be put into effect. Ricardo always believed more changes could be made than Huskisson and other political leaders were ready to propose. That Huskisson supported the repeal of the Combination Laws means only that he believed the time for it had come. Harriet Martineau said he "opened his hand one finger at a time, because the people or their rulers could not receive a whole handful of truth."[39] His support of repeal does not mean he did what Ricardo urged him to do even if we suppose (what is improbable) that Ricardo had urged him. In the last years of his life, Ricardo believed that his influence had declined, and there is reason to believe that he was right.[40]

Why the Laws Were Repealed

The Leadership of the Parties

An important reason why the laws were repealed is that the Tory Government, with the concurrence of the Whig leaders, wanted them to be. Some accounts suggest that the political leaders simply had no objection to repeal. That implies that they were indifferent or inactive. They were neither. While they did not initiate the proposal and did not take a large part in the debate or the hearings, they nevertheless approved of repeal. If they had not, it never would have carried.

In formulating economic policy, the parties were influenced by what was workable and what was fair. On neither point could the Combination Laws be defended. They had not prevented combinations from being formed, and after 1800 when the most comprehensive of all prohibitions was enacted, the combinations became more numerous than ever. Ricardo observed that the laws protected neither employers from being bullied by workers nor workers from being bullied by employers. By the standard of fairness the laws were objectionable because while they fell on employers, they fell more heavily on workers. Such, at any rate, was the leading opinion of the time.

In reaching their decision, the political leaders did not ignore economic doctrine but in this instance acted independently of it. They would be called "pragmatists" if that were not a word that too often is used when we fail to discover the principles on which men act. Here

39. Quoted by William Smart, *Economic Annals of the Nineteenth Century*, Vol. II (London: 1917), p. 290.

This is not, however, the view everyone has had of Huskisson. Some have made him out to be an opponent of classical economics, unconvincingly, in my opinion, but in a way that must be noticed. See William Atkinson, *Mr. Huskisson, Free Trade, and the Corn Laws; etc.* (London: 1840).

40. Ricardo, *Works*, Vol. VIII, p. 190.

they were influenced by the principles of workability and fairness more than by classical policy. They sometimes followed that policy and sometimes did not. Examples of the former are the following: the proposal of the Woollen Committee of 1806 to allow each weaver to use as many looms as he wished; the proposal of Viscount Sidmouth in 1813 to repeal the wage-fixing provisions of the Statute of Artificers; the repeal in 1813 of the apprenticeship provisions of that statute; the tireless efforts of Serjeant Onslow to get the usury laws repealed; the declaration of 1820 that commercial policy in the future should move toward free trade; the tariff reductions made by Huskisson in the following decade; and so on to the repeal of the Corn and Navigation Laws in 1846 and 1849.

On the other side, one can cite the recommendation of the same Woollen Committee to restrict the export of machinery and emigration of skilled workers; the Factory Acts, the first of which was an amendment to the Statute of Apprentices; the laws that regulated banking and currency, the safety of ships, the construction and operation of railroads, and the flotation of securities. Shall we add the laws that abolished the slave trade and then slavery? Desirable laws, surely, but they were just as surely restrictions on the market.

At times, the parties acted independently of classical policy. The repeal of the Combination Laws is an example. Some of the laws (as stated above) prohibited combinations in order to strengthen the wage fixing by the government. Some prohibited them in order to strengthen competition, that is, to strengthen wage fixing by the market. If Huskisson and his allies had acted on the principle of freedom of exchange, they would have repealed only the former. If they had acted to oppose that principle, they would have repealed only the latter. They repealed both, acting, as they did, on another principle, which was to do what was practical and what was fair. That they wanted to be practical, I may call on Jevons for support. Of all that was later written about repeal and the economists, his brief statement comes nearest the mark. Writing in 1882 about the state in relation to labor, he said he did not favor laws prohibiting unions because such laws do not work. "It was upon such grounds of distinct experience, rather than upon any theory of freedom of trade, that Parliament in 1824 . . . swept those mistaken laws away," he said.[41]

The party leadership did not always initiate a change in policy. At times, it responded to what others proposed or to necessity. It listened to those who believed their income would be affected by a

41. W. Stanley Jevons, *The State in Relation to Labour*, 4th ed. (London: 1910), p. 115.

change. It also listened to those who, acting not out of self-interest but in the public good as they saw it, marshalled the forces of opinion. They usually were the reformers.

The Labor Movement

Of those who believed their income would be affected by repeal, the most forthright were the workers. They, or those who spoke for them, believed that the laws held down wages and repeal would raise them. The employers might have believed just the opposite, and they too could have supported repeal out of self-interest. But they did not have a noticeable part in the campaign..Of some 150 petitions that were submitted to the Commons in 1824, almost all were from the working class and most claimed the laws held down wages. Only two were in favor of retaining the laws, and they came from employer groups.[42]

The ways in which labor saw its interest affected by repeal were not always what one would suppose. Labor did, as stated above, claim that the laws reduced its income. Also, there were groups in the working class that wanted the right to organize because the right was important in itself. But there were other groups that looked upon the right as a means to an end. That is, they believed that the workers by combining could do for themselves what the state was supposed to do for them but had not. That was to take the determination of wages away from the market.

The state had long tried to regulate the wages in particular employments. The laws by which this was done often (as stated above) prohibited combinations.[43] As late as 1823, the silk weavers petitioned

42. *Journals of the House of Commons* (London: n. d.), Vol. LXXIX, p. 19 *et passim*. The two petitions that favored retaining the Combination Laws also favored retaining the laws prohibiting the export of machinery and the emigration of artisans. A third petition favored retaining the law against exporting machinery.

The petitioning of Parliament in this way began in 1779 when groups assembled in different parts of the country and prepared a statement of the reforms they wanted made. In the nineteenth century large numbers of petitions were submitted to both Houses. (See M. F. Bond, *A Guide to House of Lords Papers and Petitions*, Record Office Memorandum No. 20, 1959.) The practice diminished late in the century, as the franchise was extended and possibly for that reason, and has been used very little in this century.

43. 1424, 3 Henry VI, cap. 1; 1542, 33 Henry VIII, cap. 9 (I); 1720, 7 Geo. I, cap. 13; 1756, 29 Geo. II, cap. 33; 1767, 8 Geo. III, cap. 17; 1771–72, 11 and 12 Geo. III, cap. 18 (I); 1771–72, 11 and 12 Geo. III, cap. 33 (I); 1773, 13 Geo. III, cap. 68; 1779–80, 19 and 20 Geo. III, cap. 24 (I); 1779–80, 19 and 20 Geo. III, cap. 36 (I); 1785, 25 Geo. III, cap. 48 (I); 1792, 32 Geo. III, cap. 44; 1807, 47 Geo. III, cap. 43.

The full text of the laws cited is in one of the following:

The Statutes of the United Kingdom of Great Britain and Ireland ["Statutes at Large"] (London: v. d.). The laws that applied only in Ireland are designated (I) and only in Scotland (S).

The Statutes at Large, Passed in the Parliaments Held in Ireland (Dublin: v. d.).

The Acts of the Parliaments of Scotland (London: v. d.).

Parliament to retain the laws by which their wages were fixed and also by which they were prohibited from combining. The petitions indicated that the workers were willing to forgo the right to organize in return for the government's fixing wages for them. The first of such petitions came from the weavers of Sudbury who were not actually covered by the law. It covered the Spitalfields workers, but they had not submitted a petition. Ricardo hinted that the workers of Sudbury were asking that wages be kept high in Spitalfields in order that employment would be maintained in Sudbury. However, a few days later a petition came from Middlesex where the law did apply.

There is additional evidence that workers wanted the state to intervene in the labor market. They themselves put forward a bill to repeal the Combination Laws. They did so before Hume took up the question, and their bill was much different from his. Theirs was drafted by a labor activist, Gravener Hensen, and was placed before Parliament in 1823 by Peter Moore, the Radical member for Coventry. The bill went far beyond repeal of the Combination Laws and specified in great detail the conditions of work and their enforcement. That was much too far for the Government but did convince it that the time had come to do something about the Combination Laws. Place believed the workers could be persuaded to support Hume's bill instead of Moore's. He also believed Moore would be no problem if Hume put him on the Select Committee where he would be outnumbered. Place was right on both points. The workers supported Hume, and Moore never attended the meetings of the committee.[44]

However, Place was wrong about something that was more important. He had told Hume, M'Culloch, and others that repeal would cause combinations to decline and in time to disappear. He had not said this to labor groups whose support he enlisted. He allowed them to believe that repeal would strengthen their organizations and on occasion encouraged the belief. He did not try to disabuse them of the belief that the Combination laws held wages down. One sees the belief expressed in many of the petitions he persuaded them to put before the House. But to the Select Committee, he said the idea was "absurd." Reformer that he was, he knew his cause was pure, and he was not fussy about his means. He also had the reformer's habit of thinking he was awfully clever with people. He sometimes was. But in the repeal

44. On Place see Wallas, *op. cit.*, pp. 209, 213.

Moore's bill was entitled "A Bill for Repealing Several Acts relating to Combinations of Workmen, and for more effectually protecting Trade and for settling Disputes between Masters and their Workpeople." It was ordered printed and appears in *Bills, Public: In Three Volumes: Volume the Second. Ireland continued, etc. Session 4 February-to-19 July 1823* (London: 1823), no continuous pagination.

campaign he did not use the labor movement as much as it used him. Once the laws were abolished, its power increased, and its activities multiplied. The act of repeal was a milestone in the development of modern trade unionism.[45]

The Reformers

Place was prominent among the radical reformers, and they took up the issue of the Combination Laws. The radicals did not constitute the entire reform movement, and not every part of it shared their views. It was an extensive and intricate collection of groups and people who meant to do good. One cannot help but respect them for their intentions and one also cannot help but notice that at times they were ridiculous. One thing about them is certain. They were influential. One part or another of the reform movement is associated with just about every important change made in the nineteenth century including every major change in economic policy and many minor changes.

In the repeal of the Combination Laws, the radicals could not have succeeded without the concurrence of the party leaders and the support of the working class. But the radicals were the first to act. They had made the Combination Laws an issue in 1799 when Burdett was their leader and spoke against the law of that year in the House. He was supported by another radical worthy, John Cam Hobhouse (later Lord Broughton).[46] The two were still in the House in 1824 and 1825. But the leadership of the group had passed to Hume. He, in turn, was prompted to act by Place, himself one of the principals of the movement. Place began to prepare the case for repeal in 1814. He persuaded M'Culloch to write against the laws, which M'Culloch did, beginning in 1818. Place prevailed on Hume to put the issue before the House in 1824 and kept Hume solidly for repeal when Place suspected the Tories of throwing sand in Hume's eyes. The two of them staged the hearings of the Select Committee, which went as planned except for the fiasco of Malthus' testimony. Place then advised Hume not to prepare a report, which was the customary thing to do, and instead to submit a set of resolutions, each of which was to contain a statement of fact so it could not easily be disputed. (Some of the "facts" had an opinion enclosed within them.) The act of repeal was written by a legislative expert, but Place managed to rewrite it. It went through the Commons without a vote, without any debate, and with

45. See the Webbs, *op. cit.*, p. 97; Thompson, *op. cit.*, p. 520; Aspinall, *op. cit.*, p. xxxi; Allen Hutt, *British Trade Unionism* (New York: 1953), p. 11.

46. Woodfall, *op. cit.*, Vol. III (June 10, 1799), p. 235.

remarkable speed. It was sent to the Lords where one of the members was Lauderdale, the economist. He favored repeal but believed it should be enacted properly. He believed the Lords should see the minutes of evidence collected by Hume's committee. If his request had been granted, the bill would have been opened to scrutiny and debate. Place feared that "sinister influences" might then prevail. He was furious with "the half-crazy Lauderdale," as he called him, and said later, "with almost incredible pains taken, Lauderdale was induced to hold his tongue. . . ." So it was that Place, after prevailing on one economist, M'Culloch, to speak out, prevailed on another to be quiet, about a law for which the economists are said to be responsible![47]

If Place was not overly scrupulous, neither was Hume. He led the House to believe that Ricardo when speaking against the Spitalfields Acts had expressly objected to the provisions that prohibited combinations when in fact Ricardo had not. He conceivably could have told Hume privately that he objected to those provisions. But that is not what Hume implied. It was that Ricardo had told the House that the prohibiting of combinations was wrong.[48] Hume also made questionable use of the testimony of the workers. When it supported repeal, he accepted it as a sincere statement of belief, as he did that of Richard Taylor before the Select Committee. When the testimony was unfavorable, he impugned it as he did the petition of the silk weavers for the retention of the Spitalfields Laws, which, the petition claimed, protected their wages. Hume insinuated that the weavers wanted the laws retained because the laws, while formally prohibiting combinations, actually promoted them.[49] To other workers, however, he represented himself as a defender of their right to combine. To employers, he was bullying if they opposed him, as he was to Thomas Osler of the Birmingham Chamber of Commerce who testified in favor of retaining the laws.[50] This occurred on March 26 (1824). On April 14 Lord Stanley put before the House a petition from Bolton in support of them. Hume rose to say that his committee had "received no evidence whatever. . . in favor of those laws."[51]

However Hume and Place may be judged, they cannot be said to have unduly protracted the proceedings in the House or to have burdened it with testimony against repeal. Liverpool and Eldon, the Tory Lords, said later they had not fully understood the law and would

47. Wallas, *op. cit.*, p. 216.
48. See above, p. 514.
49. *First Report, etc.*, p. 54; Hansard, Vol. X, p. 147.
50. *First Report, etc.*, pp. 324–25.
51. Hansard, Vol. XI, p. 409.

have voted against it if they had.[52] Huskisson said that the Commons had not understood the bill as well as it might, that the bill had gone through in a questionable way, and he took some of the responsibility on himself.[53] Another contemporary comment was that the law was "hurried through with a rapidity almost suspicious."[54] It may in fact have set a speed record. It went through three readings in the Commons in one week and received the royal assent ten days later.

An examination shows it was not the product of a Parliament at its best.[55] Of the laws repealed entirely or in part, one was the Spitalfields Law of 1773[56]—one to which Ricardo had objected. The provisions that fixed wages and prohibited combinations were repealed. This seems perfectly reasonable until one notices the act in its entirety had been repealed by the House four days earlier.[57] The law of 1799[58] was repealed in part but the clause that prohibited combinations among colliers in Scotland was retained. Actually, there was no need to repeal any of it because the entire act had been repealed in 1800 and was replaced by a general law against combinations.[59] It was repealed in 1824 (except for the arbitration provisions, which the 1824 act continued).

All in all, the law of 1824 was a muddle and had to be done over the next year. By then there was some opinion in favor of a return to prohibiting combinations, and a deputation of ship-builders worked hard to this end. The reformers no longer held the leading strings. Huskisson managed the bill in the Commons and now acted for the Government. Hume was on the new Select Committee but only as a member. Place was furious, again saw sinister influences at work, and predicted they would do their worst.[60] He was mistaken. The new bill, through the work of the Government, was much like that of 1824 but tidier. Its similarity to the earlier bill did not signify that the Government had succumbed to the reformers. The explanation is simply that the Government, and the Opposition, for some time had wanted the repeal of the laws and had allowed the reformers to make the case for it. Each side would have been amused if it had known that in the future repeal would be attributed to the classical economists, only one

52. S. Maccoby, *English Radicalism* (London: 1955), p. 525, n. 2.
53. Hansard, Vol. XII (March 29, 1825), pp. 1288–1301.
54. "Art. VII, etc.," *The Law Magazine*, XI, p. 160.
55. The formal designation of the act of repeal is 1824, 5 Geo. IV, cap. 95. See "Statutes at Large," Vol. LXIV, pp. 508–19.
56. 1773, 13 Geo. III, cap. 68.
57. 1824, 5 Geo. IV, cap. 66.
58. 1799, 39 Geo. III, cap. 56.
59. 1800, 39 and 40 Geo. III, cap. 106.
60. Wallas, *op. cit.*, p. 222.

of whom in fact had anything of consequence to say about it, and he was by no means the leading figure among them.

The law of 1825[61] contained all of the provisions of that of 1824, enlarged two of them, and added three others. In addition to prohibiting the use of coercion to influence wages, strikes, and other matters (as the 1824 act did), the later act also prohibited its being used in organizing combinations. The later act stated an action had to be brought within six months of an offense being committed and stated no Justice of the Peace could hear an action if he was a member of the trade where it originated. Neither limitation was in the act of 1824. The later act contained provisions (which the earlier act did not) that expressly stated it "shall not extend" to meetings of workmen or masters who assemble to consult and agree about wages and other conditions of work.

The act of 1825 in no sense withdrew the privileges that the act of 1824 had granted to combinations. On the contrary. The act of 1825 was, in the words of an observer of strong labor sympathies, "the starting point of a great new development in the history of English trade-unionism."[62] To one with sympathy for the grand principle of the market, the law was a great new development away from "having all things of . . . any marketable nature to find their own level." That the classical economists should be made responsible for the development surely is a mistake and is unjust to them.

UNIVERSITY OF ILLINOIS AT CHICAGO CIRCLE

61. 6 Geo. IV, cap. 129. "Statutes at Large," Vol. LXV, pp. 1066–78.
62. Aspinall, *op. cit.*, p. xxxi.

[18]

History of Political Economy 13:1

British thought on the influence of foreign trade and investment on growth, 1800–1880

Arthur I. Bloomfield, University of Pennsylvania

I. *Introduction*

A by-product of the postwar interest in the economics of growth has been the renewed attention given to the views expressed in this area by earlier writers, especially by the British classical economists and by Marx, in whose works economic development played a major role. Valuable analyses and reinterpretations have been made of nineteenth-century growth doctrines and of various aspects of the growth process as viewed by writers of that period.

One aspect of the growth process which has been almost completely neglected in these doctrinal histories has been the relations between trade and growth. This fact has recently been emphasized once again by O'Brien.[1] To be sure, the core of what has come to be known as the classical theory of international trade was based on the assumptions of given tastes, techniques, and factor supplies; and for the most part it focused on the static gains from the more efficient allocation of resources that trade made possible and on the distribution of those gains among the trading partners. Yet a careful survey of nineteenth-century British economic literature does indeed reveal considerable though widely scattered discussions and analyses of various interactions between trade and growth. Included here were analyses of the growth-stimulating effects of foreign trade on national economies, the effects of growth on the pattern of international specialization and on the volume and terms of trade, and many other interconnections.

In an earlier article I examined the views of nineteenth-century British writers on the impact of growth and technological change on patterns of comparative advantage and trade flows.[2] The present arti-

The author's address is Professor Arthur I. Bloomfield, Department of Economics, University of Pennsylvania, Philadelphia 19104, U.S.A.

1. D. P. O'Brien, *The Classical Economists* (Oxford, 1975), p. 200. This article will not examine any views that Marx might have had in the area of trade and growth. For an analysis of Marx's foreign-trade doctrines generally, see G. Kohlmey, "Karl Marx' Theorie von den internationalen Werten," *Jahrbuch des Instituts für Wirtschaftswissenschaften* 5 (1962): 18–122.

2. A. I. Bloomfield, "The Impact of Growth and Technology on Trade in Nineteenth-Century British Thought," *History of Political Economy* 10 (1978): 608–35.

cle surveys their thinking on the effects of foreign trade—and, closely related to it, foreign investment—on growth. As in the earlier paper, emphasis will fall on the period 1800–1850, with only occasional references to writings later in the century when interest had waned in the problem of growth generally. References after 1880, which has been chosen as the terminal date for this survey, will be even fewer. For expositional purposes it will be useful to distinguish the effect of exports from the effect of imports on a country's rate of growth. Much more was said about the latter than the former.

II. *The Influence of Exports on Growth*

A good deal of the literature since 1945 on the effect of exports on economic growth has focused on an analysis of the channels through which this effect has been exerted. These include backward and forward linkages, induced technological advance, increased domestic investment opportunities, multiplier-acceleration effects, economies of scale, and externalities of various kinds. Other studies have focused on factors causing different types of economies to respond differently to stimuli arising from given increases in exports. Still others have assessed the relative roles of increases in foreign demand and in domestic supply as stimuli to exports. Some have placed emphasis on the indirect growth-promoting influence of exports (and other sources of foreign exchange) in providing a means of financing the volume of imports needed to maintain targeted growth rates. A number of statistical studies of the relation between exports and growth have also been made. Last but not least, a purely theoretical literature of impressive size has developed.[3]

In degree of sophistication, these analyses of course go well beyond anything that earlier writers had to say about the impact of exports on growth. But at a more fundamental level, many of the essential ideas can be found in nineteenth-century writings and can indeed be traced back to Adam Smith's penetrating analysis of foreign trade and economic development in 1776. Some of them can be found even earlier in

3. Some indication of the extent of development of the literature on exports and growth in the past few decades is evident from the extensive bibliographies in R. E. Caves, "Export-Led Growth and the New Economic History," in J. Bhagwati, R. W. Jones, R. A. Mundell, and J. Vanek, eds., *Trade, Balance of Payments, and Growth* (Amsterdam, 1971), pp. 403–42; R. E. Caves, "Export-Led Growth: The Postwar Industrial Setting," in W. A. Eltis, M. FG. Scott, and J. N. Wolfe, eds., *Induction, Trade, and Growth* (Oxford, 1970), pp. 234–54; and I. B. Kravis, "Trade as a Handmaiden of Growth," *Economic Journal*, Dec. 1970, pp. 850–72. For representative statistical studies, see R. F. Emery, "The Relation of Exports and Economic Growth," *Kyklos*, 1967, no. 2, pp. 470–84; M. Michaely, "Exports and Growth," *Journal of Development Economics*, 1977, pp. 49–53; and B. Balassa, "Exports and Economic Growth," ibid., 1978, pp. 181–89.

the writings of other eighteenth-century economists, notably David Hume.

Briefly, Smith had argued that the main benefits of foreign trade, apart from the static allocative efficiency gains based on absolute advantage, consist in the stimulus to economic growth that trade provides. This it does in several ways. First, by widening the extent of the market, foreign trade extends the division of labor and thus leads to increased productivity, improved and more specialized processes of production, the promotion of inventions and technical advance, and, more generally, increasing returns and economic growth. Second, and much more ambiguously, foreign trade affords an outlet for 'surpluses' of particular goods above domestic requirements which, in the absence of markets abroad, would lead to reduced output and decreased employment of resources. Myint has referred to the two arguments as the 'productivity' theory and the 'vent for surplus' theory.[4] It will be helpful to draw on this distinction in the discussion that follows.

The 'productivity' theory

The 'productivity' theory was widely repeated in the nineteenth century. John Stuart Mill, for example, in discussing the indirect benefits of foreign trade, referred to "the tendency of every extension of the market to improve the processes of production. A country which produces for a larger market than its own, can introduce a more extended division of labour, can make greater use of machinery, and is more likely to make inventions and improvements in the processes of production."[5] Elsewhere he argued that the extent of the market was a key determinant of the practicability of large-scale production, which "can only be advantageous when a large amount of business is to be done: it implies, therefore, either a populous and flourishing community, or *a great opening for exportation*" (italics supplied).[6]

The same benefits of enlarged exports—namely, increased productivity, stimulation of technical advance, and achievement of economies of scale—were also stressed in one form or another by McCulloch[7] and

4. For a recent interpretation of Smith's ideas on trade and growth, see H. Myint, "Adam Smith's Theory of International Trade in the Perspective of Economic Development," *Economica*, Aug. 1977, pp. 231–48. See also A. I. Bloomfield, "Adam Smith and the Theory of International Trade," in *Essays on Adam Smith*, ed. A. Skinner and T. Wilson (Oxford, 1975), esp. pp. 467–73, for another view of Smith's ideas, including his 'vent for surplus' argument.

5. J. S. Mill, *Principles of Political Economy* [1848], Ashley ed. (London, 1909), p. 581.

6. Ibid., p. 142. See also ibid., pp. 122–31.

7. See especially John R. McCulloch, *A Treatise on the Principles, Practice, and History of Commerce* (London, 1832), p. 8.

by Torrens, Rooke, Buchanan, and others.[8] The argument was repeated later in the period by Alfred Marshall. In 1879 he wrote:

> . . . the extent to which division of labour in the production of [a commodity] can be carried, is enlarged by every extension of the foreign markets for it. . . . And it is certain that in the century which has followed the publication of Adam Smith's work England's export trade has exerted a quiet but constant influence in developing broad inventions and economies in manufacture.[9]

It is not entirely clear in all cases, however, whether the writers just cited and others who used similar arguments had in mind the effects of exports on growth or simply the once-for-all increase in productivity and real income associated with a shift from no-trade to trade. Nor, in particular, is it always clear whether reference was being made to the effects of a given increase in exports or of a continuing increase in exports. In other cases it is uncertain whether writers were referring to the effect of higher exports in promoting growth or in simply lifting a country out of recession.[10] After all, the distinction between short-term cyclical movements and long-term trends was not drawn as sharply for the nineteenth century as it is today. Even in instances where writers do seem to have had growth in mind, one cannot always be sure whether by growth they meant increases in aggregate output, in output per head, or in rates of growth.

In at least one case, however, the argument was unambiguously dynamic in character. As early as 1803 Henry Brougham had emphasized the stimulus to economic growth provided by export markets *that were continually growing*: "the extent of the market, whose demands call forth the industry, and employ the capital of a country, is of less importance than its progressive state." He regarded the market afforded by newly settled countries as particularly advantageous to the industry of

8. Robert Torrens, *An Essay on the Production of Wealth* (London, 1821), pp. 248–50; John Rooke, *An Inquiry Into the Principles of National Wealth* (Edinburgh, 1824), pp. 125–26; David Buchanan, *Inquiry Into the Taxation and Commercial Policy of Great Britain* (Edinburgh, 1844), pp. 111–13; [Anon.], "Spence on Agriculture and Commerce," *Edinburgh Review*, April 1809, pp. 56, 58; J. S. Eisdell, *A Treatise on the Industry of Nations* (London, 1839), 1:337; and J. L. Shadwell, *A System of Political Economy* (London, 1877), p. 416.

9. A. Marshall, *The Pure Theory of Foreign Trade: The Pure Theory of Domestic Values* [1879] (London, 1930), p. 13.

10. On the other hand, various writers clearly had in mind the recovery-stimulating effects of increased exports. See, e.g., [John Cazenove], *Considerations on the Accumulation of Capital* (London, 1822), p. 63; and Samuel Laing, Jr., *National Distress: Its Causes and Remedies* (London, 1844), p. 92. Simon Gray, *The Happiness of States* (London, 1815), pp. 83–87, in similar fashion stressed the depressing effect on business activity of a fall in exports.

an older country because "it continually and rapidly increases."[11]

The 'vent for surplus' theory

Smith's 'vent for surplus' argument—whatever its exact meaning—seems to have been less frequently discussed in the nineteenth century than the 'productivity' theory, and it even had a number of critics. To be sure, many writers spoke of trade as being an exchange of 'surpluses' or as providing an outlet or vent for 'surpluses',[12] but they did not explicitly tie this in with the promotion of growth. One writer went a little farther by arguing that commerce "acts as a very great stimulus to the whole of the national labour, by furnishing a vent for the surplus produce of almost every kind of . . . production." But since he noted that this in turn made possible a more extended division of labor, he may really have had the 'productivity' theory in mind.[13]

The Smithian 'vent for surplus' argument is sometimes interpreted, most notably by Myint, to mean that exports promote growth by drawing into active employment domestic resources that would in the absence of trade have been idle, underutilized, or unexploited. The only statement that I can find in the period covered which seems explicitly to capture some of the essence of this idea is the following by Lauderdale:

> . . . by promoting an interchange of commodities betwixt two countries, [commerce] becomes a most powerful agent in extending the demand for the manufactures of each, enriching the one and the other, *by exciting a quantity of industry that would otherwise have remained dormant*; but which when thus brought into activity, augments the productions of both. . . . [It is] the great cause of putting the means of increasing wealth into action.[14]

This passage, with due allowance for the ambiguity of the term 'industry,' would seem to fit this particular interpretation of the Smithian ar-

11. H. Brougham, *An Inquiry Into the Colonial Policy of the European Powers* (Edinburgh, 1803), 1: 159–60.

12. E.g., John Wheatley, *Remarks on Currency and Commerce* (London, 1803), pp. 103–4; H. St. George Tucker, *Reflections on the Present State of Great Britain* (Edinburgh, 1813), p. 51; and [Anon.], *An Inquiry Into Several Questions of Political Economy* (London, 1817), p. 27.

13. James Syme, *The Principles of Political Economy Applied to the Financial State of Great Britain* (London, 1821), p. 291. Elsewhere (ibid., p. 315) he noted that "the surplus would be lost if it could not be sent abroad and exchanged for foreign. . . produce."

14. James M. Lauderdale, *An Inquiry Into the Nature and Origin of Public Wealth*, 2d ed. (Edinburgh, 1819), pp. 353, 356 (italics supplied). He goes on to note (ibid., p. 364) that "the progress of [a country's] opulence is accelerated or retarded in proportion as the distribution of wealth in other countries creates a demand for the articles, in the production of which it excels."

gument. Even if that interpretation were not valid, Lauderdale's statement could still be regarded as an early anticipation of modern 'vent for surplus' models,[15] which unambiguously stress the activation of dormant resources through exports.

Bastable commented favorably on Smith's surplus-produce argument, but he seems to have interpreted it in a rather innocuous way. Yet in the course of his comments he noted somewhat ambiguously: "It is highly probable that the opening of new markets will stimulate industry and also bring about a better adjustment of productive force."[16] On the other hand, Ricardo, J. S. Mill, and Shadwell were critical of the argument, questioning why 'surpluses' should tend to be produced in the first place and why, if foreign markets for them were not available, the resources involved would not be transferred to the production of other goods at home for which there *is* a demand.[17] Their criticism involved the assumption of a fully employed stock of resources.

James Mill explicitly denied that foreign markets were ever needed as outlets for a country's output and thus by implication as a stimulus to the continued increase of production. Supply creates its own demand, he said, so that there will always be a domestic market for all that can be produced. In his words: "Foreign commerce . . . is in all cases a matter of expediency rather than of necessity. The intention of it is not to furnish a vent for the produce of the industry of the country, because that industry always furnishes a vent for itself."[18]

Ricardo was also quite explicit. When asked, for example, before the House of Lords Committee on the Resumption of Cash Payments, whether an increase of foreign demand tended to increase the production and wealth of a nation, he answered:

> In no other Way than by procuring for us a greater Quantity of the Commodities we desire in Exchange for a given Quantity of our own Commodities, or rather for a given Quantity of the Produce of our Land and Labour . . . . the Amount and Value of the Commodities produced, whether the Country possess Foreign Trade or not, is always limited by the Amount of Capital employed; and there-

15. R. E. Caves, " 'Vent for Surplus' Models of Trade and Growth," in R. E. Baldwin, et al., *Trade, Growth, and the Balance of Payments* (Chicago, 1965), pp. 95–115.

16. Charles F. Bastable, *The Theory of International Trade*, 4th ed. (London, 1903), pp. 20–21.

17. David Ricardo, *The Works and Correspondence of David Ricardo*, ed. P. Sraffa (Cambridge, 1951–55), 1: 294–95, 291n.; Mill, *Principles*, pp. 579–80; and Shadwell, *System*, pp. 412–4, 475.

18. James Mill, *Commerce Defended*, 2d ed. (London, 1808), p. 86. See the valuable comments on the evolution of Mill's thought on this matter by D. Winch (editor), *James Mill, Selected Economic Writings* (Chicago, 1966), pp. 27, 33–35. Winch contrasts Mill's view with Smith's "vent for surplus" approach (ibid., p. 35).

fore Foreign Trade may alter the Description of Commodities produced, but cannot increase their aggregate Value.[19]

Since Ricardo measured value in terms of labor inputs, the alleged inability of an increased foreign demand to raise "aggregate value" simply meant that it would not increase the amount of labor engaged in production, which follows from the Ricardian assumption of full employment. There were no idle resources to be activated. On the other hand, an increased foreign demand would raise real income by improving the terms of trade, and it would involve some reallocation of the fully employed stock of resources.

Malthus occasionally referred to the importance to a country of expanded foreign markets for its output. In particular, he referred to the need for foreign outlets for increased production made possible by new inventions. Thus, he wrote,

> . . . suppose that, without any extension of the foreign market for our goods, we could by means of machinery obtain all the commodities at present obtained at home, with one third of the labour now applied, is it in any degree probable that the mass of vacant capitals could be advantageously employed, or that the mass of labourers thrown out of work could find the means of commanding an adequate share of the national produce? If there were other foreign trades which by means of the capital and labour thrown out of employment, might be greatly extended, the case would be at once quite altered, and the returns of such trades might furnish stimulants sufficient to keep up the value of the national income.[20]

One could conceivably read into this and similar passages[21] elements of a 'vent for surplus' theory. But Malthus was far more interested in the potentialities offered by an increased *domestic* market in providing the needed expansion in 'effectual demand'; and he believed that the stimulation of domestic tastes and wants, in part by the introduction of new commodities through domestic and foreign trade, could make an important contribution to this end (see below).

Exports as an indirect stimulus to growth

A number of nineteenth-century British writers called attention to

19. Ricardo, *Works*, 5: 435.

20. Thomas R. Malthus, *Principles of Political Economy*, 2d ed. (London, 1836), p. 354.

21. Ibid., pp. 358–60 and passim. One might also discern traces of the 'productivity' theory in Malthus. See ibid., pp. 162–63, where he refers to the "prodigious stimulus to improvement" that would be imparted by a greatly increased foreign demand for a country's raw produce.

the *indirect* stimulus to growth that rising exports provided by making possible the financing of increasing imports. The latter were regarded, for one reason or another, as important or essential for growth. What is of interest for our purposes was not the widespread recognition of the broad truth that 'exports pay for imports,' but the incorporation into the argument of the view that imports as such are in some way significant for a country's growth. The reasons for this view, which was widely accepted at the time, will be surveyed in the next section. We are concerned here only with the argument that exports indirectly promoted growth through their effect on the volume of imports.

The argument in question was generally applied to industrial countries such as Great Britain; and the imports to which growth effects were attached were thus mainly raw materials and foodstuffs.[22] Malthus stated the argument quite bluntly. After listing a number of important commodities imported by Britain, he wrote:

> Now I would ask how we should have obtained these valuable imports, if the foreign markets for our cottons, woollens, and hardware had not been extended with the use of machinery? And further, where we could have found substitutes at home for such imports, which would have been likely to have produced the same effects, in stimulating the cultivation of the land, the accumulation of capital and the increase of population?[23]

Elsewhere, in arguing the case for agricultural protection by a manufacturing country such as Britain, Malthus contended that one risk of excessive dependence on imported primary produce was that it might be impossible to finance the increased imports needed for growth if exports slackened because of industrialization abroad or "indolence and want of accumulation" on the part of foreign customers. In such case, the country "might be unable, even with the temptation of reduced prices, to stimulate its [foreign] customers to such purchases as would

22. The same kind of argument, incidentally, has been advanced in our time in the case of those less developed countries which, because of limited external reserves, are forced to restrict their imports to those goods, mainly producers' goods, for which there are no adequate domestic substitutes. It has been argued that in such countries the volume of these imports, and thus the rate of domestic economic activity and growth, tend to be related in an important way to the level of exports (and other foreign-exchange inflows), which determine how tightly import controls will have to be applied. For discussions of such an argument, see, e.g., W. L. Hempill, "The Effect of Foreign Exchange Receipts on the Imports of Less Developed Countries," *IMF Staff Papers*, Nov. 1974, pp. 637–77, esp. 637–41; W. A. Lewis, "International Competition in Manufactures," *American Economic Review*, May 1957, pp. 578–87; and D. Wall, "Import Capacity, Imports and Economic Growth," *Economica*, May 1968, pp. 157–68.

23. Malthus, *Principles*, p. 356.

allow of an increasing importation of food and raw materials; and without such an increasing importation, it is quite obvious that the population [and wealth of the country] must become stationary."[24]

III. *The Impact of Imports on Growth*

One finds in nineteenth-century writers much more emphasis on the role of imports in promoting domestic economic growth than on that of exports. A variety of reasons were given for the growth-stimulating effects of imports. For a manufacturing country such as Britain, where the possibilities of expanded domestic agricultural output were viewed as restricted because of diminishing returns, imports of raw materials and foodstuffs were regarded by some as essential simply because they were needed to support continued increases in manufacturing production and in population. Nassau Senior, for example, expressed the opinion that the only obstacle to the continued progress of British manufactures in the future would be increasing difficulty in importing materials and food (presumably because of diminishing returns and industrialization abroad), and that if imports of raw produce could keep pace with the power of working it up, "there would be no limit to the increase of wealth and population."[25]

An extreme statement of the dependence of growth on imports of primary produce was provided by John Wheatley:

> . . . if all the corn were grown that the country could grow, and no foreign corn were admitted, the manufacturing population could never exceed what the quantity of corn reared at home could support, and, therefore, manufactures would be limited in amount as well as corn, and no further increase could be made to the wealth of the nation. But if foreign corn were admitted, an additional number of manufacturers would be maintained in proportion to the supply, and the nation would proceed in wealth according to the increase of manufactures raised.[26]

Wheatley in fact had earlier argued that this state of affairs was descriptive of the actual situation then prevailing in Britain.

24. Malthus, *Additions to the Fourth and Former Editions of an Essay on the Principle of Population* (London, 1817), p. 115. Also ibid., pp. 113–14, 130–31. The adverse consequences for Ireland's growth of its inability to purchase sufficient amounts of imports because of restrictions on its exports into England and Scotland were discussed by Rooke, *Inquiry*, pp. 134–37.

25. Nassau W. Senior, *An Outline of the Science of Political Economy* (London, 1836), p. 86.

26. John Wheatley, *Tempora Praeterita; or, More Currency and More Corn* (Cape Town, 1828), p. 25. See also John Wheatley, *A Letter to the Right Honorable Charles Watkin Williams Wynn . . . on the Latent Resources of India* (Calcutta, 1823), pp. 3–4.

The demonstration effect

There was widespread agreement that imports played an important role in the growth process by developing new wants and tastes as new foreign commodities were introduced, by stimulating people to work harder so as to acquire the goods in question, by encouraging the inventiveness and industry of domestic producers, and in other related ways. A representative statement of this 'demonstration effect' of foreign trade, recognition of which can be traced back to David Hume and even earlier, was provided by Malthus:

> The greatest of all difficulties in converting uncivilized and thinly peopled countries into civilized and populous ones, is to inspire them with the wants best calculated to excite their exertions in the production of wealth. One of the greatest benefits which foreign commerce confers, and the reason why it has always appeared an almost necessary ingredient in the progress of wealth, is, its tendency to inspire new wants, to form new tastes, and to furnish fresh motives for industry. Even civilized and improved countries cannot afford to lose any of these motives.[27]

In similar vein, John Stuart Mill spoke of the "sort of industrial revolution" brought about in a less developed country by the opening of foreign trade, which made people acquainted with new objects and induced them to work harder to gratify their new tastes "and even to save, and accumulate capital, for the still more complete satisfaction of their tastes at a future time."[28]

McCulloch, Scrope, and others argued that imports facilitate growth by enabling a country to benefit from the inventions and discoveries of other countries. Imports also give a competitive spur to domestic producers, inducing them to improve the quality of their domestic substitutes (if any), providing them with models of new goods for imitation, or otherwise stimulating their inventiveness and industry.[29] Indeed, it was argued by Joplin that imports of new products stimulate

27. Malthus, *Principles*, p. 403.

28. J. S. Mill, *Principles*, p. 581, and ibid., p. 190. For similar views, see also McCulloch, *Treatise on the Principles*, pp. 9–12; Thomas Smith, *An Attempt to Define Some of the First Principles of Political Economy* (London, 1821), pp. 85–86; Thomas Hodgskin, *Popular Political Economy* (London, 1827), pp. 165–66; [Anon.], *An Essay on the Political Economy of Nations* (London, 1821), pp. 141–44; [Anon.], *Notices on Political Economy* (London, 1821), p. 61; and Robert Hamilton, *The Progress of Society* (London, 1830), p. 295. See also Thomas Chalmers, *On Political Economy* (Glasgow, 1832), pp. 182–84.

29. J. R. McCulloch, *Principles of Political Economy* (London, 1825), pp. 121–22; and G. Poulett Scrope, *Principles of Political Economy* (London, 1833), pp. 364, 368.

their local manufacture by creating—one might even say by demonstrating the existence of—a domestic market for them. As he expressed it:

> Manufactures will seldom to any great extent, be set on foot, if the parties have not only to make the commodity, but create a market for it; and this would have to be done if the habit of consumption be prevented by restrictions upon import. All experience has in fact shewn that foreign trade has proved the best mode of giving a taste for, and introducing domestic manufactures. It introduces both knowledge and enterprise.[30]

Joplin went on to make the further perceptive observation that prohibitions on the import of foreign manufactures are much more likely to retard than to encourage the growth of the domestic industry that they are intended to promote—presumably because of the 'dynamic' effect of imports that he had just noted.

Among nineteenth-century writers, none emphasized more than Malthus the effect of the introduction of new commodities through foreign (and domestic) trade in raising the 'propensity to consume.' He argued that the introduction through imports of new goods better adapted to local tastes and wants, in exchange for goods exported which are valued less by local residents, raises the "effectual demand" for commodities generally and increases the "exchangeable value of the whole produce estimated in labour" as well as profits.[31] This in turn provides a stimulus to capital accumulation and increased production. This rather obscure argument in various forms reappears frequently in the *Principles*[32] and in other writings of Malthus.

Modern writers on economic development have tended to stress the allegedly *deleterious* consequences for growth of the demonstration effect, such as by lowering the savings ratio and inhibiting the rate of capital formation. I have been unable to find any similar view expressed by nineteenth-century writers. The demonstration effect, to the extent that it was recognized, was apparently regarded as having only a beneficial impact on growth.[33]

30. Thomas Joplin, *Outlines of a System of Political Economy* (London, 1823), pp. 150–51.

31. For brief interpretations, see G. S. L. Tucker, *Progress and Profits in British Economic Thought 1650–1850* (Cambridge, 1960), pp. 150–51; and J. Viner, *Studies in the Theory of International Trade* (New York, 1937), pp. 528–31. See also Ricardo, *Works*, 2: 388–420.

32. Malthus, *Principles*, pp. 359, 371, 383–84, 388, 396, 397, 428–29.

33. For a survey of some of the modern views and literature in this area, see G. C. Kottis, "The International Demonstration Effect as a Factor Affecting Economic Development," *Kyklos*, 1971, no. 3, pp. 455–71.

The corn model

The most impressive nineteenth-century model relating growth to imports was that developed by David Ricardo and subsequently used, in one form or another, by Torrens, McCulloch, J. S. Mill, and others. According to the model, free imports of 'corn' (grain) were regarded as a means of arresting a tendency for the rate of profit to decline with progress, and thereby of preventing an eventual cessation of the growth process that, in theory at least, would otherwise occur. Imports, by keeping up the rate of profit, would in this indirect way make continued growth possible.

The Ricardian corn model, which needs no detailed elaboration here, was designed inter alia to demonstrate that the rate of profit would tend to fall in a growing economy because of the need, in the absence of free corn imports or of agricultural improvements, to extend the margin of cultivation to less and less fertile land or to cultivate existing farm land more intensively. In either case there would be diminishing increments of output of corn, and a rise in the marginal cost of producing corn, as successive doses of capital-and-labor were applied to land. With wages per head assumed fixed at the subsistence level by the Malthusian law, profits, as a share of the total produce less rent, would fall—as would the (corn) rate of profits—with continued applications of capital and labor to land. In monetary terms, the rate of profit was shown to vary inversely with the money wage rate. Thus, as accumulation proceeded, the rate of profit would tend to fall as the money wage rose with the increase in the price of corn under the impact of diminishing returns.

In the absence of free corn imports or technical change, this process would continue until the rate of profit had fallen so low as to bring capital accumulation and with it population growth to an end, resulting in a stationary state. As Ricardo put it:

> The natural tendency of profits then is to fall; for, in the progress of society and wealth, the additional quantity of food required is obtained by the sacrifice of more and more labour. . . . The rise in the price of necessaries and in the wages of labour is however limited; for as soon as wages should be equal . . . to . . . the whole receipts of the farmer, there must be an end of accumulation; for no capital can then yield any profit whatever, and no additional labour can be demanded, and consequently population will have reached its highest point. Long indeed before this period, the very low rate of profit will have arrested all accumulation.[34]

34. Ricardo, *Works*, 1: 120. For other references, see ibid., 1: 109, 122, 290, and 4: 179. Ricardo emphasized that a stationary state as he envisaged it would not involve

At bottom, the difficulty stemmed from a shortage of land. As Ricardo noted in a letter to Malthus in December 1814: "If with every accumulation of capital we could tack a piece of fresh fertile land to our island, profits would never fall."[35]

Ricardo focused mainly on the need for getting cheap and abundant supplies of food from abroad so that money wages could be kept down and the rate of profit kept up.[36] "I never was more convinced of any proposition in Polit: Economy," he wrote to Malthus in June 1814, "than that restrictions on importation of corn in an importing country have a tendency to lower profits."[37] He was thus led to his recommendations that the Corn Laws be repealed.[38] In this way Britain would be able to draw low-cost corn supplies from abroad to meet the needs of a growing population. With money wages thus kept down and the rate of profit up, capital accumulation and economic growth could continue without hitch. Indeed, Britain "could go on for an indefinite time increasing in wealth and population"[39] so long as low-cost food and other raw produce could be freely supplied from abroad in exchange for manufactured goods.

Quite apart from the effect of imports on the rate of profit and thus on capital accumulation, another linkage between imports and growth noted by Ricardo was the direct effect of imports upon saving and thus upon investment. The argument was applied to the introduction of machinery as well as to imports. Ricardo argued that if by the application of machinery, prices generally were lowered by 20 percent, one could save as effectively as if his income had been raised by 20 percent. If by the introduction of cheap foreign goods one could save 20 percent from his expenditures, the effect would be exactly the same as if machinery had lowered their cost of production. Imports could have this effect even if (in the event they were non-wage goods) they did not raise the rate of profit. Ricardo was able to conclude that foreign trade "affords,

---

stagnation. True, net savings and investment would have ceased, but "all that is produced will be at its fair relative price and will be freely exchanged. . . . there will not be a general glut." Ibid., 9: 25.

35. Ricardo, *Works*, 6: 162 and 4: 18.

36. E.g., ibid., 4: 25, 237; 5: 137; 8: 357–58. Ricardo noted that money wages could also be kept down and profits up by a fall in the prices of commodities other than food so long as they were consumed by laborers, but not by a fall in the prices of commodities not entering into workers' budgets. Ibid., 1: 118, 132, 133.

37. Ibid., 6: 109; also 5: 33, 38.

38. Ibid., 4: 9, 263, 266; and 8: 208. Cf. O'Brien, *The Classical Economists*, p. 55: "Ricardo's *whole* system . . . was designed to prove one fundamental proposition: that unless the Corn Laws were repealed the rate of profit would decline, accumulation would cease, and the economy would cease to grow."

39. Ricardo, *Works*, 4: 179. The corn model and all other aspects of the Ricardian system are treated exhaustively in the recent work by S. Hollander, *The Economics of David Ricardo* (Toronto, 1979).

by the abundance and cheapness of commodities, incentives to saving, and to the accumulation of capital."[40]

The effect of corn imports upon domestic economic growth was also discussed by Robert Torrens in a number of his writings. In one of his earliest works,[41] for example, he argued that restrictions on the free import of corn tended to retard capital accumulation and growth. But his argument bears only a superficial resemblance to that underlying the Ricardian corn model. True, one finds here a statement of diminishing returns in agriculture and recognition that corn prices and money wages would rise as land less and less fertile is cultivated. But these were not linked to a falling rate of profit. Indeed, it was Torrens' view, for reasons not clearly stated, that in the absence of free corn imports the rate of profit would be *prevented* from falling as the margin of cultivation was extended. Conversely, he argued that with free corn imports, the higher rate of capital accumulation would lower the rate of profit,[42] which would confer "great encouragement on manufactures and commerce" and, along with lower money wages,[43] reduce prices generally and thereby improve the country's competitive position in foreign markets. The differences between all this and the Ricardian model are quite evident.

Within a few years, however, Torrens' views on the relation between trade and growth had been brought into somewhat closer conformity with those of Ricardo. In an article published anonymously in 1819,[44] he took the position that the rate of profit was determined by the quality of the soil under cultivation, the degree of skill with which labor was applied, and the proportion of the produce absorbed as

40. Ibid., 1: 131–33.

41. R. Torrens, *Essay on the External Corn Trade* (London, 1815).

42. Torrens seems to have accepted here the Smithian view that movements in the rate of profit were due to the "competition of capital." See ibid., pp. 301–2: "Let us suppose . . . from the accumulation of capital, and the consequently increasing difficulty of finding beneficial occupation for it, the profits of stock fall."

43. Profits and wages were regarded as rising and falling together rather than, as in the Ricardian scheme, moving inversely. Ibid., pp. 210–11, 224–25, 298. For Torrens' changing views on the relation between profits and wages, see the definitive study by L. Robbins, *Robert Torrens and the Evolution of Classical Economics* (London, 1958), pp. 51–57.

44. [R. Torrens], "Mr. Owen's Plans for Relieving the National Distress," *Edinburgh Review*, Oct. 1819, pp. 453–77. Key passages in this article, from among those cited here, were incorporated almost verbatim in the second and later editions of Torrens' *Essay on the External Corn Trade*. A few economists, including Viner and most recently Thweatt, have taken the position that the article, and more particularly the so-called Sismondi digression (pp. 469–75), was the work, not of Torrens, but of McCulloch. For a detailed statement of this position, see W. O. Thweatt, "The Digression on Sismondi: By Torrens or McCulloch?" *History of Political Economy* 6 (1974): 435–53. Further detailed discussion of this issue is to be found in articles by D. P. O'Brien and A. C. Darnell and by Thweatt, ibid., 12 (1980): 383–419.

wages—the first two exerting much more influence than the third. From this he was led to conclude:

> Under any given degree of skill and economy in the application of labour, the return upon capital will be determined by the quality of the land in cultivation; and as inferior soils are resorted to, the rate of profit will constantly diminish, until that stationary state is attained, in which no additional capital can be employed, and all tendency to increased population must be checked by famine.[45]

This "stationary and melancholy state, to which . . . . every country is gradually approaching," may be forced prematurely upon a country by unwise commercial regulations which, by excluding the raw produce of other countries, hasten the decline in the rate of profit and induce, along with the pressure of taxation, an export of capital. If free trade were introduced, Britain would exchange its manufactures for foreign corn, the rate of profit would rise, and this would enable Britain "indefinitely to advance in the career of improvement."[46]

Torrens elaborated further on these ideas two years later.[47] Trade had growth effects not only in 'old' countries such as Britain, but also in 'new' countries. In the former, in the absence of trade, growth is checked, and the stationary state ultimately brought on, by the increasing difficulty of procuring raw products; on the other hand, the productive powers of manufacturing industry increase because of a dense population, larger capital accumulation, and advanced division of labor. By contrast, in new and thinly peopled countries the situation is just the reverse: in the absence of trade, agriculture is highly productive because of the abundance of fertile land, but manufacturing is underdeveloped and its productivity very low. Trade between the two sets of countries, by obviating the difficulty of procuring raw produce in old countries, and of working it up into manufactures in new countries, "throws the stationary state to a greater distance"[48] in the former, while making possible a higher rate of capital accumulation and growth in the latter.[49] But Torrens did not note that should the additional post-trade demands on agriculture in new countries push them to the point of diminishing returns, the growth benefits of trade to them

45. "Mr. Owen's Plans," p. 459.

46. Ibid., p. 461; and pp. 462–63.

47. Torrens, *Essay on the Production of Wealth*, pp. 252–60.

48. Ibid., p. 253. Elsewhere (ibid., p. 257) he referred to "the ultimate limits to the progress of an old country [being] thrown to an indefinite distance, by trading with a new country."

49. Torrens liked this argument so much that he used it in some of his later writings: e.g., *Letters on Commercial Policy* (London, 1833), pp. 63–64, and *Essay on the External Corn Trade*, 4th ed. (London, 1827), pp. 121–23.

and to old countries would to that extent be counteracted.

In his later writings Torrens tended to shift away from the 'corn model' type of analysis and from unqualified support of repeal of the Corn Laws, although both continued to make occasional appearances in his works. He came to oppose unilateral tariff reduction, in keeping with his growing conviction that tariffs should be lowered only in response to reciprocal concessions by foreigners.[50] He increasingly turned his attention to the need for opening up new investment opportunities for British capital in colonial areas in order to meet the problems arising from excessive capital accumulation at home (see below).

McCulloch likewise incorporated elements of the Ricardian corn model in his discussions of economic growth and the Corn Laws. He recognized that unless cheap corn could be freely imported from abroad, food prices would rise as inferior soils were resorted to; that rising food prices would lead to rising money wages; that the rate of profit would thereby be reduced; that this would slow up capital accumulation and induce capital export; and that there was the possibility of a stationary state. For example, in 1830 he wrote:

> A government which prevents its subjects from exchanging their manufactured goods for the corn of more fertile and less densely-peopled countries, compels them prematurely to resort to poor soils at home; and profits being consequently reduced, the country is made to approach the stationary state at a period when, had the legislature acted on more enlarged principles, she might have been advancing with the same rapidity as before in the career of improvement.[51]

Nevertheless, there were also substantial differences in McCulloch's treatment compared with Ricardo's. While accepting the Ricardian view of the inverse relation between profits and wages, McCulloch usually stated the relation in terms of proportional shares rather than with reference to the rate of profit. His arguments against

50. While this and associated arguments were based predominantly on the allegedly adverse effects on a country's terms of trade of unilateral tariff repeal (or of failure to retaliate against the imposition of hostile foreign tariffs), Torrens was even here not unmindful of the effect of such actions on a country's growth. In either case the resulting shift in international demands, given Torrens' underlying assumptions, would exert a deflationary impact on the internal economy and this could have adverse implications for domestic growth. See, e.g., Torrens, *The Budget*, Letter No. II (London, 1841), pp. 36–37, and *Postscript to a Letter . . . on the Condition of England and on the Means of Removing the Causes of Distress* (London, 1843), pp. 3, 27–28; and the surveys of Robbins, *Robert Torrens*, ch. 7, and O'Brien, *Classical Economists*, pp. 189–97.

51. McCulloch, *Principles of Political Economy*, 2d ed. (London, 1830), p. 490. This passage, with its reference to the stationary state, did not appear in the first edition, nor can I find it in later editions.

the Corn Laws were based much more on the price fluctuations they caused than on their effect on the rate of profit and growth. He focused much more than Ricardo on the export of capital caused by a declining profit rate. In any case, as O'Brien has shown,[52] in the end he came to reject all of the key elements in the Ricardian corn model to the extent that he had originally subscribed to them.

The Ricardian model was essentially restated in John Stuart Mill's *Principles*.[53] No one could have been more explicit than Mill in emphasizing the dependence of continued growth in Britain upon cheap imports of food. Writing after the Corn Laws had been repealed, he noted:

> As long as food can continue to be imported for an increasing population without any diminution of cheapness, so long the declension of profits through the increase of population and capital is arrested, and accumulation may go on without making the rate of profit draw nearer to the minimum. And on this ground it is believed by some, that the repeal of the corn laws has opened to this country a long era of rapid increase of capital with an undiminished rate of profit.[54]

Nevertheless, Mill was aware that the mere absence of import restrictions might not suffice to keep up the rate of profit. For foreign exporting countries might be unable to meet Britain's rapidly growing needs for imported foodstuffs and materials unless there were great improvements in their agriculture or the application of much additional capital to the extension of cultivation. Mill was not optimistic about either occurring autonomously on the scale required. He concluded that the main hope for assuring a supply of cheap imported food sufficient to keep up the rate of profit lay in the export of British capital, which would develop, extend, and improve agriculture abroad.

Tariffs and growth

In preceding sections we have surveyed a number of arguments to the effect that imports could, in one way or another, promote domestic economic growth. Some economists, however, claimed that *restrictions* on imports, particularly on imports of manufactures, might under certain carefully prescribed conditions stimulate growth. These claims

52. D. P. O'Brien, *J. R. McCulloch: A Study in Classical Economics* (New York, 1970), pp. 291–99, 378–95.

53. Mill, *Principles*, pp. 714–15, 732–33, 736–39, and passim. Mill had also stated the essentials of the corn model in an early paper published anonymously. "The Corn Laws," *Westminster Review*, April 1825, esp. pp. 396–401.

54. Mill, *Principles*, p. 736.

generally involved use of the 'infant industry' argument for tariffs, or some variant thereof. To the extent that this argument was confined to only a few individual industries, it would scarcely deserve mention here. But a number of British writers recognized the possibility of the argument being applied to a whole range of industries, whose development in the aggregate might contribute significantly to the growth of the economy as a whole. On the other hand, little or nothing appears to have been explicitly said about the channels or mechanisms whereby protection was supposed to promote national economic development. For the most part these writers seem to have taken it for granted that protection would in fact do so.[55]

The case for tariffs for infant-industry protection, which Viner has traced back to the seventeenth century, became respectable doctrine in Britain about 1850 in view of the support given it, although carefully qualified, by John Stuart Mill. Mill regarded it as "the only case in which, on mere principles of political economy, protecting duties can be defensible." But he insisted that the protection should be temporary and should be confined to cases in which "there is good ground of assurance that the industry which it fosters will after a time be able to dispense with it."[56] He later protested that his argument was being used in defense of policies of promiscuous protectionism in Australia and other newer countries and that he had never for a moment thought of recommending a general protective policy.[57]

Although a few economists of stature, such as Cairnes, disagreed with Mill's case for infant-industry protection even with its strict limitations,[58] most leading British economists appear to have accepted it, though with reservations, as a theoretically valid argument for a tariff.[59] It was generally believed, however, that in actual practice few

55. For a modern analysis of the possible channels of influence of protection on the rate of national economic growth, see W. M. Corden, "Protection and Growth," *International Economics and Development*, ed. L. E. Di Marco (New York, 1972), pp. 181–208.

56. Mill, *Principles*, p. 922. For excellent earlier statements, see Ackoute Smyth, *Outlines of a New Theory of Political Economy* (Cork, 1828), pp. 41–42, and Edward S. Cayley, *On Commercial Economy* (London, 1830), pp. 184–85. See also John Rae, *Statement of Some New Principles on the Subject of Political Economy* (Boston, 1834), pp. 362–68.

57. J. S. Mill, *Collected Works*, vol. 16, ed. by F. E. Mineka and D. W. Lindley (Toronto, 1972), pp. 1043–44, 1150–51, 1419–20, and 1520–21.

58. John E. Cairnes, *Some Leading Principles of Political Economy Newly Expounded* (New York, 1874), p. 403 n. According to O'Brien (*J. R. McCulloch*, p. 221), McCulloch had little use for the infant-industry argument.

59. Charles F. Bastable, *The Commerce of Nations* (London, 1892), pp. 120–28, 133–37, and "Economic Notes," *Hermathena*, 1886, pp. 103–4; Henry Sidgwick, *Principles of Political Economy*, 3d ed. (London, 1901), pp. 488 ff.; Henry Fawcett, *Free Trade and Protection* (London, 1878), pp. 109–19; F. Y. Edgeworth, "The Theory of International Values," *Economic Journal*, 1894, pp. 615–16; and A. Marshall, "Some

industries could meet the strict tests that Mill, and later Bastable, laid down for justifiable infant-industry protection.

Mill, in his qualified advocacy of infant-industry protection, seems clearly to have had in mind only a few industries. Others, however, referred to the possibility of tariffs being applied to a wider range of industries with a view to promoting national economic development generally. Giffen, for example, noted that Mill's idea had been applied "by other writers to manufacturing industries generally," but did not specify who the other writers were.[60] Bastable, in fact, mentioned that the main point of protectionist theories generally was "to secure national development."[61] One of the specific arguments for protection that he discussed was an extension of the infant-industry argument into the broader doctrine that "there may be ample justification for applying a wide-reaching policy of protection that will bring the nation more rapidly through its several stages of progress, and create the immaterial capital of industrial capacity."[62] But he had little sympathy for that argument. His own view seems to have been that the acquisition of industrial skill was quite as likely to advance under free trade as under protection.[63] That the infant-industry argument could be given a wider application was also noted by Pigou in 1906,[64] who even admitted that this broader argument for protection was strong in any agricultural country possessing natural advantages for manufacturing.

IV. *Capital Movements and Growth*

It was noted in an earlier section that one of the objections raised against the Corn Laws was that they provoked an export of capital by lowering the rate of profit. Brief comments will be made here on some representative nineteenth-century British views regarding the influence of capital movements on growth and trade.

There was general agreement that capital movements were motivated by international difference in rates of profit (or interest), after allowance for risk. High rates of taxation at home were also regarded by some (including Ricardo, Torrens, and McCulloch) as a factor of importance, driving capital abroad because of their effect on the rate of

---

Aspects of Competition," [1890], in *Memorials of Alfred Marshall*, ed. A. C. Pigou (London, 1925), pp. 258–65. See also Marshall's comment in *Economic Journal*, Dec. 1903, p. 659.

60. Sir Robert Giffen, "Protection for Manufactures in New Countries," *Economic Journal*, March 1898, p. 4.

61. *Commerce of Nations*, p. 130.

62. Ibid., p. 137.

63. Ibid., p. 138. See also Bastable, *Theory of International Trade*, pp. 141–42, 147–48.

64. A. C. Pigou, *Protective and Preferential Import Duties* (London, 1906), pp. 12–22.

profit. International capital mobility was regarded as restrained by "the fancied or real insecurity of capital, when not under the immediate control of its owner, together with the natural disinclination which every man has to quit the country of his birth and connexions, and intrust himself . . . to a strange government and new laws."[65] The view that the capitalist would tend to migrate with his capital and that capital exports were restrained to some degree by love of country was expressed by McCulloch, but he was usually quick to add that "love of country has its limits" and that "the love of gain is a no less powerful and constantly operating principle."[66] Indeed, his main stress was on the high degree of international capital mobility.[67]

Discussion of the effects of capital movements on growth focused on capital-exporting rather than capital-importing countries. With regard to those effects, there were two opposing views.

The earlier nineteenth-century view stressed the allegedly detrimental effect of capital exports on growth. Ricardo, for example, was quite explicit in this respect:

> It can never be allowed that the emigration of Capital can be beneficial to a state. A loss of capital may immediately change an increasing state to a stationary or retrograde state. A nation is only advancing whilst it accumulates capital. . . . England even if she received the revenues from the Capital employed in other countries would be a real sufferer.[68]

In the chapter "On Machinery" in his *Principles*, Ricardo in similar fashion noted that the export of capital involved a much more serious discouragement to the demand for labor than the most extensive use of machinery. For while the investment of capital in improved machinery involved a diminution in the progressive demand for labor, its export to another country wholly annihilated that demand.[69]

In discussing the export of capital prompted by a falling rate of profit, Torrens in one of his earlier writings referred to the difficulties that would thereby be "occasioned by a diminution of the [wages] fund for setting labour in motion, and by whose extent, the extent of the productive industry of the country must always be regulated."[70]

65. Ricardo, *Works*, 1: 136; also 1: 247–48.

66. E.g., McCulloch, "Standard of National Prosperity," *Edinburgh Review*, March 1824, pp. 19–20; idem, "Ricardo's Political Economy," ibid., June 1818, p. 82; and idem, *Principles of Political Economy* (London, 1825), p. 385. Ricardo believed that McCulloch exaggerated the international mobility of capital (*Works*, 8: 357).

67. O'Brien, *J. R. McCulloch*, p. 194.

68. Ricardo, *Works*, 3: 274.

69. Ibid., 1: 396–97; also 5: 32.

70. Torrens, "Mr. Owen's Plans," p. 462.

McCulloch similarly noted that "the injury done to the working classes by sending abroad so large an amount of capital, or of the funds destined for the employment of labour, are of themselves conclusive reasons why the Corn Laws should be abolished."[71] Another writer, while taking a generally liberal attitude towards capital exports, claimed that they operated "to curtail the fund destined to become in the hands of the next generation the basis of national wealth."[72] West and Longfield both clearly implied that capital exports were a bad thing, but they apparently regarded this as such a self-evident proposition that they did not even bother to make clear why this was so.[73] Some authors objected to capital exports on the ground that they would foster growth in capital-importing countries at the expense of the capital-exporting ones. As early as 1805, for example, Playfair had written that "the capital of a rich country supplies the want of it in poorer ones, and . . . by degrees, a nation saps the foundation of its own wealth and greatness, and gives encouragement to them in others."[74]

On the other hand, there were those who believed, though not always for the same reasons, that capital exports would actually promote rather than retard growth in the capital-exporting countries. Indeed, from the 1830's on, this came to be the dominant view. An early statement of the changing attitude to capital exports was the following by Rooke in 1824:

> The new capital annually invested [abroad] . . . is never advanced out of the capital stock at home, but, on the contrary, tends to augment that capital stock very considerably, being remitted in the

71. McCulloch, "Abolition of the Corn Laws," *Edinburgh Review*, Sept. 1826, p. 345.

72. Joseph Lowe, *The Present State of England in Regard to Agriculture, Trade and Finance* (London, 1822), p. 341. See also [G. Poulett Scrope], "The Political Economists," *Quarterly Review*, Jan. 1831, pp. 22–23, where capital exports resulting from high taxation are alleged to reduce "the sole fund for the employment and support of labour," to impoverish all classes, and to bring on depression and decay. Scrope was later to change his views on this matter (see n. 82 below).

73. Sir Edward West, *Price of Corn and Wages of Labour* (London, 1826), pp. 142–43; and Mountifort Longfield, *Lectures on Political Economy* (Dublin, 1834), pp. 234–35.

74. William Playfair, *An Inquiry Into the Permanent Causes of the Decline and Fall of Powerful and Wealthy Nations* (London, 1805), p. 181. (But in another connection Playfair noted that capital exports would not be very harmful to the exporting country if the capital had previously been idle, although it would tend to enrich other countries. Ibid., p. 162.) Torrens also feared that the export of capital (and skill) from Great Britain would weaken its manufacturing superiority. *Essay on the External Corn Trade*, 4th ed., pp. 427–28, and passim. See also [Anon.], *A Few Observations on Some Topics in Political Economy* (London, 1825), pp. 26–27. All this was quite apart from the reservations that many writers expressed regarding the export of machinery.

> manufactures and other productive industry of the country . . . and it therefore follows, that all capital so created abroad, is the clear gain by which national wealth gradually accumulates.[75]

The stress here is on the domestic growth generated by the capital flows via increased exports. A similar point had been made a few years earlier by Thomas Smith, who argued that capital exports must be made in the form of increased merchandise exports and the interest received in the form of increased imports, both of which in his view would augment the wealth of the country concerned and make the capital left at home "more effective and of more value."[76] For this reason he denied that capital movements from one country to another would benefit the latter at the expense of the former.

In an influential paper in 1826, William Ellis contended that capital exports, far from reducing the amount of capital employed productively at home (for such exports in his view would be financed by idle savings or by additional savings stimulated by the prospect of higher profits), would actually increase the national capital. For if the capital exported went to increase the availability abroad of, say, wheat needed by the capital-exporting country, the increased production and export of the commodities required to pay for the wheat would furnish employment for additional capital and labor.[77]

The main argument emphasizing the growth-stimulating effects of capital exports was that embedded in the case for colonization developed during the late 1820's and the 1830's under the influence of Wakefield and Torrens. In view of the extensive secondary literature on nineteenth-century theories of colonization,[78] the treatment here will be brief and confined to arguments favoring capital exports.

In 1827 Torrens argued that colonization was a means of getting rid of 'surplus' capital and of lifting Britain out of a state of economic stagnation which in his view had been brought on by that surplus.[79] The problem as he saw it was that Britain had reached the state "at which her further progress in wealth and population [was] retarded, not by the difficulty of accumulating capital, but by the difficulty of employing

75. Rooke, *Inquiry*, p. 373.

76. Thomas Smith, *An Attempt*, p. 125.

77. [William Ellis], "Employment of Machinery," *Westminster Review*, Jan. 1826, pp. 128–30.

78. E.g., D. Winch, *Classical Political Economy and Colonies* (Cambridge, Mass., 1965); R. N. Ghosh, *Classical Macroeconomics and the Case for Colonies* (Calcutta, 1967); B. Semmel, *The Rise of Free Trade Imperialism* (Cambridge, 1970); Tucker, *Progress and Profits*, pp. 178–86; and Robbins, *Robert Torrens*, pp. 144–81.

79. *Substance of a Speech Delivered by Colonel Torrens in the House of Commons, 15th February, 1827, on the Motion of Sir Robert Wilmot Horton, Bart.*, 2d ed., n.d., pp. 42 ff. (The pagination of the copy at my disposal starts at p. 37.)

it beneficially."[80] In the Ricardian view, there could be no possibility of a 'surplus' of capital: when the rate of profit had fallen to a minimum and the stationary state had set in, net saving and investment would simply cease. As noted above, moreover, the Ricardian stationary state was not supposed to be a stagnant one. Torrens' theoretical innovation was to argue that even when the stationary state was reached, savings would still continue to be made—out of rent and the wages of skilled labor. Since by definition no profitable investment outlets at home existed, the excess savings, according to Torrens, would lead to economic stagnation. He concluded that a program of systematic colonization was needed to provide an outlet for the redundant capital (and population), relieve stagnation at home, and create renewed opportunities for domestic investment and growth.[81] These ideas were further developed in Part II of Torrens' *Colonization of South Australia* in 1835, a book that was much influenced by the work of Edward Wakefield, who in turn had been anticipated in part by Torrens himself.

Wakefield emphasized that in the 1830's Britain was suffering from an insufficiency of profitable investment outlets, a glut of capital, and general stagnation. Despite the low rate of profit, savings continued to accumulate, the funds being either held idle or wasted in speculative ventures abroad. Colonization was regarded as the best way to enlarge the 'field of employment' for capital, a field which did not, according to Wakefield, automatically expand as capital accumulated. Besides providing profitable outlets for British capital, colonization would remove excess population, extend markets for British manufacturers, and increase the availability of imported supplies of foreign corn.[82] (Wakefield favored repeal of the Corn Laws, but did not believe it would assure adequate supplies.) Wakefield was influenced by Adam

80. Ibid., p. 44.

81. It is not entirely clear why colonization as such was needed to promote capital export. As one writer noted: "Should capital find no profitable employment in one country, it will soon go to seek for it in another. . . . capital will not lose its uses anywhere, till every corner of the world has acquired as large a share of it as can be productively employed." John Craig, *Remarks on Some Fundamental Doctrines of Political Economy* (Edinburgh, 1821), pp. 101–2. See also John Craig, *Elements of Political Science* (Edinburgh, 1814), 2: 79–81.

82. Wakefield's economic case for colonization was laid out in most detail in his book *England and America* (London, 1833), especially vol. 2, pp. 61–262. For other supporters of colonization as a means of getting rid of 'surplus' capital (among other things), see Brougham, *Inquiry*, 1: 161 ff.; Scrope, *Principles*, pp. 375–77, 381–83, and passim; John Broadhurst, *Political Economy* (London, 1842), pp. 201–8; John Barton, *An Inquiry Into the Expediency of the Existing Restrictions on the Importation of Foreign Corn* (London, 1833), pp. 63 ff., 74–75, 83–84, 107; Herman Merivale, *Lectures on Colonization and Colonies* (London, 1861), pp. 167–85; and J. E. Cairnes, *Political Essays* (London, 1873), pp. 30–33.

Smith's view of the falling rate of profit as resulting from the increased competition of capital for employment, and also by Smith's stress on the acquisition of new markets, new territories, and new investment opportunities as means of stemming the profit decline—notions which the Ricardians had opposed.

The various strands of thought in favor of capital exports made by earlier writers were brought together in Mill's *Principles*. Mill argued for capital exports, as part of his broader case for colonization, within the framework of essentially Ricardian reasoning as to the causes of the falling rate of profit. Unlike Wakefield and Torrens, he did not explicitly take a stagnationist position. He regarded the export of capital in search of higher profits abroad as one of the principal forces counteracting the downward tendency of the rate of profit. First, it carried off "part of the increase of capital from which the reduction of profits proceeds."[83] This statement, which is suggestive of a Smithian rather than a Ricardian interpretation of the falling rate of profit, must have been something of a lapse, for elsewhere the Smithian view was specifically criticized[84] and the Ricardian view upheld. Second, the capital exported was, according to Mill, employed chiefly in developing and extending agriculture abroad, which, by assuring cheap imported food and other necessaries (assuming constant returns) served to maintain the rate of profit and also provided a field for the employment of capital at home in producing manufactures with which to pay for these imports.[85]

I can find few if any systematic discussions in nineteenth-century British writings of the economic effects of capital movements on capital-*importing* countries. It seems to have been generally taken for granted that capital imports would normally serve to promote growth in the recipient countries. For example, Mill listed among the requirements for raising living standards in less developed countries "the importation of foreign capital, which renders the increase of production no longer exclusively dependent on the thrift or providence of the inhabitants themselves . . . and by instilling new ideas and breaking the chains of habit . . . tends to create in [the population] new wants, increased ambition, and greater thought for the future."[86]

83. Mill, *Principles*, p. 738.

84. Ibid., pp. 725–27.

85. Ibid., pp. 738–39, 745. Elsewhere, however (ibid., pp. 825–26), in discussing the effects of a tax on profits, Mill seemed to imply that the export of capital was detrimental to national wealth.

86. Ibid., pp. 189–90. In discussing India's prospects, McCulloch "took it to be self-evident that capital in massive quantities was required if the productive potential of the country was to be harnessed." W. J. Barber, *British Economic Thought and India 1600–1858* (Oxford, 1975), p. 186. See also Eisdell, *Treatise*, 2: 112.

In the particular case of Ireland, however, various economists argued that capital imports on any substantial scale, even if they could be achieved, might not accomplish these ends. Indeed, Torrens asserted that instead of making things better they could make them worse. For there was little chance of an expansion of manufactures in Ireland so long as they were subject to the competition of England. Thus capital imports would have to go into agriculture, and the result of the improved modes of cultivation would be only to increase the unemployed surplus population.[87] Malthus believed that domestic demand in Ireland was too limited and the tastes of the masses too underdeveloped and inflexible to permit the profitable absorption in the near future of any large quantity of capital imports. He contended that the full development of Ireland's potential undoubtedly required immense capital, "but it can only be employed to advantage as it is gradually called for." What was required were measures to increase the will and power of the lower and middle classes to purchase domestic manufactures and foreign commodities.[88] He cautioned against any attempt to force capital into the Irish economy, a view that McCulloch shared.[89] Both men also believed that lack of security in that country in any case discouraged capital from going there.

V. *Conclusion*

The writings surveyed here provide ample evidence of the fact that nineteenth-century British economists were aware of a variety of effects that foreign trade and investment could exert on a country's rate of growth—just as they were aware, conversely, of the fact that domestic economic growth affected the pattern of a country's foreign trade and investment.

There was general recognition that increases in a country's exports tended to promote domestic economic growth, but the argument was not carried much beyond that of Adam Smith. Most of the writers concerned stressed the 'productivity' rather than the 'vent for surplus' strand in the Smithian argument, and some even criticized outright the notion of vent for surplus. A few denied that increases in exports would exert any stimulating effect at all on a country's economy. Some emphasized the indirect influence that rising exports had on domestic growth by making possible the financing of an increasing volume of

87. Speech in the House of Commons, 8 Feb. 1833, cited in R. D. C. Black, *Economic Thought and the Irish Question, 1817–1870* (Cambridge, 1960), p. 139.

88. Malthus, *Principles*, pp. 348–51.

89. [J.R. McCulloch], "Ireland," *Edinburgh Review*, Jan. 1825, p. 409, and also his testimony, *Select Committee on Ireland*, 1825 (VIII), pp. 811–12, 816. On the other hand, McCulloch believed that capital shortage played a crucial part in Irish problems. See, e.g., *Edinburgh Review*, June 1822, p. 104.

imports. The latter, indeed, were commonly regarded as more important for a country's growth than exports as such.

Imports were viewed as a stimulus to domestic growth by developing new wants and tastes and thus inducing people to work harder to satisfy those wants; by giving a competitive spur to domestic producers to develop or improve the quality of import-competing goods, and by providing them with models of new goods for imitation; and by enabling a country to increase its production potential as a result of foreign inventions and technological innovations. Of considerable influence, for a time at least, was the Ricardian corn model according to which imports promoted growth indirectly by keeping money wages down and thus preventing a fall in the rate of profit (under the impact of diminishing returns from land) that would otherwise have brought domestic investment and growth ultimately to an end. By contrast, a number of writers referred to the possibility that a *restriction* of imports, if applied to manufactures generally, could actually promote domestic growth under specified circumstances.

In these discussions of trade and growth, reference was frequently made to the impact of foreign investment on growth. One group of writers argued that capital exports tended to retard growth in the capital-exporting countries by reducing the wages fund and with it domestic investment. Another group contended that capital exports would tend to promote growth by increasing merchandise exports, by expanding the availability of imported primary produce, by getting rid of 'surplus' capital that was allegedly causing economic stagnation at home, or by any combination of these. So far as capital-importing countries were concerned, there seemed to be general agreement that foreign investment would promote domestic growth, although some economists expressed reservations about the ability of Ireland to absorb any substantial amount of foreign capital.

These various 'dynamic' notions, widely scattered throughout the nineteenth-century British economic literature—while indicative, along with other evidence not presented here, of the degree of interest shown in trade-growth problems—were never developed systematically. And in the last few decades of the century they tended to recede into the background with the flagging of interest in growth theory and growth problems generally.

I am indebted to Wilfred J. Ethier, Irving B. Kravis, and Sidney Weintraub and to two anonymous referees for helpful suggestions. I also appreciate the courtesies shown me by the librarians of the Goldsmiths Library, the British Museum, the London School of Economics, the Kress Library, the New York Public Library, and the Special Collections of the University of Pennsylvania Library.

Name Index

Pioneers in Economics

Section I: The Forerunners of Classical Economics

1. The Historiography of Economics
2. Aristotle (384–322 B.C.)
3. St Thomas Aquinas (1225–1274)
4. The Early Mercantilists
   Thomas Mun (1571–1641), Edward Misselden (1608–1634), Gerard de Malynes (1586–1623)
5. The Later Mercantilists
   Josiah Child (1603–1699) and John Locke (1632–1704)
6. Pre-Classical Economists Volume I
   Charles Davenant (1656–1714) and William Petty (1623–1687)
7. Pre-Classical Economists Volume II
   Pierre le Pesant Boisguilbert (1645–1714), George Berkeley (1685–1753), Baron de Montesquieu (1689–1755), Ferdinando Galiani (1727–1787), James Anderson (1739–1808), Dugald Stewart (1753–1828)
8. Pre-Classical Economists Volume III
   John Law (1671–1729) and Bernard Mandeville (1660–1733)
9. Richard Cantillon (1680–1734) and Jacques Turgot (1727–1781)
10. François Quesnay (1694–1774), Volumes I and II
11. David Hume (1711–1776) and James Steuart (1712–1780)

Section II: The Golden Age of Classical Economics

12. Adam Smith (1723–1790) Volumes I and II
13. Henry Thornton (1760–1815), Jeremy Bentham (1748–1832), James Lauderdale (1759–1839), Simonde de Sismondi (1773–1842)
14. David Ricardo (1772–1823)
15. Jean-Baptiste Say (1776–1832)
16. Thomas Robert Malthus (1766–1834) and John Stuart Mill (1806–1873)
17. Ramsay McCulloch (1789–1864), Nassau Senior (1790–1864), Robert Torrens (1780–1864)
18. Thomas Tooke (1774–1858), Mountifort Longfield (1802–1884), Richard Jones (1790–1855)

19. William Whewell (1794–1866), Dionysius Lardner (1793–1859), Charles Babbage (1792–1871)

20. George Scrope (1797–1876), Thomas Attwood (1783–1856), Edwin Chadwick (1800–1890), John Cairnes (1823–1875)

21. James Mill (1773–1836), John Rae (1796–1872), Edward West (1782–1828), Thomas Joplin (1790–1847)

22. James Wilson (1805–1860), Issac Butt (1813–1879), T. E. Cliffe Leslie (1827–1882)

23. Karl Marx (1818–1883)

Section III: Neoclassical Economics and its Critics

24. Johann von Thünen (1783–1850), Augustin Cournot (1801–1877), Jules Dupuit (1804–1866)

25. Leon Walras (1834–1910)

26. Carl Menger (1840–1921)

27. Eugen von Böhm-Bawerk (1851–1914) and Friedrich von Wieser (1851–1926)

28. Knut Wicksell (1851–1926)

29. Alfred Marshall (1842–1924) and Francis Edgeworth (1845–1926)

30. Gustav Schmoller (1838–1917) and Werner Sombart (1863–1941)

31. Dissenters
Charles Fourier (1772–1837), Henri de St Simon (1760–1825), Pierre-Joseph Proudhon (1809–1865), John A. Hobson (1858–1940)

32. Thorstein Veblen (1857–1929)

33. Wesley Mitchell (1874–1948), John Commons (1862–1945), Clarence Ayres (1891–1972)

34. Henry George (1839–1897)

35. Vilfredo Pareto (1848–1923)

Section IV: Twentieth Century Economics

36. Arthur Pigou (1877–1959)

37. Frank Knight (1885–1972), Henry Simons (1899–1946), Joseph Schumpeter (1883–1950)

38. Edward Chamberlin (1899–1967)

39. Michael Kalecki (1899–1970)

40. Harold Hotelling (1895–1973), Lionel Robbins (1898–1984), Clark Warburton (1896–1979), John Bates Clark (1847–1938), Ludwig von Mises (1881–1973)

41. Irving Fisher (1867–1947), Arthur Hadley (1856–1930), Ragnar Frisch (1895–1973), Friedrich Hayek (1899––), Allyn Young (1876–1929), Ugo Mazzola (1863–1899)

42. Harry Johnson (1923–1977)

43. Bertin Ohlin (1899–1979)

44. Piero Sraffa (1898–1983)

45. Joan Robinson (1903–1983) and George Shackle (1903––)

46. John Maynard Keynes (1883–1946) Volumes I and II